EIGHTH EDITION

Teaching Students with Special Needs in General Education Classrooms

Rena B. Lewis
San Diego State University

Donald H. Doorlag
San Diego State University

PEARSON

Boston   Columbus   Indianapolis
New York   San Francisco   Upper Saddle River
Amsterdam   Cape Town   Dubai   London
Madrid   Milan   Munich   Paris   Montréal   Toronto
Delhi   Mexico City   São Paulo   Sydney
Hong Kong   Seoul   Singapore   Taipei   Tokyo

Vice President and Editor in Chief: Jeffery W. Johnston
Executive Editor: Ann Castel Davis
Senior Development Editor: Hope Madden
Editorial Assistant: Penny Burleson
Vice President, Director of Marketing: Quinn Perkson
Marketing Manager: Erica DeLuca
Senior Managing Editor: Pamela D. Bennett
Senior Project Manager: Linda Hillis Bayma
Senior Operations Supervisor: Matthew Ottenweller
Operations Specialist: Laura Messerly
Senior Art Director: Diane Lorenzo
Cover Designer: Diane Y. Ernsberger

Photo Coordinator: Monica Merkel
Permissions Administrator: Rebecca Savage
Cover Image: Fotosearch
Media Producer: Autumn Benson
Media Project Manager: Rebecca Norsic
Full-Service Project Management: Norine Strang, S4Carlisle Publishing Services
Composition: S4Carlisle Publishing Services
Printer/Binder: WebCrafters, Inc.
Cover Printer: Lehigh-Phoenix Color/Hagerstown
Text Font: Berkeley

Credits and acknowledgments borrowed from other sources and reproduced, with permission, in this textbook appear on appropriate page within text.

Every effort has been made to provide accurate and current Internet information in this book. However, the Internet and information posted on it are constantly changing, so it is inevitable that some of the Internet addresses listed in this textbook will change.

Photo Credits: iStockphoto.com, pp. 2, 99, 110, 282, 329, 336; Anthony Magnacca/Merrill, pp. 6, 27, 122, 133, 148, 167, 186, 222, 224, 302, 316, 323, 344; Patrick White/Merrill, pp. 10, 57, 305; Scott Cunningham/Merrill, pp. 19, 140, 264, 278, 300; Tom Watson/Merrill, pp. 22, 95; Laura Bolesta/Merrill, pp. 24, 274 (bottom); Lori Whitley/Merrill, pp. 30, 162; Leanne Temme/Photolibrary.com, p. 50; David Napravnik/Merrill, p. 56; Jupiter Unlimited pp. 63, 80, 190, 205, 238; Jim Cummins/Corbis–NY, p. 68; Liz Moore/Merrill, pp. 73, 97; David Young-Wolff/PhotoEdit Inc., pp. 86, 242; Charles Gupton/Charles Gupton Photography, p. 115; Valerie Schultz/Merrill, p. 127; Michael Newman/PhotoEdit Inc., p. 130; BoldStock Images by Unlisted Images, pp. 135, 151; Larry Hamill/Merrill, p. 155; Shutterstock, pp. 169, 177 (top); Katelyn Metzger/Merrill, p. 179 (right); Pearson Learning Photo Studio, p. 181; David Roth/Getty Images, Inc.–Stone Allstock, p. 184; Richard Hutchings/Photo Researchers, Inc., p. 210; Ellen Senisi/The Image Works, p. 230; Mark Lewis/Getty Images Inc.–Stone Allstock, p. 250; Jan Sonnenmair/Aurora Photos, Inc., p. 272; Bill Aron/PhotoEdit Inc., p. 286; David Mager/Pearson Learning Photo Studio, p. 291; EyeWire Collection/Getty Images–Photodisc, p. 296; Ken Karp/Prentice Hall School Division, p. 319; Hope Madden/Merrill, p. 345.

Library of Congress Cataloging-in-Publication Data

Lewis, Rena B.
  Teaching students with special needs in general education classrooms / Rena B. Lewis, Donald H. Doorlag.—8th ed.
    p. cm.
  Rev. ed. of: Teaching special students in general education classrooms, c2006.
  Includes bibliographical references and index.
  ISBN 978-0-13-501490-5
  1. Inclusive education—United States. 2. Special education—United States. 3. Mainstreaming in education—United States.
I. Doorlag, Donald H. II. Lewis, Rena B., Teaching special students in general education classrooms. III. Title.
  LC1201.L48 2011
  371.9′0460973—dc22   2010002210

10 9 8 7 6 5 4 3 2

www.pearsonhighered.com

ISBN-13: 978-0-13-501490-5
ISBN-10:   0-13-501490-5

To Kendall Hope Lewis,
the newest member of our family.

Welcome to this world, Starshine.
May your life be long, joyful, and faithful to your middle name.

Dr. Rena B. Lewis earned her Ph.D. at the University of Arizona, with a major in special education and minors in psychology and systems engineering. She began in special education as a teacher of children with intellectual disabilities, although the majority of her work has been with students with learning disabilities. She served as Professor of Special Education at San Diego State University until her appointment as Associate Dean for Faculty Development and Research in the College of Education. Dr. Lewis held the Associate Dean position until her recent retirement.

A frequent contributor to the professional literature, Dr. Lewis is interested in instructional adaptations for students with special needs, classroom assessment techniques, and ways to use classroom technologies to improve literacy instruction. In addition to this book, she is co-author with Dr. James A. McLoughlin of *Assessing Students with Special Needs*, Seventh Edition. She was honored with an award by the International Reading Association for her report on research implications for teaching reading to students with learning disabilities. Her most recent research interests center around literacy interventions for highly gifted children from linguistically diverse families.

PREFACE

This book is about two things: Students with special needs and teaching. It is designed to prepare the professional educator to effectively teach the range of students found in the typical elementary or secondary classroom. It provides information about several groups of students with special needs, including those with disabilities, gifted and talented students, culturally diverse learners, and those who are English learners. In addition, it presents practical strategies for adapting standard instruction to meet the learning needs of all students in general education classrooms.

Teaching Students with Special Needs in General Education Classrooms, Eighth Edition, provides the knowledge, strategies, and instructional techniques that teachers need to address the complex and often perplexing diversity that lies behind the classroom door. All students, particularly those with special learning needs, deserve special care and special teaching. This reader-friendly, categorically organized text takes a case-based approach to contextualize the laws, organizational information, and teaching methods educators need to know to teach all children effectively. Among the new areas of focus in this edition are the important topics and trends of Response to Intervention, Universal Design, classroom assessment techniques, and the needs of English learners. The most tech-savvy text of its kind, this comprehensive new edition continues to break new ground in preparing general educators for the challenges and opportunities of the inclusive classroom. It focuses first on the creation of inclusive classrooms, second on skills for the general education teacher, and finally on effective strategies for teaching students with disabilities and other types of special needs.

 ## NEW TO THIS EDITION

From the more than 200 new references come the research, ideas, and material that informed this thorough revision.

- Chapter 4, Diversity in Today's Classrooms, discusses cultural and linguistic diversity in the U.S. as well as diversities related to race and ethnicity, religion, the makeup of families, and income.
- Chapter 18, Teaching English Learners, provides strategies for identification, assessment, and classroom adaptations such as building English vocabulary and teaching content area subjects.
- A new and updated version of Chapter 9, Assistive Technology, includes new classroom technologies, technology tools, the Internet as an instructional tool, and web-based tools for teachers.
- Expansion of Chapter 6, Encouraging Positive Classroom Behavior, to focus on the behavioral support process and positive strategies for managing behavior.

- A revised chapter—Chapter 11, Teaching Students with Intellectual Disabilities—reflects the most current recommendations on terminology and programming for this group of students.
- More coverage on the use of differentiated instruction with gifted and talented students and with other students with special needs as well.
- Increased emphasis throughout the book on the principles of accessibility and Universal Design.
- Updated information on prereferral interventions including the Response-to-Intervention model.
- The latest research on recommended practices for students with autism spectrum disorder.
- Updated information on best practices for gifted and talented students.
- **MyEducationLab** margin notes throughout the text that lead users to online, video-based assignments and lessons that deepen content comprehension.

The first four chapters of the book discuss the purposes of and rationale for inclusion, describe collaboration and the team approach, identify the major characteristics of students with special needs, and explore the various types of diversity found in today's inclusive classrooms. Many text features support the fundamental concepts presented in these initial chapters and provide the background for the chapters that follow.

 ## NEW! CHAPTER 4: DIVERSITY IN TODAY'S CLASSROOMS

This new chapter in Part I examines the diversity of present-day classrooms early in the text so that all other chapters can build on this foundation. The chapter introduces teachers to many common types of diversity, beginning with culture, ethnicity, race, and language. The chapter also explores other ways in which general education classrooms can be diverse, including religion, family makeup, and family income level and its relationship to other risk factors. Teachers learn strategies for increasing the acceptance of diversity within the classroom community through culturally responsive instruction and the promotion of academic success for all students.

Special Features

Several text features, found not only in Part I but throughout the text, are aimed at helping the teacher develop an inclusive classroom.

Students' Stories

Students' Stories, part of the case-based approach to describing inclusive classrooms, are presented at the start of each chapter to pique the reader's interest and help frame that chapter's content. These stories describe students whose special needs are related in some way to the information presented in that chapter. At the end of each Students' Stories portion of the chapter is a section called Looking Ahead that poses challenging questions about these students for readers to attempt to answer by reading the chapter.

For Your Information

For Your Information boxes in the text highlight important facts, providing an aid for comprehension and emphasizing information that will be valuable to all classroom teachers working to create an inclusive environment. Readers learn about landmark legislation for persons with disabilities, people-first language, required components of the IEP, common characteristics of autism spectrum disorder, how today's students use technology, and much more in these insightful features.

MyEducationLab

Look for MyEducationLab notes directing the reader to IRIS, comprehensive online modules offering case studies, videos, and questions that lead to a fuller understanding of reflective practice and differentiated instruction.

To enhance your understanding of inclusion, go to the IRIS Center Resources section of Topic *Inclusive Practices* in the MyEducationLab for your course and complete the Module entitled *Assessing the General Education Curriculum: Inclusion Considerations for Students with Disabilities.*

Application Activities

These end-of-chapter activities throughout the text are designed to extend the reader's understanding of the chapter. Among the activities are school and classroom observations, interviews with practicing professionals, exploration of the Internet, and critical reading of the special and general education literature.

Part II of the text addresses the skills needed by the educator, with emphasis on those of particular importance for teachers in general education classrooms. Strategies are provided for achieving four basic instructional goals: adapting instruction for learners with special needs, encouraging positive classroom behavior, promoting social acceptance, and coordinating the classroom learning environment. Also, information is presented on assistive technology and the effective use of computers and other technologies in the general education classroom. Special features found throughout the text provide coverage of practical teaching strategies and techniques.

▶ UPDATED AND REVISED! CHAPTER 9: ASSISTIVE TECHNOLOGY

This updated and revised chapter on assistive technology (AT) offers a comprehensive overview of classroom technology that can be used to promote student learning in inclusive classrooms. The chapter catalogues the various types of classroom technology, examines the advantages and disadvantages of technology use, and discusses the need for accessibility and the principles underlying Universal Design for learning. Also included are descriptions of a variety of modern technology-based tools, including educational software programs, Internet resources, and web-based tools such as Wikipedia, blogs, and RSS feeds. Among the assistive technology applications discussed in this chapter are AT for computer access, AT for access to print, AT to promote communication, and AT for physical, visual, and hearing impairments. Readers will learn about what technologies are available for their use, when to use them, and how to use them appropriately in inclusive classrooms.

Special Features

Several text features found in every chapter in the text, not only in Part II, are particularly helpful in addressing the questions and needs of the educator.

SPOTLIGHT ON TECHNOLOGY

Augmentative Communication

When students do not talk or their speech is not intelligible, an **augmentative communication** system may be used to increase their ability to communicate. There are many types of augmentative communication systems. For example, if you have a cold and find it difficult to talk, you might augment your usual means of communication by using more gestures or even writing notes rather than speaking. In classrooms, two types of systems are used most often with students with communication disorders: communication boards and electronic communication devices.

Communication Boards

Communication boards are considered a "low" technology. According to Lewis (1993),

> A communication board can be as simple as a piece of paper or cardboard with two photographs pasted on it, or as elaborate as a

Note: Image courtesy of Mayer-Johnson, LLC

▪ *Inclusion Tips for the Teacher*

These sections in every chapter answer common questions regarding inclusion practices and offer practical tips for classroom teachers. Among the dozens of topics found within this text are:

- Teaching students with special needs *and* all the others
- Explaining classroom modifications to peers
- Welcoming diverse families to the school
- Direct teaching
- Helping students evaluate websites
- Myths about ADHD
- How to reduce classroom bullying
- Determining reading levels
- Recognizing speech problems
- Facilitating smooth transitions
- What to do for seizures
- Teaching content subjects using Sheltered English

Inclusion Tips for the Teacher

Explaining Classroom Modifications to Peers

It is sometimes necessary to make changes in classroom activities so that students with special needs can succeed. For example, students with academic needs may be given special assignments or may be required to complete only part of the work assigned to the rest of the class. Those with behavioral needs may earn special rewards for good behavior. The rest of the class may become curious about why these students rate special treatment from the teacher.

Teachers can prevent problems from occurring by following these suggestions.

- Don't call undue attention to students with special needs. Treat them as you would any other student in your class.

▪ *Spotlight on Technology*

Spotlight on Technology features in every chapter consider up-to-date applications and assistive technology devices recommended for students with special needs. Among the topics of the Spotlights on Technology are computer software for struggling writers, using augmentative communication, switch access, Braille personal notetakers, software to assist language learners, WebQuests and web inquiry projects, as well as digital texts for students with reading disabilities and applications to help students develop basic reading and math skills.

▪ *MyEducationLab*

Notes throughout all chapters lead to online learning units that help pre-service and practicing teachers develop instructional skills and dispositions to take directly into inclusive classrooms.

 Go to the Building Teaching Skills and Dispositions section of Topic *Cultural and Linguistic Diversity* in the MyEducationLab for your course and complete the activity entitled *Culturally Responsive Instruction*.

STRATEGIES FOR TEACHING STUDENTS WITH DISABILITIES AND OTHER TYPES OF SPECIAL NEEDS

In Parts III and IV of the text, teaching strategies are suggested for a variety of different types of special students. Part III provides methods for teaching students with learning disabilities, intellectual disabilities, behavioral disorders, communication disorders, autism spectrum disorder, physical and health impairments, and visual and hearing impairments. This part also discusses interventions for individuals with three other types of disabilities: students with attention deficit hyperactivity disorders, severe intellectual disabilities, and traumatic brain injuries. Part IV recommends instructional techniques for those who are gifted and talented as well as for English learners.

▶ NEW! CHAPTER 18: TEACHING ENGLISH LEARNERS

This new chapter in Part IV introduces techniques and strategies for meeting the needs of English learners in the general education classroom. The chapter begins with information about how to identify students in need of English language instruction and strategies for teachers to use in assessing students' oral English skills in the classroom. The services available for this group of learners are described. Then, the chapter presents principles for adapting classroom instruction for English learners and recommends ways to put these principles into practice for two important classroom goals: building English vocabulary and teaching content subjects using Sheltered English.

Special Features

You'll find special features in every chapter, including chapters in Parts III and IV, that address the special learning needs of students in an inclusive classroom setting.

 Window on the Web

Technology can be such a powerful tool for teachers in inclusive classrooms, and to help teachers make the most of this resource, these features introduce websites that offer valuable information about special education, general education, or the teaching-learning process. Dozens of featured websites provide information on such areas such as the following:

- Intellectual disabilities
- Advocacy organizations such as CHADD (Children and Adults with Attention-Deficit/Hyperactivity Disorder) and Autism Society of America
- Websites for teachers such as Google for Educators
- Organizations for other professionals such as American Speech-Language-Hearing Association
- Physical and health conditions
- Sensory impairments
- Diversity
- Risk factors for school-aged children and youth
- Giftedness

💻 WINDOW ON THE WEB

Websites About Giftedness and Talent

Organizations Related to Gifted and Talented Education

- GT World(http://www.gtworld.org)
- National Association for Gifted Children (NAGC) (http://www.nagc.org)
- National Foundation for Gifted and Creative Children (http://www.nfgcc.org)
- The Association for the Gifted (http://www.cectag.org)
- World Council for Gifted and Talented Children (http://www.worldgifted.org)
- Supporting the Emotional Needs of the Gifted, Inc. (http://www.SENGifted.org)

Web Resources

- Hoagies' Gifted Education Page (http://www.hoagiesgifted.org)
- Uniquely Gifted: Resources for Gifted Children with Special Need (http://www.uniquelygifted.org/
- Odyssey of the Mind (http://www.odysseyofth-emind.com)

Special Programs and Research Centers

- Connie Belin and Jacqueline N. Blank International Center for Talented & Gifted Education, University of Iowa (http://www.education.uiowa.edu/belinblank/)
- Northwestern University Center for Talent Development (http://www.ctd.northwestern.edu)
- Duke University Talent Identification Program (TIP) (http://www.tip.duke.edu)
- Jacob K. Javits Gifted and Talented Students Education Program (http://www.ed.gov/programs/javits/index.html)
- National Consortium for Specialized Secondary Schools of Mathematics, Science, and Technology (http://www.ncsssmst.org)
- National Research Center on Gifted and Talented at the University of Connecticut (http://www.gifted.uconn.edu/NRCGT.html)
- The Center for Talented Youth at the Johns Hopkins University (http://www.jhu.edu/~gifted)
- College of William and Mary Center for Gifted Education (http://www.cfge.wm.edu)

MyEducationLab

Notes throughout all chapters take the reader to online Assignments and Activities that use authentic classroom video footage to help answer questions that will deepen the reader's understanding of the special needs of students in inclusive classrooms.

 Go to the Assignments and Activities section of Topic *Inclusive Practices* in the MyEducationLab for your course and complete the activity entitled *Legal Basis for Inclusion*.

SUPPLEMENTARY MATERIALS

myeducationlab

The power of classroom practice.

Teacher educators who are developing pedagogies for the analysis of teaching and learning contend that analyzing teaching artifacts has three advantages: it enables new teachers time for reflection while still using the real materials of practice; it provides new teachers with experience thinking about and approaching the complexity of the classroom; and in some cases, it can help new teachers and teacher educators develop a shared understanding and common language about teaching. . . .[1]

As Linda Darling-Hammond and her colleagues point out, grounding teacher education in real classrooms—among real teachers and students and among actual examples of students' and teachers' work—is an important and perhaps even an essential part of training teachers for the complexities of teaching in today's classrooms. For this reason, we have created a valuable, time-saving website—MyEducationLab—that provides the context of real classrooms and artifacts that research on teacher education tells us is so important. The authentic in-class video footage, interactive skill-building exercises and other resources available on MyEducationLab offer uniquely valuable teacher education tools.

MyEducationLab is easy to use and integrate into assignments and courses. Whenever the MyEducationLab logo appears in the text, follow the simple instructions to access the interactive assignments, activities, and learning units on MyEducationLab. For each topic covered in the course you will find most or all of the following resources:

Connection to National Standards

Now it is easier than ever to see how coursework is connected to national standards. Each topic on MyEducationLab lists intended learning outcomes connected to the appropriate national standards. And all of the Assignments and Activities and all of the Building Teaching Skills and Dispositions in MyEducationLab are mapped to the appropriate national standards and learning outcomes.

---

[1]Darling-Hammond, L., & Bransford, J. Eds. (2005). *Preparing Teachers for a Changing World.* San Francisco: John Wiley & Sons.

Assignments and Activities

Designed to save instructors preparation time and enhance student understanding, these assignable exercises show concepts in action (through video, cases, and/or student and teacher artifacts). They help students synthesize and apply concepts and strategies they read about in the book.

Building Teaching Skills and Dispositions

These learning units help students practice and strengthen skills that are essential to quality teaching. They are presented with the core skill or concept and then given an opportunity to practice their understanding of this concept multiple times by watching video footage (or interacting with other media) and then critically analyzing the strategy or skill presented.

IRIS Center Resources

The IRIS Center at Vanderbilt University (*http://iris.peabody .vanderbilt.edu*)—funded by the U.S. Department of Education's Office of Special Education Programs (OSEP)—develops training enhancement materials for pre-service and in-service teachers. The Center works with experts from across the country to create challenge-based interactive modules, case study units, and podcasts that provide research-validated information about working with students in inclusive settings. In your MyEducationLab course we have integrated this content where appropriate.

General Resources on Your MyEducationLab Course

The Resources section on MyEducationLab is designed to help students pass their licensure exams, put together effective portfolios and lesson plans, prepare for and navigate the first year of their teaching careers, and understand key educational standards, policies, and laws. This section includes:

- *Licensure Exams:* Contains guidelines for passing the Praxis exam. The *Practice Test Exam* includes practice multiple-choice questions, case study questions, and video case studies with sample questions.
- *Lesson Plan Builder:* Helps students create and share lesson plans.
- *Licensure and Standards:* Provides links to state licensure standards and national standards.
- *Beginning Your Career:* Educate yourself—Offers tips, advice, and valuable information on:
  - *Resume Writing and Interviewing:* Expert advice on how to write impressive resumes and prepare for job interviews.

- *Your First Year of Teaching:* Practical tips on setting up a classroom, managing student behavior, and planning for instruction and assessment.
- *Law and Public Policies:* Includes specific directives and requirements educators need to understand under the No Child Left Behind Act and the Individuals with Disabilities Education Improvement Act of 2004.

Visit *www.myeducationlab.com* for a demonstration of this exciting new online teaching resource.

Online Instructor's Manual with Test Items

An expanded and improved online Instructor's Manual includes numerous recommendations for presenting and extending text content. The manual consists of chapter overviews, objectives, outlines, and summaries that cover the essential concepts addressed in each chapter. You'll also find presentation outlines, learning activities, reflective exercises, weblinks, resources, and MyEducationLab activity suggestions. You'll also find a complete, chapter by chapter bank of test items.

The electronic Instructor's Manual is available on the Instructor Resource Center at www.pearsonhighered.com. To access the manual with test items, as well as the online PowerPoint lecture slides, go to *www.pearsonhighered.com* and click on the Instructor Resource Center button. Here you'll be able to log in or complete a one-time registration for a user name and password.

Online PowerPoint Lecture Slides

The PowerPoint lecture slides are available on the Instructor Resource Center at *www.pearsonhighered.com.* These lecture slides highlight key concepts and summarize key content from each chapter of the text.

Pearson MyTest

Pearson MyTest is a powerful assessment generation program that helps instructors easily create and print quizzes and exams. Questions and tests are authored online, allowing ultimate flexibility and the ability to efficiently create and print assessments anytime, anywhere! Instructors can access Pearson MyTest and their test bank files by going to *www.pearsonmytest .com* to log in, register, or request access. Features of Pearson MyTest include:

Premium Assessment Content
- Draw from a rich library of assessments that complement your Pearson textbook and your course's learning objectives.
- Edit questions or tests to fit your specific teaching needs.

Instructor-Friendly Resources
- Easily create and store your own questions, including images, diagrams, and charts using simple drag-and-drop and Word-like controls.
- Use additional information provided by Pearson, such as the question's difficulty level or learning objective, to help you quickly build your test.

Time-Saving Enhancements
- Add headers or footers and easily scramble questions and answer choices—all from one simple toolbar.
- Quickly create multiple versions of your test or answer key, and when ready, simply save to MS-Word or PDF format and print!
- Export your exams for import to Blackboard 6.0, CE (WebCT), or Vista (WebCT)!

▶ CONTRIBUTORS AND ACKNOWLEDGMENTS

Revisions for this eighth edition (and the seventh) were completed primarily by Rena B. Lewis, one of the co-authors of the first six editions. The contributions of Donald H. Doorlag to previous editions continue to add to the strength of this book.

Three chapter authors helped with the eighth edition, and I thank them for their willingness to share their perspectives and expertise. They are Laura J. Hall, author of Chapter 14, Teaching Students with Autism Spectrum Disorder; Kristina M. English, author of Chapter 16, Teaching Students with Visual and Hearing Impairments; and Margie K. Kitano, author of Chapter 17, Teaching Students Who Are Gifted and Talented.

I owe the greatest debt of thanks to the students and the special and general educators and educators-in-training who asked the difficult questions that prompted the writing of this book. Thanks are also due to my editors, Ann Davis, Heather Doyle Fraser, and Hope Madden, and to the reviewers: Greg Conderman, Northern Illinois University; Linda K. Elksnin, The Citadel (Emerita); Terry Gillies, Sierra Nevada College; David Majsterek, Central Washington University; Darcy Miller, Washington State University; and Rangasamy Ramasamy, Florida Atlantic University. Third, I'd like to wish special thanks to colleagues at Pearson and Norine Strang, Project Editor, and others at S4Carlisle Publishing Services who helped to birth yet another edition of this book. Last, but never least, I would like to thank Jim, the fabulous felines, and the captivating Cavaliers for continuing their support, understanding, and wondrous powers of distraction through yet another edition.

Rena B. Lewis

BRIEF CONTENTS

CONTENTS

SPECIAL FEATURES

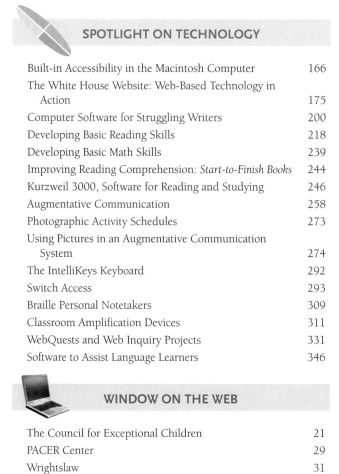

SPOTLIGHT ON TECHNOLOGY

WINDOW ON THE WEB

Introduction to Inclusive Classrooms

Success for All Students in the General Education Classroom

Tiffany

Tiffany is 8 years old and likes to swim, skate, and eat pizza. She and her two best friends, Jennifer and Sarah, walk to school together each morning. They are all in Ms. Cole's second grade class. Tiffany likes school this year, but last year was very different. Tiffany is a student with special needs; she has learning problems. In first grade Tiffany had great difficulty with reading. This year she works with the special education resource teacher for a half hour each day, and she's beginning to make progress in reading. In her second-grade class she does well in math and handwriting, and she can keep up with her classmates in spelling. Tiffany is successfully included.

Josh

Josh is a high school student who is planning to attend college when he graduates. He wants to pursue a career in chemistry or physics. This year he's taking English, American history, biology, and geometry. Josh is a student with special needs; he has a physical impairment and travels by wheelchair. Josh rides a special bus to school and attends an adapted physical education class. Josh writes and types slowly, so he sometimes needs extra time to complete tests and assignments. His grades in all his classes are excellent, and he has many friends. Josh is successfully included.

LOOKING AHEAD

Later in the chapter we will take a look at portions of the Individualized Education Programs for Tiffany and Josh. Until then, think about the questions that follow.

- What do you think is Tiffany's best subject in school?
- What types of assistance do you think Tiffany might need to succeed in the general education classroom?
- From what you know now, what are Josh's greatest strengths?
- If Josh were one of your students, what types of classroom adaptations do you think might be helpful?

Behind each classroom door lies a world of diversity. In a typical class of students, there is a wide range of abilities. Some students learn easily; others require much assistance. Some are well behaved; others, mischievous. Some are friendly; others, ill at ease with their peers. In addition, students perform differently at various times and under different circumstances. The class leader may be overcome with shyness when asked to speak at a school assembly. The student who excels in science may write and spell poorly. Addition and subtraction problems may be easy for a student, but multiplication extremely difficult. Such variations contribute to the wonder of individuality.

When students with special needs are members of a class, the range of diversity increases. Students with disabilities, gifted and talented students, and culturally and linguistically diverse students are indistinguishable from their peers in most ways. However, their learning needs may be more serious or more compelling. Such students are individuals with different personalities, preferences, skills, and needs. Like all students, they present a challenge to the teacher.

This book is for teachers who wish to learn more about students with special needs. It is also about good teaching. All students, particularly those with special learning needs, deserve special care and special teaching. This book provides teachers with the skills needed to deal with the complex and often perplexing diversity that lies behind the classroom door.

INCLUSION IN TODAY'S CLASSROOMS

Many different terms have been used to describe the practice of educating students with special needs in the general education classroom. In the 1970s and 1980s, most professionals called this approach *mainstreaming*. In the 1990s, the terms *full inclusion* and *inclusion* became more popular. However, these terms differ somewhat in meaning, and it is important to understand those differences.

Mainstreaming refers to the inclusion of students with special needs in the general educational process. (Words appearing in **boldface** in this text are defined in the Glossary.) Students are considered mainstreamed if they spend any part of the school day with general education class peers. In a typical mainstreaming program, students with special needs in general education classrooms participate in instructional and

social activities side by side with their classmates. Often they receive additional instruction and support from a special educator such as a resource teacher. That instruction may take place within the general education classroom or outside of it in a setting such as a resource room.

Students with special needs are those who require instructional adaptations in order to learn successfully. This book considers several types of students with special needs: pupils with disabilities, gifted and talented individuals, and culturally and linguistically diverse students. Also of interest are students at risk for school failure. Because of physical, cognitive, or emotional disabilities, some children and adolescents receive special education services in addition to (or, in some cases, in place of) services provided by the general educational program. Other students may not be offered special programs in their schools, but their special learning needs soon become apparent to the general education teacher.

Integration of students with special needs into the mainstream of education differs according to the needs of the individual. The amount of time these students participate in regular class activities varies from student to student. For some, the mainstream is their full-time permanent placement; for others, mainstreaming occurs for only a portion of the school day. The activities mainstreamed students take part in also vary. Some interact with typical peers primarily on a social basis; others are included in both social activities and classroom instruction. In the area of instruction, many participate in most of the general education curriculum, whereas others are mainstreamed only for selected subjects.

Mainstreaming is an educational program that varies with the needs and abilities of the student. It is characterized by the meaningful interaction of special and typical students in social activities and/or classroom instruction. Mainstreaming has been defined in many ways. In one early definition, mainstreaming was described as "temporal, instructional, and social integration" (Kaufman, Gottlieb, Agard, & Kukic, 1975, p. 5). Not only are students with special needs placed in an educational environment with typical peers for some specified amount of time (temporal integration), but they also participate meaningfully in the academic activities of the general education class (instructional integration) and are accepted as members of that class by their teacher and classmates (social integration). Integration to this extent is a real possibility for many students with special needs, particularly those with mild learning and behavior problems. However, severe disabilities may prevent some students from full participation in all instructional aspects of the general education class.

Full inclusion, a more recent term than *mainstreaming,* was introduced by professionals interested in students with severe disabilities. The full inclusion movement calls for reform of practices that exclude and segregate individuals with disabilities (Stainback & Stainback, 1985; Thousand & Villa, 1990). Advocates of full inclusion maintain that the general education classroom is the most appropriate full-time placement for all students with disabilities—not only those with mild learning and behavior problems, but also those with more severe disabilities. In the purest form of this model, students do not leave the mainstream to receive special services; instead, support is provided within the regular classroom setting.

Many special education professionals disagree with the assumption that full-time mainstreaming is the only appropriate placement for students with disabilities (e.g., Kavale & Mostert, 2003). Many argue that other options, such as resource rooms, should be available so that educational programs can be tailored to the specific needs of individual students. This is the position of the Council for Exceptional Children (CEC), the major professional organization in special education. According to the *CEC Policy on Inclusive Schools and Community Settings* (1993b),

> . . . a continuum of services must be available for all children, youth, and young adults. CEC also believes that the concept of inclusion is a meaningful goal to be pursued in our schools and communities. In addition, CEC believes children, youth, and young adults with disabilities should be served whenever possible in general education classrooms in inclusive neighborhood schools and community settings.

As discussed later in this chapter, this position is consistent with current federal laws and their requirements for placement of students with disabilities in the "Least Restrictive Environment."

Inclusion is the term most often used today to describe the placement of students with special needs in general education. *Inclusion* is a more modern term than *mainstreaming,* but, unfortunately, its meaning is imprecise. Sometimes *inclusion* is used as shorthand for *full inclusion;* at other times, it is a synonym for *mainstreaming.* It is important to determine what each speaker or writer means by the term *inclusion* because there are basic philosophical differences between the approaches of full inclusion and mainstreaming.

In this book, we use the term *inclusion* to refer to the meaningful participation of students with disabilities and other special needs in general education classrooms and programs. Although we believe that all students should be participants in the general education process, we also believe that the nature and extent of their participation should be determined on an individual basis. No one program, placement, or service arrangement meets the needs of all students.

Including students with special needs in general education programs is not a new idea. In the early days of education in the United States, classrooms served a wide variety of individuals, including some students with disabilities. The one-room schoolhouse with its range of ages and skills is an example. Kirk and Gallagher (1979) described an inclusion program that began in 1913 for students with vision losses. Students spent part of their day in the regular classroom and part in a special "sight saving class."

Today, most students with special needs begin school in general education and receive the majority of their education there. Many never leave the general education classroom. If their learning problems become apparent, some are identified as having a disability and receive special education services.

Of these, few are served in special classes and special schools. Those who do attend special classes often join their regular class peers for social activities and for instruction in nonacademic subjects such as art, music, and physical education. However, most students with disabilities are educated in general education classes, with part-time special services provided if necessary. In Fall 2004, for example, the general education classroom was the primary educational placement for more than 75% of this nation's children and youth with disabilities ages 6 to 21 (U.S. Department of Education, 2009). Consider the stories of Tiffany and Josh at the start of this chapter. Tiffany and Josh are students with disabilities who participate fully in general education while receiving special assistance in problem areas. They are examples of successfully included students.

▷ STUDENTS WITH SPECIAL NEEDS

Most discussions of inclusion concentrate on students with only one type of special need: children and adolescents with disabilities. Students who have a disability that negatively affects their school performance are served by special education, and federal laws uphold their right to a free, appropriate public education. In this book, however, we have expanded the concept of students with special needs to include three other groups with learning needs significant enough to warrant special consideration. These are (1) gifted and talented students (often served by special education, but not protected by the laws for learners with disabilities), (2) culturally and linguistically diverse students (including those who are English learners), and (3) students at risk for school failure. The special needs of these students, like those of many students with disabilities, can often be accommodated within the general education classroom.

 myeducationlab To enhance your understanding of inclusion, go to the IRIS Center Resources section of Topic *Inclusive Practices* in the MyEducationLab for your course and complete the Module entitled *Assessing the General Education Curriculum: Inclusion Considerations for Students with Disabilities.*

Students with special needs are a heterogeneous group. They may learn quickly and easily or with great difficulty. Their school behavior may be beyond reproach or frequently inappropriate. Some have sensory or physical impairments. Others stand out because of their speech, language, or culture. Despite their special needs, such students can and do learn. However, more than most students, they require good teaching to succeed in general education classrooms.

Students with disabilities may have special learning needs because of a cognitive, physical, sensory, language, or emotional disability. According to the Individuals with Disabilities Education Improvement Act of 2004 (IDEA 2004), students with disabilities include those with

mental retardation, a hearing impairment (including deafness), a speech or language impairment, a visual impairment

(including blindness), a serious emotional disturbance (referred to in this part as "emotional disturbance"), an orthopedic impairment, autism, traumatic brain injury, another health impairment, or specific learning disability, deaf-blindness, or multiple disabilities. (IDEA 2004 Final Regulations, §300.8(a)(1))

Attention deficit disorder (ADD) and attention deficit hyperactivity disorder (ADHD) are covered under other federal legislation and as types of other health impairments under IDEA.

Some of the terms that describe disabilities in federal laws are replaced or changed in common usage. For example, most special educators prefer *behavioral disorders* to *emotional disturbance*. Also, *orthopedic impairments* are often called *physical impairments*, and *mental retardation* may be referred to *cognitive* or *intellectual disability*. The term *autism* is often replaced by the term *autism spectrum disorder.*

Students with learning disabilities have adequate general intelligence and are able to succeed in many school tasks. However, because of specific disabilities in areas such as attention, perception, and memory, they experience difficulty in school. They may encounter learning problems in one or more, although usually not all, academic subjects. In contrast, students with intellectual disabilities generally are delayed in most, if not all, academic subject areas. They are characterized by a slower rate of learning and difficulty with reasoning tasks.

Students with behavioral disorders may have adequate academic achievement despite poor classroom behavior, or their behavior problems may interfere with learning. Such students may be disruptive or withdrawn, they may experience difficulty controlling their own behavior, or they may lack the skills necessary for building and maintaining interpersonal relationships with peers and adults.

Communication problems are primary in students with speech and language impairments. A student's speech may be difficult for others to understand, or language development may be delayed. Students with autism spectrum disorder experience difficulty in socialization as well as in communication. With visual and hearing impairments, the disability is sensory. Individuals with visual impairments may be blind or partially sighted; those with hearing impairments may be deaf or hard of hearing. In either case, learning takes place through the senses still available to the student.

Students with physical and health impairments may participate fully in regular class activities. However, those with limited physical mobility, such as those who travel by wheelchair, may take a less active role. Some with chronic health problems may have special needs because of prolonged school absences. In general, students with special physical and health needs can progress successfully in general education. For many of these students, their physical problems have little effect on their ability to learn.

Two other groups of individuals with disabilities are often members of general education classes: students with traumatic brain injury (TBI) and those with ADD or ADHD. Most students with TBI are members of general education classes when the accident or other trauma that causes the injury to the brain occurs, and most return to that setting after hospitalization

and rehabilitation. Students with ADD or ADHD typically remain in the general education setting while receiving assistance for problems in attention, impulsivity, and hyperactivity.

Like learners with disabilities, **gifted and talented students** are exceptional. Although they usually do not encounter school failure, their extraordinary abilities require special teaching. Gifted students are unusually bright; they may learn quickly and excel in all areas. They may be far ahead of their peers and thus require special attention and instruction. Some gifted students are creative; others may have special abilities in specific areas such as art, music, drama, and leadership. Opportunities for expression of creativity and talents can be provided within the general education classroom.

Culturally and linguistically diverse students present a different type of challenge. Although many students from diverse groups do not need special assistance to succeed in general education, some do. The customs, traditions, and values of their culture may set them apart from their peers and hinder their acceptance. Some students may be fluent speakers of English; others may be bilingual, speaking English and another language; and still others may be just beginning to acquire English language skills. If communication is difficult, learning problems may result.

Also posing a challenge to the teacher are **students at risk for school failure.** Although these students are not considered to have a disability under the law, their current performance and future welfare are threatened by a host of complex societal problems: poverty, homelessness, child abuse, and drug and alcohol abuse. They are the potential school dropouts, potential or actual delinquents, runaways, teenage parents, and suicide risks. Students at risk have very real educational needs that must be addressed if the likelihood of their failure in school is to be reduced.

Students with special needs come to the attention of their teachers when they require instructional assistance in order to succeed in school. Their needs, however, are similar to those of their peers, although probably more serious and long-standing. Every class, no matter how homogenous, has its bright and not-so-bright students, its troublemaker or behavior problem, and its student with a transitory physical impairment in the form of a broken arm or leg. Such students only enhance the range of skills and abilities within the general education classroom. To learn more about students with special needs, see the accompanying "For Your Information" box. Boxes such as these, placed throughout the book, present facts of interest to teachers.

 For Your Information

Students with Special Needs

- Although students with special needs differ in the extent of instructional adaptation they require, most have mild learning problems. Only a small proportion have severe disabilities.
- Approximately 11% of the population ages 6 to 17 is identified as having a disability (U.S. Department of Education, 2007). In a typical classroom of 30 students, there may be 3 students with disabilities.
- Many people think of physical problems when they hear the term *disability*. However, physical, visual, and hearing impairments are the least common types of disabilities. The most frequently occurring disabilities are learning disabilities, speech and language

impairments, behavioral disorders, and mental retardation/intellectual disabilities.
- It is usually not possible to tell whether students are special from their physical appearance. Typically developing students may be indistinguishable from gifted students, students with learning disabilities, and those with speech impairments.
- It is possible for a student to have more than one special need. A young child with an intellectual disability may have poor speech and language skills, a talented adolescent may have a learning disability, and a student who is blind may be gifted.

HISTORICAL PERSPECTIVES AND CURRENT PRACTICES

If identified as having a disability, being gifted, or in need of English language instruction, students may receive part-time services from a trained specialist such as a special education teacher. In some cases, that professional provides support to students (or to the teacher) within the general education classroom; in others, students leave the classroom for brief periods to receive instruction in a resource room or other setting. In either case, students with special needs remain with their peers for all general education activities in which they can successfully participate.

Not all students with special needs spend the majority of the school day in the general education classroom. Special classes (and, in some locations, special schools) are available for students with more severe disabilities whose instructional needs are different from and more intense than those of their age peers. Although educated in separate programs, these students are included in general education nonacademic and social activities whenever feasible. Also, they may increase their level of participation in the general education program as they acquire new skills and/or as professionals become more proficient at providing them the support they need to succeed in the general education classroom. The door to the general education classroom remains open to all students with special needs. This has not always been so. Inclusion, as it is known today, has had a long developmental period.

The Past

In the early days of education in the United States, students with special needs were placed in general education classes because this was the only placement available. Special services were virtually nonexistent. Students with special needs did not receive assistance from trained specialists; classroom teachers were left to cope with these students as best they could. Students considered difficult to teach, such as those with severe disabilities, were often excluded from public education.

With the growth of special education and other such services, changes occurred. Children and adolescents with severe disabilities, who had until then been denied an education, were provided with special schools. Regular class students with learning and behavior problems were removed from general education and placed in separate special classes. Because those students were having difficulty meeting the demands of the general education classroom, intensive full-time special education services were seen as the remedy. It was thought that the needs of students with disabilities could best be served by specially trained teachers in special situations, far from the general education mainstream.

Although the idea of providing special services to students with special needs was a worthwhile notion, serious problems grew out of the special class movement. It was soon discovered that full-time special education was not the answer for most students with disabilities. Many students did not require full-day services. Many were able to participate in at least some general education activities; all could benefit from contact with their peers. But students in special classes often were physically removed from the mainstream of education; special classes frequently were located in obscure places in the school building. Special class students were also segregated from their peers and often excluded from typical school activities such as assemblies. In addition, the labeling process set students with special needs further apart from their peers. In order for students to qualify for special services, it was necessary to determine the existence of a disability. Students were tested and, often on the basis of inadequate assessments, were labeled brain injured, mentally retarded, or emotionally disturbed. Labels such as these did not provide useful educational information for the classroom teacher or the special educator; worse, they attached a stigma to students with special needs.

Another major problem was the inappropriate placement of students in special classes. Students who spoke little or no English were tested in English and labeled retarded. Students from diverse cultures were compared with middle-class, Anglo American peers and were found different and, therefore, inferior. Such students were placed in special classes side by side with students with disabilities. And once removed from the general education setting, a student had little chance to return. Special class place placement was virtually permanent.

These practices were soon recognized as problems. Parent groups, such as the Arc (formerly the Association for Retarded Children) and the Learning Disabilities Association of America (formerly the Association for Children with Learning Disabilities), became active in support of appropriate services for all students with special needs. Leaders in special education began to speak out against special class abuses; the article "Special Education for the Mildly Retarded—Is Much of It Justifiable?" by Lloyd Dunn (1968) is an example. Researchers like Jane Mercer (1973) accumulated evidence that students from diverse groups were vastly overrepresented in special classes. *The Six Hour Retarded Child,* by the President's Committee on Metal Retardation (1969), found that many students acted disabled only in the school situation. Court cases were filed. The *Diana* suit (1970, 1973) attacked testing abuses with students who did not speak English; the *Larry P.* case (1972, 1979, 1984) pointed up abuses with students from diverse cultures.

As more and more information became available, the prevailing educational philosophy began to shift. With the report of the Project on Classification of Exceptional Children by Hobbs (1975, 1976), the disadvantages of labeling became apparent. Normalization, or the belief that individuals with disabilities have the right to as normal an existence as possible, became an accepted goal of special services (Nirje, 1969; Wolfensberger, 1972). The pendulum swung away from segregation of students with special needs in separate special schools and classes and toward inclusion in the mainstream of education. This viewpoint was endorsed not only by parents and professional educators, but also by state and federal laws such as Public Law 94-142, the Education for All Handicapped Children Act of 1975.

As the accompanying "For Your Information" box explains, PL 94-142 expanded the idea of normalization and applied it to school programs by requiring that students with disabilities be educated in the least restrictive environment—that is, alongside their peers without disabilities—whenever feasible. Congress enacted this law in 1975 for several reasons. At that time, about one million children with disabilities had been excluded from the public school system. Also, large numbers of students in general education classes were experiencing failure because their disabilities had not been detected. Congress concluded that less than half of the students with disabilities in the United States were receiving appropriate educational services (PL 105-17, 1997). PL 94-142 has been updated several times since its passage in 1975. In 1990, it was given a new name: the Individuals with Disabilities Education Act (IDEA). Revised in 1997 and again in 2004, the most current version is called the Individuals with Disabilities Education Improvement Act. The "For Your Information" section describes these and other pieces of federal legislation considered to be landmark civil rights laws for persons with disabilities.

 For Your Information

Landmark Legislation for Persons with Disabilities

Federal legislation has had a dramatic impact on the lives of individuals with disabilities in the United States. Some of these laws regulate the education of children and adolescents with disabilities; others guarantee the civil rights of persons with disabilities of all ages.

Legislation Related to Education

Public Law 94-142, the Education for All Handicapped Children Act of 1975, guaranteed appropriate educational services to all school-aged students with disabilities. It also required that students with disabilities be educated with general education peers to the maximum extent appropriate. The major provisions of PL 94-142 follow.

■ All students with disabilities are guaranteed a free, appropriate public education.
■ An Individualized Education Program (IEP) must be developed for each student with disabilities.
■ Parents have the right to participate in planning their children's educational program.
■ Students with disabilities are to be educated in the least restrictive environment, that is, with students not identified as having disabilities, whenever possible.
■ Tests and other assessment procedures used with students with disabilities must not discriminate on the basis of race, culture, or disability.
■ Due process procedures must be in place to protect the rights of students with disabilities and their parents.
■ The federal government provides some funding to states to help offset the costs involved in educating students with disabilities.

Public Law 105-17, the Individuals with Disabilities Education Act Amendments of 1997, introduced several key changes. This legislation

■ allowed states to serve youngsters ages 3 to 9 as children experiencing developmental delays (rather than requiring identification of a specific disability);
■ required that students with disabilities participate in state- and district-wide assessments, with accommodations as necessary, or in alternative assessments;
■ expanded IEP teams to include both special and general education teachers, when appropriate;
■ revised IEP requirements to include consideration of students' involvement with and progress in the general education curriculum; and
■ added provisions related to discipline of students with disabilities for weapons, drugs, alcohol, and injury to self or others.

Public Law 108-446, the Individuals with Disabilities Education Improvement Act of 2004 (IDEA 2004), the current special education law, includes the following provisions.

■ It brings special education into closer conformity with the No Child Left Behind (NCLB) Act by spelling out what makes special education teachers "highly qualified."
■ It continues the mandate for participation of students with disabilities in state and district assessments required by NCLB.
■ It changes the criteria for identifying students with specific learning disabilities.
■ It modifies IEPs by requiring research-based interventions (if available) and the inclusion of annual goals but not benchmarks or short-term objectives.
■ It relaxes requirements for IEP meetings (e.g., team members can be excluded from meetings if parent and school agree; meetings can be held via telephone or video conference; multiyear IEPs are allowable).
■ It permits parent and school to decide that reevaluation for special education is unnecessary.
■ It allows schools to change the placement of students with disabilities who violate the student conduct code.

Civil Rights Legislation

Section 504 of the Vocational Rehabilitation Act of 1973 applies to people of all ages. Known as the civil rights act for persons with disabilities, it provides that

no otherwise qualified handicapped individual in the United States . . . shall, solely by reason of his handicap, be excluded from the participation in, be denied the benefits of, or be subjected to discrimination under any program or activity receiving federal financial assistance.

Section 504 forbids discrimination in employment, in admissions to institutions of higher education, and in the provision of health, welfare, and other social services (Berdine & Blackhurst, 1985). Also, it entitles school-aged children with disabilities to a free, appropriate public education.

Public Law 101-336, the Americans with Disabilities Act of 1990, or ADA, is a comprehensive law designed to "provide a clear and comprehensive national mandate for the elimination of discrimination against individuals with disabilities." To this end, the ADA prohibits discrimination in employment, public accommodations (e.g., restaurants, hotels, theaters, and medical offices), services provided by state or local governments, public transportation, and telecommunications.

myeducationlab Go to the Assignments and Activities section of Topic *Inclusive Practices* in the MyEducationLab for your course and complete the activity entitled *Legal Basis for Inclusion*.

The Present

Today, the inclusion of students with special needs in general education is a reality. As Figure 1-1 shows, approximately 96% of students with disabilities are educated in regular schools (U.S. Department of Education, 2009). These students receive instruction in general education classes, resource rooms, and separate classes. The majority (about 78%) are placed in general education and receive special education services for some portion of the school day (the regular class and resource room options). Less than one-fifth are educated in separate classes within regular schools, and no more than 4% are educated in separate facilities.

There are several important differences between current practices and those of several decades ago. First, today the general education classroom is not the only service available to students with special needs, although it is viewed as the most appropriate option for many. Second, rather than being allowed to flounder and fail in the mainstream, students with disabilities are provided with aid and assistance including, when necessary, individualized instruction from a specialist.

Third, general education teachers also receive assistance from specialists. Professionals such as resource teachers or special education consultants may aid in planning educational programs for students with special needs, provide suggestions for the modification of general education classroom activities, and supply special materials and equipment. As part of the team that serves students with special needs, the general educator contributes by sharing information and ideas with parents and specialists.

According to federal law, alternative placements must be available for students with disabilities whose educational needs cannot be met in general education classes. However, such students are encouraged to interact with general education peers in any way feasible. For example, in many districts students once placed in special schools are now members of special classes located within regular schools. This greatly enhances their opportunities to interact with age peers. In addition, special classes are not viewed as permanent placements; students may reenter the mainstream at some time in the future if they are able to benefit from the general educational program.

Although school districts typically offer a range of special education services for students with disabilities, services for students with other types of special needs are less common. If available, programs for students who are gifted, talented, bilingual, or English learners are similar to those offered by special education. That is, students are educated in regular classes for a portion of their school day and receive individualized services from specialists as necessary. Most programs also provide assistance and support to the general education teacher.

BENEFITS OF INCLUDING STUDENTS WITH SPECIAL NEEDS

Many benefits accrue when students with special needs are members of general education classrooms. Students remain with their typical peers; they are not segregated from the normal activities of the school. Labeling is de-emphasized. Students leave the classroom for special help, not to see the teacher of students with

FIGURE 1-1 Educational Environment for Students with Disabilities, Ages 6–21, Fall, 2004

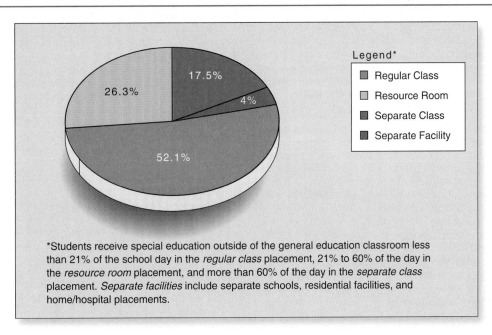

Legend*
- Regular Class
- Resource Room
- Separate Class
- Separate Facility

17.5%
26.3%
4%
52.1%

*Students receive special education outside of the general education classroom less than 21% of the school day in the *regular class* placement, 21% to 60% of the day in the *resource room* placement, and more than 60% of the day in the *separate class* placement. *Separate facilities* include separate schools, residential facilities, and home/hospital placements.

intellectual disabilities or emotional disturbance. Resource room services have aided in decreasing the stigma attached to special education because resource teachers often serve students with many different types of special needs. In addition, research indicates that students with disabilities can achieve academic success in mainstream classrooms. Success is most likely when general education instruction is individualized and when support is available not only to students with special needs but also to their teachers (Leinhardt & Pallay, 1982; Madden & Slavin, 1983; Schulte, Osborne, & McKinney, 1990).

 myeducationlab Go to the Assignments and Activities section of Topic *Inclusive Practices* in the MyEducationLab for your course and complete the activity entitled *Benefits and Challenges of the Inclusive Classroom.*

Current practices safeguard against the inappropriate placement of students in special education programs. Every effort is made to keep students with special needs in general education situations, and those students in separate, special programs are encouraged to participate in as many of the school's regular activities as feasible. For example, they should attend school assemblies, use the playground with other classes, and eat at the regular lunchtime.

General education students benefit from association with their peers with special needs. The inclusion of individuals with disabilities in school activities is a realistic introduction to

U.S. society. As the "For Your Information" box shows, typical students learn about those different from themselves and have the opportunity to learn that the differences are unimportant.

Teachers and specialists also gain when students with special needs are included in general education. Special educators are able to serve more students. Special classes usually contain

For Your Information

Students' Perceptions of Inclusion

Until quite recently, Jessica Rose attended a special school for students with multiple disabilities. Last fall, however, Jessica became a fifth grader; with support from a special education teacher, Jessica was included as a member of a grade 5 general education classroom located in a regular neighborhood school. Jessica's parents, Peggy and Tim, describe Jessica as a beautiful 9-year-old who is nonverbal, nonambulatory, and unable to feed, dress, or care for herself. Her fifth grade classmates have a somewhat different perspective. Read a sample of their responses (presented here in their original form) when they were asked at the end of the school year to describe what it was like to have Jessica in their class.

■ I feel that Jessica has changed my life. How I feel and see handicapped people has really changed. My friends used to make fun of handicaped children. When I saw Jessica I was scared and I didn't know what of. I used to think about handicaped people being really weak and if I would touch her I would hurt her but now I think diffrently.

■ Whenever I'm around Jessica I feel very special. I feel lucky to be able to interact with her. When I look at Jesse and then look at myself I look back at how I used to be. I never used to look at a disabled person without staring at them. I've learned alot from Jesse. She taught me how to accept peopl's differences. Jessica is very special to me. She's a pleasure to be around.

■ I feel like she is just a normal person. I though that I would not ever have a eperence with a handicaped but I do now. I feel lucky to have this experience. I use to feel unconferable but now I do not. I like her in our room now.

■ I think it is great that Jessica is in our room. Jessica is very fun. She laughs and smiles a lot. Sometimes she crys but that is OK. I have learned that Handicapped people are just like the others. I used to say "ooh" look at that person but now I don't I have a big heart for handicapped because they are interesting they can do things that other people can't do. I think Jessica has changed because she is with lots of other kids.

■ I like Jessica a lot and I enjoy it a lot when I hear her giggle. I feel just because she is in a wheelchair that doesn't mean she is bad. I have learned a lot about Jessica. Jessica will allways be my friend.

■ I really like having Jessica in my class. Before she came I always had thought people in wheelchairs were real weak. I was wrong. Jessica is really quite strong. I never really thought that she could have feelings because she was handicapped. She can have feelings too. She can paint with guided help. I never thought she could paint. Having Jessi in my class has taught me stuff others might never know.

■ I think that I used to be scared of handy caped people but now that Jessica came in I am not scared anymore. Because I think we should be treated equally. Because we are all the same.

■ I really like Jessica in my class. Befor I met her I never really cared about handycapt people. Jessie is really nice and I like her alot. Jessica is almost like a sister to me. I like to spend my recess playing with her. I thought a handycapt kid would never be part of my life but now one and alot more are.

Inclusion Tips for the Teacher

Teaching Students with Special Needs *and* All the Others

As a teacher in the general education program, you are responsible for the education of your students. Each of the children or adolescents in your charge has specific learning needs; each is an individual. When students with special needs are members of your class, you may feel overwhelmed. Don't! These students have specific learning needs, just like the other students in your class. They are individuals, just like their peers. Their differentness comes from the severity of their needs. They require more help in some areas than typical students do. In these areas they receive special education. In your classroom they participate in general education. Some adaptations of instructional procedures or the classroom environment may be necessary, but many "regular" students also need such changes.

Shortly after the passage of PL 94-142, Mills (1979) offered several suggestions to teachers in general education classrooms. Despite the age of these suggestions, they remain good ones, and, although they deal specifically with students with disabilities, they are equally applicable to all types of students.

- Develop the necessary skills.
- Think positively.
- Know your own strengths and weaknesses.
- Insist on in-service.
- Seek assistance.
- Utilize parents.
- Prepare your class.
- Smile.

This last suggestion deserves more explanation. Mills elaborates:

These are kids, too. They need the same love and warmth as do all children and may need a little assurance of the mainstream's desire to have them there. The other children won't accept the child with problems if the teacher isn't ready to do so. Be a leader in your own class; set the stage for a positive learning environment for all children. (p. 16)

---

only 10 to 15 individuals, whereas resource programs may serve as many as 25 to 30 students. Also, specialists are able to concentrate on the special learning needs of the student and are not forced to duplicate the efforts of the general education teacher. General educators benefit, too, from collaboration with other professionals and from the support they receive in the team approach. Specialists provide individualized help to students and are available to assist the teacher in meeting the needs of students placed in the general education classroom.

Of course, difficulties may occur in the inclusion process. General education teachers who have little experience with students with special needs may be reluctant to participate. Both typical students and their parents may be apprehensive, as may students with special needs and their parents. These problems are exacerbated when financial and personnel resources are reduced; there may be fewer special services and less assistance to teachers. Such difficulties are minimized when general education teachers are skilled in dealing with students with special needs. One purpose of this book is to help teachers develop the necessary skills. See the "Inclusion Tips for the Teacher" box to learn about meeting the needs of special students as well as those of the other pupils in the classroom.

 ### THE ROLE OF SPECIAL EDUCATION

According to federal laws, **special education** is instruction specially designed to meet the unique needs of students. That instruction can take place in a variety of settings (such as classrooms, homes, and hospitals), and it includes instruction in physical education. In his definition, Heward (1996) describes the type of instruction involved and its purposes:

Special education is individually planned, systematically implemented, and carefully evaluated instruction to help exceptional children achieve the greatest possible personal

self-sufficiency and success in present and future environments. (p. 47)

In a later work, Heward (2003) expanded this definition to include a more detailed description of the instructional methodologies used in special education:

Special education is individually planned, specialized, intensive, goal-directed instruction. . . . Special education is also characterized by the use of research-based teaching methods, the application of which is guided by direct and frequent measures of student performance. (p. 38)

Special educators serve students identified as having disabilities: students with learning disabilities, behavioral disorders and emotional disturbances, intellectual disabilities, speech and language impairments, autism spectrum disorder, physical and health impairments, traumatic brain injury, and visual and hearing impairments. Many states also provide special education services to gifted and talented students. Unless they are also disabled or gifted, culturally and linguistically diverse students are not eligible for special education; however, those who are English learners may receive services from specialists in bilingual education or from teachers of English for speakers of other languages.

Special education services are available to both students and their teachers. These services range from special consultation provided to the teacher of a student with disabilities, to special instruction delivered to a student a few minutes per day by a special education resource teacher within the general education classroom or in the resource room, to full-day special classes for students with severe and comprehensive disabilities.

Several other **related services** may be provided to students with special needs if necessary. These include psychological services for assessment and counseling, transportation, speech and language services, special physical education, rehabilitation counseling, and physical and occupational therapy. Auxiliary services such as these are available to help students with special needs derive the maximum benefit from special education.

Supplementary aids and services, in contrast, are supports provided to students with special needs to help them succeed in general education classes and other settings. Examples are special materials such as taped textbooks, equipment such as computer adaptations, and services such as peer tutoring.

Many different professionals may provide services to the same student with disabilities. For example, Tiffany, the 8-year-old student introduced earlier in this chapter, receives instruction from her second grade teacher, Ms. Cole, and from the resource teacher. Josh, the high school student, attends four different subject matter classes, sees the adapted physical education teacher, and receives special transportation services. The resource teacher coordinates his program and provides assistance to his general education teachers as necessary. In addition, the assistive technology specialist will be working with Josh to find computer adaptations to help increase his writing speed.

A team approach is used to plan and deliver the educational programs of students such as Tiffany and Josh. That team is made up of the student's classroom teacher (or teachers), any specialists who work with the student, the parent(s) of the student, and, when appropriate, the student himself or herself. Each of these individuals has an important role in planning and executing the inclusion experience. The team approach is critical in fostering communication, cooperation, and collaboration among those interested in the education of the student with special needs.

One of the functions of the team is to plan the student's educational program. As soon as a student is found to be eligible for special educational services, the team meets to make several important instructional decisions. After the student's present level of performance in important educational areas is identified, the team plans the student's program for the next year and annual goals are established. The next decisions concern placement and services. The extent to which the student is able to participate in the general education program is determined, along with any supplementary aids and services needed to support the student's participation in general education. Special education and related services are provided to meet the student's remaining educational needs. In this way, the student's needs determine the amount and kind of services and supports to be provided. Placement outside the general education class occurs only when absolutely necessary.

The educational plan devised by the team is called the **Individualized Education Program,** or IEP. It is a written plan agreed on by a team that includes the student's parents and often the student. An IEP is prepared for each student who receives special education services. The IEP is available to all team members and it is reviewed typically once a year.

A sample IEP form is shown in Figure 1-2. On this form, the team records information about the student's present performance and lists annual goals. Special education services are described, and the extent to which the student will participate in the general education program is noted. At the bottom of the form is a space for the student's parent(s) to indicate approval of the educational program and placement.

myeducationlab Go to the Building Teaching Skills and Dispositions section of Topic *Pre-Referrals, Placement and IEP Process* in the MyEducationLab for your course and complete the activity entitled *Conducting or Participating in an IEP Meeting.*

Portions of the IEPs for Tiffany and Josh appear in Figure 1-3. Included for each student are present levels of educational performance, annual goals, and the persons responsible for helping each student achieve those goals. After that come descriptions of the educational services to be provided. Note that both special education services and the amount of general education participation are specified.

General education placement is considered optimal for students with disabilities if they are capable of making progress in the standard school curriculum. As Figure 1-4 illustrates, a range of special services is available, and many of these include at least part-time placement in the general education classroom. For example, a special educator may collaborate with the classroom teacher to identify appropriate instructional adaptations for one or more students or to assist in the general education classroom by teaching lessons to a small group that includes a student with special needs. The array of special education service options is sometimes viewed as a continuum. The continuum extends from placement in general education with no special services or supports to options that serve small numbers of students with very severe needs, such as a school within a hospital for young children receiving treatment for cancer.

In selecting placements for students with special needs, it is necessary to follow the principle of **Least Restrictive Environment,** or LRE. The LRE for a student with disabilities is believed to be the appropriate placement closest to the general education classroom. As federal special education law states:

> To the maximum extent appropriate, children with disabilities . . . are educated with children who are nondisabled, and special classes, separate schooling, or other removal of children with disabilities from the regular educational environment occurs only when the nature or severity of the disability of a child is such that education in regular classes with the use of supplementary aids and services cannot be achieved satisfactorily. (IDEA 2004 Final Regulations, §300.114(a)(2))

For students unable to function successfully in a general education class, placement in a special class within a public school is less restrictive (i.e., closer to the mainstream) than placement in a separate special school. This concept does not imply that students should be placed in less intensive settings simply to bring them closer to the mainstream. Their placement must be feasible; they must have a good chance of successful performance. The goal is the least restrictive and most appropriate placement possible. For most students with disabilities, this means the general education classroom with special services for the student and teacher.

Date _____
☐ Initial IEP
☐ Annual Review
☐ Three-year Review
☐ Other _____

Orchard County Public Schools
Individualized Education Program (IEP)

Student Information
Last Name _____ First Name _____ Birth Date __-__-__
Male ☐ Female ☐ Age _____ Grade _____ Ethnicity _____
Identification Number _____ English Learner Yes ☐ No ☐
Home Language _____ Interpreter Required Yes ☐ No ☐
Address _____
School of Residence _____
School of Attendance _____
Rationale for placement, if other than student's school of residence:
_____

Parent/Guardian Information
Name _____
Address _____
Home phone _____ Work phone _____
Interpreter Required Yes ☐ No ☐

Assessment Information
Present Levels of Performance (include how disability affects involvement and progress in general curriculum)
_____
_____
_____
_____

Modifications needed in State and district wide assessment _____
_____
Why needed _____

IEP Information
Date of Next IEP _____ Date of 3-year Review _____
Primary Disability Category _____
Primary Placement _____
P.E. Type _____
Transportation _____

Special Education & Related Services; Supplementary Aids & Services; Program Modifications	Start Date	Duration	Frequency	Location

Continued

FIGURE 1-2 *continued*

Extent to which student will not participate with nondisabled students in regular class _____
_____

Explanation _____

Annual Goals and Progress Measures

_____
_____
_____
_____
_____
_____
_____
_____
_____
_____
_____

Parents/guardians will be informed of student's progress via _____
_____

As appropriate, the following factors were considered in the development of this IEP:

❑ For students whose behavior impedes learning, positive behavioral interventions, strategies, and supports
❑ For students with limited English proficiency, language needs
❑ For students who are blind or visually impaired, instruction in and use of Braille and appropriate reading and writing media
❑ Communication needs of the students
❑ For students who are deaf or hard of hearing, language and communication needs
❑ Assistive technology devices and services

Transition Services

❑ Transition service needs included in this IEP
❑ Transition service needs described in attached Individualized Transition Plan
❑ Student has been informed of his or her rights

Signatures

My due process rights have been explained to me.

❑ I consent to the IEP.
❑ I consent to portions of the IEP as described on the attached form.
❑ I do not consent to the IEP.

Parent/Guardian's Signature	Date
Student's Signature	Date
Signature of Administrator/Designee	Date
Signature of General Education Teacher	Date
Signature of Special Education Teacher/Specialist	Date
Signature/Title of Additional Participant	Date
Signature/Title of Additional Participant	Date
Signature of Interpreter	Date

Note: Developed by Tamarah M. Ashton, Ph.D., California State University, Northridge.

FIGURE 1-3   Portions of the IEPs for Tiffany and Josh

Tiffany
Current Grade: 2
Present Levels of Educational Performance
- Tiffany is in good health with normal vision, hearing, and motor abilities. She is well adjusted and gets along well with her peers.
- Tiffany's listening and speaking skills are age appropriate. She performs at grade level in math and handwriting.
- Tiffany is able to say the alphabet and identify all letters. She knows most of the consonant sounds and the short sound of *a*. Her sight vocabulary is approximately 70 words. Tiffany reads on the primer level.
- Tiffany is able to spell most of the words in the first grade spelling text (although she cannot read them all). She receives passing grades in spelling in her second grade classroom.

Annual Goals
1. By the end of the school year, Tiffany will read at a beginning second grade level with 90% accuracy in word recognition and comprehension.
   Person responsible: Resource teacher
2. By the end of the school year, Tiffany will increase her sight vocabulary to 150 words.
   Person responsible: Resource teacher
3. By the end of the school year, Tiffany will know the short and long sounds of the vowels.
   Person responsible: Resource teacher
4. By the end of the school year, Tiffany will read and spell at least 70% of the second grade spelling words.
   Person responsible: Second grade teacher
5. By the end of the school year, Tiffany will successfully complete second grade requirements in math, handwriting, science, social studies, art, music, and physical education.
   Person responsible: Second grade teacher

Amount of Participation in General Education
- Tiffany will participate in the second grade class for all subjects except reading.

Special Education and Related Services
- Tiffany will receive special instruction in reading (Annual Goals 1, 2, and 3) from the resource teacher for 30 minutes daily.

Josh
Current Grade: 10
Present Levels of Educational Performance
- Josh is unable to move his legs and has difficulty with fine-motor tasks involving eye–hand coordination. He is able to travel independently by wheelchair.
- Josh's general health is good. His hearing and vision are within normal limits. He is well adjusted and friendly and appears to get along well with his peers.
- No academic problems are apparent. Josh received As and Bs in grade 9 classes and scored well above average in group academic achievement tests.
- Josh communicates better orally than in writing because of motor difficulties. His handwriting and keyboarding are slow and require much effort.

Annual Goals
1. By June, Josh will successfully complete all 10th grade requirements, including physical education.
   Persons responsible: General education teachers, resource teacher, adapted physical education teacher
2. By June, Josh will increase his writing speed by using a computer with an adaptation such as word prediction or voice input.
   Persons responsible: Resource teacher, assistive technology specialist

Amount of Participation in General Education
- Josh will participate in regular 10th grade classes four out of five periods per day.

Special Education and Related Services
- Josh will receive special transportation services between his home and the school.
- Josh will attend an adapted physical education class one period per day.
- The assistive technology specialist will assess Josh to determine an effective computer adaptation.
- The resource teacher will provide consultation as needed to Josh's regular class teachers.

FIGURE 1-4   Placement in the Least Restrictive Environment

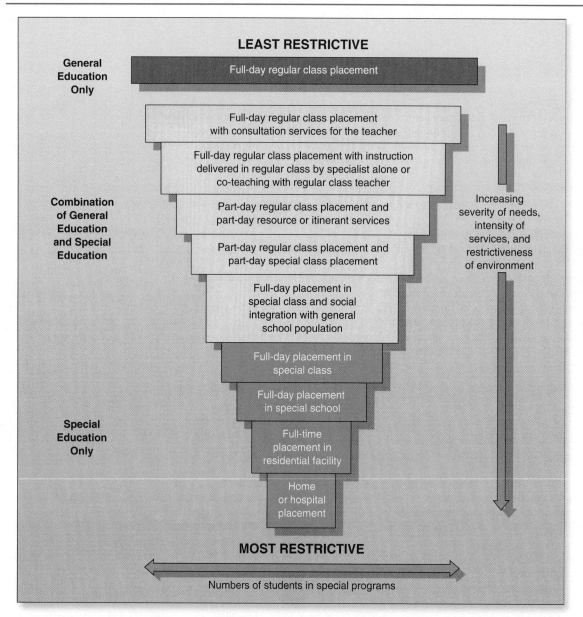

 CURRENT ISSUES AND TRENDS

Several important factors influence general education, special education, and their collaboration in the provision of services to students with special needs. The educational reform movement is one major trend. The 1980s produced a series of commission reports and recommendations aimed at improving the quality of U.S. schools. Best known among these is *A Nation at Risk: The Imperative for Educational Reform* (National Commission on Excellence in Education, 1983). This report and others calling for educational reform led to the excellence in education movement. Among the results of this movement were an increased emphasis on content area subjects (as opposed to basic skills), longer school days and years, higher expectations and grading standards, and more stringent discipline requirements.

The next wave of reforms led to the school restructuring movement and efforts to increase the decision-making powers of educators through site-based management models. At the same time, the nation's governors, led by President George H. W. Bush, agreed on six national educational goals (*America 2000*, 1990). Modified slightly, these goals became the framework for President Bill Clinton's Goals 2000: Educate America Act of 1994. The goals for the new millennium included the following.

- All children in America will start school ready to learn.
- The high school graduation rate will increase to at least 90 percent. . . .
- United States students will be first in the world in mathematics and science achievement.
- Every adult American will be literate. . . .

■ Every school in America will be free of drugs, violence, and the unauthorized presence of firearms and alcohol. . . . (National Education Goals Panel, 1997)

Goals 2000 called for a number of reforms such as drug-free schools and improved high school graduation rates. Math and science achievement was stressed, but attention was also given to universal literacy and readiness for school. In addition, the phrase *all students* was defined as including not only typical students and those who are academically talented, but also students with disabilities, those from diverse cultural and ethnic groups, those with limited proficiency in English, and those who are disadvantaged. Some progress was made toward these ambitious goals (Manzo, 1996), although none had been fully met by the turn of the century.

Another important trend of the 1990s was the standards movement. Several national professional organizations established student standards or performance indicators in subjects such as mathematics, science, history, and English–language arts. By the mid-1990s, states had developed common academic standards for their students, and most states began to link student assessment to standards (American Federation of Teachers, 2009; Olson, 2006). The standards movement sparked controversy as groups attempted to achieve consensus about appropriate educational outcomes for students. Many questions also remained about how best to ensure that students with disabilities participated in standards-based assessments (National Research Council, 1997).

The direction of educational reform shifted in 2001 with the election of George W. Bush as president. His education initiative, the No Child Left Behind Act (NCLB), continued the earlier focus on academic success for U.S. students, but shifted emphasis to greater accountability along with more state and local authority and control. In Bush's words, the four major tenets of the initiative are as follows.

■ *Increase Accountability for Student Performance:* States, districts, and schools that improve achievement will be rewarded. Failure will be sanctioned. Parents will know how well their child is learning, and that schools will be held accountable for their effectiveness with annual state reading and math assessments in grades 3–8.
■ *Focus on What Works:* Federal dollars will be spent on effective, research-based programs and practices. Funds will be targeted to improve schools and enhance teacher quality.
■ *Reduce Bureaucracy and Increase Flexibility:* Additional flexibility will be provided to states and school districts, and flexible funding will be increased at the local level.
■ *Empower Parents:* Parents will have more information about the quality of their child's school. Students in persistently low-performing schools will be given a choice. (Bush, 2001)

Despite its worthy goal of increasing student achievement, the No Child Left Behind Act of 2001 has drawn heated criticism since its enactment. The educational community has expressed frustration with the law's reliance on test scores as the sole measure of school success as well as the lack of fiscal support to help schools meet legislated mandates. The general public also is concerned. In the 39th Annual Phi Delta Kappa/Gallup Poll (Rose & Gallup, 2007) of the attitudes of U.S. citizens toward public schools, 40% of citizens polled said they had a somewhat or a very unfavorable opinion of No Child Left Behind. Moreover, 41% viewed this law as having no impact on the performance of public schools, while 21% saw its impact as negative.

Many organizations have called for changes in the law. The National Education Association (2007), for example, has developed a set of recommendations for Congress as the reauthorization of this law is debated. The three priority areas named by the NEA are:

■ Use more than test scores to measure student learning and performance.
■ Reduce class size to help students learn.
■ Increase the number of highly qualified teachers in our schools. (NEA, 2007)

The great emphasis placed by No Child Left Behind on student performance on standardized tests of academic achievement is a major area of concern in the education of students with special needs. Federal laws governing programs for students with disabilities require that these students participate along with their general education peers in state and local assessments of academic achievement. In many cases, testing accommodations or even alternative assessment procedures may be required to enable students with disabilities to participate in this type of "high-stakes" assessment. Even with such adaptations, results of a national survey by *Education Week* (Olson, 2004) suggested that a majority of teachers believe that students receiving special education would be unlikely to meet the same state standards as age peers. In a recent Gallup poll (Rose & Gallup, 2007), 72% of U.S. citizens said that students receiving special education should not be required to meet the same academic standards as their schoolmates. The Council for Exceptional Children (CEC) (2007), the leading professional organization for special education, recommended in 2007 that all students—including those with disabilities—be included in school assessments. However, it maintained that many types of assessment procedures should be employed, not only standardized tests, and that growth and progress should be considered in determining student success, not simply achievement of predetermined standards.

It is likely that there will be modifications to No Child Left Behind legislation instituted by President Barack Obama's administration. At the start of his term of office in 2009, President Obama signaled his support for education by making it one of his priorities under the American Recovery and Reinvestment Act. The Act included funding for early learning programs and programs for children with special needs, $77 billion for reforms in elementary and secondary education, and additional funding to support innovation to close the achievement gap and to improve access to college. These fiscal commitments complement the guiding principles for education policy found on the White House website:

- Focus on early childhood education.
- Reform and invest in K–12 education.
- Restore America's leadership in higher education. (*Education*, 2009)

A national trend that continues to influence education is the changing nature of the U.S. population. At the same time that reform movements have led to more rigorous educational standards, the student population has become more diverse and, in some ways, less able. Children under 18 comprise one of the poorest segments of the national population: According to the U.S. Census Bureau, in 2006, 17.4% of this group fell below the poverty line (DeNavas-Walt, Proctor, & Smith, 2007). Several general population trends are beginning to have dramatic effects on the needs of students entering general education classrooms.

The population of the United States continues to increase and with it the number of school-aged children. Public school enrollment reached 48.5 million in 2003, and it is expected to increase each year, reaching a record high of 51.2 million in 2014 (National Center for Education Statistics, 2007b). The racial and ethnic composition of the United States is also changing, and by the start of the 21st century almost one-third of the country's population was African American, Hispanic, Asian, or American Indian (Grieco & Cassidy, 2001). This increase is mirrored in the public schools, where 42% of all students were considered members of minority groups in 2004 (National Center for Education Statistics, 2007c). In addition,

the number of students identified as limited in English proficiency is growing very quickly in relation to the total school population; this group numbered more than 5 million students in 2005–2006 (National Clearinghouse for English Language Acquisition and Language Instruction Educational Programs, 2007b).

Changes such as these are likely to increase the number of students who are at risk for school failure. This suggests that educational reform efforts that divert funds away from remedial programs may be moving in the wrong direction. There is a need for more support for low-performing students and their teachers, not less (McLoughlin & Lewis, 2008).

At present, the effects of educational reform and changes in student demographics are becoming apparent in both general and special education. Special education is directing some of its efforts to the early childhood years in an attempt to reverse or at least slow the effects of disabilities on young children's readiness for school. In addition, there is movement in special education toward improving assessment procedures for students with disabilities, not only by developing new identification approaches based on students' progress within the general education curriculum, but also by enhancing the ways in which students with disabilities participate in school-mandated testing alongside their general education peers. As the future unfolds, it will become increasingly important for general and special educators to continue to collaborate in the search for the most effective ways of promoting inclusion and solving the educational problems facing students with all types of special needs—not just those with identified disabilities.

 For Your Information

People-First Language

Language is a powerful tool. When talking or writing about people with disabilities, professionals should make every effort to use language that reflects positive attitudes, not negative stereotypes. One important consideration is putting the person first, not the disability. Consider these examples from the California Governor's Committee on Employment of People with Disabilities (2005):

DON'T SAY "Mr. Lee is a crippled teacher and confined to a wheelchair."

DO SAY "Mr. Lee is a teacher with a disability. He is a wheelchair user."

The Research and Training Center on Independent Living (2001) provides several suggestions in its brochure *Guidelines for Reporting and Writing About People with Disabilities* (6th edition). Several examples are reprinted here.

- DO NOT USE GENERIC LABELS for disability groups, such as the retarded or the deaf. Emphasize people, not labels. Say people with mental retardation or people who are deaf.
- PUT PEOPLE FIRST, not their disability. Say woman with arthritis, children who are deaf, people with disabilities. This puts the focus on the individual, not the particular functional limitation. . . .
- EMPHASIZE ABILITIES, not limitations. For example: uses a wheelchair/braces, or walks with crutches, rather than confined to a wheelchair, wheelchair-bound, differently-abled, birth difference, or crippled. Similarly, do not use emotional descriptors such as unfortunate, pitiful, and so forth.*

The guidelines are updated periodically. To obtain a print copy of the latest version, contact the Research and Training Center on Independent Living, RTCIL Publications, 1000 Sunnyside Avenue, Room 4089 Dole, University of Kansas, Lawrence, KS 66045-7555. Visit *http://www.rtcil.org/products/index.shtml* to download a copy of the brochure.

*Reprinted with permission of The Research and Training Center on Independent Living (2001) from *Guidelines for Reporting and Writing About People with Disabilities* (6th ed.). Copyright 2001.

GENERAL EDUCATION TEACHERS AND STUDENTS WITH SPECIAL NEEDS

General education teachers make several contributions to the success of students with special needs. The classroom teacher is often the first professional to identify the special needs of students and to initiate the referral process. This teacher is also a source of valuable information about current school performance when students are assessed for possible special education services. As part of the inclusion team, the general education teacher participates in planning the student's educational program and in developing the IEP.

The classroom teacher's most important role is implementation of the student's general education program. This process sometimes requires adaptation of classroom procedures, methods, and/or materials to guarantee success for the student with special needs. Classroom activities should be coordinated with the special services received by the student. Also, communication between parents and professionals is crucial.

In addition, the classroom teacher may help to evaluate the student's progress not only in the general education program, but also in the areas served by specialists. Evaluation is a critical step in the educational process because it helps determine program modifications. Figure 1-5 presents the educational process, including the final step of evaluation. This diagram also provides a summary of the general education teacher's roles.

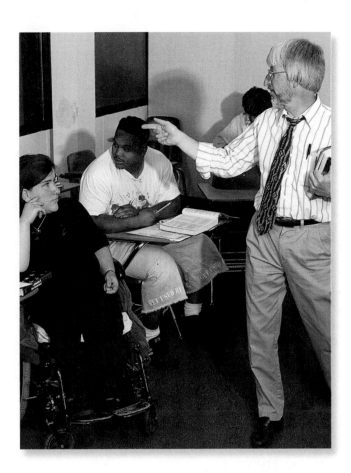

 FIGURE 1-5 The Special Education Process

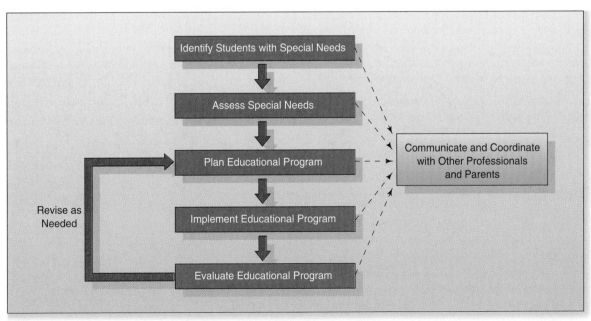

Even though these roles are not new ones for the teacher, students with special needs may require special teaching skills. The first part of this book provides basic information about inclusion in today's general education classroom. Chapter 1 has presented the concept and some of the benefits of this approach, has introduced students with special needs and special education, and has briefly described the roles of the general education teacher. Later chapters will acquaint the teacher with the team approach and the collaboration process, including some of the legal requirements for general education teachers. Readers also will explore the special needs of students with disabilities and others who may need classroom adaptations and present information about the rich diversity of today's classroom.

Things to Remember

- Most students with special needs can succeed in general education classrooms.

- *Inclusion* is the meaningful participation of students with special needs in the general educational process.

- Students with special needs include those with disabilities (learning disabilities, behavioral disorders, mental retardation/intellectual disabilities, speech and language impairments, autism spectrum disorder, physical and health impairments, traumatic brain injury, and visual and hearing impairments), gifted and talented students, culturally and linguistically diverse students, and students at risk for school failure.

- Inclusion in general education allows students with special needs to interact with typical peers. It also reduces the effects of labeling.

- Most students with special needs receive the majority of their education in general education classrooms. These students and their teachers are provided with aid and assistance to ensure their success.

- The general education teacher contributes to the success of students with special needs by participating in assessment, program planning and IEP development, placement decisions, and, most important, implementation of students' general education programs.

ACTIVITIES

Here are several activities that will help increase your understanding of the concepts presented in this chapter. Some are designed to acquaint you with the print literature or with resources on the World Wide Web. Others are explorations of current programs and practices in your local schools and community. You will find activities such as these at the end of each chapter in this text.

1. Arrange a visit to an elementary, middle, or high school. Talk with the principal or one of the staff members about the special services at the school. What types of programs are available? Is there a resource teacher who provides part-time special services to students with disabilities? If possible, visit a general education class and observe the students carefully. Can you tell which are identified as having special needs?

2. Interview several general education teachers about their perceptions of inclusion. Have they taught students with special needs in their classrooms? If so, what special learning needs did these students have? What do the teachers believe are the advantages and disadvantages of inclusion?

3. Select one or two of the major educational journals in your field. Look for articles that present useful suggestions for adapting instruction for students with special needs. You may also wish to look at some of the journals in special education. Two that feature practical articles about educating students with disabilities are *Intervention in School and Clinic* and *Teaching Exceptional Children*. Despite its title, *Teaching Exceptional Children* includes suggestions for both elementary and secondary teachers.

4. Search the Internet for information on inclusion. Visit some of the sites to get an idea of what people are saying. Are any of the sites sponsored by public schools?

5. The major professional organization in special education is the Council for Exceptional Children. Many communities

The Council for Exceptional Children

The national headquarters of the Council for Exceptional Children maintains this website for its members and others interested in special education, students with disabilities, and gifted and talented students. The site offers many types of information for its members, but general educators might be most interested in features of the Teaching & Learning Center such as "Instructional Strategies" and "Current Special Ed. Topics." The site features up-to-date news and, in its Policy & Advocacy section, information about bills now in Congress and recently passed laws. Teachers can also subscribe to the *CEC SmartBrief,* an e-mail newsletter delivered three times a week.

http://www.cec.sped.org

have local CEC chapters, and student chapters are often found at colleges and universities. The national CEC office is located at 1110 North Glebe Road, Suite 300, Arlington, VA 22201. Get in touch with your local or state CEC chapter or contact the national headquarters to learn more about this organization. (See the "Window on the Web" feature for its Internet location.) Is CEC concerned with all types of students with special needs? Are all of its members special education teachers? How does it attempt to improve educational services for students with disabilities?

CHAPTER
TWO

Collaboration and
the Team Approach

Marvin and Jake

Marvin and Jake are freshmen this year at Jefferson High. They have always been somewhat less-than-average students with minor problems in school, but they have never been referred for special services. This year, Mr. Morse, the boys' English teacher, is concerned about their school performance and decides to ask for assistance.

In English class, Marvin is uncooperative and often disruptive; he doesn't complete most of his writing assignments. Those that he does complete are usually late and of poor quality (Marvin's average grade on writing assignments is 38%). In addition, when other students in the class are bothered by Marvin's outbursts, they retaliate by commenting on his poor achievement, which leads to arguments in class and in the hall after class.

Jake also is doing poorly on his assignments, often turning them in late (Jake's average grade on assignments is 59%). He is late to class several times a week and appears to be confused about assignments. He rarely asks questions and never participates in class discussions.

The Prereferral Team

After reviewing Mr. Morse's request for assistance, the prereferral team at Jefferson High asked for more information about the academic performance and classroom behavior of both students. Mr. Morse collected data by recording daily grades and collecting samples of the boys' work. He also gathered information on how often several behaviors took place: Marvin's classroom disturbances, arguments between Marvin and his peers, Jake's late arrival to class, and Jake's participation in classroom activities. The special education resource teacher observed both students during their English classes and reviewed samples of their work.

Jake: Modifications of the General Education Program

After review of this information, the prereferral team decided that Jake's educational needs could best be met in the general education classroom, without referral to special education at this time. The team suggested that Mr. Morse establish a reward system to encourage Jake to arrive in class on time, participate in class, keep an assignment notebook with directions for his English assignments and their due dates, and complete the assignments. Mr. Morse was asked to continue collecting information about Jake's performance. The remedial English resource teacher was contacted for ideas about instructional materials for students like Jake. In addition, the special education resource teacher offered to provide periodic consultation to Mr. Morse.

Marvin: Referral to the Assessment Team

After review of the information about Marvin, the prereferral team recommended that he be referred for evaluation for special education. Mr. Morse made the referral and an assessment team was formed. An assessment plan was developed by the team, Marvin's parents' approval was obtained, and the assessments were carried out. Mr. Morse collected additional data on Marvin's in-class performance. The school psychologist and the special education resource teacher assessed Marvin's academic achievement and general ability. The school counselor visited Marvin's parents to discuss performance at home and in the community. The counselor also contacted Marvin's math, science, and history teachers to determine how he was doing in those classes.

The assessment team then met with Marvin's mother to review what had been found. Results indicated that Marvin has good general ability and is able to read at grade level. His grades in subjects other than English are passing, although quite low. Marvin's writing skills are very poor, particularly in the areas of spelling, grammar, punctuation, and capitalization. In addition, he lacks the social skills necessary for establishing interpersonal relationships, particularly with peers.

LOOKING AHEAD

Mr. Morse worked with three different teams in his efforts to meet the needs of his students Jake and Marvin. You'll learn more about each of these teams in this chapter, but before reading further, think about these questions.

- What types of classroom modifications did the prereferral team recommend for Jake?
- What other types of modifications might be possible for students with different types of needs?
- What information do you think the assessment team might have asked Mr. Morse to collect about Marvin's classroom performance?
- Mr. Morse, Marvin, and Marvin's mother all participated as members of Marvin's IEP team. What do you think each of these individuals was able to contribute?

From these results, the team concluded that Marvin qualified for special education services, and his case was sent on to the IEP team.

Marvin's IEP Team

An IEP team—composed of the vice principal, the counselor, Mr. Morse, the special education resource teacher, the school psychologist, Marvin, and Marvin's mother—then met to develop the IEP. According to the plan agreed on by the IEP team, Marvin will continue to attend his regular academic classes, including English. He will also see the resource teacher one period per day for special instruction in written expression. In addition, the resource teacher will meet at least once a week with Mr. Morse to assist in adapting Marvin's writing assignments. The school counselor will work with Marvin to develop the skills needed to get along with other students. The counselor, resource teacher, and Mr. Morse will meet with Marvin to establish a contract system to reward successful completion of classroom assignments and appropriate classroom behavior.

The IEP is to be evaluated in 6 months. In the interim, the school counselor will monitor Marvin's progress in all of his classes. Marvin and his mother agree with the IEP goals and the special services to be provided. Optimistic about the future, they believe that with help Marvin will succeed in the general education program.

Students with special needs are best served by collaborations among professionals in general education and special education, other resources within the school community, and the parents and other family members of those students. In school settings, these collaborations take place when groups of individuals work together to identify and provide the best options for students in need of extraordinary interventions. The team approach is the strategy of choice for addressing the problems of students who are struggling in school.

▶ TEAMS SERVING STUDENTS WITH SPECIAL NEEDS

Teams serving students with special needs serve one or more of the following purposes: (a) assisting teachers to meet students' needs within the general education classroom, (b) determining whether students are eligible for extraordinary services such as special education, and (c) planning, monitoring, and evaluating the provision of special education services.

In special education, federal law requires that teams, not individuals, make important decisions about services for students with disabilities. Two types of teams are mandated, the **assessment team** and the **Individualized Education Program (IEP) team**. The "For Your Information" section about requirements of IDEA 2004 describes these teams and other important mandates of the law.

Although the team approach is required by special education law, variations are seen from state to state and from district to district in the names of the teams and their specific functions. The assessment team might be called the *special services committee, special education committee, placement committee,* or *student study team.* The assessment team's responsibilities begin when an educator or parent decides to refer a student for consideration for special education services. The team develops and executes a plan for evaluating the student to determine whether he or she meets the legal criteria for those services. Once a student has been found eligible for special education services, the IEP team is charged with planning and monitoring the student's educational program plan.

This team may be called the *IEP committee* or the *educational planning team.*

The third type of team is the **prereferral intervention team**. Although federal special education law does not require this team, the prereferral intervention approach has become quite popular, and it is mandated or recommended by a majority of states (Truscott, Cohen, Sams, Sanborn, & Frank, 2005). The purpose of this approach is to assist teachers in resolving instructional and behavioral problems within the general education classroom before formal referrals are made to special education or other types of special services. This type of team might be called the *teacher assistance team, student support team,* or the *prereferral committee.*

A newer method for collaboration between general and special education is the **Response-to-Intervention (RTI)** approach. As its name implies, this approach centers around study of how well students learn when provided with various types of instructional interventions. According to McLoughlin and Lewis (2008), "the Response-to-Intervention approach, as it is described in IDEA 2004 and its regulations, is based upon an examination of the student's ability to profit from high quality instruction in order to show progress in the school curriculum" (p. 243). In effect, RTI is a prereferral approach that

For Your Information

Important Provisions of IDEA 2004

IDEA 2004, the Individuals with Disabilities Education Improvement Act, provides guidelines for many of the activities and procedures that take place in special education, including requirements for the assessment and IEP teams. IDEA is the current version of Public Law 94-142, the Education for All Handicapped Children Act of 1975, the first federal law to guarantee a free, appropriate, public education to students with disabilities. The following paragraphs discuss some of the important terms appearing in federal special education law.

- *Child find.* State and local education agencies must work actively to identify unserved students in need of special education.
- *Assessment team.* When a student is referred for evaluation for possible special education services, a multidisciplinary team is formed to plan and carry out the assessment. The specific disciplines represented on the team vary by the needs of the student, but the information gathered must be comprehensive enough for the team to make decisions about whether the student meets eligibility requirements for special education. Parents of the student must give permission for the assessment to take place, and both parents and professionals participate in determining if the student has a disability and, if so, what educational needs are present.
- *Nondiscriminatory assessment.* Assessment instruments and materials must be technically sound and administrated by trained personnel. These instruments must not penalize students for their native language, race, culture, or disability.
- *IEP team.* This group develops, reviews, and revises the IEP. Individualized Education Programs are written for all students with disabilities who receive special education services. IEPs must be reviewed and revised at least annually. The IEP team is composed of the following members: (a) the parents of the student with a disability; (b) at least one of the student's general education teachers (if the student is, or may be, participating in the general education program); (c) at least one special education teacher or special educator who provides service to students with the type of disability being considered; (d) a representative of the local education agency (LEA) who is qualified to supervise or provide special education and is knowledgeable about the general education curriculum and the school's resources; (e) an individual who can interpret the assessment results (if one is not already a member of the team); (f) at the discretion of the parent or the LEA, others with expertise regarding the student; and (g) the student with a disability, when appropriate. One of the changes under IDEA 2004 is that a team member may be excused from attending an IEP meeting if both the parent and the local educational agency give their consent.
- *Surrogate parent.* If a parent of a student with disabilities is not available to work with the school, a surrogate parent can be appointed. The surrogate parent approves the student's placement, is a member of the IEP team, and serves as an advocate for the student.
- *Due process hearing.* If the school or the parent(s) of a student with disabilities are not satisfied that the student is receiving an appropriate educational program, an impartial due process hearing can be requested. Hearings attempt to resolve disagreements regarding issues such as identification, evaluation, and educational programs and placements. Under IDEA 2004, parents and the school must meet in a resolution session to attempt to reach a settlement before a due process hearing can be held.
- *Confidentiality.* Federal laws guarantee "confidentiality in the disclosure of information that may unnecessarily identify a student as having a disability" (Strickland & Turnbull, 1993, p. 261). Parents of students with disabilities must be informed of the confidentiality requirements for personally identifiable information (e.g., name, address) and must give consent before this information can be released to anyone outside the school district. The district must maintain confidential records of each student, and these records must be accessible to parents.
- *Transition services.* By the age of 16, the IEPs of students with disabilities must include a statement of postsecondary goals and the transition services needed to meet those goals. Transition services are designed to support students as they move from the K–12 school environment to the world of work or postsecondary education or training. According to IDEA 2004, such services may include not only instruction but also community experiences, development of employment and adult living goals, and assistance in acquiring daily living skills.

---

involves both assessment and instruction. Students who do not show progress may be eligible for special education services.

IDEA 2004 permits states to use the RTI approach in identification of students with learning disabilities in place of or in addition to an older approach: identification of a significant discrepancy between ability and achievement. States may also choose to use RTI with struggling students with other types of possible special needs. Zirkel and Krohn (2008) reported that, as of October 2007, regulations in the majority of states permit districts to use RTI in the identification of learning disabilities, but do not prohibit the use of the discrepancy approach.

One other variation of the team approach is important to consider. Some students with disabilities receive accommodations within the general education classroom under Section 504 of the federal Rehabilitation Act of 1973. Section 504, intended as a civil rights law for individuals with disabilities of all ages, repeats IDEA's guarantee of a free public education but covers a wider segment of the student population. Students with attention deficit hyperactivity disorder and those with attention deficit disorder often receive services under Section 504, rather than IDEA. Salend (2008) adds that other students (such as those with health conditions such as asthma, diabetes, and epilepsy) may also be served under this act. Similar to the procedures dictated under IDEA, the team approach is used to gather assessment information, make decisions about student eligibility, and develop an individualized accommodation plan, often called a **504 accommodation plan.**

The position in this book is that general and special educators should work together when making educational decisions about all students with special needs, particularly those who are served in the general education classroom. Teams should be concerned not only with students with identified disabilities, but also with others who are struggling in school,

Prereferral Team
- Identify possible problem.
- Consider previous interventions.
- Design data collection procedures.
- Design prereferral interventions.
- Identify needed support/services to implement intervention plan.
- Coordinate implementation of prereferral interventions.
- Evaluate prereferral interventions.
- Modify interventions as needed.
- Initiate special education referral if general education interventions are not successful.

Assessment Team
- Review referral for special education.
- Review data on prereferral interventions.
- Identify team members needed to develop assessment plan.
- Design assessment plan.
- Provide assessment plan to parents and review plan.
- Obtain parents' permission to conduct assessment.
- Conduct assessment.
- Summarize assessment results.
- Conduct meeting with parents to determine eligibility.

Individualized Education Program (IEP) Team
- Identify IEP team membership needed for specific student.
- Review assessment results.
- Establish present levels of educational performance.
- Identify and select appropriate annual goals.
- Designate the appropriate placement in the Least Restrictive Environment (LRE).
- Develop plan for implementation of the IEP.
- Develop evaluation plan.
- Identify process for reporting student's progress to parents.
- Establish and monitor reevaluation plan.

with those who are gifted and talented, and with those who are culturally and linguistically diverse. For students with disabilities, federal and state laws and regulations describe the purpose, responsibilities, and makeup of the teams that make educational decisions. For students with other types of special needs, there may be no laws or regulations requiring the team approach. Despite this, this book will stress the importance of prereferral, assessment, and educational planning teams in helping all students with special needs to succeed in the general education program. Figure 2-1 summarizes the responsibilities of each of these important teams.

 ROLES OF TEAM MEMBERS

Teams serving students with special needs are composed of individuals directly involved with some aspect of delivering or supporting instruction. Included are general and special educators, some of whom may provide direct services to the student. Other professionals such as school psychologists, speech-language pathologists, and school nurses are involved

as necessary. School administrators serve as resources to the team, and the parents of the student are an important addition. Although parents typically are not professional educators, they are able to provide information about the student and thus play a significant role in the educational decision-making process. If appropriate, the student with special needs should also be encouraged to participate.

Building Principals

School principals or vice principals serve as key members of teams serving students with special needs. As administrators, they are responsible for the general education programs and often the special education programs housed within their buildings. In large elementary or secondary schools, the vice principal with supervisory responsibilities for the special education program may represent the principal on the team.

The principal often schedules and chairs the team's formal meetings. Although usually not directly responsible for implementing any portion of the student's IEP, administrators do influence the operation and effectiveness of the effort. As the educational leaders of the school, their activities, the attitudes they convey, and the support they provide can help establish the necessary school climate for developing educational programs that serve a wide variety of learners and for building successful programs that provide appropriate services for students with special needs.

Special Education Administrators

Special education directors supervise the provision of educational programs for all students with disabilities within a district. Among the programs under their direction are resource programs and special classes as well as support services to general education teachers who teach students with disabilities. Special education directors may also develop in-service training programs to help teachers work more effectively with students with special needs.

On assessment and IEP teams, special education administrators assist in the review of assessment information and help the team examine options for special education services. In some districts, these professionals serve on the team only when students are likely to require placement in more intensive service options such as separate special classes.

General Education Teachers

The involvement of general education teachers is critical because they have firsthand experience with students with special needs in their classrooms. They share ideas with parents and other professionals, and they assist in devising strategies for successful programs to serve students with special needs who are included in the general education program. If these teachers do not participate on the team, the effectiveness of the inclusion effort is compromised.

myeducationlab Go to the Assignments and Activities section of Topic *Collaboration, Consultation, and Co-Teaching* in the MyEducationLab for your course and complete the activity entitled *Teacher Collaboration*.

At the secondary level, students are served by a number of general education teachers, and the school counselor may be designated as the teachers' representative on teams serving students with special needs. The counselor collects information from each teacher about a student's classroom performance and reports to the team. The counselor is then responsible for conveying team decisions and recommendations to each of the student's teachers. Of course, it is possible (and often desirable) for secondary teachers to serve as members of the team, as in the example of Mr. Morse, Marvin's and Jake's ninth grade English teacher (see "Students' Stories").

General education teachers who have worked with students being considered for special education services can provide the team with much information. They are aware of strengths students may have, students' past responses to instructional programs and procedures, and areas in which students may require the most assistance. The presence of these teachers on the team can ensure that all important classroom information is considered. In addition, their experience with individual students may temper the interpretation of assessment results or the recommendations made by the team.

General education teachers responsible for implementing a portion of the IEP should be involved in the team's discussion of assessment results and other relevant information gathered by professionals or provided by parents. Teachers can describe their classroom programs and their perceptions of a student's ability to participate in activities in the general education class. They can also contribute to and benefit from the team's discussion of ways to adapt the general education program. As soon as the modified classroom program or the IEP

is initiated, the teacher can inform the team of the student's progress in the general education class. This input helps the team evaluate the current program in order to make any changes needed to enable the student to meet the goals established by the prereferral or IEP team.

Other General Educators

Some students with special needs may be served by general educators other than their classroom teacher. For example, when special needs of students first come to the attention of the school, general education specialists in reading, mathematics, or learning the English language may become part of the team. These professionals may assist by gathering assessment data and by providing instructional support to students who are struggling and their teachers. If students are then referred to special education, general education specialists can lend their expertise to the team about specific instructional needs and the success of various interventions.

Special Educators

In addition to general education teachers, special educators provide instructional services to students with disabilities. Those most likely to be on the teams serving students with special needs are those assigned to a classroom or office within the student's school. The special educator may be a teacher-consultant who provides assistance to general education teachers who have students with special needs in their classes. Or the special educator may be a resource room teacher who provides direct services to special students as well as consultation to their teachers. The special class teacher also may participate as a member of the team; this teacher serves students who require more intensive special education but who may be included in the general education program for selected activities.

> **myeducationlab** Go to the Assignments and Activities section of Topic *Collaboration, Consultation, and Co-Teaching* in the MyEducationLab for your course and complete the activity entitled *Related Service Providers*.

Itinerant teachers, who travel from school to school, may be specialists in the education of students with speech or language impairments, visual impairments, hearing impairments, physical or health impairments, or other special needs. One of the most common itinerant specialists is the **speech–language pathologist,** who serves students with communication disorders. These and other specialists are team members when a student likely to receive their specific services is being evaluated.

Special educators fulfill a variety of roles on the team. Often they are responsible for organizing the team, conducting the meetings, and monitoring the services provided to students with disabilities. They may observe a student in the general education class and conduct much of the educational assessment. Special education teachers explain the different types of available special services and describe in detail the support services for general education teachers. Also, these professionals help interpret assessment results and assist the team in formulating the educational plan. In the implementation of the IEP, they typically provide direct services to students with disabilities and consultant services to general education teachers.

The special educator most likely to provide instruction to a specific student should serve on the IEP team when that student's educational program is being planned. This involvement provides the special educator with the opportunity to meet the student and his or her parent(s) and teacher(s). The special educator thus becomes familiar with the student's current performance and educational needs, as well as with the views of the student's general education teacher(s), the student's parent(s), and other professionals concerned with the student's education.

Parents and Students

Parents may be reluctant to participate in the activities of teams serving students with special needs, particularly if there is a history of negative contacts with the school. They also may be apprehensive about becoming a member of a team composed mainly of professionals. It is the responsibility of the professionals on the team to encourage parents to participate and to reassure them about the importance of their involvement.

> **myeducationlab** Go to the Building Teaching Skills and Dispositions section of Topic *Parents and Families* in the MyEducationLab for your course and complete the activity entitled *Collaborating with Families*.

Educational programs are more effective for students when parents are active participants. Parents can provide the team with information about the performance of the student outside the school setting. They are also able to assist in establishing appropriate educational goals. In addition, parents contribute by identifying which aspects of the educational program can be supported or supplemented within the home. A parent's awareness of the specific program designed for his or her child and the resultant coordination between home and school can make an important difference for many students. See the "Window on the Web" box for information about the PACER Center, a website with many resources for families that include a student with disabilities.

School Psychologists

School psychologists assist the assessment team in evaluating students referred for special education services. In addition to administering tests and other assessments, psychologists may observe students in the general education classroom, interview parents, or consult with other professionals who have information about students' recent performance. Their participation on

PACER Center

The mission of the PACER Center focuses on children and young adults and their families, although teachers and others are welcome to take advantage of the resources on this site. PACER Stories is a good place to start because it opens a window into the lives of several individuals with disabilities and their families. The site offers links to a number of other worthwhile Internet destinations, including the Technical Assistance ALLIANCE for Parent Centers with links to local community resources and a new site, Kids Against Bullying, designed for teens with disabilities and their friends.

Among the most valuable resources on the PACER Center site are its publications, many of which are available to download without charge (*http://www.pacer.org/publications/specedrights.asp*). Titles include "Attending Meetings to Plan Your Child's IEP," "Drop-Out Prevention: Parents Play a Key Role," "When Billy Doesn't Do His Homework," and "Tips for Transition Planning." For parents and others who are English learners, portions of the website and key publications have been translated into Spanish, Hmong, and Somali.

The team should make every effort to include special students' parents as fully participating team members. If possible, conflicts between parents and professionals should be resolved at the team level. However, if parents do not agree with the recommendations made by the team, they may request a hearing to appeal the team's decisions. The school district also has the right to appeal if it believes that parents are not acting in their student's best interests.

Students with special needs participate in the activities of the team when appropriate. As a general rule, students who have reached adolescence are the most likely to be included. One survey (Martin, Marshall, & Sale, 2004) found that secondary students with disabilities attended 70% of IEP meetings. Students participating in team meetings should be encouraged to discuss their reactions and perceptions regarding possible educational goals and placements.

http://www.pacer.org/index.asp

---

the assessment and IEP teams also involves explanation or interpretation of assessment results.

School psychologists generally have training in counseling and classroom management. However, their responsibilities for assessing students, writing reports, and serving on several prereferral, assessment, or IEP teams throughout the district often consume most of their time. Because they are usually required to serve more than one school, they may not be available for consultation with a teacher who has an immediate concern.

School Social Workers

School social workers assist in collecting information from parents, coordinating the efforts of the prereferral or IEP teams with community agencies, and observing the student's interactions in settings outside the classroom. They are able to provide consultative services to parents, teachers, and students themselves.

School Counselors

Although counselors are most likely to be found at the secondary level, in some districts they are available for students of all ages. Counselors take on a number of roles on teams serving students with special needs and also provide direct services to these students. They assist in gathering information from teachers, school records, parents, and community agencies (particularly when school social workers are not available). Students with special needs may receive counseling or educational guidance from these professionals. Counselors at the secondary level often coordinate the educational programs for students with special needs and assume responsibility for communicating each student's progress to teachers, parents, and the student.

School Nurses

The school nurse may collect medical information regarding students with special needs; for example, nurses can screen students for possible vision or hearing problems. As team members, nurses assist in interpreting medical records and reports and also can explain the educational implications of medical information. They may provide services to students with physical impairments, those with chronic illnesses, or others needing continued medical attention. In addition, they assist parents in obtaining medical services for their children.

 To enhance your understanding of collaboration, go to the IRIS Center Resources section of Topic *Collaboration, Consultation, and Co-Teaching* in the MyEducationLab for your course and complete the Module entitled *Working with Your School Nurse: What General Education Teachers Should Do to Promote Educational Success for Students with Health Needs.*

Other Team Members

Other persons join teams serving students with special needs when their particular expertise is needed. For instance, for students with physical impairments, professionals such as **physical therapists**, **occupational therapists**, and **adapted physical education teachers** are important team members. When young students with disabilities enter school, it is important to obtain information from the **early interventionist** familiar with their progress in infant and toddler or preschool programs to facilitate their transition into the school program. For secondary students, **vocational rehabilitation counselors** may be an important addition. **Audiologists** contribute to the team's understanding of hearing losses, and medical personnel may assist when students with health impairments are being considered. **Assistive technology specialists** can advise the team regarding the selection, acquisition, and use of technological devices to increase, maintain, or improve the functional capabilities of students with disabilities. Another possible addition is the instructional aide who has worked closely with the student.

Although these professionals are included as team members as needed, the effective team involves only those individuals who are necessary for careful and complete consideration of the student's special needs. Large teams of more than five to seven members become unwieldy, and productivity declines. At minimum, however, every team should include the student's parent(s) and his or her general and special education teachers.

> ## COLLABORATION IN THE IDENTIFICATION AND PREREFERRAL STAGES

Collaboration among general and special educators, other professionals, and students and their parents takes place at many points in the process from identification of a possible special instructional need to referral for assessment to program planning and the provision of services over and above those offered to all students in the general education community. This section of the chapter discusses collaboration prior to the time a formal referral is made for evaluation for special education or other services. The first activities to be discussed are identification procedures: child find, screening efforts, and the identification of struggling students using results of state- and district-mandated achievement tests. Next are the prereferral team and prereferral interventions, the more traditional approach to making classroom changes to help students improve their school performance. The following section of this chapter presents a description of a new approach, Response to Intervention (RTI), a method

introduced in IDEA 2004 as an alternative strategy for the identification of learning disabilities.

Identification

Federal and state laws and regulations specify procedures for educational agencies to follow in the location and identification of students with disabilities. As the "For Your Information" earlier in this chapter noted, IDEA 2004 requires that all states and local education agencies engage in child find activities to locate all students with disabilities in need of special education and then to provide those students with appropriate services. States spell out district responsibilities in this area and in others such as notification of parents, due process procedures, and confidentiality of student records. A good source of information about federal laws and legal issues is the Wrightslaw website described in the "Window on the Web" feature.

One way in which schools endeavor to locate students who are in possible need of special education and other services is through **screening.** Screening procedures are methods of gathering information about a large number of individuals quickly in order to identify persons who may be in need of further study. Screening for hearing and vision problems is routine today in schools. A school nurse, hearing specialist, or other professional works with each child individually to see how well that child is able to perform on a task requiring vision or hearing ability. For example, the child may be asked to look at letters of various sizes and say the letter names. Or, to screen hearing, the student might listen through a headphone and raise his or her hand when a sound is heard. Students who have difficulty with screening tasks may then be referred for more in-depth assessment.

Screening also takes place to identify students who may be in need of assistance in learning the English language.

Wrightslaw

The Wrightslaw website features up-to-date information about current laws, legal issues, and advocacy efforts related to students with disabilities. Among the choices available are:

- Special Education/Education (e.g., Tests and Measurements for the Parent, Teacher, Advocate, and Attorney)
- Special Education Advocacy
- Individuals with Disabilities Education Act (IDEA 2004)
- Law and Legal Issues

- Free Flyers, Resources, Pubs
- Books, DVDs, and Websites

There is also an Advocacy Library, a Law Library, and a "Topics" section that provides information on a number of subjects such as Autism Spectrum, Behavior and Discipline, NCLB Laws and Regulations, Privacy and Records, and Research-Based Instruction. The site also offers a free subscription to the e-mail newsletter, the *Special Ed Advocate*.

http://www.wrightslaw.com

When students enter school, parents are asked to provide information about the language or languages spoken in the home. If a language other than English is spoken by the student or others in the family, the student may be assessed to determine how proficient he or she is in English. Those who have not yet mastered English may then be referred for educational services or programs for those learning English.

General education teachers are also involved in screening efforts. Teachers often take part in workshops or other types of training to learn more about students with special needs, including those with disabilities. Also, districts may provide information to teachers about warning signs of common learning problems, then ask teachers to identify any of their students who show similar signs. To reach a broader audience, state education agencies or local districts may run community information campaigns to help acquaint community members, including parents, with the types of special needs that children and adolescents might show and the services available in the schools to address those needs.

Testing of student achievement has become a common occurrence as states and districts have adopted standards of performance for most academic subjects and developed or adopted tests to assess how well students are progressing toward those standards. Districts may choose to use results of these "high-stakes" tests administered to all students to identify those who are lagging behind. Thus, for example, tests of reading or mathematics proficiency in the early grades become screening procedures as well as measures of academic progress. One drawback of this approach is the infrequency of such tests. As the next section of this chapter on Response to Intervention (RTI) discusses, frequent measures of school progress are preferred so that assistance can be provided promptly to students who are struggling.

Prereferral Intervention

Before considering RTI, it is important to learn about the more traditional approach called **prereferral intervention.** As the term implies, *prereferral interventions* are changes that take place in the school program prior to a formal referral.

myeducationlab To enhance your understanding of the prereferral process, go to the IRIS Center Resources section of Topic *Pre-Referrals, Placement and the IEP Process* in the MyEducationLab for your course and complete the Module entitled *The Pre-Referral Process: Procedures for Supporting Students with Academic and Behavior Concerns.*

Anyone within the school community can refer students for consideration for possible special education services. Most referrals originate with general education teachers, but many come from parents, counselors, social welfare agencies, and physicians. However, before beginning referral procedures, it is important to consider other possible options within the general education program. Research has indicated that, once students are referred for special education services, they are likely to be assessed (92%) and ultimately placed (73%) in special education (Algozzine, Christenson, & Ysseldyke, 1982). Also, Hosp and Reschly (2003) pointed out that race may play a role; these researchers concluded in their meta-analysis that African American students were more likely to be referred for special education assessment or intervention than white students.

Classroom teachers refer students for special education and other types of support services for many reasons. In one study, the most common reasons were general academic problems, difficulty in reading, and behavioral problems such as inattentiveness (Lloyd, Kauffman, Landrum, & Roe, 1991). However, before a referral is made, the teacher can try several strategies to solve the instructional problem. Because of when they are attempted, these strategies are called *prereferral interventions.*

Interventions undertaken during the prereferral stage often eliminate the need to refer students for special education or other special services. For example, a change in instructional strategies or an adaptation of the classroom learning environment may lead to improved student performance. Although not mandated by federal special education laws, prereferral interventions are required or recommended by most states (Buck, Polloway, Smith-Thomas, & Cook, 2003; Truscott et al., 2005). Typically, school personnel must document that all possible general education interventions have been attempted before a student can be formally referred for special education services.

Data Collection. When students experience difficulty with some aspect of the general education program, one of the first steps for teachers is collection of data to describe the instructional problem. This information helps to verify the existence of the problem, describe its characteristics, and determine its severity. For example, if a teacher is concerned about a student who does not seem to be working on his journal during the classroom time allotted for that activity, the teacher can observe the student to find out how often (or how long) he is off task. If the student spends half the time talking with peers rather than writing, the teacher is likely to conclude that the problem is severe enough to warrant intervention.

Collaboration with Parents and Colleagues. Once the instructional problem is described, it is often useful to confer with other professionals familiar with the student. Former teachers may be able to describe approaches that they have found effective for similar problems; current teachers can share their experiences with the student and their observations of his or her ability to meet classroom demands. Parents and other family members can also provide information about the student. In some cases, simply making parents aware of the problem is an effective intervention. For example, if the problem concerns homework, parents may decide to become more vigilant about supervising their children's homework time. Or, they may make watching television or another valued activity contingent on homework completion.

Prereferral Intervention Teams. In some districts, teachers work with individual professionals such as special education resource teachers or teacher-consultants to gather ideas for modifying classroom programs to meet the needs of students not yet referred for special education. In a more common arrangement, teachers seek assistance from teams of colleagues. These teams are known by several different names: *teacher assistance teams, student study teams, prereferral assistance teams,* and so on. They are typically composed of several general educators representing different grade levels or subject areas; other members may include an administrator such as the principal, a specialist such as a special educator, and parents. Their major role is to collaborate with teachers in solving instructional problems.

The research on teacher assistance teams and consultation services indicates that these approaches are quite successful in solving problems at the classroom level, thereby reducing the number of referrals to special education (Buck et al., 2003; Chalfant & Pysh, 1989; Hocutt, 1996; Idol, 1993; Safran & Safran, 1996). However, Burns and Symington (2002) pointed out that the empirical base for prereferral teams is weak and conflicting, although a meta-analysis found somewhat positive results for student outcomes. Other studies have found that general education teachers are generally positive about their experiences with teacher assistance teams, although they are less satisfied with student outcomes (Lane, Pierson, Robertson, & Little, 2004; Papalia-Berardi & Hall, 2007).

Idol and West (1991) emphasize the collaborative nature of the team approach. The teacher seeking assistance becomes a member of the team and participates fully in the problem-solving process, which involves six steps:

- Step 1: Entry/Goal Setting
- Step 2: Problem Identification
- Step 3: Intervention Recommendations
- Step 4: Implementation of Recommendations
- Step 5: Evaluation of the Action Plan and the Team Process
- Step 6: Follow-Up/Redesign (pp. 77–78)

For example, in step 3, the entire team (including the student's classroom teacher) brainstorms possible solutions to the instructional problem, evaluates the advantages and disadvantages of each solution, and then selects the most appropriate one.

Team deliberations are most fruitful when the teacher is able to clearly describe the student's problem and any attempts to remedy it. The student intervention checklist shown in Figure 2-2 is one method for recording this information. The teacher begins by noting the area or areas of concern (e.g., academic achievement, classroom behavior) and the steps already taken to solve the problem (e.g., student or parent conference). He or she then describes the student's present performance and current classroom procedures. At the end of the checklist, the teacher identifies the type of assistance he or she is seeking, and there is space for the team to record the results of its deliberations and the outcomes of any interventions.

Classroom Modifications. A number of prereferral intervention strategies involve changes in the instructional program of the general education class. To improve student performance, modifications can be made to any aspect of the program: the classroom curriculum, how instruction is delivered, the learning activities in which students participate, how students are graded, the physical arrangement of the classroom, and strategies for managing student behavior.

Curricular adaptations are changes in the body of knowledge and skills taught to students. One option is to retain the standard grade-level curriculum but teach only a portion of it—those areas determined to be the most important. Another option is the substitution of an alternative curriculum. In the general education classroom, this usually involves teaching the prerequisite skills that students lack or using curricular materials from a lower grade level. For example, a fifth grade teacher might use fourth grade reading materials for some students in the class.

Instructional adaptions are the most common type of classroom modification. These changes may involve any part of the teaching–learning process: the teacher's instructional methods and strategies, learning activities and instructional materials, performance requirements for students, testing and grading procedures, and grouping arrangements. Examples are as follows.

- Providing additional instruction in areas where students experience difficulty
- Structuring practice activities so that students have ample time to master one set of skills before moving on to the next
- Modifying task requirements so that students can listen rather than read or give answers by speaking rather than writing
- Giving permission for students to have extra added time to complete exams and assignments

FIGURE 2-2   Student Intervention Checklist

Name _____ Age _____ Date _____
Teacher _____ Grade _____

1. **Area(s) of Concern**
   ____ academic   ____ language   ____ gross motor   ____ hearing   ____ behavior
   ____ speech   ____ fine motor   ____ emotional   ____ physical   ____ vision
2. What kinds of strategies have been employed to resolve this problem?
   A. **Records Review and Conference**
      ____ student conference(s)   ____ review of educational records
      ____ parent conference(s)   ____ vision   ____ medical   ____ hearing
   B. **Environmental Modifications**
      ____ class seating arrangement   ____ group change   ____ other
      ____ individual seating   ____ teacher change
      ____ schedule modification   ____ teacher position in class
   C. **Instructional**
      ____ modifications in methods used with group or class
      ____ modifications in learning aids used with group or class
      ____ individual methods with regular materials
      ____ individual learning aids with regular materials
      ____ individual methods and materials different from group or class
   D. **Management**
      ____ modification in classroom management system
      ____ use of systematic group management techniques
      ____ use of individual behavior management techniques
3. What methods are currently employed to address the concern?

4. Where does this student stand in relationship to others in class, group or grade regarding systemwide tests, class average behavior, completion of work, etc.?

Student Behavior	Class or Group or Grade Behavior

5. Is the concern generally associated with a particular time, subject, or person?

6. In what areas, under what conditions, does this student do best?

7. Assistance requested (observation, materials, ideas, etc.):
   _____
   _____
   _____
   _____

Assistance provided:
Dates	Nature of Assistance	Individuals Responsible	Outcome

Permission granted by the publisher for noncommercial reproduction.

Note: Reprinted with the permission of Prentice-Hall, Inc., from *Developing and Implementing Individualized Education Programs* (3rd ed.) by Bonnie B. Strickland and Ann P. Turnbull. Copyright © 1993 by Prentice-Hall, Inc.

- Allowing students to use aids such as calculators and spell checkers
- Reducing the number of math problems students are required to solve or the number of paragraphs they must write
- Grouping of students with similar needs for instruction and change in the composition of the groups as needed

Management adaptations are changes in the classroom behavior management system. The teacher may need to provide additional instruction to all students on the rules for classroom conduct. Or he or she may need to modify the standard classroom management system if several students begin to display inappropriate behaviors. In some cases, it may be necessary to begin a systematic behavior change program for one or more students with more severe behavioral problems. For example, the teacher and student might negotiate a behavioral contract in which the student agrees to reduce his or her inappropriate behavior, and in exchange the teacher promises to provide a suitable reward.

Environmental adaptations are changes in the physical environment of the classroom. For example, a teacher may alter the arrangement of student desks and the location of learning materials in order to make classroom activities accessible to a student who uses a wheelchair. Students with visual and hearing impairments may be seated near the front of the room, if that is where instruction typically occurs. Students who act out and those who have difficulty focusing their attention may also be seated near the teacher. The classroom itself may be arranged so that there are areas for several different activities including large- and small-group instruction, independent study, work at the computer, and so on. Consult the "Inclusion Tips for the Teacher" section to learn more about the prereferral intervention planning process.

General education teachers use several different techniques to modify instruction for students with special needs. However, although teachers consider many kinds of classroom modifications valuable, they are less positive about their feasibility (Johnson & Pugach, 1990; Ysseldyke, Thurlow, Wotruba, & Nania, 1990). In general, teachers are most likely to introduce interventions that they themselves can accomplish quickly and easily within their own classrooms (Ellett, 1993; Johnson & Pugach, 1990). Some of the most common strategies are modifying assignments so they are shorter or less difficult, allowing students to respond orally on tests, and offering preferential seating (Bacon & Schulz, 1991; Munson, 1986).

General Education and Community Resources. In addition to making modifications in their own classrooms, teachers can draw on the resources of the general education program to assist students with school problems. Although different schools will have different resources available, all teachers have access to some level of support within their school, district, and community.

The use of students as instructional assistants is one example. Students act as tutors to other students, thereby increasing the amount of individualized instruction that takes place within the classroom. Peer tutoring programs are inexpensive in terms of both time and money, and research supports their effectiveness for increasing the skill levels of students with school achievement problems (Lloyd, Crowley, Kohler, & Strain, 1988). Parents, other family members, and community volunteers can also act as assistants within the classroom.

The general education program may offer a number of resources: school-wide peer tutoring or peer counseling programs, academic assistance in the computer lab, remedial programs for low-income students, reading and math labs or tutorial services, programs for students learning English, bilingual education, enrichment opportunities for students with special gifts and talents, and so on. The community may offer additional resources such as after-school programs providing homework assistance, big brother and big sister programs, sports activities and clubs, or a homework hotline staffed by tutors. School and community resources such as these provide options that teachers should consider when they select prereferral interventions for students with special needs.

A national study of prereferral intervention practices in the 50 states (Buck et al., 2003) sheds some light on the recommendations that teacher assistance teams tend to make. These recommendations span a range of different types of interventions. The most common team suggestions were instructional modifications, behavior management procedures, curricular modifications, and counseling. Other options reported by various states were placement review and change, parent training, tutoring, mentoring, and summer school services. A more recent national study (Truscott et al., 2005) reported somewhat different results, with only a handful of interventions reported as common by 20% or more of the prereferral intervention teams surveyed. Those interventions appear in Table 2-1 under the heading "Popular Interventions."

 TABLE 2-1 Recommendations of Prereferral Intervention Teams

Category	Popular Interventions	% Responding
Academic intervention	Decrease amount of work	22%
	One-on-one instruction	20%
Classroom structure change	Change seat	32%
Interdisciplinary support	Individual/group counseling	33%
	Remedial program	32%
Peer support	Peer tutor/buddy	37%

Note: From "The Current State(s) of Prereferral Intervention Teams: A Report from Two National Surveys," by S. D. Truscott, C. E. Cohen, D. P. Sams, K. J. Sanborn, & A. J. Frank, 2005, *Remedial and Special Education, 26,* 135–136. Copyright 2005 by PRO-ED, Inc. Adapted by permission.

Inclusion Tips for the Teacher

Planning Prereferral Interventions

As a member of the prereferral intervention team, the classroom teacher collaborates with colleagues to develop a plan to resolve educational problems of struggling students within the general education classroom. The first step is describing the types of problems the student may be having. Among the possible areas of difficulty are academics, classroom behavior, speech and language, hearing and vision, and physical skills and abilities. Of course, precise problem descriptions are better than general statements. The team will be better able to understand and respond to a student's needs if the teacher describes him or her as "a fourth grader having difficulty with reading and understanding second grade material" rather than "has problems in reading."

Next, the teacher should provide information about any steps already taken to learn more about the problem and to help improve the student's performance. As shown in Figure 2-2, these steps might include actions such as:

- Review of the student's school records
- Conferences with the student and/or with the student's parent(s)

- Change of the student's seat in class (e.g., away from potential distractions)
- Change of the group (e.g., reading group) in which the student is placed
- Alteration of the instructional method used with the student
- Change in the classroom management system (Strickland & Turnbull, 1993)

Along with a description of each action, the teacher needs to provide information about the results of that action. Which of the attempts to improve performance, if any, were successful?

The prereferral intervention plan can then be developed by the team using a planning form such as the one that follows. The team first decides upon the goal of the intervention, that is, what changes in student performance the team hopes to see. The second part of the form contains the details of the intervention plan. Four types of interventions are listed: academic modifications, behavioral strategies, parent/home activities, and motivational/incentive system. Space is provided to specify

---

Student: _____   Grade: _____

Teacher: _____

Intervention Goal
What observable, measurable changes do we want to see in the student? _____
_____
_____
_____

Details of Intervention Plan

Academic Modifications

What strategy/method is to be used?
How is it to be done? Where? When?
Who will do it?

Behavioral Strategies

Parent/Home Activities

Motivational/Incentives system

Data Collection Activities

How will effectiveness be assessed? _____
_____
_____

Who will collect the data? _____
_____

How often will data be collected? _____

Follow Up Plans/Procedures

How often will the team meet to monitor the plan? _____
_____

What is our criteria for success? _____
_____

Who will help the teacher implement the plan? _____
_____

General Comments

Note: From "Effective Preassessment Team Procedures: Making the Process Work for Teachers and Students" by C. K. Ormsbee, 2001, *Intervention in School and Clinic, 36,* p. 151. Copyright 2001 by PRO-ED, Inc. Reprinted by permission.

continued

what methods or strategies will be used and other pertinent information about each intervention (e.g., who will be responsible for implementation).

The next part of the plan concerns data collection activities: how the effectiveness of the intervention will be evaluated, who will be responsible for data collection, and how often data collection will occur. There are also follow-up plans for the team. These specify how often the team will meet to monitor the effectiveness of the plan, the criteria they will use for evaluation, and who will assist the classroom teacher in plan implementation. At the bottom of the form is space to record other comments as needed.

RESPONSE TO INTERVENTION (RTI) AND COLLABORATION

Similar in purpose to the prereferral intervention approach, Response to Intervention (RTI) is a newer strategy for the early solution of classroom problems. First introduced in special education law in IDEA 2004 as an alternative method for the identification of learning disabilities, RTI is now viewed as a more comprehensive approach to the collaboration of general and special education in the improvement of instruction for all students. The National Center on Response to Intervention (2008) describes the approach in this way on the home page of its website:

> Response to Intervention (RTI) is a process intended to help educators maximize student achievement through early identification of learning or behavioral difficulties. By using RTI, teachers and other school staff are able to identify challenges to student learning, provide appropriate evidence-based interventions, and monitor student progress based on achievement and other performance data. By providing information about how a child responds to evidence-based interventions and other supports, RTI enables teachers to adjust their instruction to best meet the needs of their students.

 myeducationlab To enhance your understanding of RTI, go to the IRIS Center Resources section of Topic *Pre-Referrals, Placement and the IEP Process* in the MyEducationLab for your course and complete the Module entitled *RTI (Part 1): An Overview.*

Consult the "Window on the Web" feature for information about this website and others focusing on RTI.

The RTI approach combines several key components, one of which is different levels or tiers of supports for students with different levels of need. The RTI model is often depicted as a triangle, as Figure 2-3 illustrates. At the base of the triangle is universal support for all students. The second level responds to the needs of some students with targeted interventions, while the third level provides intensive supports to a relative few individual students.

In most descriptions of RTI, the first tier or level represents high-quality instruction in the general education classroom provided by general educators. As required by federal laws such as No Child Left Behind, instruction should be based on sound scientific research to increase the probability that learning will occur. Student progress in the general education curriculum is to be monitored so that those not making adequate progress may be provided with additional support. A later chapter of this book discusses strategies such as curriculum-based measurement that teachers can use to evaluate the progress of students in their classrooms.

The second tier or level in RTI is designed to provide high-quality supplemental instruction to students who were identified as struggling in level one. This intervention may be provided to a small group of students in the classroom by the general education teacher. Another option for level two is collaboration between general and special education that results in instructional responsibilities being shared by general and special educators. Depending on the school plan, other professionals such as reading and math specialists may become involved in the RTI effort. As was the case in level one, student progress is carefully monitored to determine if interventions are successful.

The third tier or level of intervention serves students who require more intensive support than that offered in level two. Specialists such as special educators typically provide instruction at this level. Instruction takes place in a very small group or individually, and the intervention period is longer than that of level two interventions. Again, progress is monitored to determine if students are learning. If progress is not satisfactory, the student may be referred for special education assessment.

There is much variation among states and districts in how they are implementing the RTI approach. However, it is useful to consider one well-known model, the 3-Tier Reading Model from the Vaughn Gross Center for Reading and Language Arts at The University of Texas at Austin (2005) to better understand the differences among the three levels of intervention. In this model, Tier I serves all students, Tier II approximately 20 to 30% of general education students, and Tier III approximately 5 to 10%. Tier II interventions are delivered to small groups of three to five students for 20 to 30 minutes a day for a period of 10 to 12 weeks. After that time, progress is evaluated to determine which of three options is most appropriate: return to Tier I, introduction of a second Tier II intervention, or movement to Tier III. In Tier III, intervention is even more intense: Small groups of one to three students receive two 30-minute instructional sessions a day. Progress monitoring in Tier III may point to the need for a return to Tier II, a second Tier III intervention, or a referral for evaluation for special education or other services.

According to McLoughlin and Lewis (2008), "it is important to keep in mind that widespread use of the RTI approach is in its

WINDOW ON THE WEB

RTI Websites

The U.S. Department of Education supports three centers that serve educators interested in the RTI approach.

National Center on Response to Intervention

This, the newest of the three websites described here, has RTI as its sole focus. It provides a glossary of RTI terms and library of downloadable resources on RTI topics such as tiered instruction, progress monitoring, and cultural and linguistic diversity. Also available are reviews of available progress monitoring tools, an online newsletter called the *RTI Responder,* and information about services such as free webinar series on current topics (e.g., curriculum-based measurement).

http://www.rti4success.org

National Research Center on Learning Disabilities

This national center contains resources related to the assessment and identification of learning disabilities, including the RTI

approach. It offers a variety of RTI resources including a Learning Disabilities Resource Kit with downloadable information on RTI topics. The site provides information tailored specifically to a number of audiences such as teachers, parents, school psychologists, and administrators.

http://www.nrcld.org

National Technical Assistance Center on Positive Behavioral Interventions and Supports

This website has a somewhat different focus: positive behavioral interventions and supports. However, many of its resources target both academic and behavioral concerns within the general education program.

http://www.pbis.org

FIGURE 2-3   The RTI Model

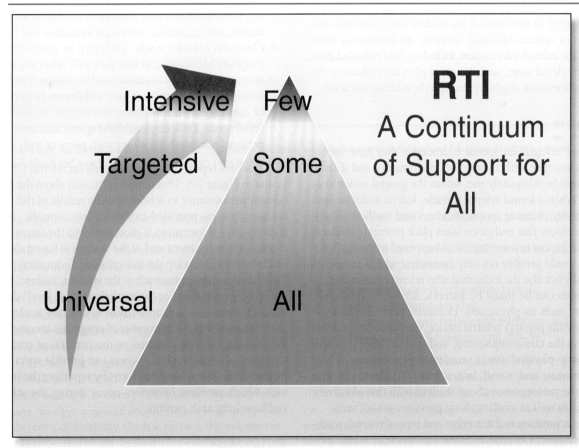

Note: From Sugai, G. (2007). *RTI: Reasons, Practices, Systems, & Considerations.* Keynote presented at the December 2007 Response to Intervention Summit, OSEP Center on Positive Behavioral Interventions & Supports, Washington, DC. Retrieved February 18, 2008, from *http://www.pbis.org/main.htm*

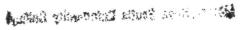

FIGURE 2-5 Formal Referral Form

Referral for Evaluation for Special Education

Directions: Complete all sections of this referral form and provide as much specific information as possible. Please return this form to the school office when it is complete.

Teacher _____ Grade/Class _____ Date _____

Student _____ Age _____ Birth Date _____

1. What is the reason for this referral?

2. How does the student's problem affect his/her ability to participate in your classroom?

3. How would you describe this student's performance compared with that of others in your class?

4. What are the student's areas of strength?

5. What are the student's areas of greatest need?

6. What steps have you taken to address the student's areas of need in your classroom? What results were obtained?

7. Use this space to include any other important information.

---

status, and motor abilities may be considered" (p. 53). Also, the law mandates that no single test or other measure can be used to determine a student's placement.

Once assessment data are gathered, the team prepares a written report and shares results with the student's parent(s). Those results are used to determine whether the student meets eligibility requirements for special education. If so, the assessment findings serve as a basis for the IEP team to design the educational program for the student and determine the most appropriate educational placement.

Under federal law, eligibility for special education services is determined by two criteria. First, it must be established that the student has a disability and, second, there must be evidence that the disability adversely affects the student's educational performance. Satisfying one criterion but not the other is not sufficient. For example, many students with school problems do not meet special education eligibility requirements because they do not have a disability. Similarly, students with a mild disability (e.g., a mild vision loss or physical impairment) would not

qualify for special education if they were not experiencing educational difficulties as a result of that mild disability.

COLLABORATION IN DESIGNING THE INDIVIDUALIZED EDUCATION PROGRAM

Once it has been determined that a student is eligible for special education, the next step is design of the Individualized Education Program. This must take place before special education can begin. The IEP is typically reviewed and modified at least annually and its content is regulated by federal law. Consult the "For Your Information" section for more information about legal requirements.

Several areas of need may be identified when the team reviews the student's present levels of performance. It may not be possible, or even appropriate, to include each of these areas in the IEP. The team determines possible annual goals for the

For Your Information

Components of the Individualized Education Program (IEP)

The required content of the IEP is specified by IDEA 2004. Because requirements are very specific, excerpts from the final regulations for the law follow. The emphasis (terms in **bold print**) has been added to identify major parts of the IEP.

Content of the IEP (§300.320(a))

(1) A statement of the **child's present levels of educational achievement** and functional performance, including—
  (i) How the child's disability affects the child's involvement and progress in the general curriculum (i.e., the same curriculum as for nondisabled children); or
  (ii) For preschool children, as appropriate, how the disability affects the child's participation in appropriate activities;

(2) (i) A statement of **measurable annual goals**, including academic and functional goals designed to—
  (A) Meet the child's needs that result from the child's disability to enable the child to be involved in and make progress in the general education curriculum; and
  (B) Meet each of the child's other educational needs that result from the child's disability;
  (ii) For children with disabilities who take alternate assessments aligned to alternate achievement standards, a description of benchmarks or short-term objectives;

(3) A description of—
  (i) **How the child's progress** toward meeting the annual goals described in paragraph (2) of this section **will be measured**; and
  (ii) When periodic reports on the progress the child is making toward meeting the annual goals (such as through the use of quarterly or other periodic reports, concurrent with the issuance of report cards) will be provided;

(4) A statement of the **special education and related services and supplementary aids and services,** based on peer-reviewed research to the extent practicable, to be provided to the child, or on behalf of the child, and a statement of the **program modifications or supports** for school personnel that will be provided to enable the child—
  (i) To advance appropriately toward attaining the annual goals;
  (ii) To be involved in and make progress in the general curriculum . . . and to participate in extracurricular and other nonacademic activities; and
  (iii) To be educated and participate with other children with disabilities and nondisabled children in the activities described in this section;

(5) An **explanation of the extent, if any, to which the child will not participate with nondisabled children in the regular class** and in the activities described in paragraph (a)(4) of this section;

(6) (i) A statement of **any individual appropriate accommodations** that are necessary to measure the academic achievement and functional performance of the child on **State and districtwide assessments . . .**; and
  (ii) If the IEP Team determines that the child shall take an alternate assessment on a particular State or district-wide assessment of student achievement, a statement of why
   (A) The child cannot participate in the regular assessment; and
   (B) The particular alternate assessment selected is appropriate for the child; and

(7) The **projected date** for the beginning of the services and modifications described in paragraph (a)(4) of this section, and the anticipated frequency, location, and duration of those services and modifications.

In addition to the required components of the IEP, several other factors must be taken into account when they apply to individual students.

Consideration of Special Factors (§300.324(2))

(i) In the case of a child whose **behavior impedes the child's learning or that of others,** consider the use of positive behavioral interventions and supports, and other strategies, to address that behavior;

(ii) In the case of a child with **limited English proficiency,** consider the language needs of the child as such needs relate to the child's IEP;

(iii) In the case of a child who is **blind or visually impaired,** provide for instruction in Braille and the use of Braille unless the IEP Team determines, after an evaluation of the child's reading and writing skills, needs, and appropriate reading and writing media (including an evaluation of the child's future needs for instruction in Braille or the use of Braille), that instruction in Braille or the use of Braille is not appropriate for the child;

(iv) Consider the **communication needs** of the child, and in the case of a child who is deaf or hard of hearing, consider the child's language and communication needs, opportunities for direct communications with peers and professional personnel in the child's language and communication mode, academic level, and full range of needs, including opportunities for direct instruction in the child's language and communication mode; and

(v) Consider whether the child needs **assistive technology** devices and services.

student, then ranks those goals in priority order. Once the most important goals have been selected, the team can decide how best to measure progress toward those goals.

The sample IEP in Figure 2-6 shows the present levels of performance for a sixth grade student as well as annual goals in written language and spelling. Although IEP formats vary from district to district, all should contain the essential components required by law.

The IEP is a formal written plan designed for and based on the specific individual educational needs of each student with disabilities. It should clearly communicate to all team members the exact nature of the student's educational program.

FIGURE 2-6 Sample IEP

Date __11/14/08__
❏ Initial IEP
☒ Annual Review
❏ Three-year Review
❏ Other _____

Orchard County Public Schools
Individualized Education Program (IEP)

Student Information
Last Name ___Cooper___   First Name ___Steven___   Birth Date ___7-23-97___
Male ☒ Female ❏ Age _11-4_ Grade _6_ Ethnicity ___white, nonHispanic___
Identification Number ___000000000___ English Learner Yes ❏ No ☒
Home Language ___English___ Interpreter Required Yes ❏ No ☒
Address ___1400 Lilac Rd. Blanchard 00000___
School of Residence _____Piper Middle School_____
School of Attendance _____Piper Middle School_____
Rationale for placement, if other than student's school of residence:
___N/A___

Parent/Guardian Information
Name ___Bob Cooper and Helen Downing-Cooper___
Address _____same_____
Home phone ___555-5555___ Work phone ___555-0000___
Interpreter Required Yes ❏ No ☒

Assessment Information
Present Levels of Performance (include how disability affects involvement and progress in general curriculum)
___Steven has average performance in all areas except written language. He scores in the below average to low average___
___range in spelling and written expression. Steven should be able to function well in general education with support___
___in written language.___

Modifications needed in State and districtwide assessment ___in assessments requiring written expression, use___
___of dictionary and thesaurus; time and a half to complete essays___

Why needed ___student requires support in written expression___

IEP Information
Date of Next IEP ___11/09___ Date of Three-year Review ___11/10___
Primary Disability Category ___specific learning disability___
Primary Placement ___regular class & resource room___
P.E. Type ___regular___
Transportation ___N/A___

Special Education & Related Services; Supplementary Aids & Services; Program Modifications and Supports	Start Date	Duration	Frequency	Location
Resource Room	11/08	1 year	1 hour, 5 days/week	Rm. 5
Consultation to general education teacher	11/08	1 year	as needed	Rm. 7
Testing accommodations in regular class, State/district assessments	11/08	1 year	as needed	Rm. 7
Assistive technology assessment re: Adaptations for written language	11/08	as needed	as needed	Rm. 5, Rm. 7

Extent to which student will not participate with nondisabled students in regular class ___one hour per day___

Explanation ___Steven will participate in spelling activities in the regular classroom and receive additional spelling instruction in the resource room. He will begin written expression assignments in the regular class and receive support in editing and revising in the resource room.___

Annual Goals and Progress Measures

1. WRITTEN LANGUAGE. Steven will write a 5-sentence paragraph with (a) correct capitalization and punctuation and (b) topic, supporting, and concluding sentences.

2. SPELLING. Steven's spelling skills will improve as evidenced by his performance in weekly spelling tests in the regular classroom.

EVALUATION. Portfolio assessment of Steven's work samples. All writing assignments and spelling tests will be graded with the criteria used for general education students.

Parents/guardians will be informed of student's progress via ___monthly progress reports and regular report cards___

As appropriate, the following factors were considered in the development of this IEP:
- ☐ for students whose behavior impedes learning, positive behavioral interventions, strategies and supports
- ☐ for students with limited English proficiency, language needs
- ☐ for students who are blind or visually impaired, instruction in and use of Braille and appropriate reading and writing media
- ☒ communication needs of the student
- ☐ for students who are deaf or hard of hearing, language and communication needs
- ☒ assistive technology devices and services

Transition Services
- ☐ Transition service needs included in this IEP
- ☐ Transition service needs described in attached Individualized Transition Plan
- ☐ Student has been informed of his or her rights

Signatures

My due process rights have been explained to me.
- ☒ I consent to the IEP.
- ☐ I consent to portions of the IEP as described on the attached form.
- ☐ I do not consent to the IEP.

Helen Downing-Cooper	11/14/08
Parent/Guardian's Signature	Date
Steven Cooper	11/14/08
Student's Signature	Date
Marianne Kemp	11/14/08
Signature of Administrator/Designee	Date
Connie Hernandez	11/14/08
Signature of General Education Teacher	Date
Edward Johnson	11/14/08
Signature of Special Education Teacher/Specialist	Date
Marsha Humphries, Advocate	11/14/08
Signature/Title of Additional Participant	Date
Signature/Title of Additional Participant	Date
Signature of Interpreter	Date

Note: Developed by Tamarah M. Ashton, Ph.D., California State University, Northridge.

IEP Responsibilities of General Educators

General education teachers have many questions about IEPs and their responsibilities in the IEP process. Some of the most commonly asked questions (and their answers) appear here.

- *Does the classroom teacher participate in the development and review of IEPs?* Under current federal law, general education teachers are required to serve on the IEP team when students they are (or will be) teaching are under consideration for special education services or when their IEP is being reviewed. When students with disabilities receive both general and special education services, the teacher in the general education classroom is expected to aid in the development of the IEP. At the elementary level, the classroom teacher is required to participate because he or she is probably the only general education teacher working with the student. At the secondary level, however, a staff member such as the school counselor is often selected to serve as the classroom teachers' representative on the IEP team.
- *Is the IEP a contract? Are teachers legally responsible for meeting each of the goals on the IEP?* The IEP is a contract because schools and agencies are legally responsible for providing the services indicated on the IEP. However, teachers are not held legally accountable for accomplishing IEP goals and objectives. Nevertheless, teachers do have the responsibility for making good-faith efforts to assist the students in accomplishing the goals stated in the IEP (Strickland & Turnbull, 1993).
- *Do IEPs cover both special education and general education programs?* The IEP must state an explanation of the extent, if any, to which the student will not participate in the general education program. Goals are written for only those portions of the school day during which students require specialized services. The IEP must also include information about supplementary aids and services and other supports and program modifications that will be provided in general education classes or other education-related settings to enable children with disabilities to be educated with nondisabled children to the maximum extent appropriate. If major adaptations are made in general education classroom procedures, then those will be reflected in IEP goals and services. However, for most students with special needs, general education goals are not needed.
- *Who is responsible for implementing the IEP?* The IEP states who is responsible for implementing the special education program to meet each of the annual goals. In most cases this will be the special educator. However, if the IEP contains general education class or even home goals, then the general education teacher or the parent may be named as one of the persons responsible.
- *Who may see the IEP?* Copies of the IEP are available to the student's parent(s) and each of the persons responsible for implementing portions of the IEP. Many districts do not distribute copies of the IEP to all teachers working with the student because of the cost of copying and because IEPs are considered confidential documents that must be stored securely. To see the IEPs of students included in the general education program, teachers should contact the special educator or their school principal.

The IEP coordinates the efforts of the team by specifying what the team is attempting to accomplish, who is responsible for implementing each component of the plan, which evaluation procedures will be used to determine the student's progress, and how the student's parent(s) will be regularly informed of progress. Development of the IEP requires the team to carefully review each student's needs. The time spent in this analysis helps to improve the quality and appropriateness of the educational experiences for students. See the "Inclusion Tips for the Teacher" section to learn more about the responsibilities of general educators in the IEP process.

> **PEARSON**
> **myeducationlab** Go to the Assignments and Activities section of Topic *Pre-Referrals, Placement and IEP Process* in the MyEducationLab for your course and complete the activity entitled *Understanding the IEP Document.*

The IEP team ensures that the student's educational program is implemented as specified in the written plan, once that plan has received parental approval. No change may be made in the services for the student unless the IEP is modified by the team and the changes approved by the student's parent(s).

Annual evaluation of the IEP is most typical, but it possible to review an IEP after a shorter time if one or more team members think the plan is in need of revision. When the IEP is reviewed, the team considers how much progress the student has made toward the annual goals. Throughout the year, the teachers who work with the student gather the assessment information required to gauge progress. Frequent data collection enables these teachers to make changes as needed in the instructional program, rather than waiting until the end of the year. Parents can also contribute to the ongoing assessment effort. It is important for them to continue their collaboration with the team and to incorporate their views of the child's progress in school into any team deliberations.

 ## TYPES OF SERVICES FOR STUDENTS WITH DISABILITIES

One of the most important components of the IEP is a description of the services the student will receive to support attainment of annual goals. Options include four types: special education, related services, supplementary aids and services, and program modifications and/or supports for school personnel.

Special education is defined by law as "specially designed instruction, at no cost to the parents, to meet the unique needs of a child with a disability." As the next section of this chapter describes, special education programs range from full inclusion with specially designed instruction provided by a special educator within the general education classroom setting to part-time, specially designed instruction in resource room settings to more intensive instructional services in special classes or even special schools or residential programs.

Some students require **related services** in order to benefit from special education. In the words of the law, related services are those supports "required to assist a child with a disability to benefit from special education." One example is transportation. A student who travels by wheelchair and who cannot board the regular school bus will not be able to benefit from the individualized instructional program that awaits at the school. Special transportation arrangements are needed to provide that student with access to special education.

There are many different types of related services, including the following.

- Transportation
- Speech-language pathology
- Audiology services for students with hearing impairments
- Psychological services
- Physical and occupational therapy
- Recreation (including therapeutic recreation services)
- Early identification and assessment of disabilities
- Counseling services (including rehabilitation counseling)
- Interpreting services for students who are deaf or hard of hearing
- Orientation and mobility services for students with visual impairments
- Diagnostic medical services
- School health and school nurse services
- Social work services
- Parent counseling and training.

Supplementary aids and services are another type of support for students with disabilities. According to the law, these are "aids, services, and other supports that are provided in regular education classes, other education-related settings, and in extracurricular and nonacademic settings, to enable children with disabilities to be educated with nondisabled children to the maximum extent appropriate." Thus, while related services allow students with disabilities to benefit from *special* education, supplementary aids and services allow students to take part in *general* education. One example is assistive technology. In the sample IEP that appeared in Figure 2-6, assistive technology assessment was one of the services planned for Steven. If that assessment shows assistive technology would help Steven with writing tasks, the technology would be provided and the assistive technology specialist would train Steven and his teacher in its use. Other examples of supplementary aids and services are peer tutors, taped textbooks for students with visual impairments, and classroom tables and desks that students who travel by wheelchair can roll under.

The fourth service type that IEPs can specify are **program modifications and/or supports for school personnel.** These options are not spelled out in the law, but their meaning appears quite clear. Program modifications are any type of change made in the general education program to support the successful progress of a student with disabilities. One example is a shortened school day for a student with a chronic illness who lacks the stamina to complete the entire day. In contrast, supports for school personnel are services provided to teachers and other school employees. Possibilities include training for teachers in how to use special devices and equipment needed by students with disabilities and part-time assistance from an instructional aide or community volunteer to help supervise classroom or recess activities.

▶ SPECIAL EDUCATION PROGRAM OPTIONS

Special education options vary in the opportunities offered to students with disabilities to participate in the general education program. In some programs, students spend the entire school day in the general education classroom (least restrictive); in others, students are excluded from any interaction with general education age peers (most restrictive). The remaining programs fall between these two extremes, providing a range of options with varying intensities of support.

The IEP team is tasked with ensuring that students are educated in the most appropriate setting that is also the Least Restrictive Environment (LRE). Although federal law requires the IEP team to address how students will "be involved in and make progress in the general education curriculum . . . [and] participate in extracurricular and other nonacademic activities" (IDEA 2004 Final Regulations, §300.320(a)(4)(ii)), full-time placement in the general education classroom is not the LRE for all students with disabilities. For some, a special class might be the LRE. Most students, however, benefit from spending at least a part of the school day in the general education classroom.

There are typically a number of special education program options for the team to consider when choosing the most appropriate, although options may differ from district to district. Possibilities range in intensity from full-time placement in the general education classroom to the rarely used options of home and hospital placement and residential schools. Families of infants and toddlers with or at risk for disabilities may participate in home-based programs; young adults with disabilities may be served in community-based vocational or transition programs.

Three major categories of placement options are available for students with disabilities, as seen in Figure 2-7. In the first, general education options, students with special needs are members of general education classes and the general education teacher takes primary responsibility for their instruction. These programs serve the greatest number of students with disabilities. In the second, special class options, students are members of special education classes, and the special education teacher takes primary responsibility for their educational program. The third, more restrictive options, serves the smallest number of students with disabilities. It is designed for students with severe, comprehensive, and specialized needs.

General Education Class Options

Full-time General Education Class. This is the least restrictive of the educational placement options. Students are not identified as having a disability. They spend their entire school day in the regular classroom; neither the students nor

FIGURE 2-7   Program Options

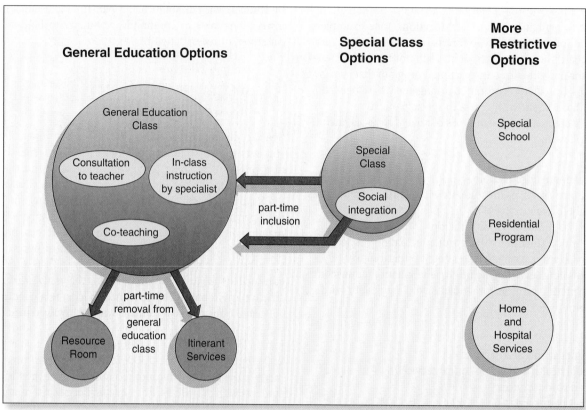

their teachers receive any direct special education services. Most students with special needs begin their educational careers in this setting and, for most, the goal of special education is to help them develop the skills needed for return to the general education classroom. For some students with more severe disabilities, however, this goal may not be realistic.

Indirect services that do not target any specific student may be provided to general education teachers and their classes. For example, teachers may receive in-service training from special educators on topics such as referral procedures or techniques for working with learning or behavioral problems. General education students may learn about different types of disabilities and acceptance of individuals different from themselves. Special educators may visit classrooms to discuss alternative communication strategies such as Braille and American sign language or to demonstrate electronic communication devices. In schools with peer tutoring or buddy programs, general education students may learn how to provide support and assistance to students with special needs.

It is important to remember that students with disabilities may not require special education services throughout their entire school career. For instance, a student with a hearing loss may have received special education services in the past but is now fitted with a hearing aid, trained to use and care for it, and able to use speechreading to supplement the information received via the hearing aid.

General Education Class with Consultation to the Teacher. Like the previous option, the student receives no direct services. However, the student's teacher does: A special educator provides consultation on the needs of students with disabilities who are included in the teacher's classroom.

Consultation can take a number of forms. A special education consultant or a school psychologist may help the teacher design and implement a positive behavioral support program for a student with behavior problems. An itinerant teacher of students with visual impairments may furnish materials such as large-print, Braille, or tape-recorded versions of class textbooks and provide the teacher with information about how best to use these resources. A resource teacher may collaborate with the teacher to modify general education reading or math instruction for a student with learning disabilities.

The goal of specialists in consultation is to assist teachers in developing the skills and confidence necessary to meet students' educational needs; it is not to evaluate classroom instruction or management. General education teachers should feel free to call on special education consultants for assistance in adapting instruction, managing behavioral problems, and promoting social acceptance of students with special needs.

General Education Class with Instruction Delivered by the Specialist. In this option, students with disabilities receive special education services within the general education classroom. Instead of leaving their classroom to visit a specialist, students remain where they are. The specialist comes to the students' class and delivers services there.

Special education services can be provided in the general education classroom by a special educator working alone or with a trained assistant. These staff members "can support integrated special students in many ways, including (a) making adaptations when needed; (b) assisting the classroom teacher in working with a student; (c) coaching nondisabled peers; (d) providing direct instruction; and (e) facilitating positive interactions among students" (Hamre-Nietupski, McDonald, & Nietupski, 1992, p. 8).

The amount of support offered depends upon the needs of the student. For students with mild learning needs, the specialist may visit the classroom each day to deliver a brief lesson to target students and peers with similar needs. Support may be needed throughout the day by students with more severe disabilities. Also, it is likely that the amount and nature of services required will change over the course of the school year. For example, as the school year goes on, the special educator may be able to decrease the amount of time spent in the classroom because a cadre of peer tutors has been trained to assist the student with special needs. Or, the need for assistance from a specialist may be reduced because the general education teacher has developed the skills and confidence necessary to work with the students with special needs in the classroom.

Benefits of this option for students with disabilities include reduction of the stigma associated with special education services, more opportunities for social interactions with age peers, and increased likelihood of continued exposure to the general education curriculum (Hamre-Nietupski et al., 1992; Wiedmeyer & Lehman, 1991). These authors also point out that the success of this type of program is dependent on ongoing collaboration between the general and special educators serving students with special needs.

General Education Class with Co-Teaching. A variation of the specialist teaching in a general education class is the co-teaching model. In this option, a general educator and a special educator co-teach a class composed of students with and without disabilities. For example, if the class includes 30 students, 20 may be typical students and 10 students may be identified as students with disabilities. The teachers share responsibility for all the students in the class, with the special educator providing specialized interventions for students with special needs, as required. Walsh and Jones (2004) reported that instruction in co-taught classrooms is more likely to reflect the general education curriculum and support the development of critical thinking skills than instruction in self-contained special education classes.

In a recent review of the research on co-teaching, Scruggs, Mastropieri, and McDuffie (2007) concluded that both general and special education teachers find co-teaching beneficial. However, special educators are most often relegated to the role of assistant rather than becoming a full partner in the educational enterprise of the general education classroom. Scruggs et al. comment that "the ideal of true collaboration between two equal partners—focused on curriculum needs, innovative practice, and appropriate individualization—has largely not been met" (p. 412).

General Education Class and Resource Room or Itinerant Services. In this option, special education services are typically provided to students in a setting outside the general education classroom. However, students continue to spend the majority of their school day in the general education class.

The resource room is usually located within the student's neighborhood school. At a regularly scheduled time each day (or several times a week), students leave the general education classroom to participate in special instruction in the resource room. Resource programs, common across the K–12 grade span, may serve a diverse group of students with disabilities (e.g., those with learning disabilities, physical impairments, mild mental retardation), or they may limit service to students with one particular disability.

Consultation services, such as those described earlier, are often provided for the general education teachers of the students enrolled in a resource room program. These services can assist the teacher and help coordinate general education and resource instructional activities.

Itinerant special education teachers travel from school to school. Again, students leave the classroom daily (or several times a week) to receive the services of itinerant teachers, such as those provided by speech-language pathologists. Whereas resource teachers generally serve students who spend the majority of their day in the general education class, itinerant teachers may also serve students educated in more intense options, such as special classes.

Resource and itinerant teachers are the special educators who serve the majority of students receiving special education services today. They supplement and support the general education program by providing assistance to students and to their teachers. Although the most usual option is for students to leave the classroom for special education services, those services may come to them when special educators (or their instructional aides) teach small instructional groups within the general education setting. In this service arrangement, the student is fully included and receives all instruction, both general and special education, within the general education classroom.

Special Classes and More Restrictive Options

Special Class and General Education Class. Special classes are located within regular elementary or secondary schools. Students receiving service in this placement option spend the majority of the school day in the special class and some time each day in the general education classroom. Participation in the general education class can vary from half a day to only a few minutes. This is the most restrictive of the educational environments in which students still spend time in the general education instructional program.

Students placed in this option need intensive special education services, and involvement in the general education program is planned in curriculum areas in which success is fairly certain. Participation in general education for such students is limited to the period of time in which they can function successfully without becoming frustrated or creating a disruption. General education teachers working with students in this option generally have consultation services available to assist them in designing and implementing appropriate instructional programs.

Full-time Special Class and Social Integration. An increased number of students with more severe disabilities are now educated on regular school campuses at all levels of education. This trend provides educators with the opportunity to integrate these students with their typical age peers whenever appropriate. Even if students do not attend academic classes, they can participate in social activities such as lunch periods, assemblies, or extracurricular and recreational activities. These activities offer students the opportunity to interact with typical peers and gain the skills needed to function independently. Some schools have a reverse inclusion program in which general education students take part in activities in the special class. These programs are particularly appropriate for preschool and early elementary students.

Full-Time Special Class. Students in this option are no longer included in the general education program; instead, they spend their entire school day in the special class. At one time, special classes were the primary special education option between general education classrooms and special schools. Their use has diminished as less restrictive programs, such as the resource room and teacher consultants, have become

popular. Today, the main goal of special classes is to provide an intensive program to develop skills that will prepare students for adulthood and, if possible, inclusion in the general education program.

Special School. Students are placed in this option on the premise that they cannot currently benefit from inclusion in the general education program. Special schools typically serve students with more severe disabilities (e.g., those with multiple disabilities, severe behavioral disorders, severe mental retardation). Although this option was quite popular in the past, concerns over the segregation of students with disabilities and their exclusion from the general education experience has led to the closing of special schools in many districts and the redistribution of students to special classes on regular school campuses (Pumpian, 1988; Sailor, Gee, & Karasoff, 1993).

Residential Program. Residential programs serve students who may require specialized educational services and medical care that cannot be provided either in public schools or by their parent(s) at home. Students may be identified as having severe behavioral disorders, severe intellectual disabilities, or multiple severe disabilities; others may be candidates for residential programs because they live in rural areas where specialized services are not available. In the residential setting, the 24-hour program permits the coordination of medical, psychological, educational, and other services.

Home and Hospital Services. A very small number of students receive their education at home or in a hospital setting. This arrangement is usually not permanent; a student might begin

Things to Remember

- Parents and professionals work together in teams to ensure that the education students receive meets their individual abilities and needs.

- Teams serving students with disabilities include general and special education teachers, school administrators, parents, students (as appropriate), and other professionals when needed.

- Federal law requires schools to identify students in need of special education services.

- After identification of a possible problem, the prereferral intervention team assists the general education teacher in making classroom changes in an attempt to solve the problem.

- The Response-to-Intervention (RTI) approach, also used prior to referral, is a newer and more comprehensive strategy for helping students meet the demands of the general education curriculum.

- Students are referred for consideration for special education services if prereferral interventions and RTI strategies do not improve their performance.

- The assessment team gathers information to determine if a student is eligible for special education services.

- If a student is found eligible, the IEP team plans his or her program, specifying annual goals, services needed (special education, related services, and supplementary aids and services), placement (with an explanation of any time spent away from the regular class), and procedures for monitoring and reporting student progress.

- Some students with disabilities are served under Section 504 of the federal Rehabilitation Act; their individualized plan for adaptations within the general education classroom is called a 504 Accommodation Plan.

- IEPs should be evaluated and revised at least annually. No placement should be considered permanent.

- General and special educators share responsibility for the education of students with disabilities who are included in general education.

- Most students with disabilities spend at least part of their school day in the general education classroom and receive part-time special education services from a resource or itinerant teacher within that classroom or in another location in the school.

the year in a general education classroom, then require hospital services followed by services in the home, but return to school before the end of the year. Students with physical and health impairments and those hospitalized because of mental health issues most often participate in this option. A teacher visits the student several times a week to provide instruction. If the student is a member of a general education class, the teacher of that class may be asked to help in choosing the student's assignments, books, and other materials.

Consult the "Things to Remember" section to review what you've learned in this chapter.

▶ **ACTIVITIES**

1. Visit a local school to find out about the school's teams that serve students with disabilities and other special needs. What are the teams called? Who serves on the teams? How often do they meet? Do they consider only students with disabilities? Gather information that will help you explain to another educator how these teams operate. If possible, obtain permission to observe a team meeting.

2. Interview a general education teacher and a special educator from the same school to find out about that school's policies for prereferral interventions for students struggling in the regular class. Does the school have a prereferral intervention team? If so, who are the members of the team? What happens when a teacher asks the team for help with a specific student? Also ask these educators if the school has begun to use the Response-to-Intervention (RTI) approach, either for all students experiencing difficulty in the general education classroom or to evaluate those with possible learning disabilities. If RTI is in use, what do the teachers think of this approach? Is it effective?

3. Read two journal articles on collaboration, the team approach, or consultation as it relates to the education of students with special needs. The journals *Exceptional Children* and *Remedial and Special Education* often address these topics. Write a brief summary and evaluation of each article you read.

4. Contact a local school district to find out what types of special education programs are offered. Are resource rooms, special classes, and other programs described in this chapter available? What about collaborations within the general education classroom such as co-teaching and in-class instruction by a specialist? How have program options changed in the past 5 years? Compare your findings with those of someone who has investigated another district. Explain why programs may vary from district to district.

5. Several organizations serve parents of special students. Two of the most prominent are the Learning Disabilities Association of America (LDA), found at www.ldanatl.org, and the Arc of the United States (formerly the Association for Retarded Citizens), found at www.thearc.org. Does your community have local chapters of these organizations? Contact a local, state, or national office of LDA or the Arc to learn the purpose or mission of these groups. Do they provide information about students with disabilities? Serve as advocates for parents? Work for better special education legislation? What should classroom teachers know about these organizations?

CHAPTER
THREE

Students with Disabilities and Other Types of Special Needs

- Jody's vision is limited. Her textbooks, worksheets, and other reading materials are in large print, and she uses a talking word processing program on the computer.
- Luis has diabetes. He takes medication to control this condition, and he carefully monitors his diet and physical activity.
- George has poor reading skills. He listens to taped textbooks for reading assignments, and he is learning to "take notes" in class with an audio recorder.
- Tom is impulsive and often leaves his seat, speaks out in class, and interrupts the work of other students. He and his teacher have set up a program to help Tom control these behaviors.
- Annette is very bright and academically far ahead of her peers. She works on special assignments in subjects that interest and challenge her.

LOOKING AHEAD

This chapter is all about the special needs of students with disabilities and others who may benefit from adaptations in the general education classroom. Before reading about these students, consider the questions that follow.

- Think about the students just described—Jody, Luis, George, Tom, and Annette. Which students have special needs in the area of academic performance?
- Which students have special emotional or classroom behavior needs? What about special social needs?
- Do any of these students show special physical needs?
- Do you think any of these students are gifted or talented? What evidence would you offer to support your opinion?

---

tudents with special needs such as those described in "Students' Stories" can succeed in the general education classroom with the assistance of the teacher and other members of the team. Because the educational needs of these students are not radically different from those of their peers, they can participate in many aspects of the general education program without special educational interventions. In areas where adaptations are necessary, support services are available to the student and to the classroom teacher. Special materials and equipment are provided, such as the large-print books needed by students with visual impairments and the taped and electronic texts needed by students with reading problems. The school nurse assists students with physical and health needs. The resource teacher works with the classroom teacher to set up behavior change programs for disruptive students

and enrichment activities for advanced students. In this way, the members of the team collaborate to meet the needs of students within the general education classroom.

 ## STUDENTS WITH SPECIAL NEEDS: AN OVERVIEW

Many students have special needs in school. Best known are those identified as having a disability, such as students with learning disabilities or those with behavioral disorders. However, this book includes other groups of students in discussions of special needs and the classroom modifications and adaptations required to address those needs. One group is made up of students who are gifted, those who are talented, and those who are both gifted and talented. Also of interest are students from culturally and linguistically diverse backgrounds, such as those students who enter school speaking a language other than English. Students at risk for school failure are also a concern; included here are truants, students at risk for dropping out of school, and those who are victims of child abuse and neglect.

The next sections of this chapter introduce each of these groups of students and provide an overview of the special needs they will face as members of the school community. It is important to recognize that most students with special needs are able to participate in general education classrooms because their learning problems are relatively mild. Teachers should

Special Needs

- A student may have a disability without being handicapped. A disability is some sort of impairment. It becomes a handicap only when it interferes with performance in some important area.
- Male students with special needs are more common than female students. No one knows exactly why this is so. It may be that males are more susceptible to the inheritance of learning problems and disabilities. Or it may be related to the cultural expectations for students of different genders.
- There is no relationship between physical impairments and intelligence. People with severe physical problems may be bright, and

individuals with intellectual disabilities may have no physical impairments.
- Most disabilities are not identified until students encounter difficulty in school. Children identified in the preschool years have serious or obvious disabilities or conditions that place them at risk for developmental delays.
- Given the right circumstances, any student could be considered culturally different. For example, a student who moves from Texas to New England will encounter new speech patterns, foods, social customs, and even sports activities.

---

also be aware that an individual student may fit within more than one group. For example, a gifted student may have a learning disability, a child who is learning English may be gifted, and students with behavioral disorders may be at risk for drug or alcohol abuse. To learn more about students with special needs, consult "For Your Information."

Students with special needs make up a sizable portion of the school community. In a collection of 100 students, there may be 9 or 10 with disabilities and 3 to 5 who are gifted. The number of students who are culturally and linguistically diverse varies from community to community depending on population patterns. The number of students at risk for school failure also varies widely from locale to locale.

STUDENTS WITH DISABILITIES

The most common disabilities identified in U.S. schools are learning disabilities, mild intellectual disabilities (also called *mild retardation*), behavioral disorders, and speech and language impairments. In contrast, physical, health, visual, and hearing impairments are relatively rare. Mild disabilities are much more frequent than severe disabilities. It is likely that at least 75% of the special education population has mild learning needs that can be met, at least in part, in a general education setting.

> **myeducationlab** To enhance your understanding of the needs of students with disabilities, go to the IRIS Center Resources section of Topic *Inclusive Practices* in the MyEducationLab for your course and complete the Module entitled *Accessing the General Education Curriculum: Inclusion Considerations for Students with Disabilities*.

It is important to note that not all disabilities are equally represented in the general education classroom. Figure 3-1 illustrates this, using terminology from federal laws (e.g., *mental retardation* in lieu of *intellectual disabilities*). As this figure shows, students with more severe and comprehensive disabilities (such as mental retardation and multiple disabilities) are more likely to be placed in separate classes and other separate environments. However, even for groups such as students with learning disabilities and those with speech or language impairments for whom inclusion is the most common practice,

some students require the more intensive, specialized services available in settings such as special classes.

Students with Learning Disabilities

Teachers often use the word *puzzling* to describe students with **learning disabilities**. These students are average, even bright, learners who encounter difficulties in specific school subjects. Because they seem capable and do learn some things quickly and easily, their failure to learn in other areas is perplexing.

> **myeducationlab** To hear a Teacher of the Year discuss helping learners who struggle, go to the Teacher Talk section of Topic *Learning Disabilities* in the MyEducationLab for your course and listen to the piece from *Pamela Herman, Alabama*.

Students with learning disabilities have at least average intelligence. Their learning problem is not due to hearing or visual impairments, physical or health impairments, or emotional disturbance. The reason for their poor school performance is much more subtle and elusive: They have difficulty processing information. **Information processing** (sometimes called *psychological processing*) refers to the way in which persons receive, store, and express information. Students with learning disabilities may have difficulty receiving information because of attention or perception problems, their memory may be poor, or they may have difficulty communicating information to others because of expressive language problems. Students with learning disabilities may use poor strategies for learning (Lenz, 2006; Robinson & Deshler, 1995; Swanson & Cooney, 1996). For example, when given a list of spelling words to learn or a textbook chapter to read, such students may simply stare at the page or read and reread it without actively engaging with its content.

Despite adequate general ability, students with learning disabilities experience school learning problems. They appear able to achieve, but their performance in school falls short of expectations. Even more perplexing than this discrepancy between expected and actual achievement is the variability of performance that characterizes individuals with learning disabilities. They are successful in some areas but have great difficulty in

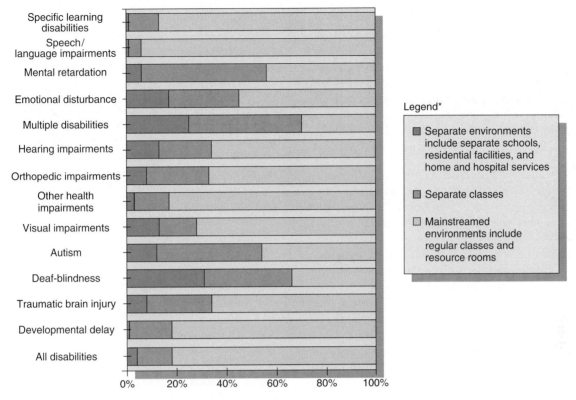

Note: From data provided in *28th Annual Report to Congress on the Implementation of the Individuals with Disabilities Education Act, Volume 1* by U.S. Department of Education, 2009, Washington, DC: Author.

others. In addition, their performance may vary from day to day; teachers often comment that students with learning disabilities appear to know something one day but forget it the next.

Many different labels have been used to describe students with learning disabilities. Although the emphasis today is on educational terminology, it is still possible to encounter medical terms such as *neurologically impaired*. Labels such as this refer to the theory that learning disabilities are due to some type of damage to the central nervous system. There are also medical terms for common academic problems: *dyslexia* (difficulty in reading), *dyscalculia* (difficulty in math), and *dysgraphia* (difficulty in writing). More recent additions to the medical terminology are *attention deficit disorder* (ADD) and *attention deficit hyperactivity disorder* (ADHD), two disorders distinct from but often associated with both learning disabilities and behavioral disorders.

Much debate has arisen over what constitutes a learning disability and how the condition should be defined. Federal special education law uses the following definition, which is an adaptation of that of an early advocacy group (National Advisory Committee on Handicapped Children, 1968):

Specific learning disability means a disorder in one or more of the basic psychological processes involved in understanding or in using language, spoken or written, that

may manifest itself in the imperfect ability to listen, think, speak, read, write, spell, or do mathematical calculations, including conditions such as perceptual disabilities, brain injury, minimal brain dysfunction, dyslexia, and developmental aphasia. Specific learning disability does not include learning problems that are primarily the result of visual, hearing, or motor disabilities, of mental retardation, of emotional disturbance, or of environmental, cultural, or economic disadvantage. (IDEA 2004 Final Regulations, §300.8(c)(10))

This definition, like most definitions of learning disabilities, excludes other disabilities and points to information processing deficits as the reason for poor school performance. In the general education classroom, students with learning disabilities may have special needs in the areas of academic, behavioral, social, and physical performance.

Academic Needs. Students with learning disabilities typically experience difficulty in one or more of the basic school subjects. Young children may enter school with poor listening or speaking skills. In the early grades, acquisition of language arts skills such as reading and spelling may prove difficult. For most elementary-aged students with learning disabilities, reading is the major stumbling block in academic achievement. However, some fare well in this area, yet have specific disabilities in other subjects such as math, written expression, or handwriting.

The basic skill problems of students with learning disabilities persist into middle school, high school, and beyond. These students may fail to acquire reading, writing, and perhaps math skills equal to those of their peers. Although able to cope with the content of secondary-level courses, many students with learning disabilities achieve poorly because of their inability to read texts and complete written assignments. Those with poor listening skills find lecture presentations a serious problem.

Behavioral Needs. Some students with learning disabilities, particularly in the elementary grades, are characterized by a high activity level. Such students may be constantly in motion and, as a result, may have difficulty paying attention to school tasks. Others who are not overactive may instead be impulsive and distractible; they, too, may have difficulty focusing their attention on appropriate aspects of the learning environment.

Older students with learning disabilities often have behavioral needs in the areas of classroom conduct and study skills. They may be unable to work independently (at least in part because of poor academic skills). Their attention span may continue to be a problem, and their organizational skills may be poor. In addition, some evidence exists of a link between juvenile delinquency and learning disabilities in adolescents (e.g., Quinn, Rutherford, & Leone, 2001).

Social Needs. The social arena is another area in which students with learning disabilities may perform poorly. Research suggests that some children and adolescents with learning disabilities have social perception deficits (e.g., Bryan, 1997). That is, they may lack the skills needed for understanding and communicating appropriate social messages (National Center for Learning Disabilities, Inc., 2007). Social communication requires not only speech but also an understanding of more subtle cues such as facial expression, vocal inflection, and body language; it becomes particularly important when students enter the peer-conscious world of the adolescent.

Physical Needs. Students with learning disabilities do not have obvious physical needs: in appearance they are indistinguishable from their peers. However, some students with learning disabilities have motor coordination problems. They may appear clumsy and may perform gross-motor skills, such as running and jumping, poorly. Fine-motor skills such as using scissors to cut, manipulating small objects, and mastering the use of pencils and pens may also be troublesome areas. In school, motor problems such as these become evident in physical education and art activities and in academic tasks requiring handwriting.

Special Services. For students with learning disabilities severe and comprehensive enough to warrant placement in separate programs, many districts offer special classes. However, the majority of students with learning disabilities remain in general education throughout their school careers and receive special services on a part-time basis from professionals such as resource teachers. Because students with learning disabilities have average ability and are able to perform as well as general education students in some areas, they are excellent candidates for inclusion.

Students with Behavioral Disorders

Behavioral disorders are a more obvious disability than learning disabilities. Students with behavioral disorders are often described by teachers as "behavior problems" or "troublemakers." They may be rowdy, unruly, disruptive, and even aggressive. Some, whose behavior does not call attention to itself as readily, may appear withdrawn or depressed. All are characterized by inappropriate school behavior. Although most students with behavioral disorders have adequate intelligence as well as acceptable hearing, vision, and physical abilities, they often show poor achievement in academic skills. Some students, however, achieve satisfactorily despite inappropriate classroom behavior.

The term *behavioral disorders* includes a wide range of disabilities. The most severe are seen in students with serious emotional disturbances, such as individuals with psychotic behavior and childhood schizophrenia; such students generally require intensive special education services and are not included in general education instructional programs. However, most students with behavioral disorders have relatively mild problems that can be dealt with successfully in general education. In fact, the special needs of many of these students are virtually identical to those of the problem student found in every classroom.

PEARSON
myeducationlab) Go to the Assignments and Activities section of Topic *Emotional and Behavioral Disorders* in the MyEducationLab for your course and complete the activity entitled *Students with Emotional and Behavioral Disorders in the Inclusive General Education Classroom.*

Even though apparently obvious, the disability of behavioral disorders is difficult to describe and define. It is necessary to decide which behaviors are appropriate and which are not. The problem is further complicated by the fact that all students behave inappropriately at one time or another in their school careers. Kauffman (1997) sidesteps some of these problems by describing students with behavioral disorders as

> those who chronically and markedly respond to their environment in socially unacceptable and/or personally unsatisfying ways but who can be taught more socially acceptable and personally gratifying behavior (p. 23).

This definition contains several important points. First, behavioral disorders are chronic and severe. The student's behavior must be inappropriate over time, not a one-time occurrence. The student's behavior problem must also be serious; it must in some way impair the student's ability to function in the school environment. Second, behaviors are judged to be inappropriate by either social or personal standards. This allows not only teachers and parents but also students themselves to determine problem behaviors. It also provides for inclusion of behaviors such as withdrawal that may be socially acceptable but are detrimental to the student. Third, the definition recognizes that behavior is learned and that students with behavioral disorders are able to acquire more acceptable responses to their environment. This point is crucial for teachers who seek to change the behavior of their students.

The definition in current special education law uses the term *emotional disturbance* rather than the term preferred today in the profession. This definition, which is based on the early work of Bower (1969), describes students with emotional disturbance as those who show at least one of the following characteristics "to a marked degree" and "over a long period of time":

a. An inability to learn that cannot be explained by intellectual, sensory, or health factors.

b. An inability to build or maintain satisfactory interpersonal relationships with peers and teachers.

c. Inappropriate types of behaviors or feelings under normal circumstances.

d. A general, pervasive mood of unhappiness or depression.

e. A tendency to develop physical symptoms or fears associated with personal or school problems (IDEA 2004 Final Regulations, §300.8(c)(14)(i))

A student need not exhibit all five of these characteristics to be identified as having an emotional disturbance; only one is necessary, although students may meet several of the criteria. This definition stresses the educational aspects of this disability by focusing on learning problems, student–teacher relationships, and school phobia problems.

The Council for Children with Behavioral Disorders (CCBD), a division of the Council for Exceptional Children, is critical of the definition found in current laws and recommends this revision:

> The term "emotional or behavior disorder" means a disability that is characterized by behavioral or emotional responses in school programs so different from appropriate age, cultural, or ethnic norms that the responses adversely affect educational performance . . . (CCBD, 2000).

According to CCBD, this definition reflects current professional knowledge and research and is endorsed by prominent mental health and education organizations.

As Heward (1996) remarks, definitions of behavioral disorders "require a child's behavior, in order to be considered disordered, to differ markedly (extremely) and chronically (over time) from current social or cultural norms" (p. 286). In the general education classroom, this means that students with behavioral disorders may have special needs in the areas of social and academic, as well as behavioral, performance.

Behavioral Needs. Children and adolescents with behavioral disorders are a heterogeneous group that exhibits a wide range of inappropriate classroom behaviors. These students may be disobedient, aggressive, or overly shy and retiring. One way to conceptualize this array of possible problem behaviors is to think about behaviors that are either externalizing or internalizing (Heward, 2006). Externalizing behaviors are consistent with those patterns of disordered behaviors described by Quay (1979) as conduct disorder and socialized aggression, whereas internalizing behaviors are consistent with the patterns described as immaturity and anxiety–withdrawal.

Students with conduct disorders are aggressive, defiant, uncooperative, disobedient, and disruptive. Their behavior is judged socially unacceptable by teachers and others in authority. Students falling under the socialized aggression dimension also are perceived as behaving inappropriately. They are socialized in that they belong to gangs, but they participate in delinquent activities such as truancy and theft. Less obvious are the internalizing dimensions of immaturity and anxiety–withdrawal. Immature students appear delayed in development; they may be passive, have a short attention span, appear preoccupied, and daydream. Students characterized by anxiety and withdrawal appear fearful, timid, depressed, and lacking in self-confidence.

Students with behavioral disorders may have difficulty following classroom rules and meeting teachers' expectations for appropriate school conduct. Although aggressive students are the ones most easily and quickly identified by teachers, withdrawn and immature students also require special help. In middle school and high school, the truancy problems of pre-delinquent and delinquent students complicate their difficulties in meeting school demands.

Social Needs. Students with behavioral disorders often have trouble establishing interpersonal relationships. Their inappropriate behaviors may make them unattractive to peers and to teachers. They may lack the social skills necessary to make and keep friends. In addition, the self-concept of students with behavioral disorders is often low, especially in individuals who are anxious and withdrawn. And the problem perpetuates itself. Students with poor social skills have few friends and their self-esteem suffers; students with low self-esteem are unwilling to risk interpersonal relationships.

Academic Needs. Students with behavioral disorders, like those with learning disabilities, often experience difficulty with basic school skills (Sabornie, Cullinan, Osborne, & Brock, 2005; Whelan, 1995). Most studies of the academic achievement of students with behavioral disorders find poor performance in reading, math, and other subjects such as written language (e.g., Lane, Barton-Arwood, Nelson, & Wehby, 2008), although there is some evidence that mathematics provides the most difficult challenge to these students (Nelson, Benner, Lane, & Smith, 2004). The precise relationship between academic underachievement and inappropriate classroom behavior, however, is difficult to assess. Students may act out or withdraw as a reaction to school failure, or problem behaviors may interfere with successful school learning. In either case, most students with behavioral disorders require instruction in both behavioral and academic skills.

Special Services. Some students with behavioral disorders require intensive special education services in special classes, special schools, and even residential facilities. Most, however, are able to participate in at least some aspects of regular classroom instruction. Some may spend part of their day in a special class and part in general education. Others take part more fully in general education class activities and receive only part-time special services. The general education classroom is usually the most appropriate placement for students with mild behavioral disorders, provided, of course, that necessary support services are available to students and teachers.

Students with Mild Intellectual Disabilities

Traditionally, the term *mental retardation* was used to describe students with comprehensive learning problems. However, professionals today often prefer the term **intellectual disabilities.** Both terms describe students with below-average intellectual ability who learn slowly and appear delayed in most areas of school performance when compared with their age peers. Tasks requiring reasoning and abstract thinking may be particularly difficult for them.

> **PEARSON**
> **myeducationlab** To enhance your understanding of the needs of students with mild intellectual disabilities, go to the IRIS Center Resources section of Topic *Intellectual Disabilities* in the MyEducationLab for your course and complete the Module entitled *What Do You See? Perceptions of Disability.*

Mental retardation is one of the oldest areas of study within the field of special education, and there is general agreement regarding the definition of this disability. According to the American Association on Mental Retardation (AAMR), now known as the American Association on Intellectual and Developmental Disabilities (AAIDD),

> Mental retardation is a disability characterized by substantial limitations both in intellectual functioning and in adaptive behavior as expressed in conceptual, social, and practical adaptive skills. This disability originates before age 18. . . . (2002, p. 8).

Less-than-average intelligence is central to the concept of intellectual disabilities. Individuals considered retarded are those whose general aptitude for learning is impaired. Intellectual functioning is assessed by intelligence or IQ tests; these measures typically contain several types of verbal and nonverbal reasoning and problem-solving tasks. General ability level is established by comparing the performance of one student with that of others of the same age. Individuals who fall within the lowest 2% to 3% are considered retarded; that is, their intellectual performance is significantly subaverage in comparison to that of their peers. However, as Heward (2006) points out, measurement of intelligence is not an exact science, and it is possible for IQ scores to change significantly over time.

In addition to limitations in intellectual functioning, students must also show impaired adaptive behavior in order to meet criteria for mental retardation. Adaptive behavior, sometimes referred to as social competence, is "the effectiveness or degree with which individuals meet the standards of personal independence and social responsibility expected for their age and cultural group" (Grossman, 1983, p. 1). It is the way in which students meet the expectations of the total social environment, not merely those of the school. Expectations for adaptive

behavior vary with the age of the student. Parents expect preschool youngsters to learn to walk, talk, and interact with family members; teachers expect school-aged children to learn to read, write, do math, and interact with peers; society expects adults to be gainfully employed and to get along in the community. Expectations also vary across cultures. For example, while American teachers expect their students to ask questions and participate in discussions, Asian parents may expect their children to be quiet and obedient and listen to adults without asking questions or challenging their authority (Cheng, 1991).

Thus, students with mental retardation are characterized by both below-average intellectual ability and deficits in adaptive behavior. A low IQ score alone is not sufficient to determine retardation; the student's learning problem must be substantiated in the home, neighborhood, and community. The problem must also become apparent during the developmental period (i.e., before age 18). Older persons whose intellectual abilities are impaired by an injury, accident, or illness are not considered mentally retarded.

Within the group of students considered mentally retarded are several levels of abilities. Students with mild retardation (or mild intellectual disabilities, the term that is used in this book), are those who are able to learn basic academic skills. The special needs of students with severe retardation are more serious and comprehensive. Students with severe disabilities may be educated in a full-day special class; such classes are typically located on regular school campuses to facilitate social interactions between students with severe disabilities and typical students. In some cases, however, students with severe disabilities are fully included in general education classes with support from special education personnel. Severe disabilities are discussed more fully in a later section of this chapter.

Many students with mild intellectual disabilities are able to participate in at least some of the instructional activities of the regular classroom. The special needs of this group, which makes up approximately 80% of the population identified as mentally retarded, are in the areas of academic, behavioral, social, and physical performance.

Academic Needs. Students with mild intellectual disabilities generally master academic skills at a slower rate than regular class students of the same age. Because they enter school somewhat behind their peers, they may not be ready to begin formal academic instruction immediately. Individuals with mild intellectual disabilities are able to acquire basic school skills, but their achievement is below grade-level expectations. Nonetheless, most such students acquire upper-elementary-level reading and math skills by the completion of their school careers (Cole, Waldron, & Majd, 2004; Heward, 2006; Kirk & Gallagher, 1979).

Some aspects of school learning are especially troublesome for students with mild intellectual disabilities. They may have difficulty focusing their attention, remembering, and transferring information and skills learned in one setting to another situation. Tasks involving abstract reasoning, problem solving, and creativity pose special problems. For example, students with mild intellectual disabilities perform less well on arithmetic reasoning tasks than on straightforward computational problems.

In the elementary years, the discrepancy between the age of students with mild intellectual disabilities and their achievement level is not great. In adolescence, the gap widens. At the secondary level, such students often participate in special programs that stress vocational training. Despite their evident learning needs, students with mild intellectual disabilities may be identified as retarded only during their school years. Outside the school environment with its academic demands, many individuals with mild intellectual disabilities do not have obvious needs.

Behavioral Needs. As a group, students with mild intellectual disabilities display more problem behaviors than their general education peers, perhaps because of their slower rate of learning. Their repertoire of classroom behavioral skills may be appropriate for their developmental level but not for their age group. Another possible factor is the low tolerance for frustration of many students with mild intellectual disabilities. Repeated failure in school and social situations contributes to this decreased capacity for handling frustration.

Social Needs. Students with mild intellectual disabilities may not be socially accepted by their age peers. Lacking social skills, they may be rejected or ignored. This difficulty in establishing interpersonal relationships may be the result of the apparent immaturity of students with mild intellectual disabilities. Their social skills are not well developed in comparison with those of their age peers, and their problem behaviors may make them unattractive. Also, the play and leisure interests of these students may be inappropriate for their age.

Physical Needs. Not all individuals with mild intellectual disabilities have special physical needs; indeed, some excel in the physical area. However, as a group, these students are somewhat deficient in motor skills. When compared with their age peers, they perform less well in tasks requiring agility, coordination, strength, and dexterity (Bruininks, 1977). In addition, youngsters with mild intellectual disabilities show visual problems and hearing losses more frequently than do typical students.

Special Services. Students with mild intellectual disabilities are educated in a range of settings. Some are placed in a special class but may attend general education programs for nonacademic activities. Others are members of general education classes for the majority of the day while receiving part-time special education services. As with all special students, decisions regarding the amount of inclusion for pupils with mild intellectual disabilities must be made on an individual basis.

To learn more about intellectual disabilities as well as other types of disabilities, visit the National Dissemination Center for Children with Disabilities described in "Window on the Web."

WINDOW ON THE WEB

National Dissemination Center for Children with Disabilities

The National Dissemination Center for Children with Disabilities is funded by the U.S. Office of Special Education Programs to provide information to the nation on the following topics.

- Disabilities in infants, young children, and youth
- IDEA, which is the law authorizing special education
- No Child Left Behind (as it relates to children with disabilities)
- Research-based information on effective educational practices

The Dissemination Center takes the place of an earlier information service, the National Information Center for Children and Youth

with Disabilities, but retains many of its features as well as new resources.

Visit the site to subscribe to its electronic newsletter ("News You Can Use"), learn about publications related to disabilities (e.g., Questions Often Asked by Parents about Special Education Services), and consult the Center's resources on topics such as Disabilities, Laws, Research, and News. There are separate resource pages for families and communities, early intervention providers, school and administrators, and state agencies. The website is available in both English and Spanish.

http://www.nichcy.org

Students with Other Disabilities

Many general education classrooms include students with disabilities other than learning disabilities, behavioral disorders, and mild intellectual disabilities. Among these are students with speech and language impairments, physical and health impairments, traumatic brain injury, and the sensory disorders of visual and hearing impairments. Students with ADD and ADHD are also frequently served in general education settings. Students with autism spectrum disorder and those with other severe disabilities participate in general education programs in some districts; in others, they receive more comprehensive special education services.

Communication Disorders. Among the most common of all disabilities are **speech and language impairments.** According to Van Riper's (1978) classic definition, speech is considered abnormal "when it deviates so far from the speech of other people that it calls attention to itself, interferes with communication, or causes the speaker or his [or her] listeners to be distressed" (p. 43). Articulation disorders, or difficulty with the production of sounds, are the most typical speech problem, especially in young children. Other possible trouble areas include voice problems and disorders of fluency, such as stuttering.

Speech is the production of sounds for the communication of oral language. Oral language includes not only the expression of messages by speaking but also the reception of messages by listening. Students with language impairments may experience difficulty in either or both areas. Some students show an overall delay in language development. Others have particular difficulty with a specific component, such as grammatical structure (syntax) or the meaningful aspects of language (semantics).

In the general education classroom, students with speech and language impairments have special academic and social needs. In addition to receiving special help from speech-language pathologists, they may require instruction in listening skills, vocabulary, grammar, and oral expression. In the social area, students with communication problems may find interpersonal encounters stressful. Such students may need assistance in order to become full participants in classroom social interactions.

Physical and Health Impairments. This group of students is relatively small (less than 1% of the school-aged population) but extremely diverse. **Physical and health impairments** encompass a multitude of different conditions and disabilities that range from mild to severe and from invisible to obvious. According to Sirvis (1982), this group includes individuals with *functional limitations* "related to physical skills such as hand use, trunk control, mobility" (p. 384) and individuals with *medical conditions* that affect strength and stamina.

Students with physical impairments include those with missing limbs, spinal cord injuries causing paralysis, and conditions such as muscular dystrophy. Two of the most common physical problems are cerebral palsy and epilepsy. Cerebral palsy is a motor impairment caused by damage to the brain; it results in difficulty with coordination. Epilepsy is a convulsive disorder; students with epilepsy may have seizures during which they lose consciousness and motor control. Examples of health problems that may affect school performance are diabetes, cardiac conditions, asthma, hemophilia, and cancer.

In the general education classroom, students with physical and health impairments may encounter few difficulties; if special needs do arise, they are likely to be in the areas of physical, academic, and social performance. Special services may be provided by adaptive physical education teachers or other motor specialists; school nurses help with students needing special diets, medication, or activity restrictions. For students with physical mobility problems (such as individuals who walk using crutches or those who travel by wheelchair), the physical environment of the school may need to be modified to allow access. Instructional materials are adapted for students whose physical problems make writing difficult. Although students with physical and health impairments are not poor achievers as a group, those with chronic medical conditions may miss much school and may fall behind their peers as a result. Social acceptance is another possible problem area, particularly for students with conspicuous disabilities.

Attention Deficit Hyperactivity Disorder. Lerner, Lowenthal, and Lerner (1995) describe this disorder as a "condition characterized by developmentally inappropriate attention skills, impulsivity, and, in some cases, hyperactivity" (p. 4). In its definition of **attention deficit hyperactivity disorder (ADHD),** the American Psychiatric Association (1994) differentiates three subgroups: predominantly inattentive, predominantly hyperactive-impulsive, and combined (i.e., showing inattentiveness, hyperactivity, and impulsivity). ADHD appears to be quite common; the U.S. Department of Education (1991) estimates that 3% to 5% of the school-aged population has significant educational problems related to ADHD. Students with ADHD may experience difficulty in academic achievement in addition to their behavioral problems.

Students with ADHD are served in both general and special education settings. Students with ADHD can receive adjustments in the general education program under Section 504 of the Rehabilitation Act of 1973 (U.S. Department of Education, 1991). In addition, IDEA includes students with ADHD under the disability category "other health impairment." According to the regulations for IDEA 2004, this category contains students with

> . . . limited strength, vitality or alertness, *including a heightened alertness to environmental stimuli*, that results in limited alertness with respect to the educational environment. . . . [italics added] (IDEA 2004 Final Regulations, §300.8(c)(9)).

Students with ADD or ADHD fit that portion of the definition related to "heightened alertness." Some students also meet eligibility qualifications for disabilities such as learning disabilities or emotional disturbance and receive special education and related services under those categories.

Traumatic Brain Injury. Traumatic brain injury was recognized as a distinct disability separate from other physical impairments by the 1990 IDEA. The National Head Injury Foundation Task Force defines traumatic brain injury as "an insult to the brain, not of a degenerative or congenital nature, but caused by an external physical force that may produce a diminished or altered state of consciousness which results in impairment of cognitive abilities" (as cited in Tucker & Colson, 1992, p. 198). The most common causes of head injuries in school-aged individuals are motor vehicle accidents, falls, sports injuries, and, in some parts of the country, assaults (Mira & Tyler, 1991). Students with traumatic brain injury often have physical, academic, and social-behavioral needs. Such students receive educational services in hospital settings, at home, and in a variety of school placements, including general education classrooms.

Sensory Disorders. Another small group of students with disabilities includes those with **visual impairments** and **hearing impairments.** Many school-aged individuals are able to see and hear normally despite visual and hearing problems; their difficulties either have responded to medical treatment or are corrected by devices such as eyeglasses or hearing aids. Such students are not considered to have a disability. Only those whose senses remain impaired after treatment and correction are identified as having a visual or hearing impairment.

Students with visual impairments may be **blind** or may have **low vision.** Individuals who are blind receive so little information through the eyes that they must learn through their other senses; for example, they may use the sense of touch to read Braille. Students with low vision, although visually impaired, are able to use their residual vision to learn. In the general education class, students with visual problems may have physical, academic, and social needs. They may require assistance in learning to move about the school and classroom environments; itinerant or resource teachers assist by teaching these students basic orientation and mobility skills. Specialists also locate and provide any special materials and equipment needed for academic instruction; some examples are large-print books, Braille materials, raised or embossed maps, tape recorders and taped textbooks, magnification devices, and computers with speech output. In the social area, students with visual impairments may need encouragement to interact with sighted peers.

Students with hearing impairments may be **deaf** or **hard of hearing.** Individuals who are hard of hearing hear well enough to understand speech, usually with the assistance of a hearing aid. Students who are deaf, however, receive so little information through the ears that the sense of hearing is not useful for speech comprehension. In the general education classroom, students with hearing impairments may have special physical, academic, and social needs. Difficulty in speech and language development is one of the major educational problems associated with hearing loss. Students with hearing impairments may require classroom adaptations in order to use the skills taught by special educators.

For example, sitting near the front of the classroom helps in hearing or speechreading the verbal instructions of the teacher.

Some students with hearing impairments communicate with speech; others use a manual communication system such as sign language. Interpreters may accompany some students who are deaf to the classroom, particularly at the secondary level; interpreters are hearing individuals who translate the spoken word into manual signs and vice versa. Students with hearing losses may be academically delayed in subjects related to language, such as reading, spelling, and written expression; they may receive special instruction from a resource or itinerant teacher in these areas. Speech and language problems may also inhibit the social interaction of students with hearing losses. If they communicate via speech, articulation problems may make them difficult to understand; those who use manual communication may be isolated from peers unless the peers have also acquired basic signing skills.

Autism Spectrum Disorder. Kauffman (1997) calls **autism spectrum disorder** a "pervasive developmental disorder" because it affects all areas of functioning and is identified before a child reaches 3 years of age. Individuals with this disorder have difficulty engaging in interactions with other people; experience marked delays in language development; may use echolalic speech (i.e., instead of responding to a question, the person with autism echoes or repeats the question); and engage in behaviors such as tantrums, repetitive activities, and stereotyped movements (Kauffman, 1997; Lovaas & Newsom, 1976).

Experts often disagree about autism. Some maintain that it is a severe behavioral disorder; others suggest it is a severe disorder of language or a type of health impairment (Heward & Orlansky, 1992). Because of this controversy, autism was designated as a separate disability under 1990 IDEA. Clearly, students with this disorder have special needs in all areas: behavioral, social, academic, and physical performance. These students are often served in special schools or classes. In recent years, some students with autism spectrum disorder have been placed in general education classes as part of the full inclusion movement. When that occurs, special education personnel must provide comprehensive support services in the regular classroom to assist the general education teacher and increase the probability that the student will benefit from the inclusion experience.

Severe Disabilities. Students with severe disabilities have the most serious and comprehensive needs of all the individuals served by special education. Such students have severe intellectual disabilities and/or show significant developmental delays; their cognitive disabilities are often accompanied by physical, health, communication, and sensory impairments. The U.S. Department of Education describes students with severe disabilities as those

> who because of the intensity of their physical, mental, or emotional problems, or a combination of such problems, need highly specialized educational, social, psychological,

and medical services beyond those which are traditionally offered by regular and special education programs, in order to maximize their potential for useful and meaningful participation in society and for self-fulfillment. (*Federal Register,* 1988, p. 118, as cited in Heward, 1996)

In the past, students with severe disabilities were served in special schools and residential programs. Today, however, these students typically attend special classes in regular schools. Like students with autism spectrum disorder, students with severe disabilities are fully included in general education classes in some districts.

In working with special educators and others who serve students with disabilities, one of the first things that most general educators notice is terminology. Because special education is a technical field, many terms are used to describe disabilities. Abbreviations, designed as shortcuts in communication, are also used abundantly. However, statements like "Joel has been identified as being BD and LD, and his IEP says the RR is the LRE for him" certainly do not further communication.

Translations of some of the common abbreviations used in special education are listed in the "For Your Information" feature.

Causes of Learning Problems

For most special students, the cause, or **etiology**, of their learning problem is unknown. Although a host of causative agents has been identified, it is often impossible to state with certainty which was responsible for the disability of a particular student.

Causes can be classified according to when they occurred in the life of the individual: prenatal (before birth), perinatal (during the birth process), or postnatal (after birth). An example of a prenatal cause is rubella or German measles. If contracted by a woman during the first 3 months of her pregnancy, rubella can lead to hearing, visual, physical, and cognitive impairments in the fetus as it develops. Oxygen deprivation during the birth process is a perinatal cause, whereas a head injury sustained in an automobile accident at 3 years of age is a postnatal cause.

Another view of etiology is the dichotomy of hereditary and environmental factors. Some types of deafness are inherited, and

---

For Your Information

Making Sense of Special Education Abbreviations

Special educators are sometimes accused of speaking in jargon and "alphabet soup." Here are some of the abbreviations commonly used in discussions of students with disabilities. If you hear one that is not on this list and you fail to understand its meaning, stop the speaker and ask for an explanation. Remember that communication can occur only if the listener is able to comprehend the speaker's message.

ADA	The Americans with Disabilities Act of 1990
ADD	Attention deficit disorder
ADHD	Attention deficit hyperactivity disorder
BD	Behavioral disorder; often used synonymously with *emotional disturbance* (ED) or *serious emotional disturbance* (SED)
DHH	Deaf and hard of hearing
ED	Emotional disturbance
FAPE	Free and appropriate public education; refers to the basic guarantee of federal special education laws such PL 94-142, the Education for All Handicapped Children Act, and the Individuals with Disabilities Education Act (IDEA) and its amendments
HH	Hard of hearing
HI	Hearing impairment
ID	Intellectual disabilities
IDEA	The Individuals with Disabilities Education Act of 1990
IDEA 2004	The Individuals with Disabilities Education Improvement Act of 2004
IEP	Individualized Education Program
LD	Learning disability; also called *specific learning disability* (SLD) and *language and learning disability* (LLD)

LLD	Language and learning disability
LRE	Least Restrictive Environment
MMR	Mild mental retardation
MR	Mental retardation
NCLB	The No Child Left Behind Act of 2002
OHI	Other health impairment; refers to health disorders
OI	Orthopedic impairment; refers to a physical impairment involving the skeletal system
PH	Physical handicap; an older term that refers to physical impairment
PL	Public Law, as in PL 94-142
POHI	Physical and other health impairment
RR	Resource room
RTI	Response to Intervention; a method for identifying students in need of special education by evaluating their achievement when provided high-quality instruction
SC	Special class, also called *special day class* (SDC)
SDC	Special day class
SED	Serious emotional disturbance; used in federal law to refer to emotional disturbance (ED)/behavioral disorders (BD)
SH	Severely handicapped; often used to describe individuals with severe retardation and/or multiple serious disabilities
SLD	Specific learning disability
TBI	Traumatic brain injury
VI	Visual impairment

---

there is some indication that reading problems tend to run in families. Environmental causes of learning problems include poor nutrition, lack of sensory stimulation, and inadequate instruction.

The causes of learning problems are of interest for two reasons: treatment and prevention. Medical research has developed treatments for some known etiologies and preventive techniques for others. For example, the Salk vaccine has virtually eliminated the crippling disease of polio in the United States, and progress is being made in the use of gene therapy for conditions such as muscular dystrophy. In education, the emphasis is on environmental causes of learning problems. Research indicates that providing appropriate early educational experiences for children with special needs may lessen or prevent later learning problems (Casto & Mastropieri, 1986; White, Bush, & Casto, 1986). Education itself is one of the environmental influences on students, one that can precipitate learning problems. Poor or inappropriate instruction has been cited as a major factor in the development of school problems. Reynolds and Birch (1982) contend that "most pupil behaviors called learning disabilities and behavior disorders are best acknowledged as the consequences of failure to provide enough high quality individualized instruction" (p. 237). A more optimistic viewpoint is that high-quality instruction has the power to enhance the achievement of all students, including those who enter the classroom challenged by special needs.

 GIFTED AND TALENTED STUDENTS

In addition to typical students, general education classrooms usually contain not only students with disabilities but also individuals with special gifts and talents. **Gifted and talented students,** who are estimated to make up 3% to 5% of the school-aged population, may be exceptionally bright (i.e., gifted), have special talents in areas such as art or music, or be both gifted and talented. One definition of this group is found in federal law:

> The term *gifted and talented children* means children and, whenever applicable, youth who are identified at the preschool, elementary, or secondary level as possessing demonstrated or potential abilities that give evidence of high performance capabilities in areas such as intellectual, creative, specific academic, or leadership ability, or in the performing and visual arts . . . (Section 902, PL 95-561, Gifted and Talented Children's Act of 1978)

Gifted students are characterized by above-average performance on measures of intellectual performance; they may excel academically in all subjects or be particularly advanced in one. Some have creative ability that allows them to produce unusual or novel solutions to problems. Talented students may excel in leadership, drama, art, music, dance, or other areas.

Many states provide special educational opportunities for this diverse group of students. Some gifted individuals are allowed to enter school early and accelerate quickly through the curriculum, perhaps skipping one or several grades. Others attend special schools or classes. Most common, however, is regular class placement with part-time special services either in a resource setting or through special enrichment activities such as seminars or after-school programs.

In the general education classroom, gifted and talented students may have special academic and social needs. Those who are advanced academically benefit from special learning projects and assignments to help them continue their development. Some, however, although bright, may achieve poorly in relation to their potential; for example, they may be unmotivated, lack prerequisite skills, become bored with what they perceive as elementary-level instruction, or fail to achieve because a disability interferes with their performance. Students who are creative and talented may be academically advanced or typical of individuals their own age; whatever their academic ability, they require guidance to develop their talents. Some gifted and talented students have excellent social skills; others, especially those with extraordinary abilities, may need assistance in relating to their age peers. It is also possible for special populations to overlap. A culturally diverse student with a disability may also be identified as gifted, and some gifted youngsters may be at risk for school failure.

 CULTURALLY AND LINGUISTICALLY DIVERSE STUDENTS

In most cities and towns in the United States today, **culturally and linguistically diverse students** are members of general education classrooms alongside their typical peers and those with special learning needs. Culturally diverse individuals are those reared in a culture that is at variance with that found in the school or different from the dominant culture in the United States. These students face at least two sets of expectations—those of the home and those of the school—and many times these expectations are discrepant. Included within this group are linguistically diverse students; these youngsters may speak languages other than English or be bilingual, speaking English and the language of the home. Some culturally and linguistically diverse students have special learning needs; others do not.

---

myeducationlab Go to the Building Teaching Skills and Dispositions section of Topic *Cultural and Linguistic Diversity* in the MyEducationLab for your course and complete the activity entitled *Culturally Responsive Instruction*.

Students who speak little or no English are likely to be members of diverse cultures. They are at an extreme disadvantage in school if both their language and experiential backgrounds set them apart from their peers. Some schools offer such students bilingual education, in which they develop English language skills while learning more about their own culture and the culture of the United States. Students from diverse backgrounds include Native Americans and Alaskan natives, Asians and Pacific Islanders, African Americans, and Hispanics. African Americans and Hispanics are the two most prevalent diverse groups in the United States today. Within the Hispanic group are individuals of Mexican, Cuban, Puerto Rican, or other Spanish culture or origin. Some diverse students are bilingual, some may be considered culturally diverse, but many are English-speaking members of the dominant American culture.

Culturally diverse students are those whose background and experiences differ from those of their peers. Cultural differences must be defined in terms of local norms. For instance, a Christian student may be perceived as culturally different in a predominantly Jewish community; a student who speaks with a Boston accent may appear out of place among residents of the Deep South.

Students with ethnic, linguistic, and cultural backgrounds different from those of their peers add diversity and variety to the general education classroom. However, they may have special academic and social needs. Those still developing skills in understanding and speaking English may experience difficulty with academic instruction. Others may fail to meet teacher expectations because of different entry-level skills or different cultural values and motivational systems. Social acceptance may be withheld by peers unaccustomed to cultural variations.

 STUDENTS AT RISK
FOR SCHOOL FAILURE

Another important consideration for teachers of general education classes are **students at risk for school failure.** Students can be at risk for many reasons. They may live in an impoverished family with inadequate housing, poor nutrition, and little or no medical care; with their basic needs in jeopardy, such students often have few resources left to devote to school learning. Others may be slow learners who, although they do not have disabilities, learn at a pace that falls somewhat below grade-level expectations. Some students are unmotivated to achieve in school, and as a result their academic performance is less than satisfactory. Older students with a history of poor school achievement may become truant or contemplate leaving school. According to a recent report from *Education Week* ("Diplomas Count 2008: School to College," 2008), about 30% of students who enter the ninth grade drop out before graduating from high school four years later.

Every classroom contains students at risk for school failure, although it is difficult to determine precisely how many general education students fit within this category. Many types of students can be considered at risk. Among these are potential school dropouts, students with violent or suicidal behaviors, those who use or abuse alcohol or other drugs, teenage mothers, victims of child abuse or neglect, those with eating disorders, and delinquents.

At-risk students often have needs in the area of academic performance; they may fail to achieve, show little interest in instructional activities, or achieve at levels far below their potential. Some students may also show special needs in the area of behavior; they may exhibit inappropriate behavior in the classroom or begin to develop very serious problems such as drug and alcohol abuse, gang activity, and delinquency. Social acceptance may be a problem, particularly for students who fail to meet the school's expectations for achievement and the peer group's expectations for behavior.

Factors that place students at risk for school failure are discussed throughout this book along with strategies, recommendations, and suggestions to help teachers respond. To learn more about these risk factors, consult "Window on the Web" for a list of websites offering information and resources for students, their parents, their teachers, and the community.

 WINDOW ON THE WEB

Websites About Risk Factors for School-Aged Children and Youth

Child Abuse and Neglect
- Prevent Child Abuse America (*http://www.preventchildabuse.org*)
- Child Welfare Information Gateway (formerly the National Clearinghouse on Child Abuse and Neglect Information and the National Adoption Information Clearinghouse) (*http://www.childwelfare.gov/can/*)

Delinquency and School Violence
- National School Safety Center (*http://www.schoolsafety.us*)
- National Youth Violence Prevention Resource Center (*http://www.safeyouth.org*)
- Office of Juvenile Justice and Delinquency Prevention, U.S. Department of Justice (*http://www.ojjdp.ncjrs.org*)

Dropping Out of School
- Students at Risk: Working Together to Reduce the Dropout Rate and Increase the Graduation Rate (*http://www.studentsatrisk.org/*)
- National Dropout Prevention Centers (*http://www.dropoutprevention.org*)

Suicide
- American Foundation for Suicide Prevention (*http://www.afsp.org*)

- Youth Suicide Prevention Program (*http://www.yspp.org*)
- Centers for Disease Control and Prevention: Understanding Suicide (*http://www.cdc.gov/Features/Suicide/*)

Substance Abuse
- Center for Substance Abuse Prevention (CSAP) (*http://prevention.samhsa.gov*)
- Stop Underage Drinking (*http://www.stopalcoholabuse.gov*)
- National Institute on Drug Abuse, National Institutes of Health (*http://www.nida.nih.gov*)

Teen Pregnancy and Sexually Transmitted Diseases
- The National Campaign to Prevent Teen and Unwanted Pregnancy (*http://www.thenationalcampaign.org*)
- National Center for HIV/AIDS, Viral Hepatitis, STD, and TB Prevention (*http://www.cdc.gov/nchhstp*)

Eating Disorders
- National Eating Disorders Association (*http://www.nationaleatingdisorders.org*)
- National Association of Anorexia Nervosa and Associated Eating Disorders (*http://www.anad.org*)

TYPES OF SPECIAL NEEDS

It is common practice to divide students with special needs into separate groups or categories such as students with learning disabilities, those with intellectual disabilities, and so on. In the classroom, however, the special needs of these students are often so similar that distinctions among categories become blurred. It also becomes difficult to differentiate between students with identified disabilities and some of their peers with similar learning problems.

Academic needs are common. The acquisition, mastery, and application of school skills prove difficult for many students with special needs and for many of their classmates. Children are expected to enter school with listening, speaking, and other readiness skills. In the primary years (grades 1, 2, and 3), the basic skills of reading, writing, and mathematics are taught; at the intermediate level (grades 4, 5, and sometimes 6), students learn to use these skills to acquire information in content areas such as science and social studies. In middle school and high school, the focus of the curriculum shifts to the content areas; mastery of basic skills is assumed. For many students, this assumption is unwarranted; they are not able to read, write, and calculate at the level expected in the secondary grades. Those who have acquired rudimentary basic skills may fail to acquire content area knowledge and concepts. Still others may require alternatives to the general education curriculum; their major educational need may be career education with an emphasis on vocational training.

Classroom behavior needs frequently occur among students with special needs and their general education peers. Elementary school students are expected to obey their teacher and others in authority, adhere to the rules of classroom conduct, and get along with their peers during instruction and in less structured situations such as lunch and recess. These expectations are also true for secondary students. In addition, however, they are assumed to have developed the study skills and work habits necessary for independent learning. Many students require assistance in meeting these expectations for classroom behavior.

Students may also have special *physical needs.* Children are expected to enter school with intact visual, hearing, and physical abilities. Those with sensory losses cannot participate in many classroom activities designed for sighted and hearing students. Many students, including those with physical and health impairments, cannot walk, run, or play games and sports as well as their general education peers. They have special needs in the area of physical development.

Special students and others often have *social needs.* Young children are expected to know how to make friends with their classmates. Instruction is often presented in group situations that require students to interact with both their teacher and peers. Many school activities are at least partly social in nature; personal interactions take place during lunch, recess, assemblies, and field trips and in clubs, organizations, and sports teams. Social skills become increasingly important as individuals approach adulthood; secondary students are expected to build and maintain friendships and begin establishing interpersonal relationships as preparation for courtship and marriage. Because they may appear to be different in some ways, students with special needs may have difficulty gaining acceptance from their regular class peers. Students with poor social skills (whether they are identified as having special needs or not) need instruction and training in this area.

Most students require assistance in one or more of these areas at some time during their school careers. Students with special needs are no exception. However, with this group of students, it is possible to predict some of the areas in which they are likely to encounter difficulty. As shown in Table 3-1, it is probable that all will have special academic and social needs. Some may also have needs in the areas of classroom behavior and physical development. This table depicts only the typical needs of groups of students; it is certainly possible

T A B L E   3 - 1   Typical Difficulty Areas of Students with Special Needs

Types of Students	TYPES OF NEEDS			
	Academic	Classroom Behavior	Physical	Social
Learning disabilities	X	X	X	X
Behavioral disorders	X	X		X
Intellectual disabilities	X	X	X	X
Speech/language impairments	X			X
Physical/health impairments	X		X	X
Visual/hearing impairments	X		X	X
ADHD/ADD	X	X		X
Autism spectrum disorder	X	X	X	X
Severe disabilities	X	X	X	X
Gifted/talented students	X			X
Diverse students	X			X
Students at risk	X	X	X	X

for students with speech and language impairments to display problem behaviors or for students with physical impairments to require no special academic assistance.

There are many similarities among students with special needs and between this group of students and their general education peers. This is particularly true in relation to students with mild disabilities: learning disabilities, behavioral disorders, and mild intellectual disabilities. These students make up perhaps 5% to 7% of the school population. They are physically indistinguishable from their regular class peers and are usually not identified as having special needs until they experience failure in school. They begin school in general education classes and receive the majority of their education in mainstreamed situations. It has long been accepted that students with mild disabilities cannot be differentiated by the causes of their learning problems, the methods found effective in their instruction, or their behavioral characteristics (Hallahan & Kauffman, 1976). All have academic, behavioral, and social needs that may require adaptations in general education classrooms.

However, recent research points to differences among the three groups in terms of the amount and types of support required for successful school performance (Sabornie, Evans, & Cullinan, 2006). Caffrey and Fuchs (2007) report that students with learning disabilities are more likely to have success on inductive reasoning tasks and generalization of conceptual knowledge to new tasks than students with mild intellectual disabilities. Results of the study by Sabornie et al. (2005) indicate that students with learning disabilities surpass those with mild intellectual disabilities in academic achievement, while students with behavioral disorders evidence greater difficulty than students in the other two groups in the area of behavior. Research findings such as these underscore the need to consider all students as individuals, rather than as members of homogeneous groups with identical instructional needs.

When adaptations are made for students with special needs, general education teachers often wonder how to explain these changes to the rest of the class. Students may wonder why others are receiving special treatment. Ideas for handling this situation are listed in the "Inclusion Tips for the Teacher" box.

 Inclusion Tips for the Teacher

Explaining Classroom Modifications to Peers

It is sometimes necessary to make changes in classroom activities so that students with special needs can succeed. For example, students with academic needs may be given special assignments or may be required to complete only part of the work assigned to the rest of the class. Those with behavioral needs may earn special rewards for good behavior. The rest of the class may become curious about why these students rate special treatment from the teacher.

Teachers can prevent problems from occurring by following these suggestions.

- Don't call undue attention to students with special needs. Treat them as you would any other student in your class.

- When special assignments are necessary, give them privately. Then, when the class is working on individual assignments, the student with special needs will not be conspicuous.
- Group students with similar learning needs together. If a student with a disability requires extra instruction in reading, set up a small group that includes peers with similar needs. If students with special needs have difficulty following class rules, consider beginning a behavior program for the entire class.
- When class members have questions, answer them promptly and honestly. Acknowledge that you are individualizing assignments and activities so that everyone in the class can learn successfully. A matter-of-fact response will usually satisfy curiosity and allay any feelings of resentment.

ASSESSMENT OF SPECIAL LEARNING NEEDS

Assessment is the process of gathering information about students to make important educational decisions (McLoughlin & Lewis, 2008). In special education and other supplementary school services, it is necessary to determine whether students meet certain legal requirements before services can begin. In special education, for example, students are considered eligible for services only if they have a disability and if that disability has a negative effect on school performance. That is, students must experience difficulty in school, and that difficulty must be attributable to a disability.

Classroom Assessment

General educators play many roles in the assessment process. It was discussed earlier in this text that the classroom teacher typically is the person who refers students for special education and other types of assessment. In addition, teachers collect all sorts of information about their students. Some of the assessment strategies that classroom teachers use most often are

- observations of students as they engage in academic activities and social interactions;
- analysis of students' errors and correct responses on work samples such as homework assignments, tests, essays, and math papers;
- administration of quizzes and exams to assess student progress toward instructional goals; and
- interviews with students to learn more about their attitudes, viewpoints, and the strategies they use to interact with classroom tasks.

These techniques are **informal assessment** strategies. Unlike formal, norm-referenced tests, their purpose is not to compare one student's performance to that of others of the same age or grade. Instead, they are considered **curriculum-based assessments** because they focus on students' mastery of the instructional goals addressed in the general education classroom.

Another example of an informal data collection technique is **portfolio assessment.** Portfolios are simply collections of student work gathered over time; however, students are responsible for selecting their best work for inclusion in the portfolio and for evaluating their own progress (Grady, 1992). Teachers evaluate the contents of a portfolio with the same informal techniques used to analyze other types of student work samples.

One major reason for the collection of data is to evaluate the effectiveness of instruction. When done systematically, this is called **clinical teaching** (McLoughlin & Lewis, 2008). It is also the assessment phase of the Response-to-Intervention (RTI) approach discussed earlier in this text. First, the teacher gathers data about student performance on the task in question. Then, an intervention is introduced and data collection continues. Any of the informal assessment strategies described earlier can be used in clinical teaching: observation, analysis of student work samples, quizzes, and so on. The intervention is considered successful if results indicate that student performance has improved.

Curriculum-based measurement (CBM) is an informal assessment strategy used in special education to monitor student progress (Deno, 1985, 1987; Shinn & Hubbard, 1993). It is easy to use and sensitive to small changes in students' skill levels, which makes it a useful measurement technique for clinical teaching. In CBM, the teacher collects very brief samples of important student behaviors. For example, to assess oral reading skills, students read aloud for 1 minute while the teacher (or an assistant) records the number of words read correctly. This "probe" is administered frequently (e.g., two or three times each week), and results are graphed to provide a visual record of the student's progress. In clinical teaching, this graph is inspected to determine whether desired changes occurred when the new intervention was introduced.

Assessment for Program Eligibility

When students are referred for special education assessment, a multidisciplinary team is formed to plan the process of gathering information about the need for extraordinary services. **Norm-referenced tests** are typically used for this type of assessment. These tests provide information about a student's status in relation to other students of the same age or grade; this type of comparison is needed to determine whether a student's problem is severe enough to warrant special educational intervention.

The tests are administered by trained specialists to one student at a time. Group administration procedures are not used because they can depress the performance of students with special learning needs. Group tests require students to read, write, and attend to test tasks for a relatively long period of time. On individually administered tests, a student's knowledge of science can be separated from his or her reading skills because the tester reads the questions to the student; also, if the student's attention wavers, the professional can help the student refocus on the task at hand.

No matter what disability is suspected, the team will collect information on three major areas of functioning.

1. *Intellectual performance.* Tests of intellectual performance, sometimes called *intelligence* or *IQ (intelligence quotient)* tests, are used to assess the student's skills in reasoning and problem-solving tasks. These measures do not determine innate potential; instead, they assess a student's aptitude for academic tasks (McLoughlin & Lewis, 2008).
2. *Academic achievement.* At the beginning of assessment, tests that include several academic subjects (e.g., reading, spelling, composition, mathematics, content area knowledge) are administered to identify broad areas of need. Then, more specific measures (e.g., a test of reading skills) are used to pinpoint areas of difficulty.
3. *Area of disability.* In special education assessment, it is necessary to establish the existence of a disability. For instance, in intellectual disabilities, the team will study intellectual performance and adaptive behavior. In learning

disabilities, the focus is on information processing or on response to instruction in the RTI approach, and in behavioral disorders, the focus is on severe and long-standing conduct disorders. Federal laws provide regulations for determining eligibility, and states and school districts supplement these with additional guidelines.

To help teachers become better acquainted with the tests and other data collection procedures used in special education, common assessment tools and techniques are discussed throughout this book. However, this book places most of its emphasis on the types of assessment tools that teachers find useful in the classroom. These are typically informal assessments—measures and strategies devised by teachers to answer specific questions about the academic, social, physical, and behavioral needs of their students. The measures also tend to be curriculum-based rather than norm-referenced; that is, their purpose is to compare a student's performance to the demands of the local curriculum and the expectations in a particular classroom.

▶ **SKILLS FOR GENERAL EDUCATION TEACHERS**

General education teachers play an important role in the prevention and treatment of school learning problems. With appropriate instruction, students with disabilities and others with special learning needs can experience success in the general education classroom. The next chapters of this book focus on the major skills needed by teachers to assess student needs and adapt instruction, manage behavior, promote social acceptance, and coordinate the learning environment of the classroom. These skills are simply good teaching procedures; they can be used with any student, special or not. Good teaching skills focus on the needs of the student (rather than any particular disability), and they are based on the following four assumptions about students with special needs and the teaching–learning process.

All Students Can Learn

Despite any special needs they may have, all individuals are able to acquire new skills and absorb new information and attitudes. Students learn at different rates, and the same person may learn some things more quickly than other things. Although much is known about different groups of students with special needs, it is impossible to accurately predict the specific areas in which they will experience difficulty. However, we do know that they *can* and, with proper instruction, *will* learn.

Learning Is Determined by Changes in Behavior

Learning is a process of change. Students acquire new skills, become more proficient in previously learned skills, and learn to perform in certain ways. Teachers evaluate students' progress by their behavior; that is, they observe students' overt responses and infer that learning has occurred. Students demonstrate that they have learned academic, classroom conduct, and social skills in many ways; they may display new behaviors, a greater number of appropriate behaviors, or fewer inappropriate behaviors. Teachers monitor the learning process by noting what students say in class discussions, what they write on assignments and exams, and how they act in the many situations of the school day.

Teaching Involves Arrangement of the Environment

If learning is the change of student behaviors, then teaching is the arrangement of the learning environment to maximize the chance that desired behaviors will occur. In instruction, teachers have control over two important factors: the **antecedents** and **consequences** of student behaviors. An antecedent is anything that precedes or comes before a behavior; typical teaching activities such as lectures, small-group discussions, text readings, and written assignments are all instructional antecedents that can be manipulated to enhance learning. Consequences, or events that follow behaviors, include grades, teacher praise or scolding, and rewards (remember gold stars?) and punishments; these, too, are powerful tools that can be used to facilitate learning. Just as students learn at different rates, they also respond differently to instructional antecedents and consequences. Although there is no one sure-fire teaching method, material, or reward system, empirical evidence suggests that some instructional procedures are more effective than others. For example, direct systematic instruction methods that focus on skill development have been found useful for teaching basic academic skills (Adams & Carnine, 2003; Stevens & Rosenshine, 1981). As federal special education dictates, instructional strategies with research supporting their effectiveness should be selected whenever possible.

Data Collection Increases Teaching Efficiency

Because the options to choose from in setting up an instructional system of antecedents and consequences are almost unlimited, it is important to approach the task systematically. The first step, after precisely describing the desired student behavior, is selecting the appropriate instructional strategy. That strategy should be based on sound instructional principles and, whenever possible, have ample research support. The teacher collects information about the behavior before instruction and also during the instructional intervention. If the behavior changes in the desired way, the intervention is considered successful; if it does not, the teacher proceeds to a more complex or intensive instructional strategy. In this way, instructional decisions are made on the basis of data rather than on guesses or hunches; teaching becomes more efficient, with the end result that students learn more. This data-driven approach to instruction is particularly beneficial for students who encounter difficulty in learning.

To review these major points and others, consult the "Things to Remember" section.

Things to Remember

- Both students with special needs and their regular class peers may require support in the general education classroom. Special needs occur in the areas of academic, classroom behavioral, physical, and social performance.

- Students with special needs, as a group, typically experience difficulty in academic and social areas; some students also have special behavioral and physical needs.

- Information about special needs is more useful to the teacher than knowledge of the student's categorical label.

- Causes of learning problems are important if they help in treatment or prevention.

- Appropriate instruction can prevent some learning problems and help to overcome others.

- Teachers arrange the learning environment to produce changes in the behavior of students.

- Data-driven instruction is efficient and effective in teaching students with special needs the behaviors needed to succeed in the general education classroom.

ACTIVITIES

1. Disabilities are not the same as handicaps. However, some disabilities interfere with the performance of tasks required by certain professions. For example, consider blindness for a painter or deafness for a musician. Are there any disabilities that would interfere in the profession of teaching? If so, what are they? What disabilities would a teacher be able to overcome? Be prepared to discuss your answers to these questions.

2. Interview two or more general educators about the students they teach. How many students with disabilities are included in their classrooms? What types of special needs do these students have? Do other children in the classroom have similar needs? What kinds of classroom modifications have the teachers made to accommodate the special needs of these students?

3. Many special education journals concentrate on one disability. For instance, the Council for Exceptional Children publishes *Behavioral Disorders*, *Education and Training in Developmental Disabilities*, and *Learning Disabilities Research and Practice*. Select one or two of these journals and look at several recent issues. Did you find any articles on the inclusion of students with special needs in general education?

4. Search the World Wide Web for information about one of the disabilities discussed in this chapter. What kinds of sites did you locate? Are they sponsored by professional organizations? Parent groups? Districts or schools? Individuals?

5. A person's culture affects many perceptions. Talk with someone from a culture different from yours and compare your experiences. You might discuss foods, dress, manners, or traditional celebrations or holidays. Also, compare the ways in which different cultures view the birth of a child with a disability. Are persons with disabilities treated differently by different cultures?

Skills for the General Education Teacher

PART

II

CHAPTER
FIVE

Adapting Instruction

- Eleanor, a fourth grader, reads at the beginning third grade level.
- Patrick can solve math computation problems with ease, but he has trouble with word problems.
- Erin's handwriting is barely legible, and the assignments he turns in are wrinkled, messy, and full of crossed-out words.
- Although Patty seems to understand the information presented in chemistry class, she has failed every quiz this semester.
- Ian's essays contain excellent ideas, but his spelling, grammar, and punctuation are atrocious.
- Billy is habitually late to class, and he often forgets to do his homework.
- Dan's vocational skills are good, but he'll have difficulty completing job applications.

LOOKING AHEAD

This chapter focuses on the academic difficulties faced by some students in general education classrooms. As you read this chapter to learn about strategies to assist these students, think about the questions that follow.

- Each of the students just described has some sort of academic problem. In what school subject—or subjects—would you expect them to need assistance?
- What could you do to find out more about Patrick's difficulties with word problems? Erin's illegible handwriting? Billy's tardiness and poor homework record?
- What adaptations might be useful to help Patty communicate her knowledge of chemistry? To help Ian better communicate his ideas?

This chapter helps teachers develop a set of skills important for meeting the needs of all of the students in their classroom. These are the skills needed for adapting instruction for students with special needs and others in the classroom who may require some type of assistance to benefit fully from the opportunities available in general education. To begin, read the "Students' Stories" to meet several students who are encountering difficulty meeting the academic demands of the general education curriculum.

Students such as the individuals described in the "Students' Stories" have special needs in the area of academic performance. For them to succeed in the general education classroom, it may be necessary to adapt instructional procedures. To do this, teachers should be familiar with the typical **academic problems** of students with special needs and their peers and strategies for adapting instruction to meet the needs of all students. Strategies for collecting assessment information about academic performance and for making accommodations in tests of academic skills are also discussed in this chapter.

ACADEMIC PROBLEMS IN THE CLASSROOM

Students can experience difficulty with academic instruction at any age and in any subject. Such students come to the attention of their teachers when their classroom performance does not meet teacher expectations. Elementary teachers often describe students with academic problems as "achieving below grade level" in one or more subjects. Secondary teachers, however, take note of students who receive poor or failing grades in specific courses, such as English, biology, U.S. history, art, or woodworking.

School learning involves the acquisition of both knowledge and skills. Students are expected to absorb vast amounts of information in academic subjects and to develop and sharpen their thinking and learning skills. Problems can occur in any one of the three stages of learning: acquisition, maintenance, and generalization. **Acquisition** is initial learning, **maintenance** is the recall of previously learned material, and **generalization** is the application or transfer of learned material to similar situations and problems. Students may require more time to absorb new knowledge and learn new skills, have difficulty sustaining performance over time, or fail to apply old learning to new situations.

Teachers evaluate student responses to determine whether learning is occurring as expected. Students respond in the classroom in a number of ways: oral answers to teacher questions, participation in class discussions, in-class assignments and homework, and quizzes and examinations. Academic problems

Educational Resources Information Center (ERIC)

If you're looking for information about some aspect of education, ERIC is a good place to start. ERIC is the Education Resources Information Center, which, according to its website, is an "online digital library of education research and information" and "is sponsored by the Institute of Education Sciences (IES) of the U.S. Department of Education."

The online version of ERIC includes a searchable database of more than 1.2 million ERIC entries dating back to 1966. Each entry contains information about author, title, and source as well as a brief abstract. An exciting new feature of this online service is access to full-text versions of recently published documents (including articles published in a limited number of journals). This free service replaces the former system where users were required to purchase print or microfiche copies of ERIC documents or visit libraries that had already made these purchases.

http://www.eric.ed.gov

---

are suspected if one (or more) of the following response patterns is evident.

- *High number of incorrect responses.* The majority of the student's responses are incorrect, or the student's accuracy rate falls below the criterion set by the teacher. For example, George solves only 6 out of 10 subtraction problems correctly; the teacher's criterion is 90% accuracy.
- *Low number of responses.* The student fails to respond to a significant number of questions, problems, or activities. For example, Jack answers only 7 of the 15 questions at the end of the chapter.
- *Inconsistent responses.* The student's responses to the same question, problem, or activity vary in correctness from time to time. For example, Thelma writes all 20 spelling words correctly on the Wednesday practice quiz but scores only 40% on the test on Friday.

Of course, if many students within the class show response patterns such as these, the first step would be to evaluate classroom instructional procedures.

Inappropriate response patterns can be seen in any school subject. One typical trouble spot is **basic skills;** listening, speaking, reading, writing, and mathematics often are difficult for students to acquire, maintain, and generalize. The written language skills of reading and writing are built on the oral language skills of listening and speaking. Students may have trouble with the reception of information (listening and reading), the expression of information (speaking and writing), or all aspects of the communication process. The development of basic skills is a high-priority instructional goal in the elementary grades. Students with special needs may experience difficulty with the rote aspects of these skills (e.g., word recognition, handwriting, spelling, mathematics facts and computation) or with the more conceptual aspects (e.g., reading comprehension, written expression, mathematical problem solving).

At the secondary level, instruction centers on **content-area subjects** rather than basic skills. The academic curriculum is organized according to bodies of knowledge: English (including both composition and literature) and other languages; science (biology, chemistry, physics); higher math (algebra, geometry, trigonometry); the social sciences (history, social studies, geography); and other areas such as art, music, and physical education. However, academic problems in basic skills may persist; students may not have acquired or maintained adequate reading, writing, and mathematics skills, or they may be unable to apply these skills to the acquisition of new information. Students may also have difficulty learning the skills, knowledge, concepts, and principles associated with a particular content area. Poor organizational and study skills may also interfere with student performance.

Preparation for the **transition** from adolescence to adulthood is another aspect of school learning in which academic problems can arise. Hasazi, Furney, and Hull (1995) defined *transition* as a "series of purposeful activities designed to ensure that students have the skills, opportunities, and supports needed to locate and maintain employment, to pursue postsecondary education and training, to participate in the social fabric of the community, and to make decisions about their lives" (p. 420). Transition planning is required by federal law for students with disabilities; it is also an important concern for many other students with special needs. One aspect of transition planning is specific vocational training experience at the secondary level. Another is the application of basic skills and content-area information to the solution of daily life problems, such as reading menus, making change, and selecting appropriate items to purchase. Students may have difficulty in the acquisition of specific vocational skills, such as keyboarding, mechanical drawing, or welding. They may also have difficulty in the generalization of basic work habits, such as punctuality and task completion, and the application of school learning to job and community situations.

Because academic instruction is one of the major goals of U.S. education, academic problems are a concern to classroom teachers at all levels. However, as Montgomery (1978) pointed out, not all variations in student performance are learning problems:

Johnny reads with his book turned sideways, or kneels instead of sitting on his chair, or wears his jacket in class. Do we "fix" him or let him be? Before we can answer that question realistically we must ask, "Is it a problem for Johnny—or for us?" Does it hamper Johnny's learning, or do we see it as a problem because of our own preoccupation with things being normal, with Johnny acting like everyone else? (p. 112)

THE INSTRUCTIONAL PROCESS

Students with disabilities and other types of special needs have the necessary skills to participate in many classroom activities. They may take part in all instructional aspects of the general education program, or they may be included only for selected subjects. The decision is made on the basis of three factors: the student's skills in the subject area, the amount of instructional support required to ensure the student's active participation, and the usefulness or functionality of the academic subject for the student. When students are included only for those subjects that are useful to them and in which successful performance is probable, the general education curriculum is appropriate; that is, *what* is taught need not be modified by the classroom teacher. However, it is often necessary to alter instructional procedures, that is, *how* skills and information are taught to special students.

Much is known today about what teachers can do to have positive effects on student performance. This knowledge comes from a large body of research on teaching behaviors, sometimes known as the *teacher effectiveness literature* (e.g., Brophy & Good, 1986; Medley, 1982; Rieth & Evertson, 1988; Rosenshine & Stevens, 1986; Weil & Murphy, 1982). The major factors found to have a positive influence on student achievement are listed here (Weil & Murphy, 1982).

- Teachers maintain an *academic focus* in selecting classroom activities and directing classroom work.
- Teachers maintain *direction and control* in the management of the classroom learning environment.
- Teachers hold *high expectations* for the academic progress of their students.
- *Students are accountable* for the satisfactory completion of classroom work.
- Students work together, showing *cooperation* rather than competition.
- The affective climate of the classroom learning environment is *not negative*.

Among the most critical concerns in fostering student achievement are the quantity and pace of instruction (Brophy & Good, 1986). Both concerns are related to an opportunity to learn. Learning increases when more time is devoted to academic pursuits and when students are actually engaged in learning during that time. Learning also increases when students move through the curriculum at a brisk pace, provided that students maintain a high rate of successful performance.

Both quantity and pace of instruction can be enhanced by active teaching. In active teaching, "the teacher carries the content to the students personally rather than depending on the curriculum materials to do so" (Brophy & Good, 1986, p. 361). The teacher directs the learning experience, and students "spend most of their time being taught or supervised by their teachers rather than working on their own (or not working at all)" (p. 361). Active teaching has been called many things, including **direct teaching,** direct instruction, and **explicit instruction** (Spear-Swerling & Sternberg, 2001). In direct teaching, the teacher demonstrates appropriate strategies for the performance of the learning task, allows maximum opportunity for students to respond, and

provides systematic and frequent feedback on their task performance (Archer, Gleason, Englert, & Isaacson, 1995; Archer, Gleason, & Isaacson, 1995).

Lloyd and Carnine (1981) called this *structured instruction*, or the "carefully organized manipulation of environmental events designed to bring about prespecified changes in learners' performance in skill areas of functional importance" (p. viii). It is **individualized instruction,** designed to meet the needs of each student. This does not mean that instruction must be individualized in the sense that it is delivered by one teacher to one student. Stevens and Rosenshine (1981) view instruction as individualized when a high proportion of student responses is correct. Good instruction can occur in large groups, small groups, or one to one; the criterion is student success.

According to Hardman, Drew, and Egan (2005), effective instruction for students with disabilities and other special needs has three characteristics:

- *Individualization.* A student-center approach to instructional decision making
- *Intensive instruction.* Frequent instructional experiences of significant duration
- *The explicit teaching of academic, adaptive, and/or functional life skills* (p. 44)

Heward (2006) agreed, but added three other characteristics: specialized instruction, research-based methods, and instruction guided by student performance. Table 5-1 presents Heward's schema with explanations of each of the characteristics.

myeducationlab Go to the Assignments and Activities section of Topic *Instructional Practices and Learning Strategies* in the MyEducationLab for your course and complete the activity entitled *Differentiating Instruction.*

Differentiated instruction is the term commonly used today to describe individualization within the general education environment (Council for Exceptional Children, 2006–2007; Tomlinson, 2000; Wormeli, 2003). Tomlinson identified four aspects of classroom instruction that teachers can differentiate in an attempt to meet the needs of additional learners:

1. *Content*—what the student needs to learn or how the student will get access to the information;
2. *Process*—activities in which the student engages in order to make sense of or master the content;
3. *Products*—culminating projects that ask the student to rehearse, apply, and extend what he or she has learned in a unit; and
4. *Learning environment*—the way the classroom works and feels.

Related to the differentiation of instruction is the principle of **Universal Design** or, as it is sometimes called, Universal Design for learning (Hall, Strangman, & Meyer, 2003). Although often discussed in relation to technology, this principle is relevant to all aspects of education (Cawley, Foley, & Miller, 2003; Edyburn, 2004). Most simply, universal design is "an approach to the design of all products and environments to be usable by

TABLE 5-1 Characteristics of Effective Instruction for Students with Disabilities

Dimension	Defining Features
Individually planned	■ Learning goals and objectives selected for each student based on assessment results and input from parents and student ■ Teaching methods and instructional materials selected and/or adapted for each student ■ Setting(s) where instruction will occur determined relative to opportunities for student to learn and use targeted skills
Specialized	■ Sometimes involves unique or adapted teaching procedures seldom used in general education (e.g., constant time delay, token reinforcement, self-monitoring) ■ Incorporates a variety of instructional materials and supports—both natural and contrived—to help student acquire and use targeted learning objectives ■ Related services (e.g., audiology, physical therapy) provided as needed ■ Assistive technology (e.g., adapted cup holder, head-operated switch to select communication symbols) provided as needed
Intensive	■ Instruction presented with attention to detail, precision, structure, clarity, and repeated practice ■ "Relentless, urgent" instruction (Zigmond & Baker, 1995) ■ Efforts made to provide incidental, naturalistic opportunities for student to use targeted knowledge and skills
Goal-directed	■ Purposeful instruction intended to help student achieve the greatest possible personal self-sufficiency and success in present and future environments ■ Value/goodness of instruction determined by student's attainment of outcomes
Research-based methods	■ Recognition that all teaching approaches are not equally effective ■ Instructional programs and teaching procedures selected on basis of research support
Guided by student performance	■ Careful, ongoing monitoring of student progress ■ Frequent and direct measures/assessment of student learning used to inform modifications in instruction

Note: From Heward, *Exceptional Children*, Table 1.8 "Dimension and defining features of special education instruction," p. 44, © 2006. Reproduced by permission of Pearson Education, Inc.

everyone, to the greatest extent possible, regardless of age, ability, or situation" (Center for Universal Design, 2004). An early example familiar to most is the curb cut. Although curb cuts make it easier for individuals who travel by wheelchair to negotiate curbs and cross the street, they also assist many others such as persons pushing baby strollers, toddlers learning to climb up and down steps, students pulling backpacks on wheels, and people who walk with a cane or crutches.

When the principles of universal design are incorporated into the development of the curriculum and learning materials, the flexibility needed to accommodate diverse learners is built in. CAST, the Center for Applied Technology (2003), describes this approach:

> The central practical premise of UDL [Universal Design for Learning] is that a curriculum should include alternatives to make it accessible and appropriate for individuals with different backgrounds, learning styles, abilities, and disabilities in widely varied learning contexts. The "universal" in universal design does not imply one optimal solution for everyone. Rather, it reflects an awareness of the unique nature of each learner and the need to accommodate differences, creating learning experiences that suit the learner and maximize his or her ability to progress.

In most cases, however, the principles of universal design do not guide the development of educational approaches and strategies. Instead, when students with special needs are members of general education classrooms, it is often necessary to adapt curriculum, modify instructional procedures, or change the ways in which students demonstrate how much they've learned. Teachers individualize instruction, differentiate to meet various students' needs, and make accommodations in how information is presented and the ways in which students respond. See the "Inclusion Tips for the Teacher" section for examples of ways to differentiate instruction for students with special needs.

Teachers can make changes at any point in the instructional process in order to enhance the learning of their students. As shown in Figure 5-1, instruction takes place in a series of steps involving both teacher and student(s) and progressing from the active direction of the teacher (teaching) to the active involvement of the student(s) (learning). There are five steps: curricular choice, presentation, practice, mastery, and application.

1. *Selection of the learning task.* To make this curricular decision, the teacher considers the scope and sequence of the general education curriculum, the skills and information already acquired by the student, and the student's current interests and learning needs. The learning task represents the goal of instruction, and successful performance of this task is the desired student behavior.

Inclusion Tips for the Teacher

Differentiated Instruction

Differentiating instruction is a way to turn the thinking of universal design for learning (UDL) into classroom practice. Although many approaches to differentiating can be found in books and on websites, thinking of it in terms of ways to change (1) the content students learn, (2) the processes through which they learn it, and (3) the products they produce to demonstrate their learning can be helpful. After you review these examples, try to think of several of your own to add to each category.

Differentiating Based on Content

- Assess students' knowledge prior to instruction so that those who already understand key concepts can be given alternative tasks and those who lack even background knowledge can be readied for the core instruction.
- Students with significant intellectual disabilities may learn just three key ideas or concepts from among ten concepts that other students are learning.

Differentiating Based on Process

- All students are taught how to use a Venn diagram to describe how characters in a short story are similar and different.

Students practice using stories of varying levels of difficulty in terms of reading level and character complexity.
- Some students complete the math lesson using manipulatives or calculators while others complete the lesson without these tools.

Differentiating Based on Product

- Students demonstrate their knowledge of the novel just read in any of several ways: Some make a poster that would advertise the novel if it were made into a major motion picture, some create an alternative ending to the story, and some complete Internet research about the period in history in which the novel occurred.
- Some students write essays to respond to items on their tests. Some students dictate their answers or make lists of bullet points so that they can express their ideas more efficiently.

Differentiation can occur in literally thousands of ways; your challenge as an educator, regardless of the students you teach, is to find those approaches that will have the most positive impact on your students' learning outcomes.

Note: Friend, *Special Education, 2e,* "Differentiating Instruction for Diverse Learners," p. 24, © 2008. Reproduced by permission of Pearson Education, Inc.

2. *Presentation to the student of the material necessary for task performance.* The teacher uses procedures such as lectures, in-class activities, and reading assignments to provide the student with the skills and information required for the task. The teacher may model or demonstrate the skill or explain new information by presenting rules, principles, and examples. Then the teacher gives directions for the performance of the task. The student's role at this stage is to give adequate attention to instruction and feedback to the teacher if instruction is unclear.

3. *Practice of the learning task.* The student first performs the task under the close supervision of the teacher (guided practice). Gradually the teacher's guidance is withdrawn, and the student performs independently (independent practice). The teacher's role is to monitor student performance and provide feedback to the student regarding the adequacy of task performance. In guided practice, feedback is immediate, whereas in independent practice, it is delayed. If a high proportion of student responses is incorrect, the teacher returns to the presentation step. Presentation and practice lead to the acquisition of skills and information.

4. *Mastery of the learning task.* At some later time, the student performs the task independently, and the teacher monitors student responses. If performance is not adequate, it may be necessary to return to the practice steps or even to the presentation steps. Mastery is determined by maintenance of previously acquired learning.

5. *Application of previous learning.* The student performs tasks similar to the original learning task. If the teacher notes poor performance at this step, it may be necessary to reteach the original task through presentation and practice or to devise a new instructional sequence in which generalization of skills or information is taught directly. Application generalizes previous learning.

The teacher directs instruction by selecting the desired student behavior, arranging instructional antecedents, and providing consequences such as feedback regarding performance accuracy. Even though the teacher is the instructional manager, student factors that influence learning must also be considered. Several of these are described in Table 5-2. In addition, the principles of teaching discussed in the following sections should guide the instructional process.

Before proceeding, it is important to differentiate between direct (or explicit) instruction and an alternative approach, **discovery learning**. In discovery learning, information and skills are not taught directly. Instead, the teacher arranges the learning environment and students explore that environment as they attempt to discover the facts, concepts, principles, and skills that make up the school curriculum. Discovery approaches are considered constructivist because students are expected to construct their own knowledge by building on the prior knowledge they bring to the learning task (Cegelka, 1995a). For example, many proponents of the whole-language approach to reading and writing instruction recommend discovery learning (Gersten &

FIGURE 5-1 Instruction

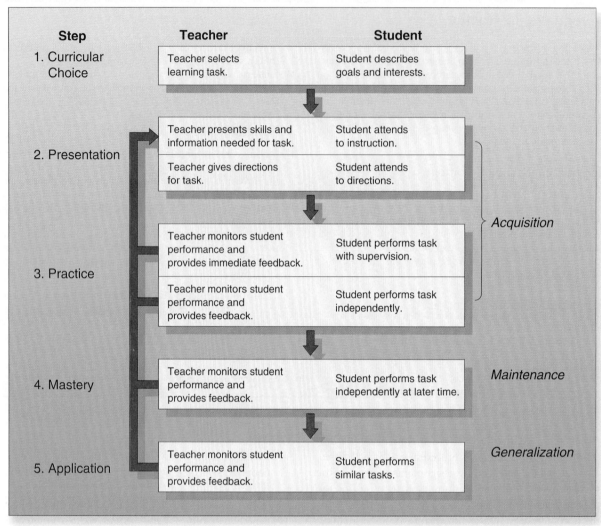

Step	Teacher	Student	
1. Curricular Choice	Teacher selects learning task.	Student describes goals and interests.	
2. Presentation	Teacher presents skills and information needed for task.	Student attends to instruction.	Acquisition
	Teacher gives directions for task.	Student attends to directions.	
3. Practice	Teacher monitors student performance and provides immediate feedback.	Student performs task with supervision.	
	Teacher monitors student performance and provides feedback.	Student performs task independently.	
4. Mastery	Teacher monitors student performance and provides feedback.	Student performs task independently at later time.	Maintenance
5. Application	Teacher monitors student performance and provides feedback.	Student performs similar tasks.	Generalization

 TABLE 5-2 Factors That Facilitate Learning

Factor	Principle
Meaningfulness	A student is more likely to be motivated to learn things that are meaningful to him or her.
Prerequisites	A student is more likely to learn something new if he or she has all the prerequisites.
Modeling	A student is more likely to acquire a new behavior if he or she is presented with a model performance to watch and imitate.
Open communication	A student is more likely to learn if the medium used in the learning situation is structured so that the teacher's messages are open to the learner's inspection.
Novelty	A student is more likely to learn if his or her attention is attracted by relatively novel presentations.
Active appropriate practice	A student is more likely to learn if he or she takes an active part in practice geared to reach an instructional objective.
Distributing practice	A student is more likely to learn if practice is done in short periods over time.
Fading	A student is more likely to learn if instructional prompts are withdrawn gradually.
Pleasant conditions and consequences	A student is more likely to learn if the instructional conditions are pleasant.

Note: From *Teaching Exceptional Children* by N. A. Carlson. Copyright 1980 by Council for Exceptional Children (VA). Reproduced with permission of Council for Exceptional Children (VA) in the formats Textbook and Other book via Copyright Clearance Center.

Dimino, 1993; Keefe & Keefe, 1993; Mather, 1992). Students are expected to become proficient readers and writers by "exposure to and participation in many experiences involving written language" (Richeck in Lerner, Cousin, & Richeck, 1992, p. 227), not through direct teaching.

Unfortunately, some students do not succeed in programs in which discovery learning is the norm (Adelson, 2004; Gersten & Dimino, 1993). In fact, Mayer (2004) asserted that "there is sufficient research evidence to make any reasonable person skeptical about the benefits of discovery learning" (p. 14). Students with mild disabilities and others at risk for academic learning problems are more likely to succeed when instruction is presented using the principles of direct teaching (King-Sears, 1997; Vergason & Anderegg, 1991). As Morsink and Lenk (1992) pointed out, effective instruction of students with special needs can take place in any setting, general education or special, if teachers "(a) engage in teacher-directed instruction, (b) provide students with opportunities for active academic responding, (c) use high rates of contingent reinforcement, and (d) adapt teaching strategies to accommodate individual differences" (p. 36).

One of the cornerstones of the No Child Left Behind Act, the federal education law, is that schools employ proven educational methods. According to the ED.gov website, "*No Child Left Behind* puts emphasis on determining what educational programs and practices have been proven effective through rigorous scientific research" (*Overview, Four Pillars of NCLB,* 2004). In special education, there is a substantial body of research on instructional methodologies (Mainzer, Deshler, Coleman, Kozleski, & Rodriguez-Walling, 2003). Vaughn, Gersten, and Chard (2000) synthesized this body of research and drew these conclusions:

> . . . instructional practices that are visible and explicit, interactive between students and teacher and between students and students, controlled for task difficulty, and include strategies to guide student learning result in the greatest student achievement. (cited in Mainzer et al., p. 8)

Research findings on instruction in general education are less definitive, although the U.S. Department of Education is attempting to rectify this. One of the first steps is the establishment of the What Works Clearinghouse described in the "Window on the Web" feature.

 PRINCIPLES OF INSTRUCTION

The sections that follow present the most important principles of instruction. These principles should guide teachers as they make decisions when planning, implementing, evaluating, and modifying instruction for the students in their classrooms.

Select Appropriate Learning Tasks

Selection of the learning task is a critical instructional decision. No matter how excellent the teaching procedures, instruction will not be effective if the task selected is inappropriate for the learner. Task selection is even more critical for students with special needs because they may learn new information and skills more slowly than their peers. The teacher should choose the most important portions of the general education curriculum as target behaviors. In making these decisions, priority should be given to skills and information that are useful both now and in the future. Special educators often use the term *functional* to refer to such learning tasks, whereas general educators may talk about *authentic* tasks.

In addition, tasks should be described as precisely as possible. Some, such as Mager (1984), advocate the use of instructional objectives, which are statements of the desired student behavior in specific, observable terms. They spell out the conditions under which the behavior should occur and the criterion for successful performance of the behavior. Objectives help clarify the goals of instruction. Unlike broad goals such as "Students will become better readers," instructional objectives are stated with precision: "When presented with a 100-word passage from a book or story written at the grade 3 level, students will read the passage aloud with no more than 5 word recognition errors."

Writing Instructional Objectives

An objective, according to *Webster's New Collegiate Dictionary*, is "something toward which effort is directed; an aim, goal, or end of action." In education, objectives clearly state the aim of instruction. Their purpose is to direct the teacher in the selection of instructional activities.

Writing clear and useful instructional objectives is not an easy task. One common mistake is confusing objectives with goals. Goal statements are less specific than objectives; they generally describe only the behavior of interest and the direction in which the behavior should change.

> *Goal:* By the end of the school year, Jaime will increase his sight word vocabulary.
>
> *Goal:* Next semester Susie will be absent from school fewer days.

Instructional objectives, in contrast, are much more detailed. They include specific information about the exact behavior in question, the conditions under which the behavior should occur, and the criterion for successful performance of the behavior (Mager, 1984).

> *Objective:* When given a simple job application form,
>   *(conditions)*
>   Jack will write his complete name and address
>   *(behavior)*
>   in legible handwriting with no errors in spelling.
>   *(mastery criterion)*

One of the most important (and most difficult) steps in writing objectives is stating student behaviors in observable and measurable terms. The statement "Louise will write her name" is observable, but "Henry will know the meaning of all new vocabulary words" is not. Look at the lists of words below. The "observables" are action verbs; you can easily see whether someone is writing or walking. The "nonobservables" cannot be seen; it is not possible to see whether someone is understanding, knowing, or appreciating.

Observables	Nonobservables
Write a letter	Understand subtraction
Point to the answer	Know state geography
Say the alphabet	Appreciate sculpture
Read aloud from the text	Realize the importance of budgeting
Raise a hand to volunteer	Differentiate hand tools
Look at the teacher	Attend to class lectures
Name the U.S. presidents	Perceive the main idea
Draw a triangle	Draw conclusions

After the desired student behavior is identified, the teacher chooses instructional activities to present the skills and information required for task performance. Most teachers use commercial programs and supplement them with teacher-made materials and activities. The teacher must be sure that ready-made programs present all necessary skills and information and do not include extraneous or irrelevant material. The teacher must also consider current performance level when placing a student in a program sequence. For example, grade 9 texts may not be appropriate for ninth graders who read at the seventh grade level. Students should be placed in educational programs at a level at which they can succeed, that is, at their instructional level.

Break the Learning Task into Teachable Subcomponents

Tasks often require several skills or many different kinds of information for successful performance. Sometimes, particularly with commercial education programs, **task analysis**—the breaking down of tasks into smaller subtasks—is necessary. When the components of the task are identified, they can be presented to students in a systematic fashion.

First, the prerequisites for learning the task should be considered. For example, students who have not learned to solve multiplication problems will encounter difficulty when trying to calculate the area of a room. If necessary prerequisite skills are not present, instruction should begin with them. Next, the learning task is divided into subtasks. The subtasks may be a series of sequential steps or a collection of important subskills. An example of a task that can be broken into steps is addition of three-digit numbers; first the numbers in the ones column are added, then the numbers in the tens column, and finally the numbers in the hundreds column. Other tasks made up of a sequence of subtasks include building a model and locating a reference in the library. Writing a friendly letter is a task that can be divided into component subskills: handwriting (or keyboarding), spelling, capitalization, punctuation, and paragraph writing. Other such tasks are telling time, making change, and reading with comprehension.

The identification of subtasks and subskills allows the teacher to make decisions about the order in which skills and information will be presented. With tasks that are sequential in nature, subtasks are generally taught in the order in which they occur. With tasks made up of several components, the easier subskills are presented first. For example, in cursive writing instruction, simpler letters, such as lowercase *a* and *o,* are taught before more difficult letters, such as uppercase *F* and *G.*

Use Systematic Instructional Procedures

Effective instruction follows the demonstration-prompt-practice model. After the teacher presents a demonstration or explanation of the skills and information necessary for performance of the learning task, students attempt to perform the task with prompts or assistance from the teacher. Students then practice the task independently. In other words, presentation is followed by guided practice, then independent practice.

In **demonstration,** the teacher may model the performance of new skills. If factual information is being presented, the teacher may simply tell students the new material. For example, in mathematics instruction, teachers can model appropriate performance by stating a fact or a rule, performing a task as students watch and listen, or asking one student a question while others observe (Lloyd & Keller, 1989). When information is conceptual, principles and examples are used to aid in explanation (Kameenui & Simmons, 1990). In one method (Close, Irvin, Taylor, & Agosta, 1981), the teacher presents new concepts directly, then cites relevant examples; guided practice is provided when students answer direct questions, and then the teacher repeats and summarizes the original presentation.

In the prompt or **guided practice** stage, students are given opportunities to perform the task under the supervision of the teacher. This should occur before independent practice to ensure that students do not practice incorrect responses. In guided practice, the teacher gives immediate feedback to students regarding the accuracy of their responses; correct responses are confirmed, and incorrect responses are corrected. This step can be done individually, with small groups, or with the entire class. For example, the teacher can present new material to the class and then conduct a short question-and-answer session with all students. Stevens and Rosenshine (1981) recommend this technique and advocate the use of factual questions and whole-group unison responses.

In **independent practice,** the teacher continues to provide students with feedback or knowledge of results. Because this form of practice usually takes place in individual work sessions in class or as homework assignments, the time delay between student performance and feedback from the teacher is greater.

Direct teaching is another important feature of effective instruction. Skills are taught directly, and teaching activities are designed to be as close to the instructional goal as possible. For example, if the goal is for students to read words aloud, the teacher does not include activities such as matching words with pictures, looking up words in the dictionary, or writing sentences using the words. Instead, the teacher models, and students practice, reading words aloud.

Two other major considerations are maximizing the number of student responses and monitoring the accuracy of student performance. First, because students learn by responding, it is important to maximize the number of response opportunities available to each student. The goal is as many student responses as possible within given time limits. Second, because students learn by receiving information about the quality of their responses, it is important to monitor student performance by the frequent collection of data. Teachers (and students themselves) should collect information about the number and accuracy of student responses; this should occur frequently, even daily, but at a minimum once a week. This information provides feedback

Inclusion Tips for the Teacher

Direct Teaching

If you wish to teach spelling skills, here is one direct instruction method you can use. Be sure to select words that the students know the meaning of and can read. Then teach spelling.

Teacher: Let's spell the word *avalanche.* Watch me. (Teacher writes a word on the board and says letter names.) *A-v-a-l-a-n-c-h-e, avalanche.* Everyone say that with me.

Teacher and students: *A-v-a-l-a-n-c-h-e, avalanche.*

Teacher: Right. *Avalanche* is spelled *a-v-a-l-a-n-c-h-e.* Now, everyone, write *avalanche* on your paper.

Students: (Students write word.)

Teacher: Did you write *a-v-a-l-a-n-c-h-e, avalanche?* Good! Everyone say it with me.

Teacher and students: *A-v-a-l-a-n-c-h-e, avalanche.*

Teacher: *Avalanche* is spelled *a-v-a-l-a-n-c-h-e.* Now, turn your paper over and write *avalanche.*

Students: (Students write word.)

Teacher: Did you write *a-v-a-l-a-n-c-h-e, avalanche?* Good spelling.

This presentation requires only 2 or 3 minutes. In this short time the teacher has modeled the spelling of the word for the class once by writing it and five times orally. Students have spelled the word twice orally, have written it twice, and have been provided with immediate feedback each time. In just a few minutes each student in the class can be provided with several response opportunities.

to both students and teachers. If the total number of student responses or the proportion of correct responses becomes low, the teacher can modify the instructional procedures.

Effective instructional strategies can be incorporated into any type of teaching situation for any age learner. Rosenshine and Stevens (1986) suggested that teachers follow six fundamental steps in the instructional sequence:

1. Review, check previous day's work (and reteach, if necessary)
2. Present new content/skills
3. Guide student practice (and check for understanding)
4. Feedback and correctives (and reteach, if necessary)
5. Independent student practice
6. Weekly and monthly reviews. (p. 379)

This sequence is based on the demonstration-prompt-practice model; it is easily adapted to any subject matter area and is equally appropriate for elementary and secondary students.

Archer and Gleason (1989) suggested that lessons based on the demonstration-prompt-practice model be divided into three important components.

1. *Opening of the lesson.* The teacher gains the attention of the students and reviews any skills or knowledge areas critical to the content of the lesson. Then, he or she states the goal of the lesson and tells why the skill to be learned is important and when and where it will be used.
2. *Body of the lesson.* The teacher models the new skill and provides two types of guided practice: prompt and check. First, the teacher uses prompting to assist students in

performing the new skill. Second, the teacher checks the students' progress by having them perform the new skill without assistance. According to Archer and Gleason (1989), with simpler skills, "MODEL, PROMPT, and CHECK can occur in quick succession (e.g., '*This word is against. Say the word with me. What word?*')" (p. 5).
3. *Close of the lesson.* The teacher ends the lesson by reviewing the critical information presented and providing a preview of the next lesson. Then students are assigned work for independent practice.

Figure 5-2 presents a checklist developed by Polloway, Patton, and Serna (2008) to help teachers gauge how well their lessons follow the guidelines for systemic (or structured) instruction. Note that the checklist is organized around the key word PURPOSE (e.g., Prepare the student, have the student Understand) as an aid for remembering the steps in this instructional model.

Consider Both Speed and Accuracy

In selecting and describing learning tasks, teachers should determine whether the instructional goal is rapid or accurate performance. This decision influences both presentation and practice.

For most learning tasks, particularly those that involve skills, both speed and accuracy are desired. The teacher demonstrates rapid, accurate performance; students practice for accuracy first and then speed. It is imperative in skill acquisition to provide practice that ensures that students acquire

 FIGURE 5-2 The PURPOSE Checklist for Evaluating Instruction

Did the instructor:

_____ **P**repare the student to learn the skill?
_____ Define the skill?
_____ Discuss different situations where the skill could be used?
_____ Have the student **U**nderstand and learn the skill steps?
_____ Define each skill step?
_____ Give rationales for each skill step?
_____ Give examples of how each skill step should be performed?
_____ Have the students **R**ehearse the skill correctly?
_____ Model the skill for the students?
_____ Have the students research the skill?
_____ Have students **P**erform a self-check of the skill?
_____ Have each partner check to see if the skill user performed all steps and rehearsed the skill until each student reached criterion?
_____ Have the students perform a self-check of their performance?
_____ Help the students **O**vercome any skill performance problems?
_____ Have the students **S**elect other situations where the skill can be used?
_____ Have the students **E**valuate any skill performance areas outside the teaching setting?

Note: From *Strategies for Teaching Learners with Special Needs* (9th ed.) by Edward A. Polloway, James R. Patton, and Loretta Serna (p. 69). Copyright 2008 by Pearson Education, Inc. Reprinted with permission.

both accuracy and speed. If skills such as reading and writing are performed slowly, their usefulness decreases.

In skill acquisition, initial practice activities emphasize accuracy. Research suggests that students should achieve a 70% to 90% success rate during guided practice and at least a 90% success rate during independent practice (Englert, 1984; Rieth & Evertson, 1988; Rosenshine & Stevens, 1986). However, instruction should not stop with achievement of accuracy; further guided practice stressing speed should be given. This approach helps develop automatic responses that are both quick and accurate and also helps prevent students from acquiring slow response habits.

Maximize Engaged Time

Engaged time refers to the minutes and hours during which students are actively involved and participating in instruction. During that time they are "on task," whether that means listening to the teacher, observing a science experiment, answering the teacher's questions, reading, or writing. As engaged time increases, learning increases.

Students are engaged in learning for only certain portions of the school day because many noninstructional activities intrude. Even during time allocated for instruction, student attention may be directed elsewhere (Bulgren & Carta, 1992). In one study (Karweit & Slavin, 1981), actual instruction in elementary mathematics classes accounted for only 81% of the scheduled instructional time, and students were found to be engaged during only 68% of the time scheduled for instruction. Student inattention accounted for the greatest loss of learning time.

 Go to the Building Teaching Skills and Dispositions section of Topic *Intellectual Disabilities* in the MyEducationLab for your course and complete the activity entitled *Choral Responding*.

Similar results are reported by other researchers. In a study of general education classrooms, although 78% of class time was allocated to instruction, students with special needs were actively engaged only 63% of that time (Rich & Ross, 1989). Christenson & Ysseldyke (1986) compared regular classes

and resource rooms and found that, regardless of the setting, students with learning disabilities and their peers spent less than 30 minutes of a 95-minute instructional period actively responding to academic tasks.

Student engagement can be increased in several ways. First, teachers should make full use of scheduled instructional time. Other activities such as clerical and housekeeping chores should not be done during the time allotted to teaching and learning. Make every minute count!

Second, teachers should emphasize instruction rather than independent practice. Research indicates that students show much higher engagement rates in teacher-led activities than in seatwork tasks (Rieth & Evertson, 1988).

Third, instruction should be designed to engage student attention. Materials and activities should be selected so that they are attractive, interesting to students, and at an appropriate level of difficulty. The length of the lesson should be neither too short nor too long; if the lesson is too long, student interest and attention may decline. The pace of instruction should be brisk. While not rushing students, the teacher should ensure that instruction proceeds at an energetic tempo with few pauses, hesitations, interruptions, or opportunities for boredom.

Fourth, engagement increases when students are required to respond. Students should be provided with as many response opportunities as possible; students actively involved in asking and answering lesson-related questions are engaged in learning. Maximum response opportunities that result in high proportions of correct responses are basic to successful instruction.

Group responding is one way to increase the number of active student responses. In **choral responding,** all of the students in the group respond in unison to questions posed by the teacher. Heward, Courson, and Narayan (1989) recommend including several brief (5- to 10-minute) choral response sessions throughout the school day for different academic subjects. The questions asked should require short answers (no more than three words), and only one correct response should be possible.

Response cards are another method to promote group responding (Heward et al., 1996). Instead of answering orally, students hold up a card with the response they believe to be correct; for example, students might choose between a true card and a false card or among cards saying *carnivore, herbivore,* or *omnivore.* A variation is the "pinch card" (p. 5). The card contains several responses (e.g., 25%, 50%, 75%, and 100%), and the student pinches or points to the location of one of those responses. A third technique is group writing. The teacher asks a question or poses a problem (e.g., "What does the word *democracy* mean?"), and each student writes his or her response. Class members then discuss their answers and make corrections as needed.

Feldman and Denti (2004) advocated for what they call "high-access instruction," that is, instruction that promotes the active participation of all students in the classroom. Among the common low-access teaching practices not recommended by these authors are having students raise their hands to answer questions, allowing students to blurt out answers without being called on, and round-robin reading where only one student is actively engaged in reading at a time. Instead, Feldman and Denti recommended high-access instructional strategies such as choral responding, thumbs up if you know, partner techniques such as Think-(Write)-Pair-Share, peer tutoring, and random questioning with 3 × 5 name cards.

Englert (1984) suggested several ways to increase the amount of class time allocated to learning and methods for promoting student engagement during allocated learning time. The teacher checklist shown in Figure 5-3 summarizes these suggestions. For instance, teachers should spend at least 80% of class time in instructional activities and interact with 70% or more of their students each hour.

Give Clear Task Directions

For students to succeed, the directions for the learning task must be clearly stated and understandable. Before giving directions, the teacher should be sure that students are paying attention. Directions can be presented orally, in written form, or both. If directions are complicated and contain a number of steps, they should be broken down into subsets. For example,

teachers who say, "Get out your math book and a sheet of paper, turn to page 46, do the even-numbered problems in Section A, the odd-numbered problems in Section C, and the first three story problems at the top of page 47" will likely find that their directions are not followed.

Directions can be simplified by presenting only one portion at a time and by writing each portion on the chalkboard as well as stating it orally. When using written directions, the teacher must be sure that students are able to read and understand the words and comprehend the meaning of the sentences. Also, directions should be presented immediately preceding the learning task (Rosenkoetter & Fowler, 1986). Students beginning an assignment at 10 A.M. are not likely to recall or follow the directions given by the teacher at 9:30 A.M.

Teachers can determine whether directions are clear by attending to feedback from students. Puzzled expressions and failure to follow the directions are immediate cues that directions are unclear. If students are asked to repeat the directions to the teacher, misunderstandings become apparent. Clear directions are an important part of effective instruction, and clarity is one of the teacher characteristics most valued by students.

FIGURE 5-3 **Are You Making Optimal Use of Class Time?**

Respond to each item in terms of the extent to which it describes yourself: (1) not at all descriptive, (2) descriptive to a small extent, (3) descriptive to a moderate extent, (4) descriptive to a large extent, (5) descriptive to an extremely large extent.

Competencies	Performance Evaluation
Allocated Time	
1.1 Maximizes time in instruction by continually scheduling students in direct instruction (e.g., interacts with 70% or more of the students per hour).	1 2 3 4 5
1.2 Minimizes time in non-instructional activities (e.g., spends 80% or more of class time in instructional activities).	1 2 3 4 5
1.3 Keeps transition time between lessons short (e.g., no more than 3 minutes between change of students and activity; no more than 30 seconds when a change of activity only).	1 2 3 4 5
1.4 Established procedures for lessons that signal a clear beginning and end.	1 2 3 4 5
1.5 Gains all students' attention at the beginning of the lesson and maintains student attention during lesson at 90% level.	1 2 3 4 5
1.6 Prepares students for transitions in advance by stating behavioral expectations and informing students that lesson is drawing to a close.	1 2 3 4 5
Engaged Time	
2.1 Maintains students' attention during seatwork at 80% levels or higher.	1 2 3 4 5
2.2 Monitors seatwork students continuously through eye scanning.	1 2 3 4 5
2.3 Circulates among seatwork students between lessons to assist students and to monitor progress.	1 2 3 4 5
2.4 Maintains seatwork accuracy at 90% level or higher.	1 2 3 4 5
2.5 Tells rationale for seatwork and communicates the importance of the assignment.	1 2 3 4 5
2.6 Provides active forms of seatwork practice clearly related to academic goals.	1 2 3 4 5
2.7 Sets seatwork and assignment standards (neatness, accuracy, due dates).	1 2 3 4 5
2.8 Uses tutoring (e.g., peer, volunteers, aides) and other specialized instructional technology to increase opportunity for active academic responding during seatwork.	1 2 3 4 5
2.9 Establishes procedures for early finishers, students who are stalled, and those seeking help.	1 2 3 4 5
2.10 Schedules time to review seatwork.	1 2 3 4 5
2.11 Requires that students correct work and make up missed or unfinished work.	1 2 3 4 5
2.12 Gives informative feedback to students in making written or verbal corrections.	1 2 3 4 5

Source: From "Measuring Teacher Effectiveness from the Teacher's Point of View" by C. S. Englert, 1984, *Focus on Exceptional Children,* 17(2), p. 9. Copyright 1984 by Love. Reprinted by permission

Providing Students with Feedback

- When students respond correctly, tell them! A simple "Yes," "Right," "Good," or "Correct" lets a learner know that the answer was on target.
- If a student's response is correct but hesitant, the teacher should provide process feedback. The response is confirmed and the teacher explains why it was correct. For example, the teacher might say, "Yes, John, that's correct. The first word in every sentence begins with a capital letter."
- If students give incorrect responses, again they should be told. The teacher can say "No" or "Not quite." If the teacher believes a student answered incorrectly because he or she did not understand the question or was not paying attention, the question should be repeated.
- The next step is the use of a **correction procedure**. After making the student aware that the response was incorrect, the teacher should help the student produce the correct answer. The teacher can model the correct response.

Teacher: Spell *this*.
Student: *T-h-e-s*.
Teacher: No, *this* is spelled *t-h-i-s*. Spell *this*.
Student: *T-h-i-s*.
Teacher: Right!

With some learning tasks a prompt can be given.

Teacher: Read this word: *shut*.
Student: *Cut*.
Teacher: Not quite. The first sound is *sh*. Read it again.
Student: *Shut*.
Teacher: Good reading.

Or the task can be made easier.

Teacher: Who was the first president of the United States?
Student: Lincoln.
Teacher: No. Was it George Washington or Thomas Jefferson?
Student: Washington.
Teacher: Correct.

Knowledge of results is a powerful tool for helping students learn. However, when students make errors, feedback alone is not sufficient. To help students learn the correct response, correction procedures must also be used.

Provide Consequences for Successful Task Performance

In most classrooms, a variety of consequences are available for the teacher's use. Successful task performance may be followed by teacher attention, praise, special privileges, or awards. Unsuccessful performance, in contrast, may result in the loss of teacher attention and praise or other unpleasant consequences. Because behaviors followed by pleasant consequences are more likely to occur again, teachers should make a systematic effort to reward successful task performance.

One powerful consequence is feedback to the student or **knowledge of results.** The student responds, and the teacher comments about the accuracy of the response; correct answers are confirmed, and incorrect answers are corrected. Students provided with information about the acceptability of their responses tend to modify their performances to increase the number of correct responses. Eventually they begin monitoring their own performances rather than relying on teacher feedback. Suggested ways of providing feedback are listed in the "Inclusion Tips for the Teacher" material.

In addition to knowledge of results, other consequences can be used. Teachers can reward successful task performance with attention, praise, and compliments; with letter or number grades; with recognition of the student's accomplishment before peers or parents; and with awards, privileges, and special activities.

Consequences, like instructional antecedents, are powerful tools for promoting successful classroom performance. However, consequences must be used systematically. They should follow behaviors as closely in time as possible, especially when

students are in the acquisition stage of learning. Consequences should also be used consistently. Behaviors confirmed as correct and rewarded on one day should receive the same consequences on the next day.

Check for Maintenance and Generalization

The majority of the time spent in instruction is devoted to acquisition of skills and knowledge. However, if students are to use what they have learned in later school and life situations, maintenance and generalization are also important. Teachers cannot assume that tasks performed successfully today will also be performed successfully next week, next month, or next semester. Acquisition does not guarantee maintenance. Skills and information, particularly those that are verbal in nature, are forgotten if not practiced. To enhance maintenance, task performance should be monitored over time, and practice should be provided when necessary.

Generalization cannot be assumed, either. Students may perform quite well on one task but be unable to transfer their learning to a similar task. For example, words spelled correctly on a spelling test may be misspelled in a book report or essay. Generalization is crucial because there is insufficient time to teach all the possible situations in which particular skills and information may be needed. Teachers can promote transfer by evaluating its occurrence; if necessary, the teacher can demonstrate how skills and information are used in many different situations and then provide students with practice in generalization.

If Change Is Needed, Try the Least Intrusive Intervention First

Data on student performance may indicate the need for a change in instructional procedures. Student responses may be infrequent, inconsistent, or less accurate than desired. To increase the likelihood of successful performance, the learning task should be made easier—by changing teaching procedures, modifying materials and activities, or altering task requirements. Several ways of accomplishing this are described later in this chapter.

However, unsuccessful performance should not result in the immediate substitution of an alternate task. First, the original task should be modified in an attempt to increase response accuracy. The simplest, least dramatic changes should be tried first; for instance, task failure may be due to insufficient practice or poor understanding of the directions. Intense interventions such as radically different instructional procedures, new materials and activities, or abandonment of the original task should be used only when all other options have been exhausted.

The principles of instruction presented here apply to learners of all ages and all ability levels. However, it is possible for teachers to use effective instructional techniques but to apply these techniques unequally with different groups of students. Research indicates that teachers treat high achievers and low achievers quite differently. For example, in one study (Alves & Gottlieb, 1986), general education teachers interacted less frequently with students with disabilities than with their classmates without disabilities. Students with disabilities also were asked fewer questions by their teachers and received less feedback on their performance. For instruction to be truly effective, it must address the needs of all students within the classroom.

▶ **METHODS FOR GATHERING DATA ABOUT INSTRUCTION**

Information about student performance helps the teacher make instructional decisions. For example, data are gathered to determine the student's current level of academic performance before instruction begins. Such information aids in planning the educational program and placing the student in the correct portion of the instructional sequence. During instruction, data are used to evaluate student progress and to explore reasons for poor performance; this information helps to determine whether instructional adaptations should be made.

Although many types of assessment techniques are available, in most cases informal assessment rather than formal testing is the method of choice for gathering information about a student's classroom performance. One approach to informal assessment is **curriculum-based assessment (CBA)**, defined as "a procedure for determining the instructional needs of students based on the student's ongoing performance in existing course content" (Gickling & Thompson, 1985, p. 206). That is, the curriculum of the student's classroom is used as the yardstick by which to measure educational progress. Results of such assessments have immediate instructional applications (Pemberton, 2003). Skills that the student has not yet mastered become the next goals in the instructional sequence. The sections that follow provide principles for gathering useful information about student performance.

Determine the Student's Current Levels of Performance

Before beginning instruction, teachers are interested in determining what skills have already been acquired by the student. The group achievement tests given routinely to students in many school districts are one source of this information. Measures such as the *Metropolitan Achievement Tests,* the *California Achievement Tests,* and the *Stanford Achievement Tests* provide information about level of performance in basic skills such as reading and mathematics. For example, results may indicate that a sixth grade student is performing at a fifth grade level in reading comprehension, a sixth grade level in mathematics, and a fourth grade level in written language.

Because student achievement levels change over time, only recent achievement test results are of interest. However, even recent test data should be considered with caution because test tasks may differ from classroom learning tasks. Also, some students—particularly those with special needs—do not perform to the best of their ability on tests administered in group settings. In general, standardized measures such as group achievement tests are not the best source of information about current levels of performance for this group of students. In fact, federal law requires that test modifications be made whenever necessary for students with disabilities who participate in the group achievement tests administered on district-wide or statewide basis to their general education peers. A later section of this chapter discusses principles for making test accommodations for these students.

Using the principles of the Response-to-Intervention approach, teachers can review the results of group achievement tests to identify students who might need supplemental instruction or interventions such as special education. Stone, Cundick, and Swanson (1988) recommended selecting the 5th percentile as a cutoff point. Percentile rank scores indicate the percentage of a test's norm group that a particular student's performance equals or exceeds. Thus, a student scoring at the 5th percentile would show achievement equal to or better than 5% of norm group peers (and worse than 95% of that group). Reynolds, Zetlin, and Wang (1993) recommended a somewhat different procedure, "20/20 Analysis." Results of group achievement tests are studied to identify two groups of students who benefit from adaptations of the general education program: (a) students with learning problems, defined as students who fall in the lowest 20% (i.e., below the 20th percentile); and (b) high achievers, defined as students who fall in the highest 20% (above the 80th percentile).

Informal measures such as placement tests, inventories, and criterion-referenced tests provide the most useful information about current levels of student performance. For example, the placement tests found in many commercial educational programs and textbook series assess the student's skill levels and provide information about where in the educational program the student should begin. If these measures are not available, the teacher can devise informal assessments such as inventories and criterion-referenced tests.

Inventories are measures that sample a variety of different skills and information within a subject matter area. They are designed to estimate the approximate level of student functioning. For instance, an informal math inventory would not assess all aspects of a mathematics curriculum. However, it might include a range of problems sampling knowledge of basic number facts, skills in basic operations (addition, subtraction, multiplication, and division), and ability to solve problems requiring regrouping. Student performance on this inventory would give the teacher some information about which skills have been acquired and which have not. An informal handwriting inventory appears in Figure 5-4; this measure provides general information about current levels of performance in the skill area of handwriting.

 FIGURE 5-4 **Handwriting Inventory**

Print your name on the line below.

_____
- -

Fill in the missing letters.
_____
a _ c d _ f g _ i j _ l _ n o _ q r _ t u _ w _ y

Print the uppercase (capital) letter that goes with each of the lowercase (small) letters below.

a A

b _____   f _____   d _____

g _____   r _____

Copy this sentence in your best printing.

Foxes and rabbits are quick, but turtles are slow.

_____

Write your name in cursive on the line below.
_____
- -

Finish writing the cursive alphabet.

a b c _____

Write the following words in cursive.

dog _____   like _____   and _____   the _____

Write this sentence in your best cursive handwriting.

At the zoo you can see lions and tigers, elephants, bears, and monkeys.

_____
_____

For more specific data, more precise measures are necessary. **Criterion-referenced tests** assess whether students have mastered the educational goals stated in instructional objectives. The teacher selects an objective, sets up the necessary conditions, and determines whether students are able to perform well enough to meet the criterion for acceptable performance. For example, to determine mastery of the objective "Students will write the names of at least 45 of the states with no errors in spelling," the teacher simply directs students to write the names of each of the states. Responses are acceptable if they are state names and if they are spelled correctly. Students with fewer than 45 correct responses have not yet met the objective and should receive further instruction.

Evaluate Progress

Information about student performance during instruction provides the teacher with feedback about the effectiveness of teaching procedures. Before instruction begins, it is important to pretest students to establish a performance baseline. This initial performance then becomes the reference point for evaluating progress in the instructional program.

Systematic observation is a useful and flexible technique for monitoring academic progress and a variety of student behaviors. As explained later in this text, observation is a flexible technique that can be used with a variety of student behaviors. In academic instruction, observation generally focuses on the number of responses made by the student and the proportion (or percentage) of correct responses. Figure 5-5 presents an example in which the teacher observed Juan's performance on science assignments for a 1-week period. Although Juan answered all the questions, the proportion of correct responses never rose above 50%. Thus, the teacher will modify instruction in an attempt to increase response accuracy.

Curriculum-based measurement is also an effective strategy for monitoring student progress (Deno, 1985, 1987; Fuchs, 1986, 1987; Howell, Fox, & Morehead, 1993). Deno and Fuchs (1987) describe the procedures needed to establish a system of curriculum-based measurement in the classroom. The teacher decides what to measure and how to measure it, then formulates a specific instructional goal and objective. In the example provided by Deno and Fuchs, the goal is as follows:

> In 19 weeks, when presented with stories for 1 minute from Level 2-SRA series, Michael will read aloud 80 words with no more than 6 errors. (p. 13)

The accompanying objective is to increase the number of words Michael reads correctly by an average of 2.6 words per week.

The teacher assesses this student's progress by having him read randomly selected passages from his reading text for 1-minute periods. These data are collected frequently, at least twice a week. The student's performance is graphed (see Figure 5-6), and his progress is compared with the aimline, a diagonal line extending from his baseline performance to the instructional goal (marked with an *X* on the graph).

Another approach to monitoring student growth is the use of **rubrics** to determine progress toward curricular standards. Airasian (1996) explains that rubrics are "brief, written descriptions of different levels of student performance" (p. 154). These levels can be indicated by numerical values (e.g., 1 through 5) or by descriptive labels such as *excellent, very good, good, average*, or *needs improvement*. The teacher (or other rater) evaluates the student's work and determines where within the descriptive framework that work falls. Figure 5-7 shows two sections of a rubric for evaluating student essays, the sections on Writing Conventions and Organization. In using this rubric, the teacher would need to decide which descriptions are most accurate. For example, a student's work might make sense (a rating of 4 in the Organization section), but show errors in the use of writing conventions (a rating of 2).

Analyze Reasons for Task Failure

When task performance is unsatisfactory, the student's responses can be analyzed to help locate problem areas. Called **error analysis**, this technique involves scoring each response as correct or incorrect and then looking for error patterns. For example, a student may solve only 8 of 22 addition problems

 FIGURE 5-5 Observations of Academic Performance

Student: _____Juan_____
Subject: _____Science 9_____
Task: ___Homework Assignments___

Day	Number of Questions	Number of Responses	Number of Correct Responses	Percentage of Correct Responses
Monday	7	7	3	43%
Tuesday	9	9	4	44%
Wednesday	6	6	3	50%
Thursday	10	10	5	50%
Friday	8	8	3	38%

FIGURE 5-6   Curriculum-Based Measurement

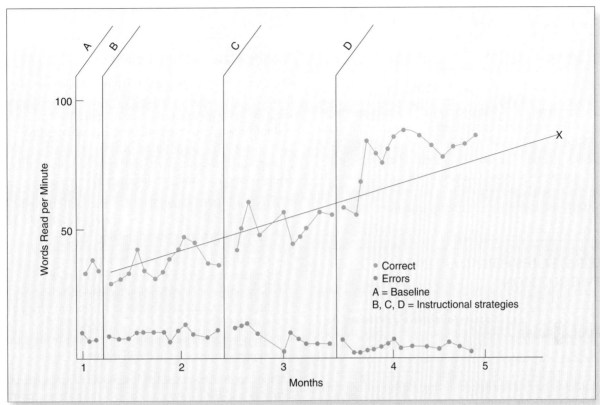

Source: From "Developing Curriculum-Based Measurement Systems for Data-Based Special Education Problem Solving" by S. L. Deno and L. S. Fuchs, 1987, *Focus on Exceptional Children, 19*(8), p. 15. Copyright 1987 by Love. Reprinted by permission.

FIGURE 5-7   Excerpts from a Rubric for Evaluating Student Essays

Writing Conventions

Rating	Description
5	The use of writing conventions is very effective. No errors evident. These conventions are fluid and complex: spelling, punctuation, grammar usage, sentence structure.
4	The use of writing conventions is effective. Only minor errors evident. These conventions are nearly all effective: spelling, punctuation, grammar usage, sentence structure.
3	The use of writing conventions is somewhat effective. Errors don't interfere with meaning. These conventions are somewhat effective: spelling, punctuation, grammar usage, sentence structure.
2	Errors in the use of writing conventions interfere with meaning. These conventions are limited and uneven: spelling, punctuation, grammar usage, sentence structure.
1	Major errors in the use of writing conventions obscure meaning. Lack of understanding of spelling, punctuation, grammar usage, sentence structure.

Organization

5	Clearly makes sense.
4	Makes sense.
3	Makes sense for the most part.
2	Attempted but does not make sense.
1	Does not make sense.

Source: Tombari & Borich, *Authentic Assessment in the Classroom*, Rubric for Evaluating Student Essays, p. 176, © 1999. Reproduced by permission of Pearson Education, Inc.

correctly; by systematically analyzing the student's responses, the teacher may find that all errors involved problems requiring regrouping and that the student was using an inappropriate strategy, such as failing to carry:

$$\begin{array}{r} 42 \\ +39 \\ \hline 711 \end{array}$$

If student performance is poor (few responses are made, or most of the responses are incorrect), analyzing the task rather than the specific student errors may be helpful. With task analysis, the task is broken down into component parts, and then students are asked to perform each of the parts. In this way, the subtasks that are causing the most difficulty can be identified, and instruction can begin with those areas.

 ## STRATEGIES FOR ADAPTING INSTRUCTION

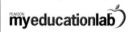 Go to the Assignments and Activities section of Topic *Assessment* in the MyEducationLab for your course and complete the activity entitled *Using Assessment to Drive Instruction*.

When students have difficulty acquiring skills and information, the teacher adapts instruction to better meet the students' needs. Teachers can modify instructional materials and activities, change teaching procedures, or alter the requirements of the learning task. Several of the specific strategies for instructional adaptations appear in Figure 5-8. These should be used in an attempt to improve student performance before more involved modifications are made. Note that the strategies are arranged in numerical order from 1 to 10. Number 1 should be tried before number 2, number 2 before number 3, and so on. Of course, before these methods are used, teachers should be sure that the learning task is at an appropriate level of difficulty for the student.

Modify Materials and Activities

The first type of adaptation to try is modification of instructional materials and activities. The learning task remains the same; what is changed is the way in which the necessary skills and information are presented to the student. Three possible strategies are the clarification of task directions, addition of prompts to the learning task, and correction of specific student errors (items 1, 2, and 3 in Figure 5-8).

Clarify Task Directions. Students may perform tasks poorly if the directions for the task are unclear. Several changes can make directions more understandable.

- Give directions both orally and in writing.
- Restate oral directions in simpler language.
- Give only one or two oral directions at a time.
- Be sure students are able to see directions written on the chalkboard.
- Keep written directions on the student's reading level.
- Explain any new or unfamiliar terms.

After giving directions, the teacher should demonstrate task performance and then answer any questions students may have.

Add Prompts. Prompts or *cues* are any features added to learning tasks that assist students in task performance. Prompts can be verbal, visual, or physical and can either call attention to the cues already available in the learning task or introduce an artificial cue system.

Prompts are often used to make critical features of the learning task more noticeable. For example, if students confuse

 ## FIGURE 5-8 Adapting Instruction

IF students experience difficulty in task performance,
TRY these adaptations of . . .
Materials and activities:
1. Clarify task directions
2. Add prompts to the learning task
3. Teach to specific student errors
Teaching procedures:
4. Give additional presentation of skills and information
5. Provide additional guided practice
6. Make consequences for successful performance more attractive
7. Slow the pace of instruction
Task requirements:
8. Change the criteria for successful performance
9. Change task characteristics
10. Break each task into smaller subtasks
BEFORE selecting an alternate task.
IF NECESSARY, substitute a similar but easier task or a prerequisite task.

addition and subtraction symbols, teachers might circle the symbols, make them larger, write them in red, or remind students to "check each problem to see whether you add or subtract." If students read aloud without attending to punctuation, punctuation marks can be underlined, highlighted, or color coded to make them stand out.

Artificial prompts can also be added to learning tasks. In handwriting instruction, for instance, guidelines are provided to assist beginning writers. Another example is the use of underlining; teachers who underline important words and phrases on the board are providing prompts. Teachers can also give verbal prompts or reminders; for example, before students begin to write a paragraph, the teacher might say, "Remember to begin each sentence with a capital letter."

Any learning task can be made easier by the use of prompts. However, as students learn, it is important to withdraw the prompts from the task, fading them gradually (as shown in Figure 5-9) to maintain successful student performance.

Teach to Specific Student Errors. If students make consistent errors that affect overall task performance, the teacher should focus on the correction of those errors. This approach is effective if a few types of errors account for the majority of incorrect responses. For example, if a student writes the cursive alphabet correctly with the exception of the letters *m* and *n*, these letters should be singled out and taught directly. Or if oral reading is characterized by frequent repetitions ("I want . . . I want to go to the . . . I want to go to the store . . . I want to go to the store to buy . . ."), the teacher should attempt to correct this error. However, if task failure is the result of several types of errors (or too few responses), it is probably necessary to modify the procedures used in teaching.

FIGURE 5-9 Fading Prompts from the Learning Task

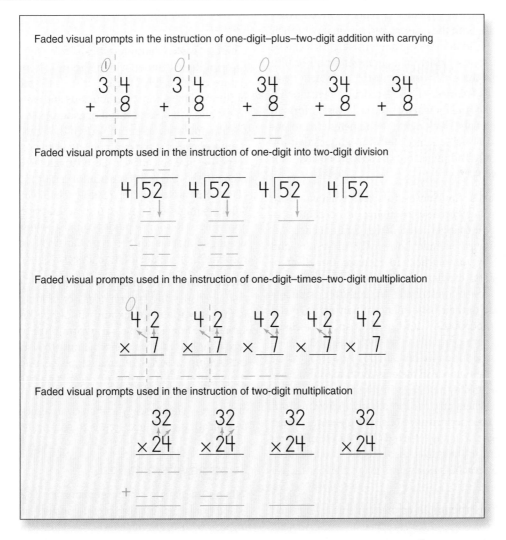

Source: Fading Prompts from the Learning Task: Reprinted with permission of Merrill, from *Teaching the Mildly Handicapped in the Regular Classroom* (2nd ed., p. 107) by J. Affleck, S. Lowenbraun, and A. Archer. Copyright © 1980 Merrill Publishing Company, Columbus, Ohio.

Change Teaching Procedures

If modification of instructional activities and materials does not result in successful performance, the next step is to adapt the teaching procedures. Strategies include giving additional presentations, providing additional practice, changing the consequences, and slowing the pace of instruction (items 4, 5, 6, and 7 in Figure 5-8).

Give Additional Presentation of Skills and Information. An additional presentation of the skills and information necessary for task performance may be appropriate. With this strategy, the teacher demonstrates skills and explains information. A repetition of the original presentation may produce the desired results. However, the teacher must usually provide a more complete (or simpler) explanation, additional examples, or several instances in which the skill is modeled.

Provide Additional Guided Practice. Poor task performance may be improved by additional guided practice. The teacher can increase the amount of practice by requiring more student responses, lengthening practice sessions (although not to the point of student fatigue), or scheduling extra sessions throughout the school day. To make practice more effective, teachers can increase both the amount and the quality of their feedback to students. To increase the amount, feedback can be given after every response rather than after every third or fifth answer. To increase the quality of feedback, the teacher can describe important features of the student's behavior in addition to telling the student whether the task was performed correctly. The statement "That's right. You remembered to put a period at the end of the sentence" tells the student that the response was accurate and points out the specific behavior for which praise is given.

Make Consequences for Successful Performance More Attractive. This strategy involves changing the consequences of the behavior rather than its antecedents. Consequences for successful performance include knowledge of results and rewards supplied by the teacher. To increase the effect of knowledge of results, teachers can improve the quality of feedback, as previously described. In addition, students become more aware of their performance if they are involved in data collection procedures. They can place an *X* or a check mark beside each correct response on their assigned papers and then plot their performance on a graph.

The reward system in use in the classroom may also need to be altered. Students may require incentives to begin or complete a task. And teachers may need to reward approximations toward successful task performance (e.g., 60% accuracy, then 70%, etc., until the criterion is achieved). The nature of the rewards used by the teacher may also require modification; things perceived by teachers as rewards may be less attractive to students.

Slow the Pace of Instruction. If changes in antecedents and consequences do not produce acceptable performance, slowing the pace of instruction may be necessary. The learning task and the time allotted for instruction remain the same, but less material is presented and practiced. For example, the teacher may demonstrate telling time to the hour and to the half hour in two separate sessions rather than one. If this strategy is unsuccessful, the teacher should consider altering the requirements of the learning task.

Alter Task Requirements

The learning task itself can be modified to enhance student success. Possible strategies are changing task criteria, changing task characteristics, and breaking the task into smaller subtasks (items 8, 9, and 10 in Figure 5-8).

Change the Criteria for Successful Performance. The criteria for successful performance generally address three aspects of the task: quantity, speed, and accuracy. The requirements for each can be reduced. The number of questions, problems, or activities to be performed can be reduced. The time limits imposed can be increased so that speed demands are relaxed, or a lower accuracy rate can be accepted. However, the teacher should maintain reasonable accuracy requirements to ensure that the student is learning the task.

Change Task Characteristics. Task characteristics include the conditions under which the task is performed and the nature of the behavior itself. If the task requires students to perform from memory without aids and assistance, the teacher might allow the use of aids. For example, students may be able to solve multiplication problems if they can use an aid such as a multiplication table or a pocket calculator. Presentation and response modes can also be changed. A task's presentation mode is the way it presents information; for example, many classroom tasks require reading skills. Instead of reading, students might listen to lectures and tapes or watch television and videos. Response modes can also be modified. Instead of writing, students might type, answer orally, record their responses, or dictate them to a peer.

Break Tasks into Smaller Subtasks. If alteration of task characteristics and criteria does not produce success, the task is probably too complex and should be broken into smaller subtasks. For example, if writing (or dictating or tape recording) an essay is overwhelming to a student, the teacher can set up a series of smaller tasks: selection of a topic, preparation of an outline or organizational map, writing the title, formulation of the topic sentence for the first paragraph, and so on. This strategy is the last in a series of instructional modifications; the next step is to substitute an alternate task.

Select an Alternate Task

When student performance remains poor despite instructional adaptations, the teacher should consider replacing the learning task with an alternate task. Two choices are possible: a similar but easier task or a prerequisite task.

Substitute a Similar but Easier Task. The teacher can select an alternate task similar in nature to the original task but easier for students to perform. For example, if students are unable to cope with the history textbook (even in taped form), the teacher can substitute another text that covers the same material but in less depth and at an easier reading level. This allows students to proceed at their own levels and rates while remaining in the same general subject area as their peers.

Substitute a Prerequisite Task. The most drastic intervention available to the general education teacher is replacement of the original learning task with a prerequisite task. For example, if students with poor basic skills are unable to solve algebraic equations (even with the aid of a calculator), the teacher may substitute instruction in math facts and the operations of addition, subtraction, multiplication, and division. This strategy should be the last employed in the general education classroom because it involves the most radical change from typical classroom procedures. Students whose needs cannot be met with this strategy are candidates for special education services.

The most comprehensive instructional modification that can be made is change of the curriculum. This often occurs when students with severe disabilities are included in general education classes as part of their special education program. In most cases, the educational goals for students with serious learning needs address areas such as socialization and communication skills, rather than academic performance. For students such as these, instructional adaptations usually include the substitution of an alternative curriculum. For example, a student with severe disabilities might participate in the same lesson on volcanoes as others in the class, although the instructional goal for that student relates to learning to work with others, rather than science.

▶ MAKING TEST ACCOMMODATIONS

When students with special needs are members of general education classrooms, it is often useful to consider adapting not only instruction but also the procedures used to assess student learning. Adaptations are particularly important when students with disabilities participate alongside their general education peers in state-wide or district-wide tests of academic achievement. These "high-stakes" tests, usually administered on an annual basis, are part of the national movement toward higher performance standards for students and greater accountability for schools, districts, and state educational agencies.

Federal special education law requires that IEP teams address how students with disabilities will participate in state-wide or district-wide measures of academic achievement. Three options are possible. First of all, students may simply take the same tests as their grade-level peers under identical conditions; no changes or modifications are made. Second, students with disabilities may participate in the same assessments as their regular class peers but with one or more changes or accommodations to increase the probability of success. One common example of a test accommodation is an increase in the amount of time allowed to complete a particular section of a test. The third and most drastic option open to the IEP team is to determine that the general education achievement test is not appropriate for a student and that his or her educational progress should instead be measured by an alternate assessment procedure. That alternate assessment is then selected or developed by the IEP team.

The second option, test accommodations, is likely the most common for students with disabilities who are included in general education classes. Elliott, Kratochwill, and Gilbertson (1998) defined testing accommodations as "a change in the way that a test is administered or responded to by the person tested" (p. 10). Because of the many types of accommodations possible, several attempts have been made to come up with category systems to simplify discussion of the possibilities.

For example, Erickson, Ysseldyke, Thurlow, and Elliott (1998) and Landau, Vohs, and Romano (1998) described similar systems. Each addressed four basic types of test accommodations:

- Timing and/or scheduling accommodations
- Setting accommodations
- Presentation accommodations
- Response accommodations

Timing/scheduling modifications involve extending time limits for a test, allowing a student to take frequent breaks, or scheduling the test over several days rather than one. Setting accommodations include changes such as administration of the test to a small group rather than a large group or a change in the location of the test. Presentation accommodations include modifications such as providing test materials in a different format (e.g., large print, Braille) and reading the test aloud to a student. In contrast, when the test's response mode is changed, students may be allowed to answer orally rather than write on an answer sheet.

Although many different types of accommodations are available, states and districts vary in the modifications they permit for students with disabilities. The most typical types of changes, allowed by more than half of the 50 states ("State-wide Assessment Programs," 1998), follow:

- *Presentation:* Large print, Braille, sign language
- *Setting:* Small-group administration, separate testing session
- *Timing/scheduling:* Flexible scheduling, extra time, multiple testing sessions

Less common were alterations in response mode. Only 12 states allowed students to tape record their responses and 21 permitted the use of word processors. A more recent review of state policies

TABLE 5-3 Strategies for Making Assessment Accommodations

Type of Accommodation	Examples
Directions/instructions	Use simpler language when providing directions; repeat the directions as needed by the student.
Demonstrations	Show the student what to do before he or she is required to do it.
Time limits	Extend the time limits or remove them altogether.
Presentation mode	Change the way in which information is presented; for example, students could listen to a question rather than read it.
Response mode	Change the way in which answers are given; for example, students could answer orally rather than write.
Aids	Permit students to use aids such as paper and pencil or calculators.
Prompts and cues	Provide prompts during assessment; for example, begin the first task for the student or remind him or her to complete all parts of the question.
Feedback	During assessment, confirm to students that answers are correct; indicate which answers are incorrect.
Positive reinforcement	Praise students for attending to the assessment task; reward them for correct answers.
Physical location	Have the student work in a different part of the classroom or in a different room altogether.

Note: McLoughlin & Lewis, *Assessing Students with Special Needs*, pp. 98–99, © 2008 Pearson Education, Inc. Adapted by permission of Pearson Education, Inc.

for test accommodations revealed a similar pattern with one exception. Forty-three states allowed dictation of responses to a scribe, an alternate response mode (Bolt & Thurlow, 2004; Thurlow, House, Boys, Scott, & Ysseldyke, 2000). It is hoped that restrictions on types of accommodations in high-stakes testing will continue to become less stringent as states and districts become more familiar with the process of making assessment modifications.

Students with special needs are more likely to succeed in general education classrooms when teachers adapt instruction and make accommodations in assessment. These accommodations make sense not only for state-wide and district-wide testing but also for the types of assessments used routinely in classroom situations. Table 5-3 lists ideas for adapting assessment procedures in the general education classroom.

This chapter has presented important principles and strategies for teaching and adapting instruction and assessment to meet the needs of students in general education classrooms who experience difficulty at some point in the learning process. Before going on, check "Things to Remember" to review what you have learned.

Things to Remember

- Students may experience academic problems during any of the three stages of learning: acquisition, maintenance, and generalization.

- Effective instruction is individualized, intensive, and explicit.

- Differentiated instruction is a technique used in general education to individualize the learning process for all students within the classroom.

- In systematic instruction, teachers select the learning task based on students' needs, present the content and skills needed for task performance, and provide practice until tasks are mastered.

- Classroom assessment data provide information about current levels of functioning, rates of progress, and reasons for task failure.

- When students are not making adequate progress, teachers introduce the least intrusive instructional modification first.

- Adapt instruction by first changing materials and activities, then altering teaching procedures, and finally modifying task requirements.

- Use substitution of an alternate learning task, the most drastic instructional change, only as a last resort.

- Students with special needs may benefit not only from adaptations in instruction but also from accommodations in assessment procedures.

► ACTIVITIES

1. Arrange to observe in a classroom, and explain to the teacher that you are interested in seeing how much of the school day is actually devoted to instruction. Observe and keep a record of classroom activities for an hour or so. How much time is spent in large-group instruction? Small-group instruction? Supervision of students' independent work? Noninstructional duties?

2. Ways of adapting instruction include changing the characteristics of the task and the performance criteria. Try your hand at modifying this objective.

   When given a page of 25 math problems, the student will write the correct answers to at least 20 problems within 5 minutes. Describe how you would alter the task for each of the modifications listed here. The first one is done for you.

Modification	Altered Task
Reduce quantity	Give only 20 problems
Reduce speed	
Reduce accuracy	
Change presentation mode	
Change response mode	

3. Explain why substitution of an alternate learning task should be the last instructional modification attempted.

4. Several educational journals offer suggestions to teachers about adapting instruction for students with special needs. Examples are *Teaching Exceptional Children, Focus on Exceptional Children,* and *Intervention in School and Clinic.* Find an article that interests you and summarize its recommendations.

CHAPTER
SIX

Encouraging Positive Classroom Behavior

Classroom behavior problems such as those described in the following "Students' Stories" are not rare occurrences. They are a sampling of the behaviorial issue that teachers face daily in the general education classroom.

- Henry is late for class at least twice a week.
- Maxine hasn't completed an assignment this semester.
- Several times each day, John interrupts the teacher's lecture by talking and making noises.
- Pablo argues and fights with other students in the classroom.
- During independent study time, Tanisha looks around the room and watches other students or writes notes to her friends.
- Ashley doesn't ask questions in class; in fact, the only talking she does is at lunch with her two close friends.
- Willie is seldom in his seat. He seems to be constantly on the move, and he holds the class record for the longest round-trip to the pencil sharpener.

LOOKING AHEAD

Behavior problems are one of the most common difficulties students with special needs experience in general education classrooms. Before reading about strategies for addressing these problems, think about the questions that follow.

- Each of the students described here appears to be having difficulty meeting classroom behavioral demands. Would you predict that these students also have special needs in the area of academic performance?
- Which students exhibit behavior that is likely to interfere with classroom instructional activities and disrupt their classmates' learning?
- Which students show behaviors that are likely to interfere only with their own learning?
- Do you think students such as John, Pablo, and Ashley have difficulty making friends? What evidence would you offer to support your opinion?

BEHAVIOR PROBLEMS IN THE CLASSROOM

Behavior problems are commonplace. They are exhibited not only by students with special needs but also by typical students of all ages and at every grade level. Some behaviors call attention to themselves only in the classroom; others may require attention at recess, in the school lunchroom, on the way to and from school, at home, and in the neighborhood.

The behavior problems of students frequently contribute to their placement in special education programs. When students with special needs are included in general education classrooms, their teachers are often concerned that their problem behaviors will interfere with the operation of the classroom. In addition, such behaviors may hinder the special students' academic achievement and may have a negative effect on their acceptance by others.

Two major types of behavior problems are of concern to the teacher: inappropriate classroom behavior and poor study skills. Behaviors that interfere with classroom instruction, impede social interaction with teacher and peers, or endanger others are considered **classroom conduct problems.** Examples of inappropriate classroom behaviors are talking out, fighting, arguing, being out of one's seat, swearing, and avoiding interactions with others. Immature and withdrawn behaviors also fall under this category. Behaviors that interfere with students' academic performance or the teacher's ability to assess academic progress are considered **study skill problems.** Typical study skill problems include failure to complete assignments, poor attention during lectures or class discussion, failure to follow directions, and poor management of study time.

Problem behaviors are exhibited in one of three ways: low rate of appropriate behaviors, high rate of inappropriate behaviors, or absence of the appropriate behavior from the student's repertoire. Different management strategies are linked to each type of problem behavior.

- *Low rate of appropriate behaviors.* Students exhibit appropriate behaviors but not as frequently as expected or required. For example, a student may be able to complete homework assignments but chooses to do so only 10% to

Behavior Problems

- In a recent Gallup poll (Bushaw & Gallup, 2008), the general public identified lack of discipline as the second biggest problem faced by schools today. The only problem considered more pressing was lack of funding.
- Seventeen percent of new teachers in the elementary grades and 23% of those in the secondary grades report that their biggest challenge is maintaining classroom order and discipline, according to a recent MetLife Survey of the American Teacher (Markow & Martin, 2005).
- A recent report from the National Center for Education Statistics and the Bureau of Justice Statistics (Dinkes, Kemp, & Baum, 2009) revealed that in 2007 almost one-third of students said that they had been bullied at school during the school year. However, the same report suggests that the percentage of school principals who perceive bullying as a frequently occurring discipline problem has decreased from 1999–2000 to 2005–2006.
- One older study (Rubin & Balow, 1978) reported that 60% of elementary school children are identified by at least one of their teachers as having a behavior problem.

- In effective classrooms, teachers provide instruction in both academics and social behavior to maximize the time students spend on learning tasks, increase student achievement, and decrease the need to focus primarily on classroom management (Kauffman, 2001; Pacchiano, 2000; Sutherland & Wehby, 2001).
- Students with poor social behaviors do not achieve as well academically as peers with appropriate social skills (Lane, Barton-Arwood, Nelson, & Wehby, 2008). Improving performance in personal interactions and task-related social skills increases both academic performance and social acceptance (Zirpoli & Melloy, 2001).
- The behaviors that are appropriate in the classroom are determined by the teacher, the policies of the school, and the beliefs of the community. A behavior that one teacher considers inappropriate may be totally acceptable to another.

20% of the time. Also, students may behave appropriately in one setting but not in another. For instance, a student with disabilities may work well in the resource room but may find it difficult to work in a small-group setting in the general education classroom. To alleviate these problems, the teacher sets up a systematic program to increase the occurrence of appropriate behaviors or to help students generalize behaviors from one situation to another.

- *High rate of inappropriate behaviors.* Inappropriate behaviors that are troublesome to teachers occur frequently or for long periods of time. Examples include students who are out of their seats 30 to 40 times per day, those who talk during 50% to 60% of the class lecture, and those who use profanity 5 to 10 times in one class period. To overcome these high rates of inappropriate behavior, teachers attempt to decrease the frequency or duration of the undesired behavior by increasing appropriate behaviors that are incompatible. For instance, to decrease running in the classroom, the teacher can work to increase the frequency of walking.
- *Absence of the appropriate behavior from the student's repertoire.* Students may not yet have learned the appropriate behavior for social interaction or classroom functioning. The age or grade level of a student is not an accurate predictor of behavioral competence; it is necessary to consider each student individually. For instance, sixth graders may not know how to start a conversation or how to organize their time to ensure completion of assignments. To remedy this, the effective teacher directly teaches the new behavior (conversation skills or time management), provides instruction on when and how the behavior is to take place, and carefully builds practice and review opportunities into the instructional sequence (Cullinan, 2002; Emmer, 1981; Olson & Platt, 1996).

Behavior problems do not occur in isolation. The way in which the classroom learning environment is arranged and the actions of others can promote, initiate, or reinforce inappropriate behaviors. If classroom behavior problems are to be understood and managed, not only the behavior of the target student but also that of the teacher and peers must be examined. For example, a sarcastic comment from a teacher can initiate a verbal retort from the student. Classmates who laugh at the clowning or wisecracks of their peers ensure that similar behaviors will recur.

Students behave inappropriately when they have not learned correct responses—or when they have found that acting inappropriately is more rewarding than acting appropriately. Such behavior problems *do* respond to instruction. According to one point of view, behavior problems belong to the teacher, not the student. This viewpoint holds that it is not the students who fail; instead, educators have failed to develop acceptable student behaviors. Opinions about and results of research into student behavior in the schools are presented in the accompanying "For Your Information" feature.

 THE BEHAVIORAL SUPPORT PROCESS

Current thinking about problem behavior of students in elementary and secondary classrooms centers on behavioral support rather than behavior management. Behavioral support is viewed as a school-wide process, one that is positive in nature, and one that is based, when necessary, on functional behavioral assessment and behavioral intervention plans. The paragraphs that follow explain each of these concepts.

The modern term **behavioral support** is preferred to the more traditional term *behavior management* because it places emphasis not on the student exhibiting the behavior, but rather on the ways in which the instructional environment can be manipulated to support the encouragement or development of appropriate behavior. Chitiyo and Wheeler (2009) defined the related term *positive behavior support* as a "proactive approach to managing challenging behavior that emphasizes the readjustment of environments, teaching of replacement behaviors, and manipulation of consequences to reduce or eliminate the targeted behaviors" (Wheeler & Richey, 2005)" (p. 58). These authors also suggested that the behavioral support approach is less punitive than the behavior management approach.

Behavioral support is the foundation of the **schoolwide positive behavior supports (SWPBS)** approach to school discipline. This approach, like the Response-to-Intervention (RTI) model discussed in earlier chapters, seeks to prevent problems whenever possible and, when problems do occur, to identify them as early as possible and offer appropriate interventions. Simonsen, Sugai, and Negron (2008) described SWPBS as "a proactive, systems-level approach that enables schools to effectively and efficiently support student (and staff) behavior" (p. 33). Like RTI, the SWPBS model includes three levels or tiers of interventions:

1. School/classroom-wide system for all students, staff, and settings
2. Specialized group systems for students with at-risk behavior
3. Specialized individualized systems for students with high-risk behavior (Simonsen et al., p. 33)

Check out the "Window on the Web" feature for more information about the federally funded center on positive behavioral supports.

In the SWPBS model, students receive support at the first level, sometimes called the *primary tier.* This tier is implemented for all students and in all settings in the school. Table 6-1 describes the strategies used in the primary tier to set up a system that prevents school behavior problems and responds quickly to minor behavioral difficul ties.

Like their counterparts in RTI, the second and third tiers of SWPBS are designed not for all students, but rather for those few unable to succeed with only the supports available in the first tier. The second tier provides support to small groups of students while the third tier supports individuals with more serious behavioral concerns.

The assessment and intervention approaches used in tiers two and three are more intensive than those used in primary tier approaches. **Functional behavior assessment (FBA),** an assessment approach described later in this chapter, is the strategy used to gather information about the student's behavior and the context in which it occurs. The intervention plan that is based on this type of assessment is called the **behavioral intervention plan (BIP)** or sometimes the *positive behavioral support plan.* As current federal law requires, for each student identified as eligible for special education services, the IEP team must "consider the use of positive behavioral interventions and supports" if "behavior impedes the child's learning or that of others."

TABLE 6-1 Strategies for Implementing Primary Tier Schoolwide Positive Behavior Supports

- Establish a small number of positively stated **expectations.**
- Define the expectations in the context of **routines/settings.**
- Develop **scripted lesson plans** to teach expectations.
- Increase **active supervision** in classroom and nonclassroom settings.
- Establish a continuum of strategies to **acknowledge appropriate behavior.**
- Establish a continuum of strategies to **respond to inappropriate behavior.**
- Develop a **staff reinforcement system.**
- Develop an **action plan** to guide roll-out and **implement.**

Note: From "Schoolwide Positive Behavior Supports: Primary Systems and Practices" by B. Simonsen, G. Sugai, and M. Negron, 2008, *Teaching Exceptional Children, 40*(6), p. 35. Copyright 2008 by CEC. Reprinted by permission.

PRINCIPLES OF BEHAVIOR SUPPORT

Students who exhibit inappropriate behaviors require a classroom behavioral support program that is systematic, consistent, and concerned with both the prevention and the improvement of problem behaviors. This system should provide for group management, yet be flexible enough to allow individualization for the problems of one specific student.

> **myeducationlab** Go to the Assignments and Activities section of Topic *Classroom/Behavior Management* in the MyEducationLab for your course and complete the activity entitled *School-Wide Positive Behavior Support*.

Behavioral support and management follow many of the same principles used in adapting academic instruction. Teachers state precise goals, break behaviors into teachable subcomponents, institute systematic intervention procedures, and collect data to monitor student progress. Whereas instruction deals primarily with academic skills, behaviorial support is concerned with classroom conduct and study skills; in both, the teacher arranges the classroom environment to produce changes in student behavior. The following paragraphs present principles to follow in setting up a systematic behaviorial support program.

Remember That Behaviors Are Learned

At-risk and high-risk behaviors are learned behaviors that have developed from the student's experiences and reinforcement history. Sometimes called *operant behaviors*, they are under the voluntary control of the individual. Because behaviors are learned, students can learn new ways of acting; present behaviors can be replaced or supplemented. The learning of new behaviors occurs at different rates for different students, and instructional procedures affect individuals differently. This individuality is particularly important for students with special needs, who may require extra time or additional practice. They are certainly capable of acquiring new behaviors, but may need a more systematic program than that provided to their general education peers.

Take into Consideration a Behavior's Antecedents and Its Consequences

Behaviors do not happen in isolation. They are affected by the events that precede them and the consequences that follow them. Antecedents and consequences are both important in the management of behavior. New skills can be taught, or current behaviors can be modified, by either altering antecedent events or conditions or by manipulating consequences. The "Inclusion Tips for the Teacher" section suggests questions for teachers to ask to learn more about the antecedents and consequences of a behavior of interest.

As a general rule, if antecedents are contributing to the behavior, teachers should first alter the antecedent conditions and then consider changing the consequences. For example, if students fail to follow directions, the first step may be to alter the directions. A change from "Get back to your seat!" to "Would you please return to your seat?" may produce the desired behavior.

According to Walker (1995), "Simultaneous manipulation of antecedent(s) and consequences is probably the most effective method for changing behavior" (p. 59). The physical organization of the classroom, the procedures established for movement within the classroom, and the quality of the instructional program all play important roles in determining the frequency of behavior problems. Careful arrangement of such things as physical space, student seating, storage of instructional materials, and student traffic patterns can greatly reduce the potential for disruptions of instructional activities and the occurrence of behavioral problems. Appropriate instructional programs and streamlined classroom procedures are also likely to reduce behavior problems.

Inclusion Tips for the Teacher

Questions to Ask About Antecedents and Consequences of Behaviors

Barnhill (2005) advises teachers to ask questions to learn more about target behaviors, that is, behaviors of interest. Those question follow, with questions about antecedents first, then questions about consequences.

- Does the child demonstrate any other behavior prior to the target behavior?
- When, where, with whom, and in what conditions is the target behavior least likely to occur?

Questions About Antecedents

- When does the target behavior usually occur?
- Where does the target behavior usually occur?
- Who is present when the target behavior occurs?
- What activities or events precede the target behavior?
- What do people say or do immediately prior to the target behavior?

Questions About Consequences

- What happens after the target behavior occurs?
- What do you do when the target behavior occurs?
- What do other people do when the target behavior occurs?
- What changes after the target behavior?
- What does the child get after the target behavior?
- What does the child get out of or avoid after the target behavior?

Note: From "Functional Behavioral Assessment in Schools" by G. P. Barnhill (2005), *Intervention in School and Clinic, 40*, p. 137, 139. Reprinted with permission of SAGE Publications, Inc.

Use Reinforcement to Increase the Probability That a Behavior Will Occur

Behaviors followed by reinforcers are more likely to occur again. A student who receives praise from the teacher for raising her hand to speak in class is more likely to raise her hand the next time she wishes to contribute something. This is an example of **positive reinforcement**; the behavior is followed by the presentation of a pleasant (or positive) event that makes the behavior more likely to recur. Examples of positive reinforcers are praise, special privileges, positive notes to students and parents, early dismissal for lunch, and special awards. Positive reinforcement is a powerful tool for supporting appropriate behavior.

Although less favored, negative reinforcers also increase the probability that behaviors will recur. In **negative reinforcement,** the behavior is followed by the *removal* of an aversive (unpleasant or punishing) event or condition. A student who completes his homework to stop the nagging of his teacher and parents is being negatively reinforced; that is, the desired behavior, finishing the assignment, is followed by the removal of the aversive event, nagging, and is thus more apt to recur in the future. The student who stops talking to classmates and begins working to stop the frown of the teacher is also being negatively reinforced. Negative reinforcement should not be confused with punishment; negative reinforcers *increase* the occurrence of a behavior by removing something that is aversive. However, because it is a negative approach, negative reinforcement may produce avoidance, escape, or aggressive behaviors on the part of the student (Zirpoli & Melloy, 2001).

Reinforcement is most effective when the reinforcer is clearly associated with the specific behavior and is presented closely following that behavior. The effect of reinforcing a student with immediate praise for entering class on time is much greater than complimenting the student at the end of the day. Reinforcement should be immediate, systematic, realistic, and meaningful to students in order to be effective.

Remove Reinforcers or Introduce Aversives to Decrease the Probability That a Behavior Will Occur

The strength of a behavior decreases when it is followed by an aversive event or when it stops being followed by a reinforcer. The student whose peers laugh when he mutters profanities will likely decrease this activity if peers stop laughing. Tardiness will decrease if students lose privileges for each minute they are late; the same is true for students who lose use of the family car because they come home after curfew.

Extinction is the removal of reinforcers that have previously followed the behavior. If the objective is to decrease an inappropriate behavior that has been reinforced in the past, the reinforcer is withheld. For example, the teacher may wish to decrease the number of times Mike talks out in class. If the teacher has been reinforcing Mike's out-of-turn responses by attending to them, this positive reinforcer must be withdrawn; the teacher should ignore Mike's comments until Mike raises his hand.

Although extinction procedures will reduce and eliminate a behavior, their use may be somewhat frustrating. A teacher may be unable to identify or control all classroom reinforcers. In addition, the effect of extinction procedures is not always immediate; the student's undesirable behavior may even increase temporarily before it decreases. For example, the frequency of Ann's tantrums might increase until she realizes the teacher's attention can be gained only by exhibiting appropriate behaviors.

Some inappropriate behaviors should be ignored from the outset (e.g., occasional calling out, brief whispering). Behaviors falling into this category are (1) those of short duration that are not likely to spread or persist, (2) minor deviations from classroom rules, and (3) behaviors in which a reaction from the teacher would interrupt a lesson or draw undue attention to the behavior. Procedures that decrease behaviors more rapidly (such as punishment or overcorrection) should be considered if the behavior to be reduced is harmful to others (such as fighting) or if it causes a major disruption of the classroom (such as yelling or stealing).

The presentation of an aversive event following a behavior is called **punishment.** Examples of punishers are verbal reprimands, criticism, and low grades. Two of the milder punishment procedures often used in the general education classroom are response cost and time-out. In **response cost,** an inappropriate behavior is followed by the loss or withdrawal of earned reinforcers or privileges. In **time-out,** the student is removed from an event that is reinforcing, or reinforcement is withdrawn for a specified period of time.

Time-out may involve contingent observation (viewing from the "sidelines"), exclusion time-out (excluding students from observing or participating in activities without leaving the

room by, for example, turning their chair toward the wall or placing it behind a screen), or temporary removal from the room. Time-out is effective only if it is carefully planned and systematically implemented and if its effects are carefully evaluated and documented (Cuenin & Harris, 1986; National Association of State Directors of Special Education, 1991). Also, it is important to note that some districts, schools, and states do not permit the use of time-out procedures or require that parents give signed permission before their use (Intervention Central, n.d.).

Punishment is a negative procedure that can rapidly decrease a behavior. However, it should be used only if more positive approaches are not appropriate or feasible. Before punishment is used with students with special needs, teachers should carefully check district and state policies and regulations. In addition, the permission of parents should always be obtained because punishment can harm students' self-concept and can produce avoidance, escape, or aggressive behaviors.

Punishment is most effective if it is combined with positive reinforcement. This combination brings about more rapid and effective changes than the use of either procedure alone (Walker, 1995). For example, a student who runs in the classroom will learn appropriate behavior more quickly if he or she receives both positive reinforcers (such as praise and extra recess time) for walking and also punishers (such as loss of earned free time or verbal reprimands) for running.

Identify Consequences That Are Meaningful to Students

To have the desired effect on behavior, consequences must be meaningful to the student. This is true for both positive and negative consequences. A consequence that is positive for one person may be negative for another. For example, going to the school library may be positive for the book lover, but not for the sports addict; watching a football game may be a negative activity for those who like to play tennis or visit museums. In addition, the effect of a specific consequence on an individual can change under different conditions. Earning a dessert for completing classwork is reinforcing to a student under most conditions; however, an offer of a banana split for doing the dishes would not be appealing even to the most avid dessert lover who had just eaten a huge meal.

Educators often assume that students are motivated by grades; however, for many students with special needs, grades are aversive. They have received poor grades in the past that may have triggered ridicule from their peers and negative feedback from their parents and teachers. For students with a history of school failure, grades are no longer positive consequences, and other reinforcers must be found.

It is possible to misinterpret the potential effects of a consequence. For example, a teacher may use verbal reprimands as an aversive consequence for inappropriate behavior. However, the teacher's attention may be a positive reinforcer for the student, regardless of the nature of the attention. Also, verbal praise from a teacher may have the effect of a punisher; for instance, praise from a teacher may be distasteful if given in front of a student's middle school peers.

Consequences must have meaning to their recipients. For instance, most teachers would soon tire of receiving grades instead of paychecks for their work. Pay is not bribery; it is the presentation of a meaningful reinforcer for hard work. Because the paycheck is negotiable, teachers can choose which secondary reinforcers they wish to purchase.

Beware of Noneducational Interventions

Every so often, "miracle" cures, methods, or treatments will appear on the market promising dramatic improvement for students in need of behavioral support. Many of these interventions are noneducational in nature and most lack objective data supporting their effectiveness. For example, special diets, nutritional supplements, medications, and therapies (e.g., relaxation therapy) may claim to produce solutions to academic and behavioral problems.

Teachers should exercise great caution when considering such approaches. Like any good consumer, teachers should be aware of products and interventions that appear to be too good to be true. Many of these purported panaceas are medical-type or pseudo-medical interventions with no empirical backing. However, it is important to note that some medical approaches have been found effective with students with behavioral needs. One prominent example is the use using psychotropic medications in the management of behavioral problems such as those of students with ADHD (Kollins, Barkley, & DuPaul, 2001; Ryan, Reid, & Ellis, 2008).

▶ METHODS FOR GATHERING DATA

Gathering data about the classroom behavior and study skills of students is an essential component of a behavioral support program. Typically called **functional behavioral assessment** (or simply *functional assessment*), this systematic process is aimed at providing sufficient information to educators to allow them to (1) understand the factors contributing to the problem behavior and (2) plan the positive behavioral interventions necessary to bring the problem behavior under control (McLoughlin & Lewis, 2008).

Functional behavioral assessment focuses not only on the behavior of the student but also on the reasons for and factors influencing that behavior. Ryan, Halsey, and Matthews (2003) suggest that educational teams consider not only the environment in which the behavior takes place but also the functions that behavior serves for the student. Important aspects of the environment are the antecedents and consequences of the behavior as well as setting events (i.e., events that take place earlier in time) (Ryan et al., 2003); the two primary functions of problem behavior are "(1) to obtain something or produce a desired effect, or (2) to escape or avoid something" (Walker, 1995, p. 78). Ryan et al. provided the example of Johnny, a student who screams obscenities when given a writing task. This happens most often when Johnny has had little sleep (the setting event). The consequence for Johnny is that he is sent to the hallway, thereby avoiding the writing task.

Many different types of informal methods are used in functional behavioral assessment to gather information about behaviors of interest. McLoughlin and Lewis (2008) explained:

> Two techniques are always included: direct observation of the student in order to fully describe the behavior in question, and interviews with persons knowledgeable about the student and the behavior. In some cases, other techniques are also used. Examples are record reviews (e.g., medical and educational histories), task and work sample analyses, and curriculum-based assessments. . . . (p. 284)

General education teachers may take part in functional behavioral assessment by participating in interviews and providing the educational team with samples of student work. However, even more important is the teacher's role in the collection of classroom observational data. Teachers use such data to determine students' current levels of performance, to identify antecedents and consequences that may influence behavior, to identify settings in which the behavior is likely to occur, to determine the effectiveness of the intervention program, and to communicate progress to students and parents. Knowledge of progress can be a strong reinforcer for students.

Direct Observation of Behavior

The most useful method for gathering information about classroom behavior and study skills is the direct observation of student behavior. Observations are usually conducted in the classroom setting by the teacher, an aide, or a trained volunteer; in some cases, students can be trained to collect information about other students or about their own performances.

Although teachers observe students every day, such observations are usually not precise or systematic; general impressions do not provide enough information for planning intervention programs. Instead, direct observations should be carefully planned and should follow the steps outlined in the following paragraphs.

Specify the Behavior to Be Observed. The first task is to specify the behavior of interest to the teacher. This behavior should be described with as much precision as possible. If it is stated clearly, two or more observers will be able to agree on whether the student has produced the behavior. Imprecise descriptions of behaviors make them difficult to observe and measure. The statements "Jack is hyperactive," "Mario is nasty," "Judy is restless," and "Sam has poor study habits" lack specificity and

leave much to the interpretation of the observer. Descriptions such as "Louis hits other students," "Wen-Chi leaves her seat frequently," "Candy talks out without raising her hand," and "José doesn't turn in his homework assignments" are more precise.

At times, teachers may wish to collect data on the overall performance of a student in order to identify specific problem behaviors. Sulzer-Azaroff and Mayer (1977) suggested narrative recording or sequence analysis for this purpose. In **narrative recording**, the observer describes all the behaviors displayed by the student during the observation period; this record is then analyzed to determine whether there is any pattern in the student's behaviors. **Sequence analysis** is more systematic; the observer describes each behavior and attempts to identify its antecedent and consequence. Table 6-2 presents a portion of a sequence analysis of John's behavior during instruction. Examination of the events that precede and follow a behavior yields much more information than is obtained in a simple observation.

However, narrative recording and sequence analysis may not be practical ways for general education teachers to collect data. The teacher may be unable to undertake such a detailed observation while managing all of the other activities in the classroom. One solution is to have someone other than the teacher conduct the observation; this person could be an instructional aide, an adult volunteer, a special education teacher or consultant, or even a peer tutor. Another technique is to develop a simpler observation system. In any event, when the task is to identify problem behaviors, it is important to consider not only the behavior itself, but also the effect of antecedents and consequences on it.

Select a Measurement System. As soon as a behavior has been identified and described, the system to observe and measure the behavior can be selected. There are several different types of behaviors, and their nature influences the kind of measurement system chosen. One type is that of permanent products such as completed assignments, worksheets, and essays, which are available for review at a later time. Other behaviors are more transitory; they must be observed at the time of the occurrence. Examples include fighting, verbal outbursts, stealing, and being out of one's seat. These behaviors may be discrete (i.e., like writing and talking, they have a definite beginning and ending), or they may be continuous (e.g., studying). Some transitory behaviors can be converted into permanent products if they are audio- or videotaped for later study.

Several methods of recording data are possible during an observation.

TABLE 6-2 Example of a Sequence Analysis

Time	Antecedent	Behavior	Consequence
9:05	Teacher asks the class a question.	John raises hand.	Teacher calls on Bill.
9:07	Teacher asks question.	John yells answer.	Teacher reprimands John.
9:11	Teacher asks question and reminds students to raise hands.	John raises hand.	Teacher calls on John and compliments him for raising his hand.

1. *Permanent product or work sample analysis.* A sample of the student's work is evaluated, and information such as the number of problems correct is recorded.
2. *Event recording.* The number of times a behavior occurs within a time interval is noted; for example, the teacher counts the number of times a student leaves her seat during one class period.
3. *Duration recording.* The length of time a behavior occurs is recorded; for example, the teacher times how long a student takes to complete an assignment.
4. *Interval recording.* The occurrence or nonoccurrence of a behavior is noted within a specific time interval; for example, the teacher might observe that Bill was reading his science book during only two of the five 3-minute observation periods.

Which method to use depends on the type of behavior and the kind of data that will be most useful to the teacher. Also, the system must be easily implemented by the observer. Table 6-3 describes several kinds of information that result from the different recording systems: percentage, frequency, duration, and interval data.

Permanent product recording and **event recording** produce frequency data that can be converted into percentage data. Percentages and frequencies are appropriate measures for academic, classroom, and study skills behaviors. A teacher might be interested in the percentage of words read correctly or the percentage of time students spent on a task. Frequency data indicate the number of occurrences of a behavior. To compare frequencies, the teacher should be sure that observation periods are equal in length and that the student has the same opportunity to produce the behavior during each observation period. For example, results would be misleading if a student's questioning behavior during the teacher's lecture were compared with that student's questioning behavior during a discussion period.

Frequency data gathered during unequal observation periods can be more easily compared if they are transformed into rate information, which is simply the number of times a behavior occurs within a certain period (e.g., 8 times per minute; 17 times per hour). Examples of rate data are the number of math problems completed correctly per minute or the number of tantrums per day. Rate and percentage data are easy to compare. For instance, it is possible to compare the percentage of correct responses or the rate of reading words from one day to the next even if the student does not read the same number of words per day.

Duration recording is useful if the length of time the student engages in a behavior is of interest. For example, teachers might note the amount of time students require to line up for lunch or the time a student takes to begin work after the teacher gives directions. Duration can be reported in actual time units (e.g., "Katie cried for 14 minutes"; "Elijah now starts his work within 15 seconds after the teacher gives his group the assignment") or as a percentage (e.g., "Ralph was out of his seat 10% of the school day").

Interval recording is particularly useful for the teacher of a general education class because it does not require that

T A B L E 6 - 3 Measures of Behavior and the Types of Information Yielded

Measure	Derived From	Example	Application
Percent	Number of units correct out of number of total units recorded	8 math problems correct out of 10 total math problems: $\frac{8}{10} \times 100 = 80\%$ accuracy	When a measure of accuracy is of concern without regard for time or proficiency
Frequency	$\frac{\text{Count of behavior}}{\text{Observation time}}$	12 handraises in a 6-minute observation period: $\frac{12}{6} = 2$ handraises per minute	When it is desired to know how often a distinct behavior occurs within a period of time
Duration	Direct measure of length of time	A child tantrums for 15 minutes	When the total length of time a continuous behavior occurs is desired
Intervals	Number of fixed time units in which behavior occurred or didn't occur	Children are observed for 30 seconds; the observer records whether or not the behavior occurred during the interval. Observers then repeat the process. Usually data are expressed in terms of the percentage of intervals during which behavior occurred. $\frac{5 \text{ intervals}}{10 \text{ intervals total}} \times 100 = 50\%$ of intervals	When total duration is not possible and an estimation of the occurrence of continuous behavior is desired

Note: From "An Applied Behavioral Analysis Research Primer for Behavioral Change Personnel" by M. A. Koorland and D. L. Westling, 1981, *Behavioral Disorders, 6,* p. 166. Copyright 1981 by the Council for Children with Behavioral Disorders, The Council for Exceptional Children. Reprinted by permission.

FIGURE 6-1   Observations Using Momentary Time Sampling

Student(s) observed:	Entire class
Behavior observed:	Number of students on task, working on independent assignment or actively participating in assigned group activity
Measurement system:	Momentary time sampling (observer determines the number of students on task at the end of each interval)
Length of interval:	5 minutes
Time of measurement:	Reading instruction time (9:00–9:52 a.m.)
Data recorded:	Number of students on task/Number of students in class (percentage can be calculated for each observation or for the entire period)
Results:	Over the entire time scheduled for reading instruction, 62% of the students in the class were on task. However, the percentage of students on task decreased as the class progressed.

Observation Time	Data	Observation Time	Data
9:05	24/30 = 80%	9:30	18/30 = 60%
9:10	27/30 = 90%	9:35	15/30 = 50%
9:15	24/30 = 80%	9:40	12/30 = 40%
9:20	21/30 = 70%	9:45	15/30 = 50%
9:25	21/30 = 70%	9:50	9/30 = 30%

Class totals:	186/300 = 62%

students be observed continuously. McLoughlin and Lewis (2008) described several of the different interval recording systems:

> With these techniques, the observer determines whether a behavior occurs during a specified time period. The class day, period, or activity is broken down into short intervals of a few minutes or even a few seconds, and a record of the presence or absence of the target behavior is kept for each interval. These techniques can also be used with discrete behaviors if a complete record of every occurrence is not necessary.

Several variations of interval recording and time sampling are available:

- *Whole-interval recording.* The student is observed for the entire interval, and the observer notes if the target behavior occurs continuously throughout the interval. Observation intervals are very brief, usually only a few seconds.
- *Partial-interval time recording.* The student is observed for the entire interval, but the observer notes only if the behavior occurred at least once during the interval. Again, time intervals are very brief.
- *Momentary time sampling.* The student is observed only at the end of each interval; at that time, the observer checks to see if the behavior is occurring. Intervals are usually longer—3, 5, or even 15 minutes—making this a more convenient method for classroom teachers. However, it is less accurate than [whole- or partial-] interval recording techniques because much of the student's behavior goes unobserved. (pp. 109-110)

Figure 6-1 provides an example of the use of momentary time sampling with an entire class. In this example, the teacher was interested in determining what percentage of the class was on task during reading instruction. The same observation system could also be used with individual students or small groups.

Decide Who Will Observe and How Often Observations Will Occur. Observers must be able to record data accurately and consistently. If the teacher is the only adult in the classroom, the kind and frequency of observations that are possible may be limited. However, teachers can record data while conducting instruction or while assisting students; devices such as clipboards, data sheets, stopwatches, and counters are helpful. Some behaviors can be self-recorded if students are monitored by the teacher and reinforced for accurate recording. For more information about conducting observations in the general education classroom, see the suggestions in the "Inclusion Tips for the Teacher."

The frequency of observations depends on several factors, including the availability of the student, the type of behavior being observed, the observation system, and the availability of the observer. Data collection should occur frequently, but observations usually require only a short period each day. The observation must be long enough to obtain an accurate picture of the student's behavior. The time of day or the length of the observation should be adjusted if the teacher believes that this sample of behavior is not typical. Observations that occur for shorter periods over several days provide more accurate data concerning student behavior than monitoring efforts that occur over one or two longer time periods (Walker, 1995).

Inclusion Tips for the Teacher

Conducting Observations in the Classroom

Although teachers may be concerned that they do not have the time necessary to conduct observations of a student or students in their classroom, there are techniques that can make the observation process feasible even during instruction. Teachers don't need to stop teaching to observe; in fact, it's almost impossible to teach without observing. Try the following strategies for including systematic observation into your classroom routines.

1. Carry a small card such as an index card; on it list the names of one or two students of interest and the problem behaviors you wish to observe (e.g., hitting, being out of their seats, talking to others). Place a tally or check mark on the card (and possibly the time of the behavior) each time the behavior occurs. Start this system with one or two students and gradually expand it as your skills improve.

2. For each in-class assignment, have students record the time they begin and the time they finish. With this information, you can determine the frequency of responses, the accuracy, and the rate. Students can also note the times they leave and return to their desks; then the total amount of time in-seat each day or each period can be calculated.

3. Carry a stopwatch to measure the duration of behaviors. For example, start the watch each time Lurlene leaves her seat, and stop it when she returns. Continue this (without resetting the watch) and time each occurrence of the behavior. At the end of the observation period, note the total amount of time recorded.

4. To count behaviors without interfering with the operation of the class, use wrist counters (golf counters), supermarket counters, paper clips moved from one pocket to another, navy beans in a cup, and other inexpensive devices.

5. Have a seating chart in front of you as you talk to the class. Place a tally or check mark by a student's name for each behavior of interest, such as asking a question, talking out, or answering a question correctly.

6. Recruit volunteers to observe in the classroom. Older students, parents, senior citizens, college students, or other students in the class can be excellent observers. If the teacher has developed a method to record the data and clearly stated the behavior to be observed, a nonprofessional should be able to conduct the observation.

Collect and Graph Baseline Data. Before any intervention is begun, baseline data are collected under the natural conditions of the classroom. Baseline data are generally gathered for at least 5 days to ensure that the extremes of the behavior have been established. These data, recorded on a graph, are used to determine the rate or magnitude of the problem, to suggest possible interventions, and later to set the standard for evaluating the effectiveness of instruction. Baseline data may indicate that the behavior believed inappropriate is not as frequent or intense as hypothesized; if so, a behavior change program is not necessary. When the teacher is sure that the desired behavior is not part of the student's repertoire or when a behavior is injurious to the student or others, baseline data need not be collected.

Graphing of data allows the teacher and student to easily see the behavior and its rate of occurrence. Graphs can present baseline data, progress during intervention, and later the maintenance of behavior after intervention has been discontinued. Graphs are an excellent way to communicate progress to parents and other educators. Figure 6-2 presents an example of a graph that could be used in the classroom.

Collect Data During Interventions. Data collected during the intervention phase help the teacher determine whether the intervention is having the desired effect on behavior. It is then possible to decide whether the intervention should continue as originally developed or be modified to improve its effectiveness.

Intervention data should be gathered for a minimum of 5 days. Longer data collection periods permit a more careful evaluation of the program's effectiveness. Figure 6-2 shows information collected by the teacher about Elsie's completion of assignments. During the intervention phase, Elsie was rewarded with 3 minutes in the game center for each assignment she finished on time; this was the only way Elsie could earn time in the game center—an activity she enjoyed very much. After 1 week, Elsie's teacher decided that the intervention was working and that it should be continued.

POSITIVE STRATEGIES FOR MANAGING AND IMPROVING BEHAVIOR

The most effective interventions for at-risk and high-risk behaviors are based on student performance data; these programs help students learn new behaviors, increase or maintain appropriate behaviors, and decrease inappropriate behaviors. Because classroom and study skills are learned behaviors, many of the principles of instruction presented earlier remain applicable.

The goal in positive behavior support and management is to establish a learning environment in which students are accepted as individuals but in which there are definite guidelines for acceptable classroom conduct. Students understand the need for behavioral guidelines and accept them if they are applied fairly, equally, and consistently.

Managing and improving classroom behavior is a systematic process of identifying expected student behaviors, analyzing student performance to see whether it meets expectations, and implementing interventions when necessary. Figure 6-3 presents the step-by-step process for teachers to follow to plan, develop, implement, evaluate, and revise behavioral interventions. This model for classroom behavioral support is based on the same principles as those underlying the schoolwide positive behavior supports model. These principles form the basis for the recommendations of

FIGURE 6-2   Graphing Baseline and Intervention Data

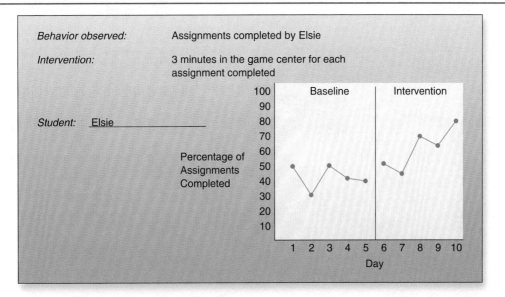

Behavior observed: Assignments completed by Elsie

Intervention: 3 minutes in the game center for each
                         assignment completed

Student: Elsie

FIGURE 6-3   Systematic Behavioral Support Model

1. State the behavioral expectations for all students.
2. Determine whether students meeting expectations are receiving reinforcement to encourage maintenance of these behaviors.
3. Determine whether some students do not meet expectations. If so, do they know and understand the expectations? Do they have the prerequisite skills for the behaviors?
4. For students with inappropriate behaviors, identify target behaviors to be achieved.
5. Select an observation system, and collect baseline data on each behavior.
6. Analyze data to determine the need for an intervention program.
7. If data indicate the need for an intervention, determine whether the target behavior needs to be learned, increased, or decreased.
8. Select (or design) the intervention that uses the most positive approach.
9. Implement the intervention.
10. Collect data on student performance.
11. Analyze the data to determine the need to continue, modify, or terminate the intervention. Take required action.
12. When the behavior is at the desired level and is no longer dependent on the intervention, continue to collect maintenance data and return to step 4.

the recent *Reducing Behavior Problems in the Elementary School Classroom: A Practice Guide* from the U.S. Institute of Education Services (Epstein, Atkins, Cullinan, Kutash, & Weaver, 2008).

■ *Recommendation 1.* Identify the specifics of the problem behavior and the conditions that prompt and reinforce it.
■ *Recommendation 2.* Modify the classroom learning environment to decrease problem behavior.
■ *Recommendation 3.* Teach and reinforce new skills to increase appropriate behavior and preserve a positive classroom climate.
■ *Recommendation 4.* Draw on relationships with professional colleagues and students' families for continued guidance and support.

■ *Recommendation 5.* Assess whether schoolwide behavior problems warrant adopting schoolwide strategies or programs and, if so, implement ones shown to reduce negative and foster positive interactions. (p. iii)

The need for intervention can be reduced through preventive planning. Expectations for behavior should be communicated to students; students who meet expectations should receive positive reinforcement. If intervention is needed, the least intrusive approach should be attempted first; often a change in seating, a careful explanation of class rules, a demonstration of the expected behavior, or a mild reprimand in private can eliminate the problem. Intensive behavior support programs should be used only when less dramatic methods have been found to be unsuccessful.

Establish Behavioral Expectations and Communicate Them to Students

Students do not always know or understand the expectations of the teacher in a specific classroom situation. Although more able students may be capable of interpreting expectations from environmental cues (e.g., teacher signals, behavior of other students), students with behavioral problems often do not interpret these cues. They need specific direction and instruction to know how they are expected to act. Effective classroom managers have been found to be skilled in establishing classroom rules and procedures that communicate behavioral expectations to students (Doyle, 1986; Gable, Hester, Rock, & Hughes, 2009). Research results suggest that effective teachers take the following steps.

1. *Establish classroom rules and procedures at the start of the year.* Effective managers do not wait until problems occur; they anticipate potential problems prior to the beginning of school.
2. *Introduce rules and procedures on the first day of the class.* When rules and procedures are communicated to students immediately (from the beginning of the first day of school), they need not guess what the expectations are. Information overload is avoided by introducing the most essential rules and procedures first and presenting others as they are needed. The rules are posted or given to students as a handout, and new students are immediately oriented to the classroom expectations when they arrive in class.
3. *Explain rules and procedures clearly and teach them deliberately to students as part of a system for classroom operation.* A rationale is provided and instruction continues until the students have the rules and procedures mastered.
4. *Make rules and procedures concrete, functional, and explicit so that they contribute to the accomplishment of work and the order of the classroom.* The statements should be few, clear, and plainly stated. They should indicate the desired behavior (e.g., "Work quietly at your desk," "Respect other people's property") rather than all the undesired behaviors (e.g., "Don't talk when you are working at your desk," "Don't write on the desks").
5. *Associate rules and procedures with clear signals that indicate when students are to carry out or stop specific behaviors or activities.* For instance, the teacher may use a specific phrase (e.g., "Please close your books and straighten your materials") to indicate that it is time to stop the current activity and quietly prepare to move to the next class or activity. In addition, the teacher may need to remind students about acceptable conduct prior to activities that are likely to elicit inappropriate behaviors (e.g., "You may sharpen your pencil but remember not to talk to others").
6. *Demonstrate or model rules and procedures and then allow students to rehearse them.* The teacher demonstrates both the correct and incorrect forms of the behavior (e.g., sitting at a desk, getting to the pencil sharpener). The demonstration enables the students to discriminate the dimensions of the behavior. Students are then given an opportunity to practice the required behavior. Mastering rules and procedures is similar to learning academics; it requires teacher instruction and feedback combined with student practice.
7. *Design rules and procedures to anticipate possible classroom interruptions or problems and to manage these situations.* For example, students may be expected to continue working when classroom visitors enter the room or to stop all activities immediately and line up quickly and quietly when there is a fire drill. Although these events may occur infrequently, expectations should be established and practiced.

8. *Monitor closely how well students follow rules and procedures.* Appropriate behavior is reinforced, and inappropriate behavior is stopped promptly. The teacher must be able to enforce the rules and procedures that are specified; failure to do so diminishes or eliminates their effectiveness. Rules should be modified or eliminated if they prove to be ineffective, unenforceable, or no longer needed.

> **myeducationlab** Go to the Building Teaching Skills and Dispositions section of Topic *Classroom/Behavior Management* in the MyEducationLab for your course and complete the activity entitled *Establishing Classroom Rules and Routines.*

Prevent Inappropriate Conduct by Monitoring Behavior and Providing Feedback

To prevent behavior problems from occurring, teachers must be aware of the behavior of their students at all times and provide them with feedback regarding their performance. This process is as important in developing and maintaining appropriate classroom conduct and study skills as it is in providing academic instruction.

Two important skills related to preventing behavior problems have been identified by the research on effective teaching: (1) the ability to direct the activities of one group while simultaneously monitoring one or more other groups, and (2) the ability to direct the activities of those students who are not involved in the lesson being conducted by the teacher (Englert, 1984). The first skill requires that teachers position themselves so that they can visually scan the entire class in order to observe and make eye contact with students not involved in the lesson. The second skill involves more than observation; it requires that the teacher respond to student behavior with verbal or nonverbal signals (e.g., frown, finger point, head nod) that will redirect the student to the assigned task. Effective managers do this without interrupting the lesson they are conducting.

> **myeducationlab** To examine a challenging case, go to the IRIS Center Resources section of Topic *Classroom/Behavior Management* in the MyEducationLab for your course and complete the Case entitled *Encouraging Appropriate Behavior.*

The combination of providing positive attention for appropriate behavior and ignoring inappropriate behavior is frequently advocated for decreasing behavior problems. However, it is more effective to use positive attention for appropriate behavior together with the careful use of **negative attention** (i.e., a verbal or nonverbal response indicating disapproval) for inappropriate behavior (Jones & Eimers, 1975; Jones & Miller, 1974). This combination can be implemented without interfering with the activities of the classroom if teachers follow certain guidelines.

1. *Identify potentially disruptive behaviors at an early stage.* The teacher anticipates the need to act by observing student actions that are likely to lead to inappropriate behaviors.
2. *Develop a repertoire of quick, low-intensity gestures and verbalizations that signify that a student is not following the accepted guidelines.* For example, the teacher may say "John" (student's

name) or "That's all" to get the student's attention and identify the current activity as inappropriate.

3. *Establish physical proximity to the disruptive student and orient yourself toward the student.* This strategy may involve the teacher moving closer to the student and facing him or her to signal that the teacher is aware of, and does not approve of, the student's behavior. At the same time, the teacher maintains direction of an instructional group. Teacher movement around the room and a tight horseshoe arrangement of desks faciliate the use of this procedure.
4. *Promptly respond to inappropriate student behavior.* The teacher uses negative attention to interrupt the student's disruptiveness before it can produce approval or attention from peers.
5. *With negative attention, use a facial expression and tone of voice that is consistent with disapproval.* It is important to communicate to the offending student that the teacher is registering disapproval.
6. *After negative attention, provide immediate reinforcement and attention when the student displays the appropriate behavior.* This identifies the accepted behavior and reaffirms that appropriate behaviors are reinforced and inappropriate behaviors are punished.
7. *If necessary, use prompting to elicit the desired behavior, and then reinforce the student immediately.* Effective teachers actually require misbehaving students to practice the appropriate behavior until they have exhibited it at the established criterion level; these teachers often drill students until they perform the behavior automatically.

Reinforce Appropriate Behavior

It would be wonderful if all students behaved appropriately in school because their teachers expected them to or because it was intrinsically rewarding. However, this expectation is simply not realistic for many students. Teachers need to help students learn that accomplishments themselves can be rewarding. To do this, a powerful tool—reinforcement—is available.

When appropriate behaviors occur, they should be rewarded. To be effective, the reinforcer should follow the desired behavior. Rewards should not be provided when students promise to exhibit the behavior at some time in the future. Only performance is rewarded. If the student behaves appropriately, then the reward will occur. Appropriate behaviors should also be reinforced immediately. Reinforcers are most effective when delivered immediately after the occurrence of the behavior. For example, if the target behavior is completion of assignments, the student should be reinforced when handing in his or her paper. The reinforcer would lose its effect if it were delivered several hours later, after the teacher had corrected the paper.

> **myeducationlab** Go to the Assignments and Activities section of Topic *Classroom/Behavior Management* in the MyEducationLab for your course and complete the activity entitled *Positive Behavior Support in the Classroom.*

When students are learning new behaviors, each occurrence should be reinforced. *Continuous reinforcement* rewards

TABLE 6-4 Intermittent Reinforcement Schedules

	Fixed	Variable
Ratio	Reinforcement is delivered contingent on a *fixed* number of occurrences of the target behavior.	Reinforcement is delivered contingent on an *average* number of occurrences of the target behavior.
Interval	Reinforcement is delivered after a *fixed* interval of time has elapsed, contingent on the occurrence of target behavior during the interval.	Reinforcement is delivered after an *average* interval of time has elapsed, contingent on the occurrence of a target behavior during the interval.

From: Behavior Management (5th ed., p. 317) by Thomas J. Zirpoli, 2008, Upper Saddle River, NJ: Pearson Prentice Hall. Copyright 2008 by Pearson Education Inc. Reprinted by permission.

an appropriate behavior every time it happens. This is the most effective schedule for establishing a new behavior or for increasing the occurrence of an infrequent behavior. As soon as the behavior has become established, the reinforcers can be delivered according to one of the intermittent schedules described in Table 6-4; *intermittent reinforcement* requires less attention than the continuous schedule. If reduction in reinforcement is gradual, the student will eventually maintain the desired behavior with little reinforcement. Schedules of reinforcement should move from continuous to fixed interval/ratio and then to variable interval/ratio. With variable schedules, students are less able to predict when reinforcement will occur because reinforcers are given after an average period of time (interval) or after an average number of responses (ratio). For example, a variable ratio of 1:10 may deliver the reinforcer after 8 responses, then 7, then 13, as long as the average is 1 reinforcer for every 10 responses.

Provide Reinforcers That Are Valued by Students

Reinforcers of little value to students soon lose their effect. The simplest method of finding out what students perceive as rewarding is to ask them. The teacher might interview students or provide them with a set of questions to answer (e.g., "What is your favorite school activity? Book? Movie?"). Another method of gaining this information is to observe how students use their free time.

It is also important to use a variety of reinforcers. Of the many types available, those that have strong effects on behavior are preferred. Following are several types of reinforcers found to be useful in the classroom.

1. *Social reinforcement.* Social attention or interaction with teachers and peers is a strong reinforcer for most students. It is easy to deliver and is naturally available in the school environment. It can be provided immediately after the occurrence of the desired behavior, and the effects can be generalized to other settings. When social reinforcement is provided, the teacher should tell the student the reason for the reward. The teacher can say (or write on the student's paper), "Good reading," "Nice job on the assignment," "I like the way you lined up for recess," or "Your handwriting is very easy to read." The teacher can also try smiles and, for younger students, a pat on the back; these and other forms of positive attention are easy to give, free, and the supply is unlimited.

2. *Activity reinforcers.* Activities are also strong reinforcers. Any activity that the student enjoys can serve as a reward for the performance of a less desired task. This approach is known as the **Premack principle.** If Joe finishes his math, then he can feed the gerbil. If the class works quietly all morning, then they will get to see a movie after lunch. Other examples of activity reinforcers are spending time in the listening center, watching television, reading comics or magazines, and helping the teacher. These reinforcers are readily available in the school and involve minimal cost.

3. *Tangible reinforcers.* Objects such as certificates, notes to parents, toys, and school supplies can also serve as reinforcers for students. However, tangible reinforcers should be used only after social and activity reinforcers have proved too weak to support the occurrence of the behavior. When tangible reinforcers are delivered, they should always be accompanied by a social reinforcer; over time, the tangible reinforcer can be gradually faded so that it is replaced by just the use of the social reward. Disadvantages of tangible reinforcers include their cost (in terms of money or time to prepare) and a possible loss of effectiveness if they are provided too frequently. In addition, many parents and educators disagree with their use. Because they are not universally available, their effects may not generalize to other school settings.

4. *Edible reinforcers.* The use of edibles should be considered only if social, activity, and tangible reinforcers have been found ineffective. Edibles have disadvantages similar to those of tangible reinforcers. If edibles are used, their presentation should always be paired with the delivery of a social reinforcer.

5. *Negative reinforcers.* Unlike other forms of reinforcement, negative reinforcers are removed when the desired behavior occurs. For example, the teacher can eliminate 2 math problems for each 10 that are completed correctly. Or the teacher's frown can disappear when students begin working. Like the more positive reinforcers, these have a place in the classroom. When negative reinforcers produce the desired behavior, the student should be rewarded. For example, when the student begins to work, the teacher can stop frowning and praise the student for working.

The variety of reinforcers available in the classroom is limited only by the teacher's imagination. Other examples appear in the "Inclusion Tips for the Teacher" section. Remember,

Reinforcers for Classroom Use

Here are several examples of different types of reinforcers appropriate for use in school settings. Social and activity reinforcers have special appeal because they are usually available at no cost to the teacher.

	Social	Activity	Tangible	Edible

Elementary-aged students	Smile
	Pat on back
	Positive comments:
	  "Good job," "I like
	  the way you raised
	  your hand," "You really
	  pay attention"
		Helping teacher
		Popcorn party
		Being team leader
		Reading with a friend
		Time in the computer center
		Choosing game for P. E.
		Extra minutes of recess
		X minutes of free time
		Eating lunch with teacher
			Toys
			Crayons
			Pencils
			Erasers
			Paper
			Art materials
			Books
			Stars
			Good note to parents
				Fruit/Vegetables
				Cereal
				Cake
				Nuts
				Popcorn
				Ice cream
				Sandwich
				Milk

Adolescents	Signal or gesture of
	  approval
	Handshake
	Positive comment on
	  appearance
	Positive comments:
	  "Great job," "Best
	  work I've seen,"
	  "Great to see you
	  working so well"
		Field trip
		Free time
		Early lunch
		Choosing class activity
		Listening to tape for X minutes
		Attending a concert
			Pens
			Paper
			Rental of tapes/CDs
			School supplies
			Sports equipment
			Magazines
			Posters
			Positive note home
				Teacher buys lunch
				Popcorn
				Chips
				Juice
				Candy
				Fruit/Vegetables
				Soft drinks

however, that social, activity, tangible, and edible reinforcers are rewards only if they are valued by the student.

Use Token Economies to Deliver Reinforcers

In a **token economy,** students are presented with tokens rather than reinforcers after the occurrence of a desired behavior. Such a system can be used with one student, small groups, or the entire class. Students collect the tokens—such as poker chips, gold stars, or points—and later trade them for backup reinforcers listed on a reinforcement menu. Tokens should be delivered as soon as the desired behavior has occurred and should always be paired with a social reinforcer. In setting up a token economy, the teacher should do the following.

- Specify the behaviors that earn tokens.
- Use tokens that are appropriate for the students.
- Develop and post a menu that includes a variety of reinforcers and a wide range of costs—students should be able to "cash in" for either high- or low-cost reinforcers.
- Allow students to help in developing the menu.
- Revise the menu regularly to ensure variety.
- Use a record system that is clear and cannot be sabotaged by students (who might add points or take the tokens of others).
- Give students frequent opportunities to cash in (daily or at least several times per week).
- Set up a cash-in system that takes a minimal amount of time and does not disrupt the operation of the class.
- Provide clear rules to staff for distribution of tokens.
- Gradually reduce the value of the tokens to increase reliance on more natural reinforcers.

Token systems have been shown to be effective with general education students and students with special needs (Smith, Finn, & Dowdy, 1993), and they are easily understood by teachers and students. The menu allows students to select their own rewards. Also, token systems accommodate students who have difficulty waiting for their reinforcers; they can cash in when they want to. When the token economy is first set up, students tend to cash in frequently; however, as they grow accustomed to this system, they are able to wait for longer periods.

With Older Students, Use Contingency Contracts

Contingency contracts are written agreements between the student and teacher that indicate what the student must do to earn a specific reward. These agreements, like most contracts, are negotiated; both parties must accept the terms. Because they involve negotiation and require students to assume responsibility for fulfilling their part of the bargain, contracts are probably best for older students.

Homme, Csanyi, Gonzales, and Rechs (cited in Blankenship & Lilly, 1981) provided the following rules for developing contracts in the classroom.

1. The contract payoff (reward) should be immediate.
2. Initial contracts should call for and reward small approximations.
3. Reward frequently with small amounts.
4. The contract should call for and reward accomplishment rather than obedience.
5. Reward the behavior after it occurs.
6. The contract must be fair.

FIGURE 6-4 Contingency Contract

Official Contract

Effective Dates: From _____ to _____

This contract involves an agreement between _____ and

_____
(Teacher/Parent)

_____ . This agreement will be reviewed on the following
        (Student)

date(s) _____ and can be renegotiated at any time by

agreement of both parties.

When _____ (Student) does the following: _____

_____

_____

then _____ (Teacher/Parent) will: _____

_____

_____

According to this agreement the teacher/parent will provide the agreed-upon reinforcers to the student only if he or she fulfills his or her part of the contract. If
the student does not fulfill his or her part of the agreement, the reinforcers will be
withheld.

Teacher/Parent Signature _____   Date _____

Student Signature _____   Date _____

---

7. The terms of the contract must be clear.
8. The contract must be honest.
9. The contract must be positive.
10. Contracting as a method must be used systematically. (p. 235)

A sample contract form, providing space for recording the agreement that has been negotiated between the student and the teacher, is shown in Figure 6-4. A good contract identifies the responsibilities of both parties and the consequences if the terms are not fulfilled. In one example provided by Polloway, Patton, and Serna (2008), the student contracts to "do twenty multiplication problems every day for a week during my math period" to earn the privilege of "play[ing] basketball outside for fifteen minutes" (p. 107).

Teach Behaviors by Shaping

Shaping is the reinforcement of successive approximations or small, progressive steps toward the desired behavior. The technique of shaping is used to teach new behaviors or increase the occurrence of behaviors exhibited infrequently. For example, shaping can be used with a student who completes only one or two assignments per week, when the desired behavior is eight assignments per day. First, a target of one completed assignment per day is established. This is reinforced until the student regularly finishes the daily work. Then the target is raised to two, then three assignments, and so on, as the student progresses toward the ultimate goal of eight assignments per day. For the student who completes no assignments, the beginning target might be a few problems or items of each assignment; this goal would be gradually increased toward the classroom goal of eight completed assignments per day.

Use Modeling to Improve Student Behavior

Modeling involves the reinforcement of another individual, the model, for exhibiting the desired behavior in the presence of the target student. The target student is then reinforced when he or she imitates the modeled behavior. For example, the model seated near the target student might be reinforced for studying; the teacher clearly identifies the reason for the reinforcement by saying, "I like the way you are working quietly in your seat." When this behavior is imitated by the target student, he or she is also rewarded.

Consider Involving Peers in Behavioral Programs

Involving class members in implementing programs designed to improve student behavior can be effective. Students can often provide strong reinforcers for the behavior of their peers, and in many cases they are able to monitor and respond to behaviors that the teacher might miss. The use of peers can involve either individual or group programs.

Group contingencies involve establishing a criterion level for the entire group, and the distribution of reinforcement to individual class members is based on the performance of the entire group. For example, a teacher concerned with the high number of talk-outs (average of 45 per day) could establish a system in which the entire class earns 5 minutes of extra recess if there were no more than 20 talk-outs the previous day. As the students improve, the teacher can gradually reduce the number of talk-outs accepted (e.g., they might be reduced by 1 each week).

Team-based contingencies involve grouping students into teams that compete against each other. As with group contingencies, individual students can help or hurt their team. A teacher wishing to increase the amount of homework completed might establish a prize based on the percentage of assignments completed for the week. The prize (i.e., consequence) could be awarded in one of several different ways: (1) Only the team with the highest percentage wins, (2) each team wins that reaches a percentage higher than a preset criterion (e.g., 95%), or (3) the prize earned by each team is based on the percentage of assignments completed by that team (e.g., a team completing 50% of the assignments earns 30 minutes in the computer area, whereas the team that completes 100% earns 1 hour). Greater changes are usually achieved by dividing groups into teams than by concentrating on whole groups.

Another way of involving peers is to have group members share in the consequences earned by a particular student. A withdrawn student in a general education class might earn points for each social interaction with a peer. Peers might seek to increase their interactions with that student if the entire class receives an extra minute of recess for every 10 points earned by the student. Similarly, a student who is easily distracted might experience fewer interruptions from classmates if they are all earning reinforcers for increases in the student's on-task behavior.

Peers can be trained to reinforce students such as the withdrawn or distractible students described earlier. They might provide the reinforcement for such students, especially if they earn reinforcers for the other student's performance. They might also be used to record the other student's performance (e.g., actual interactions or the amount of on-task behavior); these data may be more accurate than teacher-collected data.

Although such programs can be effective, teachers must consider several factors before involving peers in interventions. First, all the students involved must be able to perform the desired behavior. Otherwise, students may be subjected to potential physical or verbal abuse. Second, individual students should not be able to subvert the efforts of the group. Third, students should not be able to do the work required of others in order to improve the performance of their group. The interactions resulting from these programs can be very reinforcing to the students involved, and they often lead to improved transfer of behaviors and to positive interactions outside the typical classroom setting. As with other interventions, careful planning increases the likelihood of success.

Involve Students in Managing Their Own Behavior

Students can be directly involved in managing their own behavior by (1) participating in setting goals, (2) self-monitoring, or (3) assisting in the intervention itself by evaluating their own performance and rewarding themselves for appropriate behavior (Davies & White, 2000; Graham, Harris, & Reid, 1998; Prater, 1994; Reid, 1996). If they learn techniques that help improve their behavior in one setting, they can often transfer those skills to other settings.

Teachers can identify several areas in which students need to improve their behavior. The students themselves, especially those at the secondary level, can help to set goals for improvement in these areas, or they can choose other areas of need. Assisting in identifying goals increases students' active involvement in improving their own behavior.

Self-monitoring can take a number of forms. Students may simply be required to judge whether they are "working" at the end of each 5- to 10-minute segment of the class period or at the time a teacher-set buzzer rings. They might also record and graph their daily spelling performance, the number of times they leave their desk, or the length of time they are away from their desk each day. In addition, the number of talk-outs or the number of social interactions they initiate can be recorded by the students. Self-monitoring needs to be supervised by the teacher, with reinforcement provided for accuracy; reinstruction should be provided if the data are not consistent with those collected by the teacher. Self-monitoring decreases the demands on the teacher for collecting data, and it also makes students acutely aware of their own behavior.

---

myeducationlab Go to the Assignments and Activities section of Topic *Classroom/Behavior Management* in the MyEducationLab for your course and complete the activity entitled *Self-Monitoring*.

A variety of interventions can be self-administered by students. They can learn to evaluate and self-reinforce their own performance in class. For example, they might give themselves points or check marks for improving their spelling performance or for reducing the amount of time they are out of their seats during a day. Self-punishment might involve deducting points for talking out in class or failing to complete a homework assignment. Other approaches might involve teaching students a strategy to use in resolving various kinds of problems they encounter. Students might be taught to ask specific questions or to make specific self-statements (i.e., **self-instruction**) to help themselves develop problem-solving skills (e.g., "What am I supposed to do? What is my plan? How do I do it?"). A combination of these various approaches (e.g., self-instruction followed by self-reinforcement) can actively involve students in improving their own behavior. It also increases the chance of the intervention's success and the generalization of newly learned skills to other situations.

Involve Parents in Behavior Management Programs

Parents are often willing and helpful participants in behavior management programs. They can provide continuation of the intervention program at home; for instance, parents can reinforce students for time spent doing homework. They can also assist by providing reinforcers for the school behavior of their children. For example, if students earn a certain number of points in school, parents can provide a special activity, such as a camping trip, or a gift, like a baseball glove or doll.

Positive notes to parents from teachers can be reinforcing both for students and for parents. Many parents of special students have received few good reports from school. A note from a teacher praising the accomplishments of a student can increase the level of praise that the student receives at home.

Before involving parents in intervention programs, teachers should be sure that the parents are willing and able to implement procedures consistently. If home and school programs are not well coordinated, the effectiveness of both may decrease. Consistency can be improved by providing some parent training or with frequent communication between parents and teachers. Englert (1984) provided several suggestions for improving classroom behavior support techniques. The checklist in Figure 6-5 summarizes these suggestions.

Thank you for reading to the end of this chapter. When you complete your review of "Things to Remember" and the activities that follow, you may want to reward yourself with a short break or a favorite beverage.

FIGURE 6-5   Are You Managing the Classroom Effectively?

Respond to each item in terms of the extent to which it describes yourself: (1) not at all descriptive, (2) descriptive to a small extent, (3) descriptive to a moderate extent, (4) descriptive to a large extent, (5) descriptive to an extremely large extent.

Competencies

Classroom Set-up and Organization

1.1	Arranges physical space and instructional materials to minimize disruptive movement around classroom and to facilitate easy access to high-use materials.	1	2	3	4	5
1.2	Establishes and implements minimally disruptive traffic patterns and procedures.	1	2	3	4	5
1.3	Establishes and implements procedures for nonacademic class business (e.g., tardiness, material use, movement in and out of room, distributing materials, talk among students, bathroom breaks).	1	2	3	4	5
1.4	Establishes and implements procedures for academic business (e.g., seatwork procedures, obtaining help, volunteer behavior during small group, learning centers, set-up and takedown of lessons).	1	2	3	4	5

Teaching Rules and Procedures

2.1	Communicates clearly what behavior will be tolerated and what will not.	1	2	3	4	5
2.2	Gives behavior reminders and statements of desired behavior in advance of activity.	1	2	3	4	5
2.3	Clearly introduces rules, procedures, and consequences at beginning of school year and whenever needed.	1	2	3	4	5
2.4	States rules, posts rules, and provides discussion of rules at the time of their introduction.	1	2	3	4	5
2.5	Presents examples and non-examples of rules and procedures.	1	2	3	4	5
2.6	Requires student rehearsal of rules and procedures.	1	2	3	4	5
2.7	Monitors rule compliance and provides specific behavioral feedback.	1	2	3	4	5
2.8	Consequates rule noncompliance by stopping inappropriate behavior immediately and requiring students to practice the procedure until it is performed automatically.	1	2	3	4	5

Maintaining Rules and Procedures

3.1	Positions self in the room to provide high degree of visibility (e.g., can make eye contact with all students).	1	2	3	4	5
3.2	Scans constantly and makes eye contact with all students on an equal basis.	1	2	3	4	5
3.3	Detects disruptive behavior early and cites rule or procedure in responding to disruptive behavior.	1	2	3	4	5
3.4	Reinforces appropriate performance through specific praise statements (e.g., states specific behaviors).	1	2	3	4	5
3.5	Administers praise contingently.	1	2	3	4	5
3.6	Includes students in the management of their own behavior.	1	2	3	4	5
3.7	Uses nonverbal signals to direct students when teaching other groups of students.	1	2	3	4	5

Note: From "Measuring Teacher Effectiveness from the Teacher's Point of View" by C. S. Englert, 1984, *Focus on Exceptional Children, 17*(2), p. 5. Copyright 1984 by Love. Reprinted by permission.

Things to Remember

- To be successful members of the general education classroom, students may need to increase some behaviors, decrease others, and learn new ways of acting.

- Classroom behavior problems interfere with instruction and social interactions; study skills problems affect a student's academic performance.

- Intervention may be necessary if there is a low rate of appropriate behavior, a high rate of inappropriate behavior, or an absence of the appropriate behavior from the student's repertoire.

- Behavior is learned and can be taught; it is increased by reinforcement and decreased by the removal of reinforcers or the introduction of aversive events.

- Behaviors do not occur in isolation; their antecedents and consequences must be considered.

- Direct observation of student behavior provides the most useful data for classroom teachers.

- Class rules and procedures make students aware of the expectations for behavior.

- Methods of using reinforcers to change behavior include token economies, contingency contracts, and group contingencies.

- Preventing behavior problems involves careful monitoring of students, reinforcement of appropriate behaviors, and use of negative teacher attention for potentially disruptive behavior.

- Students can participate in self-management of behavior by setting goals, monitoring their own performance, or implementing interventions such as self-reinforcement or self-instruction.

- Effective reinforcers are those valued by the students.

ACTIVITIES

1. Collect observation data on an individual (friend, student, teacher) during five separate observation periods. Be sure you have identified a specific behavior to observe (such as being on task). Record and graph the data using a format similar to the one presented in this chapter. When you are finished, show your graph to another individual. Can that person interpret your data? Can you speculate about what antecedents and consequences contribute to the observed occurrence of the behavior? Describe an intervention you might use if you wished to change the behavior.

2. Interview both a special educator and a general education teacher. Obtain information about the approaches they advocate for managing students in the general education classroom. What do they consider to be problem behaviors? According to the teachers, are special techniques needed for students with special needs, or are the behavior problems of all students managed in generally the same way? Ask the teachers to describe how they use student performance data in behavior change programs. Do they collect data before beginning a program? During the program? How do they decide when a program is working? When it needs to be changed?

3. Develop a set of rules for a classroom you have recently observed. Describe the class and establish five to eight rules using the guidelines stated in the chapter. Explain specifically how you would implement these rules at the beginning of a school year. Identify potential problems you might experience in implementing your rules, and describe how you would deal with these problems.

4. Read and summarize two articles that discuss token economies, contracting, or one of the other techniques described in this chapter. Journals such as *Remedial and Special Education, Journal of Applied Behavior Analysis, Education and Treatment of Children,* and *Journal of Positive Behavior Interventions* often feature articles on these topics.

5. Consider different viewpoints on classroom discipline. Contact local school districts to learn about their policies. Also, get in touch with a national teachers' organization, such as the American Federation of Teachers or the National Education Association. Compare the policies of local districts with those of the professional organization you contacted. What changes would you make in these policies? Why would you make these changes?

6. Develop a reinforcement menu for a school-aged student. Begin by interviewing the student or observe the student in different situations. Then develop a menu that includes at least 10 items, ranging in cost (points) from cheap to expensive. Describe how a general education teacher could use this menu when implementing a behavior change program.

SEVEN

Promoting Social Acceptance

- Hector has been included in a general education class for over a month, but he still eats lunch alone.
- Jackie, who travels by wheelchair, is the only girl in her fifth grade class who hasn't been invited to a birthday party yet this year.
- June dislikes talking in class because the other students make fun of her speech.
- Even though Matt's classroom behavior has improved, his teacher is reluctant to have him join the class for assemblies and field trips.
- Maria's American history teacher wants her to read the text like everyone else rather than listen to special tapes.
- The school janitor is irritated because Hank's crutches leave marks on the floors of the classroom, halls, and bathroom.
- Mike attends a class for students with severe disabilities at his neighborhood school. Although members of his class eat in the lunchroom, attend assemblies, and use the playing fields and the gym for physical education, students in the general education program avoid social and verbal interactions with Mike and his classmates.
- Several of the parents of Tim's classmates are concerned about his mild seizures; they wonder whether Tim's condition is contagious.

LOOKING AHEAD

Consider the questions that follow as you read this chapter about helping students with special needs become socially included in the general education classroom.

- Sometimes students need help to make friends with their classmates. What suggestions could you offer to the teachers of Hector, Jackie, and Mike?
- Sometimes students are not accepted because their peers, teachers, or other adults have limited understanding of their special needs. How would you go about rectifying that situation for Maria, Hank, and Tim?
- How could you help June feel more comfortable about speaking in class? Would your plan include working with June's classmates?
- What ideas could you share with Matt and his teacher so that Matt could participate with his class in school assemblies and field trips?

Students with special needs participating in general education programs often suffer rejection during their school years. They may be rejected by their general education peers, their teachers, or the parents of their classmates. This lack of acceptance has a negative effect on both their self-concept and their school performance (Heron & Harris, 2001; Schumaker & Hazel, 1984). To be truly effective, a general education program that includes students with special needs must make provisions for improving the social skills of these students and enhancing their social integration (Allsopp, Santos, & Linn, 2000; Hughes, 1999; Maag & Webber, 1995). This holds true not only for students with disabilities who enter the general education class from a special program, but also for those who have never left the mainstream setting.

SOCIAL PROBLEMS IN THE CLASSROOM

Many students with special needs encounter difficulty when interacting socially with general education peers and teachers. One source of this difficulty can be the behavior of the student with special needs (Swanson & Malone, 1992). However, at least equally important are the attitudes and feelings of the general population. When general education teachers and students are unfamiliar with individuals with disabilities and others with special needs, this lack of knowledge can create fear and prejudice.

Students with special needs may fail to conform to the expectations of school and society. They may not look or act the same as other students. For teachers and peers with little knowledge about and experience with students with special needs, these differences can create apprehension, distrust, and even hostility. The abilities, talents, and needs of the student with special needs are frequently overlooked.

Some students with special needs can be easily identified; their appearance or their actions are visibly different. One example is the student who travels by wheelchair. Others have no observable signs, but stand out when their performance falls below expectations. For instance, students with learning disabilities may be indistinguishable from their peers until they are asked to read or write or do math.

Throughout their school careers, students with special needs encounter failure. When placed in the general education classroom, they may be apprehensive about attempting activities. This fear of failure and feeling of incompetence may cause them to withdraw. This withdrawal can contribute to their rejection and make it difficult for even the most effective and creative teacher to provide an appropriate learning situation (Gresham, 1984; Meisgeier, 1981; Pavri & Luftig, 2000).

Students with special needs can be as delayed in their social development as they are in other areas (Leffert & Siperstein, 2003; Odom, McConnell, & Chandler, 1994). Thus, poor social skills can be another factor in their rejection (Hollinger, 1987). Many students with special needs are not as capable as their general education peers of initiating and sustaining appropriate social relationships. For example, the research of Tur-Kaspa and Bryan (1994) found that students with learning disabilities were lacking in the language skills necessary for effective social communication. Students with disabilities may fail to develop appropriate social skills because they have fewer friends and are rated significantly lower in sociometric status than their peers (Asher & Taylor, 1981; Drabman & Patterson, 1981; McIntosh, Vaughn, & Zaragoza, 1991; Ray, 1985). Or it may be that they have difficulty using social cues; some misperceive their social standing and feel that they are better accepted by peers than they actually are (Heron & Harris, 2001). According to Bryan and Bryan (1977), students with learning disabilities exhibit more aggressive or negative behaviors, are less accurate in interpreting nonverbal communications, and "emit a lot [of] nasty statements to their peers" (p. 142). Drabman and Patterson described students with special needs as "opposing peers, displaying disruptive behavior and exhibiting withdrawal behavior" (p. 48). It is difficult to determine the cause of the problem: Friendless students have little opportunity to develop social skills, and those with poor social skills are unlikely to form friendships.

These problems may increase at the secondary level. In adolescence, social interaction with peers becomes extremely important. For students with disabilities who have received special educational programming throughout the elementary grades, the transition to the secondary-level general education environment can be difficult. Students with disabilities may not only lack a common experiential background with general education students but also be delayed in the acquisition of important social skills (Siperstein, Parker, Bardon, & Widaman, 2007). These obstacles, combined with the barriers to acceptance in the general education class, magnify the difficulty of promoting the social acceptance of secondary students with special needs.

Research indicates that general education students and teachers do not consistently accept the student with disabilities (e.g., Bryan, 1997; Drabman & Patterson, 1981; Gans, 1985; Pavri & Luftig, 2000; Sabornie & Kauffman, 1985; Sale & Carey, 1995). Teachers and peers are more likely to ignore social interactions initiated by students with disabilities. And teachers are more critical of their behavior, provide fewer praise statements, and consider them less desirable as students (Cook, 2001; Heron & Harris, 2001); this is especially apparent if the students are boys (e.g., Schlosser & Algozzine, 1980; Slate & Saudargas, 1986; Stitt et al., 1988).

One factor that influences teacher attitudes is labeling. When students are identified by a negatively perceived label (e.g., *learning disabilities, mental retardation/intellectual disabilities*), teachers are less able to objectively observe, rate, and plan appropriate interventions for their behavior (Campbell, Dodson, & Bost, 1985). Although the effects of labeling on social acceptance have not been consistently supported by research (Gottlieb & Leyser, 1981), evidence is adequate to caution against reliance on labels for educational information. For instance, Gillung and Rucker (1977) found that teachers expected less from students who were labeled than from unlabeled students with identical behaviors. Alves and Gottlieb (1986) reported that teachers involved students with disabilities in fewer academic exchanges; these students were asked fewer questions and were given less feedback than their peers without disabilities. In a study conducted by Reschly and Lamprecht (1979), students' labels lowered the initial expectations of teachers; however, as teachers spent more time with students with special needs and observed their behavior, expectations became more realistic. Thus, labels can be misleading and can have a negative effect, at least on the initial acceptance of students with special needs by their teachers.

Another factor that can contribute to the rejection of students with disabilities by general education teachers and administrators is a lack of special training and experience (Heron & Harris, 2001; Maag & Webber, 1995; Martin, 1974). Some teachers fear that they do not have the skills necessary for teaching students with special needs. Others may feel that working with these students is not as gratifying as working with typical individuals. Teachers with negative attitudes toward students with special needs can convey these feelings to all the individuals in the class and thereby further reduce the chance for successful inclusion programs (e.g., Garrett & Crump, 1980; Heflin & Bullock, 1999; Heron & Harris, 2001).

A portion of the problem related to the attitudes toward students with special needs can be attributed to former special education practices. For some time, special classes were virtually the only special education service available for students with disabilities. Special educators advocated that these students be removed from the mainstream and entrusted to the care of a specialist in a separate class setting. As a result, general education teachers were not encouraged to attempt to meet the needs of students with disabilities within the mainstream

setting. At present, however, a variety of part-time special education services are available for both students with special needs and their general education teachers. In addition, inclusion is now common practice, and training programs for general education teachers often require some level of preparation in dealing with the needs of students with disabilities ("Special Needs, Common Goals," 2004). One important aspect of effective special education programs is ensuring that the collaboration and consulting role of the special educator helps teachers in general education classes realize that students with disabilities can successfully participate in general education settings for a portion of the school day that is appropriate for each student.

The parents of students with disabilities may also contribute to the social problems of their children. Parents can be overly protective and restrict a student's involvement in normal social activities, which thereby reduces the opportunities for acquiring friends and fosters a limited experience base. Parents reluctant to allow their child to experience failure can actually be increasing the probability that failure will occur in future social interactions. In addition, the parents of general education students can influence the acceptance of students with special needs. Some may resist inclusion in the general education program if they believe that it will reduce the quality of their children's education. Other parents may discourage their children from interacting with the students with disabilities in the class. These negative attitudes are often based on limited information about, and limited experience with, students with special needs.

▶ PRINCIPLES FOR ENHANCING SOCIAL ACCEPTANCE

When rejected by general education teachers and peers, students with special needs may perform more poorly, both socially and academically. The self-concept of rejected students can be affected. In addition, because they are not encouraged to participate in classroom activities, rejected students may fall further behind in all skill areas. Simply including students with disabilities in general education classes does not guarantee their social acceptance or their acquisition of improved social skills (Guetzloe, 1999; Heflin & Bullock, 1999; Miller, 2003; Sale & Carey, 1995; Vaughn, 1995). In most cases, the general education teacher must participate in developing and implementing a systematic program to improve the students' social skills and to increase their social integration. Effective inclusion programs require that educators pay attention to the social needs as well as to the academic, behavioral, and physical needs of their students (Gresham, 1984; York, Vandercook, MacDonald, Heise-Neff, & Caughey, 1992). The principles described in the following paragraphs assist in planning and implementing a successful program for social acceptance.

Change Attitudes with Information

Attitudes are extremely important. The attitudes of the teacher have a significant effect on the attitudes of the students within the class; negative feelings toward students with disabilities can be communicated by the teacher (Cartledge, Frew, & Zaharias, 1985; Garrett & Crump, 1980; Simpson, 1980). Teachers should realize that their words and actions provide a model for students; they should attempt to convey a positive attitude that encourages acceptance of the student with special needs. Attitudes are affected by information. When students and adults increase their knowledge about students with special needs, their attitudes improve (Donaldson & Martinson, 1977; Handlers & Austin, 1980; Simpson, 1980). Information dispels misconceptions and clarifies misunderstandings; prejudice and fear decrease. Teachers and peers in the general education class become more accepting as they learn more about the abilities and problems of students with special needs (Fiedler & Simpson, 1987; Simpson, 1980).

Knowledge about students with disabilities can be gained in many ways. Students and teachers can read or view films, DVDs, and television programs about students with special

Getting to Know People with Disabilities

Have you ever wondered about how to interact with a person with disabilities? Here are several suggestions.:

- Converse with an individual with disabilities in spirit, content, and approach as you would with anyone else.
- When you think someone with a disability may need assistance, ask, "Do you need help? How should I help you?"
- Do not shout at blind persons. They have lost their vision—not their hearing.
- Do not "talk over" or provide the words for someone who stutters or speaks with difficulty. Be patient and listen, and let the person speak for himself.

- Always face a person with a hearing impairment. Be sure the person can see your lips; speak clearly without exaggerating lip movements.
- Speak directly to a person with a disability. Do not direct your conversation to an attendant, assistant, or nearby companion as if the person with a disability did not exist.
- Do not call special attention to a person with disabilities. Approach her as another person who happens to have a disability—not as a disability that belongs to a person.

Note: From "Some Social Tips for Non-Disabled Folks," *Report from Closer Look,* Spring 1981, p. 5. Adapted by permission.

needs. Also, simulations of disabilities can be used to increase understanding; however, a recent review of research with adults participating in disability simulations found only small effects (Flower, Burns, & Bottsford-Miller, 2007). Visits to special education settings can be arranged, or students and adults with disabilities can be interviewed or invited to the general education classroom. Even higher levels of exposure can be gained if teachers volunteer to accept students with special needs in their classes or if general education students are encouraged to work as peer tutors with students with special needs. As more is learned about individuals with disabilities, they appear less different, more familiar, and more acceptable. See the "Inclusion Tips for the Teacher" box for some suggestions on how to get to know individuals with disabilities.

Recognize the Similarities Between Special and General Education Students

Teachers and students may form opinions about the abilities of a student with special needs solely on the basis of physical appearance, labels, or occasional behaviors. Assumptions made by teachers are extremely important because they may influence instructional expectations for the student. A student's looks or assigned label is an insufficient database for programming decisions or for predicting the characteristics of his or her personality. Although it is easy to jump to conclusions, more information is necessary before educational plans and predictions can be made. What is needed is specific assessment information about the student's skills and abilities and an opportunity to observe the student in the classroom. Knowledge that a student has a visual impairment, for example, can raise the anxiety level of the teacher. More pertinent is information that, although the student reads Braille materials, she is able to participate in class discussions, benefit from lectures, and interact socially with her classmates. When the team determines that students are able to benefit from placement in the general education classroom, those students do not need to be protected by the teacher. They should be included in as

many activities as feasible and treated like any other student in the classroom—that is, as individuals.

Teachers often talk about the behaviors and characteristics of the students with disabilities in their classrooms. However, in most cases the academic problems and inappropriate behaviors of students with special needs are also evident in many of their "normal" peers. If teachers were to list the typical behaviors, traits, and concerns of general education students, they would find that these are also typical of students with special needs. As Turnbull and Schulz (1979) stated, "A difference is only a difference when it makes a difference. . . . [C]hildren [with disabilities] have far more similarities than differences with the [children without disabilities]" (p. 48).

Prepare Students in the General Education Class for the Inclusion of Students with Disabilities

Sometimes students in the general education program are isolated from interactions with students with disabilities. These general education students may never have met a person with a disability unless an individual with special needs is among their family, friends, or neighbors. This limited knowledge and experience can lead to the development of prejudice and nonaccepting attitudes and a natural discrimination against individuals who are different. Evidence suggests that "discriminatory responses may exist as relatively normal patterns of behavior" (Simpson, 1980, p. 2).

 Go to the Assignments and Activities section of Topic *Inclusive Practices* in the MyEducationLab for your course and complete the activity entitled *Exploring Inclusion.*

The attitudes of students in the general education class can be improved and their acceptance of students with disabilities increased (Donaldson, 1980; Fox, 1989; Guralnick, 1981; Johnson & Johnson, 1984; Richardson, 2000; York et al., 1992). Before students with disabilities are placed in the general education class, activities should be conducted to

provide information and skills to general education students. For example, students can learn about disabilities and gain skills in assisting students with special needs in the classroom. Such experiences also benefit students with disabilities who never leave the general education classroom. This training can be provided by general educators or general and special educators working together.

Prepare Students with Disabilities for Inclusion

One of the reasons for rejection of some students with disabilities is their lack of social skills. In many cases, students with disabilities should be provided with specific training in the social skills needed to function successfully in school and the community (Brady & McEvoy, 1989; Cartledge et al., 1985; Gresham, 1984; Hollinger, 1987; Schumaker & Hazel, 1984; Weiner & Harris, 1997). Students with special needs are able to acquire appropriate social behaviors; however, this is not likely to occur if students are only provided with opportunities to interact with peers and adults. Specific instruction, including modeling, imitating, coaching, and practice, is usually necessary (Allsopp et al., 2000; Elliott & Gresham, 1993; Lane, 1999) and can be provided in either the special or the general education classroom. In fact, the most successful social skills interventions are those that are structured for individuals or small groups and designed to be conducted over long-term periods (McIntosh et al., 1991).

> **PEARSON myeducationlab** Go to the Assignments and Activities section of Topic *Inclusive Practices* in the MyEducationLab for your course and complete the activity entitled *Special Education Characteristics, Attitudes, and Impacts.*

Prepare Parents for the Inclusion of Students with Disabilities

Parents of both typical students and those with disabilities can make important contributions to the social acceptance program. The attitudes they convey to their children influence their children's viewpoints, the teacher's efforts, and the school program. Parents often have concerns about students with disabilities being involved in the general education program because they are uncertain about the effects on their children. Informing parents about the needs of students with disabilities, the purpose of the program, and the impact on their children will help gain their support. It is important for parents to realize that after students leave school, they will all be members of the community. The school program helps prepare them for this involvement.

▶ METHODS FOR GATHERING DATA

Data collection is important in promoting social acceptance just as it is in instruction and support of classroom behavior. Assessment information can determine the current attitudes and social behaviors of students and teachers. If the effectiveness of a social acceptance program is to be evaluated, data should be collected both before and after the program is implemented. In addition, continuous monitoring of progress allows program modifications to be made.

Information about social skills and acceptance can be gathered from many sources: general education students and those with special needs, general and special education teachers, other professionals, and parents. Various methods are used in assessment. Sociometric measures provide information about how students with special needs are perceived by general education peers. Teacher opinions can be obtained in interviews or teacher ratings or rankings of class members. Self-concept measures are used to see how students with special needs feel about themselves. For example, students might be asked to look at descriptions (such as "makes friends easily" and "seems to lack confidence") and choose those that best fit them (Smith, 1982). Or, students could be asked to indicate their agreement with statements such as "I feel that I am very good at my schoolwork" and "I often forget what I learn" (Hadley, Hair, & Moore, 2008).

In addition, the observational techniques described in a previous chapter assist in identifying the types of social behaviors exhibited by students with special needs in their interactions with teachers and peers. McLoughlin and Lewis (2008) described a variety of assessment devices useful in a social acceptance program. These include measures of self-concept, attitudes toward school, interactions with teachers, and peer relationships.

One of the most popular methods for gathering data about acceptance and rejection of students with special needs is the **sociometric measure.** Sociometric devices, which measure the attitudes of group members toward one another, are often recommended for determining how well students with special needs are accepted by peers (Kauffman, 2001;

Polloway & Patton, 1993). Results can serve as an overall index of the social skill development of students with disabilities (Cartledge & Milburn, 1995; Luftig, 1989). These devices are relatively simple, quick to administer, and easy to interpret. However, it is important to note that although they provide an overall measure of the acceptance of students, they do not identify specific behaviors or skills that require intervention (Foster, Inderbitzen, & Nangle, 1993).

Several different types of sociometric measures are used. Students can be asked to nominate favorite peers, rate their classmates, or choose between pairs of students. According to McLoughlin and Lewis (2008), the nomination method is the most common. They offered this description.

> Students nominate the peers they would most or least like to associate with in some activity. Several activities appropriate for the students' age are presented: playing a game, working on a class art project, attending a school assembly, and so forth. For example, students can be asked to respond to questions such as:
>
> 1. Name the students in this class you would most (least) like to play with during recess.
> 2. Name the students you would most (least) like to sit next to in class.
> 3. Name the students you would most (least) like to work with on a class assignment. (p. 296)

In the rating scale method, all students in the class are rated on the same items. For example, students might be asked to rate from 5 (a lot) to 1 (very little) how much they would like to work on a group science project with student A, student B, student C, and so on (Asher & Taylor, 1981).

The nomination method tends to be a measure of friendship, whereas rating scales tend to assess the student's level of acceptance. General acceptance of students with special needs by their peers is probably a more appropriate instructional goal than an increase in the students' number of friendships. This point should be considered when selecting a sociometric device (Asher & Taylor, 1981).

Before using sociometric methods to gather data about social acceptance, teachers should consider school and district policies. These methods involve the collection of confidential information, and some schools allow their use only with parental permission. Results should be treated with caution; when students are asked to rate other students, they should be encouraged to keep the nature of their responses confidential. Also, it is important that teachers not share overall ratings with students, particularly those who may already have a poor self-concept (McLoughlin & Lewis, 2008). Sociometric devices also tend to lose their sensitivity to changes in the behavior of children over 10 years old. Finally, they provide little diagnostic information regarding which social skills should be taught, and, if used too frequently, they may actually contribute to the rejection of some students (Schumaker & Hazel, 1984).

Direct observation techniques are helpful in assessing and monitoring the specific social skills exhibited by students with special needs (e.g., Prasad, 1994) and the behaviors of teachers and peers toward these students. Direct observation can take place in analogue settings (i.e., simulated situations, such as role playing or a contrived play setting) or a natural environment. This functional behavioral assessment technique attempts to identify factors that predict, trigger, or maintain particular behaviors by examining what is occurring in the setting and the antecedent and consequent factors that contribute to the occurrence of the behavior. This information is essential in developing appropriate interventions (Sugai & Lewis, 1996). Frequent data collection is important to ensure that the initial assessment is valid and to evaluate interventions to provide a measure of the timeliness of program modifications. Data can be recorded on a graph to allow analysis of behavioral changes over time. Examples of appropriate targets for direct observation include the frequency of positive statements made by the teacher to the student with special needs or the number of social interactions between the student with disabilities and a peer in general education.

Rating scales and checklists are also useful in collecting information about a student's performance. Typically, these measures list specific behaviors that are likely to occur in a particular setting. The teacher completes the checklist or rating scale following an observation of the student. For example, a student may be observed participating in an instructional group and then rated on a number of classroom behaviors (e.g., "The student attends to the teacher's instructions. The student raises his or her hand before responding. The student maintains eye contact when talking with the teacher."). The teacher can simply check the items that describe the student's behavior or rate the quality of the behaviors observed (i.e., from "inappropriate" to "appropriate" on a five-point scale).

Behavioral rating scales may also offer a broader set of items that provide more general descriptions of behaviors (e.g., "The student participates appropriately in an instructional group"). A person who knows the student well (a teacher, parent, peer, or even the student in question) reads each description and then rates the student on a numerical scale (e.g., from 1 to 7). Checklists and rating scales permit the collection of consistent information from several different observers to assess the skill level of the student, identify problem behaviors, or assess the student's progress.

Parents can aid in gathering data by reporting on their child's social interactions in the home, neighborhood, and community. They can also keep a record of the comments the student makes about school or self. This information can reflect changes in the student's self-concept or attitudes toward school.

Figure 7-1 presents a checklist for evaluating the social environment of the classroom. It can be used to assess not only teacher behavior but also peer behavior and the curriculum. Use this measure to find out about the social climate of your classroom.

FIGURE 7-1 Social Environment Checklist

Teacher's Behavior

Direct Influence

- Can the teacher specifically state both appropriate and inappropriate student classroom behaviors he/she would like to increase or decrease?
- Does the teacher frequently follow appropriate behavior with encouragement and praise?
- Does the teacher refrain from punishing and criticizing students and rather consistently withdraw his/her attention following inappropriate behaviors?
- Does the teacher objectively record (tally, tape-record, use counter) and evaluate the frequency and consequences of his/her behaviors to document the effects they have on student behavior?
- Does the teacher clearly specify the classroom guidelines, responsibilities, and limitations for students?

Indirect Influence

- Has the teacher continued to grow by adapting teaching plans to meet the needs of each group of students?
- Is the teacher aware of any personal, social, racial, or mental prejudices and does she/he attempt to overcome these through objective teaching and evaluation methods?
- Has the teacher devised a method of getting the students' perceptions and feedback on the teacher and the class (questionnaire, suggestion box)?
- Does the teacher encourage and reinforce self-expression and participation from all the members of the class?

Peer Behavior

- Can the teacher identify the classroom leaders, followers, and isolates?
- Can the teacher identify the peer-group norm base and stereotypes that are held by the class?
- Can the teacher identify and redirect inappropriate peer attention (laughing at a class clown, picking on a . . . child [with a disability]) to promote more constructive activities?
- Does the teacher attend to the problems of the quiet, withdrawn children as much as to the acting-out problem children?
- Does the teacher use concrete activities and arrangements to maximize the social acceptance and participation of all the children?
- Do the classroom physical arrangements (seating plan) and group activities consider both the elimination of behavior problems and enhancement of social relationships?

Curriculum

- Does the curriculum encourage high levels of student independence and initiative?
- Does the curriculum present a balanced emphasis on students' personal social development and academic skill development?
- Does the curriculum provide challenging new ideas that require students to develop skills in analytic and evaluative thinking?
- Is the curriculum enhanced with a motivational system that guarantees that each child will have a successful learning experience?
- Does the curriculum require participation and interaction from the teacher and students?
- Does the curriculum encourage interaction and cooperation among the students?
- Is the subject content relevant to the interests and backgrounds of the students?
- Is an effort made to meaningfully relate the concepts covered in class to everyday experiences?
- Does the curriculum provide ample opportunity for student enrichment by frequently introducing new and different ideas and problems?
- Is motivation enhanced through liberal use of teacher praise and encouragement?
- Are students with special skills allowed or encouraged to share their expertise with their classmates?
- Is an attempt made to incorporate student ideas and suggestions into the instructional program?

Note: Reprinted with permission of Merrill, an imprint of MacMillan Publishing Company, from *Evaluating Educational Environments* (pp. 120–125) by R. M. Smith, J. T. Niesworth, and J. G. Greer. Copyright © 1978 Merrill Publishing Company, Columbus, Ohio.

 ## STRATEGIES FOR PROMOTING ACCEPTANCE OF STUDENTS WITH SPECIAL NEEDS

Teachers can use several methods to increase the likelihood that students with disabilities will be socially accepted. These methods are directed toward students and teachers in general education, parents, and students with special needs themselves. Although general educators are typically responsible for

implementing these strategies, special educators are available to provide the necessary assistance.

Inform General Education Students About Disabilities

Increasing their knowledge about individuals with disabilities improves the attitudes of general education students and teachers (e.g., Donaldson, 1980; Fiedler & Simpson, 1987;

Handlers & Austin, 1980; Schultz & Torrie, 1984). Students should be informed about disabilities, preferably before students with special needs enter the general education classroom. Instruction can take many forms. Teachers can present information directly to younger students; more advanced classes can conduct some of their own research. Some teachers may develop texts and workbooks to use with their students (Schultz & Torrie, 1984); others may use commercially developed materials. Special educators such as the resource teacher can direct general education teachers and students to other sources of information about disabilities. For example, many books, films, instructional materials, websites, and even television programs discuss various types of disabilities.

The goal of instruction is to increase awareness of both the abilities and the potential limitations of students with disabilities. The teacher can introduce the concept of individual differences and point out that each person is unique, with a distinct array of strengths and weaknesses. At the same time, the similarities between general education students and students with special needs should be emphasized (Schulz & Turnbull, 1983). Typical disabilities should be identified and discussed; students should learn why some individuals require special assistance. It is also possible to describe typical special education services and compare these with the general education program. The lives of famous people with disabilities, such as Helen Keller and Franklin D. Roosevelt, can be studied. Class discussions provide the opportunity for students to exchange information, experiences, and feelings about people with disabilities. Teachers should direct these discussions and clarify or correct any misperceptions or misinformation.

Provide General Education Students with Experiences with Individuals with Disabilities

Attitudes of general education students are also affected by meeting and interacting with individuals with disabilities. One way to provide this experience is to invite adults with special needs to the classroom; students can listen to the viewpoint of the person with a disability and then ask questions. Another method is to visit special education programs such as the resource room or special class located within the school. Older students can also be given assignments to interview an adult with a disability. The teacher should guide all of these experiences by ensuring that students prepare appropriate questions prior to visits, interviews, and discussions.

Simulation is another way of experiencing disabilities. Simulations assist general education students in understanding the problems experienced by individuals with special needs and thereby may improve the general education students' level of acceptance (Aiello, 1979; Handlers & Austin, 1980; Israelson, 1980). Some possible simulation activities are traveling around the school in a wheelchair, wearing a blindfold during lunch or art, using earplugs to limit hearing, and attempting to communicate without speaking. For younger children, puppets with various disabilities provide a type of simulation; students can talk with the puppets or become the puppeteers (Binkard, 1985). See the accompanying "Window on the Web" feature for a description of an innovative approach to disability awareness using puppetry. All simulations should be carried out in a businesslike manner. Following the activities, students should write or talk about their experiences to ensure that they have no misconceptions.

Literature can also be used to provide experience with people with special needs Ashton-Coombs & James, 1995; Dyches & Burrow, 2004; Orr et al., 1997). A wealth of fiction, biography, and autobiography about individuals with special needs is available; much is appropriate for students to read or listen to. The accompanying "Inclusion Tips for the Teacher" material provides several suggestions. See Figure 7-2 for additional recommendations drawn from recent articles about using literature to promote understanding of disability and other differences.

WINDOW ON THE WEB

Kids on the Block

Kids on the Block is a disability awareness organization that began in 1977, shortly after the passage of the original Education for All Handicapped Children Act. It develops programs for

Note: Used with permission from The Kids on the Block, Inc., http://www.kotb.com

children related to disabilities, medical and educational differences, and social and safety concerns. Among the topics are cerebral palsy, childhood cancer, learning disabilities, gifted and talented children, sexual abuse prevention, AIDS/HIV, and children of divorced parents. These programs are brought to life by large puppets, the Kids. Community groups, schools, hospitals, and other organizations form puppet troupes that bring the Kids to audiences across the United States and in several other countries.

Visit the Kids on the Block website to learn more about this organization, the puppets it creates, and its programs. The site also provides links to Kids on the Block puppet troupes, the Kids on the BLOG on MySpace, and a newsletter, *Keeping Up with the Kids.*

http://www.kotb.com

Inclusion Tips for the Teacher

Children's Literature About Disabilities

Children's literature is one way for students to learn more about disabilities and other special needs. The books listed below are organized by general disability areas, and recommended ages appear at the end of each brief description.

Learning Disabilities, Learning Differences, and Attention Problems

The Don't-Give-Up Kid and Learning Differences by J. Gehret (Fairport, NY: Verbal Images Press, 1996). The story of Alex, a young boy with reading problems who wants to become an inventor. (primary grades)

Little Monster at School by M. Mayer (Green Frog Publishers, 1978). Little Monster has school friends including Yally. Yally isn't good at reading or math but he can draw better than anyone else. (primary grades)

Shelley, the Hyperactive Turtle by D. M. Moss (Rockville, MD: Woodbine House, 2006). Shelley, unlike other young turtles, cannot sit still. (primary grades)

Josh: A Boy with Dyslexia by C. Janover (Bloomington, IN: IUniverse, 2004). Josh, a boy with a learning disability, begins fifth grade in a new school. (intermediate grades)

What Do You Mean I Have a Learning Disability? by K. M. Dwyer (New York: Walker, 1991). Jimmy, a 10-year-old, learns that he is not stupid and that he can succeed in school. (intermediate grades)

Mental Retardation/Intellectual Disabilities and Severe Disabilities

Where's Chimpy? by B. Rabe (Niles, IL: Albert Whitman & Company, 1991). Misty, a young girl with Down syndrome, has lost her favorite toy, her stuffed monkey. (primary grades)

Making Room for Uncle Joe by A. B. Litchfield (Niles, IL: Albert Whitman & Company, 1984). Uncle Joe, an adult with Down syndrome, comes to live with Amy, Beth, and Dan. (intermediate grades)

I'm the Big Sister Now by M. Emmert (Niles, IL: Albert Whitman & Company, 1989). Michelle Emmert tells the story of her older sister Amy, a teenager with severe disabilities. (intermediate grades)

Physical and Health Problems

Books Featuring Heroes and Heroines Who Travel by Wheelchair

Nick Joins In by J. Lasker (Chicago: Albert Whitman & Company, 1980). (primary grades)

Arnie and the New Kid by N. Carlson (New York: Puffin, 1992). (primary grades)

Our Teacher's in a Wheelchair by M. E. Powers (Chicago: Albert Whitman & Company, 1986). (primary grades)

Books About Specific Disorders

Even Little Kids Get Diabetes by C. W. Pirner (Chicago: Albert Whitman & Company, 1994). (primary grades)

There's a Little Bit of Me in Jamey by D. M. Amadeo (Chicago: Albert Whitman & Company, 1989). The story of Jamey, a young boy with leukemia. (intermediate grades)

How It Feels to Live with a Physical Disability by J. Krementz (New York: Simon & Schuster, 1992). (intermediate grades/middle school)

Visual and Hearing Impairments

Handtalk Birthday by R. Charlip, M. B. Miller, and G. Ancona (New York: Aladdin Books, 1991). A storybook in words, photos, and sign language that includes the signs for numbers. (primary grades and up)

A Cane in Her Hand by A. B. Litchfield (Chicago: Albert Whitman & Company, 1977). The story of Valerie, a young girl with low vision who learns to use a cane to help her travel from place to place. (primary/intermediate grades)

I'm Deaf and It's Okay by L. Aseltine, E. Mueller, and N. Tait (Chicago: Albert Whitman & Company, 1986). A young boy tells about his life and the problems he experiences because he is deaf. (primary/intermediate grades)

Words in Our Hands by A. B. Litchfield (Chicago: Albert Whitman & Company, 1980). Michael, Gina, and Diane's mother and father are deaf. Michael tells about the family's move to a new town. (intermediate grades)

Structure Interactions Between Typical Students and Students with Disabilities

Classroom and other interactions between general education students and students with disabilities have a greater chance for success if teachers provide guidelines. If the general education student's initial contact with a peer with disabilities is purposeful and occurs in a well-structured situation, positive attitudes are more likely to develop. Four techniques that may be helpful in structuring interactions are cooperative learning experiences, group rewards, special friendship programs, and peer or cross-age tutoring programs.

In **cooperative learning**, general education students and students with special needs work together as a team to complete activities or assignments (Maag & Webber, 1995). These teams, which operate in mainstream settings, are small groups of students with a range of abilities (i.e., low-, moderate-, and high-achieving individuals). According to several research reviews (e.g., Gottlieb & Leyser, 1981; Johnson & Johnson, 1980; Johnson, Johnson, & Stanne, 2000), cooperative learning is superior to both competitive learning and individualistic learning. In competitive situations, students attempt to outdo each other; in individualistic situations, the achievement of each student is unrelated to that of any other student. Cooperative learning increases the opportunity to experience success for the student with special needs (Slavin, 1995; Snell & Brown, 1993), it provides practice in school skills (Foyle & Lyman, 1990), and the social interactions involved promote the development of the social skills of the student with a disability (Andersen, Nelson, Fox, & Gruber, 1988; Fad, Ross, & Boston, 1995; Goodwin, 1999; Johnson & Johnson, 1989) and

In recent years, there have been several articles published about strategies for using literature to help general education students gain a better understanding of disabilities and other types of diversity. Citations for some of these articles are listed below along with a sampling of the books recommended in each. The disability, difference, or diversity highlighted in the books is also noted.

"More Bang for the Book: Using Children's Literature to Promote Self-Determination and Literacy Skills" by M. Konrad, S. Helf, and M. Itoi (2007). *Teaching Exceptional Children,* 40(1), 64–71.

- *Egg-Drop Blues* by J. T. Banks (2003). Dyslexia.
- *Matthew Pinkowski's Special Summer* by P. Quinn (1991). Deafness, learning problems.
- *Tru Confessions* by J. Tashjian (2007). Developmental delay.

"Books That Portray Characters with Disabilities: A Top 25 List for Children and Young Adults" by M. A. Prater and T. T. Dyches (2008). *Teaching Exceptional Children,* 40(4), 32–38.

- *Al Capone Does My Shirts* by G. Chodenko (2004). Autism.
- *Hank Zipzer Series* by H. Winkler (2006). Learning disabilities.
- *The View from Saturday* by E. L. Konisburg (1996). Orthopedic impairment.

"Teaching Students About Learning Disabilities Through Children's Literature" by M. A. Prater, T. T. Dyches, and M. Johnstun (2006). *Intervention in School and Clinic,* 42, 14–24.

- *My Name Is Brain Brain* by J. Betancourt (1993). Dyslexia.
- *It's George* by M. Cohen (1988). Difficulty writing.
- *Dicey's Song* by C. Voight (1982). Learning disability, mental illness.

"Fictional Characters with Dyslexia: What Are We Seeing in Books? by J. L. Altieri (2008). *Teaching Exceptional Children,* 41(1), 48–54.

- *Thank You, Mr. Falker* by P. Polacco (1998). Dyslexia.
- *Sarey by Lantern Light* by S. Beckhorn (2003). Dyslexia.
- *The Worst Speller in Jr. High* by C. Janover (2000). Dyslexia.

"Religious Diversity in Schools: Addressing the Issues" by C. R. Whittaker, S. Salend, and H. Elhoweris (2009). *Intervention in School and Clinic,* 44, 314–319.

- *Sam I Am* by I. Cooper (2006). Judaism and Christianity.
- *Holidays Around the World: Celebrate Ramadan and Eid Al-Fitr* by D. Heiligman (2006). Islam.
- *Las Posadas: An Hispanic Christmas Celebration* by D. Hoyt-Goldsmith (1999). Christianity.

their acceptance by peers in general education (Slavin, 1987; Slavin, Madden, & Leavey, 1984).

The teacher plays an important role in establishing and guiding the cooperative learning approach. Gottlieb and Leyser (1981) outlined the following steps for the teacher to carry out:

a. teacher specifies the instructional objectives;
b. selects the group size most appropriate for the lesson;
c. assigns students to groups and assures that the small groups are heterogeneous with (students [with and without disabilities] in the same group);
d. specifies a structured role within the cooperative groups for the . . . students (with disabilities);
e. makes the requirements for the . . . child (with disabilities) reasonable;
f. provides appropriate materials to the groups;
g. explains the task and the cooperative goal structure;

h. trains . . . (all students) in helping, tutoring, teaching, and sharing skills; and

i. observes interactions. (p. 67)

It is important to consider that learners with disabilities may require some additional special preparation or support to allow them to participate effectively in cooperative learning activities (Johnson & Johnson, 1989). The student with special needs may require preparatory coaching or instruction in the social or academic skills required to participate in a group. Other students may need instruction on how to best teach or encourage their group member with disabilities. Descriptions of various methods of using cooperative learning in the classroom, plus highlights of research findings, are provided in Figure 7-3.

 FIGURE 7-3 Cooperative Learning Approaches

Cooperative learning methods are aimed at reducing student isolation and perceived hostile climates that exist in highly competitive classrooms, and at increasing students' ability to interact and work with other students toward common goals.

The most widely used cooperative learning methods include

- **Student Teams-Achievement Divisions** (STAD)—Students assemble in teams of four or five members mixed according to achievement level, gender, and ethnicity to master the material covered in a lesson just presented by the teacher. Subsequently, they individually take a quiz on that material. The team's overall score is determined by the extent to which each student *improved* over his or her past performance. The team demonstrating the greatest improvement is recognized in a weekly class newsletter.
- **Teams-Games-Tournament** (TGT)—The procedure in TGT is the same as that used in STAD, but instead of taking quizzes, the students play academic games in tournaments with other members in the class whose past performance was similar to their own. The team score is also based on individual improvement. The balance[s] of the groups involved in the tournament are maintained by weekly adjustment of group members based on their performance.
- **Team-Assisted Individualization** (TAI)—Teams of elementary or middle school math students are established and evaluated in the same manner as in STAD and TGT. This procedure uses placement tests to determine each student's individualized level and they proceed at their own rate. Teammates check each other's instructional work and help each other with problems. Student performance is based on individual tests and team rewards are based on the number and accuracy of units completed each week. TAI is based on a specific set of materials and its individualized features make it very appropriate for heterogeneous groups.
- **Cooperative Integrated Reading and Composition** (CIRC)—A comprehensive program for teaching reading and writing that involves pairs of students from different reading groups using basal readers and working on decoding, vocabulary, writing, spelling, and comprehension activities. Teacher instruction is provided to a team while others are working on individual activities and is usually followed by team practice, preassessments for the team, and tests. Tests are not taken until the team members determine their teammate is ready.
- **Jigsaw**—Students meet in five- or six-member teams. The teacher gives each student an item of information the student must "teach" to the team. Students are then individually tested for their mastery of the material. **Jigsaw II** is the same, except that students obtain their information from textbooks, narrative material, short stories, or biographies. The class is then quizzed for individual and team scores.
- **Learning Together**—After the teacher has presented a lesson, students work together in small groups on a single worksheet. The team as a whole receives praise and recognition for mastering the worksheet.
- **Group Investigation**—This is a more complex method, requiring students to accept greater responsibility for deciding what they will learn, how they will organize themselves to master the material, and how they will communicate what they have learned to their classmates.

These methods share four positive characteristics. (1) The cooperation required among students prevents one student from doing most of the work for the others. (2) In spite of the cooperative nature of the groups, each student must learn the material in order to improve his or her own score and the team score. (3) Even low achievers who may not contribute greatly can receive recognition since scores are based on individual improvement, however small, over past performance. (4) Students are motivated to cooperate since they receive not just a grade on a piece of paper, but public recognition from the teacher and the class.

Cooperative learning methods have positive effects in several areas. They contribute significantly to student achievement—to an equal extent in both elementary and secondary schools; in urban, suburban, and rural schools; and in diverse subject matter areas.

Schools with racially or ethnically mixed populations do not necessarily have better intergroup relations based solely on student proximity. However, when dissimilar students work together in small groups toward a common goal and are allowed to contribute equally, they will learn to like and respect one another.

Cooperative learning methods also increase acceptance and understanding among students with disabilities and their nondisabled classmates. They also have a positive effect on student self-esteem.

Students who participate in cooperative learning like school more than their peers who are not allowed to work together; they are better able to interact appropriately with others and to understand another person's point of view.

Note: From "Synthesis of Research on Cooperative Learning" (Highlights), by Robert E. Slavin, 1981, *Educational Leadership, 38*(8), p. 659. Copyright 1981 by ASCD. Reprinted with permission. Learn more about ASCD at *http://www.ascd.org.*

A second method of structuring interactions is to use group rewards. The teacher sets up a system in which students can earn classroom reinforcers when (1) general education students interact positively with students with disabilities, (2) a student with special needs performs a desired behavior, (3) class members reinforce a student with behavior problems for an appropriate behavior, or (4) class members ignore a student's inappropriate behaviors. Class members pool their earnings, and the entire class is rewarded. These approaches lead to an increase in the number of positive interactions with students with special needs and thereby help to improve the attitudes of general education students (Heron & Harris, 2001; Salend, 1987).

A third technique is to encourage the development of friendships through communication, social interactions, and recreational activities involving typical students and students with disabilities (Searcy, 1996). As friends, students are encouraged to provide support and assistance to others. For example, this support may involve assisting students with physical or visual impairments in their travels around school or providing a student with severe disabilities the opportunity to learn and practice age-appropriate skills while participating in games or verbal interactions with others (Falvey, Grenot-Scheyer, & Bishop, 1989).

Programs designed to promote friendships vary greatly in their structure. Teachers may reinforce natural interactions, provide students with information or skills related to their interactions, or establish more structured programs that actually provide training for general education students in how to assist and develop interactions with students with disabilities (Campbell, 1989; Perske & Perske, 1988). These programs may build peer support by (1) fostering proximity of students with disabilities with their general education peers, (2) encouraging the development of support and friendship, (3) teaching support and friendship skills, (4) fostering respect for individual differences, and (5) providing a positive model for appropriate interactions (Searcy, 1996; Stainback, Stainback, & Wilkinson, 1992). The implementation of programs that encourage friendships becomes especially important as more students with disabilities spend increasing amounts of time in general education programs.

The use of students as tutors is a fourth approach. General education students can help students with disabilities as peer tutors (working with age-mates or classmates) or cross-age tutors (working with younger tutees). General education students gain in experience and information by working with students with special needs, and students with disabilities benefit from the instruction and the modeling provided by the general education tutor. Tutoring programs have demonstrated their effectiveness in many situations (Gumpel & Frank, 1999; Heron & Harris, 2001; Jenkins & Jenkins, 1985; Krouse, Gerber, & Kauffman, 1981; Maag & Webber, 1995; Maheady, Sacca, & Harper, 1988; Strain, 1981a, 1981b). Students have been found to be effective teachers with individuals who are withdrawn, students with acting-out behaviors, and those with academic needs. Tutors should receive specific training prior to their service, be provided with structured and carefully prescribed lessons, meet frequently with their tutee, and be continually monitored with needed reinforcement and reinstruction provided by the teacher. In addition, peer tutors should be warned that they may be rejected at first but that this response will most likely diminish as instruction proceeds (Doorlag, 1989; Gable, Strain, & Hendrickson, 1979).

Students with disabilities can also serve as peer or cross-age tutors. These experiences can provide the student with special needs with new status, increased acceptance by other students in the school, opportunities to develop social skills, and practice and improved performance in academic skill areas (Cochran, Feng, Cartledge, & Hamilton, 1993; Tournaki & Criscitiello, 2003). For instance, a student with special needs may help a classmate practice spelling words, or a sixth grade student with a learning disability may enjoy practicing third grade math if this occurs during the tutoring of a third grade student. Students with disabilities serving as tutors should be provided the same type of training and assistance suggested for other tutors. These students often benefit more than their tutees from this educational experience (Osguthorpe & Scruggs, 1986). See the "Inclusion Tips for the Teacher" box for more ideas about how teachers can help general education students accept their peers with special needs.

Improve the Social Skills of Students with Disabilities

For many students with special needs, the development of appropriate social skills improves their chances of gaining social acceptance and succeeding when they are included in the general education program (Heron & Harris, 2001; Leffert & Siperstein, 2003; Maag & Webber, 1995; Nelson, 1988; Sugai & Lewis, 1996; Zaragoza, Vaughn, & McIntosh, 1991). According to Drabman and Patterson (1981), students with disabilities who are included in general education classrooms should "display as many positive characteristics as they can to facilitate acceptance by nonexceptional peers" (p. 54). Social skills are best developed through direct instructional procedures, following the same principles as academic instruction and provided as a regularly planned component of the instructional day (Maag & Webber, 1995; Sugai & Lewis, 1996; Sugai & Tindal, 1993).

Initially, the teacher describes why the skill is needed, how the skill is performed, when it is to be used, and what its specific components are. Appropriate social behaviors are modeled for the student with special needs by the teacher and peers or by videotapes and films. The student is then questioned about the skill and the steps involved in it and is provided with the opportunity to practice the new behaviors. It is important that the teacher make use of prompts, praise, and corrective feedback during each step of the instruction. Providing multiple examples of how the skill is used and opportunities to practice in other settings improves the chance that the skills learned in the classroom will generalize to other settings (Cartledge & Milburn, 1995; Elliott & Gresham, 1993; Farmer & Cadwallader, 1999; Maag & Webber, 1995; Sugai & Lewis, 1996; Winget & Kirk, 1991).

Inclusion Tips for the Teacher

Enhancing Social Acceptance

- Be open and honest with your students. Don't avoid answering questions.
- Discuss disabilities with your class.
- Invite guest speakers—parents of children with disabilities or adults with disabilities.
- Read books to your class about people with disabilities.
- Hold class discussions. Allow students to ask questions and explore feelings.
- Emphasize how much alike we are, rather than how different we are.
- Take the mystery away from adaptive aids such as wheelchairs, braces, and hearing aids by exposing children to them and providing explanations of how they work.

- Try simulation exercises such as a blind walk or a soundless movie.
- Encourage a buddy system.
- Arrange for students without disabilities to work with special students as helpers or tutors.
- Look for ways to capitalize on the strengths of the student with disabilities and provide status and recognition through athletics, drama, the school newspaper, chorus, or as peer tutors.
- Locate and view media. . . on individuals with disabilities.

Note: From *Teaching Handicapped Students in the Mainstream* (2nd ed.), by A. L. Pasanella and C. B. Volkmor. Copyright © 1981 by the University of Southern California and by Macmillan College Publishing Company, Inc.

Instructional materials are available to assist in the teaching of social skills. Examples of programs designed for elementary-grade students are listed here.

- *Skillstreaming the Elementary School Child: New Strategies and Perspectives for Teaching Prosocial Skills*, by McGinnis and Goldstein (1997)
- *The Walker Social Skills Curriculum: The ACCEPTS Program*, by Walker, McConnell, Holmes, Todis, Walker, & Golden (1988)

Equivalents of these programs are available for older learners.

- *Skillstreaming the Adolescent: New Strategies and Perspectives for Teaching Prosocial Skills* by Goldstein & McGinnis (1997)
- *The Walker Social Skills Curriculum: The ACCESS Program* by Walker, Todis, Holmes, and Horton (1988)

These programs provide teachers with guidelines and activities for teaching social skills at the middle and high school levels.

Programs such as these typically cover several social skills areas. They often include checklists or rating scales designed to assess student behavior and identify appropriate areas in which to begin social skills instruction. For example, the *ACCEPTS* program offers a placement test that is designed to assess the five areas covered in the program: classroom skills (e.g., attending to teachers, following rules), basic interaction skills (e.g., maintaining eye contact, speaking in a moderate tone), getting along skills (e.g., sharing, assisting others), making friends skills (e.g., being clean and neat, complimenting others), and coping skills (e.g., appropriately expressing anger, ignoring teasing). This program includes specific lesson plans and scripts for the teacher to follow for each of the skill areas taught. Optional videotapes provide both positive and negative examples of the student behavior taught in each lesson, or the teacher can reenact these scenes from the description provided.

The advantages of programs such as *ACCEPTS* and *ACCESS* are that their structured lessons permit them to be implemented readily by the teacher with a minimal amount of preparation because the lessons have been designed and field tested by individuals with experience in teaching social skills. Others, such as the *Skillstreaming* programs, are more flexible; they provide less structured guidelines for lessons, behavioral steps for each skill, a general lesson format, and suggested learning and homework activities.

Another method for developing social skills is the use of **cognitive training** approaches. These methods focus on improving behavior by changing the thinking strategies of the student in order to develop skills that can be used in a variety of settings with a minimum of external support. Students are involved as active participants in the program—they are aware of the behaviors targeted for change, receive training in how the change program will operate, and are actively involved in the intervention (Graham, Harris, & Reid, 1998; Henker, Whalen, & Hinshaw, 1980).

Cognitive training programs teach students strategies such as how to (1) use a sequence of steps to deal with a problem (self-instruction), (2) consider several solutions to a situation (problem solving), (3) collect and record data on their performance and evaluate the consequences of each alternative used (self-monitoring/self-evaluation), or (4) reinforce themselves for acceptable performance (self-reinforcement). It is important for students to be provided with adequate instruction and practice in the use of cognitive training approaches; implementation of this type of program requires that teachers reward students for accurate evaluation of their own behaviors (Zirpoli & Melloy, 2001).

Cognitive training is an efficient approach because it allows teachers to train students to become responsible for portions of their instructional program; the teacher then assumes a monitoring role. A typical cognitive training program to teach social problem solving includes the following components.

- Problem definition (specifically define the problem)
- Goal statement (identify what you want to accomplish)
- Response delay (determine ways to stop and think before you act)
- Determine alternatives (identify as many solutions to the problem as possible)
- Consideration of consequences (evaluate the different consequences that may follow each alternative solution)
- Decision making/implementation (implement the alternative selected as most appropriate)
- Review of results (provide a self-evaluation and correct errors in strategies used in order to improve results in the future)
- Provision reinforcement (provide yourself a "pat on the back" for improving)

Introduce Students with Disabilities to the General Education Program According to Their Individual Needs

Adjustment can be made easier for the student with special needs who is entering the mainstream (and for the teacher and students in the general education class) if inclusion is carefully planned and occurs gradually. For instance, the first step can be an informal meeting between the student with disabilities and the general education teacher. Then the student can visit the classroom when general education students are not present. The next approximation can be participation in a nonacademic activity, such as music or art. These first steps are important because they allow the student to become acquainted with the new teacher, students, and classroom before academic demands are made. They also help the teacher learn about the new student and begin to plan effective instructional and social acceptance programs. It is important to note that not all students with disabilities require a gradual introduction into the general education program; this must be determined on an individual basis as part of the planning for the implementation of the student's Individualized Education Program (IEP).

Upgrade the Teacher's Information and Skills

At present, some but not all of the states require teachers to complete course work related to the inclusion of students with disabilities before they receive a teaching certificate or credential ("Special Needs, Common Goal," 2004). Because of this, some teachers have limited knowledge of and experience with students with special needs. Their teacher preparation program may have provided only a minimal amount of training in working with these students, and they may not have had the opportunity to learn about students with special needs through in-service training.

> **myeducationlab** Go to the Assignments and Activities section of Topic *Inclusive Practices* in the MyEducationLab for your course and complete the activity entitled *Impact of Teachers' Attitudes on Students in the Inclusive Classroom.*

Because of the strong relationship between attitudes and information, teachers should be sure they have adequate knowledge about students with disabilities and the appropriateness of different educational interventions (Gable, Laycock, Maroney, & Smith, 1991; Heflin & Bullock, 1999). The strategies recommended for informing general education students about disabilities (e.g., visitations, simulations, readings, films, websites, discussions) are also appropriate for teachers. For example, several films have featured characters with disabilities: *Scent of a Woman, My Left Foot, Forrest Gump, Lorenzo's Oil, Philadelphia,* and *Rain Man* (Smith, Polloway, Patton, & Dowdy, 2008). Educators can direct their own study or request assistance in getting this information and training from resources available in their district or region.

Although teachers often have support available from special educators, it is "essential that the [general education] teacher assume primary 'ownership' and accept responsibility for the education of a student with disabilities, just as he/she does for all students on the class list" (Putnam, 1992, p. 132). To carry out this responsibility effectively, teachers should strive to upgrade their own skill levels. For example, research indicates that teachers make more negative comments to students with disabilities, ask them fewer questions, and provide them with less feedback. This affects the attitudes of students in the general education class as well as the self-concept and achievement of the student with special needs. Because it is important to provide positive support for the appropriate behaviors of students with disabilities, teachers should assess their own behavior. They can count the different types of statements they make (e.g., positive, negative, instructional) and determine which are made most frequently to students with special needs. Teachers can collect these data by self-recording while the class is in progress or by using observers or tape recorders.

Communicate with and Involve Parents

Parents should be informed of the purpose of implementing inclusion programs and the effects these programs will have on their child's education. Parents of students with disabilities may be concerned that their child will be rejected by students and teachers in the general education program. They also may regret the loss of the special attention and services provided in the special education program. In addition, they may fear that their child will experience failure when included in the mainstream. On the other hand, parents of typical students in the general education class often believe that students with disabilities require a great deal of the teacher's attention and that the amount of instruction their children receive will be reduced. They may also be concerned that the behavior of a student with special needs will have a negative effect on the behavior of their children.

> **myeducationlab** Go to the Assignments and Activities section of Topic *Parents and Families* in the MyEducationLab for your course and complete the activity entitled *Effective Communication with Parents.*

Many of the apprehensions of parents can be eliminated if they are provided with accurate information concerning the inclusion of students with disabilities in the general education program. For example, the parent–teacher organization can feature programs on the needs of special learners, pamphlets explaining inclusion can be sent to all parents, and the acceptance of students with special needs can be a topic of discussion at parent–teacher conferences. Parents of students with disabilities will receive specific information at the meeting of the IEP team. Students in the general education class can assist by communicating accurate information about students with special needs to their parents.

Teachers should communicate regularly with parents to ensure that they remain informed. Parents of students with disabilities often hear from the school only when their children behave inappropriately; they receive limited information about accomplishments and successes. In addition, students with special needs may convey distorted reports of classroom occurrences to their parents; for example, they may say that "all" the students in the general education class pick on them. Parents of general education students also need direct communication from the teacher; they may have misconceptions about inclusion because their children talk about only the negative acts of students with special needs. Parents of all students should be informed that they are important to their children's program and should be encouraged to visit the classroom if they have questions (Heron & Harris, 2001).

According to Kroth (1981), parents should be recognized as their children's major teachers, with professionals considered consultants to the parents. With appropriate assistance, parents can improve their skills in working with their children, help professionals assist the students at school, and aid students and other parents in understanding and working with their special children (Binkard, 1985).

Communications with parents should include information about specific events and activities (Edgar & Davidson, 1979). Professional terms such as *inclusion, mainstreaming,* and *Least Restrictive Environment* should be avoided; educators should use words everyone understands. Communication should take place regularly so that parents keep in touch with the program, are informed of current events, and begin to accept and support the inclusion of students with disabilities. Figure 7-4 presents the opinions of the parent of a student with special needs about issues that teachers should consider when working with parents. Although the original statement was directed to special education teachers (Roland, 1989), it contains information that all individuals working with the parents of students with special needs should contemplate.

In this chapter, several techniques for promoting the social acceptance of students with disabilities in the general education classroom have been described. Consult the checklist in Figure 7-5 to review factors important in preparing to serve students with special needs. This chapter's "Things to Remember" feature reviews ways to enhance social acceptance of students with disabilities.

 FIGURE 7-4   **A Parent of a Special Student Speaks to Educators**

The following recommendations to teachers about working with parents of students with special needs were written by Peggy Roland, who is "the mother of a 12-year-old daughter with education difficulties" (Roland, 1989, p. 3). While the statement was originally directed to special education teachers, it contains concerns and advice that should be considered by others working with special students and their parents.

I'd like to express a few thoughts on behalf of the parents of your students.

Please be frank and *honest* with us. We need the information you have to share and we respect your professional advice and expertise. It may be painful for us to listen to what you have to say but inside we feel relief just hearing something. Our path has been, and always will be, long, but knowing you are there helps.

Please respect us, our children, our families, but above all, the feelings and thoughts that we have shared with you. You may believe we are unrealistic, opinionated, or guilty of ignoring the obvious, but it is probably the best we can manage at the moment. Tomorrow, perhaps even an hour from now, we may express very different feelings.

"They laugh so as not to cry." Such true words! Tears come easily and frequently and they are as much a surprise to us as they are to you. Don't be embarrassed or feel guilty when we cry. Take it as a sign of our humanness and feelings of safety that we react so when we're with you. Many people in the outside world understand neither our laughter nor our tears.

The same is true when we lash out or act defensive. Anger comes with the pain. That anger has no focal point so you may bear its brunt very undeservedly. For that we apologize. Do try to understand that it is usually not directed at you personally but rather at a situation which makes us feel very helpless and, often, very alone. Lashing out may be our overreaction to knowing we can't change the way things are.

Your work and continuing efforts on behalf of our disabled children mean more to us than we can ever explain. Without you, our children would not have achieved the sense of self-worth, the academic and physical success, the societal acceptance they have achieved. Without you, our families would be in more upheaval and distress. Please try to understand that our lives may be just a little different from the average; we have learned to take life one day, sometimes one hour at a time and to be aware and appreciative of the smallest steps while still maintaining our sense of humor and balance.

We are part of this vast thing called life and you are a most important and integral part of our lives. Thank you for being there and helping us establish and maintain a quality of life appropriate for *all* the members of our family.

We look forward to another year of working together!

Note: From "A Parent Speaks to Special Educators" by P. Roland, August 1989, *Exceptional Times*, p. 3.

Teachers and parents must be committed to carrying out the least restrictive alternative concept for children with disabilities. If individuals with disabilities are ever to be fully accepted in our society, this integration should occur as early and widely as possible. Educators should be willing to put forth their best efforts to make a general education class experience rewarding and enriching for students with disabilities. Special class teachers can do much to make these successes happen when students are included in the mainstream program.

The key to a successful experience in the mainstream is preparation. The checklist below can serve as a guide for the special class teacher in preparing not only the students with disabilities, but also the other people who must support the effort to include these students in the mainstream. Before placing each student with disabilities in a mainstreamed setting, the teacher should examine and work on each element of the checklist, until most, if not all, of the "yes" boxes can be checked.

1. Student with disabilities:

   Yes   No

   ____ ____   Is familiar with rules and routine of the general education classroom?

   ____ ____   Follows verbal and written directions used in the general education classroom?

   ____ ____   Remains on-task for adequate time periods?

   ____ ____   Has expressed a desire to participate in the general education class setting?

   ____ ____   Reacts appropriately to teasing, questions, criticism, etc.?

   ____ ____   Student's IEP objectives match instructional objectives in the general education class?

2. General education teacher:

   Yes   No

   ____ ____   Has been given rationale for activities related to including student with disabilities in the mainstream and asked to cooperate?

   ____ ____   Has information about the needs, present skills, and current learning objectives of the student with disabilities?

   ____ ____   Has been provided with special materials and/or support services as needed?

   ____ ____   Has prepared class for including student with disabilities in the mainstream?

   ____ ____   Has acquired special helping skills if necessary?

   ____ ____   Will be monitored regularly to identify any problems that arise?

3. Typical general education peers:

   Yes   No

   ____ ____   Have been informed about the participation of the student with disabilities and about his/her disability(ies) (if appropriate) with the opportunity to ask questions?

   ____ ____   Have been asked for their cooperation and friendship toward the student with disabilities?

   ____ ____   Have learned helping skills and praising behaviors?

4. Parents of the student with disabilities:

   Yes   No

   ____ ____   Have received verbal or written information about plan to include student with disabilities in the mainstream?

   ____ ____   Have been asked to praise and encourage child's progress in the general education and special education class(es)?

5. Parents of the typical general education peers:

   Yes   No

   ____ ____   Have been informed about the plan to include student with disabilities in the mainstream at PTA meetings, conferences, or through other vehicle, and asked for their cooperation?

6. School administrator:

   Yes   No

   ____ ____   Has been informed about specifics of plan to include student with disabilities in the mainstream?

   ____ ____   Has indicated specific steps she or he will take to encourage and support these activities?

Note: From "Helping Teachers Integrate Handicapped Students into the Regular Classroom" by J. C. Dardig, 1981, *Educational Horizons, 59*, pp. 124–130. Copyright 1981 by *Educational Horizons*. Adapted by permission.

Things to Remember

- Because rejection can damage both self-concept and academic performance, programs designed to include students with disabilities in general education should emphasize the social acceptance of these students.

- Students with special needs may be rejected if they do not look or act like their peers; another contributing factor is that some students with disabilities have poor social skills.

- Attitudes are very important; the attitudes of teachers influence the attitudes of their students.

- Attitudes are affected by information; the more teachers and peers know about students with disabilities, the more likely they are to accept them.

- General education students, students with special needs, and parents should be prepared for programs that include students with disabilities in the mainstream.

- Sociometric measures are often used to find out how students with special needs are perceived by their peers.

- Functional behavioral assessment and behavioral rating scales and checklists are used to help assess a student's social skill performance, identify problem areas that may require instruction, or assess the student's progress.

- Instruction about disabilities, experiences with people with special needs, and structured interactions with students with disabilities can be provided to help general education students (and teachers) gain information.

- Students with special needs can learn appropriate social skills; however, it is usually necessary to provide specific instruction in this area.

- Parental support for the inclusion program can be increased by explaining the purpose of the program, letting parents know how it will affect their children, encouraging parents to participate, and keeping parents informed through frequent communication.

ACTIVITIES

1. Visit a general education classroom that includes students with disabilities. Select one student with special needs and one general education peer to observe. Watch each of these students for approximately 30 minutes, and collect information about the number of times each of the following interactions occurs: The student talks to other students, the student talks to the teacher, other students talk to the student, the teacher talks to the student. Compare your results for the two students. Do you find any differences? Does one seem to be better accepted by the peers and teacher than the other?

2. Interview a student with a disability who spends part of the school day in a general education setting. How does the student feel about the inclusion experience? Does he or she feel comfortable in the general education class setting? How positive does the student perceive the attitudes of the teacher and general education class peers to be? Does he or she feel accepted or rejected? Summarize your findings, and use them to prepare a list of questions you might use to interview another student.

3. Read all (or a portion of) one of the books about disabilities, differences, and diversity recommended in the articles featured in Figure 7-2. In your view, does this book accurately portray the characters it presents? Is social acceptance an issue for any of the characters in this book? How might you use this book with general education students to heighten their knowledge and acceptance of individual differences?

4. Talk with special and general education teachers from two different schools about ways to improve the social acceptance of students with disabilities. What suggestions can they offer? What have they tried in the past that has worked? Ask about activities for teachers, students, parents, and staff members such as secretaries, custodians, and bus drivers.

5. Design a classroom activity that you could use to help general education students be more accepting of students with special needs. First, decide on a specific goal, and then describe the methods you would use to reach this goal. Include ideas about how you would go about implementing this program in your classroom and how you would evaluate its effectiveness.

6. Locate one of the social skills training programs mentioned in the chapter (e.g., *ACCEPTS, Skillstreaming the Adolescent*) and use the program to teach a lesson on a specific skill to one or more of your friends, colleagues, or students. Write a short report on your experience, and describe specifically how you would use the lesson (or its techniques) with a student with a disability included in a general education classroom.

Coordinating the Classroom Learning Environment

This chapter helps teachers develop a set of skills important for meeting the needs of all of the students in their classroom. These skills allow teachers to coordinate the classroom learning environment, including not only the arrangement of the physical environment but also the organization of the instructional environment and the resources available within the classroom and the school. To begin, read the "Student Stories" to meet several students who are encountering difficulty in the general education classroom.

- Karen is blind. She uses a cane for mobility and carries a portable Braille notetaking device with her to each of her ninth grade classes. In some classes, the desks are too small to hold all of her materials.
- Axson is a middle schooler who travels by wheelchair. His teacher wonders where he'll be able to "park" when there are assemblies in the school auditorium.
- Ariela is quite shy. Her classroom is arranged in neat rows and she chooses to sit in the last seat in the last row.
- Peter is very distractible and has trouble paying attention to his work in his noisy classroom.
- Louie wants to be in the same reading group as his best friend Alberto, but Alberto's far ahead of him in reading.
- Sergio can't resist talking to the other third grade boys as they pass his desk to turn in their work.
- Every day, Benjamin looks forward to working with Gramps, his class's Volunteer Grandfather.

LOOKING AHEAD

Think about the following questions as you read this chapter to learn more about coordinating the classroom learning environment.

- The physical environments of schools and classrooms can help or hinder learning. What suggestions could you offer to the teachers and principals of students like Karen and Axson?
- How classrooms are arranged can affect achievement, opportunities for social interactions, and disruptive behavior. What seating arrangement would you recommend for a shy student like Ariela? Distractible students like Peter and Sergio?
- Community volunteers, like Benjamin's Gramps, are an important classroom resource. Peer tutors are another. What types of classroom duties do you think would be most appropriate for adult volunteers? Peer tutors?

COORDINATION SKILLS FOR THE TEACHER

In general education classrooms, the teacher is responsible for not only instruction but also the arrangement, management, and coordination of the total learning environment. Teachers structure the physical environment in which learning takes place and set up the instructional environment within these physical surroundings. To do this, teachers coordinate many types of resources: time, people (including students as well as instructional personnel), and educational materials and equipment. Management skills aid in the successful coordination of the general education classroom.

Classroom management is "what teachers do to help make student life in the classroom pleasant, meaningful, safe, and orderly" (Stephens, 1980). Stephens outlined six classroom management elements that teachers should consider.

- *Demographics,* the group's composition
- *Physical environment,* the use of the room and its furnishings
- *Time,* the amount of time available in the class and the teacher's and students' use of it
- *Student encouragement,* ways that students are reinforced for performance
- *Provisions for interacting,* among the students and with teachers
- *Differentiating instruction,* the extent to which and how the instruction is individualized (p. 4, bullets added)

The management skills of the teacher have been found to be related to the amount of student learning; good managers are more able to adapt instruction to student needs, particularly in heterogeneous classes (Evertson, Sanford, & Emmer, 1981). This chapter describes several of the factors to consider in managing the total learning environment. Included are principles for arranging the physical environment, organizing the instructional environment, using educational technologies, and coordinating time and other resources.

The teacher can structure the learning situation in many different ways. He or she receives a room, students, curriculum guidelines, and some standard instructional materials (such as grade-level textbooks); all other factors are under the teacher's control. Because there is a great deal of freedom in the selection of options, teachers should be aware of the reasons underlying their choices.

Many teachers, in arranging the physical and instructional environments, select options that reflect their own preferences as learners. Depending on the needs of the students in the classroom, this approach may or may not be successful. Teachers should be familiar with many different ways to structure the learning environment so that management decisions can take into account not only the preferences of the teacher but also those of the students.

Teacher magazines and websites are good sources of ideas for setting up a classroom, classroom coordination strategies, and techniques for improving classroom organization. Visit the "Window on the Web" to learn about some of these valuable resources.

▶ ARRANGING THE PHYSICAL ENVIRONMENT

The **physical environment** is made up of the classroom and its furnishings. The nature of the physical environment and its arrangement have an effect on the behavior of both teachers and students (Smith, Neisworth, & Greer, 1978). For example, environmental constraints make it difficult to teach running skills in a closet, demonstrate cooking and food preparation techniques in a gymnasium, or supervise small-group discussions in a large auditorium with fixed seats. Environment exerts the greatest influence on the nonacademic performance of students. Reviews of research conclude that classroom characteristics affect attitudes and social behavior but have little impact (with the exception of seating arrangements) on student achievement (Doyle, 1986; Weinstein, 1979). In the following paragraphs, several principles are offered for consideration in arranging the physical environment of your classroom. Keep in mind that some aspects of the physical environment, such as classroom seating arrangements, are easy to modify; others, such as the size of the classroom and the colors of its walls, are less amenable to change.

 To examine a challenging case, go to the IRIS Center Resources section of Topic *Classroom/Behavior Management* in the MyEducationLab for your course and complete the Case entitled *Effective Room Arrangement.*

Ensure a Safe and Barrier-Free Environment

A primary concern with any environment is the safety of its inhabitants. Although this is important for all students, students with physical and sensory impairments require special precautions. For example, books, other objects, and clutter on the classroom floor are hazards for students with balance problems or poor eyesight. Students with limited mobility may need help to move out of the school quickly during fire drills; students who are deaf may need visual cues in order to react in emergency situations.

Another major consideration is **access** to the school and classroom. Many of the newer school buildings are designed to be barrier free; that is, **architectural barriers** are avoided to allow individuals with disabilities entry to and use of the facility. Buildings have elevators and ramps, stairs have handrails for persons with crutches or canes, doorways are wide enough to allow wheelchairs to pass through, and bathroom facilities are specially designed. Drinking fountains, lockers, vending machines, trash cans, towel dispensers, and telephones are installed so that they can be easily reached by a person in a wheelchair. In older schools that do not have these features, it may be necessary to make modifications to allow access to students with disabilities.

The environment of the classroom should also be free of barriers. The room should be arranged to allow easy travel between desks and tables. Instructional materials should be placed within reach, and storage space should be provided for special equipment such as magnification devices, crutches, and adapted keyboards for computers. In addition, bookshelves, chalkboards, whiteboards, and bulletin boards should be conveniently located and low enough to permit their use by students in wheelchairs.

Make the Working Conditions Pleasant

A pleasant physical environment is one that is both comfortable and attractive. The comfort of students and teachers depends on factors such as temperature, ventilation, lighting, and noise level. Classroom temperature should be moderate; hot or cold environments may hinder performance. Ventilation should be adequate so that the room is not stuffy. All work areas should be well lighted and free from glare; some students with visual impairments may require special lighting. Windows permit natural illumination but may offer distractions to students; these distractions can be avoided by building windows above eye level or by temporarily drawing the blinds or drapes. Noise can also distract students from their work or interfere with their ability to hear others speak. Soundproofed walls, carpeting, acoustical ceiling tiles, and drapes all help to decrease unwanted environmental sounds (D'Alonzo, D'Alonzo, & Mauser, 1979). Although some aspects of the physical environment are difficult to change (e.g., a poor heating or cooling system), it is possible to make classrooms more comfortable by additions such as heaters, fans, and lamps for additional lighting (Murdick & Petch-Hogan, 1996).

myeducationlab To enhance your understanding of room arrangement, go to the IRIS Center Resources section of Topic *Classroom/Behavior Management* in the MyEducationLab for your course and complete the Module entitled *Accommodations to the Physical Environment: Setting up a Classroom for Students with Visual Disabilities.*

The attractiveness of the learning environment is important. Attractive classrooms help improve attendance, participation, and attitudes toward instruction (Weinstein, 1979). One aspect of aesthetic appeal is the use of color. Smith et al. (1978) cautioned against dark or bright colors for classroom walls, recommending that "wall surfaces should be light in tone and subdued though not drab in hue, so that they can better function as a pleasant background for whatever is placed on them or occurs in front of them" (p. 134). The room decor also affects its attractiveness. Furnishings, bulletin boards, pictures, posters, mobiles, and displays of educational materials and equipment all contribute to visual appeal. These stimuli should be interesting and enjoyable to look at without being sources of distraction.

Obtain Appropriate Furniture and Special Equipment

Classroom furniture should be comfortable, attractive, durable, and functional. The primary furnishings of most classrooms (with the exception of specialized classes such as auto mechanics and home economics) are chairs and tables or desks. Chairs should be the correct size; students should be able to sit comfortably with their backs supported and their feet on the floor. Tables and desks should be level and should provide adequate writing space and leg room. Special tables and desks may be needed by persons using wheelchairs.

Students with visual, hearing, and physical impairments often require special classroom equipment. Students may bring with them some types of special equipment: wheelchairs, canes, braces, crutches, hearing aids, and eyeglasses. Other types are furnished by the special education teacher. For example, students with visual impairments may use a Braille notetaker or a slate and stylus to write, an abacus or talking calculator for math, and optical aids and magnification devices. Those with hearing losses may need amplification equipment. Students with physical impairments may require lapboards for writing, automatic page turners for reading, or special standing tables.

Arrange Space Functionally

Classroom space should be divided into performance areas or zones to accommodate routine activities and tasks (Mercer & Mercer, 2005). Stowitschek, Gable, and Hendrickson (1980) suggested that, in planning the room arrangement, teachers consider typical student groupings, storage needs for materials and equipment, and procedures for distribution and collection of materials and student work.

When the room is divided into separate areas, one essential consideration is space for instruction. Usually at least two areas are needed: one for large-group instruction and another for small-group instruction. Desks and chairs can be arranged in many different ways for large-group instruction. Typical patterns are straight rows, clusters of desks, and configurations in the shape of horseshoes, crescents, circles, and squares. Arrangements for small-group instruction can use chairs only, both tables and chairs, or clusters of desks. Figures 8-1 and 8-2 present examples of various arrangements for large- and small-group instruction.

It is interesting to note that elementary grade teachers today favor cluster arrangements of desk and chairs rather than the more traditional classroom arrangement by rows. In a study reported by Patton, Snell, Knight, and Gerken (2001), small-group clusters were used in more than 75% of the classrooms observed and by over 90% of the teachers surveyed. The researchers suggested that "contemporary teachers believe that this type of seating arrangement contributes directly to student's educational growth through the effects of socially facilitated learning."

In some classrooms, small-group instructional areas are set up for specific subjects or activities. For example, in classrooms that use learning centers or stations, separate areas may be set

FIGURE 8-1 Arrangements for Large-Group Instruction

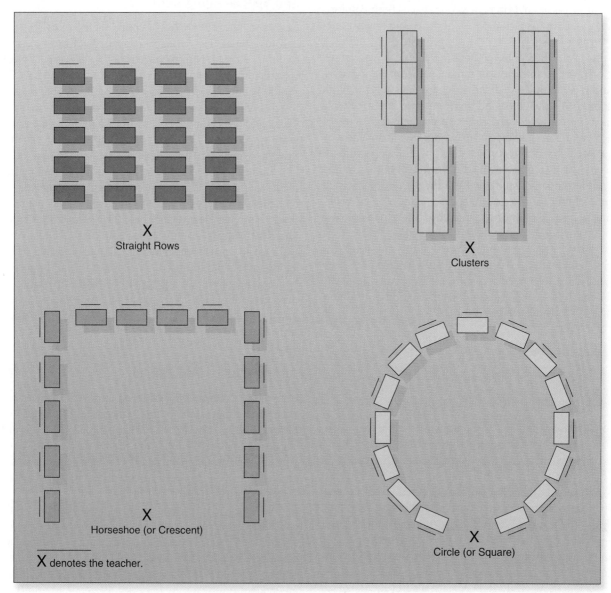

Straight Rows

Clusters

Horseshoe (or Crescent)

Circle (or Square)

X denotes the teacher.

up for math, language arts, and science. These areas can be used by the teacher for direct instruction or by students for independent study or self-instructional activities. Mercer and Mercer (2005) recommended a separate area for each subject. This might be appropriate even at the secondary level; for example, a classroom in which English is taught could be divided into writing, literature, free reading, and listening areas.

In addition to instructional areas, each student should have an individual work space. Usually the student's desk is the space where he or she works independently and takes part in large-group instruction. Students should have storage space in their desks or, if tables are used instead of desks, in cupboards, cabinets, or bookcases. Care should be taken to ensure that individual work areas are relatively quiet and private. Some students may benefit from separate work areas. Cubicles, carrels, booths, and partitions can be used to set up private

office areas for students who are easily distracted or who have difficulty sustaining attention.

Teachers also need a work and storage area, which is usually the teacher's desk. Some teachers do not use their desks as a work area during school hours; they may move from place to place throughout the classroom or station themselves in one of the small-group instructional areas. The classroom should be arranged so that the teacher can visually monitor students' activities throughout the school day. Stainback, Stainback, and Froyen (1987) advised that "the teacher should be able to make a visual sweep of the room and detect when students need assistance and what social interactions are occurring" (p. 12).

Other areas can be incorporated into the classroom if desired. A separate storage location may be needed if materials and equipment are not housed in learning centers. Some teachers set up a specific location at which students pick up

FIGURE 8-2   Small-Group Arrangements

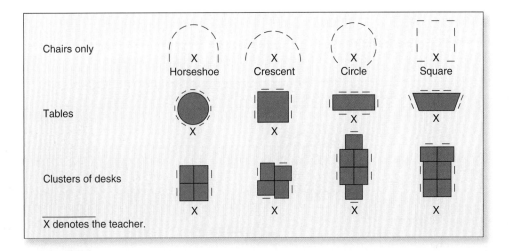

their work for the day and return completed assignments. Classroom computers may be placed at the back or side of the room, so that students can use them without disturbing the work of others. Another option is a free-time or recreational area with games, tapes, books, and other types of reading materials. Time in this area can be used as reinforcement for appropriate behavior, completed work, or accurate performance.

The plan for an elementary grade classroom in Figure 8-3 includes areas for several types of activities. Student desks are clustered for either large- or small-group instruction. There are listening centers and study carrels, a partitioned area for quiet study or games, and a small carpeted area with beanbag chairs. Three tables are available for small-group work, and storage space is ample and conveniently located. Many possibilities for flexibility exist; the placement of desks and tables can be easily changed and the portable chalkboard can serve as a temporary partition.

The relationship among the different areas within the classroom should be carefully planned. The major concerns are provision of separate areas for different instructional purposes, careful design of classroom traffic patterns, and minimization of density (Doyle, 1986). It is also important to arrange classroom space to encourage smooth and quick transitions between instructional activities (Rieth & Evertson, 1988). Among the factors to consider are the following.

1. *Sound.* Separate quiet areas from noisy areas.
2. *Convenience.* Store equipment, supplies, and materials near where they are used; locate instructional groups near the chalkboard.
3. *Student traffic patterns.* Make traffic patterns direct; discourage routes that lead to disruptions (e.g., students distracting others when turning in assignments or moving to new activities). Also, make sure that traffic areas are uncluttered and wide enough to accommodate the flow of student traffic, particularly during transitions from one activity to another (Stainback et al., 1987).

4. *Teacher mobility.* Use an open room arrangement so that you can move quickly and easily to any location. This allows you to "respond to student needs as well as to potential behavior problems" (Cegelka, 1995b, p. 139).
5. *Flexibility.* Ensure that all classroom activities can be accomplished; make areas multipurpose or use different arrangements for different tasks. Stainback, Stainback, and Slavin (1989) recommended classrooms with "areas that can be opened, closed, or screened off depending on the needs of students when working on different tasks" (p. 140).
6. *Density.* Arrange student seating so that personal space is preserved; avoid crowding. High density can reduce attentiveness and increase dissatisfaction and aggressiveness (Doyle, 1986; Zentall, 1983).

When arranging classroom space, the teacher should not consider it permanent. New arrangements should be tried as often as necessary to increase the effectiveness of the learning environment. As Polloway and Patton (1993) commented, "every teacher should periodically review why the room is arranged as it is. There is no one best way to arrange a classroom, but some ways are clearly superior to others" (p. 59).

Consider Educational Goals in Making Seating Arrangements

How students are arranged in relationship to each other can affect their academic performance, classroom behavior, and social interactions. Achievement is related to seat position: in classrooms arranged in rows, students sitting in the front center seats participate more, are more attentive, and spend more time on task according to the review of research by Weinstein (1979). This finding may be due to the availability of more cues from the teacher (e.g., increased eye contact, better reception of nonverbal messages) (Doyle, 1986). It may also be due to self-selection if students choose their own seats or to the tendency of teachers to seat low achievers farther away

FIGURE 8-3   Classroom Plan

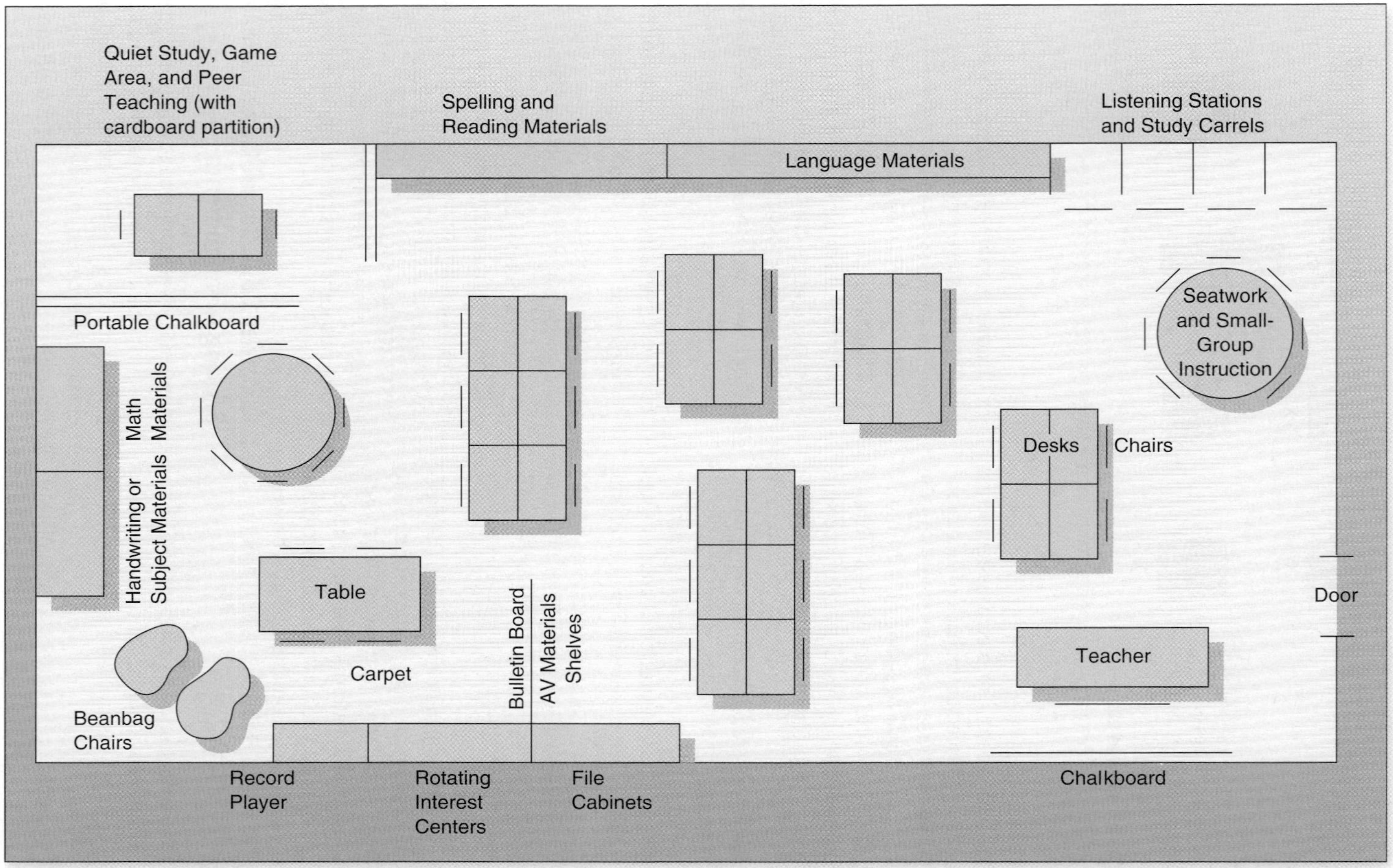

Quiet Study, Game Area, and Peer Teaching (with cardboard partition)

Listening Stations and Study Carrels

Language Materials

Spelling and Reading Materials

Seatwork and Small-Group Instruction

Desks   Chairs

Teacher

Chalkboard

Door

Portable Chalkboard

Math Subject Materials

Handwriting or Subject Materials

Bulletin Board   AV Materials   Shelves

File Cabinets

Rotating Interest Centers

Carpet

Table

Record Player

Beanbag Chairs

Note: Reprinted with permission of Merrill, an imprint of Macmillan Publishing Company, from *Teaching Students with Learning Problems* (3rd ed., p. 85) by C. D. Mercer and A. R. Mercer. Copyright © 1989 Merrill Publishing Company, Columbus, Ohio.

from the teacher's desk than high achievers (Alves & Gottlieb, 1986). However, low achievers improve academically as their seats are moved from the back to the front of the classroom (Heron & Harris, 1993). This improvement is attributed to closer proximity to the teacher and the stimuli to which they should attend.

Seating also influences classroom behavior. Axelrod, Hall, and Tams (1972) found that study behaviors improved when students were seated in rows rather than in groups around tables. To prevent behavior problems, inattentive or disruptive students are placed near the teacher; those who argue or fight are separated. Disruptive students improve their behavior when grouped with well-behaved students (Stainback et al., 1987). In some cases, teachers may move students to separate areas, away from their peers. Students who act out or display serious inappropriate behaviors may be removed to a time-out area. Those who are easily distracted can be seated in individual study carrels or booths. However, teachers should consider all possible alternatives before physically isolating students from others in the classroom.

Social interaction can be facilitated by seating arrangements. Smith et al. (1978) note that interaction increases when students are seated close to each other or opposite one another. Heron and Harris (1993) observe that verbal communication tends to move across tables rather than around them. They recommend seating a low-verbal student across from a high-verbal student to enhance performance. In this arrangement, the low-verbal student is better able to receive the verbal messages and the facial and gestural cues of the peer model.

▶ ORGANIZING THE INSTRUCTIONAL ENVIRONMENT

The **instructional environment** of the classroom includes the procedures, routines, materials, and equipment used by the teacher to increase student performance. The teacher organizes the curriculum, groups students, and sets up delivery systems for the presentation and practice of skills and information. This structure directly affects nonacademic performance as well as student achievement. Students actively involved in appropriate instruction are less likely to exhibit problem behaviors and more likely to feel good about their competence. Several principles are important to consider in arranging the instructional environment.

Organize Curricular Skills and Information

Although the scope and sequence of the general education curriculum are usually well specified, the teacher may have the opportunity to arrange the skills and information in different ways. The traditional organization follows academic subjects; this is most apparent at the secondary level, where the curriculum is broken down into separate courses. At the elementary level, skills and information can also be divided into different subjects, such as language arts, mathematics, social studies, and science.

An alternate way of organizing the curriculum is the unit approach, which cuts across subject matter areas (Polloway & Patton, 1993). In this approach, content is organized around **thematic** or **instructional units.** Unit teaching has been described as a generic instructional approach that integrates instruction "on academic and social skills, with information structured around a common theme building on the previous experience of students" (Meyen, 1981, p. 3). Topics of interest and importance to students become the vehicle for teaching academic skills. For instance, Meyen (1981) suggested experiential themes, such as transportation, the community, leisure time, and the newspaper. The teacher organizes the unit around a central theme and includes activities in each of the core areas: communication skills, math, social competencies, safety, health, and vocation.

Many teachers use thematic units as a supplement to the standard curriculum. While continuing instruction in specific academic subjects, they also introduce activities related to a special topic or interest area. Examples are space travel, February holidays, contributions of African Americans, and endangered species. This approach is more common at the elementary level but can also be adapted for secondary-aged students.

If units are carefully planned to ensure the inclusion of several important academic skills, they become a valuable addition to the instructional environment. Units include a variety of different activities, and the teacher can tailor instruction to the needs of the individual students. In addition, the use of themes that interest and motivate students can increase their willingness to participate in academic activities.

Another method of organizing curriculum is the blending or integration of academic subjects. For example, at the

elementary level, the whole language approach integrates the language arts of listening, speaking, reading, and writing (Lapp & Flood, 1992). Skills are taught in the context of authentic communication tasks, not as separate (and isolated) subjects (Westby, 1992). Writing across the curriculum is another example. In this approach, secondary students are expected to practice their writing skills in all subjects, not just in English classes.

Group Students for Instruction

Before instruction can begin, the teacher must decide how to group students. Two factors must be determined: group size and group type. The number of students per group can vary from one (in a tutoring situation) to the entire class. Class size is a factor in instruction; it has been noted that student achievement increases as the number of students in the class decreases (Glass & Smith, 1978). However, this does not necessarily mean that classes of 30 or more students should always be broken into several groups for instruction. Using the whole class as a group is an efficient way of presenting new material, if that material is appropriate for all of the students (Brophy & Good, 1986). Also, providing guided practice for the entire class at once is an effective use of time. For instance, if the time allotted for mathematics is 1 hour, the teacher can spend only 2 minutes with each of 30 individual students or can devote the entire period to the class as a whole.

When it is necessary to present different material to different students, small groups are appropriate. Small groups are necessary in beginning reading instruction and in highly heterogeneous classes (Brophy & Good, 1986). Also, smaller groups can lead to greater student participation (Mercer & Mercer, 2005). Small groups generally range in size from three to seven or eight individuals. For some students, individual instruction is needed; this can be presented by the teacher or other instructional personnel, such as peers, aides, and volunteers.

The criterion used to group students often determines the size of the group. The most typical criterion is homogeneity: Students of similar ability, at similar levels, or with similar skills are placed in one group. For example, a placement test might be given to pinpoint each student's current instructional level and the results used to form instructional groups. A **skill-specific group** is made up of students requiring instruction in the same skill area. This type of homogeneous grouping, although temporary because skill needs change, is the most effective means of individualizing instruction.

Heterogeneous grouping can also be used for instruction. In this type of group, lower functioning students are provided with models (Smith et al., 1978); for example, students with articulation problems can benefit from hearing the more appropriate speech of their peers. Also, heterogeneous grouping can be used to promote the development of social skills (Bossert & Barnett, 1981). In groups with a range of skills represented, Affleck, Lowenbraun, and Archer (1980) recommended individualizing by using the same task to develop different skills. For example, having students read a short story can be used for instruction in several types and levels of comprehension skills. Today, this approach would be called *differentiation of instruction*.

Flexible grouping is the practice of using several kinds of grouping formats at different times; this allows all students to interact with one another (Schubert, Glick, & Bauer, 1979). Although skill-specific grouping remains the most effective for the purpose of instruction, several of the other methods suggested by these authors may be appropriate for nonacademic and social activities. Examples are grouping by common interests, grouping by choice, proximity grouping, alphabetical grouping, and grouping by counting off. Ford (2005) recommended flexible grouping as a strategy for differentiation of instruction.

Set Up Systems for Monitoring Practice

Teachers provide opportunities for practice after new material is presented. During practice, student performance is monitored, either directly by the teacher or through the use of **self-instructional learning materials.** With self-instructional materials, students receive feedback from the materials themselves and thus are able to practice independently without the assistance of the teacher. This approach frees the teacher for other activities, such as direct instruction.

Among the different forms of self-instruction are self-correcting materials and mediated instruction. Self-correcting materials are those that provide the student with the correct answer so that responses can be checked for accuracy. For example, math fact flashcards with the problem on one side and the answer on the other allow immediate feedback. Teachers can also prepare answer keys for independent practice activities and encourage students to check and correct their responses. Mercer and Mercer (2005) pointed out that this works well with students who have a history of academic failure because they are able to make (and correct) mistakes privately. See the "Inclusion Tips for the Teacher" material for more information about self-correcting materials.

Mediated instruction is any procedure that includes the use of media. For example, many computer software programs provide programmed instruction or practice activities with immediate feedback and correction of errors. Another example is the use of audiotapes for self-instruction. As de Grandpre and Messier (1979) suggested, teachers can develop self-instructional tapes to aid secondary students in reviewing material before exams. The student listens to a tape-recorded question, stops the tape, writes an answer, and then continues the tape to find out whether the response is correct. The tape directs the student to correct any errors immediately.

A **learning center** is a common way to organize self-instructional materials for independent classroom practice. A learning or interest center is "an area especially designed for auto-instructional use by the student" (Berdine & Cegelka, 1980, p. 212). Centers provide independent work for one or several students in one or several skill areas. A typical arrangement is by academic subject; for example, many elementary classrooms contain centers for language arts, mathematics, science, and social studies.

Inclusion Tips for the Teacher

Self-Correcting Instructional Materials

With instructional materials that are self-correcting, students receive immediate feedback on the accuracy of their responses. Some of the most common teaching tools contain self-correcting features. For example, at the end of many textbooks are the answers to all or some of the questions and problems.

Teachers can also design self-correcting materials to meet the needs of specific students. One example of an easy-to-make device that can be used for almost any school subject is suggested by Mercer and Mercer (2005):

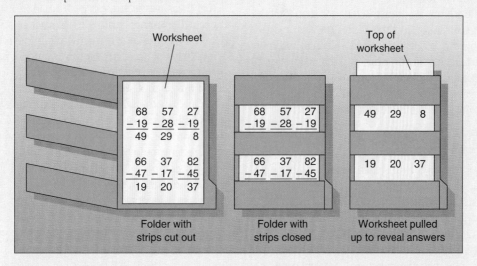

Note: Reprinted with the permission of Merrill from *Teaching Students with Learning Problems,* 7th ed., by Cecil D. Mercer and Ann. R. Mercer (p. 65). Copyright © 2005 Prentice Hall, Inc.

Strips are cut in one side of a manila folder, which then is laminated. Worksheets containing problems and answers are inserted into the folder so that only the problem is presented. The student uses a grease pencil or a felt-tip pen to write the responses under each problem. Then the worksheet is pulled upward, and the answers appear in the strip.

Flashcards are another example of a self-correcting material. The question or problem appears on one side of the card and the other side contains the answer. Like the folder device, flashcards are easy to make and can be adapted for many different subjects. Also, students can use flashcards for independent practice or for review with a peer.

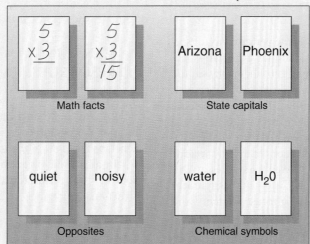

When students use self-correcting materials for class assignments, teachers often ask how to prevent them from merely copying down the correct answers. Here are three ways to avoid this problem.

■ Within each activity or assignment, include a few questions or problems for which the answer is not provided. These items serve as probes to determine whether students can transfer skills to questions for which the answers are not supplied.

■ Have students correct each other's work. Students can trade assignments, or one or two individuals can be selected to be graders for the period or the day.

■ Distribute answer keys only after students have completed their work; be sure, however, that the feedback occurs as soon after completion of the assignment as possible.

Learning centers should be based on specific instructional objectives, house all necessary media and materials, and provide clear and simple directions for student activities. Pretests allow students to select appropriate activities; several kinds and levels of activities should be included in each center. Another important component is a record-keeping system; for example, checklists can be used to note which activities each student has completed. Student progress is measured by posttests or other evaluation devices.

Learning centers can be constructed so that practice activities are individualized or, as King-Sears (2007) suggested, differentiated according to learner need. Centers promote independence, free teachers for other duties, and encourage students to work cooperatively. Like other types of self-instructional systems, they also provide students with immediate feedback on the adequacy of their performance during practice.

Provide Guidelines for Student Behavior

Classroom rules and routines help structure the learning environment. Many students need guidelines for behavior and benefit from consistently enforced rules. As was discussed in the chapter on encouraging positive classroom behavior, rules for classroom conduct are helpful for students of any age. Madsen, Becker, and Thomas (1968) recommended that classroom rules be short and to the point, few in number, and phrased positively (e.g., "Keep your hands to yourself" rather than "Don't hit others"). Affleck et al. (1980) added that rules should be simple, clearly stated, and directly enforceable by the teacher. Classroom rules should be explained to students and reviewed frequently.

 myeducationlab To examine a challenging case, go to the IRIS Center Resources section of Topic *Classroom/Behavior Management* in the MyEducationLab for your course and complete the Case entitled *Norms and Expectations.*

Structure can also help the academic performance of students. When consistent classroom routines are established, students are aware of what they should do, where they should be, and how they should act. For example, the teacher may establish a specific time and place in the classroom for turning in assignments. Some teachers provide each student with a daily assignment card that spells out each of the activities that must be completed. Secondary teachers can establish a routine pattern of assignments (e.g., quiz on Wednesdays, essay due on Fridays) and provide students with a weekly assignment sheet (Raison, 1979). It is also possible to use student work folders that contain the schedule for the day, assignments to be completed, answer keys, and check-off sheets to record finished tasks (Eaton & Hansen, 1978).

Another way to provide structure is through the use of prompts and models. Somewhere in most elementary grade classrooms is a model of the alphabet for students to consult if they have difficulty remembering how to form letters. This technique can be used in most other subjects. For example, procedures for division, alphabetizing, or constructing a paragraph can be written on the board. These prompts help students to function independently.

Use Systematic Record-Keeping Procedures

A great many sources of data are available to the teacher in the general education classroom, and it is easy to become overwhelmed by masses of information. However, by using systematic record-keeping procedures, the teacher can collect sufficient information to make informed instructional decisions.

Teachers generally collect and record two types of data: activities completed (e.g., math workbook, pages 32–34) and actual measures of student performance on tests, quizzes, and other achievement indices (e.g., science test, 75%). Keeping detailed records of every activity completed by every student is probably not necessary. However, student performance should be measured in each major subject area at least once per week and more often if students are encountering difficulty.

One way to make data collection simpler is to enlist the aid of students. After correcting their academic work, they can record their scores or the number of correct responses. For example, each student could be provided with a daily assignment sheet. As students complete each activity, they check their answers with the key provided, record their own score, and then correct their mistakes. Students can also learn to graph their scores so that they and their teacher can easily see progress from day to day.

Systematic record keeping requires consistency. Teachers should decide what data will be collected, how frequently, and what methods will be used for recording. It is best to begin gradually, perhaps with one or two subjects per week. The record-keeping system should be one with which the teacher is comfortable. Some teachers use computer-based grade books. Others favor traditional print grade books or loose-leaf notebooks divided into sections by academic subjects, a file folder for each instructional group, or a 5- × 8-inch index card for each student. The most important factors are that data are collected regularly, recorded in a systematic fashion, and then utilized to determine whether instructional modifications should be made.

▶ MANAGING TIME AND OTHER RESOURCES

When the physical and instructional environments have been arranged and the teacher begins to implement the classroom educational program, coordination skills become crucial. The teacher, as manager of the total learning environment, supervises the allocation, organization, and use of essential learning resources: time, educational materials and equipment, and instructional personnel.

Manage Instructional Time Effectively

Time is a valuable and irreplaceable resource; its effective use is essential in the classroom and in other areas of a teacher's busy life. **Time management,** however, is a skill that most teachers and other professionals need to improve. Several key time management points appear in the accompanying "Inclusion Tips for the Teacher" box.

In the classroom, teachers manage time by establishing a daily schedule. A schedule divides the day into segments and allots specific amounts of time to different activities. Time

Inclusion Tips for the Teacher

Time Management

1. *Set goals.* What are your long-term goals? What are your goals for the next semester? Consider all aspects of your life: professional, personal, social, family, and community.

2. *Establish priorities.* Which of your goals are most important? Separate your goals into those of high value, moderate value, and low value.

3. *Analyze present time use.* Are you using your time to reach your high-priority goals? Keep a log or diary for a few days and see.

4. *Eliminate time wasters.* Spend your time on priority tasks that lead to high-priority goals.

5. *Recognize the difference between "urgent" and "important."* Urgent tasks are those that demand immediate attention; they may or may not be important tasks that lead to your high-priority goals.

6. *Don't procrastinate.* Instead, break large tasks into smaller, manageable tasks. Begin a smaller task immediately.

7. *Make a daily list of things to do.* Make one list and update it daily; be sure to assign a priority to every item on the list.

8. *Begin with high-priority tasks.* Completion of these tasks will reap the most benefit; low-priority tasks can be postponed.

9. *Ask yourself, Is this the best use of my time right now?*

Note: Suggestions from *Getting Things Done* by E. C. Bliss, 1978, New York: Bantam Books; *Get It All Done and Still Be Human* by T. and R. Fanning, 1979, New York: Ballantine Books; *How to Get Control of Your Time and Your Life* by A. Lakein, 1974, New York: New American Library; *Working Smart* by M. LeBoeuf, 1980, New York: Warner Books; and *How to Put More Time in Your Life* by D. Scott, 1981, New York: New American Library.

---

should be scheduled so that student engagement in important learning tasks is maximized (Englert, 1984). The highest priority tasks should be given the most time, and noninstructional activities should be kept to a minimum.

Several suggestions for scheduling, presented by Mercer and Mercer (2005), are appropriate for both the elementary grade teacher, who schedules the entire school day, and the secondary grade teacher, who schedules several different class periods. Among these suggestions are the following recommendations.

- Schedule for maximum instructional time.
- Proceed from short work assignments to longer ones.
- Alternate highly preferred with less preferred tasks.
- Provide a daily schedule for each student.
- Schedule assignments that can be completed in a school day.
- Provide time cues.
- Plan a variety of activities. (pp. 74–75, bullets added)

The Premack principle is also important to consider when designing an instructional schedule. According to Polloway and Patton (1993), this principle is "often called 'grandma's law' because it is reminiscent of the traditional dinner table remark, 'If you eat your vegetables, then you can have dessert'" (p. 102). Thus, schedule highly preferred activities after less preferred activities. For example, if students finish their assignments, then they can select a free-time activity.

It is usually best to begin with a structured schedule that includes several short activities. As students progress, the activities can become longer, and more choices can be offered. The schedule should be shared with students and remain consistent from day to day, providing a guideline to help students know what they should be doing at any time during the day.

Select Learning Materials Wisely

Instructional materials, media, and equipment are other resources that teachers manage, and a major consideration is their selection. Few teachers have unlimited funds, and budgets

for materials must be used wisely. Smith et al. (1978) recommended the evaluation of both the technical and practical aspects of instructional materials. One important technical factor is whether the material has been validated, that is, proven to be effective for its recommended use. Practical considerations include the cost of the material, the number of students with whom it can be used, the strength of its physical construction, and its portability. According to Goodman (1978), characteristics such as difficulty level, presentation sequence, input modes, and modes of response should also be considered. The evaluation guide that appears in the next "Inclusion Tips for the Teacher" addresses several important factors to take into account when evaluating instructional materials.

Teachers often design their own teaching materials if commercial ones are unavailable or too costly. When time and effort are devoted to the production of new instructional tools, the teacher should be sure to make materials that will last. As Cohen and Hart-Hester (1987) advised, "Never make a material twice; make it durable from the start" (p. 57). For example, elementary grade teachers can laminate supplementary math problem worksheets; secondary grade teachers may wish to keep a file, notebook, or CD with class handouts or directions for homework assignments. In addition, teacher-designed materials should be saved for several years. A worksheet or activity from last year, although not useful this year, may be just the thing that is needed next year.

Commercial materials as well as those made by teachers should be stored within the classroom so that they can be easily located and retrieved by students and teachers alike. Mercer and Mercer (2005) recommend the use of a filing system for organization; materials are organized by subject area (e.g., reading) and then by skill (e.g., comprehension). Another possibility is a skill file system designed for student use, with practice materials sequenced according to the skills and skill tests included (Stowitschek et al., 1980). In addition, the books *Stephanie Winston's Best Organizing Tips* (Winston, 1995) and *Taming the Paper Tiger*

(Hemphill, 1997), although not written specifically for educators, give several suggestions that can be used in establishing a management system for classroom materials.

Recruit, Train, and Supervise Instructional Personnel

In many cases, teachers do not have instructional aides, and they may view themselves as the only human instructional resource in their classrooms. However, two excellent sources of assistance are available to every teacher: peer tutors and adult volunteers.

Peer tutors are students who assist by teaching other students. They can come from the same class or can be older, more advanced students (usually called *cross-age tutors*). Peer tutoring approaches with good research support include class-wide peer tutoring (Maheady, Harper, & Mallette, 2003) and its variant, Peer-Assisted Learning Strategies (Fuchs, Fuchs, & Burish, 2000; Fuchs et al., 2001). In the class-wide peer tutoring arrangement, students within a general education class provide tutoring support to each other. Maheady et al. described class-wide peer tutoring as "a form of intra-class, reciprocal peer tutoring in which pupils alternated tutor and tutee roles during each session" (p. 1).

Students can learn to perform many instructional duties: They can be scoring monitors and check others' assignments; teach specific skills to individuals in need of extra help; or deliver reinforcers such as points, verbal praise, and feedback (Jenkins & Jenkins, 1985; Stowitschek et al., 1980). Ehly and Larsen (1980) and Utley, Mortweet, and Greenwood (1997) concluded from reviews of research that peer tutoring produces learning gains not only for the learner but also for the tutor. Thus, although tutoring is generally used to provide extra assistance to low-functioning students, such students also can improve their skills by becoming tutors. For instance, a sixth grader with special needs might be assigned as a cross-age tutor in a second grade classroom. This experience could provide motivation and recognition to the older student while benefiting both individuals academically. Krouse, Gerber, and Kauffman (1981) cautioned that tutoring programs should ensure that the student who is tutored is not stigmatized.

Adult **volunteers** can also provide instructional assistance. Platt and Platt (1980) describe a program that recruited parents and retired persons to help in the schools. Each volunteer was asked to specify areas of interest; choices included working with students on a one-to-one basis, working with small groups, performing clerical duties, and supervising activities outside the classroom.

Training must be provided for instructional personnel, whether they are adults or students (Carroll, 2001). In one program (Heron, Heward, & Cooke, 1980; Parson & Heward, 1979), tutors were taught four skills: preparing learning materials, prompting student responses, praising correct answers, and plotting the results of the tutoring session. Teachers must also supervise and monitor the performance of tutors and volunteers. They can meet with their assistants before instruction or provide written directions. Each assistant should be observed frequently, and further training should be provided as needed. Consult the "Inclusion Tips for the Teacher" box for additional information about peer tutors and adult volunteers.

This chapter has presented several principles for the arrangement, management, and coordination of the classroom learning environment. Before going on, check "Things to Remember" to review coordination skills.

Inclusion Tips for the Teacher

Peer Tutors and Adult Volunteers

Peer tutors and adult volunteers are valuable instructional resources. They assist the teacher by taking responsibility for some of the more routine duties in the classroom. One of the first steps in beginning a peer tutoring or adult volunteer program is specification of the duties that these assistants will assume. Remember when choosing tasks that it will be necessary to train tutors and volunteers to perform them.

Student tutors can be trained to perform a variety of tasks, including the following.

- Provide students with feedback about response accuracy
- Correct written assignments
- Deliver reinforcers such as verbal praise and points in a token economy
- Teach specific skills to individuals or small groups of students
- Supervise independent activities such as learning centers
- Administer simple assessments

Adult volunteers can be trained to perform any of the duties suggested for student tutors. They can also do the following.

- Supervise small groups of students in the classroom, at lunch, during assemblies, and so on

- Collect and record data on student performance
- Assist in the preparation of instructional materials
- Perform routine clerical duties
- Help with classroom housekeeping chores

When selecting duties for peer tutors, keep in mind that they are students. Choose tasks that relate directly to school learning; save clerical and housekeeping chores for adult volunteers.

Another important consideration is the system that the teacher will use to communicate with tutors and volunteers after these classroom assistants are trained. Hammill and Bartel (1986) suggested using a notebook that contains three different forms.

- *Tutor's lesson plan* a description of the instructional activities, procedures, and amount of time to be spent on each
- *Tutor's log sheet* a reporting form for the tutor to record student performance data and any observations about the tutoring session
- *Teacher's note* a page for the teacher to give feedback to the tutor, praise good performance, and suggest ideas for changes

Things to Remember

- Teachers arrange, manage, and coordinate the learning environment.
- The physical environment of the classroom should be safe, barrier free, comfortable, and attractive.
- Arranging classroom space by functions helps structure the environment for students with special needs and other class members.
- The instructional environment of the classroom affects both achievement and nonacademic performance.

- Large-group instruction is an effective use of time; homogeneous skill-specific groups are optimal for individualized instruction.
- Self-instructional learning materials help students monitor their own independent practice activities.
- Daily schedules assist in time management; time should be scheduled to maximize student involvement in important learning tasks.
- Peer tutors and adult volunteers can be effective classroom assistants.

ACTIVITIES

1. Several educational journals offer suggestions to teachers about managing the classroom learning environment. Examples are *Teaching Exceptional Children, Focus on Exceptional Children,* and *Intervention in School and Clinic.* Find an article that interests you and summarize its recommendations.

2. Visit a school, university, shopping mall, or library to check its accessibility. Are there architectural barriers that would deny access to some individuals with disabilities? Watch for curbs, stairs, and steep inclines. If ramps are provided for wheelchairs, try traveling by this route. Is it less direct? Are information signs (e.g., signs on restrooms, elevators, telephones) provided in raised print and Braille?

3. Develop a daily schedule for students in an early elementary classroom and another for students in middle school. In what ways are these schedules different? How do students' ages and instructional needs influence how the school day should be organized?

4. Talk with teachers who have used peer tutors or adult volunteers in their classrooms. How were the classroom assistants selected or recruited? Were they provided with a training program? How did the teacher communicate with these helpers? Ask the teachers to discuss the advantages of tutors and volunteers. Are there any disadvantages?

CHAPTER
NINE

Assistive Technology

- David, a sixth grade student, likes creative writing but dreads trying to find and fix all of the spelling errors he makes. For him, a word processor is almost a necessity.
- Although he has poor vision, Gustavo is able to surf the 'Net; his computer has a large-screen display with magnification.
- Julie wears her technology—her hearing aids—to school every day.
- Jimmy plays math games on the computer to practice his multiplication facts.
- Because Gariella's speech is difficult to understand, she "talks" in class with the help of her electronic communication device.
- Phuoc drives his power chair by manipulating a joystick, and he "types" by talking to his computer.

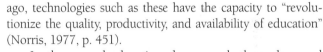

LOOKING AHEAD

In this chapter, you'll learn about strategies for using technology to enhance the general education experience for students with special needs. As you read, think about these questions.

- Each of the students described here uses some type of technology. From what you know now, do you believe these technologies help students bypass or compensate for a disability or special need?
- Computers are likely the most common technology found in schools today. What barriers might standard computers present to students like Gustavo who have vision problems? To students like Phuoc who have physical limitations?
- Assistive technologies are specifically designed for persons with disabilities. Some of the students described here are using assistive devices, and some are not. In your judgment, which students are using off-the-shelf rather than assistive technologies? What are some of the advantages (and disadvantages) of off-the-shelf devices?

The technology of education, in a broad sense, includes all of the techniques, strategies, and approaches used in classrooms to engage learners in the instructional process. More common, however, is to use the term **educational technology** to refer to equipment and media with potential for contributing to student learning. Examples are traditional technologies such as television, radio, film, tape recorders, and calculators as well as more modern technologies such as computers, video, the Internet, and hybrid devices that combine phones, audio players, electronic calendars, and other applications. As one author suggested more than three decades

ago, technologies such as these have the capacity to "revolutionize the quality, productivity, and availability of education" (Norris, 1977, p. 451).

In the general education classroom, both modern and traditional technologies can play a role in the individualization of instruction and enhancement of the standard curriculum for learners with diverse needs. Even more important for students with disabilities are recent breakthroughs in the development of **assistive technology,** that is, technology designed specifically to address the special needs of this group of individuals. For example, assistive technology can help students with visual impairments who cannot see the words on a computer screen to hear them read aloud. Other students, unable to type using a computer keyboard, can use voice recognition technology to "write" by speaking into a microphone. This chapter explores the various types of educational technology, with emphasis on assistive technology, and the ways in which these tools can best be put to use in the general education classroom.

TYPES OF TECHNOLOGY

Technology has great potential for assisting teachers in the educational process, particularly as they work with students with special needs (Edyburn, 2000; Lewis, 2000). Although

Technology in Today's Classrooms

To obtain an overview of technology in today's classrooms, consider these highlights of a report from the National Center for Education Statistics of the U.S. Department of Education on how U.S. children and adolescents use technology.

- *Most children and adolescents use . . . technologies.* About 90% of children and adolescents ages 4–17 (47 million people) use computers, and about 59% (31 million persons) use the Internet.
- *Use begins at an early age.* About three-quarters of 5-year-olds use computers, and over 90% of teens (ages 13–17) do so. . . .
- *There is a "digital divide."* Computer and Internet use are divided along demographic and socioeconomic lines. . . .
- *Disability, urbanicity, and household type are factors in the digital divide. . . .* 5- through 17-year-olds without a disability are more likely to use computers and the Internet than their disabled peers, and children and adolescents living outside of central cities are more likely to use computers than those living in central cities. . . .
- *There are no differences between the sexes in overall computer or Internet use rates. . . .*
- *More children and adolescents use computers at school (81%) than at home (65%). . . .*
- *Use of home computers for playing games and for work on school assignments are common activities. . . .*
- *Home is the most common location for Internet access, followed by school. . . .*

- *Many disadvantaged children and adolescents use the Internet only at school. . . .*
- *Considering all locations, use of the Internet for work on school assignments, e-mail, and games are common activities.* (DeBell & Chapman, 2003a, pp. iv–vii)

A more recent report from the same governmental agency (Wells & Lewis, 2006) provides updated information about some of the newer technologies.

- In 2005, 97% of public schools with Internet access used broadband connections . . .
- Forty-five percent of public schools with Internet access used wireless connections in 2005 . . .
- In 2005, 15% of all public school instructional rooms had wireless Internet connections . . .
- In 2005, 19% of public schools provided hand-held computers to students or teachers for instructional purposes . . .
- In 2005, 10% of public schools lent laptop computers to students . . .
- In 2005, nearly 100% of public schools with Internet access used various technologies or procedures to control student access to inappropriate material on the Internet . . . (Wells & Lewis, 2006, pp. 5–9)

Note: From *Computer and Internet Use by Children and Adolescents in 2001: Statistical Analysis Report* (pp. iv–vii) by M. DeBell & C. Chapman (2003a). U.S. Department of Education, National Center for Education Statistics: Washington, DC. Retrieved August 17, 2004, from *http://nces.ed.gov/pubsearch/pubsinfo.asp?pubid=2004014.* This material is not copyrighted. Also from *Internet Access in U.S. Public Schools and Classrooms: 1994–2004* (NCES 2007-020) by J. Wells & L. Lewis (2006). U.S. Department of Education, National Center for Education Statistics: Washington, DC. Retrieved March 18, 2009, from *http://nces.ed.gov/pubsearch/pubsinfo.asp?pubid2007020.* This material is not copyrighted.

---

technology is not a panacea for the ills of education, when used appropriately, it can help teachers differentiate instruction in the general education classroom. Among the technologies now available for classroom use are computers, the Internet and World Wide Web, film and video, and assistive technologies such as electronic communication aids and talking calculators designed specifically for people with disabilities.

One way to think about technology is to consider the ways in which it can be used. In this schema, three major types of technology, described here, are typically found in schools today.

- *Instructional technology.* This term refers to any type of device with the capacity to support the teaching–learning process; examples are classroom computers, VCRs and DVD players, and educational television.
- *Technology tools.* These are hardware devices and/or software programs or applications that help students and teachers to accomplish educational tasks; examples are word processing programs and handheld electronic spellcheckers.
- *Assistive technology.* This technology is specially designed to aid individuals with disabilities; examples are alternative computer keyboards for students with physical needs and talking wristwatches for students who are blind.

These types of technology are now a common feature of schools and classrooms in the United States. This represents a great increase in the availability of computers and other technologies in classrooms within the past few decades. In the 1980s, fewer than 40% of U.S. school districts owned computers (Quality Education Data, Inc., 1985). By the 1990s, more than 2.5 million computers were being used for public school instruction, with a national average of one computer for every 19 students (Market Data Retrieval, as cited in Kinnaman, 1992). By 2002, the ratio of students to instructional computers was 4.8 to 1, and 99% of public schools had access to the Internet (DeBell & Chapman, 2003b). According to the U.S. Department of Education (DeBell & Chapman, 2003a), "Computers and the Internet recently passed a milestone; both are now used by a majority of Americans" (p. 1). To learn more about how school-aged individuals use these technologies, check out the "For Your Information" section.

▶ **ADVANTAGES AND DISADVANTAGES OF TECHNOLOGY**

Computers and other technologies are versatile tools that can be used for a variety of educational purposes. They offer several potential advantages including these four.

- *Technology allows individualization of instruction.* A case in point is the computer. Computers are also called personal computers (PCs) because they are intended for use by one person; they are a technology for individuals. If there were 30 students in a classroom, each sitting at a computer, these students could be engaged in activities in 30 different content areas. Or they could all be working on the same content, but each at the skill level appropriate for his or her level of learning. In addition, most computer programs allow learners to proceed at their own pace.
- *Technology motivates students.* Novelty is an important factor in motivation, and technology is still a new enough instructional medium to excite students' interest. In addition, students often perceive technology-based learning activities as more like play than work. Another motivating feature, particularly for students with learning needs, is that many software applications provide feedback to the learner in a nonjudgmental manner. If the student makes an error, the application might simply say, "Not quite, Olivia. Try again."
- *Technology allows new types of learning and new ways of accomplishing old tasks.* With computers, teachers can provide students with a variety of learning experiences not usually possible in a traditional classroom setting. For example, with applications called simulations, students might learn to manage a small business, command troops in a Civil War battle, conduct a series of chemistry experiments, or travel to Jupiter. By interacting with the **World Wide Web,** students can move beyond classroom walls to visit the White House, see NASA's latest expedition, learn about current exhibits at the Smithsonian, check the status of the stock market, and interact with students in classrooms throughout the world.

> **PEARSON** **myeducationlab** Go to the Assignments and Activities section of Topic *Intellectual Disabilities* in the MyEducationLab for your course and complete the activity entitled *Assistive Technology.*

Computers also provide new ways of doing old tasks. With word processing programs, for example, writing becomes a somewhat different process. As soon as the writer has entered text into the program, that text can be modified and manipulated quickly and easily. The writer can add or delete words or phrases, change the order of sentences or paragraphs, format the text in many different ways, and even add graphics. This flexibility makes writing an easier task for students because errors are less difficult to correct.

- *Technology helps students with special needs bypass or compensate for disabilities.* Computers and other technologies permit many students with special needs to bypass physical or sensory limitations so that they can take part in general education classroom activities. For example, a student who is paralyzed and able only to nod his head can "type" on a computer by using a special switch mounted on the headrest of his wheelchair. Or a student who is blind can use a computer to translate her Braille essay into regular print that

her teacher can read. Computers can also help students compensate for their difficulties in basic academic skills. Students who spell poorly, for example, can write with a word processor, then use a spelling checker program to help locate and correct misspelled words.

There are also potential disadvantages to classroom technology use. Computers are only as good as the software applications they run or the websites to which they connect. Selection of appropriate instructional activities is critical. Not all technology-based learning tasks use sound principles of instruction. Although a wide selection of educational software applications is now available and the Internet offers a vast supply of potential resources, it may not be possible to find an application or website that fits the content, level, and interest needs of a particular student. In addition, most applications do not provide field-test data to support their effectiveness.

Another potential area of difficulty is access to computer equipment and other technologies. A school may have a limited supply of state-of-the-art computers; and, if computers aren't available in the classroom, teachers may need to schedule their students in a central computer lab or media center for a limited time each week. In addition, technology quickly becomes outdated as new versions are introduced, and applications designed to run on newer computer systems may not work on older ones. Another major consideration is cost. Technology is not an inexpensive addition to the teacher's instructional arsenal.

▶ UNIVERSAL DESIGN AND ACCESSIBILITY

Accessibility is often discussed in relation to environmental barriers. A school is not accessible if the water fountain is too high for students who travel by wheelchair to reach it to get a drink. A community center is not accessible to all citizens, young and old, if stairs must be climbed to enter the building. Other barriers limit access by presenting information in only one way. For example, print restaurant menus are not accessible to persons who are blind or those who have not learned to read. Likewise, auditory portions of films shown at local movie theaters are not accessible to individuals who are deaf or have difficulty hearing.

> **PEARSON** **myeducationlab** Go to the Assignments and Activities section of Topic *Instructional Practices and Learning Strategies* in the MyEducationLab for your course and complete the activity entitled *Universal Design.*

For education to be accessible to all learners, barriers must be removed from not only the physical environment of the classroom but also the instructional environment. The principles of **Universal Design** (sometimes called *universal design for learning*) promote classroom accessibility. Although most often associated with technology, these principles apply to all aspects of the educational process, including curriculum, instruction, assessment, and the physical environment of the school. Universal design has been described as "an approach to the design of all products and environments to be usable by everyone, to the greatest extent possible, regardless of age, ability, or situation" (Center

Built-in Accessibility in the Macintosh Computer

According to the Apple website (*www.apple.com/accessibility/*), "for more than 20 years, Apple has provided new and innovative solutions for people with disabilities." One of the best examples is the Macintosh computer, which provides built-in access features for individuals with several different types of disabilities.

"Universal Access" is the name of one of the applications built into the Macintosh computers. Located within System Preferences, the Universal Access screen looks like this:

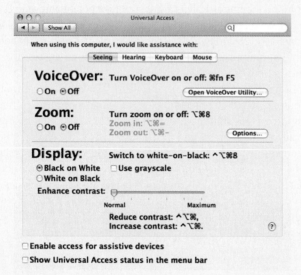

Note: Screen shot reprinted with permission of Apple Inc.

In Universal Access, individuals are able to select the type or types of help they would like. As shown near the top of the screen display, the choices are assistance with seeing, hearing, the keyboard, and the mouse.

Built-in features that provide *assistance with seeing* include VoiceOver, Zoom, and Display. The VoiceOver option, when activated, will read all text on the screen aloud, including menus, dialogue boxes, and all other aspects of programs with which users must interact. With this feature, blind persons can hear what is on the computer screen and make choices by typing on the keyboard. For those individuals who do not need all portions of the screen display read aloud, the Macintosh offers synthesized speech. (This option, called "Speech," is also found in the System Preferences panel.) For example, if a writer wants to hear what he or she is writing with a word processing application, that text can be read aloud as it is entered and later in the editing stage. Or the speech option can be turned on if a reader needs assistance with reading the text on a webpage. The Zoom option for individuals who have difficulty seeing assists by increasing the size of the display on the computer screen. For instance, it is possible to zoom in with 20x magnification. With the Display option, the color of the display can be changed (e.g., white letters on black) and the contrast enhanced.

Among the adaptations for persons who need *assistance with hearing* are volume controls and the use of visual flashes (instead of an auditory signal) when a program alert takes place. An important option is iChat, a built-in conferencing application in which persons can communicate with each other across distances using not only text and speech and other types of audio but also video. Thus, with iChat, deaf individuals can talk with one another not only by typing text but also by using sign language.

There are several modifications that can be made for those who require *assistance with the keyboard, mouse, and trackpad.* For example, individuals who encounter difficulty using the mouse can activate MouseKeys and move the pointer around the screen by pressing on the numeric keypad. For those persons who are adept at using the mouse (or another pointing device), an on-screen keyboard can be added to the display so that users enter text by clicking on individual keys with the mouse. Other adaptations for the standard keyboard are slow keys (for those who make unintended keystrokes), adjustments for the rate at which keys repeat (for those who might hold a key down too long), and sticky keys (for those who have difficulty holding down more than one key at a time).

There are many additional built-in accessibility features on the Macintosh computer and also on other Apple technologies. Examples for the Macintosh are speech recognition, spelling and grammar checking, and built-in applications providing access to a dictionary, thesaurus, and encyclopedia. One example of other Apple technologies is the iPod Nano (fourth generation) with spoken menus, allowing those who cannot see (or read) print menus to hear them read aloud. Others are the iPod shuffle with VoiceOver that reads aloud the names of the user's playlists and speaks the name of the artist and the song that is playing and the iPhone 3G S with a screen-reader and full-screen magnification.

---

for Universal Design, 2004). According to CAST (1999–2009), the nonprofit Center for Applied Special Technology,

> Universal Design for Learning is an educational approach with three primary principles:
>
> - *Multiple means of representation,* to give diverse learners options for acquiring information and knowledge
> - *Multiple means of action and expression,* to provide learners options for demonstrating what they know
> - *Multiple means of engagement,* to tap into learners' interests, offer appropriate challenges, and increase motivation

Technology can help to provide multiple options for students who experience difficulty with standard classroom tasks.

For example, an audio recording of a book or chapter might be helpful for students unable to read the print version. However, the best way to promote accessibility would be to employ the principles of universal design in the creation of educational approaches, strategies, and materials. Introducing universal design features in the development of a technology, a learning material, or a curriculum increases accessibility for all and reduces the need for after-the-fact adaptations.

One example of an educational tool with built-in universal access features is the Macintosh computer. Consult the "Spotlight on Technology" to learn how this technology offers multiple alternatives for students who experience difficulty with vision, hearing, reading, and motor skills.

In the 2004 IDEA Act, the federal government took an important step toward ensuring accessibility of instructional materials for students with disabilities by establishing **NIMAS,** or the National Instructional Materials Accessibility Standard. This portion of the special education law requires that print instructional materials be available not only in print but also in electronic files that can be converted to formats accessible to students with different types of disabilities. The law specifies the electronic format and defines print materials as not only textbooks but also related core materials used in the classroom. Examples of specialized formats into which print materials might be converted are Braille, audio, digital text, and large print.

▶ CLASSROOM INSTRUCTIONAL TECHNOLOGIES

As noted earlier in this chapter, technology is available to almost every student in today's public schools. The computer is the most common technology and interacting with the Internet is the most common use (DeBell & Chapman, 2003a; Wells & Lewis, 2006). When the population of U.S. households is considered, the picture of technology use broadens. According to a recent study by the Pew Research Center (2007), 78% of the population say that cable or satellite television is a regular household expense, 74% report cell phones, and 65% Internet service. This picture mirrors that of U.S. schools except in relation to cell phones. As Norris and Soloway (2009) reported, "Mobile technologies such as cell phones, digital music players, and handheld gaming devices are by and large banned from America's K–12 schools."

Computers are used in classrooms for many different instructional purposes. Although these purposes include what was called in the early days of classroom technology use "computer-assisted instruction," today's teachers and students are more likely to use computers as tools rather than as providers of tutorials. It is important to understand these various purposes, however, and how they are related to the type of software or application that the computer or other technology presents to the user. **Application,** the more modern term, is likely the better word to use today instead of software. Instructional applications, though once a scarce commodity, are available in the thousands across the school curriculum and across the age span. Applications are available for computers in the form of computer software and via the World Wide Web; they are also available on cell phones and other types of handheld devices.

myeducationlab) Go to the Building Teaching Skills and Dispositions section of Topic *Visual Impairment* in the MyEducationLab for your course and complete the activity entitled *Using Technology to Support Learning.*

Table 9-1 presents information about several common types of instructional applications. Tool applications are not included here because they are discussed in the next section of this chapter. Along with each application type (e.g., tutorial, practice, simulation) is a description of its instructional purpose as well as examples of computer software applications, applications on websites, and/or iPhone applications.

When selecting technology applications for classroom use, teachers need to consider a number of factors including students' instructional needs, the usefulness of the application's content, and the mode of instruction the application offers. Also important are the types of demands the application places upon the student, over and above the instructional content. There are five areas of concern.

1. *Technology use demands.* Before using any type of applications, students must learn to operate the computer or other technology upon which the application runs. More complicated applications may pose problems for young or inexperienced technology users.
2. *Academic demands.* One academic skill may be needed to profit from an application, even if the application addresses a different skill. For example, math, science, and social studies applications often require students to read text or to type in correctly spelled words. Demands such as these may be major barriers for students with learning problems.
3. *Physical demands.* Students respond in many applications by typing on the keyboard or moving the mouse. Keyboarding responses range from pressing any key (a response mode used in discovery programs for preschoolers) to typing words or connected text. However, some students with physical impairments may require assistive devices to enter information without using either the keyboard or mouse.
4. *Speed demands.* Some applications present information quickly and students cannot regulate the speed with which information appears on the screen; other programs require students to respond within a time limit. When

Application Type	Description	Examples
Tutorial	Tutorials present content that is new to the learner. They introduce and explain new skills or information, then supervise the learner's first attempts to practice and apply this new material.	*Typing Tutor* (software); *Learn 2 Type* (*www.learn2type.com*); *Spanish 101 24/7 Tutor* (iPhone ap)
Practice	Practice applications review material previously introduced, giving practice so performance can improve. Most provide immediate feedback; many impose speed demands.	*Math Blaster* (software); *Flashcards* (*www.aplusmath.com*); *300+ Sight Words* (iPhone ap)
Simulation	Simulation applications provide experience in situations difficult or impossible to duplicate in classrooms. Students practice critical thinking and problem analysis.	*The Oregon Trail* (software); iPhone aps: *The Oregon Trail, Herod's Lost Tomb*
Discovery/ exploration	Students are encouraged to explore a rich learning environment. No attempt is made to teach specific content and there are no right or wrong answers.	*Living Books Library* (e.g., *Arthur's Birthday Party*) (software); iPhone aps: *Wheels on the Bus, iZoo*
Educational games, puzzles	Educational games and puzzles include traditional board, card, and paper-and-pencil games as well as adventure games and puzzles.	*Scrabble* (software); *Imaginext Dinosaurs Puzzle* (*www.fisher-price.com*); iPhone aps: *Monopoly, Chicktionary*

applications are under user control, the student controls the pace and spends as much time as needed on any one part of the program.

5. *Accuracy demands.* Applications differ in how they handle errors. In some, students can type responses, then make corrections before signaling that they have finished; in others, the first response typed is considered the final response. Also, some programs provide prompts when responses are close to correct ("Did you mean to type *yes* instead of *yse?*").

The teacher should weigh all of these factors before making a decision about the worth of an instructional application. No application will be perfect in every respect. Instead, it is necessary to weigh the advantages and disadvantages to determine whether an application will be a useful addition to the instructional resources already available in the classroom.

 TECHNOLOGY TOOLS

Technology tool applications help students and teachers to accomplish tasks. The most common tools are word processors and e-mail programs. **Word processors** are tools for writing any type of text; e-mail programs, to be discussed in the next section, combine word processing capabilities with tools for sending, receiving, storing, and searching e-mails.

In schools, word processors are the tool applications used most widely not only by students but also by teachers. Word processors present the writer with the technological equivalent of a blank sheet of paper—an empty screen—and then provide a system for entering text onto that screen. Their main value, however, is the ease with which that text can be changed and manipulated. The writer can correct errors quickly and

easily, alter the sequence and format of the text, and then store what has been written for later use.

Today's word processors routinely offer such features as spelling checkers, thesauruses, and the ability to import photos and other graphics, video, and Internet links. Programs specially designed for younger children may provide simpler operation and large-sized text. Others have the capacity to talk so that students can hear the text they have written read aloud.

Idea processors are another type of application tool often used in education. Sometimes called *concept mapping programs* (Puckett, 2004), these tools help students and teachers generate, manipulate, and organize their thoughts and ideas, usually in a visual format. Perhaps the best known examples are the *Inspiration* program and the version for younger students, *Kidspiration*. Figure 9-1 presents an illustration of how *Inspiration* might be used in science to foster understanding of the various forms of energy.

Database programs assist in the organization and management of large bodies of information; in effect, they create a computer-based filing system. The user determines the type of information to be stored and the exact data to be included in each record. The major value of such a record-keeping system is that, once the information has been stored, it can be sorted and retrieved quickly and easily. For example, it would be easy to retrieve the names of students with September birthdays from a classroom database storing names and birthdates.

Integrated productivity packages typically offer both a word processor and database (as well as other features such as **spreadsheets** for manipulating numerical information). The best known integrated productivity tool collection is *Microsoft Office*. School versions of this package typically include a word processor, spreadsheet, an e-mail program, and a presentation

FIGURE 9-1   Science Concept Map Using *Inspiration*

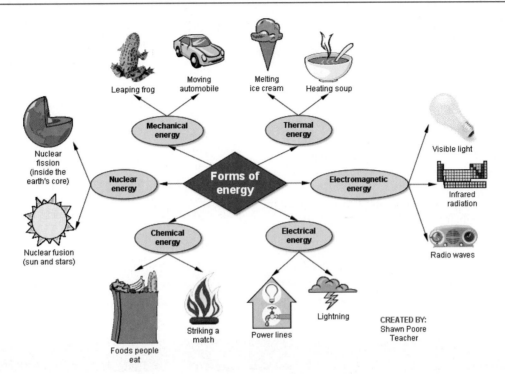

Note: Reprinted with permission from the *Inspiration* website (*http://inspiration.com/Examples/Inspiration*)

tool. The **presentation tool**, PowerPoint, assists students and teachers in organizing and displaying many types of information (text, still and animated graphics, video, and sound) as computer- or web-based presentations.

Creativity tools aid in the design, development, and presentation of many different creative products including graphics and other types of visual arts, music, photographs, and movies. Also available are creativity tools for the development of web pages, websites, and web-based learning activities.

Among the software tools designed specially for teachers are those that help manage information about students. Examples are gradebook programs, software for managing and evaluating student portfolios, and programs to help in the development of IEPs for students with disabilities. Also available are tools for preparing instructional materials such as programs to generate crossword puzzles and word finds, special word processing fonts for creating handwriting practice activities, and programs that generate math fact worksheets.

Some of the most useful tools for educators and students are not computer applications. One example is the handheld spelling checker used in many classrooms. With the Franklin Spelling Ace®, for instance, students type in their best guess of a word's spelling and the aid provides them with a list of possible alternatives. Similar devices include electronic dictionaries, thesauruses, and foreign language aids. Other tools include reading devices such as the Kindle-style e-reader or those in the LeapFrog series for preschool and elementary grade children.

Also of interest are **personal digital assistants (PDAs)**, handheld devices that offer a range of capabilities including scheduling, note taking, storage of information such as addresses, and wireless transmission of information. Two of the most popular PDAs, the BlackBerry and the iPhone, offer both phone and Internet access alongside the more standard features. In some schools, teachers use PDA technology to record information about student progress and performance. For more information about educational applications of PDAs, visit the K12 Handhelds website at http://www.k12handhelds.com. That website suggests 101 uses for PDAs in education, including helping teachers keep their own schedules, track student progress on specific skills, take and store digital photos, and record voice notes.

THE INTERNET AS AN INSTRUCTIONAL TOOL

Perhaps the biggest change in educational technology in the past 10 years is the entry of the Internet into the classroom. As a recent National Center for Education Statistics study (Wells & Lewis, 2006) reported, in 2005 virtually every public school in the United States had Internet access, and that access was by broadband connection. Wireless access was available in close to half of the schools (45%). Also, almost 100% of schools with Internet access were concerned enough about safeguarding students from inappropriate content that access was controlled in some way.

The Internet is a worldwide computer network. Begun in the 1970s as a U.S. military research project (Posth, 1997), it has evolved into a communication system that today reaches literally millions of people across the globe. The World Wide Web (WWW) is not quite the same as the Internet. According to the online encyclopedia Wikipedia (2009), the web is "an application built on top of the Internet" that has "enabled the spread of information over the Internet through an easy-to-use and flexible format." Sites on the web are multimedia; they often include not only text but also graphics, photos, music, voice, sound effects, video, and even live camera feeds.

The range of information available on the web is truly astounding. Information about almost any subject can be found, and it is possible to use the web for a variety of purposes including online shopping; "visiting" another state, another country, or even another planet; communication with family, friends, and professional colleagues; and getting up-to-the-minute news and weather, to name but a few possibilities. Among this vast array of options are valuable instructional resources for general education teachers who serve students with disabilities and other special needs. If you need a refresher course on basic web browsing skills, consult the "For Your Information" box that follows.

Search Strategies

One of the most powerful features of the World Wide Web is the user's ability to search all of its public websites. With just a few keystrokes, teachers and students have the ability to shift

---

For Your Information

Basic Techniques for Web Browsing

Website Addresses

Website addresses are everywhere. Turn on the TV, read a newspaper or magazine, pick up a catalog, or listen to the radio and you'll find something like

> http://www.anyschool.edu

This address of a site on the World Wide Web is called a *URL* (pronounced "U-R-L") or Uniform Resource Locator. The first part of the address is a command. The letters *http* stand for HyperText Transfer Protocol. The letters *www* stand for World Wide Web, and the middle portion of the address (*anyschool* in the example above) is a short name for the website. The last three letters indicate the type of site. For example, education sites are designated *edu*, government sites *gov*, sites of organizations *org*, and commercial sites *com*. When a URL is read aloud, a period in the address is read as "dot."

When the URL for a website is known, it is easy to access that site. The user logs onto the web, starts up a *web browser* software program (e.g., Internet Explorer, Firefox, Safari), and opens a website. Usually that involves typing the URL in its entirety.

It is often possible to determine the URL of a company or organization by making an educated guess. For example, the URL for the software publisher Broderbund is *http://www.broderbund.com*. Sometimes, however, the guessing strategy does not work. For example, the web address for the Council for Exceptional Children is not *http://www.cec.org*, as would be predicted. Instead, it is *http://www.cec.sped.org*. When a URL is not available or predictable, it is necessary to search the web, a procedure that will be explained in a later section.

Navigating the Web

When a user first starts up a web browser software program, that program goes directly to a *home page*. A home page can be any website. When purchased, programs are typically set to the website of their publisher. This can be changed to any other site. For example, a teacher might want the school's website to be his or her home page.

Most web pages contain *links* that allow movement to other locations, either within the same website or to other sites. When text is underlined or printed in boldface type (e.g., **bold**), that signals that it is linked to something else.

Links are also found in graphics. In many websites, the first page contains a graphical menu that allows users to go to the section of the site in which they're interested. That graphical menu could be a menu bar with words describing the parts of the website, a drawing depicting the site, or a series of photos. In most cases where there are graphical links, text links are also provided, although these may be in very small print.

In a typical session on the web, a user begins with one website, selects links within that site, and then moves to another site either by selecting a link in the first site or by typing in another URL. This process is usually repeated several times.

At some point in the session, the user may want to return to one of the pages visited previously. To return to the last page visited, the *Back command* is used. In contrast, the *Forward command* moves the user forward. Another method is to use the special history menu in the web browser program (e.g., the Go menu in Internet Explorer or the History menu in Firefox). That menu lists the sites visited in the session and any one can be selected. It also lists Home as an option, if the user wants to return to the home page.

Bookmarks are another important feature of most web browsers. A bookmark records the URL of a website so that it can easily be accessed in the future. Whenever users find an interesting website, they can go to the Bookmark menu and choose the command to add a bookmark. The name of the website will then be listed on the Bookmark menu, and selecting that name will move the user to the website. The bookmark file can be edited, and it can be saved so that it can be shared with others.

through literally millions of web pages to locate information about a specific topic. That topic can be very broad (e.g., educational reform) or quite narrow (e.g., hearing ear dogs for people with hearing impairments). It can be professional in nature or relate to more personal concerns (e.g., Hawaiian vacations, clogged toilets, the care and feeding of gerbils).

To search the web, the user goes to one of the many sites that provide search services. According to the Search Engine Watch website (Johnson, 2009), the top two choices for search services are google.com and yahoo.com. The basic procedure for searches is quite simple. The user types in a descriptor (e.g., disability), clicks on "search," and the search service generates a list of "hits," that is, websites that match the descriptor. That list contains links to each of the matching sites and usually brief descriptions of them. In most cases, the most relevant sites (the ones with the closest match to the descriptor) appear first in the list.

The search engine in each service works a bit differently, and this results in varying numbers of hits from one service to another. For example, on a recent search for *disability,* the approximate number of hits reported by Google was 56 million, by MSN Live Search 34 million, and by AOL Search 314 million.

Search services typically provide information about how they search the web so that users can make informed choices about which service to select for a specific purpose.

One problem that often occurs is that a search produces too many hits. Search services offer different ways of handling this problem, but most allow users to modify their search terms to narrow the scope of their search. For example, with Google's Advanced Search feature, it is possible to search for web pages that include *all* of the terms in the search query (e.g., searching for pages that include these terms in any order: "baseball," "girls," and "home runs"). Other possibilities are searching for exact phrases, searching for pages that include at least one of several search terms, and searching for pages that do not include specific terms.

The web is a rich source of valuable resources for teachers and students alike. To locate these resources, it would be possible to search the web using a descriptor such as "websites for teachers." A recent Google search with these search terms resulted in nearly 7 million hits. This number could be reduced by adding additional descriptors such as age or grade levels or specific school subjects (e.g., reading, math, history, music). For information about several useful sites, consult the "Window on the Web" feature.

 WINDOW ON THE WEB

Websites for Teachers

Federal Resources for Educational Excellence (FREE)

This site provides access to thousands of teaching and learning resources compiled by dozens of federal agencies and organizations including the Library of Congress, NASA, the Smithsonian Institution, the National Gallery of Art, the U.S. Mint, and the Centers for Disease Control and Prevention. New resources are added daily. Resources can be accessed by subject (e.g., arts and music, history and social studies, math) or by searching the entire collection. It is also possible to browse collection of animations, primary documents, photos, and videos.

http://www.ed.gov/free/

PBS TeacherSource

Sponsored by the Public Broadcasting System (PBS), this site contains educational resources, some with connections to PBS programming, that include "lesson plans, teaching activities, on-demand video assets, and interactive games and simulations." The site can be searched by keyword or the teacher can choose a subject (e.g., the arts, science and technology), a grade range, and a topic. For instance, if a teacher selected "social studies," "grades 3–5," and "community and citizenship," some of the resources that might be identified are "A Nation of Many Cultures," "Fight for Freedom," and "All Aboard the Campaign Train!"

http://www.pbs.org/teachers/

Kathy Schrock's Guide for Educators

Part of the website of the Discovery Channel, this site describes itself as a frequently updated "categorized list of sites useful for enhancing curriculum and professional growth." Teachers can access information by selecting from more than 20 different subjects (from Agricultural Education to World Info & Languages) and by choosing one of the many "Teacher Helpers" (e.g., Assessment & Rubrics). Other features include "Sites of the Week," "Theme of the Month," search tools, and links to Discovery School activities such as Brain Boosters, Clip Art, Puzzlemaker, and Science Fair Central.

http://school.discovery.com/schrockguide/

Education World

Education World is a commercial site full of useful tools and information for teachers and administrators. The site menu includes areas such as Lesson Planning, Administrator's Desk, School Issues, Professional Development, Technology Integration, and More Resources. New resources are added frequently. For example, on one visit to the site, among the new additions were a lesson of the day using an online tool for a class time-telling competition and a review of the Listening Adventures activities on the Carnegie Hall website.

http://www.education-world.com/

Teacher Planet

Another commercial site, Teacher Planet, contains collections of lesson plans for teachers, theme units, worksheets, teacher tools, rubrics, and much more. The site's home page features a calendar with the current month's holidays and special events noted, and instructional resources are linked to each special date.

http://www.teacherplanet.com

Evaluating Websites

One of the primary advantages of the web, the vast number and variety of the resources it offers, is also its major disadvantage. It is quite easy for students and their teachers, overwhelmed with the quantity of Internet resources, to fail to pay sufficient attention to a much more important concern: the quality of web-based information. Because anyone can publish a website and there are no referees to determine if the information presented is even true, the World Wide Web is truly a "buyer beware" information marketplace.

Several excellent guides are available for use by teachers and other professionals in evaluating the quality of web-based resources. The Cornell University Library presents a number of evaluation resources on its website at http://www.library.cornell.edu/olinuris/ref/research/webeval.html. One example is the set of five criteria that Kapoun (1998) suggested for evaluating websites. These criteria are:

- accuracy,
- authority,
- currency,
- objectivity, and
- coverage.

In Kapoun's discussion of these criteria, he urged users to examine web pages with an attitude of skepticism. In Kapoun's words, "View any Web page as you would an infomercial on television. Ask yourself why was this written and for whom?"

Like their teachers, students also need to develop skill in evaluating web content. Schrock (2009) has designed a set of tools for students to use as they begin to learn how to critically evaluate websites. Guides are available for elementary grade, middle school level, and secondary school level students as well as Spanish language versions of all three guides. Another resource is the Web Site Evaluation Form designed in 2001 by Ron Goral and Joanne Lenburg of the Madison Metropolitan School District in Madison, Wisconsin. That form appears in the "Inclusion Tips for the Teacher" section.

▶ WEB-BASED TOOLS FOR TEACHERS

A number of web-based technology tools have the capability of being valuable resources for teachers and their students. Several but certainly not all of these tools are described in this section. Also, it is important to point out that new potentially useful tools become available almost on a daily basis. Thus, any discussion of exemplary tools becomes dated as soon as it is prepared.

Communication Tools

Perhaps the best known web-based tool is **e-mail**. E-mail, or electronic mail, is a quick, easy way to communicate with others who have access to the Internet. E-mail is provided as part of most educational and commercial Internet services.

E-mail addresses take this format:

pqsmith@longhornelem.edu

The first part of the address specifies the person. This person can be found at (signified by the symbol @) a particular school or district, and this location is an educational institution. Like URLs, e-mail addresses from businesses or commercial Internet providers end in *com* (e.g., mrchips@aol.com). E-mail addresses from other countries end in a country code such as *ca* for Canada and *jp* for Japan.

Sending e-mail is quite simple. First, it is necessary to have one of the following: an e-mail software program such as Outlook or Eudora, an online e-mail service such as Google Mail or Yahoo! Mail, or the e-mail application furnished by a commercial Internet provider. The user chooses "New Message." Then, in most e-mail systems, the user will be asked to provide three types of information:

To:

From: myname@myschool.edu

Subject:

Message:

After "To" the teacher types in the e-mail address of the recipient. It is usually possible to type more than one address here so that the same message can be sent to several recipients. This is a very useful feature when it is necessary to share information across a group of individuals. The "From" space is often filled in automatically by the e-mail program. "Subject" typically is a brief description of the content of the message, and the "Message" area is where the electronic communication is typed. In many e-mail systems, it is possible to attach computer files to e-mail messages. All sorts of files can be attached, including word processed documents and photos. For example, at many universities, students turn in their written assignments via e-mail.

When users open their e-mail program, they learn whether or not they have received new mail. Usually this information is provided in a list or table that indicates who sent the message, when the message was sent, and the subject. This allows users to scan their incoming mail and decide whether or not to read it. Once a message has been opened and read, the user typically has several options: replying to the message, forwarding a copy of the message to someone else, printing a copy of the message, and saving or discarding the message. Saved messages can be stored within the e-mail program for later retrieval. In addition, most e-mail systems provide an electronic address book where users can record the e-mail addresses of persons with whom they correspond.

E-mail is likely one of the technology-based communication tools that is most often used by teachers, students, and other citizens. However, new communication methods are gaining popularity. One is **web-based conferencing**, sometimes called *web-based chats*. With this tool, two or more people can communicate in real time using text alone or text

Helping Students Evaluate Websites

Web Site Evaluation Form

Site Name: _____

Site Address/URL: http:// _____

(Respond to all questions below. Leave blank any question that does not apply.)

Consider WHO is responsible for the web site:
- Does the publisher appear to be knowledgeable about the content?   ____ YES   ____ NO
- Does the publisher qualify as an authority or expert on the topic?   ____ YES ____ NO
- Can you contact the publisher from the site?   ____ YES ____ NO
- Is the site's sponsor identified?   ____ YES ____ NO

Consider WHAT is the content/subject matter of the web site:
- Does the content appear to be accurate? Error free?   ____ YES ____ NO
- Is the information presented in an objective manner, with a minimum of bias?   ____ YES ____ NO
- Is there real depth-of-content (vs. information that is limited and superficial)?   ____ YES ____ NO
- Are links from the site appropriate and/or supportive of the content?   ____ YES ____ NO
- Does the content have educational or informational value?   ____ YES ____ NO

Consider WHERE the web site resides:
- What type of domain is this site?   ____.gov ____.com ____.edu ____.org ____.net ____.biz Other _____
- Is this a personal page with a "~" or ".name" in the URL?   ____ YES ____ NO

Consider WHEN the web site was last updated:
- Is the information current?   ____ YES ____ NO
- Does the site provide information on when it was last updated?   ____ YES ____ NO
- Does a current date matter?   ____ YES ____ NO

Consider HOW the main page looks and functions:
- Is the page easy to understand and use?   ____ YES ____ NO
- Is the page well organized?   ____ YES ____ NO
- Does the page load in a reasonable amount of time?   ____ YES ____ NO
- Do all of the links work?   ____ YES ____ NO
- Is the page free from (excessive amounts of) advertising?   ____ YES ____ NO

Consider WHY the web site exists:
- Is the site trying to
  - sell something?   ____ YES ____ NO
  - inform?   ____ YES ____ NO
  - persuade?   ____ YES ____ NO
- Is the web site appropriate for your target audience?   ____ YES ____ NO
- Is the Internet the best place to find this information (vs. books, journals, etc.)?   ____ YES ____ NO

Comments:

Name/School: _____

Date: _____

Note: Website Evaluation Form developed by Ron Goral and Joanne Lenburg, 2001. Copyright 2001–2003 Madison Metropolitan School District, Madison, Wisconsin. Retrieved November 6, 2004, from *http://www.madison.k12.wi.us/tnl/detectives/evalform.htm*

supplemented with live video feeds. This tool is available through free online tools such as Google Mail and from commercial sources such as gotomeeting.com. **Text messaging** is a similar tool, but one in which communication does not necessarily take place in real time. One person texts a message to another (or to several others); recipients can access that message as soon as it is received or later when they check their mobile phone or computer. **Twitter** is a text messaging system where users answer the question "What are you doing?" using less than 140 characters of text. Accessible via the web (twitter.com) or a mobile phone, Twitter allows its members to follow other members, which might include friends, family, and colleagues as well as organizations such as NASA and the Library of Congress and popular culture icons such as Oprah Winfrey and American Idol.

Information Sources

In contrast to the communication tools just discussed, the next group of web-based tools are content-rich information sources. One example is **Wikipedia** (wikipedia.org), a free online encyclopedia with articles in dozens of languages; in English, the number of articles available is almost 3 million. However, the most interesting feature of Wikipedia is how its articles are written and updated. According to the Wikipedia website:

> Wikipedia is written collaboratively by volunteers from all around the world. Anyone with internet access can make changes to one of the largest reference web sites, attracting at least 684 million visitors yearly by 2008. There are more than 75,000 active contributors working on more than 13,000,000 articles in more than 260 languages.

At the end of most Wikipedia articles is a list of references and notes, and many of the words and phrases within articles are linked to other articles within Wikipedia and to other websites. When articles are not well documented, Wikipedia posts this warning: "This article does not cite any references or sources. Please help improve this article by adding citations to reliable sources. Unverifiable material may be challenged and removed."

Blogs, or web logs, are another web-based information source. A blog is "a frequent, chronological publication of personal thoughts and Web links" (marketingterms.com). Blogs are made up of journal entries arranged in chronological order, with the most recent appearing first. In many cases, the creator of the blog will include references to other websites and, in some, readers are able to respond to the blogger's message with their own comments. Google offers a website for searching for blogs on specific topics (blogsearch.google.com). Mathews (2009) identified two sources of education-related blogs that are useful to teachers:

- Top 100 Education Blogs (http://oedb.org/library/features/top-100-education-blogs)
- Education Blogs in Yahoo (http://dir.yahoo.com/Education/News_and_Media/Blogs/)

Podcasts are similar in many ways to blogs. Podcasts usually are recorded as a series but, instead of being based in text, podcasts are audio or video files. The term *podcast* was first used to describe files that could be downloaded into the free program iTunes for use on an iPod. At present, podcasts can be played on computers and as well as on the iPod and other mobile devices. Good examples of podcast series can be found on the website of any news organization. The website of the *New York Times*, for instance, offers a number of podcasts including "Front Page," "Backstory," "Book Review," "Only in New York," and "Your Money."

E-mail mailing lists (also called *Listservs*) are e-mail newsletters to which users can subscribe. E-mail newsletters from both online and brick-and-mortar stores are perhaps the types of listservs most familiar (and perhaps most irritating) to most users. However, there are many valuable e-mail mailing lists such as those that most professional organizations offer as a service to their members to keep them updated about what the group is doing. For example, the Council for Exceptional Children publishes the e-mail newsletter *CEC SmartBrief;* the Division for Learning Disabilities, part of CEC, publishes *TeachingLD News.* Most e-mail newsletters allow users to unsubscribe at any time, although the directions for doing this are often found in small print at the very end of the e-mail message.

Information Management

Keeping track of new information as it becomes available on the web is a very difficult task. One way to make that task easier is by using **RSS feeds.** RSS, according to Wikipedia, is "most commonly translated as 'Really Simple Syndication.'" RSS feeds allow users to be notified when new items appear on a favorite website or new entries appear in a favorite blog.

For example, a person might be interested in keeping up with all of the news that the cnn.com website offers on technology. To do that, the user selects "Tools & Widgets" from the bottom of the cnn.com home page, then "RSS Feeds" from the next page. This brings the user to a new page that lists more than a dozen RSS feeds that can be selected including one called "Technology." The user is given a web address (in this case, http://rss.cnn.com/rss/cnn_tech.rss) which is to be copied into an application called an RSS reader. RSS readers are built into many web browsers, and both Yahoo.com and Google.com offer free RSS readers. After subscribing to CNN's Technology RSS feed, when the user opens the RSS reader, he or she will see headlines about the latest news about technology and be able to read more by clicking on the links provided. One particularly useful RSS feed for educators comes from FREE (free.ed.org), the Federal Resources for Educational Excellence website described in the "Window on the Web" feature on page 171.

Delicious is another useful tool for managing web-based information. According to delicious.com, "Delicious is a social bookmarking service that allows users to tag, save, manage, and share web pages from a centralized source." Membership in Delicious is free, and members are provided with space on the website to store their collection of bookmarks (i.e., addresses of favorite websites). This allows members to access their bookmarks from any computer; teachers who have bookmarked interesting websites at school only to have to bookmark them again at home will appreciate this feature. When a bookmark is added to a member's collection, he or she is asked to provide "tags" to describe the content of the bookmarked site. For example, a member might use these tags to describe the NASA website: space, nasa, shuttle, rocket, astronomy.

Tags are a valuable feature because they can be used to search the member's bookmark collection. Even more important, an individual can find out more about a topic by searching the tags in the bookmark collections of all members of Delicious. If a teacher is looking for websites with information about photosynthesis, for instance, he or she could search Delicious for bookmarks with that tag. In a recent search, more than 1500 bookmarks were found tagged with the term *photosynthesis*. This ability to share information among users makes Delicious not only a valuable information management site but also one that promotes networking.

Networking Sites

Networking sites are designed to facilitate communication among site members. In the case of **social networking** sites, that communication is primarily social. Examples of this are the well known MySpace and Facebook sites. MySpace is described on its website as "a place for friends." Facebook's website says that it "helps you connect and share with the people in your life." A recent news article (Wayne, 2009) reported that these social networking sites (as well as online video sites) have become even more popular than e-mail.

There may be some educational value to social networking sites for teachers interested in popular culture and politics in particular. For example, the Republican National Committee has a Facebook page, and the Democratic Party and the Libertarian Party each have pages on both Facebook and MySpace. Consult the "Spotlight on Technology" to learn how the White House is taking advantage of these and other web-based communication and networking tools.

Two other networking sites of interest are YouTube and Flickr. **YouTube** is a free membership site where members can upload videos and search for and view videos of other members. According to its website, "YouTube is a free online video streaming service that allows anyone to view and share videos that have been uploaded by our members." One of the most useful features of this site is the ability to conduct searches; the user types in a word or phrase and the search engine scans the description of each video for matches. YouTube offers many videos with educational value, including a large collection of "how-to" videos. Among the skills that can be learned are how to bowl, crochet, write a five-paragraph essay, play guitar, read a map, speak Japanese, rock climb, and go bird watching.

Flickr is a site similar to YouTube except that it features still photographs rather than videos (although video uploads are possible). Its website calls Flickr "the best online photo management and sharing application in the world." Basic membership is free. Members upload their photos, add descriptive tags (like the tags used in Delicious), decide who can see each photo, and determine the copyright status of each photo. Access to photos can be open to anyone or limited to

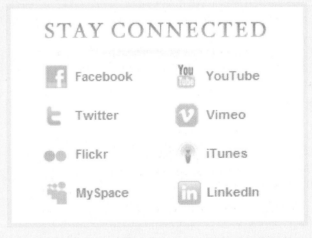

Google for Educators

This website provides a number of Google tools to educators along with ideas about how to use those tools in the classroom. The website says:

> At Google, we support teachers in their efforts to empower students and expand the frontiers of human knowledge. That's why we've assembled the information and tools you'll find on this page.

The site's home page features a series of brief articles about recent projects and news. On the righthand side is a location where teachers can sign up to receive the Google Teacher e-mail newsletter. On the left is a menu offering these choices: Tools for your classroom, Classroom activities, Classroom posters, Google Teacher Academy, and Teacher Community.

When teachers select "Tools for your classroom," they see the screen that appears below. Among these tools are Geo Education with Google Earth, Google Sky, and Google Maps; iGoogle, a homepage that teachers can tailor to their own needs by adding RSS feeds and other applications; Blogger, a free application allowing teachers to write their own blogs; Docs, a writing program where teachers (or students) can collaborate on the same writing project; and Picassa, a photo-sharing application. To learn more about these and other tools, visit the Google for Educators website and explore.

http://www.google.com/educators/index.html

only the member, the member and family, and/or the member and designated friends. Members can reserve all rights for a photo or make it available for use by others by selecting one of the Creative Commons options. For instance, a member might allow noncommercial use of his or her photo as long as attribution is given. For more information about Creative Commons licensing, visit the website at creativecommons.org.

Members of Flickr can search the photo collections of others as long as those members have indicated that their photos can be viewed by anyone. Members can also join groups organized around specific topics and interests. For example, a recent search for "history" located more than 11,000 Flickr groups. Among these groups are History USA, Australian History and British Heritage, 20th Century Black History, and Peruvian Images (History & Culture).

Google, best known for its popular search engine and its Google Maps application, offers an ever-increasing number of free web-based tools including a Google site for educators. Read the "Window on the Web" for more information about Google resources for teachers.

ASSISTIVE TECHNOLOGY AND THE GENERAL EDUCATION CLASSROOM

If the principles of universal design were followed in the development of all the learning materials, activities, and technologies in the general education classroom, students with disabilities would have access to the same instructional resources as their classmates without disabilities. Because this is not the case, assistive technology plays an important role to play in today's classrooms.

As discussed earlier in this chapter, assistive technology, or AT, is any type of technology designed specifically for use by persons with disabilities. Although *AT* is a commonly accepted term, Edyburn (2003) argued that "technology-enhanced performance" (p. 20) would be a better way to describe the process by which technology assists persons to bypass or compensate for disabilities.

Federal laws for students with disabilities require that schools consider the possible need for assistive technology devices and services when developing IEPs. An assistive technology device, according to federal law, is defined as

> any item, piece of equipment, or product system, whether acquired commercially off the shelf, modified, or customized, that is used to increase, maintain, or improve the functional capabilities of a child with a disability. [PL 108-446, Section 602 (1)]

In contrast, an assistive technology service is "any service that directly assists a child with a disability in the selection, acquisition, or use of an assistive technology device" [PL 108-446, Section 602 (2)]. In a recent investigation of AT use by students receiving special education services, Quinn, Behrmann, Mastropieri, Bausch, Ault, and Chung (2009) reported that students with multiple disabilities, those with orthopedic impairments, and those with learning disabilities were the most frequent users of AT. Half or more of these students received the related services of speech–language pathology and occupational therapy; however, fewer than one-third received assistive technology services.

There are many ways to categorize the types of assistive technology available today, including the system that groups technologies by disability category (e.g., AT for students with learning disabilities, AT for students who are deaf). A more useful method is classification by the type of barrier the technology is designed to bypass or overcome and/or by the type of access the technology is designed to promote. Examples often seen in the literature are AT for computer access, AT for access to print, AT to promote communication, and AT for mobility, visual, and hearing impairments.

AT for Computer Access

Access to standard computers may be a problem for individuals with physical impairments or those with severe vision losses. Assistive technologies allow these persons as well as those with other types of disabilities to interact with computers. Among the most common adaptations are alternatives to the standard computer keyboard and to the standard computer monitor.

Sometimes all that is necessary is a simple adaptation to the standard keyboard or an alternative method for typing on that keyboard. For example, a student who is partially paralyzed but has good control of head and neck muscles might be able to type using a headpointer, a device like a hat or headband with a pointer attached. The student positions the pointer on the key to be typed and then depresses that key. A keyguard can be used with a student with tremor. Keyguards are covers that fit over the standard keyboard with holes cut out so that a student can reach down and press one key without touching the keys around it.

Another option is replacement of the standard keyboard with an alternate keyboard. That keyboard may be larger or smaller or different in shape from the regular keyboard. The ergonomic keyboard shown in Figure 9-2 is one example.

There are also a number of keyboards designed as assistive devices. These keyboards often require less pressure to activate their "keys." Those like the IntelliKeys keyboard shown in Figure 9-3 have one flat, touch-sensitive surface that is a programmable input device. The surface is divided into "key" areas that can represent various keyboard configurations. Examples are the standard keyboard, keys in alphabetical order, or pictures "keys" for young children.

Touch screens are another way to bypass the standard keyboard. Instead of typing, the student simply touches the area of the screen where the chosen response is shown. However, touch screen devices do not allow access to all applications. More useful for tasks such as writing are technologies such as speech recognition devices. With these devices, the student simply speaks into a microphone to enter information; the speech recognition application translates the spoken word into text on the screen. With some systems, however, users must first "train" the device to recognize their individual voices; each individual's vocabulary is then stored for use with any software.

FIGURE 9-2   An Ergonomic Keyboard

FIGURE 9-3   IntelliKeys Keyboard

Note: Used with permission of IntelliTools, Inc.

There are other options for students with very severe physical impairments. One, the switch, is shown in Figure 9-4 in which a young child presses the large round switch to communicate with the computer. Switch input is possible for individuals who are able to make any type of consistent movement. That movement might be moving the head from side to side, moving a hand or elbow back and forth, moving a foot up and down, or even wrinkling an eyebrow. In addition, eye gaze systems can be used by persons able to move only their eyes.

Switches work with a limited number of applications unless another type of technology is added. That technology places a virtual keyboard on the computer monitor, and the individual selects "keys" by a process known as **scanning.** If the on-screen keyboard is arranged in alphabetical order, the letters might be highlighted in that order (e.g., first the letter *A* is highlighted, then the letter *B*, and so on). The person decides which letter to select, then presses the switch when it is highlighted. The scanning process will be familiar to cell

FIGURE 9-4   Switch Input, an
Alternative to the Standard Keyboard

Note: Photo courtesy of Don Johnston, Inc.

phone users who must use the phone's number keys to add the names of friends and family to the phone's directory. To "type" the letter *A*, for example, the user presses the 2 key; to type *B*, the same number key is pressed twice. Whether using a switch or a standard cell phone, scanning is a laborious process.

AT for Access to Print

Print is a barrier to several groups: young children who have not yet learned to read, older students who have difficulty reading, and persons who are blind or have so little sight that reading print is not an option. When access to print is a problem, it may be necessary to use alternative output devices to bypass or enhance the computer's visual display. One of the most common solutions is to add auditory output in the form of speech to the visual display. Speech synthesizers are built into many modern computers. For example, the Macintosh computer allows on-screen text to be read aloud in any application including word processors and web browsers.

Speech synthesizers use voice chips that store phonemic rules; words are built or synthesized from phonemes as letters are typed in, and mispronunciations can occur when words do not follow phonemic rules. Synthesized speech typically sounds somewhat robotic, although it is usually clear enough to be intelligible to students. Many of the newer multimedia programs use digitized (rather than synthesized) speech. This higher quality, more natural sounding speech is produced by recording actual speech and storing it as part of the application. Unfortunately, digitized speech requires so much memory that it is not feasible for applications like word processors that allow users to enter any text they wish.

Individuals who are blind or have limited sight may need additional assistance. If students cannot see the screen, they cannot see what they are writing and they cannot see any of the on-screen

control options such as menus and dialog boxes. To access that level of information, a different application is needed: screen readers. These applications have the capability to read aloud text that appears anywhere on the screen, including commands and controls. To see why screen readers are so necessary, put on a blindfold and try to open a word processor, begin a new file, type a paragraph or two, edit your work, and save it.

Applications similar to screen readers are available for students who can see but have reading problems. One example is the Kurzweil Reader from Kurzweil Educational Systems. This technology allows teachers to scan print materials so that they can be read aloud by the Kurzeil Reader on the computer; other features include a set of study tools such on-screen highlighting, bookmarks, and voice notes. Other examples are the Reading Pen from Wizcom, a device that reads print words aloud, and the latest version of the Kindle, an electronic reading device with synthesized speech that can read an entire book or a portion aloud.

AT to Promote Communication

Some students are unable to speak, or their speech is very difficult to understand. To bypass this problem, communication aids are used. Communication aids allow students to "talk" by simply pointing or pressing a button. For example, a simple communication board may be a piece of cardboard with pictures, letters, or words on it; a student could point to a picture of a glass to indicate thirst or use an alphabet to spell out greetings or requests.

Electronic communication aids are more sophisticated because they "talk." One type of electronic communication device uses prerecorded speech. Spoken messages are recorded by a family member, teacher, or peer; to "speak," the student simply selects one of the available messages (see Figure 9-5). Other communication devices contain speech synthesizers. The student may spell out words by typing on the device's keyboard or messages may be preprogrammed so that they can be activated by pressing a single key or a switch. When a word or phrase has been entered, the synthesizer pronounces it.

AT for Physical, Visual, and Hearing Impairments

AT for Physical Impairments. Mobility is a major need of some students with physical impairments. Some students use standard wheelchairs; they propel these chairs with their hands and arms. Others, with limited strength or movement in their upper bodies, use power chairs (or scooters) equipped with motors and batteries. Power chairs are usually controlled by a joystick that the student operates by moving his or her hand, arm, foot, head, or chin.

Braces and prosthetic devices such as artificial limbs are aids that strengthen or replace portions of the body. In recent years, the design of these devices has improved, and lighter and stronger materials have been used in their construction. These changes have made braces and prosthetic devices more comfortable and attractive, which increases the likelihood that

FIGURE 9-5 Electronic Communication Aid

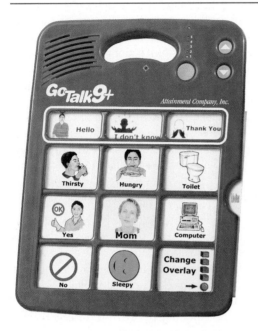

FIGURE 9-6 Print Enlarger

Note: Photo courtesy of Attainment Company.

their owners will wear them. Among the newer developments are prostheses that use microprocessors (such as those found in computers) to improve mobility and motor control (e.g., Lake & Miguelez, 2003).

In the classroom, students with physical limitations who have difficulty writing often use computers and calculators with print output. Audio recording devices serve several purposes: recording class lectures, "reading" taped texts, and recording assignments or exams so they don't have to be written. Manual or electronic page turners assist students by holding a book in an open position for reading; to turn the page, the student activates the device with a chin or mouth movement.

AT for Visual Impairments. Students with visual impairments can use the sense of hearing to learn by listening with the assistance of audio aids. For example, students can gain access to print information by listening to audio recordings of books, magazines, and textbooks. Sometimes tapes use compressed speech; in this mode, the spoken word is speeded up so that large amounts of information can be reviewed in less time. Audio recording devices can also be used to record lectures or class notes so that information is available for later access. A talking calculator resembles a regular pocket calculator, but it provides both a visual and an audible display. When a key is pressed or a calculation completed, the calculator speaks.

One type of modification often used with students with visual impairments who retain some useable residual vision is magnification. For example, a regular computer monitor might be replaced with a large-screen monitor if it enlarges the image sufficiently for it to be visible to the student. Magnification devices called *low-vision aids* resemble small

telescopes or magnifying glasses; they are used to read print and look at visuals such as drawings and maps. Closed-circuit television systems are used to enlarge reading materials; the book or paper is placed on a platform and a video camera projects its image to a monitor that looks like a television screen (see Figure 9-6). Print is greatly enlarged, and the student can control the size and brightness of the display and whether the image is black on a white background or white on a dark background.

Devices that translate print to some other communication mode are designed for students unable to use sight for reading. Most devices convert printed material to synthesized speech. However, some convert print to a tactile image. For example, the Focus Braille Displays from Freedom Scientific convert information on the computer screen into a tactile Braille display.

AT for Hearing Impairments. Several technologies assist students with hearing impairments to communicate with each other and persons in the hearing world. Hearing aids have become smaller and more versatile as a result of transistors and printed circuits. According to the National Institute on Deafness and Other Communication Disorders (2007b), there are three basic types of hearing aids: (1) behind-the-ear aids, (2) in-the-ear aids, and (3) canal aids, which fit into the ear canal. Canal aids, the smallest aids, are not recommended for young children.

Cochlear implants have become quite common for some individuals with serious hearing losses. The implants consist of a tiny external microphone, signal processor, and transmitter that are attached to a receiver implanted in the mastoid bone behind the ear, just under the skin. Electrical signals are transmitted from the receiver to the intact auditory nerve in the inner ear, bypassing the damaged cochlea or sensory organ. This system converts sounds to electrical signals that are transmitted to the brain for interpretation (Lowenbraun & Thompson, 1986). Although this option is not appropriate for all individuals, it does provide an option to many persons with profound hearing losses, particularly adults who have lost their hearing within the past 2 or 3 years. Also, the National Institute on Deafness and Other Communication Disorders (2007a) reports that the most common age for children to receive cochlear implants is between 2 and 6 years, the developmental period when speech and language skills are acquired by hearing children.

However, the use of cochlear implants has not been without controversy (D'Antonio, 1993; National Association of the Deaf, 2000). Representatives of the Deaf community have objected to the use of implants as a method to "fix" deafness, especially for children who are not yet old enough to decide for themselves if they wish to belong to the Deaf culture or the hearing culture.

Telecommunication Devices for the Deaf (TDDs) allow persons who are deaf or others who are nonverbal to communicate on the telephone. These devices resemble a portable computer; the individual types a message on the keyboard and looks at a visual display for the response. Some TDDs also have printers so that a record of the telephone conversation can be made. The Americans with Disabilities Act requires that all companies providing phone services also provide relay services to allow TDD users and hearing persons to communicate; in effect, the relay operator acts as a translator. When the hearing person speaks, the operator types the message for the TDD user; when the TDD

user types a response, the operator reads it aloud. Devices for individuals who are hard of hearing amplify telephone conversations through the handset of the telephone.

Closed captioning allows students with hearing impairments to enjoy regularly scheduled television programs. Written captions transmitted along with the television signal are decoded by a special device and projected onto the screen. The Americans with Disabilities Act requires that all televisions sold in the United States contain built-in decoding devices. Open captioned films and television programs provide captions visible to all viewers and do not require a special decoder. Amplification devices using infrared transmission facilitate television use for viewers who are hard of hearing.

Other types of assistive devices include the following.

- Visual alerting systems for the telephone, doorbell, alarm clock, fire alarm, and smoke detector (these use bright strobe lights to attract attention)
- Amplification systems in classrooms, cinemas, theaters, auditoriums, and other public facilities, for use with or without hearing aids
- Tactile or vibrating devices for speech therapy, alarm clock systems, and paging systems

Clearly, computers are only one of the many technologies that can facilitate inclusion of students with disabilities in school and in the community. Assistive technologies such as the ones described in the preceding paragraphs also help

 WINDOW ON THE WEB

Assistive Technology Resources

Closing the Gap

The Closing the Gap organization offers publications, online resources, and a yearly conference on applications of assistive technology for persons with disabilities. Its magazine, *Closing the Gap,* is published six times a year and includes an annual *Resource Directory;* both the magazine and directory are available in print and online. The online version is called *Solutions,* and 14-day trial subscriptions are free. Subscribers are able to peruse the current issue of the magazine, search its archives, search the online AT product database, and find links to producers of AT and organizations related to AT.

http://www.closingthegap.com

CAST (Center for Applied Special Technology)

In the past, this not-for-profit organization was best known for *Bobby,* a free program designed to evaluate websites for their accessibility for persons with disabilities. Unfortunately, *Bobby* is no longer available. CAST's current focus is on universal design for learning (UDL), and the CAST website is a treasure trove of information on universal design. Among the available resources are tutorials on UDL, tools such as UDL Self-Check and UDL Lesson Builder, and online versions of publications such as *Teaching Every Student in the Digital Age* (Rose & Meyer, 2002). In addition, a new

version of the *WiggleWorks* PreK-3 reading program developed by CAST and Scholastic is once again available; included are both software-based and print books appropriate for beginning and early readers.

http://www.cast.org

Alliance for Technology Access (ATA)

The Alliance for Technology Access (ATA) describes itself as "a national network of community-based resource centers, product developers, vendors, service providers, and individuals" with the mission of increasing assistive technology use by individuals with disabilities. Its website contains several useful features such as Success Stories and Video Success Stories that introduce individuals with disabilities and tell how AT has affected their lives. In the Family Place in Cyberspace on the ATA website are resources for families. Examples are We Can Play/¡Podemos jugar!, ideas for play activities in English and in Spanish; Access Transition, suggestions for students transitioning from public school to adulthood; and AT in K12, information about integrating technology into educational programs. The website also provides information about the latest edition of the ATA resource book, *Computer Resources for People with Disabilities.*

http://www.ataccess.org

students to bypass or compensate for disabilities that could interfere with their ability to succeed in the general education classroom. In addition, new technologies continue to emerge. For more information about resources on assistive technology, see the "Window on the Web" feature.

Web Accessibility

Web accessibility is just as important to students with disabilities as accessibility to other types of learning tools and materials. Because the web is a somewhat new instructional medium, it's important to think about the types of accessibility problems that people might encounter when navigating it. The Alliance for Technology Access (ATA) describes several types of barriers that might hinder access.

- *Vision barriers.* Information on the web usually requires reading text on the screen. This can be a barrier for people with low vision, for whom the text is too small, and for people who cannot see the text at all.
- *Hearing barriers.* Some websites contain audio clips or QuickTime movies that include an audio component. These can produce a barrier for people who have hearing impairments.
- *Learning or cognitive barriers.* In some cases, the content itself is a barrier. Some people with disabilities have difficulty reading or understanding print material that appears on web pages. Others have difficulty understanding the message being conveyed by the graphics.
- *Physical barriers.* The web uses a Graphical User Interface (GUI), which essentially means that the user points and clicks in order to navigate a web page, using Windows or a Mac. This, with most browser software, requires the use of a mouse, but some people with disabilities find the mouse to be a barrier.
- *Economic barriers.* Understanding the technological capabilities of the visitor to your site can help in designing accessible sites. (Alliance for Technology Access, n.d.)

The Alliance for Technology Access also recommends strategies for overcoming each of these barriers. Visit the ATA site at *http://www.ataccess.org* and look for the feature on Web Accessibility in the Related Resources portion of the site.

▶ TEACHING WITH TECHNOLOGY

Bringing computers, software and other applications, assistive technology, and the World Wide Web into the classroom is only the first step in effective technology use. What must also occur is an integration process in which technology is "fully included" into the instructional activities of the classroom. Technology is an instructional tool like textbooks and chalkboards. If it is to be used effectively, the teacher must consider it as one of the many resources available to assist in the teaching–learning process. The "Inclusion Tips for the Teacher" box presents the basic principles to consider when integrating computers and other technologies into the general education classroom. These principles underscore the need to consider technology as a tool for accomplishing important educational tasks, not as an end in itself.

 Go to the Assignments and Activities section of Topic *Hearing Loss and Deafness* in the MyEducationLab for your course and complete the activity entitled *SmartBoards for Students with Hearing Impairments.*

This chapter has focused on strategies for the effective use of AT and other technologies in the general education classroom. Consult "Things to Remember" to review the primary concerns in classroom technology use.

▶ ACTIVITIES

1. Visit a school and observe how teachers use technology in instruction. Find out where computers are located (in classrooms, a central computer lab, the library or media center, or a combination of these arrangements), what types of software are available, and what learning activities students accomplish with computers. How do students interact with the web? What types of assistive technologies are being used in classrooms?

2. Observe a classroom or lab in which students are using technology. Are students actively involved in the learning task or does their attention wander? Do they appear excited about learning? Watch the interactions among students. Is any cooperative learning taking place?

Inclusion Tips for the Teacher

Principles for Integrating Technology

1. Start with the curriculum, not the technology. The needs of individual students and the curriculum designed to meet those needs should drive the selection of technologies and the ways in which they are used.

2. Take advantage of the motivational value of technology, but don't limit its use to that of a reward or a leisure time activity. Technology has too much value as a teaching tool to ignore its use in instruction.

3. Use technology to reinforce skills taught by the teacher. Technology can present guided practice activities, monitor students' responses, and provide students with immediate feedback.

4. Select technology activities that match the goals of instruction and the skill levels of individual students. No matter how dazzling the technology or how superb the instructional strategy, teaching an irrelevant skill is a waste of time.

5. Take advantage of the customization options that some technologies offer. Features such as the ability to control content and instructional parameters make it easier to adapt learning activities to students' needs.

6. Monitor students' work at the computer or with other technologies with the same diligence used to monitor other types of classroom work. If performance data are collected by the technology, use that information in making instructional decisions.

7. Use technology to present new information to students. Although technology is certainly not the only instructional strategy available for this purpose, it does provide teachers with an additional resource for introducing new material.

8. Enrich and extend the curriculum through technology. Technology opens doors to experiences that students can't access in other ways, and these experiences can expand both the depth and breadth of the standard curriculum.

9. Teach students to use technologies as tools, then provide opportunities and encouragement for practice. Technology can help students bypass or compensate for disabilities, empowering them to achieve greater levels of independence.

10. Extend the benefits of technology to teachers. Technology is truly mainstreamed when it becomes an important tool not only for students but also for teachers.

Note: From *Special Education Technology: Classroom Applications* by R. B. Lewis. Copyright © 1993 by Brooks/Cole Publishing Company, Pacific Grove, CA. Reprinted by permission of Wadsworth Publishing Co., a division of Thomson Learning: *www.thomsonrights.com*. Fax 800 730-2215

Things to Remember

- Technology, including both computers and the Internet, is a common feature of U.S. schools and classrooms.

- Three types of technology support education: instructional technology, technology tools, and assistive technology.

- Assistive technology is technology that is specially designed for persons with disabilities.

- Advantages of technology include its capacity for individualizing instruction, motivating students, and allowing new types of learning; technology can also help bypass or compensate for disabilities.

- The principle of universal design suggests that all types of learning activities should be developed with sufficient flexibility so that they are accessible to all learners.

- Technology tools include word processors, e-mail programs, idea processors, presentation tools, and creativity tools, among others.

- The Internet offers many learning opportunities to students including a wealth of information resources and the ability to communicate with others throughout the world.

- Assistive technology can provide computer access, increase access to print, promote communication, and help students with physical, visual, and hearing impairments bypass or compensate for the effects of disabilities.

- Web accessibility is just as important as the accessibility of any other learning tool.

- Technology does not reach its potential until it is fully integrated into the instructional life of the classroom.

3. Use the information presented in this chapter to find out more about assistive technologies that might be useful for persons with different types of special needs. Be sure to consult one or more of the assistive technology resources described in the chapter's "Window on the Web" feature on AT.

4. Several professional organizations are concerned with technology in education, but one that focuses on individuals with disabilities is the Technology and Media (TAM) Division of The Council for Exceptional Children. Visit TAM's website (*http://www.tamcec.org*) to find out about the services it provides.

PART

III

Strategies for Teaching Students with Disabilities

CHAPTER
TEN

Teaching Students with Learning Disabilities and Attention Deficit Hyperactivity Disorders

Jane

Jane is a seventh grader with a learning disability; she has great difficulty remembering what she has learned, particularly in the area of written language. It took Jane several years to acquire basic reading and spelling skills; now, she can read fourth grade material with adequate word recognition and good comprehension, and in spelling she performs at the third grade level. This year in seventh grade, Jane attends general education classes for all subjects except English; during that period, she visits the special education resource teacher for reading and spelling instruction. With the help of her seventh grade teacher, Mr. Henry, Jane is earning passing grades in math, science, and social studies. Classroom adaptations for Jane include digital textbooks and modified exams and assignments.

Danny

Danny is a student with learning disabilities who is 8 years old and in second grade. Although Danny can read and spell quite well for his age, he has difficulty with handwriting and math. His printing is large and uncoordinated, and he has trouble staying within the lines. Several of his letters and numbers are written incorrectly; for example, he confuses b and d, n and u, and 6 and 9. In math, Danny has learned some of the basic addition facts but has not yet begun subtraction. His math papers are messy and difficult to read; the margins are irregular and the columns of numbers poorly aligned. Danny visits the resource teacher for an hour each day for special help in math and handwriting. During the rest of the day, Danny participates in the activities of his second grade class. Mrs. Rose, his second grade teacher, provides him with extra practice in math facts to help him progress more quickly. She also modifies his handwriting assignments so that he can complete them successfully.

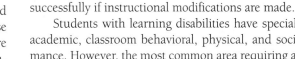

LOOKING AHEAD

We will learn more about assessments for Jane and Danny later in this chapter and we'll have a look at Jane's IEP. The majority of the chapter, however, provides suggestions for adapting and improving academic instruction for students such as these. As you read, keep these questions in mind.

- From what you know right now, what are Jane's areas of strength? Areas of need?
- Although Jane is in seventh grade, she reads at the fourth grade level. What types of adaptations might be needed for her to take part in seventh grade science and social studies instruction?
- If you were Danny's second grade teacher, what types of modifications might you use for his handwriting assignments?
- Does Danny's poor handwriting interfere with his ability to do math? How could you separate out those two skill areas?

A learning disability is a perplexing condition. Students with learning disabilities are of average intelligence and learn some things quickly and easily. However, because of deficits in attention, perception, and memory, they acquire other skills only with extreme difficulty. Students with learning disabilities may read well yet spell poorly. Or they may fail a written test but be able to answer every question correctly on an oral exam. These students with special needs are often members of general education classes; they can participate successfully if instructional modifications are made.

Students with learning disabilities have special needs in academic, classroom behavioral, physical, and social performance. However, the most common area requiring adaptation of classroom procedures is academic instruction. Students like Danny need extra help in acquiring basic skills; reading, handwriting, spelling, written expression, or math can be trouble areas. Older students, such as Jane, benefit from assistance in content-area subjects. Class requirements may need to be modified in science, social studies, and English courses to help students compensate for poor basic skills.

This chapter explores the characteristics of students with learning disabilities and provides methods for the general education teacher to use in gathering data, teaching basic skills, and modifying content-area instruction. In addition, the last section of this chapter suggests strategies for instructional modifications for another group of learners who often experience academic difficulties: students with attention deficit hyperactivity disorder (ADHD).

► INDICATORS OF LEARNING DISABILITIES

For students with learning disabilities, the general education teacher is a vital member of the inclusion team. Classroom teachers are usually the first to notice signs of learning disabilities and refer students for special education assessment. In addition, general educators assist in gathering assessment information and in coordinating special services. Check the "Window on the Web" to learn about some of the Internet resources about learning disabilities.

The legal definitions of learning disabilities and other disabilities were discussed earlier in this book. However, a learning disability is one of the most difficult disabilities to define. Debate over definitional issues has continued since the passage of PL 94–142, and new definitions of learning disabilities have been proposed.

One example is the definition of the National Joint Committee on Learning Disabilities (1994), a coalition of organizations concerned with this disability:

> *Learning disabilities* is a general term that refers to a heterogeneous group of disorders manifested by significant difficulties in the acquisition and use of listening, speaking, reading, writing, reasoning, or mathematical abilities. These disorders are intrinsic to the individual and presumed to be due to central nervous system dysfunction. . . . Even though a learning disability may occur concomitantly with other handicapping conditions . . . or environmental influences . . . it is not the direct result of those conditions or influences.

A more recent definition is that of the National Center for Learning Disabilities (2001):

> A learning disability (LD) is a neurological disorder that affects the brain's ability to receive, process, store and respond to information. The term learning disability is used to describe the seeming unexplained difficulty a person of at least average intelligence has in acquiring basic academic skills. These skills are essential for success at school and work, and for coping with life in general. LD is not a single disorder. It is a term that refers to a group of disorders.

Common to both of these definitions of learning disabilities and to most others is an extreme difficulty in the acquisition of basic school skills despite adequate intellectual ability.

Students may be identified as having a learning disability at any age, but most are noticed during the early elementary grades. There are two major indicators of learning disabilities. First, students appear capable but experience extreme difficulty in some area(s) of learning. This is a discrepancy between expected and actual achievement. For example, a young child might be verbal and appear bright, but be very slow to learn the alphabet, write his or her name, and count to 20. The second indicator is variation in performance; that is, there is a discrepancy among different areas of achievement. A fourth grader might perform well in math, but read and spell poorly. Or a 10th grader might be a good science student except when required to express ideas in writing. In addition to these two main indicators of learning disabilities, teachers should watch for several other

signs that are listed in the "Inclusion Tips for the Teacher" box. Although it is unlikely that any student would display all of the characteristics presented at his or her age or grade level, most students with learning disabilities exhibit at least one or two.

Poor **learning strategies** may also be a sign of learning disabilities (Clark, 2000; Lerner & Johns, 2009; Mercer & Pullen, 2005; Reid, Hresko, & Swanson, 1996). Learning strategies are the methods students use to plan, begin, and complete learning tasks; students with learning disabilities tend to use less effective strategies than average achievers. For example, with memory tasks, average achievers rehearse the information they are trying to commit to memory, whereas students with learning disabilities do not. This difference in performance led Torgesen (1977) to call students with learning disabilities *inactive learners* because they fail to become actively involved in the learning task. In contrast, Swanson (1989) suggested that these students are not passive but "*actively inefficient learners*" (p. 10).

Many school districts have developed checklists to help general education teachers identify students with learning disabilities, and several commercial measures such as the *Learning Disability Evaluation Scale* (McCarney, 1996) are also available. A teacher can use this rating scale to screen students for learning disabilities in academic areas (e.g., listening, thinking, speaking, reading, writing, spelling, mathematical calculations) and in areas such as attention, auditory discrimination, visual perception, fine-motor skills, and memory. A newer measure, the *Learning Disabilities Diagnostic Inventory* (Hammill & Bryant, 1998), asks teachers to rate student

performance in six areas: listening, speaking, reading, writing, mathematics, and reasoning.

 ## ASSESSMENT PROCEDURES

If prereferral interventions have not been successful in solving classroom learning problems, students are referred for special education assessment. Parents are notified of the reasons for referral and are presented with an assessment plan prepared by the multidisciplinary team. If consent is given for special education evaluation, the team begins to collect information about the student.

> **myeducationlab** To enhance your understanding of RTI, go to the IRIS Center Resources section of Topic *Learning Disabilities* in the MyEducationLab for your course and complete the Module entitled *RTI (Part 2): Assessment.*

Assessment is an information-gathering process that includes both formal testing and informal procedures such as observation, inventories, and work sample analyses. In the assessment of learning disabilities, information is collected about the student's current intellectual functioning, academic achievement, and performance in areas related to the disability: information processing and strategies for learning. Figure 10-1 presents a portion of the special education assessment report for Jane, one of the students introduced at the beginning of this chapter.

Intellectual functioning is assessed by intelligence tests such as the *Wechsler Intelligence Scale for Children–Fourth*

Inclusion Tips for the Teacher

Signs of Learning Disabilities

The signs of learning disabilities that follow are written for parents but are equally useful for teachers and other professionals. These signs appear on the LD OnLine website (http://www.ldonline.org), a service of the public television station WETA in Washington, DC.

Preschool

- Speaks later than most children
- Pronunciation problems
- Slow vocabulary growth; often unable to find the right word
- Difficulty rhyming words
- Trouble learning numbers, alphabet, days of the week, colors, shapes
- Extremely restless and easily distracted
- Trouble interacting with peers
- Difficulty following directions or routines
- Fine motor skills slow to develop

Grades K–4

- Slow to learn the connection between letters and sounds
- Confuses basic words (*run, eat, want*)
- Makes consistent reading and spelling errors including letter reversals (*b/d*), inversions (*m/w*), transpositions (*felt/left*), and substitutions (*house/home*)
- Transposes number sequences and confuses arithmetic signs (+, −, ×, /, =)
- Slow to remember facts
- Slow to learn new skills; relies heavily on memorization
- Impulsive; has difficulty planning
- Unstable pencil grip
- Trouble learning about time
- Poor coordination; unaware of physical surroundings; prone to accidents

Grades 5–8

- Reverses letter sequences (*soiled/solid, left/felt*)
- Slow to learn prefixes, suffixes, root words, and other spelling strategies
- Avoids reading aloud
- Trouble with word problems
- Difficulty with handwriting
- Awkward, fist-like, or tight pencil grip
- Avoids writing assignments
- Slow or poor recall of facts
- Difficulty making friends
- Trouble understanding body language and facial expressions

High School Students and Adults

- Continues to spell incorrectly; frequently spells the same word differently in a single piece of writing
- Avoids reading and writing tasks
- Trouble summarizing
- Trouble with open-ended questions on tests
- Weak memory skills
- Difficulty adjusting to new settings
- Works slowly
- Poor grasp of abstract concepts
- Either pays too little attention to details or focuses on them too much
- Misreads information

For another view of the indicators of LD, visit the website for the National Center for Learning Disabilities (*http://www.ncld.org*). The Learning Disabilities Checklist presented there is organized by skill areas (e.g., language, reading, math) rather than by age/grade levels.

Note: Reprinted with permission from the LD OnLine website, a service of the public television station WETA in Washington, DC. Retrieved from *http://www.ldonline.org/ldbasics/signs*

Edition (WISC–IV) (Wechsler, 2003). This is an individual test, appropriate for students age 6 to 17, that is administered by the school psychologist. Several intelligence quotient (or IQ) scores are obtained. The test average (or mean) is 100; scores between IQ 85 and 115 are considered to be within the average range of performance, and those between IQ 70 and 85 are considered low average (McLoughlin & Lewis, 2008). In this interpretation system, approximately 68% of the population falls within the average range of performance, 14% show low average performance, and 2% show below average performance. *WISC–IV* results include a total test score called the Full Scale IQ, and four composite scores. These are Verbal Comprehension, Perceptual Reasoning, Working Memory, and Processing Speed. As the report in Figure 10-1 indicates, Jane scored within the average range in most areas, although her performance fell in the low average range in Working Memory.

Most states require students to achieve an IQ score in the low average range or above to qualify for special education services for learning disabilities. This criterion is based on the assumption that students with learning disabilities show a discrepancy between average intellectual performance and poor academic skills.

This discrepancy notion has been challenged in the past few years (Vaughn & Fuchs, 2003). Recommended instead is the use of failure to learn as the defining characteristic of learning disabilities. In the Response-to-Intervention (RTI) model, learning disabilities would be indicated if students failed to progress when provided with instructional programs judged effective (Fuchs, Mock, Morgan, & Young, 2003; McNamara & Hollinger, 2003; Vaughn & Fuchs, 2003; Vaughn, Linan-Thompson, & Hickman, 2003). It is important to note that the current federal law, IDEA 2004, specifically states that schools are not required to document a discrepancy. Instead, schools "may use a process that determines if the child responds to a scientific, research-based intervention" (P.L. 108–446, Section 614 (b) (6) (B)).

FIGURE 10-1   Special Education Assessment Results

Student: Jane   **Age:** 13 years, 2 months   **Grade:** 7

Intellectual Performance

The *Wechsler Intelligence Scale for Children–Fourth Edition (WISC-IV)* was administered to Jane by Ms. Ducharme, the school psychologist. Jane performed within average range on all scales of the *WISC-IV* except the Working Memory scale where her score fell in the low average range of performance. These results indicate that, overall, Jane shows average capabilities for academic learning. However, short-term memory may be a weak area for Jane.

Verbal Comprehension	108
Perceptual Reasoning	98
Working Memory	75
Processing Speed	95
Full Scale	94

Academic Performance

Mr. Ross, the resource teacher, administered the *Peabody Individual Achievement Test–Revised/Normative Update.* On that measure, Jane showed average performance in Mathematics, Reading Comprehension, and General Information (a measure of content-area knowledge). However, her performance fell within the low average range in Reading Recognition and Spelling. She earned these standard scores:

General Information	98
Reading Recognition	82
Reading Comprehension	88
Mathematics	101
Spelling	72
TOTAL TEST	84

Jane scored at the fourth-grade level in decoding, as measured by the Reading Recognition subtest. Spelling, at grade 3, was her weakest area. These results are consistent with the observations of Mr. Henry, Jane's seventh-grade teacher. Despite average intellectual performance, Jane continues to experience difficulty in some academic tasks.

Learning Abilities and Strategies

To find out more about Jane's memory skills, Ms. Ducharme administered portions of the *Woodcock-Johnson III Tests of Cognitive Abilities.* Jane's performance was within the low average range on tests of Long-Term Retrieval and tests of Short-Term Memory. Mr. Henry notes that Jane appears to comprehend grade 7 material but has great difficulty committing facts to memory. Mr. Ross, Jane's resource teacher, reports that Jane is beginning to learn strategies for memorizing information but is not yet able to use these strategies consistently. These teacher observations and test results point to a learning disability in the area of memory and the need for continued instruction in strategies for learning and recalling academic information.

After general ability level has been determined, academic achievement is assessed. One commonly used measure is the *Peabody Individual Achievement Test–Revised/Normative Update (PIAT–R/NU)* (Markwardt, 1998). It is administered individually by the school psychologist or the special education resource teacher and is appropriate for students in kindergarten through grade 12. The *PIAT–R/NU* assesses several areas of school achievement, and results include grade scores, age scores, percentile ranks, and standard scores. *PIAT–R/NU* standard scores, like the IQ scores on the *WISC–IV,* have a mean of 100; the range of average performance extends from standard score 85 to 115.

Jane's *PIAT–R/NU* results also appear in Figure 10–1, and variation is seen among the different academic areas: Jane's achievement is average in math, reading comprehension, and general information, but low average in reading recognition and spelling.

The third area of assessment is information processing. Several newer measures are available such as the *Developmental Test of Visual Perception* (2nd ed.) (Hammill, Pearson, & Voress, 1993), *Motor-Free Visual Perception Test* (3rd ed.) (Colarusso & Hammill, 2003), *Developmental Test of Visual-Motor Integration* (5th ed.) (Beery & Beery, 2004, 2006), and *Test of Memory and Learning* (Reynolds & Bigler, 1994). More comprehensive measures such as the *Woodcock-Johnson III* (Woodcock, McGrew, & Mather, 2001) and the *Detroit Tests of Learning Aptitude* (4th ed.) (Hammill, 1998) provide information about students' functioning in areas such as memory, processing speed, auditory and visual processing, and attention. Tests are often supplemented with results of informal assessments such as observations of the student's strategies for learning. In Jane's case, a memory problem is indicated by test results and her teachers' observations.

Once it has been established that a student is eligible for special education services, the team begins to gather information about educational needs. The general education teacher can provide valuable assistance at this point in the assessment

FIGURE 10-2 Informal Assessment

Student: Danny   **Age:** 8 years, 4 months   **Grade:** 2

Criterion-Referenced Test of Basic Addition Facts

Objective: When presented with any 20 one-digit plus one-digit basic addition facts problems (e.g., 1 + 1, 4 + 3, 8 + 5), the student will write the correct answer to at least 18 problems within 2 minutes.

Test and Student's Responses:

1 +4 **5**	5 +2 **7**	3 +3 **6**	(9 +4 **14**)	0 +7 **7**	(2 +7 **8**)	4 +5 **9**
(8 +1 **10**)	5 +6 **11**	3 +5 **8**	7 +0 **7**	(3 +8 **12**)	4 +2 **6**	9 +7 **16**
6 +3 **9**	(8 +9 **16**)	1 +1 **2**	(6 +8 **15**)	2 +8 **10**	(7 +9 **14**)	

Criterion for Acceptance Performance: 18 correct responses in 2 minutes

Student's Score: 13 correct responses in 2 minutes

---

process. For example, for Danny (the second grader described at the beginning of this chapter), specific data about math and handwriting performance must be collected. Formal tests are available, but more specific information is obtained from informal measures.

The general education teacher might decide to devise an informal procedure for a particular student. As shown in Figure 10-2, Danny's teacher prepared a criterion-referenced test of addition facts to assess current math skills; results indicate that Danny has not yet mastered the basic facts of addition. The teacher might also wish to obtain a sample of Danny's handwriting and analyze it to locate typical error patterns.

Other assessment procedures available to the classroom teacher are informal inventories, curriculum-based measurement, direct observation, and classroom tests. Also useful are the results from recently administered group achievement measures and placement tests for educational materials and programs. One area of special need for many students with learning disabilities is reading. The "Inclusion Tips for the Teacher" box suggests several ways to assess reading in the

classroom. These include methods to determine students' reading levels and to measure the readability of textbooks and other instructional materials.

Inclusion Tips for the Teacher

Determining Reading Levels

To ensure effective instruction, the teacher must match reading materials to the skills of students with special needs. There are several ways to accomplish this.

Oral Reading Sample

To check oral reading skills, the teacher can simply have the student read a portion of a textbook or other reading material aloud. If the student can read at least 95% of the words and successfully answer at least 75% of the comprehension questions the teacher asks, it is likely that the text is appropriate for the student (Kirk, Kliebhan, & Lerner, 1978). Oral reading samples should be collected in a private setting so that students are not embarrassed by the errors they make.

Cloze Procedure

With the cloze procedure, students can read silently or orally. This procedure is a valuable (and quick) way to determine whether class textbooks in subjects such as science, history, or shop are written at an appropriate level for students. The student reads a short passage in which every fifth (or seventh or *n*th word) has been replaced with a blank. The student must insert appropriate words in the blanks. If at least 44% to 57% of the missing words are correctly supplied, the passage is at the student's instructional level (Bormuth, 1968; Burron & Claybaugh, 1977).

Informal Reading Inventories

Another approach is to first determine the instructional reading level of the student and then select materials written at this level. Informal reading inventories (IRIs) are useful for this purpose. These measures contain several reading passages and comprehension questions for each passage. The student reads (usually aloud) and answers the questions; results are used to determine three reading level scores: independent, instructional, and frustration.

According to McLoughlin and Lewis (2008), materials at the student's Independent Level can be read easily without assistance from the teacher, those at the Instructional Level are more difficult but appropriate for classroom reading instruction, and those at the Frustration Level are too difficult for the student. Students are expected to show 90% to 100% accuracy in comprehension at the Independent Level, 75% to 90% accuracy at the Instructional Level, and less than 75% accuracy at the Frustration Level (Kirk et al., 1978).

Three popular IRIs that are available commercially are the *Analytical Reading Inventory* (8th ed.) (Woods & Moe, 2007), the *Classroom Reading Inventory* (10th ed.) (Silvaroli & Wheelock, 2004), and the *Ekwall/Shanker Reading Inventory* (4th ed.) (Shanker & Ekwall, 2000); all are appropriate for students reading between the primer and grade 8 or 9 reading levels. It is important to remember that published IRIs may focus on a different set of reading skills than those emphasized by the classroom reading series or other instructional materials.

If a student achieves an instructional reading level of grade 6 on an IRI, then books at that reading level will generally be appropriate for instruction. However, that student may not be able to read a sixth grade science text. Grade levels of content-area texts refer to subject matter, not reading level, and such texts often require above-grade-level reading ability. For example, a fourth grade social studies book can have a reading level of fifth, sixth, or even seventh grade.

Readability Measures

To select instructional materials that are appropriate for students with special needs, the teacher must match the reading levels of students with those of texts and other materials. A readability formula or graph can be used to discover the reading level of the books in a classroom. There are many readability measures that teachers can use to determine the reading level of materials such as textbooks (e.g., Dale & Chall, 1948; Flesch, 1951; Spache, 1953).

One relatively quick and easy method is that suggested by Fry (1968). It is appropriate for use with materials that range from first grade to college levels; extended versions are available for preprimer and primer materials (Maginnis, 1969) and reading matter at college and graduate school levels (Fry, 1977). Use the Fry readability graph and its accompanying directions to discover the approximate reading levels of texts, supplementary reading materials, newspapers and magazines, and any other type of reading matter you might use in your classroom. Once potentially appropriate materials have been identified by readability analyses, their suitability for particular students can be determined by oral reading samples or the cloze procedure.

Directions: Randomly select 3 one-hundred-word passages from a book or an article. Plot average number of syllables and average number of sentences per 100 words on graph to determine the grade level of the material. Choose more passages per book if great variability is observed and conclude that the book has uneven readability. Few books will fall in [the] blue area but when they do grade level scores are invalid.

Count proper nouns, numerals and initializations as words. Count a syllable for each symbol. For example, "1945" is 1 word and 4 syllables and "IRA" is 1 word and 3 syllables.

Example	Syllables	Sentences
1st Hundred Words	124	6.6
2nd Hundred Words	141	5.5
3rd Hundred Words	158	6.8
AVERAGE	141	6.3
READABILITY 7th GRADE (see dot plotted on graph)		

Expanded Directions for Working Readability Graph

1. Randomly select three (3) sample passages and count out exactly 100 words beginning with the beginning of a sentence. Do count proper nouns, initializations, and numerals.

2. Count the number of sentences in the hundred words, estimating length of the fraction of the last sentence to the nearest 1/10th.

3. Count the total number of syllables in the 100-word passage. If you don't have a hand counter available, an easy way is to simply put a mark above every syllable over one in each word; then, when you get to the end of the passage, count the number of marks and add 100. Small calculators can also

continued

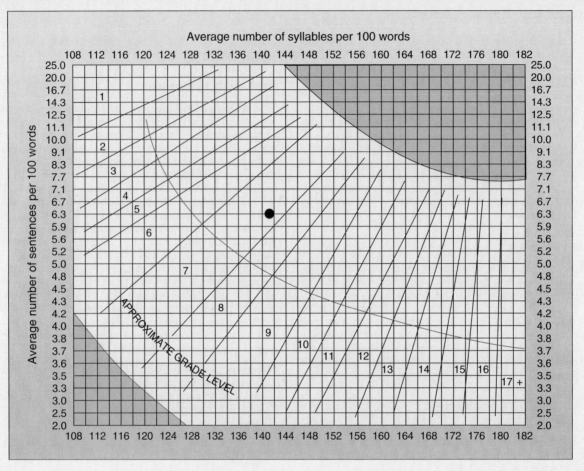

Average number of syllables per 100 words

Average number of sentences per 100 words

APPROXIMATE GRADE LEVEL

be used as counters by pushing numeral "1," then pushing the "+" sign for each word or syllable when counting.

4. Enter graph with average sentence length and average number of syllables; plot dot where the two lines intersect. Area where dot is plotted will give you the approximate grade level.

5. If a great deal of variability is found in syllable count or sentence count, putting more samples in the average is desirable.

6. A word is defined as a group of symbols with a space on either side; thus, "Joe," "IRA," "1945," and "&" are each one word.

7. A syllable is defined as a phonetic syllable. Generally, there are as many syllables as vowel sounds. For example, "stopped" is one syllable and "wanted" is two syllables. When counting syllables for numerals and initializations, count one syllable for each symbol. For example, "1945" is 4 syllables and "IRA" is 3 syllables, and "&" is 1 syllable.

Note: From "Fry's Readability Graph: Clarifications, Validity, and Extension to Level 17" by E. Fry, 1977, *Journal of Reading, 21*, 242–252. Reproduction permitted. No copyright.

SPECIAL SERVICES

When assessment is complete, the team meets to plan the student's IEP. Figure 10-3 presents portions of the IEP for Jane. Like most students with learning disabilities, she is a general education student who leaves her classroom for only a short time each day for special education services.

Go to the Assignments and Activities section of Topic *Learning Disabilities* in the MyEducationLab for your course and complete the activity entitled *Impact of Disabilities*.

Although the resource room is the most typical placement for students with learning disabilities, some districts provide self-contained special classes for those with comprehensive learning needs. In addition to part- or full-day special education, many students with learning disabilities receive assistance in oral language development from speech–language clinicians. Some receive counseling from the school psychologist, social worker, or counselor; those with motor problems may attend special physical education classes. For the general education teacher, consultant services are available to assist in including students with learning disabilities. To learn more about this group of students, consult the "For Your Information" feature.

FIGURE 10-3   IEP Goals and Services for Jane

Annual Goals

1. By the end of the school year, Jane will read sixth grade material with adequate word recognition skills and comprehension.
   Person responsible: Resource teacher
2. By the end of the school year, Jane will correctly spell all words on a high-frequency word list such as the Dolch list.
   Person responsible: Resource teacher
3. By the end of the school year, Jane will correct her spelling errors by using the dictionary or a word processing program with a spelling checker.
   Person responsible: Resource teacher
4. Jane will successfully complete all requirements for seventh grade math, science, and social studies.
   Person responsible: Seventh grade teacher

Amount of Participation in General Education
Jane will attend all seventh grade classes in general education with the exception of English.

Special Education and Related Services

1. Jane will receive special education services from the resource teacher (annual goals 1, 2, and 3) for one period daily.
2. The resource teacher will provide consultation to Jane's seventh grade teacher as needed (annual goal 4).

 For Your Information

Students with Learning Disabilities

- Students with learning disabilities make up about 4.2% of the school-aged population (U.S. Department of Education, 2009).
- Learning disabilities are the most common disability; in fall 2004, 46.4% of students ages 6 through 21 who were served in special education were identified as having learning disabilities (U.S. Department of Education, 2009).
- Four times as many boys are identified as having learning disabilities as girls (Lerner & Johns, 2009).
- Reading is one of the academic skills in which students with learning disabilities experience difficulty most frequently. Other common problem areas are math, spelling, handwriting, and written expression.
- Current findings in brain research suggest that reading disabilities have a neurological basis (Lerner & Johns, 2009; Shaywitz, 2003).
- Among the most typical behavioral characteristics of students with learning disabilities are hyperactivity, impulsivity, and disorders of attention (Tarver & Hallahan, 1976).

- Terms such as *dyslexia* (a difficulty in reading) and *dyscalculia* (a computational difficulty) are sometimes used in reference to learning disabilities. Medical terms such as these do little to describe the learning problem. Instead of calling a student dyslexic, it is better to say he or she has a learning disability in the area of reading.
- Most students with learning disabilities are in general education classrooms for the majority of the school day and receive part-time special education services in areas of need. For example, in fall 2004, approximately 87% of the students identified as having learning disabilities in the United States were served in regular classrooms (U.S. Department of Education, 2009).
- Among the famous people in history believed to have learning disabilities are Winston Churchill, Thomas Edison, Albert Einstein, Nelson Rockefeller, Leonardo da Vinci, and Woodrow Wilson. Famous people today include Tom Cruise, Jay Leno, and Whoopi Goldberg (Gorman, 2003).

 CLASSROOM ADAPTATIONS

Academic instruction is the primary area in which adaptations are made for students with learning disabilities in the general education classroom; the next sections of this chapter focus on methods for meeting their academic needs. Some students with learning disabilities also require assistance in classroom behavior; methods for teaching study skills and controlling disruptive behavior can be found in earlier chapters. Ways to increase social acceptance for students who have difficulty relating to classmates was also discussed earlier.

 Go to the Assignments and Activities section of Topic *Learning Disabilities* in the MyEducationLab for your course and complete the activity entitled *Differentiated Instruction for Students with Learning Disabilities.*

Two approaches are available for the instruction of students with learning disabilities. In the **remediation** approach (sometimes called the *remedial* approach), the teacher instructs the student in skills that are areas of need. For example, extra assistance in spelling might be provided to a fourth grader who spells at the second grade level. **Compensation,** on the other hand, attempts to bypass the student's weaknesses. For instance, to compensate for the reading and writing problems of a high school student, the teacher might administer class tests orally. Remediation techniques are used to teach basic skills and are most appropriate for elementary-aged students. Compensation techniques bypass deficiencies in basic skills in order to teach content-area subjects; they are used most commonly in the late elementary grades, middle school, and high school.

The following sections of this chapter present several remediation techniques and compensatory strategies. Methods of teaching basic skills to younger students and methods for adapting content-area instruction are included. In the latter section, secondary teachers can find ideas for modifying assignments and exams, using taped texts, and compensating in other ways for the academic difficulties of students with special needs.

▶ TEACHING BASIC SKILLS

Reading, handwriting, spelling, written expression, and math are often called basic skills; these "tool" subjects, once acquired, are used in the acquisition of new information and concepts. Although most students learn the rudiments of basic skills in the early elementary grades, students with special needs may not. They may require additional instruction in order to progress. In general, basic skills instruction is provided to students with special needs by the general education teacher if it is a part of the classroom curriculum. Some students may receive tutoring in some skills as part of their special education program, but most will take part in at least some of the basic skills instruction in the regular classroom. The general education teacher can enhance the learning of students with special needs by modifying the techniques used to teach basic skills. Three adaptations are recommended: providing prompts, giving additional instruction, and allowing extra guided practice.

 myeducationlab To enhance your understanding of how to teach basic skills, go to the IRIS Center Resources section of Topic *Learning Disabilities* in the MyEducationLab for your course and complete the Module entitled *Providing Instructional Supports: Facilitating Mastery of New Skills*.

Prompts are features added to learning tasks; they are particularly helpful for students with learning disabilities and others who have difficulty focusing attention on relevant instructional cues. Prompts also structure the task and help the student know exactly what to do. Danny could use the prompts in Figure 10-4 to help improve his printing.

Providing additional direct instruction and allowing extra guided practice are adaptations that aid students with poor recall. To ensure successful learning, the teacher should break down the subject matter into small steps and present it as slowly as necessary. Several practice opportunities should be available; the teacher can monitor performance during practice, enlist the aid of a peer tutor or adult volunteer, or use self-correcting materials. The basic math self-instructional materials in Figure 10-5 can help Danny learn addition facts.

Reading

Word recognition and comprehension are two very important subskills of reading. Word recognition is the ability to decode printed symbols; decoding is accomplished by sight if the word is familiar or by analysis of the word's phonetic components or its structure (roots, prefixes, suffixes, etc.). Reading comprehension—the ability to understand what is read—involves knowing the meanings of individual words, following the sequence of events in a passage, detecting the main ideas, drawing conclusions, and making inferences.

Two major approaches are used to teach reading skills: the **code-emphasis approach** and the **meaning-emphasis approach.** According to Mercer and Mercer (2005), code-emphasis programs teach decoding first, then comprehension; instruction in decoding stresses the regular relationships between letters and sounds. In contrast, meaning-based programs emphasize comprehension from the start; students practice decoding by reading common words.

The whole-language approach to reading instruction is an example of a meaning-emphasis program. In this approach, reading is not broken down into separate skill areas; thus, skills such as decoding are not taught separately. Instead, reading is integrated with the other language arts of listening, speaking, and writing (Lapp & Flood, 1992). According to McLoughlin and Lewis (2008), in whole-language classrooms students read whole texts (not fragments) from authentic literature, and instruction emphasizes meaningful interaction with those texts, not development of isolated skills.

An extensive body of research now exists to guide how teachers go about delivering instruction in reading. First of all, research results clearly suggest that explicit code-emphasis programs are more effective than implicit meaning-emphasis programs, particularly for students with special needs and those at risk for learning problems (Chall, 1967, 1977, 1983, 1989, 2000; Rankin-Erickson & Pressley, 2000; Snow, Burns, & Griffin, 1998; Spear-Swerling & Sternberg, 2001; Stahl & Miller, 1989; Vaughn, Gersten, & Chard, 2000). Two additional evidence-based recommendations for reading instruction concern the development of phonological awareness and reading fluency. **Phonological awareness,** a readiness skill for younger children, has been defined as "the ability to recognize that the words we hear are composed of individual sounds within the word" (Lerner, 2003, p. 257). **Reading fluency,** a skill area more pertinent to older readers, is the ability to read text both quickly and accurately.

In the general education classroom, code-emphasis programs provide beginning readers with a systematic method of decoding unfamiliar words. Students learn decoding strategies and then practice with words that can be read using these strategies. Code-based reading materials feature a controlled vocabulary, that is, one limited to words that can be read by students who have mastered the strategies taught in the program.

Materials based on the **phonics** method represent the code-based approach to reading. Students first learn the

FIGURE 10-4   Prompts for Basic Skills Instruction

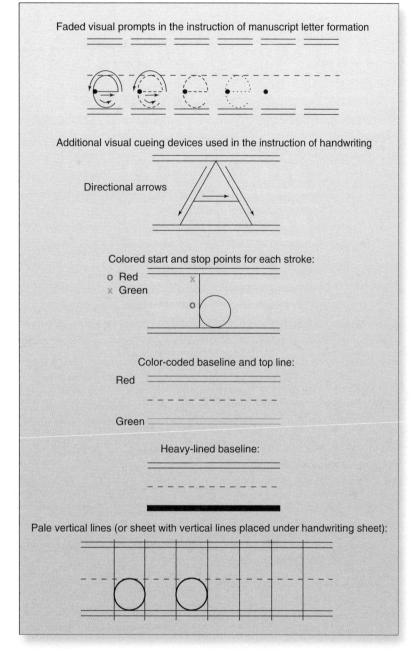

Note: Reprinted with permission of Merrill/Prentice Hall, an imprint of Macmillan Publishing Company, from *Teaching the Mildly Handicapped in the Regular Classroom* (2nd ed., p. 108) by J. Affleck, S. Lowenbraun, and A. Archer. Copyright © 1980 Merrill Publishing Company, Columbus, Ohio.

sound for each letter (phoneme–grapheme combinations) and practice reading phonetically regular words; later, other types of words are introduced. Linguistic methods are an adaptation of the phonics approach; reading instruction begins with phonetically regular word families such as *at, bat, cat, rat,* and *sat.*

Reading programs that begin with a controlled vocabulary help students acquire skills quickly and gain confidence in their ability to decode print; however, students eventually must make the transition to a more conventional vocabulary

selection. One way to accomplish this is to teach students to read common words that appear with high frequency in the English language. Because many of these words are irregular and therefore not readily decodable with phonics strategies, they are often taught as sight vocabulary. The *Dolch Basic Sight Word List* (Dolch, 1953) is one example of a high-frequency word list; an updated version of the Dolch list (Johnson, 1971) is shown in Table 10-1. Simms and Falcon (1987) suggested dividing this word list into categories for instruction. Categories might include self words (e.g., *I, me*),

FIGURE 10-5   **Materials for Independent Practice**

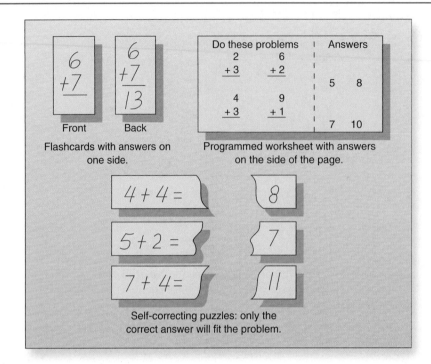

Flashcards with answers on one side.

Programmed worksheet with answers on the side of the page.

Self-correcting puzzles: only the correct answer will fit the problem.

moving words (*come, play*), size words (*big, little*), and question words (*who, when*).

Reading is a problem area for many students with special needs, not only those with learning disabilities. Some have difficulty learning (or applying) word recognition skills; others fail to understand what they have read despite adequate decoding skills. Still others require assistance in both word recognition and comprehension. The following suggestions for modifying reading instruction for students with special needs include examples of prompts and ways to enhance the practice of reading skills.

- Add cues to help students decode troublesome words; for example, mark long vowels (sēēd) cross out silent letters (māk¢), and divide words into syllables (dis-crim-i-nāt¢).
- Provide markers for students who lose their place while reading. They can move their finger along under the line of print or use an index card with an arrow for a guideline; cards with windows can be placed on the page to expose only a few words at a time.

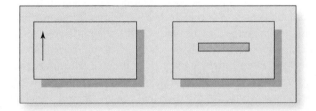

- To enhance reading comprehension, tell students the purposes for reading and what to look for in the passage.

For example, they might read a story to discover the main characters and the sequence of events, or a textbook chapter to learn important facts and main ideas. **Advanced organizers** that provide an overview of the passage to prepare students for what they will be reading are an effective strategy for increasing comprehension (Graham & Johnson, 1989). Mercer and Mercer (1993) suggest giving students a list of questions to guide their reading and the page numbers of the text on which answers can be found.

- Use peer tutors and volunteers for sight word drill.
- Provide high interest–low vocabulary reading materials to aid in the practice of silent reading. These materials appeal to students who read at a lower grade level than expected for their age; examples appear in Table 10-2. Other good resources are *Easy Reading: Book Series and Periodicals for Less Able Readers* (2nd ed.) (Ryder, Graves, & Graves, 1989) and *High Interest Easy Reading: An Annotated Booklist for Middle School and Senior High School* (7th ed.) (Phelan, 1996).
- Make audio recordings of texts or stories; students can read the passage while listening to correct word pronunciation and phrasing of sentences.
- Use computer software to help teach basic reading skills. Many multimedia programs talk, allowing students to develop sight vocabulary as they read and listen to stories, poems, and other texts.
- Provide practice in reading comprehension with materials such as the *Specific Skill Series* (Boning, 1998). This

TABLE 10-1   High-Frequency Word List

Preprimer	Primer	First	Second	Third
1. the	45. when	89. many	133. know	177. don't
2. of	46. who	90. before	134. while	178. does
3. and	47. will	91. must	135. last	179. got
4. to	48. more	92. through	136. might	180. united
5. a	49. no	93. back	137. us	181. left
6. in	50. if	94. years	138. great	182. number
7. that	51. out	95. where	139. old	183. course
8. is	52. so	96. much	140. year	184. war
9. was	53. said	97. your	141. off	185. until
10. he	54. what	98. may	142. come	186. always
11. for	55. up	99. well	143. since	187. away
12. it	56. its	100. down	144. against	188. something
13. with	57. about	101. should	145. go	189. fact
14. as	58. into	102. because	146. came	190. through
15. his	59. than	103. each	147. right	191. water
16. on	60. them	104. just	148. used	192. less
17. be	61. can	105. those	149. take	193. public
18. at	62. only	106. people	150. three	194. put
19. by	63. other	107. Mr.	151. states	195. thing
20. I	64. new	108. how	152. himself	196. almost
21. this	65. some	109. too	153. few	197. hand
22. had	66. could	110. little	154. house	198. enough
23. not	67. time	111. state	155. use	199. far
24. are	68. these	112. good	156. during	200. took
25. but	69. two	113. very	157. without	201. head
26. from	70. may	114. make	158. again	202. yet
27. or	71. then	115. would	159. place	203. government
28. have	72. do	116. still	160. American	204. system
29. an	73. first	117. own	161. around	205. better
30. they	74. any	118. see	162. however	206. set
31. which	75. my	119. men	163. home	207. told
32. one	76. now	120. work	164. small	208. nothing
33. you	77. such	121. long	165. found	209. night
34. were	78. like	122. get	166. Mrs.	210. end
35. her	79. our	123. here	167. thought	211. why
36. all	80. over	124. between	168. went	212. called
37. she	81. man	125. both	169. say	213. didn't
38. there	82. me	126. life	170. part	214. eyes
39. would	83. even	127. being	171. once	215. find
40. their	84. most	128. under	172. general	216. going
41. we	85. made	129. never	173. high	217. look
42. him	86. after	130. day	174. upon	218. asked
43. been	87. also	131. same	175. school	219. later
44. has	88. did	132. another	176. every	220. knew

Note: From "The Dolch List Reexamined" by D. D. Johnson, 1971, *The Reading Teacher, 24,* pp. 455–456. Copyright 1971 by the International Reading Association. Reprinted by permission of D. D. Johnson and the International Reading Association.

program includes activities for skills such as using context clues, locating answers, following directions, identifying main ideas, and drawing conclusions. A source of ideas for other activities for comprehension practice is *Locating and Correcting Reading Difficulties* (8th ed.) (Shanker & Ekwall, 2002).

▪ To increase reading fluency, have students reread a passage several times. **Repeated readings** increase both speed and accuracy, which helps students master a selection before attempting more difficult selections. In addition to improving fluency, repeated readings also increase comprehension (O'Connor, White, & Swanson, 2007; Therrien, 2004). Sindelar (1987) commented that "mastery is seldom achieved with a single reading, especially for students experiencing difficulty in learning to read" (p. 59).

▪ Teach students strategies for approaching comprehension tasks. In one study (Jenkins, Heliotis, Stein, & Haynes, 1987), students improved their comprehension of stories by learning to name the most important person (*Who?*) and the major event (*What's happening?*) in each paragraph.

▪ Another strategy, the SQ3R method (Robinson, 1961), can help students improve their comprehension of expository reading materials such as content-area textbooks. (*SQ3R* stands for *Survey, Question, Read, Recite,* and *Review.*) Expository text is usually more difficult to understand than narrative text (i.e., stories). In the SQ3R method, students begin by surveying the passage to get a general idea of its contents. Students ask questions about the text, then read to find the answers. The answers are recited without reference to the text, and then the entire passage is reviewed.

TABLE 10-2   High Interest–Low Vocabulary Reading Materials

Title	Publisher	Reading Grade Level	Interest Grade Level
American Adventure Series	Harper & Row	3–6	4–8
Basic Vocabulary Books	Garrard	2	1–6
Bestsellers	Globe Fearon	2–4	6–12
Breakthrough Series	Allyn & Bacon	2–6	6–12
Checkered Flag Series	Field Educational Publications	2–4	7–12
Childhood of Famous Americans Series	Bobbs-Merrill	4–5	7–9
Cowboy Sam Series	Benefic Press	PP–3	1–6
Dan Frontier Series	Benefic Press	PP–4	1–7
Deep Sea Adventures	Field Educational Publications	2–5	3–11
Everyreader Series	McGraw-Hill	6–8	5–12
Fastback Collection	Globe Fearon	4–5	6–12
First Reading Books	Garrard	1	1–4
Focus on Reading	SRA	1–6	3–12
Folklore of the World Books	Garrard	2	2–8
Interesting Reading Series	Follett	2–3	7–12
Jim Forest Readers	Field Educational Publications	1–3	1–7
Junior Science Books	Garrard	4–5	6–9
Morgan Bay Mysteries	Field Educational Publications	2–4	4–11
Morrow's High Interest/Easy Reading Books	William Morrow	1–8	4–10
Mystery, Adventure, and Science Fiction Collections	Steck-Vaughn	2–4	5–12
Mystery Adventure Series	Benefic Press	2–6	4–9
Pacemaker Classics	Globe/Fearon	3–4	5–12
Pacemaker Story Books	Xerox Education Publications	2	7–12
Pal Paperback Kits	Xerox Education Publications	1–5	5–12
Perspectives Set	High Noon Books	3–4	6–12
Phoenix Everyreaders	Phoenix Learning Resources	4	4–12
Pleasure Reading Books	Garrard	4	3–7
Power Up! Series	Steck-Vaughn	2–5	6–8
Racing Wheels Series	Benefic Press	2–4	4–9
Reading for Concepts Series	McGraw-Hill	3–8	5–12
Reading Reinforcement Skilltext Series	SRA	1–5	1–8
Reading Skill Builders	Reader's Digest Services	1–4	2–5
Sailor Jack Series	Benefic Press	PP–3	1–6
Scoreboard Series	High Noon Books	2	6–1
Space Science Fiction Series	Benefic Press	2–6	4–9
Sports Mystery Stories	Benefic Press	2–4	4–9
Spotlight on Literature	SRA	3–6	6–12
Sprint Libraries	Scholastic	1–3	3–6
Super Kits	Warner Educational Services	2–5	4–12
Teen-Age Tales	D. C. Heath	4–6	6–11
Tom & Ricky Mystery Series	High Noon Books	1	4–9
Top Picks	Reader's Digest Services	5–7	5–12
Trailblazers Series	High Noon Books	2	4–9
True Tales	Steck-Vaughn	3	4–12
Turning Point	Phoenix Learning Resources	1–4	7–12
What Is It? Series	Benefic Press	1–4	1–8

Note: Reprinted with the permission of Merrill/Prentice Hall from *Teaching Students with Learning Problems,* (7th ed.) by C. D. Mercer and A. R. Mercer (p. 312). Copyright © 2005 by Prentice-Hall, Inc.

■ **Reciprocal teaching** is an instructional approach developed by Palinscar and Brown (1988) that involves four interrelated strategies. Teachers help students develop comprehension skills and the ability to monitor their own comprehension by involving students in dialogues about texts. Lerner and Johns (2009) describe the four strategies: "*summarizing* the content of a passage, *asking questions* about a central point, *clarifying* the difficult parts of the material, and *predicting* what would happen next" (p. 115).

- The book *Strategies That Work: Teaching Comprehension to Enhance Understanding* (Harvey & Goudvis, 2000) suggests teaching young readers six strategies to enhance comprehension skills. These strategies are
  - Making connections between the text and the reader, the text and the world, and the text and other texts;
  - Asking questions about the text;
  - Visualizing what is happening in the text;
  - Making inferences from the text;
  - Determining importance in text; and
  - Synthesizing information.

Handwriting, Spelling, and Written Expression

Writing skills are built on reading skills, and many students with special needs require extra assistance in this area (Saddler, 2004). One important subskill is handwriting, the mechanical process of forming letters and words. The goal in handwriting instruction is for students to write legibly and with sufficient speed. Usually students learn manuscript writing (printing) first, then they are introduced to cursive writing in the middle elementary grades. For students who experience difficulty with forming and spacing letters, cursive writing may be less demanding. For example, in printing, the letters *b* and *d* require a similar motor pattern and are easily confused; in cursive, they are written quite differently.

Students who fail to make a complete transition from printing to cursive writing often continue forming capital letters in manuscript while writing the rest of the word in cursive. If legibility and speed are not affected, this style is acceptable. In fact, many of the special cursive alphabets developed for students with handwriting problems contain print-style capitals; in addition, letters and words are written almost vertically with little slant. One example is the D'Nealian handwriting system (Thurber, 2001). In the modified alphabet proposed by Spalding and Spalding (1986), after students learn to form manuscript letters and five connecting strokes, the transition to cursive can be made with ease.

Spelling is the arrangement of letters to form words. Because English is not a completely phonetic language, many words cannot be spelled the way they sound. Although consonants have fairly reliable phoneme–grapheme correspondence, vowel letters take on several different sounds; for example, the letter *a* produces distinct sounds in *at, ate, all*, and *father*. For this reason, teaching spelling solely by phonics is probably not the best practice, particularly for students who learn words slowly. Although phonics skills should be a part of the spelling curriculum, words that appear frequently in written language should also be stressed; see, for example, the high-frequency word list in Table 10-1 earlier in this chapter. Combining basic instruction in phonics (with emphasis on consonant sounds) and instruction in spelling common words as well as words selected by the student is a practice that produces an excellent individualized spelling program.

When a formal classroom spelling program is used, lessons can be modified for students with special needs as necessary; for instance, reducing the number of words to be learned each week is a common practice (Graham et al., 2008). Teachers should carefully monitor the words included in each lesson. For example, if lists include similar words, such as *receive* and *piece*, students may become confused and, as a result, acquire few new spelling words.

Written expression is the process of putting one's thoughts down on paper. Several skills are needed: the mechanics of writing, such as handwriting, spelling, punctuation, and capitalization; language skills such as knowledge of word meanings and syntax (grammar); and thinking skills such as organization, sequence, and logic. Although written expression used to be "the neglected basic skill" (Freedman, 1982, p. 34), it is now considered an important part of the language arts curriculum. However, it is important to remember that, for many students with special needs, written language skills—like their counterparts in reading—must be taught directly.

Several ideas for teaching spelling, handwriting, and composition in the general education classroom are listed here, along with examples of prompts and suggestions for practice activities. Also, see the "Spotlight on Technology" feature for information about using computers to teach writing skills.

- Help students who are poor spellers begin to use the dictionary as an aid; provide them with a minidictionary or "My Words" booklet that contains high-frequency words and words that they often misspell.
- Use the test–study–test method for spelling instruction (Graham & Miller, 1979). Begin with a pretest to identify words students have already mastered, then focus study activities on the words they need to learn. Students also should correct their own spelling tests under the teacher's direction. In a review of research on strategies for teaching spelling skills, Graham and Miller concluded that this approach is "the single most important factor in learning to spell" (p. 10).
- Provide handwriting prompts such as those shown earlier in this chapter in Figure 10-4. Fade the prompts as quickly as possible.
- Review rules for capitalization and punctuation before students begin writing; post rules on the bulletin board.
- Use instructional tapes for the practice of high-frequency and phonetically irregular spelling words. Students listen to the word, attempt to write it, and listen again to hear the correct spelling.
- For students who form letters slowly and laboriously, use newsprint and felt-tip pens for handwriting practice. When students write slowly on newsprint, the ink spreads, making individual letters indecipherable. Students must increase speed in order for their handwriting to be legible.
- Provide many different opportunities to practice written expression. Have students keep a daily journal, write three-sentence stories, compose a note to a friend each day, or describe an event or person. At first, keep writing activities brief; encourage clarity and accuracy.
- Teach writing as a multistage process. Isaacson (1987) described three stages: prewriting (or planning), writing, and rewriting (or revising). Mercer and Pullen

Computer Software for Struggling Writers

Writing has been described as a schizophrenic activity because the writer must assume two roles, that of an author and that of a secretary (Smith, 1982). Students with learning disabilities have particular difficulties with the secretarial aspects of writing: handwriting, spelling, capitalization and punctuation, usage, and grammar. Another problem area for students with learning disabilities is the planning stage of writing, which requires generating and organizing ideas.

Word processing programs and other writing tools may help alleviate some of these problems (Lewis, 1993, 1998, 2000b; MacArthur, 2009). One of the major advantages of word processors is that writers can easily manipulate the text to organize, revise, and improve it. Spelling checkers, present in most word processors, help in the correction of spelling errors. Another advantage is that the writer's final product is printed; it is neater and easier to read than a handwritten paper. This is very important for students with learning disabilities and others with poor handwriting. As one teacher commented about a student who had learned to use a word processor, "Now, even with hunt and peck, his written assignments are done willingly, on time, and *I can read them!!!*" (Lewis, Dell, Lynch, Harrison, & Saba, 1987, p. 61).

Draft:Builder

The *Draft:Builder* program supports three stages of the writing process: generating and organizing ideas, adding notes, and preparing the first draft. The examples illustrate these stages. The first step in writing a report about *Frankenstein* is to list and organize the main ideas. As the tab at the top of the screen indicates, this stage is called Outline. The student adds ideas to the outline on the left, and a visual map appears on the right.

Note: Photo courtesy of Don Johnston, Inc.

It is easy to move information around and to add and delete. Also, speech is available throughout *Draft:Builder;* to hear text read aloud, the student clicks on the Speak button.

In the second stage, Notes, the student begins to add information to the outline. In the example, the student is adding two notes to expand the information about the doctor as inventor.

Note: Photo courtesy of Don Johnston, Inc.

In the third stage, Draft, the student is able to move notes from the outline into the first draft of a story or essay. The student can make changes to the draft here, then move the text to a word processing program for editing and preparation of the final draft.

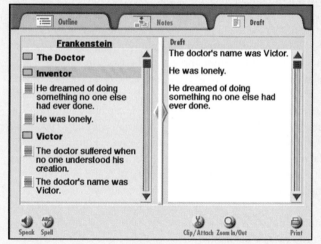

Note: Photo courtesy of Don Johnston, Inc.

Write:OutLoud

Write:OutLoud is one of the many word processing programs designed for classroom use. It has three major advantages for students with special needs. It's easy to learn and easy to operate. It talks; that is, it has the ability to read aloud whatever the student has written. And, third, it contains a spelling checker that also talks.

In *Write:OutLoud,* students can easily change the size and color of the letters and the color of the background. It is also possible to add graphics as the sample report on Rosa Parks, the freedom fighter, illustrates.

Note: Photo courtesy of Don Johnston, Inc.

One of the most powerful features of this program is its ability to read text aloud. *Write:OutLoud* can be set to speak text automatically as it is entered. Choices include hearing each letter name, each word, each sentence, and/or each paragraph. Students also have the option of hearing any portion of the text read aloud after they've finished writing. To do that, they simply select the text they want to hear and click on the button with the speaker. It is important to note that it is also possible for speech to be turned off.

The spelling checker in *Write:OutLoud* works like a typical spelling checker. When the student chooses Spell Check, the program scans the text to locate spelling errors. When a misspelling is identified, students see the misspelled word in a sentence (which can be read aloud) and several possible alternatives. Each alternative can be read aloud, a useful feature for students who may have problems reading.

Co:Writer

Co:Writer is a word prediction program. It works with other programs, such as word processors, to reduce the amount of typing students must do. Word prediction programs were originally developed for individuals with physical impairments to reduce the motor demands of the writing task. However, these programs

have also been found useful with students with learning disabilities and others who have difficulty spelling (Lewis, Ashton, & Kieley, 1996).

When students are writing with a word processor, they activate *Co:Writer* by pressing the "+" key. A window pops up (see the example) and the student begins writing. When the first letter of a word is typed, *Co:Writer* attempts to predict the word the student wants to enter in the document.

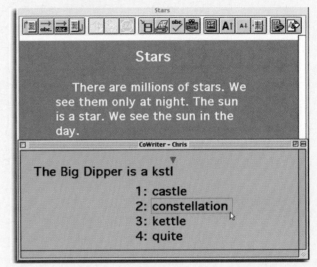

Note: Photo courtesy of Don Johnston, Inc.

Here, the student is writing about the stars and wants to use the word *constellation*. When the writer typed a somewhat phonetic version of the word (*kstl*), the program predicted *castle, constellation, kettle,* and *quite.* The student can hear any of these words read aloud and, if one is correct, select it by clicking on it or typing its number. If the list of suggested words does not contain the word the student wants, he or she types another letter and another set of words is predicted.

Draft:Builder, Write:OutLoud, and *Co:Writer* were developed by the Don Johnston company (*http://www.donjohnston.com*). *Co:Writer* is also available for use with the portable NEO keyboards available from Renaissance Learning (*http://www.renlearning.com*).

(2005) identified five: prewriting, drafting, revising (making changes in content), editing (correction of errors), and publishing. Whatever process model is used, provide guided practice at each stage. At the prewriting stage, for instance, students can engage in a variety of activities to generate ideas and gather information for writing. Students can think about the topic, read, or research ideas; they can observe or interview others or listen to speakers, watch demonstrations, or take part in field trips (Tompkins & Friend, 1986; Whitt, Paul, & Reynolds, 1988).

- Give students a format for writing compositions or essays. For example, have them list the main ideas they wish to present and formulate a title. The main ideas are then converted to topic sentences for paragraphs, and supporting sentences are added.

- **Mapping** is another strategy to help students organize their ideas for writing. Students list the key words and ideas they have identified for the topic they will write about, then draw a map showing the relationship between the main topic and key words (Tompkins & Friend, 1986). Figure 10-6 shows a map developed by a group of students for a report on scorpions.

- Teach students specific strategies for planning the content of their writing. For narratives, Graham and Harris (1989) suggested the CSPACE strategy:

C	character
S	setting
P	problem or purpose
A	action
C	conclusion
E	emotion

FIGURE 10-6   Organizational Map for an Essay on Scorpions

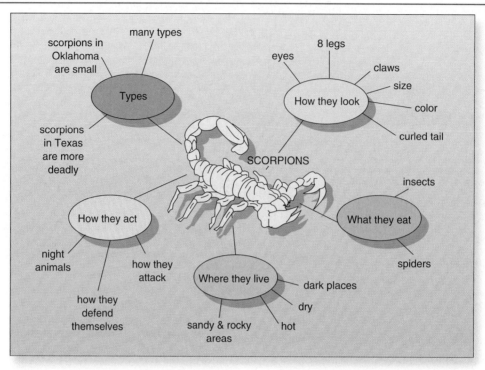

The TREE strategy (Graham & Harris, 1989) is used when planning opinion essays:

T	topic
R	reasons
E	examples
E	ending

■ Include structured activities for the revising stage of writing. One possibility is the formation of writing groups in the classroom. Each student reads his or her composition aloud to the group, and peers comment on specific strengths in the writing; the writer then asks for help (e.g., "Did the ending make sense?") (Tompkins & Friend, 1986). Students can also evaluate their own work using guides like the self-edit think sheet described by Englert and Raphael (1988). With this guide, students

> first look back at their papers, star the parts they like best, and anticipate readers' questions by putting question marks next to the unclear parts. Next, they rate the extent (e.g., "yes," "sort of," "no") to which they answered the text structure questions (e.g., Did I . . . "Tell what was being explained?" "Tell what materials you need?" "Make the steps clear?" etc.). (p. 518)

■ Also teach strategies for locating and correcting writing errors. Schumaker, Nolan, and Deshler (1985) recommend the COPS strategy:

C	capitalization
O	overall appearance
P	punctuation
S	spelling

■ Teach students to use word processors for writing. See the "Spotlight on Technology" earlier in this chapter for word processing tools that assist students in the drafting, revising, and editing stages of writing.

■ Teach students what to do when spelling checkers in word processing programs detect a misspelling but cannot suggest the correct alternative. Spelling checkers are able to supply the correct word for spelling errors only about 50% of the time for students with learning disabilities (MacArthur, Graham, Haynes, & DeLaPaz, 1996). One reason for this is that students' spellings are often far from accurate and the program is unable to "guess" the word the student is attempting to write. Ashton (1997) suggests the CHECK strategy. This strategy helps students make systematic changes in their word (altering the beginning letter, consonants, and vowels), attend to the words suggested by the program, and remain persistent.

C	Check the beginning sound
H	Hunt for the correct consonants
E	Examine the vowels
C	Changes in word lists may give hints
K	Keeping repeating steps 1 through 4

Math

Many students with special needs require extra assistance in math (Geary, 2004). Within the area of math are two important subskills: computation and reasoning. Computation is based on the prerequisite skills of number concepts, reading and writing numerals, and counting. It includes mastery of number facts in the basic operations (addition, subtraction, multiplication, and division) and knowledge of **algorithms,** the procedures for performing operations. For example, in the algorithm for adding 2 two-digit numbers such as 25 and 48, it is necessary to begin with the right-hand or ones column (5 + 8 = 13); if the sum of the ones column is more than 9 (in this case 13), then the ones portion (3) is written in the ones column, and the tens portion (1) is carried over to the tens column.

In math reasoning, computation skills are used to solve problems. A typical classroom example is the word or story problem in which students are presented with a situation and asked to find a solution. Some students find these difficult because poor reading skills interfere with their understanding of the problem; others have trouble separating essential from superfluous information, determining the appropriate algorithm, and computing the answer.

In recent years, problem solving has become a more important part of the math curriculum as a result of reform efforts led by the National Council of Teachers of Mathematics (NCTM) (Woodward, 2004). For example, the NCTM (1989, 2000) recommended that students be actively engaged in authentic problem-solving tasks beginning in the early grades. Students who perform poorly in math reasoning tasks should receive extra instruction and practice in this area.

Ways of modifying math instruction in the general education classroom are presented here. Prompts to aid students in computation and reasoning and suggestions for classroom practice activities are included.

- Add visual prompts to help students solve computation problems.
- For students who have trouble spacing math problems and writing numbers, use paper that has been marked off in squares, or add guidelines so that students write within boundaries.
- Include only a few problems per page if students appear confused by several problems or if they have difficulty finishing their work.
- Use self-instructional materials for drill in number facts; see Figure 10-5 for ideas for materials that can be made by teachers. Or select one of the many software programs for math drill and practice.
- Work toward automatic recall of number facts. Facts are automatic when students no longer need to rely on counting strategies; their responses are quick, accurate, and consistent. To develop **automaticity** (also called *fluency*), Hasselbring, Goin, and Bransford (1987) suggested introducing no more than two or three facts and their reciprocals at a time. Timed drills are used for practice, with the goal being a 1-second response time.
- Manipulative objects help some students learn basic number concepts and relationships; for example, use beans, blocks, or poker chips to teach counting, the relationship of multiplication to addition, and so on.
- Provide verbal prompts to assist in the application of algorithms; for instance, Affleck et al.(1980) recommended the following for two-digit multiplication: "Multiply by the ones column first. Remember to line up the numbers carefully. Remember to cross multiply" (p. 109).
- Use real situations for word problems. For example, the students' own performance data or the number of points earned for appropriate behavior provide material for practice problems.
- Help students begin to analyze story problems by identifying the key words that often (but not always) signal the different operations. Mercer and Mercer (1989) called these "clue words" and gave these examples:

Addition: Altogether, sum, and, plus, finds
Subtraction: Left, lost, spent, remains
Multiplication: Rows, groups, altogether
Division: Share, each, cost per month (p. 254)

- Set up a class store, bank, or stock exchange, and devise different activities for practice in math reasoning.
- Landi (2001) suggested using a four-part problem-solving strategy based on the work of Montague (1992). In this strategy, students learn to (1) paraphrase the problem, (2) visualize the problem (e.g., by making a diagram), (3) hypothesize about the procedures needed to solve the problem, and (4) estimate the answer to the problem. In contrast, Montague, Warger, and Morgan (2000) presented a more elaborate strategy, Solve It!:
  - Read (for understanding)
  - Paraphrase (your own words)
  - Visualize (a picture or a diagram)
  - Hypothesize (a plan to solve the problem)
  - Estimate (predict the answer)
  - Compute (do the arithmetic)
  - Check (make sure everything is right) (p. 111)

▶ MODIFYING CONTENT-AREA INSTRUCTION

In the late elementary grades, the curriculum shifts in emphasis from the acquisition of basic skills to the use of these tool subjects to gain other types of information. Content areas such as English, science, health, history, and social studies begin to dominate the curriculum. In high school, most courses are content subjects, and great variety is seen—foreign language, art, music, business, automotive technology, home economics, physical education and sports, agriculture, driver education, and so on.

Content-area instruction assumes that students have mastered the basic skills of reading, writing, and math. For many students with special needs, this is simply not the case. For these students to benefit from instruction, modifications must be made. Two types of changes are recommended: changing the criteria for task performance and altering the characteristics of content-area tasks. Task criteria include speed and accuracy demands and the amount of work required. Task characteristics, in contrast, refer to the basic skills necessary for performance.

Compensatory strategies are used with older students to enhance their chances of success. The most common strategy is the replacement of written language requirements with oral language requirements. Instead of reading and writing, students listen and speak; they use areas of strength to compensate for poor basic skills.

The following paragraphs describe several of the task demands that cause difficulty for students with special needs in content-area instruction; suggestions for modifications are also presented.

Reading Assignments

Students whose reading level is less than expected for their grades often find content subjects unmanageable. They may be unable to read textbook assignments, or they may be able to read only slowly and with great effort. To help such students acquire the information presented in assigned readings, teachers can try the following modifications.

- *Reduce the amount of reading required.* Permit students to read only part of the assignment or to concentrate on the most important elements, such as headings, italicized words, and chapter previews and summaries.
- *Substitute materials written on a lower reading level.* For example, use a sixth grade history text for tenth graders. Many remedial reading versions of content subject texts are available from commercial publishers.
- *Present the information through another medium.* Possible methods are lecture; class discussion; visual aids such as photos, maps, and slides; audiovisual aids such as movies, videotapes, and television; resource people who can be interviewed; peer tutors and volunteers who act as readers; and audiotapes of reading material. One of the most useful modern adaptations is digital text (Cavanaugh,

2006). See the "Inclusion Tips for the Teacher" section to learn more about this important resource.

Written Assignments and Exams

Because they may be unable to read directions and questions, students with reading problems find written assignments and exams troublesome. For these students, the adaptations previously suggested can be used. For students who perform poorly in writing despite adequate reading skills, try the following modifications.

- For students who work slowly, reduce the length of the written task or extend the time limits.
- Allow students with poor handwriting to print or write with a word processor.
- Provide poor spellers with a dictionary or a list of commonly misspelled words.
- Consider a dictionary designed for poor spellers, available in most bookstores. In this dictionary, students look up words by their phonetic spellings to find the correct version. The Franklin Spelling Ace® is an electronic version of a poor speller's dictionary. It is a small, portable device; the student types in a phonetic spelling (e.g., *reseve* for *receive*), and a list of possible options is generated: *resolve, receive, reserve,* and so on.
- Permit students to write using a word processor with a spelling checker program to help identify and correct spelling errors.
- Design assignments and exams so that writing requirements are minimized. For example, use multiple-choice and completion formats rather than essays.

 Inclusion Tips for the Teacher

Bookshare: Digital Texts for Students with Reading Disabilities

Poor reading skills are a major stumbling block for many middle and high school students, particularly those with learning disabilities in the area of reading. Grade-level texts may be too difficult for these students to read with ease and adequate comprehension. Or they may read so slowly that they are unable to absorb the same amount of material as their peers.

Bookshare offers one solution to this problem. Bookshare is an online repository of digital texts that students with print disabilities can access free of charge. With digital texts, students see the text on the screen of a computer or other device and hear that text read aloud with synthetic text-to-speech. Although synthetic speech sounds somewhat robotic, it allows students to hear every word read aloud. In addition to students with learning disabilities, Bookshare also serves students with visual impairments and physical disabilities.

Membership in Bookshare is free of charge to U.S. schools and individual students with qualifying disabilities. Adults in the United States and individuals outside the country can purchase memberships for a modest set-up fee and monthly charge. All members, however, must demonstrate eligibility resulting from a visual impairment, physical disability, learning disability, or reading disability. In school settings, one of the best ways to ensure that students with print disabilities and their teachers gain access to Bookshare is to discuss this type of accommodation as part of the IEP planning process.

Among the digital texts available from Bookshare are NIMAS books. Under NIMAS, or the National Instructional Materials Accessibility Standard established by IDEA 2004, publishers of print instructional materials must make those materials accessible to students with disabilities as electronic files, which can then be converted into several different formats. The National Instructional Materials Accessibility Center (NIMAC) is the repository for those files.

Here is a sampling of the types of texts available on the Bookshare website (*http://www.bookshare.org*):

- NIMAS books for U.S. K–12 public schools
- Caldecott Award winners
- Newbery Award winners
- *New York Times* best sellers
- Young Reader's Choice Award winners
- Selected newspapers and magazines
- National Education Association's List of Kids' Top 100 Books
- Teacher Recommended Reading (by grade level)
- *Time Magazine's* All-Time 100 Novels

For more information about the availability of digital texts for the students with learning disabilities in your classroom, contact the resource specialist or special education teacher in your school or your district's special education department.

- Have students who are unable to compose and write at the same time compose using an audio recorder and then transcribe what they have dictated.
- Have students respond through a medium other than writing. Two possible methods are telling answers to peer tutors or volunteers who write them for the student and giving oral responses to the teacher.

Math Skills

Content-area subjects often require that students have rudimentary math skills. Basic facts and algorithms are necessary for success in algebra, geometry, trigonometry, home economics, and automotive technology. In some areas, such as higher math and vocational classes, computation skills are essential. Classes like English, history, and social studies can demand quantitative reasoning; for instance, graphs and charts are often used to convey important information.

The most common adaptation for students with poor math skills is the use of aids. Students can rely on facts tables for basic computation or use calculators for problems requiring more complex operations. This compensatory strategy is a useful one, and many adults also rely on electronic aids. However, simply providing students with calculators probably will not result in successful performance. Students need to learn how to operate calculators, estimate what the answer should be, and check their results.

By allowing students with special needs to use compensatory strategies for reading assignments, written work and exams, and math skills, the general education teacher helps bypass basic skills deficits in order to facilitate content-area instruction. Many students with special needs rely on compensatory procedures their entire lives. Consider the words of Nelson Rockefeller, a former governor of New York and later vice president of the United States, who had a learning disability:

If it helps a dyslexic child to know that I went through the same thing . . .

But can conduct press conferences today in three languages . . .

And can read a speech on television . . .

(Though I may have to rehearse it six times . . .

(With my script in large type . . .

(And my sentences broken into segments like these . . .

(And long words broken into syllables) . . .

And learned to read and communicate well enough to be elected Governor of New York four times. . . . (Rockefeller, 1976, p. 14)

▶ ADAPTING INSTRUCTION FOR STUDENTS WITH ATTENTION DEFICIT HYPERACTIVITY DISORDERS

Students with attention deficit hyperactivity disorder have many of the same needs as students with learning disabilities and others with academic learning problems. However, unlike students with learning disabilities, students with ADHD may experience difficulty in most, if not all, school subjects. Problems with inattention, distractibility, impulsiveness, and hyperactivity affect all areas of learning. For some students with ADHD, these problems cause serious delays in academic achievement; for others, the effects are less severe.

Students with ADHD are identified by the behaviors they display. The definition currently accepted by most professionals is that of the American Psychiatric Association (1994). Figure 10-7 presents the major elements of the definition included in the fourth edition of that organization's *Diagnostic and Statistical Manual of Mental Disorders* (often called the *DSM–IV*). See the "Inclusion Tips for the Teacher" box to learn more about attention deficit hyperactivity disorders.

FIGURE 10-7 Definition of ADHD

The American Psychiatric Association (1994) identifies several characteristics that may indicate attention deficit hyperactivity disorder. These characteristics must appear before age seven, persist for at least six months, be present in more than one environment (e.g., home, school, work), and cause "clinically significant distress or impairment in social, academic, or occupational functioning" (p. 84).

The first set of characteristics relates to inattention and the second to hyperactivity-impulsivity. Three classifications are possible: predominantly inattentive, predominantly hyperactive, or combined. For example, a student who shows six or more of the inattention characteristics but fewer than six of the hyperactivity-impulsivity characteristics would be identified as having ADHD, Predominantly Inattentive Type. The two sets of characteristics follow.

Inattention

Six (or more) of the following symptoms of **inattention** have persisted for at least 6 months to a degree that is maladaptive and inconsistent with developmental level:

Inattention

(a) often fails to give close attention to details or makes careless mistakes in schoolwork, work, or other activities

(b) often has difficulty sustaining attention in tasks or play activities

(c) often does not seem to listen when spoken to directly

(d) often does not follow through on instructions and fails to finish schoolwork, chores, or duties in the workplace (not due to oppositional behavior or failure to understand instructions)

(e) often has difficulties organizing tasks and activities

(f) often avoids, dislikes or is reluctant to engage in tasks that require sustained mental effort (such as schoolwork or homework)

(g) often loses things necessary for tasks or activities (e.g., toys, school assignments, pencils, books, or tools)

(h) is often easily distracted by extraneous stimuli

(i) is often forgetful in daily activities

Hyperactivity-Impulsivity

Six (or more) of the following symptoms of **hyperactivity-impulsivity** have persisted for at least 6 months to a degree that is maladaptive and inconsistent with developmental level:

Hyperactivity

(a) often fidgets with hands or feet or squirms in seat

(b) often leaves seat in classroom or in other situations in which remaining seated is expected

(c) often runs about or climbs excessively in situations in which it is inappropriate (in adolescents or adults, may be limited to subjective feelings of restlessness)

(d) often has difficulty playing or engaging in leisure activities quietly

(e) is often "on the go" or often acts as if "driven by a motor"

(f) often talks excessively

Impulsivity

(g) often blurts out answers before questions have been completed

(h) often has difficulty waiting in turn

(i) often interrupts or intrudes on others (e.g., butts into conversations or games) (pp. 83–84).

Note: Reprinted with permission from the *Diagnostic and Statistical Manual of Mental Disorders,* Fourth Edition, Text Revision. Copyright © 2000 by the American Psychiatric Association.

 Go to the Assignments and Activities section of Topic *Attention Deficit Hyperactivity Disorder* in the MyEducationLab for your course and complete the activity entitled *Common Characteristics of Attention Deficit Hyperactivity Disorder.*

As explained earlier in the book, federal special education law recognizes ADHD as a disability under the "other health impairment" category. Students with ADHD who do not meet criteria for special education may be eligible for services under Section 504 of the Rehabilitation Act of 1973. Such services typically include adaptations in general education programs. The U.S. Department of Education (1991) gives these examples of possible classroom modifications.

providing a structured learning environment; repeating and simplifying instructions about in-class and homework assignments; supplementing verbal instructions with visual instructions; using behavioral management techniques; adjusting class schedules; modifying test delivery; using tape recorders, computer-aided instruction, and other audiovisual equipment; selecting modified textbooks or workbooks; and tailoring homework assignments. (p. 7)

Interventions for students with ADHD are often multimodal (Lerner & Lowenthal, 1993; Lerner, Lowenthal, & Lerner, 1995; Reeve, 1990; Trout, Lienemann, Reid, & Epstein, 2007). That is, they include not only instructional adaptations but also behavior

Inclusion Tips for the Teacher

Myths About ADHD

Read the myths below, then check the facts. Note that ADD, as used here, is synonymous with ADHD.

Myth: Attention Deficit Disorder (ADD) does not really exist. It is simply the latest excuse for parents who do not discipline their children.

> *Fact:* Scientific research tells us ADD is a biologically based disorder that includes distractibility, impulsiveness, and sometimes hyperactivity. While the causes of ADD are not fully understood, recent research suggests that ADD can be inherited and may be due to an imbalance of neurotransmitters—chemicals used by the brain to control behavior—or abnormal glucose metabolism in the central nervous system. Before a student is labeled ADD, other possible causes of his or her behavior are ruled out.

Myth: Children with ADD are no different from their peers; all children have a hard time sitting still and paying attention.

> *Fact:* Before children are considered to have ADD, they must show symptoms that demonstrate behavior greatly different from what is expected for children of their age and background. They start to show the behaviors characteristic of ADD between ages three and seven. . . . These behaviors are persistent and occur in many different settings and situations. Furthermore, the behavior must be causing significant social, academic, or occupational impairment for the child to be diagnosed educationally as having ADD.

Myth: Only a few people really have ADD.

> *Fact:* Estimates of who has ADD range from 3 to 5 percent of the school-age population (between 1.46 and 2.44 million children). While boys outnumber girls by 4:1 to 9:1, experts believe that many girls with ADD are never diagnosed.

Myth: Medication can cure students with ADD.

> *Fact:* Medicine cannot cure ADD but can sometimes temporarily moderate its effects. Stimulant medication such as Ritalin, Cylert, and Dexedrine is effective in 70 percent of the children who take it. In these cases, medication causes children to exhibit a clear and immediate short-term increase in attention, control, concentration, and goal-directed effort. Medication also reduces disruptive behaviors, aggression, and hyperactivity.

However, there are side effects and no evidence for long-term effectiveness of medication. For example, recent studies show that medication has only limited short-term benefits on social adjustment and academic achievement. While medication can be incorporated into other treatment strategies, parents and teachers should not use medication as the sole method of helping the child.

Myth: The longer you wait to deal with ADD in students, the better the chances are that they will outgrow it.

> *Fact:* ADD symptoms continue into adolescence for 50–80 percent of the children with ADD. Many of them, between 30 and 50 percent, still will have ADD as adults. These adolescents and adults frequently show poor academic performance, poor self-image, and problems with peer relationships.

Myth: There is little parents and teachers can do to control the behavior of children with ADD.

> *Fact:* Teachers and parents have successfully used positive reinforcement procedures to increase desirable behaviors. A behavioral modification plan can give the child more privileges and independence as the child's behavior improves. Parents or teachers can give tokens or points to a child exhibiting desired behavior—such as remaining seated or being quiet—and can further reward children for good school performance and for finishing homework. Mild, short, immediate reprimands can counter and decrease negative and undesirable behaviors. Students with ADD can learn to follow classroom rules when there are pre-established consequences for misbehavior, rules are enforced consistently and immediately, and encouragement is given at home and in school.

Myth: Students with ADD cannot learn in the regular classroom.

> *Fact:* More than half of the children with ADD succeed in the mainstream classroom when teachers make appropriate adjustments. Most others require just a part-time program that gives them additional help in a resource room. Teachers can help students learn by providing increased variety. Often, altering features of instructional activities or materials, such as paper color, presentation rate, and response activities, helps teachers hold the attention of students with ADD. Active learning and motor activities also help. ADD students learn best when classroom organization is structured and predictable.

Note: From *Attention Deficit Disorder: Beyond the Myths* developed by the Chesapeake Institute, Washington, DC, as part of a contract from the Office of Special Education Programs, U.S. Department of Education. No copyright.

---

management programs and medical treatment. Strategies for modifying instruction are discussed here.

The major approach to adapting instruction for students with ADHD is to increase the structure of the classroom learning environment. In addition, the teacher attempts to decrease the sources of distraction within the classroom and, at the same time, make learning materials and activities more powerful so they will attract and sustain students' attention. Lerner and Lowenthal (1993) provided several specific suggestions drawn from the work of Abramowitz and O'Leary (1991) and Ysseldyke, Algozzine, and Thurlow (1992).

- Place the youngster in the least distracting location in the class. This may be in front of the class, away from doors, windows, air conditioners, heaters, and high-traffic areas. It may be necessary for the child to face a blank wall or be in a study carrel to enable the child to focus attention.

- Surround the student with good role models, preferably peers that the child views as significant others. Encourage peer tutoring and cooperative learning.

- Maintain a low pupil–teacher ratio whenever possible through the use of aides and volunteers.

 Go to the Building Teaching Skills and Dispositions section of Topic *Attention Deficit Hyperactivity Disorder* in the MyEducationLab for your course and complete the activity entitled *Maintaining On-Task Behavior*.

WINDOW ON THE WEB

Online ADHD Resources

This website is sponsored by CHADD (Children and Adults with Attention-Deficit/Hyperactivity Disorder), a national non-profit organization providing education, advocacy, and support for individuals with ADHD. The CHADD website offers information and resources to adults with ADHD, parents, health and medical professionals, educators, and attorneys and advocates. In addition, visitors to the site can become a member of CHADD, consult a professional directory, join an online community, learn about conferences and training opportunities, and visit the online store. CHADD publishes *Attention* magazine six times a year; members can read the entire magazine online and visitors can browse the table of contents and read selected articles.

www.chadd.org

The National Resource Center on AD/HD

The National Resource Center on AD/HD, a program of CHADD that is supported by funding from the U.S. Centers for Disease Control and Prevention, provides a website with resources in English and in Spanish. Designed for children and adults with ADHD, the website includes topics such as diagnosis and treatment, dealing with the legal and insurance systems, educational issues, and how to live with ADHD—a feature specifically targeted to adults with the disorder. Visitors to the website can view a list of frequently asked questions, as well as submit questions directly to health information specialists. Visitors to the website can sign up for a free electronic newsletter.

www.help4adhd.org

- Avoid unnecessary changes in schedules and monitor transitions; the child with ADD often has difficulty coping with changes. When unavoidable disruptions do occur, prepare the student as much as possible by explaining the situation and what behaviors are appropriate.
- Maintain eye contact with the student when giving verbal instructions. Make directions clear, concise, and simple. Repeat instructions as needed in a calm voice.
- Combine visual and tactile cues with verbal instructions since, generally, multiple modalities of instruction will be more effective in maintaining attention and in increasing learning.
- Make lists that will help the student organize tasks. Have the student check them off when they are finished. Students should complete study guides when listening to presentations.
- Adapt worksheets so that there is less material on each page.
- Break assignments into small chunks. Provide immediate feedback on each assignment. Allow extra time if needed for the student to finish the assignment.
- Ensure that the student has recorded homework assignments each day before leaving school. If necessary, set up a home-school program in which the parents help the child organize and complete the homework.
- If the child has difficulty staying in one place at school, alternate sitting with standing and activities which require moving around during the day.
- Provide activities that require active participation such as talking through problems or acting out the steps.
- Use learning aides such as computers, calculators, tape recorders, and programmed learning materials. They help to structure learning and maintain interest and motivation.
- Provide the student opportunities to demonstrate strengths at school. Set up times in which the student can assist peers. (pp. 4–5)

Reeve (1990) added these recommendations.

- Help the child get started with individual seat work. Have the child verbalize to you what the task is and how he or she is to approach it. Check back periodically to see if the child is still on track.
- Make frequent contact with the child by touching or speaking the child's name. Be sure that you have his or her attention before speaking. . . .
- Give the child extra time to work on assignments or exams, without criticism or fanfare. . . .
- If note taking is a problem, arrange to have a more attentive classmate share notes by photocopying or using carbon paper; or give the child your notes.
- Use multiple choice or one-to-one oral tests to assess the child's mastery of content.
- Give regular feedback and praise successes. (p. 75)

Finally, Bender and Mathes (1995) presented these suggestions for organizing the classroom.

- Use a physically structured classroom rather than an "open" classroom. Having walls and a door will block out distractions in the hallway.
- Seat students away from noise. Be cognizant of auditory as well as visual distractions. Seat students away from the door and from auditory distractions.
- Place desks away from each other. Space desks one arm or leg length apart. . . .
- Provide two desks for each student with ADHD. Students with ADHD may stand up and leave their desk without realizing why. Provide a second desk for them to go to when this happens, and acknowledge to the class that the student has a right to change desks when he or she wishes.
- Alternate activities to eliminate desk fatigue. Provide activities that encourage active responding, such as working at the board, "Simon Says," or standing or sitting to indicate a "yes" or "no" answer. (p. 229)

For additional ideas, see Brown, Ilderton, and Taylor (2001), Carbone (2001), or Stormont (2008). For tips for parents, consult *Identifying and Treating Attention Deficit Hyperactivity Disorder:*

A Resource for School and Home (U.S. Department of Education, 2008), a pamphlet available for downloading from the Department of Education's website (*http://www.ed.gov/rschstat/research/pubs/adhd/adhd-identifying.html*). The "Window on the Web" feature describes the website of CHADD, an organization for parents and families of individuals with ADHD. This site is a rich source of ideas for classroom adaptations.

In this chapter, you have learned about ways to adapt classroom instruction for students with learning disabilities and those with ADHD. Check the "Things to Remember" feature to review ways to meet the needs of students with learning disabilities and others with academic learning problems.

Things to Remember

- The most common area in which adaptations are made for general education students with learning disabilities is academic instruction; these students may require assistance in acquiring basic skills and/or learning content-area information.

- Major indicators of learning disabilities are a discrepancy between expected and actual achievement, variation in performance, and difficulty learning despite adequate instruction.

- In assessment of learning disabilities, information is gathered about intellectual performance, academic achievement, information processing abilities, and strategies for learning; the general education teacher assists by collecting classroom performance data.

- Two approaches to the instruction of students with learning disabilities are remediation and compensation. The goal of remediation is the improvement of weaknesses; compensatory strategies, on the other hand, bypass or make up for weaknesses by using the strengths of the student.

- Remediation is used to teach younger students the basic skills of reading, handwriting, spelling, written expression, and math.

- In basic skills instruction, three adaptations are recommended: prompts, extra instruction, and additional guided practice.

- With older students, compensatory strategies are used to bypass basic skill deficiencies in order to teach content-area subjects.

- In content-area instruction, reading assignments, written work and exams, and math demands are modified by changing task criteria and characteristics.

- The most common compensatory strategy is the substitution of oral language tasks for reading and writing tasks.

- Inattention, distractibility, impulsiveness, and hyperactivity are indicators of ADHD.

- Instruction is modified for students with ADHD by increasing the structure of the learning environment and by eliminating distractions that compete with academic tasks for students' attention.

ACTIVITIES

1. Visit a special education resource room that serves students with learning disabilities. Observe the students and talk with the teacher. In what school subjects do students experience the most difficulty? What subjects are taught by the special education teacher? In what instructional activities do these students participate in the general education classroom?

2. Select one of the special education journals that focuses on learning disabilities. Choose from the *Journal of Learning Disabilities*, *Learning Disabilities Research & Practice*, and *Learning Disabilities: A Multidisciplinary Journal*. Look through recent issues for articles that present inclusion suggestions. Collect ideas for making instructional adaptations in the general education classroom.

3. Among the websites described in this chapter's "Window on the Web" features are those of two large parent organizations, the Learning Disabilities Association (LDA) and CHADD (Children and Adults with Attention-Deficit/Hyperactivity Disorder). Visit these sites, then compare them with that of the Division for Learning Disabilities (DLD), a professional organization that is part of the Council for Exceptional Children. Which sites have information for parents? Teachers? Both?

4. Pretend that you are a student with learning disabilities enrolled in a college course. You are doing quite well but anticipate that you will have trouble on the final exam. You fear that you won't be able to finish in the allotted 2 hours. How would you explain this to your instructor? What alternatives or instructional modifications could you suggest?

5. If possible, review one of the word processing programs described in "Spotlight on Technology" feature in this chapter. What are the program's major advantages for students with learning disabilities? Do you see any drawbacks? Would the program be equally effective for elementary and secondary students? If these programs are not available, try using your own word processor to check the spelling of the following sentences written by a sixth grader with learning disabilities.

   The student wrote:

   once a upon a time ther was some gis and women in the woods. thes man and women are like cavmen.

   The student read:

   Once upon a time there was some girls and women in the woods. These men and women are like cavemen.

   Did your spelling checker find all of the errors? Was it able to suggest the correct spelling?

CHAPTER
ELEVEN

Teaching Students with Intellectual Disabilities

Judy

Judy is a fourth grade student with a mild intellectual disability. In most areas of academic and social development, 10-year-old Judy performs like a student who is 7 or 8. Her reading and math computation skills are at the second grade level, and her spelling skills are at the first grade level. At home, most of Judy's playmates are younger than she is; she enjoys interacting with first and second graders but doesn't appear interested in the more advanced games and activities of her age-mates. At school, Judy spends most of her day in a regular fourth grade classroom and she has made friends with several of her classmates. In the morning, the special education resource teacher comes to Judy's classroom to teach reading to Judy and four other students. In the afternoon, Judy visits the resource room for instruction in spelling, handwriting, and written expression. Judy receives instruction from Mrs. Thomas, her fourth grade teacher, in math, art, music, and physical education. To help Judy succeed in fourth grade math, Mrs. Thomas modifies assignments and exams and provides Judy with extra practice in computational skills. Also, Judy's math program includes practice in the application of basic skills to daily life problems. For instance, she is learning to add and subtract money and to make change.

Joe

Joe is a high school student with a mild intellectual disability who is 15 years old and in the ninth grade. Joe wants to learn a marketable skill in high school so that he can get a job when he graduates. Because his basic academic skills are at approximately the fifth grade level, Joe attends special education classes in Basic English and Basic Math. He is also enrolled in Career Exploration, a special education course that surveys several job options and provides instruction in general vocational skills, such as punctuality, job-related social skills, work completion, and filling out job applications.

Joe attends two general education classes—Automotive Technology I and Physical Education. With the assistance of his general and special education teachers, Joe is earning passing grades in auto tech. Ms. Frye, Joe's reading teacher, provides tapes of textbooks so that Joe can keep up with reading assignments. Mr. Nash, the auto tech teacher, adapts the written assignments for Joe and allows him to take quizzes and exams orally. In addition, Joe's Career Exploration teacher works closely with Mr. Nash to ensure that Joe acquires the basic work skills important in auto shops. If Joe continues to succeed in his vocational education class, next year he will advance to Automotive Technology II.

LOOKING AHEAD

Later in this chapter you will see portions of Judy's special education assessment results as well as her IEP. You will also learn strategies for helping students like Judy and Joe to learn important academic skills and work habits—and to apply those skills and habits to real-life problems. As you read this chapter, think about how you might answer these questions.

- What are Judy's areas of strengths at school and at home? How would you describe her social development in relation to other 10-year-olds?
- Judy will be entering middle school quite soon. In what areas would you anticipate she will need the most support in making the transition?
- Joe wants to get a job when he graduates from high school. What academic skills will he need to successfully pursue his vocational plans? What general work habits will be the most important for him to learn?

Intellectual disabilities are comprehensive disabilities. They affect not only school learning, but also the development of language, social, and vocational skills. Students with intellectual disabilities are able to learn, but their learning proceeds more slowly than that of students with average ability. Consequently, students with intellectual disabilities often perform at a level expected of younger students. At age 6, pupils with mild intellectual disabilities may act like average 4-year-olds; at age 10, their school achievement may resemble that of second or third graders. Because it is difficult for these students to learn quickly, it is crucial that instruction focus on important areas that will help them become self-supporting adults. For most students with mild intellectual disabilities, much of this instruction occurs in the general education classroom. With the aid and assistance of general and special educators, students with mild intellectual disabilities can successfully participate in many classroom activities.

Students with mild intellectual disabilities have special needs in academic, classroom behavioral, physical, and social performance and may require individualized assistance from special educators in several of these areas. In addition, when students with mild intellectual disabilities are included in regular classes, the general education teacher must often modify classroom procedures for academic instruction. Younger students like Judy, who is described in the "Students' Stories" section, may need extra help in basic skills such as reading, math, and spelling; such students may also require help in learning to generalize skills from one situation to another. In middle school and high school, students like Joe often continue their study of basic skills and begin to acquire important career skills; when included in general education, they may participate in regular vocational education classes. Throughout the school years, instruction for youngsters with mild intellectual disabilities focuses on the development of basic academic skills and the application of these and other skills to career preparation.

This chapter describes the characteristics of students with mild intellectual disabilities. It also presents methods for the general education teacher to use in gathering data, teaching functional academic skills, and improving students' general work habits. Most students with intellectual disabilities have mild disabilities. Students are considered to have a severe intellectual disability when their limitations are moderate or severe, rather than mild. Students with severe intellectual disabilities are often members of special classes located in neighborhood schools; some are included in regular classrooms.

The final section of this chapter addresses this group of learners and suggests ways to promote the inclusion of students with severe intellectual disabilities as members of the school community and to adapt classroom instruction to meet severe learning needs. To become more familiar with intellectual disabilities, consult one of the resources described in the accompanying "Window on the Web" feature.

 ## INDICATORS OF INTELLECTUAL DISABILITIES

The general educator is an important member of the inclusion team for students with mild intellectual disabilities. These students usually begin their education in the general education classroom and are referred for special education assessment when they are slow to acquire basic academic skills. The classroom teacher plays a role not only in instruction, but also in identification and referral; in addition, general education services are coordinated with the services of special educators such as the resource teacher.

 To hear a Teacher of the Year discuss teaching students with intellectual disabilities, go to the Teacher Talk section of Topic *Intellectual Disabilities* in the MyEducationLab for your course and listen to the piece from *Ann Marie Taylor, South Carolina: I Teach to be Part of the Solution.*

Students are generally identified as having mild intellectual disabilities during the first few years of school. There are two main indicators of mild intellectual disabilities. First, although such students are able to learn, their rate of learning is slow. Because of this, their level of development resembles that

Students with Mild Intellectual Disabilities

- Intellectual disabilities are one of the most common disabilities; in fall 2004, 9.3% of the students served in special education programs were identified as having intellectual disabilities (U.S. Department of Education, 2002).
- There is still concern today about the overrepresentation of students from some racial/ethnic groups in special education programs for individuals with mild intellectual disabilities (Artiles & Trent, 1994; Chinn & Hughes, 1987; Janesick, 1995). According to a study by Harry (cited in U.S. Department of Education, 1996), African American students made up 16% of the U.S. school population but 35% of students identified as having mild intellectual disabilities.
- The President's Committee for People with Intellectual Disabilities (formerly the President's Committee on Mental Retardation) (2004) estimates that approximately 3% of the population has an intellectual disability.
- Individuals with mild intellectual disabilities account for approximately 87% of persons with any type of intellectual disability (The Arc, 2002).

- For most persons with mild intellectual disabilities, the cause of the disability is unknown (Hallahan & Kauffman, 1988; Morrison & Polloway, 1995; Smith, 2004).
- According to Kirk and Gallagher (1979), students with mild intellectual disabilities are those who are able to profit from academic instruction; the IQ range associated with this group is 50 to 70 or 75, which is equivalent to that of adults with mental ages of 7.5 to 11 years (Becker, Engelmann, & Thomas, 1975).
- During their school years, students with mild intellectual disabilities acquire basic academic skills up to approximately the sixth grade level; as adults they can achieve the necessary social and vocational skills to become at least minimally self-supporting (President's Committee on Mental Retardation, 1975; The Arc, 2002).
- The most typical special education placement for students with mild intellectual disabilities is part-time service in a resource room or special class. During the remainder of their school day, they are included with age peers in the general education classroom (Blake, 1981; Heward, 2006).

of younger children. For example, a second grade student may be just beginning to learn to say the alphabet, count, and write his or her name. The second indicator is that most areas of development are delayed. Unlike students with learning disabilities, individuals with intellectual disabilities perform poorly on most tasks when compared to peers. Their disability is comprehensive; it impinges on performance at school, at home, in the neighborhood, and in the community. These students fail to meet age expectations in intellectual and language development, academic achievement, social competence, and prevocational skills.

Students with mild intellectual disabilities, although characterized by slower learning rates, are able to profit from many of the instructional activities in the general education classroom. These individuals make up the great majority of all persons with intellectual disabilities. Heward (2006) provided this optimistic description of the effects of mild intellectual disabilities:

> Many children with mild [intellectual disabilities] are not identified until they enter school and sometimes not until the second or third grade, when more difficult academic work is required. Most students with mild [intellectual disabilities] master academic skills up to about the sixth grade level and are able to learn job skills well enough to support themselves independently or semi-independently. (p. 146)

Students with mild intellectual disabilities learn in the same ways that average students do. However, some types of learning cause them particular difficulty. For example, reading comprehension skills appear more difficult for students with mild intellectual disabilities than reading recognition skills. Similarly, such students are less successful with math problem solving than math computation (Thomas & Patton, 1990). Evidence also suggests that students with mild intellectual

disabilities have memory and attention problems and difficulty applying learned skills to new situations (Drew, Logan, & Hardman, 1992; Forness & Kavale, 1993; Turnbull, Turnbull, Shank, & Smith, 2004).

These and other indicators of mild intellectual disabilities can be noticed by the general education teacher. Students who learn slowly, perform at a level appropriate for younger individuals, and show consistent delays in several areas are prime candidates for referral for special education assessment. Consult the "For Your Information" material to learn more about students with mild intellectual disabilities.

 ASSESSMENT PROCEDURES

When intellectual disabilities are suspected, the multidisciplinary team meets and prepares an assessment plan. According to McLoughlin and Lewis (2008), it is important to collect information about at least three areas of current performance: academic achievement, intellectual functioning, and adaptive behavior. However, there is some variation in the specific guidelines that states use to determine eligibility for public school services for students with intellectual disabilities. States differ in the IQ scores used as cutoffs for determining eligibility. Also, although impaired adaptive behavior is generally accepted as an important indicator of intellectual disabilities, not all states include this area in their definition of this disability (Bruininks, Thurlow, & Gilman, 1987; Patrick & Reschly, 1982). Therefore, teachers must become aware of the specific guidelines in force in their states and school districts.

When individuals are referred for consideration for special education services for students with intellectual disabilities, academic achievement is measured to determine whether

FIGURE 11-1 Special Education Assessment Results

Student: Judy **Age:** 10 years, 5 months **Grade:** 4

Academic Performance

Judy was administered the standard achievement battery of the *Woodcock-Johnson III* by Mrs. Simeon, the resource teacher. These results were obtained:

Area	Grade Score	Standard Score	Percentile Rank
Broad Reading	1.8	68	2
Broad Mathematics	2.8	73	3
Broad Written Language	1.6	62	1

Judy's skills fall in the low average to below average range of performance in all areas, a result confirmed by her fourth grade teacher, Mrs. Thomas. Judy's grade scores indicate performance at the grade 1 to grade 2 level. In Broad Reading, she earned a percentile rank of 2, which indicates that her performance was equal to or better than that of only 2 percent of her age peers in the test's norm group. In Broad Written Language, she achieved a percentile rank of 1. Her performance was somewhat better in Math, where she earned a percentile rank of 3. These results indicate serious achievement problems in three basic skill areas, with the most severe problems occurring in reading and written language skills.

Intellectual Performance

The *Wechsler Intelligence Scale–Fourth Edition* was administered to Judy by Mr. Henry, the school psychologist. Judy's intelligence quotient (IQ) scores were as follows:

Verbal Comprehension	64
Perceptual Reasoning	61
Working Memory	58
Processing Speed	60
Full Scale	59

All IQ scores fall within the below average range. These results point to the possibility of mild intellectual disabilities.

Adaptive Behavior

Mrs. Simeon interviewed Judy's parents to learn more about Judy's performance at home and in community situations. The *Scales of Independent Behavior–Revised* were used for this purpose, with the following results:

Area	Standard Score
Motor Skills	82
Social Interaction and Communication Skills	65
Personal Living Skills	68
Community Living Skills	72

Judy's adaptive behavior, as reported by her parents, fell in the below average range of performance in two areas, Social Interaction and Communication Skills and Personal Living Skills. This finding, along with the results of other measures and the information provided by Judy's classroom teacher, supports the conclusion of mild intellectual disabilities. Intellectual performance is below average, adaptive behavior appears to be impaired, and academic achievement falls within the low average and below average ranges.

there is an educational performance problem. The *Peabody Individual Achievement Test–Revised/Normative Update (PIAT-R/NU)* (Markwardt, 1998) can be administered, or the team can select another individual measure, such as the achievement portion of the *Woodcock-Johnson III (WJ III)* (Woodcock, McGrew, & Mather, 2001).

The *WJ III*, which is generally administered by the school psychologist or special educator, is appropriate for students from age 2 through adulthood. Its standard battery assesses reading, oral language, mathematics, written language, and academic knowledge. Grade and age scores, standard scores, and percentile rank scores are available for each subtest and each academic skill area. The mean (or average) standard score on the *WJ III* is 100, and scores between 85 and 115 are considered to be within the average range of performance. The assessment results in Figure 11-1 show that Judy, introduced at the beginning of this chapter, is performing below grade level expectations in all academic subjects assessed by the *WJ III*.

Another major step in assessment is the determination of the student's general ability level. This is particularly important if mild intellectual disabilities are suspected because below average intellectual performance is one of the criteria for this disability. The *Wechsler Intelligence Scale for Children–Fourth Edition (WISC–IV)* (Wechsler, 2003) is usually used to assess global ability in school-aged children. Judy's assessment results in Figure 11-1 include *WISC–IV* scores; all IQs fall below 70, which indicates current functioning in the below-average range.

Adaptive behavior is a third consideration in assessment when intellectual disabilities are suspected. According to the most recent definition by the American Association on Intellectual and Developmental Disabilities (American Association on Mental Retardation, 2002), it is important to document not only below average intellectual performance but also impaired adaptive behavior. Measures such as the *AAMR Adaptive Behavior Scale–School* (2nd ed.) (Lambert, Nihira, & Leland, 1993) and the *Scales of Independent Behavior–Revised (SIB–R)* (Bruininks, Woodcock, Weatherman, & Hill, 1996) can be used to gather information about the student's social competence.

On the *AAMR* scale, teachers and others rate the student's performance in areas such as independent functioning, physical development, economic activity, language development, and numbers and time; the scale is appropriate for use with students ages 3 to 21. The *SIB–R*, designed for preschool through adulthood, uses interviews with parents, teachers, or others to gather information about current functioning levels. This measure assesses several different aspects of adaptive behavior: Motor Skills, Social Interaction and Communication Skills, Personal Living Skills, and Community Living Skills. Several types of scores are available, including standard scores and percentile ranks. The case of Judy in Figure 11-1 illustrates a student with low performance in two areas of adaptive behavior.

If a student is found to perform below age expectations in academic achievement, general intellectual ability, and adaptive behavior, the team may decide that the student is eligible for special education services for students with intellectual disabilities. The next step is to determine the precise educational needs of the student. All members of the team, including the student's parent(s), have valuable information to contribute; however, the general education teacher is probably the person most knowledgeable about the student's current academic skill levels. Before an educational program for a student with mild intellectual disabilities can be planned, information is needed about current school performance and the student's ability to use basic academic skills to solve daily life problems. Also, the prevocational and career skills of the student must be considered. Teachers can develop informal assessments for this purpose, or they can choose from commercially available measures, such as the criterion-referenced tests by Brigance.

BRIGANCE® inventories are available for a wide range of age levels:

- *Diagnostic Inventory of Early Development–II* (Brigance, 2004) for children from birth to developmental age 7,
- *Diagnostic Comprehensive Inventory of Basic Skills–Revised* (Brigance, 1999) for grades prekindergarten through 9,
- *Employability Skills Inventory* (Brigance, 1995a) for grades 3 through high school, and
- *Life Skills Inventory* (Brigance, 1995b) for secondary students and adults.

A special feature of the two *BRIGANCE®* inventories for older students is their coverage of basic academic skills not only in isolation but also as applied to daily life and vocational areas. Table 11-1 lists some of the functional skills subtests that teachers can choose from each of these measures.

The *BRIGANCE®* inventories allow teachers to determine which skills have been mastered by the student and which must still be taught. Each criterion-referenced test includes simple directions for administration and scoring, plus a recommended instructional objective for the skill. These objectives, if appropriate for the student, can aid the team in preparation of the IEP.

T A B L E   1 1 - 1   Selected Functional Skills Subtests from the *BRIGANCE®* Inventories

Inventory	Area	Selected Subtests
Life Skills Inventory	Speaking and Listening Skills	Personal Data Response
	Functional Writing Skills	Forms Requiring Personal Data
	Words on Common Signs and Warning Labels	Signs That Direct, Community Signs, Medicine Labels and Warning Labels on Other Containers
	Telephone Skills	Basic Telephone Skills
	Money and Finance	Equivalent Values of Coins and the Dollar Bill, Makes Change
	Food	Restaurant Vocabulary, Labels on Packaged Food
	Clothing	Personal Clothing Sizes, Clothing Labels
	Health	Basic Medical Vocabulary, Effects of Drugs
Employability Skills Inventory	Career Awareness and Self-Understanding	Job Interests and Attitudes
	Job-Seeking Skills and Knowledge	Job Interview Questions
	Reading Skills	Words Found on Employment Forms, Warning and Safety Signs, Warning Labels
	Pre-employment Writing	Simple Application for Employment
	Math Skills and Concepts	Uses a Calendar, Measures with Inch Ruler, Future Time on Clock

Note: From the *BRIGANCE® Life Skills Inventory* and from the *BRIGANCE® Employability Skills Inventory.* Copyright 1995 by Curriculum Associates. Reproduced by permission of the publisher.

 SPECIAL SERVICES

Individualized education programs for students with mild intellectual disabilities usually contain several annual goals. Typical areas of instruction are reading, math, oral language, written language, and vocational preparation and other types of transition services. Special education services can be provided by the resource teacher or, for students with severe delays, the teacher of a special class. Others such as the speech–language clinician and the adapted physical education teacher often provide support services for children and adolescents with mild intellectual disabilities.

> **myeducationlab** To hear a Teacher of the Year discuss teaching students with intellectual disabilities, go to the Teacher Talk section of Topic *Intellectual Disabilities* in the MyEducationLab for your course and listen to the piece from *Conney Dahn, Florida: I Want My Students with Severe Disabilities to Graduate and Get a Job.*

These students with special needs are included in general education programs to the maximum extent appropriate. Some may participate in only nonacademic classroom activities such as art, music, and physical education; others, like Judy and Joe, are included in academic programming. A portion of Judy's IEP in Figure 11-2 shows that, although Judy visits the resource room for an hour each afternoon, the majority of her instruction takes place in the fourth grade classroom.

 Go to the Assignments and Activities section of Topic *Intellectual Disabilities* in the MyEducationLab for your course and complete the activity entitled *Paraprofessional Support.*

CLASSROOM ADAPTATIONS

Classroom instruction is the primary area in which adaptations are made for students with mild intellectual disabilities in general education programs; this section focuses on methods for meeting the special academic needs of these students. Some individuals with mild intellectual disabilities also require assistance in the area of classroom conduct. Elsewhere in this book there are strategies for controlling disruptive behaviors and suggestions for increasing the social acceptance of students with special needs who have difficulty relating to classmates.

Habilitation is the major approach to the education of mainstreamed students with mild intellectual disabilities. The goal is not to remediate or compensate for skill deficiencies; instead, instruction is directed toward the development of the crucial skills necessary for successful adulthood. Habilitation is the process of becoming capable or qualified; for students with mild intellectual disabilities, this means the acquisition of skills that are important for daily life, citizenship, and a future career. Because these students learn more slowly than their age peers, their educational program must concentrate on the most crucial and functional skills.

 FIGURE 11-2 IEP Goals and Services for Judy

Annual Goals

1. By the end of the school year, Judy will read grade 2 material with adequate word recognition and comprehension.
   Person responsible: Resource teacher
2. By the end of the school year, Judy will correctly spell a minimum of 100 high-frequency words.
   Person responsible: Resource teacher
3. By the end of the school year, Judy will legibly print all lower- and uppercase manuscript letters.
   Person responsible: Resource teacher
4. By the end of the school year, Judy will write simple sentences and personal information, such as her name, address, and telephone number.
   Person responsible: Resource teacher
5. By the end of the school year, Judy will perform math computation problems at grade 3.5 level.
   Person responsible: Fourth grade teacher
6. By the end of the school year, Judy will achieve minimum competencies in math application skills such as time, money, and measurement.
   Person responsible: Fourth grade teacher
7. Judy will successfully complete minimum requirements for fourth grade art, music, and physical education.
   Person responsible: Fourth grade teacher

Amount of Participation in General Education
Judy will receive instruction in the regular fourth grade class for the entire day except for 1 hour in the afternoon.

Special Education and Related Services

1. The resource teacher will provide special education services to Judy for 1 hour each morning in the fourth grade classroom (goal 1) and for 1 hour each afternoon in the resource room (goals 2, 3, and 4).
2. The resource teacher will provide consultation for Judy's fourth grade teacher as needed.

Transition and **career education** services are one way of conceptualizing the habilitation process for students with mild intellectual disabilities. According to the Council for Exceptional Children (1993a), career education and transition are "the totality of experiences through which one learns to live a meaningful, satisfying work life." Brolin (1986) expanded this definition:

> Career education is not simply preparation for a job. It is also preparation for other productive work roles that comprise one's total career functioning. This includes the work of a homemaker and family member, the participation as a citizen and volunteer, and the engagement in productive leisure and recreational pursuits that are of benefit to oneself and others. (p. vii)

Kokaska and Brolin (1985) identified three major curriculum areas important in preparing for adulthood: daily living skills, personal–social skills, and occupational skills; specific competency areas are listed in Figure 11-3. In the system described by Cronin and Patton (1993), life skills are organized into six major domains: employment–education, home and family, leisure pursuits, personal responsibility and relationships, emotional–physical health, and community involvement.

FIGURE 11-3 **Important Competencies for Adulthood**

Daily Living Skills
Managing family finances
Selecting, managing, and maintaining a home
Caring for personal needs
Raising children—family living
Buying and preparing food
Buying and caring for clothing
Engaging in civic activities
Utilizing recreation and leisure
Getting around the community (mobility)

Personal-Social Skills
Achieving self-awareness
Acquiring self-confidence
Achieving socially responsible behavior
Maintaining good interpersonal skills
Achieving independence
Achieving problem-solving skills
Communicating adequately with others

Occupational Skills
Knowing and exploring occupational possibilities
Selecting and planning occupational choices
Exhibiting appropriate work habits and behaviors
Exhibiting sufficient physical-manual skills
Obtaining a specific occupational skill
Seeking, securing, and maintaining employment

Note: Reprinted with permission of Merrill, an imprint of Macmillan Publishing Company, from *Career Education for Handicapped Individuals* (2nd ed., pp. 46–47) by C. J. Kokaska and D. E. Brolin. Copyright © 1985 Merrill Publishing Company, Columbus, Ohio.

One important factor to consider in a transition and career education program is the sequence in which competencies are presented. Kokaska (1980) recommended the following progression for students with special needs:

- career awareness (kindergarten onward)
- career exploration (Grade 6 onward)
- career preparation (Grade 6–7 onward)
- career placement, follow-up, and continuing education (Grade 10 onward) (p. 38)

In the last two stages, career preparation and career placement, students may have the opportunity to participate in supervised job placements on the school campus and in the community. Community-based training is an important component of career preparation for students with mild intellectual disabilities because it promotes the generalization of work skills to actual work environments.

Transition and career education training can be infused into the general education classroom curriculum in several ways. First, by providing academic skill instruction, the general education teacher emphasizes one important component of career preparation: literacy. Being able to read and write at functional levels is essential for most work and many life tasks. Second, the classroom teacher can help students by providing instruction and practice in the application of basic school and work skills to life problems. Such assistance is particularly important for students with mild intellectual disabilities, who often have difficulty generalizing skills and information from one situation to another. Third, a portion of the general education curriculum can be devoted to career awareness and exploration. At the secondary level, much of the curriculum is already career oriented; students learn specific job skills in vocational classes, and in college preparatory courses students acquire skills and information necessary for further training.

The following sections present methods for teaching students with mild intellectual disabilities in the general education classroom. Included are ways to teach functional academic skills and techniques for improving students' general work habits.

 TEACHING FUNCTIONAL ACADEMICS

Students with mild intellectual disabilities need special help to acquire the basic skills of reading, handwriting, spelling, written expression, and math. Typically, they receive instruction in these areas from the special education teacher; many students also participate in instructional activities in the general education classroom. In teaching basic skills to persons with mild intellectual disabilities, the classroom teacher will find the techniques recommended for students with learning disabilities useful. Academic instruction can be adapted by providing prompts, giving additional instruction, and allowing extra guided practice. For students who learn slowly and require much repetition and practice, computers can be a useful tool for learning academic skills. See the accompanying "Spotlight on Technology" material for information about software programs that help develop basic reading skills.

myeducationlab Go to the Assignments and Activities section of Topic *Intellectual Disabilities* in the MyEducationLab for your course and complete the activity entitled *Functional Curriculum*.

The need to provide instruction and practice in skill generalization is a major consideration when teaching students with mild intellectual disabilities. These students have difficulty applying skills and information learned in one situation to a new but similar problem or situation. For example, a student might add and subtract whole numbers easily when given a worksheet of computation problems, but be unable to apply this skill to adding and subtracting coins. For this reason, educational programs for students with intellectual disabilities focus on **functional skills,** that is, skills required for the satisfactory performance of everyday life tasks. Basic skills instruction must go beyond textbooks and workbook pages; it must extend into the real world if students with intellectual disabilities and other special needs are to use tool subjects to solve the problems of everyday life.

Two major strategies are used for teaching functional academic skills. In one, the **unit approach,** instruction in several basic skill areas is integrated around a central theme of interest and value to the students; this approach is probably best used with younger students. In the other approach, reading, writing, and math are taught as separate subjects, but functional practice activities are designed to promote generalization of skills to life problems.

SPOTLIGHT ON TECHNOLOGY

Developing Basic Reading Skills

Computers can be used to develop reading skills in children just beginning to learn to read and in older students with difficulties in reading. For this to occur, it is necessary to use software that talks. The programs described here offer high-quality digitized (prerecorded) speech.

Phonics Instruction with *Simon S. I. O.*

Simon S. I. O. ("Sounds It Out") from Don Johnston, Inc. (http://www.donjohnston.com) is designed to help students learn the sounds that correspond to letters. This sequential program contains more than 50 levels, and levels are based on word families. For example, in Stage 1 of *Simon S. I. O.*, the first level is based on the *at* word family and introduces the sounds associated with the letters *b* and *r*. Level 20 of Stage 1 is based on the *eed* word family; it introduces the sounds associated with *w* and *sp*.

Among the activities in *Simon S. I. O.* are identifying the first sound of words, the last sound, and both sounds; spelling words; reading words aloud and recording them; and finding a word when it is pronounced. As these examples show, the screen display is consistent from activity to activity.

Note: Courtesy of Don Johnston, Inc.

Simon, the tutor, appears in the upper left-hand corner. He gives instructions and provides feedback on the student's responses. The "pronouncer" (a small speaker beneath Simon) reads the words and sounds aloud. Help is always available, and the student can move from one activity to another using the activity bar at the top of the screen.

Developing Phonics and Spelling Skills with *WordMaker*

WordMaker (http://www.donjohnston.com) is an interesting program that provides students with opportunities to practice phonemic awareness, manipulate letters, spell words, sort words by rhyme, and see what they have learned as a word wall. In the sample screen, the student hears a word, in this case *sun,* and must drag letters to the blanks to spell the word. To find out whether the word is spelled correctly, the student clicks on the check mark in the upper right-hand corner.

In later activities, the screen shows a similar task without picture cues. For example, the student might be asked to select from

Note: Courtesy of Don Johnston, Inc.

Note: Courtesy of Don Johnston, Inc.

several available letters to spell the word *glow*. *WordMaker* keeps a record of student progress, and the words the student learns are presented on a word wall that can be printed.

Learning Sight Words with the *Edmark Reading* Program

Originally designed as a print program, *Edmark Reading* is now available as a software program (*http://www.riverdeep.net/edmark/*). The program focuses on teaching beginning reading skills, with emphasis on words from the high-frequency Dolch list. Level 1 of the program teaches 150 words and Level 2 teaches 200 additional words. The instructional sequence is very systematic, with numerous opportunities for learners to practice skills. Among the lesson formats are Prereading (i.e., matching), Word Recognition, Word Practice, and Stories.

Increasing Reading Fluency with *Read Naturally*

Read Naturally is a program designed to increase students' reading fluency and comprehension. Available in both print and software editions (*http://www.readnaturally.com*), *Read Naturally* encourages faster, more accurate reading via three strategies: modeling, repeated reading, and progress monitoring. To begin, the student reads a brief nonfiction passage on the screen and clicks on difficult words. In the software version, the program determines the number of words read correctly (i.e., those not marked as difficult) within a 1-minute time period. This is called a "cold" timing. The student reads along as the passage is read aloud by a narrator, and finally practices the passage without the narrator's assistance (see the sample screen). Before the student can "pass" a passage, he or she must reach goal, have three or fewer errors, read with expression, and answer all questions correctly.

Note: Used with permission from Read Naturally, St. Paul, MN.

The Unit Approach

Instructional units allow the teacher to present functional academics in a meaningful context. First, an important life theme is selected; then, basic skills are presented, and practice opportunities related to the theme are provided. Meyen (1981) provided two examples. The first unit, "Time," is intended for intermediate grade students. Basic skills instruction and practice are included within subtopics such as recreation, seasons, measurement, money, and holidays. The second unit, "Home Safety and Maintenance," is also for intermediate grade students. It features subtopics such as basic first aid, emergencies, and drugs and poisonous substances.

Many unit themes would be appropriate for students with special needs and other members of general education classes. For example, "Becoming a Consumer" is a topic that could be adapted to varying skill, age, and interest levels. For younger students, this unit could be used to teach basic money skills, such as identifying coins and bills, adding and subtracting amounts of money, and making change. For older (or more capable) students, appropriate consumer skills are reading advertisements, comparison shopping, and installment buying. Other flexible unit themes are transportation (e.g., riding the school bus, using public transportation, driving a car), getting a job (e.g., chores at home, the want ads, job applications and interviews), and money management (e.g., budgeting your allowance, using the automatic teller machine and bank, handling paychecks and taxes).

Functional Practice Activities

The classroom teacher can design practice activities in any basic skill area so that they relate to daily life problems. One source of ideas for functional activities is a transition and career education curriculum, such as the one outlined earlier in Figure 11-3. The key factor to be kept in mind when developing practice tasks is their relevance to life and work activities. Of course, the teacher must also consider the students' skill levels and the amount of supervision required during student practice.

Reading is an excellent skill to practice with everyday materials. Activities can focus on reading for information or reading as a leisure activity. Some examples of reading materials appropriate for functional activities are listed here.

- Signs commonly found in buildings and in the community (e.g., *Women, Men, Stop, Do Not Enter*)
- Community and student newspapers and magazines

- Menus for quick-service and regular restaurants
- Schedules for classes, television, movies, buses, and trains
- The telephone book
- Advertisements for consumer goods and jobs
- Directions for building models, assembling toys, or completing forms
- Labels on foods, medicines, and clothing

Figure 11-4 lists important career and vocational words suggested by Schilit and Caldwell (1980); practice of words such as these is appropriate for secondary students.

Many daily life activities can be used to practice handwriting, spelling, and written expression. The tasks that follow emphasize writing as a means of practical communication.

- Making a shopping list or a things-to-do list
- Leaving a note for a friend or family member
- Writing a text or an e-mail message
- Writing a postcard, invitation, or friendly letter
- Completing a job application form
- Ordering something online by completing an order form
- Writing a business e-mail or letter
- Applying for a Social Security number or a driver's permit
- Writing down a telephone message for someone

The skill area of math also offers numerous opportunities for functional practice. Computation ability is often required in everyday life, particularly in tasks involving time, money, and measurement. Examples follow.

- Making a purchase
- Budgeting an allowance or paycheck
- Comparison shopping
- Using a checking or savings account
- Using a credit card
- Applying for a loan
- Selecting and preparing food
- Using measurement, as in reading a thermometer, determining a person's weight and height, and measuring the length and width of a room
- Using time, as in telling time, using a calendar, and computing time (e.g., "If it takes 20 minutes to walk to school, at what time must you leave home to arrive at school at 8:00 A.M.?")

Functional tasks often require more than one basic skill. For instance, in planning and cooking a meal, several skills are needed: reading (ads, labels, cooking and preparation directions), writing (shopping list), and math (buying foods, measuring ingredients, computing cooking times). When tasks such as these are used with students with special needs, the teacher should be sure that the students are proficient in all necessary skills; that is, a math practice activity should be designed so that low reading skills are not an obstacle.

 FIGURE 11-4 Important Career and Vocational Words

1. rules	26. supervisor	51. entrance	76. withholding
2. boss	27. vacation	52. responsibility	77. vote
3. emergency	28. apply	53. hospital	78. break
4. danger	29. fulltime	54. hourly rate	79. cooperation
5. job	30. income	55. schedule	80. dependable
6. social security	31. quit	56. instructions	81. money
7. first-aid	32. check	57. save	82. physical
8. help-wanted	33. careful	58. union	83. hazardous
9. safety	34. dangerous	59. credit	84. net income
10. warning	35. employee	60. elevator	85. strike
11. signature	36. layoff	61. punctuality	86. owner
12. time	37. take-home-pay	62. rights	87. repair
13. attendance	38. unemployed	63. hours	88. alarm
14. absent	39. cost	64. payroll	89. gross income
15. telephone	40. deduction	65. attitude	90. manager
16. bill	41. fired	66. reliable	91. reference
17. hired	42. closed	67. work	92. uniform
18. overtime	43. parttime	68. caution	93. hard-hat
19. punch in	44. correct	69. license	94. authority
20. directions	45. foreman	70. poison	95. training
21. paycheck	46. time-and-a-half	71. office	96. holiday
22. wages	47. worker	72. power	97. late
23. appointment	48. buy	73. qualifications	98. personal
24. income tax	49. raise	74. earn	99. tools
25. interview	50. on-the-job	75. transportation	100. areas

Note: From "A Word List of Essential Career/Vocational Words for Mentally Retarded Students" by J. Schilit and M. L. Caldwell, 1980, *Education and Training of the Mentally Retarded, 15,* p. 115. Copyright 1980 by The Council for Exceptional Children. Reprinted with permission.

Differential Grading

Report cards are a major way for teachers to inform parents of their children's progress in school. However, with students with special needs, grading performance in general education classes is often difficult. How should the teacher grade Judy, who is included in the fourth grade class but is successfully completing math assignments at the third grade level? Here are some alternatives.

1. State the student's current grade level in the academic subject, and grade the student's performance at that grade level.

   Judy, Grade 4

   Math grade level: <u>3</u>

   Math performance at grade 3 level: <u>B</u>

2. State the student's current grade level in the academic subject, and grade the student's work behaviors rather than skill performance.

   Judy, Grade 4

   Math grade level: <u>3</u>

   Works independently: <u>B</u>

   Completes assignments: <u>B+</u>

   Neatness: <u>B</u>

3. State the student's IEP goals and objectives in the academic subject, and indicate which have been met and which still require work.

   Judy, Grade 4

   Goal: By the end of the school year, Judy will perform math computation problems at the 3.5 grade level. <u>in progress</u>

   Objectives:

   a. Judy will add and subtract two-digit numbers with regrouping with 90% accuracy. <u>achieved</u>

   b. Judy will write multiplication facts with 90% accuracy. <u>achieved</u>

   c. Judy will multiply two-digit numbers with regrouping with 90% accuracy. <u>in progress</u>

   d. Judy will write division facts with 90% accuracy. <u>in progress</u>

Other options include replacing traditional letter grades with simplified grading systems such as pass/fail or satisfactory/needs improvement (McLoughlin & Lewis, 2008). Teachers also can assign multiple grades in a subject area; for example, the student might earn one grade for reading achievement and another for effort in reading activities (Banbury, 1987).

When students with mild intellectual disabilities are included in general education for basic skills instruction, the assignment of grades is often difficult. Students can be working hard and making progress, but their performance may remain at a lower level than that expected for their grade placement. Alternatives for grading students with special needs are suggested in the "Inclusion Tips for the Teacher" box. See the article by Salend and Duhaney (2002) for more information.

 ## IMPROVING GENERAL WORK HABITS

Work habits can be viewed as the behaviors a person exhibits when presented with a task to perform. Many work behaviors apply to all types of tasks. For example, no matter what type of work is involved, it is necessary to begin work promptly, stay on task, and complete the task. Important not only on the job but also in school and daily life, work habits are a necessary part of the curriculum for children and youth with mild intellectual disabilities. Kokaska and Brolin (1985, pp. 157–160) identified these important work behaviors.

- Following directions
- Working with others
- Working at a satisfactory rate
- Accepting supervision
- Recognizing the importance of attendance and punctuality
- Meeting demands for quality work
- Demonstrating occupational safety skills

Several of these skills are just as important for classroom success as they are for vocational endeavors.

General education teachers can help students develop and improve their general work habits in three ways. First, the acquisition of work habits must be accepted as a valuable educational goal. Second, students must receive instruction and practice in specific work behaviors. Third, good work performance must be reinforced. The following paragraphs suggest ways to promote three general work habits.

Attendance and Punctuality

These work habits are key ingredients in successful school and job performance. Students with poor attendance and those who are frequently tardy may fall behind their classmates in important school skills. Adults whose work records show frequent absences and late arrivals may find themselves unemployed. Attendance and punctuality are typically expected by teachers but are not addressed directly in instruction. For many students with special needs, these work habits must become part of the curriculum so that students are taught the behaviors, provided with practice opportunities, and rewarded for successful performance. To teach these work habits, the teacher first communicates to students that attendance and punctuality are important. One way to do this is to incorporate these behaviors into the class rules. For example, the rule for punctuality might be "When the bell rings, be in your seat." It is also necessary to explain why attendance and punctuality are important for students (and for employees). To do this, the teacher might lead the class in a discussion of the disadvantages of being tardy for school (or work).

When students are aware of the teacher's expectations, appropriate work behaviors can be rewarded. There are

several ways to reinforce students for attending class and arriving on time.

- Keep a record of attendance and punctuality. At the end of each week, allow students with good records to participate in a special free-time activity.
- Have students keep a log of their own attendance and punctuality. This can be done in the form of a journal or graph or even with a time clock.
- Present a certificate or award to students with good attendance. Begin gradually by rewarding students who come to school each day for 1 week.
- Encourage punctuality by scheduling a favorite activity at the beginning of the class period.
- Use individual contracts for students who are chronically absent or habitually late. Negotiate the terms of the contract so that acceptable performance is followed by a privilege, activity, or reward that the student values.

Work Completion

A second important work behavior critical for school and job success is task completion. Students and employees are expected to complete their work assignments. In school, the teacher must be sure that learning tasks are appropriate for the skill levels of the student. Kolstoe (1976) offered the following suggestions for teachers of students with intellectual disabilities.

- The tasks should be uncomplicated. . . .
- The tasks should be brief. . . .
- The tasks should be sequentially presented. . . .
- Each learning task should be the kind in which success is possible. . . .
- Learning tasks should be applied to objects, problems, and situations in the learner's life environment. (p. 27)

When tasks are at an appropriate level for the learner, the teacher can concentrate on building work completion skills. Students should first be told that they are expected to finish their work. Then, task completion should be reinforced by the teacher. Ways to encourage and reward work completion are identified here.

- Make free-time activities contingent on work completion. For example, tell students, "If you finish your work, then you may listen to a CD or read a magazine."
- Have students record the number of tasks they complete each day. They can then graph the data and see how they progress from day to day.
- For students who are overwhelmed by lengthy assignments, break the work into several short tasks. Reward these students after the completion of each short task.
- Begin gradually with students who rarely complete tasks. First, expect and reward one task per day, then two tasks, and so on.

Working with Others

In many situations at school and on the job, people must work closely with one another. This interaction necessitates communication, cooperation, and civility. Job-related social skills are particularly important for youngsters with mild intellectual disabilities because, as Kokaska and Brolin (1985) noted, one of the most common reasons for job failure is the inability to get along with coworkers and supervisors.

 Go to the Assignments and Activities section of Topic *Intellectual Disabilities* in the MyEducationLab for your course and complete the activity entitled *Life Skills for Transition Beyond School.*

Practice in working with others can begin at any age. In most general education classrooms, students have many opportunities to work with peers. Besides the most typical examples of group instruction and class discussions, the teacher can design special projects to be completed by teams of students: for example, preparing group science reports, writing a class newspaper, putting up a bulletin board, or planning a class field trip.

When students work in groups, the teacher must often provide instruction and guidance in important interpersonal skills. Students need to learn to share work materials, work quietly with others, be polite to coworkers, and complete tasks by working cooperatively. These skills can be practiced in any classroom and, once acquired, are among the most valuable of all general work habits for student and adult workers alike.

By helping students with special needs learn functional academic skills and work habits, the teacher is providing them with important tools that they will use for the rest of their lives. Consider the story of Bill Yore, as told by Kokaska and Brolin (1985). Bill, a young man who was in special education programs all his life, graduated from high school at age 19, and was selected by his classmates as one of the commencement speakers. In his speech, Bill said:

> It isn't easy competing with other kids, even when you are normal much less handicapped. But, the love and the patience were there for 19 long years. And, tonight I am proud to stand here and say that I am that boy—almost condemned to an institution. True, I am not an A student. But neither am I a dropout. I may never go to college but I won't be on the welfare rolls either. I may never be a great man in this world, but I will be a man in whatever way I am able to do it. (p. 386)

STRATEGIES FOR WORKING WITH STUDENTS WITH SEVERE INTELLECTUAL DISABILITIES

The educational needs of students with severe intellectual disabilities are more complex than those of students with mild intellectual disabilities. There is a greater degree of intellectual limitation, and poor intellectual performance may be accompanied by physical impairments, sensory impairments, or even emotional disturbance. According to Pumpian (1988), "individuals are typically identified as severely [disabled] . . . when the severity and/or multiplicity of their [disabilities] . . . pose major challenges to them, their families, and society in general in nearly all aspects of growth, development, and functioning" (p. 181).

> **myeducationlab** Go to the Assignments and Activities section of Topic *Intellectual Disabilities* in the MyEducationLab for your course and complete the activity entitled *Down Syndrome*.

Until quite recently, such students were educated almost exclusively in special schools and residential facilities; prior to the passage of PL 94-142, many were denied the opportunity to participate in public education in any form. However, within the past two decades, advances in research and changes in educational philosophy have led to increased participation of students with severe intellectual disabilities in public school life. During the 1999–2000 school year, for example, approximately 94% of the students with intellectual disabilities in the United States attended regular schools in which special education services were delivered in a general education classroom, resource room, or special class (U.S. Department of Education, 2002). Although many of these students were identified with mild intellectual disabilities, a significant number had been identified as having severe intellectual disabilities.

Although many students with severe intellectual disabilities now attend regular schools, physical proximity is not sufficient to guarantee their successful integration into the school community. Falvey et al. (1989) identified several other factors that must be considered. In an optimal program, students with severe intellectual disabilities would attend neighborhood schools with age peers; however, no school would enroll a disproportionate number of students with severe intellectual (or other) disabilities. Special educators and support staff would be available to provide students with an appropriate instructional program. And the school would be both physically and socially accessible to students with severe intellectual disabilities.

Social accessibility refers to the availability of opportunities for interaction between students with and without disabilities. When students with severe intellectual disabilities are members of a special class within a regular school, they should have the same access to school functions and activities as others within the school community. For example, they should arrive at and depart from school at the same times and places as other students, they should attend school assemblies and social events, they should eat lunch at one of the regular lunchtimes, and their recess or physical education activities should be scheduled similarly to those of other classes.

According to The Arc's (2009) position statement on inclusion, "All Americans gain when people with intellectual and/or developmental disabilities are fully included in their communities." This position statement also maintains that children should:

- Live in a family home;
- Grow up enjoying nurturing adult relationships both inside and outside a family home;
- Learn in their neighborhood school in a regular classroom that contains children of the same age without disabilities;
- Participate in the same activities as children without disabilities;
- Play and participate with all children in community recreation; and
- Have the opportunity to participate in an inclusive spiritual life.

Research supports the benefits of integration, not only for students with severe intellectual disabilities, but also for their peers without disabilities. Positive interactions occur between these groups of students, and typical students begin to develop more positive attitudes toward individuals with disabilities (Brinker, 1985). Parents of students with severe intellectual disabilities also report satisfaction (McDonnell, 1987). Few reported that their children were mistreated or isolated; most said that their children had made or will make friends at school with peers without disabilities.

In addition to providing opportunities for interaction, it is also possible to set up structured programs that facilitate the building of relationships between students with and without disabilities. One approach is a peer tutoring program in which general education students are trained as tutors for students with severe intellectual disabilities (e.g., Kohl, Moses, & Stettner-Eaton, 1983). Special class students benefit from positive peer models and the additional instructional resources, while typical peers develop an understanding of and appreciation for individual differences. Tutors may also gain social status among their general education classmates (Sasso & Rude, 1988). A more innovative approach is the "Special Friends" program of Voeltz (1980, 1982). In this program, the relationship between peers with and without disabilities is social rather than pedagogical; the outcome is the building of new friendships and a positive change in the attitudes of general education students.

Full Inclusion

In the past several years, advocates for students with severe intellectual disabilities have taken the position that all students should be members of general education classrooms (Kennedy & Horn, 2004; Stainback & Stainback, 1988, 1990, 1992; Stainback, Stainback, & Forest, 1989; Thousand & Villa, 1990). Called *full inclusion,* this movement encourages full-time general education placement for students with severe intellectual disabilities and others with identified special education needs. The general education teacher becomes responsible for the education of all students, although special educators and other staff are available to support students and teachers as needed. When a student with severe intellectual disabilities is fully included, general and special educators collaborate to ensure that the following occur:

a. The student's natural participation as a regular member of the class
b. The systematic instruction of the student's IEP objectives
c. The adaptation of the core curriculum and/or materials to facilitate student participation and learning (Neary, Halvorsen, & Smithey, 1991, p. 1)

According to Voltz, Brazil, and Ford (2001), "the concept of inclusion implies a sense of belonging and acceptance" (p. 24).

 Go to the Assignments and Activities section of Topic *Intellectual Disabilities* in the MyEducationLab for your course and complete the activity entitled *Students with Mental Retardation in the Integrated Inclusion Classroom.*

One of the major goals of full inclusion is the development of friendships between students with and without disabilities. Opportunities for social interactions increase when students with severe intellectual disabilities are full-time members of general education classrooms. Also, students without disabilities can be directly involved in the full inclusion effort. For example, Forest and Lusthaus (1989) recommended two strategies: circles of friends and MAPS. A circle of friends is a network of students who volunteer to offer friendship to a student with disabilities; see the "Inclusion Tips for the Teacher" box to see how a circle works.

MAPS stands for Making Action Plans (York, Doyle, & Kronberg, 1992); it was originally called the McGill Action Planning System (Lusthaus & Forest, 1987; Vandercook, York, & Forest, 1989). It is a team approach to planning the inclusion process. Members of the team include the student, parents (and perhaps other family members), professionals, and the student's circle of friends. In the MAPS process, the team addresses seven major questions:

1. What is the individual's history?
2. What is your dream for the individual?
3. What is your nightmare?

Inclusion Tips for the Teacher

Circles of Friends

Forest and Lusthaus (1989) provided this example to describe the establishment of a circle of friends for May, a student with disabilities who is going to join a seventh grade general education class.

In September, a few days before May Russell would be attending her new seventh grade classroom, an integration consultant visited the class to speak with the students. She asked them the following series of questions. The students' actual responses are included here, too.

Consultant (C)

C—"Hi, I've come to talk to you about May, who is coming to your class next week. You met her last week when she visited with her mother. For years May has gone to a segregated school or been in a self-contained life skills class. What does that mean?"

Students (S)

S—"Places for retarded people."

"Schools for kids who are really bad."

"Like the one near my house where all the wheelchairs go."

C—"Well, May is coming here and I'll tell you a secret. Everyone is really scared. Her mother and father are scared. Mr. Gorman [teacher] is scared. Mr. Cullen [principal] is scared. I'm scared. Why do you think all of us are so scared?"

S—"You all think we'll be mean to her."

"You think we'll tease her and be mean to her."

"You think she'll be left out."

C—"There are some things we don't want you to do when she arrives. What do you think these are?"

S—"Don't treat her like a baby."

"Don't pity her."

"Don't ignore her."

"Don't feel sorry for her."

C—"Why are we doing this? Why is May coming to this class?"

S—"Why not? She's our age, she should be here."

"How would you feel if you were 12 and never were with kids your own age?"

"It's dumb for her not to be here."

"She needs friends."

"She needs a boy friend."

C—"What do you think we want you to do?"

S—"Treat her like one of us."

"Make her feel welcome."

"Help her make friends."

"Help her with her work."

"Call her and invite her to our parties."

C—"I want to switch gears for a few minutes and ask you to all do an exercise with me called 'circle of friends.' I do this very same thing with teachers and parents and I think you are all grown up enough to handle it."

(The consultant handed out a sheet with four concentric circles on it. After the first circle, each circle was a little larger and farther away from the center of the page where a stick person was drawn.)

C—"There are four circles. On each circle you are to list people you know. I want you to think about whom you would put in your first circle. These are the people closest to you, people you really love. You can do this privately or in pairs, and you can tell us or keep it private."

(The consultant filled in her own circles on the chalkboard while the students did theirs at their seats. When finished, the facilitator shared her circles and then asked for volunteers to share theirs.)

S—"O.K. In my first circle I put in my mom, my dad, Matt who is my best friend, and Stacey—that's my Mom's best friend and she often helps me when I have a problem."

C—"Why did you put those people in your first circle?"

S—"They are people I feel close to. I love them."

C—"What do you do with the people in circle one?"

S—"I share my secrets, I can be myself, I go to them when I'm hurt, I trust them, I love them."

C—"Now let's do circle two—these are people you really like but not enough to put in circle one."

S—"I put in my dog and my two best friends Tim and Todd, and my teacher Mr. Gorman. I put them in because I can do everything with them and we have fun together and we visit a lot."

C—"The third circle is groups of people you like or people you do things with, like Scouts, swimming, hockey, etc."

S—"I have lots—I'm in Boy Scouts, my church, my Sunday school, this class, my street hockey group, and my family is like a group."

C—"The last circle is for people you pay to be in your lives, like your doctor, dentist, and so on."

S—"I put in my doctor and my eye glass doctor, that's all."

C—"Now I want you to think about a person's circle. Here's a fantasy person named Sebastian. He's your age (12) and his circle looks like this. He only has his Mom in circle one and the rest of his circles are empty except for circle four, which is filled with doctors, social workers, therapists, etc. Think hard for a few minutes because this is real serious. How would you feel if your life looked like Sebastian's?"

(This is a list of responses from the seventh grade students in the brainstorming session.)

S—"Lonely, depressed, unwanted, terrible, disgusted, like what's the use of living, I'd want to commit suicide, like dying, awful, crazy, hurt, nobody cares, angry, furious, mad."

C—"How do you think you'd act?"

S—(Again, a list of responses from the brainstorming.) "I'd hide and keep my head down all day, I'd hit people, I'd cry all day, I'd hate everyone, I'd kill myself, I'd want to kill others, I'd steal, I'd curse and spit, I'd fight."

C—"O.K, I want to wind this up for today and I'll be back in a few weeks to see what's happening. Remember, I came and we started talking about May who will be in your class soon. Well, right now her life looks a bit like Sebastian's imaginary circle. So why did I do all this?"

continued

S—"To help us understand about all the new kids who are coming into our classes—about how they must feel."

C—"What I'd like is for a group of you to act as a welcome committee and another group to act as a telephone crew. I want a phone caller for each day of the week. Do you think that's a good idea?"

S—"Wow, yeah—what a neat idea!"

C—"Remember, friends don't develop overnight. This is just the start. Not all of you will be May's friends—though all of you can be 'friendly.' My dream and hope is that out of this great class May will have at least six friends who will do things with her in school and most of all after school and on weekends. This won't happen fast, but I bet it will happen. Who wants to help?"

Note: From "Promoting Educational Equity for All Students" by M. Forest and E. Lusthaus in *Educating All Students in the Mainstream of Regular Education* (pp. 47–49) by S. Stainback, W. Stainback, and M. Forest (Eds.), 1989. Copyright 1989 by Paul H. Brookes, P.O. Box 10624, Baltimore, MD 21285-0624. Reprinted with permission from Dr. Marsha Forest, Inclusion Press, 416-658-5363 or fax 416-658-5067, Web page *http://inclusion.com*.

4. Who is the individual?
5. What are the individual's strengths, gifts, and abilities?
6. What are the individual's needs?
7. What would the individual's ideal day at school look like and what must be done to make it happen? (Vandercook et al., 1989, pp. 207–208)

When students with severe intellectual disabilities are included in general education classrooms, it is often necessary to adapt instructional procedures. One concern is the curriculum (Wolfe & Hall, 2003). Giangreco, Cloninger, and Iverson (1990) presented four alternatives. First, the student with severe intellectual disabilities can participate in the same learning activities with the same goals as other students in the class. Second, in a multilevel curriculum, the student can work in the same curriculum area as classmates, but at a different level. For example, while peers work on algebraic problems, a student with severe intellectual disabilities might practice addition and subtraction skills (York et al., 1992). Or, while classmates read a book and write a book report, a student with severe intellectual disabilities might listen to a story on tape, tape-record reactions to the story, and draw a picture illustrating the story (Wehman, 1997).

Third, in curriculum overlapping, all students participate in the same learning activities but pursue goals in different subject areas. Giangreco and colleagues (1990) provide this example:

> Suppose students are in science lab learning about properties of electricity. A student with special needs may be involved in these activities for the primary purpose of pursuing objectives from other curriculum areas (e.g., communication, socialization) such as following directions, accepting assistance from others, or engaging in a school job with a nonhandicapped peer. (as cited in Thousand & Villa, 1990, p. 15)

The fourth option is an alternative curriculum. This is recommended for use only when it is impossible to address a student's educational goals within the general education classroom setting.

Vandercook and York (1990) have developed the Regular Classroom Integration Checklist to help teachers assess progress toward full inclusion of students with severe intellectual disabilities. As can be seen in Figure 11-5, that checklist is divided into four sections. The first, "Go with the Flow," is used to determine whether all students follow the same classroom routines. "Acting Cool" is concerned with participation in class activities, "Talking Straight" with communication, and "Looking Good" with personal appearance. Items receiving a "no" response should be addressed by the team when it meets to discuss ways to improve the inclusion process.

Research is beginning to emerge about the effect of full inclusion on students with severe intellectual disabilities, their families, their peers, and their teachers. In a review of inclusion research, Hunt and Goetz (1997) summarized their conclusions in these six guidelines.

1. Parental involvement is an essential component of effective inclusive schooling. . . .
2. Students with severe [intellectual] disabilities can achieve positive academic and learning outcomes in academic settings. . . .
3. Students with severe [intellectual] disabilities realize acceptance, interactions, and friendships in inclusive settings. . . .
4. Students without disabilities experience positive outcomes when students with severe [intellectual] disabilities are their classmates. . . .
5. Collaborative efforts among school personnel are essential to achieving successful inclusive schools. . . .
6. Curricular adaptations are a vital component in effective inclusion efforts. . . . (pp. 25–26)

However, in one study, less than half of parents of students with severe intellectual disabilities said they believed that full inclusion would be a good idea for their child (Palmer, Fuller, Arora, & Nelson, 2001). In addition, it is important to note that very little research has focused on the academic achievement of fully included students with severe intellectual disabilities or the ways in which the general education curriculum should be adapted for these students (Hunt & Goetz, 1997; Nietupski, Hamre-Nietupski, Curtin, & Shrikanth, 1997). Despite this, Werts, Wolery, Snyder, and Caldwell (1996) reported that special and general educators are in full agreement about the types of supports general education teachers need to make full inclusion programs successful. Three supports were identified as

FIGURE 11-5   Inclusion Checklist

Directions: Record a "y" for yes and an "n" for no on the blank preceding each item. If the answer to any of the items is "no," your team may wish to consider whether any changes should be made and what those changes might be.

Go with the Flow:

_____ Does the student enter the classroom at the same time as classmates? _____

_____ Is the student positioned so that she or he can see and participate in what is going on? _____

_____ Is the student positioned so that classmates and teachers may easily interact with him or her (e.g., without teacher between the student and his or her classmates, not isolated from classmates)? _____

_____ Does the student engage in classroom activities at the same time as classmates? _____

_____ Does the student make transitions in the classroom at the same time as classmates? _____

_____ Is the student involved in the same activities as his or her classmates? _____

_____ Does the student exit the classroom at the same time as classmates? _____

Acting Cool:

_____ Is the student actively involved in class activities (e.g., asks or responds to questions, plays a role in group activities)? _____

_____ Is the student encouraged to follow the same classroom and social rules as classmates (e.g., hugs others only when appropriate, stays in seat during instruction)? _____

_____ Is the student given assistance only as necessary (assistance should be faded as soon as possible)? _____

_____ Is assistance provided for the student by classmates (e.g., transitions to other classrooms, within the classroom)? _____

_____ Are classmates encouraged to provide assistance to the student? _____

_____ Are classmates encouraged to ask for assistance from the student? _____

_____ Is assistance provided for the student by classroom teachers? _____

_____ Does the student use the same or similar materials during classroom activities as his or her classmates (e.g., Tom Cruise notebooks, school mascot folders)? _____

Talking Straight:

_____ Does the student have a way to communicate with classmates? _____

_____ Do classmates know how to communicate with the student? _____

Continued

FIGURE 11-5 *continued*

_____ Does the student greet others in a manner similar to that of his or her classmates? _____

_____ Does the student socialize with classmates? _____

_____ Is this facilitated? _____

_____ Does the student interact with teachers? _____

_____ Is this facilitated? _____

_____ Do teachers (e.g., classroom teachers, special education support staff) provide the same type of feedback (e.g., praise, discipline) for the student as for his or her classmates? _____

_____ If the student uses an alternative communication system do classmates know how to use it? _____

_____ If the student uses an alternative communication system do teachers know how to use it? _____

_____ Is the system always available to the student? _____

Looking Good:

_____ Is the student given the opportunity to attend to his or her appearance as classmates do (e.g., check appearance in mirror between classes)? _____

_____ Does the student have accessories which are similar to his or her classmates (e.g., oversize tote bags, friendship bracelets, hair jewelry)? _____

_____ Is the student dressed similarly to classmates? _____

_____ Is clothing that's needed for activities age appropriate (e.g., napkins instead of bibs, "cool" paint shirts)? _____

_____ Are personal supplies or belongings carried or transported discreetly? _____

_____ Is the student's equipment (e.g., wheelchair) kept clean? _____

  Given the opportunity (and assistance as needed):

_____ Is the student's hair combed?

_____ Are the student's hands clean and dry?

_____ Does the student change clothing to maintain a neat appearance?

_____ Does the student use chewing gum, breath mints, breath spray?

Note: From "A Team Approach to Program Development and Support" by T. Vandercook and J. York in *Support Network for Inclusive Schooling* (pp. 117–118) by W. Stainback and S. Stainback (Eds.), 1990. Copyright 1990 by Paul H. Brookes, P.O. Box 10624, Baltimore, MD 21285-0624. Reprinted with permission.

most critical: sufficient training, support from a team of professionals, and additional personnel to provide assistance in the general education classroom.

In this chapter you have learned ways to adapt classroom instruction to help students with mild intellectual disabilities learn functional academic skills and basic work habits. You have also learned more about students with severe intellectual disabilities and strategies for increasing their participation as members of the school community. Consult "Things to Remember" to review ways to help students with intellectual disabilities succeed in the general education classroom.

Things to Remember

- Academic instruction is the most common area in which adaptations must be made in the general education classroom for students with mild intellectual disabilities. They require assistance in acquisition of basic skills and work habits and in the application of these skills to daily life and career situations.

- Major indicators of mild intellectual disabilities are a slow rate of learning and consistent delays in most areas of development.

- In assessment of mild intellectual disabilities, information is gathered about academic achievement, intellectual performance, and adaptive behavior. The general education teacher assists by collecting classroom performance data.

- The major approach to the education of students with mild intellectual disabilities is habilitation; instruction is directed toward development of the critical skills necessary for successful adulthood.

- Transition and career education services are one way to view habilitation of students with mild intellectual disabilities; in this approach, students are prepared for adult life by instruction in functional academic, daily living, personal–social, and vocational skills.

- When students with mild intellectual disabilities participate in general education classes for basic skills instruction or vocational education, the teacher assists by teaching functional academic skills and improving the general work habits of the students.

- Two approaches to teaching functional academics are instructional units and functional practice activities; both help students generalize learned skills to daily life and vocational situations.

- General work habits important for school and later employment include attendance and punctuality, work completion, and working with others. The general education teacher promotes the development of these skills in students with mild intellectual disabilities with instruction, guided practice, and reinforcement of appropriate performance.

- Students with severe intellectual disabilities may attend special classes within regular schools or be fully included in general education classrooms. Both options offer opportunities for interactions between peers with and without disabilities and participation in age-appropriate school activities.

ACTIVITIES

1. Visit a special education classroom, either a resource room or a special class, that serves students with mild intellectual disabilities. Observe the students and talk with the teacher. In what school subjects do students experience the most difficulty? What subjects are taught by the special education teacher? Are transition and career education services part of the curriculum? Find out how many of the students are included in general education for at least part of the school day. Do they participate in academic instruction in the regular classroom? In nonacademic subjects such as music and art? In social activities?

2. Select one of the special education journals that focuses on intellectual disabilities. Choose from the *American Journal on Intellectual and Developmental Disabilities, Education and Training in Developmental Disabilities,* and *Intellectual and Developmental Disabilities.* Look through recent issues for articles containing suggestions that classroom teachers can use. Collect ideas for teaching functional academics and for incorporating transition and career education skills into the general education curriculum.

3. Make a list of the questions you have about intellectual disabilities and the inclusion of students with intellectual disabilities in general education classrooms. Visit at least five websites to find answers to your questions. Start with the sites described in this chapter's "Window on the Web" and use the links they provide to locate other resources. In your opinion, which sites are most valuable for teachers?

4. Imagine that you are a general education teacher with several students with mild intellectual disabilities in your class. Design an instructional program to improve the general work habits of all your students. What work habits will you include in your program? How will you explain the program to the class? How will you implement the program? Outline a method for evaluating your program.

5. Contact local school districts to find out how students with severe intellectual disabilities are served. Do students attend special classes located in regular neighborhood schools? Are students fully included in general education classes? Visit an integrated site and observe how students with severe intellectual disabilities participate in school life. If the school has a full inclusion program, use the checklist in Figure 11-5 to guide your observation.

CHAPTER TWELVE

Teaching Students with Behavioral Disorders

Jake

Jake is 15 years old, in the eighth grade, and identified as a student with behavioral disorders. He is often late for classes and, as soon as he does arrive, he draws attention to himself by his restlessness and constant activity. He frequently argues with teachers, other students, and even the few friends he has in his neighborhood. At present, Jake attends general education classes for social studies, English, physical education, and shop; he also spends two periods a day in the resource room. The special education teacher works with Jake to improve his math and reading performance, study skills, and classroom behavior. Jake's academic progress is adequate when he completes his work; however, Jake often argues with the teacher over the assignment and begins to work only when the class period is almost over. These conduct problems are evident in all classes except shop. Jake is never late to his shop class; he enjoys working on small motors and reading books that will help him build the go-cart that is his project for the year.

Tina

Six-year-old Tina is a first grade student who is small for her age. At school, she seldom talks to other children and withdraws when others try to talk to her. She speaks with the teacher, but only in a very soft voice. Tina plays alone during recess; her favorite classroom activity is art, and she enjoys painting. Tina's full-day placement is in the general education classroom; in addition, she visits the speech–language clinician twice a week, and once a week she spends a half hour with the school social worker. Tina's parents are concerned about her lack of social relationships. At home, she spends her time drawing and watching television rather than playing with the neighborhood children. Tina's teacher is also concerned. Although Tina's written class work is of average quality, she does not participate in class discussions and refuses to respond orally in class.

Mike

Mike is a 9-year-old fourth grader who displays serious behavioral problems with his teachers, other school personnel, and the students at his school. He always appears to be agitated and is described by adults at the school as aggressive and a bully. Mike gets into at least one fight on the playground each week, he has temper tantrums when he doesn't get his way, and in class he is extremely uncooperative; he repeatedly interrupts classroom instruction and refuses to complete assigned schoolwork. He has displayed similar behaviors since he came to the school in the first grade. While Mike is considered to be quite capable academically, he continues to fall farther and farther behind in academic areas because of his pattern of conflict with adults and other children.

LOOKING AHEAD

Later in this chapter, you will have an opportunity to review observational data on Jake's classroom performance and see portions of the IEP written for him. This chapter focuses on strategies for controlling disruptive behaviors in the classroom and teaching students better study skills. As you read about these options for helping students with behavioral disorders, consider these questions.

- Jake shows a number of problem behaviors in the classroom. If you were Jake's teacher, with which behaviors would you be most concerned? How might you go about gathering more information about these behaviors?
- Contrast the classroom behavior of Tina with that of Jake. What do you see as Tina's most important challenge? How could you go about helping her to meet that challenge?
- Mike's behavior is quite different from that of Jake, although both might be considered disruptive in the classroom. What techniques would you use to learn more about Mike's school conduct problems?

The behavior problems of the three students described in the "Students' Stories" section—Jake, Tina, and Mike—are equally perplexing to their classroom teachers, even though the problems of each are quite different. Jake, Tina, and Mike are all capable of meeting the academic demands of the general education classroom, yet their behaviors interfere. Jake's difficulty is his conduct in the classroom; his tardiness, poor work habits, and argumentativeness prevent successful performance. Tina, however, is withdrawn; she attends to her work but refuses to engage in social interaction. Mike's conduct leads him to encounter problems throughout the school; his aggression and defiance interfere with his academic progress and his acceptance by adults and his peers. These students present three examples of the many types of behavioral disorders that can be found in the general education classroom.

Many attempts have been made to define the term *behavioral disorders;* however, there is no common agreement on any one definition. One reason for this is that no single pattern of behaviors identifies a student as having a behavioral disorder. Instead, many student behaviors can be indicative of a behavioral disorder, ranging from high levels of aggression to extreme withdrawal. In schools, the prereferral team studies the needs of each student, explores possible adjustments in the general education program, and then decides whether to assess the student to determine eligibility for special education services.

Students with behavioral disorders can have special needs in several areas, such as classroom behavior, social skills, and academic instruction. In classroom behavior, the student's problem can lie in school conduct or the application of appropriate study skills. For example, students with poor conduct may disregard class rules or disrupt instructional activities; those with poor study skills may not pay attention to classroom instruction, may fail to complete assignments, or may work hastily and carelessly. Students with social skill problems may have difficulty getting along with their peers or the teacher and other adults. In academic instruction, students with behavioral disorders, like students with learning disabilities and those with mild intellectual disabilities, may require extra assistance to learn and apply basic school skills (Pierce, Reid, & Epstein, 2004). Other students can have more serious problems, such as involvement in drug abuse or severe depression, that could lead to suicide.

This chapter focuses on the needs of students with behavioral disorders. It includes ways to identify such students in the general education program, techniques for collecting useful assessment data, and methods for improving both classroom conduct and study skills.

 ## INDICATORS OF BEHAVIORAL DISORDERS

Teachers in general education classrooms are typically the first professionals to bring students with behavioral disorders to the attention of the prereferral team. These students can be identified at any age, but they are most likely to be noticed at the middle or upper levels of elementary school. Male students are more often identified as having behavioral disorders than are female students (U.S. Department of Education, 2002). Although both males and females can exhibit acting-out or withdrawn behaviors, boys are typically referred for aggressive behaviors and girls for withdrawal.

There are three major indicators of a behavioral disorder. According to Nelson (1993), a student's behavior "may be judged disordered (1) if it deviates from the range of behaviors for the child's age and sex which significant adults perceive as normal; (2) if it occurs very frequently or too intensely; or (3) if it occurs over an extended period of time" (p. 549). These indicators can be used by the classroom teacher and the planning team to study a student's need for special education services.

Another important sign is academic underachievement. Many students with behavioral disorders experience difficulty coping with the academic demands of the classroom. They may read poorly and have trouble in math and other basic school subjects. In many cases, there is overlap between this group of students and those with learning disabilities; inappropriate classroom behaviors can be either the cause or result of poor academic performance.

 ## WINDOW ON THE WEB

CCBD and Other Web Resources on Behavioral Disorders

Council for Children with Behavioral Disorders

This is the website for the Council for Children with Behavioral Disorders (CCBD), one of the divisions within the Council for Exceptional Children. The site features information about the organization's professional journal (*Behavioral Disorders*), its journal for practitioners (*Beyond Behavior*), and online versions of recent newsletters. Also available are updates on CCBD's advocacy efforts, teacher resources on a variety of topics (e.g., reading instruction, social skills training), and links to other websites related to behavioral disorders.

http://www.ccbd.net/

Other Web-Based Resources

Other web resources related to behavioral disorders that include the following.

- **The Behavior Homepage** (*http://www.state.ky.us/agencies/behave/homepage.html*) is a useful site for teachers featuring information about school safety, behavioral interventions, and strategies for teaching academics.
- **DisciplineHelp** (*http://www.disciplinehelp.com*) is a site describing itself as "a reference for handling over 117 misbehaviors at school and home."
- **Special Education Resources on the Internet (SERI)** (*http://seriweb.com*) presents a collection of web-based resources on a variety of topics including behavior disorders.

Other frequently mentioned characteristics of students with behavioral disorders are hyperactivity, distractibility, and impulsivity. When these behaviors occur together (or in some combination), the label *attention deficit hyperactivity disorder* (ADHD) is often used to describe the student's difficulty in maintaining attention to task. These characteristics are highly interrelated; the child who is hyperactive is likely also to be distractible and impulsive. These attributes are associated not only with students with behavioral disorders but also with other groups of special students, such as individuals with learning disabilities and those with mild intellectual disabilities. In fact, one study reported by the U.S. Department of Education (2002) found distractibility and impulsivity to be the two most common problem behaviors of students receiving special education services.

As with most educational problems, speculation about the medical etiology does not contribute useful information to educators for planning instructional programs. However, many students with ADHD can benefit when they receive an appropriate type and dosage of psychostimulant medication such as Ritalin (methylphenidate), Dexedrine (dextroamphetamine), or Cylert (pemoline). Although these medications do not remediate academic problems or teach new behaviors, it has been demonstrated that they can help improve behavior and facilitate learning by making the student more teachable. When students are receiving medication, it is important that teachers provide the physician with information about how the medication is influencing behavior and whether any side effects are apparent in the school setting; an inappropriate dosage may actually impair learning. Because the medications used with students with ADHD or other behavioral disorders are constantly changing, it is important for the parents and teachers of these students to review information on potential effects (Ryan, Reid, & Ellis, 2008). Articles such as those by Forness, Walker, and Kavale (2003) and Kollins et al. (2001) provide important information on the use of these medications and their potential effects on the behaviors of the students.

The many indicators of behavioral disorders cannot be distilled into one hard-and-fast rule that tells teachers when to refer a student for consideration for special services. Thus, guidelines for identification may be useful. First, all students exhibit inappropriate behavior at some time during their school careers. Such behavior should be considered a possible problem only when it interferes with a student's academic performance, relationships with teachers or peers, or the operation of the instructional program. Second, the behaviors of concern should occur consistently over an extended period of time. In most cases, one instance of an unacceptable behavior is not sufficient to warrant the attention of the teacher. However, if the behavior in question is extreme (e.g., one that could lead to the injury of another student), then just one occurrence may be justification for a referral.

Another guideline suggests that the nature of the inappropriate behavior be considered. The actions of students with behavioral disorders will differ from what teachers expect of typical students. The difference can lie in the frequency of the inappropriate behavior; such students may talk out in class not once or twice a period but once or twice a minute. They may have more intense reactions; a student may become extremely upset over an incident that most students would treat lightly. Or behaviors may be of longer duration; instead of quickly calming down after a disagreement, a student may remain upset throughout the school day.

Several other indicators of behavioral disorders appear regularly in the professional literature. These include descriptors such as *disobedient, defiant, attention seeking, irritable, anxious, timid, preoccupied,* and *passive.* Although these terms suggest student behaviors that may concern teachers, they have limited value because they are subjective and can be interpreted differently. Before clear communication can occur, a careful definition of terms is needed;

 ## For Your Information

Students with Behavioral Disorders

- Research suggests that 3% to 6% of school-aged students have behavioral disorders, although current programs for students with behavioral disorders serve slightly under 1% of the school-age population (Kauffman, 2001).
- Students identified as having behavior disorders make up about 8% of the total of all students receiving special education services (U.S. Department of Education, 2009).
- Students with behavioral disorders are found in both elementary and secondary schools; at least 50% of the public school programs for students with behavioral disorders are at the secondary level (Grosenick & Huntze, 1980).
- Nelson (1993) stated that "although studies do not consistently find more boys than girls with behavior problems, boys tend to be overrepresented in programs for behaviorally disordered children as much as ten to one" (p. 542).
- The majority of students with behavioral disorders spend most of their school day in the general education classroom.
- Many children in need of mental health services do not receive appropriate care until their problems have become so extreme that they require residential treatment (Knitzer, 1989).

- According to Nelson, Stage, Dupphong-Hurley, Synhorst, and Epstein (2007), the risk factors that best predict emotional and behavioral disorders in young children are "difficult child (i.e., temperament, parent management skills, interaction between temperament and parent management skills), destroys own toys, and maternal depression" (p. 367).
- Most students with behavioral disorders encounter problems in the general education classroom because they lack appropriate social and study skills. Instruction in these areas will lead to skill improvement that will enhance their chances for success when they are included in the general education program (Sugai & Lewis, 1996).
- The intelligence level of students with behavioral disorders does not vary significantly from that of the general school population. However, these students fall behind their peers in academic achievement, and the gap seems to widen as the students progress through school, unless they receive high-quality academic instruction.

what one teacher considers "hyper" or attention seeking may be perfectly acceptable to another. It is also important to look at the reasons for student behaviors that suggest such labels: A student who is passive may be tired, and one who is anxious and irritable may be concerned about the illness of a family member.

Different professionals hold varying views on what constitutes typical and disordered behavior. Such behavioral expectations influence teachers' decisions about which students should be referred for consideration for special services. If a teacher prefers a quiet and orderly classroom in which students remain seated at their desks, an active student may be perceived as a problem. However, this student may fit quite well in a classroom in which student activity, movement, and interaction are encouraged by the teacher. Prior to initiating a referral, the teacher should attempt all possible interventions in the general education class. Often this is accomplished with the assistance of a special education consultant.

The problems of substance abuse and suicide are gaining increasing attention from educators. **Substance abuse** is the voluntary intake of chemicals with adverse social and physical consequences. Alcohol and various other drugs (e.g., narcotics, depressants, marijuana, cocaine) can cause side effects that have a detrimental impact on the student's ability to perform appropriately in the school environment. For example, teachers may observe changes in the student's ability to attend to instruction; temperament; work quality; attitudes toward school, parents, or peers; or self-concept (Coleman, 1986; Kerr & Nelson, 2002). For more information about this problem, consult Figure 12-1.

 FIGURE 12-1   Signs of Alcohol and Other Drug Use

Signs of alcohol and other drug use [AOD] vary, but there are some common indicators of AOD problems. Look for changes in performance, appearance, and behavior. These signs may indicate AOD use, but they may also reflect normal teenage growing pains. Therefore, look for a series of changes, not isolated single behaviors. Several changes together indicate a pattern associated with use.

Changes in Performance:
- Distinct downward turn in grades—not just from Cs to Fs, but from As to Bs and Cs
- Assignments not completed
- A loss of interest in school; in extracurricular activities
- Poor classroom behavior such as inattentiveness, sleeping in class, hostility
- Missing school for unknown reasons
- In trouble with school, at work, or with the police
- Increased discipline problems
- Memory loss

Changes in Behavior:
- Decrease in energy and endurance
- Changes in friends (secrecy about new friends, new friends with different lifestyles)
- Secrecy about activities (lies and avoids talking about activities)
- Borrows lots of money, or has too much cash
- Mood swings; excessive anger, irritability
- Preferred style of music changes (pop rock to heavy metal)
- Starts pulling away from the family, old friends, and school
- Hostile or argumentative attitude; extremely negative, unmotivated, defensive
- Refusal or hostility when asked to talk about possible alcohol or other drug use

Changes in Appearance and Physical Changes:
- Weight loss or gain
- Uncoordinated
- Poor physical appearance or unusually neat. A striking change in personal habits
- New interest in the drug culture (drug-related posters, clothes, magazines)
- Smells of alcohol, tobacco, marijuana
- Frequent use of eye drops and breath mints
- Bloodshot eyes
- Persistent cough or cold symptoms (e.g., runny nose)
- Always thirsty, increased or decreased appetite, rapid speech
- AOD paraphernalia (empty alcohol containers, cigarettes, pipes, rolling papers, baggies, paper packets, roach clips, razor blades, straws, glass or plastic vials, pill bottles, tablets and capsules, colored stoppers, syringes, spoons, matches or lighters, needles, medicine droppers, toy balloons, tin foil, cleaning rags, spray cans, glue containers, household products)

Note: From "School-Based Alcohol and Other Drug Prevention Programs: Guidelines for the Special Educator" by D. L. Elmquist, 1991, *Intervention in School and Clinic, 27*(1), p. 14. Copyright 1991 by PRO-ED, Inc. Reprinted with permission.

FIGURE 12-2 Signs of Danger and Imminent Risk of Suicide

Signs of Danger

- Engaging in dangerous risk-taking behaviors
- Sudden changes in peer friendships or relationships or unhealthy peer relationships
- Withdrawing or isolating from friends and/or family
- Self-mutilation (e.g., cutting or burning that is uncharacteristic of the student's identified disability)
- Sudden mood changes or personality shifts
- Challenges with sexual or gender identity (e.g., students who identify as gay, lesbian, bisexual, or transgender or who are questioning their sexuality or gender identity)
- Being a bully or a victim of a bully
- Depression
- Sudden decline in academic performance or achievement
- Uncharacteristic difficulty concentrating or thinking
- Changes in eating patterns or sleeping patterns (either exceptionally more or less than typical)
- Substance use or abuse (including alcohol and illegal substances, or abuse of prescription medication)
- Preoccupation with the feelings of others
- Unusual interest in morbid themes, death, or dying
- Atypical promiscuous or sexual behavior

Signs of Imminent Risk

- Preoccupation with suicide and/or death in writing, poetry, or artwork
- Direct statements about suicide (e.g., "I'm going to kill myself")
- Indirect statements about suicide (e.g., "Don't bother grading my test, I won't be here to pick it up," "It won't matter anymore," "Sometimes I just don't want to wake up")
- Isolating behaviors
- Expressing helplessness, hopelessness, or that life is meaningless
- Giving away belongings or "setting affairs in order"
- A rapid change in mood from depression to contentment or happiness (may indicate that the student has made a decision and regards suicide as a way to escape pain)
- Dropping out of activities that had been important
- Seeking or gaining access to a weapon or other means of harming oneself

Note: From "Suicide and Students with High-Incidence Disabilities: What Special Educators Need to Know" by C. A. Wachter & E. C. Bouck, 2008, *Teaching Exceptional Children, 4*(1), p. 68. Copyright 2008 by the Council for Exceptional Children. Reprinted with permission.

Suicide is one of the leading causes of death in adolescents; it occurs more frequently in males, although females have a much higher rate of suicide attempts (Kauffman, 2001). It is often associated with feelings of depression and hopelessness and is more likely to occur among active drug and alcohol abusers. Educators should not attempt to deal with such students without outside assistance. However, teachers should be alert to the problem and aware of resources within the school and community for suicide prevention and crisis intervention. Figure 12-2 presents signs of danger related to suicide as well as signs of imminent risk.

Students with severe behavioral disorders are less likely to be found in general education classroom programs. Disabilities such as **autism spectrum disorder** and psychiatric disorders such as **bipolar disorder** are typically identified in the preschool years or early grades. School districts generally provide special programs in which these students spend the majority of their time in special classes or special schools. If students with severe behavioral disorders are returned to the general education program, they and their teachers receive a great deal of support from special educators. To learn more about classroom accommodations and interventions for students with bipolar disorders, consult the 2008 article by Killu and Crundwell.

 ## ASSESSMENT PROCEDURES

When behavioral disorders are suspected, and the behavior problems exhibited by a student do not respond to the interventions available in the general education classroom, the student is referred to the assessment team to determine eligibility and need for special education services. Parents are notified of the referral and the team's plans for special education assessment. When parents grant permission, the team can begin to collect formal assessment information.

 To hear a Teacher of the Year discuss teaching students with behavior disorders, go to the Teacher Talk section of Topic *Emotional and Behavioral Disorders* in the MyEducationLab for your course and listen to the piece from *Kimberly Kyff, Michigan: Establishing Relationships with Students Who've Given Up Hope.*

As with students with learning disabilities and mild intellectual abilities, several major areas are addressed in the special education assessment of students with behavioral disorders. Academic performance is one; measures such as the *Peabody Individual Achievement Test–Revised/Normative Update* (Markwardt, 1998) and the *Woodcock–Johnson III* (Woodcock, McGrew, & Mather, 2001) help determine whether reading, spelling, and math are areas of need. Intellectual ability is another area of concern; tests such as the *Wechsler Intelligence Scale for Children–Fourth Edition* (Wechsler, 2003) provide information about intellectual functioning. In many states, students must perform within an average IQ range to be considered for programs for individuals with behavioral disorders.

A third major concern is classroom behavior. Information about the student's typical patterns of behavior is gathered from teachers and parents. Interviews can be conducted, or the team can consider results from behavior checklists and rating scales. The *Behavior Rating Profile* (2nd ed.) (Brown & Hammill, 1990) uses the input of teachers, parents, peers, and students themselves to determine whether students have significant difficulty in home behavior, school conduct, or relationships with peers. With the *Behavior Evaluation Scale–Third Edition* (McCarney & Arthaud, 2005), teachers rate the frequency of five types of behaviors: Learning Problems, Interpersonal Difficulties, Inappropriate Behavior, Unhappiness/Depression, and Physical Symptoms/Fears.

Direct observation is the best source of data for planning behavioral change programs. Observation gives the teacher specific information about the current behavior of the student and later serves as a basis for evaluation of student progress. Because a variety of measurement systems are available, the teacher can select or design one to generate the type of data needed to plan appropriate interventions for any particular student.

Assessment of student behavior is most effective when specific behaviors are pinpointed and accurate information is collected about the occurrence of these behaviors. In the case of Jake, the eighth grader described at the beginning of this chapter, Mr. Johnson, Jake's English teacher, was particularly concerned about two of Jake's problem behaviors: tardiness and failure to complete assignments on time. To gather more data about these behaviors, Mr. Johnson set up the observation system shown in Figure 12-3. Each day Mr. Johnson noted the number of minutes that Jake was late to class (duration recording), the number of assignments that were due, and the number of assignments that Jake completed on time (event recording). The results of this observation were then used as a basis for developing and evaluating the intervention plan for Jake.

If Jake's behavior were more severe (e.g., aggressive behaviors), it would also be important to conduct a functional behavior assessment to collect information on (1) the elements in the setting that influence the behavior (e.g., the presence of particular students; recess versus classroom; individual versus group interactions) and (2) specific events that occur before

FIGURE 12-3 Observational Data

Student:	Jake
Behaviors Observed:	Number of minutes late to class Number of assignments completed on time/number of assignments due
Setting:	English 8, Period 3

Day	Number of Minutes Late	Assignments Completed/ Assignments Due	Percentage of Assignments Completed
1	10	0/5	0
2	5	1/4	25
3	2	1/2	50
4	7	0/3	0
5	11	0/4	0
6	4	2/6	33
7	4	1/4	25
8	6	0/2	0
9	3	0/2	0
10	8	0/3	0

and after the behavior (i.e., antecedents and consequences). This information on factors that contribute to the occurrence of the behavior would be essential in designing an appropriate intervention.

In some cases, it is not necessary to collect new assessment information. For example, Tina's first grade teacher was also concerned about specific behaviors. The teacher considered gathering data on the frequency of Tina's interactions with other students and her participation in class discussions. However, an observation period was not really necessary because Tina never exhibited these behaviors. Instead, the teacher decided to begin the intervention program at once.

Mike's case was reviewed by the prereferral team and his interactions at home, in the classroom, and on the playground were carefully examined to determine the factors that were influencing his behavioral problems. Observations by the school psychologist and the special education teacher determined that interactions between Mike and adults, both in school and at home, tended to be quite negative. Moreover, as Mike's resistance to adult direction and the level of his acting-out behavior increased, the adults interacting with him tended to become even more coercive.

The initial interventions with Mike involved improving the ways in which the adults in Mike's life interacted with him: increasing the precision of the directions given to Mike, avoiding angry exchanges with him, and increasing positive feedback to Mike for those appropriate behaviors that he did exhibit. In addition, the prereferral team worked with his teacher to implement social skills instruction that focused on improving Mike's skills in (1) avoiding situations in which he typically became angry and (2) learning adaptive strategies for coping with these situations.

 SPECIAL SERVICES

If assessment results indicate that an individual is eligible for services for students with behavioral disorders, the team meets to design the IEP. Most students identified as having behavioral disorders remain in the general education classroom for at least a portion of the school day. As shown in Figure 12-4, Jake will participate in four general education classes and receive special education services from the resource teacher for two periods each day. In addition, consultation services are available to Jake's general education teachers.

> **myeducationlab** Go to the Assignments and Activities section of Topic *Emotional and Behavioral Disorders* in the MyEducationLab for your course and complete the activity entitled *Individual Interventions: Problem-Solving Model.*

Other professionals can also provide support to students with behavioral disorders. In addition to the special instruction provided for the student by the resource teacher, the resource teacher or another consultant may be available to assist the student's general education classroom teacher. Students can also visit the school psychologist, school counselor, or school social worker for regular counseling sessions. Some students and their families can be referred to community agencies that offer family counseling or other appropriate services.

Although most students with behavioral disorders are educated in the general education class, those with severe disabilities may attend special classes or special schools. In extreme cases, residential or hospital settings may be the most appropriate placement.

 FIGURE 12-4 IEP Goals and Services for Jake

Annual Goals

1. By the end of the school year, Jake will complete and return to the teacher all assignments at the time they are due.
   Persons responsible: Resource teacher, eighth-grade teachers
2. By the end of the school year, Jake will arrive on time to classes at least 4 out of 5 days per week.
   Persons responsible: Resource teacher, eighth-grade teachers
3. By the end of the school year, Jake will remain in his seat during class time unless he is given permission to leave.
   Persons responsible: Resource teacher, eighth-grade teachers
4. By the end of the school year, Jake will reduce the number of his arguments with teachers and other students to less than two per week.
   Persons responsible: Resource teacher, eighth-grade teachers
5. Jake will continue to perform at the eighth-grade level or above in reading and math.
   Person responsible: Resource teacher

Amount of Participation in General Education
Jake will attend the general education eighth-grade social studies, English, physical education, and shop classes.

Special Education and Related Services
1. Jake will receive special education services from the resource teacher (annual goals 1, 2, 3, 4, and 5) for two periods daily.
2. The resource teacher will provide consultation to Jake's eighth-grade teachers as needed to accomplish annual goals 1, 2, 3, and 4.

▶ CLASSROOM ADAPTATIONS

When students with behavioral disorders are included in the general education program, the classroom teacher may find it necessary to make program adaptations in three areas: classroom behavior, social skills, and academic instruction. The techniques and strategies described for students with learning disabilities and mild intellectual disabilities are also applicable to students with behavioral disorders. See the "Spotlight on Technology" feature for additional ideas for teaching math skills, an area in which students with behavioral disorders often experience difficulty.

myeducationlab To enhance your understanding of behavioral disorders, go to the IRIS Center Resources section of Topic *Emotional and Behavioral Disorders* in the MyEducationLab for your course and complete the Modules *Addressing Disruptive and Noncompliant Behaviors (Part 1): Understanding the Acting Out Cycle,* and *Addressing Disruptive and Noncompliant Behaviors (Part 2): Behavioral Interventions.*

This chapter offers suggestions for improving students' social skills as well as methods for helping them develop appropriate classroom conduct and study skills. Although these strategies are suggested for students with behavioral disorders, they can be used with equal success with any student, special or typical, who disrupts classroom activities or has not yet acquired effective study skills.

Several approaches have been advocated for use with students with behavioral disorders. Some of these strategies assume that it is necessary to determine what is wrong with the student and study the student's past for possible causes; for example, the history of the student's family and his or her early childhood experiences might be investigated. This approach offers little aid to the classroom teacher in dealing with problem behaviors encountered daily in the classroom. The teacher is most effective in controlling behavior problems if the emphasis is on the current status of the student and if information is gathered about the status of the student's observable behaviors and the factors that influence these behaviors. This chapter adopts the same viewpoint.

In systematic management of behavior, the teacher first identifies the behavior(s) of interest, collects data on their current status, examines the factors that may contribute to the occurrence of the behaviors, designs and institutes an intervention program, and then collects additional data to evaluate the effectiveness of the intervention and determine whether it should be continued, modified, or abandoned. There are three possible instructional goals:

- Increase the occurrence of an appropriate behavior.
- Decrease the occurrence of an inappropriate behavior.
- Teach a new behavior that is presently absent from a student's repertoire.

Examples of these goals are increasing the number of times Johnny comes to class on time, decreasing the number of times Jess leaves his seat during class, and teaching Elena a new study strategy, such as skimming a chapter for major ideas before reading it.

Teachers must assume that students with behavioral disorders can learn the appropriate behaviors expected of all students in the general education classroom. The teachers who work directly with students with special needs hold the primary responsibility for planning and carrying out interventions to change problem behaviors. Although others, such as the psychologist or counselor, can provide some assistance, the general education teacher spends the majority of the school day with the student and is therefore responsible for bringing about improvement in classroom behavior.

Many students who exhibit behavioral disorders at school may also display some of these behaviors at home. It can be very helpful to involve parents by informing them of the interventions that are being implemented at school and to consider providing them with suggestions regarding activities they may use at home. Concerned parents are generally open to suggestions regarding dealing with difficult behaviors. These recommendations can be communicated at conferences, through written suggestions, at specific training meetings, or through suggested readings.

The remainder of this chapter presents several ways to handle disruptive behavior in the classroom and help students acquire effective study skills. Before selecting one of these interventions (or designing an alternative), the teacher should carefully consider each of the following questions.

1. Can the intervention be carried out in the classroom? That is, is it feasible? Consider the type of problem (e.g., tardiness versus drug abuse), the age of the students involved, the resources within the classroom (e.g., availability of an aide, the experience and training of the teacher), the factors that contribute to the occurrence or maintenance of the behavior (e.g., attention of the teacher or peers, instructional situation versus recess), and the structure of the classroom.
2. Can the intervention be implemented consistently? If it cannot, another strategy should be selected.
3. How will data be collected to assess student progress? Can this be done consistently?
4. Do students have the prerequisite skills necessary to learn the appropriate behavior? If not, what skills must be taught?

Developing Basic Math Skills

Math software is plentiful. In fact, it is likely that more programs are available for math than for any other academic subject. It is important to note that these programs tend to focus on the practice of basic math skills rather than the development of more advanced skills such the solution of quantitative problems. For students who require assistance in developing basic math skills, however, drill programs are often appropriate.

Practicing Math Facts: *Turbo Math* and *Math Blaster* Programs

The *Turbo Math* series (*http://www.nordicsoftware.com*) includes *Turbo Math Facts* for grades K–6 and *Turbo Math Maniacs* for grades 2–12. Both offer practice in addition, subtraction, multiplication, and division. Also, both offer incentives for successful performance: Students earn money or points so that they can take part in a race (with race cars in *Facts* and motorcycles in *Maniacs*). These programs track student performance so that teachers can monitor how well students are progressing.

Multiplication Activity from Turbo Math Facts

Note: Courtesy of Nordic Software

The *Math Blaster* series (*http://www.knowledgeadventure.com*) includes a number of programs, all featuring an arcade-game format as an incentive. This series also offers teachers the ability to select the types of activities students will engage in, and data are collected to allow assessment of students' progress. Among the *Math Blaster* programs are:

- *Math Blaster: Master the Basics (Ages 6–12)*: addition, subtraction, multiplication, division, problem solving, mental math
- *Math Blaster Ages 5–7*: counting, telling time, money, measurement, basic operations
- *Math Blaster Ages 6–8*: addition, subtraction, simple fractions, charts and graphs
- *Math Blaster Ages 7–9*: addition, subtraction, multiplication, and division; fractions, decimals, and percent; basic geometry
- *Math Blaster Ages 9–12*: equations, estimation, fractions, decimals, and percents

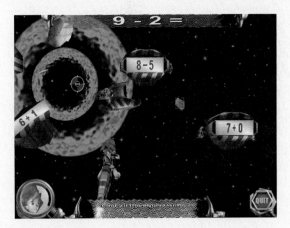

Math Blaster: Mastering the Basics

Note: Used with permission from Knowledge Adventure, www.Knowledgeadventure.com

Increasing Math Fluency: *FASTT Math*

FASTT Math (*http://www.tomsnyder.com*) is designed to help students develop fluency in basic math facts. Appropriate for grades 2 and up, this program focuses on addition, subtraction, multiplication, and division facts as well as multidigit problems.

FASTT Math

Note: Used with permission from Scholastic, Inc.

Algebra and Beyond

Software is also available to help students with the more advanced math skills that are part of the high school curriculum. Among the choices are *Math Blaster PreAlgebra* and *Math Blaster Algebra; Cosmic Geometry* from the Mighty Math series (*http://www.riverdeep.net/Edmark*); and *Algebra World, Geometry World,* and *The Trigonometry Explorer* (*http://www.mathrealm.com*).

5. Are dangerous behaviors involved that require immediate elimination or remediation? If not, which intervention being considered is the most positive and the least intrusive?

6. How can students be involved in the intervention? Can they record their own performance data? Help to develop contingency contracts? Serve as models or recorders for other students?

7. What reinforcers are meaningful to the student(s) for whom the program is designed? Is it possible to use these reinforcers with the program?

8. What resources are needed? Does the intervention require teacher time? Aide time? Reinforcers? Are these available?

9. What other factors must be considered? For example, must the physical arrangement of the classroom be changed? Must peer tutors be recruited and trained?

10. What criteria and evidence will be used to determine the success or failure of the program? What alternative interventions can be used if the original program fails?

▶ CONTROLLING DISRUPTIVE BEHAVIORS

One of the most common concerns of classroom teachers is the student who disrupts the instructional process. Whether identified as in need of special education or not, students with conduct problems call attention to themselves by arriving late, talking out in class, moving about the classroom, and interacting poorly with others. These inappropriate behaviors indicate poor social skills or poor general work habits. The following sections concentrate on what to do with students who have acquired inappropriate work habits or social skills that interrupt classroom activities.

 myeducationlab To enhance your understanding of behavioral disorders, go to the IRIS Center Resources section of Topic *Emotional and Behavioral Disorders* in the MyEducationLab for your course and complete the Modules *Addressing Disruptive and Noncompliant Behaviors (Part 1): Understanding the Acting Out Cycle*, and *Addressing Disruptive and Noncompliant Behaviors (Part 2): Behavioral Interventions*.

Tardiness

Students who arrive late begin the school day or class period at a disadvantage. Tardiness affects the performance of these students and interrupts and distracts the teacher and other students. Most students are late occasionally; however, frequent tardiness is an inappropriate behavior that must be resolved so that the student can become an active classroom participant. Suggestions for decreasing tardiness are presented next. Before implementing one of these plans, though, the teacher must be sure to collect data on current performance.

- Reward students for arriving on time. For example, students who arrive before the late bell rings can be given tickets for a raffle or have the opportunity to copy answers from the board for a couple of quiz questions. More structured programs may provide points or tokens redeemable for reinforcers. Criteria can be set up to encourage improvement in arrival time. For example, students can earn five points if they arrive on time and two points if they arrive less than 5 minutes late. Gradually reduce the number of minutes students are allowed to arrive late until it is possible to earn points only by being on time.

- Help students analyze the skills or steps required to arrive on time. For example, determine the times they should leave home, arrive at school, and be in the area of the classroom. Use this task analysis to establish a program to help students gradually master the skills needed for punctuality.

- Place a sign-in sheet at the door so students can record their name and time of arrival. Students who are late can leave tardy slips or excuses in an envelope attached to the sign-in sheet. The teacher can review these at a time that does not disrupt other classroom activities (Emmer, Evertson, Sanford, Clements, & Worsham, 1989).

- Schedule activities that students enjoy at the start of the class period. Allow only those students who are on time to class to participate.

- Set up contracts with students to specify the consequences of tardiness and punctuality. Be sure to identify clearly the criteria for success, who will keep the records, and the reinforcers that the students can earn. Students can record their own data if teachers periodically verify their accuracy.

- Discuss student tardiness with parents. Alert them to the extent of the problem, and encourage them to support the school's rules and to require—and reinforce—punctuality at home.

- Encourage parents to provide their children with watches so that students can keep track of time. If this is not possible, help students locate public clocks that they can consult.

- Arrange with parents to provide rewards at home. When students meet the punctuality criteria, they receive the rewards.

- Set up a system in which tardy students lose an equal number of minutes in a favorite activity.

- Group students into teams, and provide special reinforcers each week for the team with the best punctuality record.

- Assign peer tutors to help students get from class to class or from playground to classroom on time. As students develop appropriate skills, reduce the amount of assistance.

- Provide additional grade points for on-time arrival. For example, a student might earn five bonus points on an assignment if the assignment is started at the beginning of class.

- When students arrive on time, allow them to choose where they will sit. That is, use classroom seating preferences as reinforcers.

When any one of these interventions is implemented in the classroom, the teacher must continue to collect data on student performance to ensure that the program is effective. An alternative should be selected only after the intervention has been consistently implemented over a period of time, modifications have been made, and collected data have proved that the intervention is not working.

Verbal Outbursts

When students talk out in class, they disrupt the orderly flow of classroom activities. The teacher is distracted, and the work of other students is interrupted. Examples of verbal outbursts considered inappropriate by most teachers are answering out of turn, making irrelevant comments, arguing with the teacher or peers, and chatting with classmates during instruction. The following strategies are used to decrease the occurrence of this problem behavior.

- Establish clearly stated classroom rules regarding student verbal interactions. State the specific circumstances under which students are permitted to talk (e.g., when asked a question by the teacher, when asking the teacher a question after being called on, during assigned group work), and model the acceptable and unacceptable voice levels for each occasion. Teach these rules and provide students with opportunities to practice with teacher supervision and to obtain feedback that provides recognition for appropriate interactions and correction of inappropriate behaviors.
- Reinforce students who are good behavioral models for others, that is, those who speak out in class only at appropriate times or when teacher permission has been granted. Make the reinforcers strong enough so that students with problem behaviors will consider changing their ways. Teachers might try reinforcers such as early departure for recess or lunch, first place in line, or a certain number of minutes in a special activity.
- Recognize and reinforce problem students when they exhibit an appropriate behavior that is incompatible with the inappropriate verbal behavior, such as raising their hands and gaining recognition before answering questions in class. Clearly identify why the reinforcer is provided. For example, the teacher might say, "I like the way you raised your hand before you talked. You may take this book to the office for me." A statement such as this identifies the appropriate behavior and provides both a social reward and an activity reinforcer. Often these students are used to gaining recognition only when they exhibit inappropriate behaviors.
- Set up a system in which a loss of points results if students talk out. List the cost of talking out on the reinforcement menu or the student contract.
- Have students record the number of times they talk out in class each day. They can graph the data each day for a week and then compute the weekly total. Their goal for the next week is to decrease the number of times they talk out. Provide reinforcers if they meet their targets.
- Set up time periods in which students receive reinforcers for not talking out. Start with short time segments and gradually increase these to longer periods. You might begin with 5-minute periods, then 10-minute periods, and so on until students are able to refrain from making verbal outbursts for an entire class period or activity.
- If classroom noise (caused by several loud students) becomes a problem, use an obvious verbal signal such as "Stop talking!" or flick the classroom lights on and off to alert students to be quiet.

Excess Activity: Moving About the Classroom

A familiar conduct problem is the active student who moves about the classroom at inappropriate times. Such students leave their seats during instruction and interrupt the teacher's attempt to present information. They also move about when they have been assigned independent work tasks at their desks, interfering with their own academic progress and also disturbing the work of others. Some students remain at their desks but are constantly in motion; they wiggle and squirm in their seats, bounce up and down, tap their desks with their fingers, and kneel on their chairs.

Active behaviors such as these are described by some as hyperactivity. However, this label does not specify an observable behavior that can be counted or measured in any way. "Hyper" behaviors can be improved, but first they must be pinpointed and described in appropriate, observable terms. Consult the suggestions here for ways to decrease the occurrence of inappropriate activity in the classroom.

- Find out whether students fully understand the class rules about when they should remain in their seats and when they can move about the room. Demonstrate appropriate in-seat and transition behaviors, and clarify any misinterpretations the students may have. Reteach and provide practice for any rules the students do not remember. Briefly remind students of the rules before a transition time. As needed, provide reinforcement and correction.
- Provide frequent reinforcers for appropriate behavior; for example, students might receive rewards for remaining in their seats during instruction. If students are permitted to share reinforcers with other students seated nearby, these peers will often encourage the target students to behave appropriately.
- Record the amount of time the student is out of his or her seat; reduce time in a favorite activity by an equal amount or provide for a loss of points for each minute away from the desk.
- Allow opportunities for movement. Set up a system in which students can earn the chance to move about the room or travel to other parts of the school. For example, running errands to the office can serve as a reinforcer.
- Use extinction to reduce the occurrence of inappropriate movement. That is, provide no attention or reinforcement for inappropriate behaviors, but reward appropriate ones.
- Anticipate student movement and arrange to be near students when they are most likely to leave their seats. Often the proximity of the teacher, or a reminder provided by the teacher, will prevent inappropriate movement.
- Have students record their own in-seat behavior. They can begin with 5- or 10-minute intervals and note whether they remain seated during this time; if they leave their seats during the interval, they do not receive a check mark for that time period. At first, students can be reinforced for each successful interval. Then requirements are gradually increased so that students must perform successfully in 8 out of 10 intervals to earn reinforcers. The requirements are increased until expectations are consistent with those for all students in the class.

■ Use a timing device to check student behavior. This can be a timer or a tape recording with preset random signals. When the signal is heard, reinforce students only if they are exhibiting appropriate behavior. Be sure to vary the number of minutes between signals so that students are not aware of when their behavior will be observed.

Social Relationships

Many students have difficulty getting along with others. This type of classroom conduct problem can be characterized by either aggressive behaviors or withdrawal; in either case, students do not establish and maintain satisfactory social relationships with teachers and peers. Examples of aggressive behaviors are fighting, swearing, arguing, refusing to follow directions, and antagonizing others. Withdrawn students, in contrast, may have limited interactions with teachers and peers and may avoid both physical proximity and verbal communication.

The following suggestions can help improve the social behaviors of students in the classroom.

■ Provide students with examples of nonaggressive behaviors that can be used in situations that might lead to aggression. One way to do this is with good models; these can be adults, peers such as classmates or peer tutors, or films and videotapes.
■ Use role playing to help students practice nonaggressive responses. Simulations provide students with an opportunity to learn appropriate behaviors before encountering difficult situations in daily life.

■ Teach students acceptable responses to verbal or physical attacks. Options include calling for assistance, leaving the area, or saying something nonaggressive, such as "You played well in the softball game yesterday" or "I like the car I saw you driving after school." If students have not learned options such as these, they may react by fighting back or verbally attacking the aggressor. They need to learn a range of alternative responses and know which are appropriate for use in which situation.
■ Incorporate strategies for reducing **bullying** in the classroom and other parts of the school environment. The "Inclusion Tips for the Teacher" section provides suggestions.

◆ **Inclusion Tips for the Teacher**

How to Reduce Classroom Bullying

Migliore (2003) presents these strategies for reducing classroom bullying.

1. Lead a class discussion on bullying.
2. Write a specific no-bullying policy into your classroom rules.
3. Teach social skills routinely through specific lessons and in conjunction with other activities throughout the day.
4. Teach students how to avoid being a victim and what to do if they are victimized.
5. Support students who speak out about bullying or who seek extra adult help.
6. Use extra effort to include all students in class activities.
7. Reinforce responsible, positive behaviors whenever possible.
8. Use a confidential "message box" for student suggestions or comments on classroom concerns.
9. Always model respectful behavior toward students.
10. Make sure that situations that have the potential of becoming aggressive are closely supervised.
11. Intervene immediately with an approach that matches the incident if bullying occurs.
12. Insist that the bully make amends if the incident involves a specific targeted victim.
13. Arrange your class schedule to minimize chaos.
14. Provide many ways to gain recognition in your classroom.
15. Have a clear process to report bullying.
16. Enlist students in no-bullying activities.
17. Encourage administrators and faculty members to write a no-bullying policy into the school handbook.
18. Plan an in-service meeting for all staff members to address bullying.
19. Involve parents with your no-bullying efforts.
20. Use the PTA to publicize the school's no-bullying policy. (pp. 172–176)

Note: From "Eliminating Bullying in Your Classroom," by E. T. Migliore, *Intervention in School and Clinic, 38*(3) 172–176. Reprinted with permission.

- Reinforce students who substitute appropriate, nonaggressive responses for the aggressive behaviors they previously exhibited. For example, provide a special reinforcer when students spend the lunch period or recess playing a game rather than arguing, fighting, or name calling.
- Use extinction for inappropriate verbal behaviors such as swearing, arguing, and teasing. Supply reinforcers for other students in the classroom to encourage them to ignore this type of problem behavior.
- Provide a penalty or punisher when a student exhibits an inappropriate behavior. This action might be removing the student to a setting without reinforcement (time-out), taking away activity time or other reinforcers earned (response cost), or introducing an aversive such as scolding or notification of parents. This type of intervention should be used sparingly, but it is sometimes necessary to stop a problem behavior quickly. Punishment, when used, should be administered immediately each time the inappropriate behavior occurs. Punishment is most effective when used in conjunction with positive reinforcement of appropriate behaviors. In fact, Walker (1995) indicates that the combination of teacher praise, token reinforcement, and response cost "represents the most powerful and potentially effective intervention for changing the behavior of acting-out children" (p. 197).
- Carefully review the social skills of withdrawn students, and determine their specific strengths and weaknesses. Provide instruction in important areas of need, such as how to greet others or what to do to start and participate in a conversation with others.
- Encourage the social interaction of withdrawn students with reinforcement techniques. Reinforcers can be used with the withdrawn student to encourage interaction, but, especially at first, it may be better to reinforce the student's peers. Focusing a great deal of attention on the withdrawn student at the start of the intervention may cause further withdrawal and avoidance of interactions.
- Include the withdrawn student in a classroom group assigned to complete a project or activity. Furnish specific activities that lead to interactions. For example, in completing worksheets, each student can be given a different portion of the materials needed to answer the questions. Provide reinforcers to the entire group when the target student is an active participant.
- Pair a withdrawn student with a peer tutor, cross-age tutor, or adult volunteer. The tutor or volunteer should model appropriate social interactions and reinforce the target student for like behaviors.

It is important to note that students with more severe antisocial, violent, or acting-out behavioral problems (e.g., hostility or aggression toward others, a willingness to commit rule infractions or to violate social norms, defiance of adult authority) may require more intensive interventions to deal with their problem behaviors. Typically, special education programs have specialists or consultants available to assist general education teachers in designing and implementing these interventions. In addition, there are many resources that provide detailed descriptions of strategies and interventions to deal with more severe challenging behaviors. For ideas about one important area of concern, see the "Inclusion Tips for the Teacher" section on preventing violence in the schools.

Inclusion Tips for the Teacher

Preventing School Violence

According to the findings from a government study of violence in U.S. schools (Miller & Chandler, 2003), "in 1999–2000, 71% of public elementary and secondary schools experienced at least one violent incident" (p. 6). It is interesting to note that the most common incident was physical attacks or fights without a weapon (64% of all schools) followed by threats of attacks without a weapon (52%). Serious violent incidents were less common, ranging from 11% of schools reporting at least one threat of a physical assault with a weapon to 1% or less of schools reporting robberies with a weapon or rape.

Two government publications are designed to help teachers, parents, and the entire school community reduce the number of violent incidents in schools. The first, *Early Warning, Timely Response: A Guide to Safe Schools* (Dwyer, Osher, & Warger, 1998), identified characteristics of schools that are safe and responsive to all children. Such schools:

- Focus on academic achievement
- Involve families in meaningful ways
- Develop links to the community
- Emphasize positive relationships among students and staff
- Discuss safety issues openly

- Treat students with equal respect
- Create ways for students to share their concerns
- Help children feel safe expressing their feelings
- Have in place a system for referring children who are suspected of being abused or neglected
- Offer extended day programs for children
- Promote good citizenship and character
- Identify problems and assess progress toward solutions
- Support students in making the transition to adult life and the workplace. (pp. 3–5)

Copies of this guide can be downloaded from the website of the National Association of School Psychologists (*http://www.nasponline.org/resources/crisis_safety/*).

The second publication is called *Safeguarding Our Children: An Action Guide* (Dwyer & Osher, 2000). It describes a comprehensive three-level approach to preventing school violence: building a schoolwide foundation, responding to warning signs with early intervention, and providing intensive interventions to troubled children. Copies of this guide in both English and Spanish can be downloaded from the website of the U.S. Department of Education at (*http://www.ed.gov/admins/lead/safety/actguide/index.html*).

TEACHING STUDY SKILLS

Students with poor study habits are at a distinct disadvantage in the general education classroom (Archer & Gleason, 1995; Heron & Harris, 2001). They may have difficulty maintaining attention in class, staying on task, organizing their work, or producing accurate responses. These problems have grave effects on academic performance and hinder a teacher's instructional effort. With students who fail to complete assignments, assessing current skill levels and progress is difficult because few work samples are available. As these students fall farther and farther behind their classmates, teachers become frustrated, and the probability increases that classroom conduct problems will occur.

Teachers have not typically taught study skills in a systematic fashion. However, programs such as *Skills for School Success* (Archer & Gleason, 1994) for grades 3 to 6 or *Advanced Skills for School Success* (Archer, 1992) for grades 7 to 12 provide teachers with a method, and the materials, to teach students a wide range of school and study skills such as organizing a notebook, keeping a calendar, writing neat papers, and completing assignments. Skills such as these should be in-cluded as part of the school curriculum; they should be taught directly with opportunities for guided and independent practice. The sections that follow discuss strategies to promote several important study skills; included are ideas to help students increase their ability to maintain attention, organize their work, and respond accurately. Another way to improve study skills is to increase reading comprehension. See the "Spotlight on Technology" feature for more information.

Maintaining Attention

Students with classroom behavior problems often spend a great deal of instructional time engaging in off-task behavior; their attention is not directed toward the appropriate classroom activity. They may stare into space, watch other students, doodle on their papers, or attend to stimuli that are irrelevant to the instructional task. Such students do not make effective use of independent study time. Instead of maintaining attention on the specific task, they attend to other features of the environment. Or their attention span is brief, and they shift attention from the instructional task to some other aspect of the classroom. Some engage in disruptive behaviors and interrupt

---

SPOTLIGHT ON TECHNOLOGY

Improving Reading Comprehension: *Start-to-Finish Books*

Start-to-Finish Books is a large collection of accessible books for students who struggle with reading. The Gold Library of *Start-to-Finish* features "considerate text" written at the grade 2/3 level. Vocabulary has been simplified to increase comprehension and sentences are shorter and less complex. Each book comes in three formats: a paperback book, an audiotape, and a computer version. The computer version provides support by reading text aloud with word-by-word highlighting. The screen below from *Liddy and the Volcanoes* shows a short text, a graphic, and commands such as the Speak button.

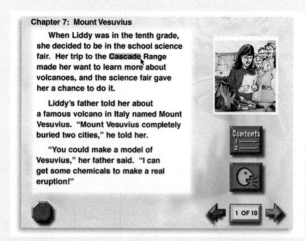

Note: Courtesy of Don Johnston, Inc.

The Gold Library contains more than 50 individual titles. They are grouped into series such as Classic Adventures (e.g., *Treasure Island*), Classic Literature (e.g., *Romeo and Juliet*), A Step into History (e.g., *Rosa Parks: Freedom Fighter*), Natural Disasters (e.g., *Liddy and the Volcanoes*), Sherlock Holmes Mysteries, Ancient History, and Overcoming the Odds: Sports Biographies. Each book contains 10 to 12 chapters with approximately 100 to 150 words per page. At the end of each chapter, students take a comprehension quiz. Results are stored so that teachers can see records of student progress.

The Blue Library of the *Start-to-Finish Book* collection features longer books with more difficult text (grade 4/5) for more mature readers. More text appears on the screen and fewer graphics are used. Several titles are available including those from the series Myths and Legends (e.g., *Greek Myths*), Classic Adventure (e.g., *Call of the Wild*), and The World Around Us (e.g., *Jane Goodall and the Chimpanzees of Gombe*).

The Gold and Blue Libraries also include books that provide struggling readers with grade-level content with "considerate text." According to the website, the *Start-to-Finish Core Content* series "offers engaging, standards-based informational texts written at two levels and delivered in three media formats." Titles include *Native Americans in the Time of Lewis and Clark, Robot Explorers on Mars, Adaptation and Change on the Galapagos Islands,* and *William Shakespeare and His Times.*

Another component of *Start-to-Finish Books* is a series called *Literacy Starters*. Designed for readers with limited skills, each *Literacy Starter Set* contains three brief books, one with emergent-level text, one with transitional text, and one with conventional text. Among the *Literacy Starter Set* series available are *Sports—Safety & Success; Plants—Science & Surroundings;* and *Early Settlers—Changes & Challenges.*

the concentration of others. One of the following strategies might help students improve their on-task behavior.

- Before presenting important verbal information to students, use a cue to alert them, such as "Listen," "Ready?" or "It's time to begin the lesson!" Establish a standard way of beginning lessons, and use the signal word or phrase only at times when you wish to obtain everyone's attention.
- Make teacher attention or other reinforcers contingent on attending behavior. Students with severe attention problems will need strong reinforcers provided immediately. This approach is much more effective than scolding students for not attending.
- When presenting information to students, seat them in a semicircle or U-shaped formation to ensure that all students can maintain visual contact with the teacher.
- Provide clear directions. Students with attention problems may be unable to follow long sets of directions with several steps. Simplify the directions and provide reinforcement when students complete each step. Avoid directions such as "Everyone return to your seat, get out your science book, turn to page 28, and answer the first five questions." Instead, start with the first step ("Everyone return to your seat") and provide reinforcement when students comply.
- Present lessons at a brisk pace. Time spent on unimportant points or skills already mastered by the group can contribute to student inattention.
- Continually monitor whether students are attending to the lesson. Be prepared to modify your instructional approach if students seem confused or inattentive or if the material is too difficult.
- Use physical proximity to encourage attention. When students start to shift attention from the task, move closer to them.
- Reduce the predictability of your actions by varying the presentation of lessons. Ask different kinds of questions, vary the intonation of your voice, and let students know that they may be asked questions at any time.
- Provide students with individual work areas in which there are few distractions. These can be cubicles, carrels, or study booths. Be sure to consider both visual and auditory distractions when selecting an appropriate place for student offices.
- Hold students accountable for attending to the lesson and learning the material presented. Periodic teacher checks of students' understanding with techniques such as random questioning can increase student involvement.
- Simplify instructional materials so that only relevant information remains. For example, pictures or drawings can be distracting in reading materials.
- For students who have poor reading skills or difficulty understanding what they read, consider using computer software that assists with study skills as well as reading comprehension. To learn more about one example of this approach, Kurzweil 3000, consult the "Spotlight on Technology."

Organizational Skills

Some students lack the ability to plan ahead. They are unorganized and use class time poorly. Such students can miss the important parts of task directions, fail to ask appropriate questions about assignments, and neglect to bring pens, pencils, and other necessary equipment to class. At test time, they are not prepared and have difficulty using the time allotted for the test effectively. The following suggestions may help students learn to plan ahead and become more organized.

- To help students budget their time, develop a schedule that divides the class period into short segments, each a few minutes in length. Make a list of activities to be finished during each time segment, and reinforce students when these tasks are completed. Gradually allow students to help in devising the daily schedule until this is an independent activity. As students learn to complete their work, make reinforcers more difficult to earn. For example, reinforcement might be delivered only after the satisfactory completion of work for two intervals rather than one.
- State directions for assignments and classroom work clearly and concisely; include only essential information. Alert students well ahead of time to work that is due and provide older pupils with a weekly schedule of assignments.
- Assist students in organizing their materials. This may involve teaching them how to organize their desks or how to set up a notebook. Student notebooks should contain a calendar, a place for recording assignments due, and sections for notes and assignments for each subject or class; they can also hold materials such as paper, pencils, pens, and rulers. The teacher should check notebooks periodically and reinforce or reinstruct students as necessary. Parents should be informed of the notebook requirements and encouraged to compliment students for organizing their work.
- Present directions for assignments and class work both verbally and in writing. Students can practice by first listening to directions and taking notes and later checking their accuracy with written directions.
- Begin with work directions that have only a few steps. Reinforce students for following each step. Gradually increase the standards for success; the time period allowed for task completion can be shortened, or the accuracy criterion raised. When students are able to follow simple directions, introduce ones that are more complex.
- Teach students to ask appropriate questions about directions and assignments by providing a model. The model can be a demonstration by the teacher or a written set of questions to ask when a task is unclear. Allow students to practice asking questions about hypothetical assignments.
- Prepare students for reading assignments by teaching strategies to help them approach tasks in an organized manner. For example, provide students with guidelines

Kurzweil 3000, Software for Reading and Studying

If an individual cannot see, how can that individual read a print book, newspaper, or magazine? One solution to that problem was provided in the mid 1970s by Ray Kurzweil's company, Kurzweil Computer Products. The solution was the first "print-to-speech reading machine, including the first omni-font optical character recognition (OCR), the first text-to-speech synthesizer, and the first CCD flat bed scanner" (Kurzweil Technologies, 2009). In the mid 1990s, that "reading machine" was redesigned to meet the needs not only of persons with visual limitations but also of persons with learning disabilities and others who experience difficulty learning from print.

Today, the Kurzweil 3000 software program allows students who struggle with reading to access any printed text by hearing it read aloud. The basic procedure requires the teacher or other professional to scan the document of interest first, before it can be "read" by the Kurzweil program using optical character recognition technology. When the print document has been converted into an electronic file in Kurzweil format, it can be read aloud. Kurzweil software is able to read some other electronic formats including PDFs and RTFs, and it is compatible with the Mozilla Firefox browser, allowing access to text on the web. To hear text read aloud, the student simply places the cursor at the start of the text to be read and clicks the forward button on the Reader panel:

The most important feature of the Kurzweil 3000 is that it makes any text accessible, including all of the print resources available to peers in the general education classroom. Other features make this program even more useful for students with reading problems and those with poor study skills.

- The "voices" that read the text aloud are quite natural sounding and easy to understand.
- When text is read aloud, that text is highlighted on the screen.
- Highlighting uses two colors. The default configuration is one color for the whole sentence and another for the word being read aloud, although that configuration can be modified as needed.
- Students can ask the program for the definition of any word, its synonyms, and its division into syllables.

- Built-in study tools allow students to highlight important text, add annotations, place bookmarks, and create summaries and outlines.
- A word processor with spell checking and word prediction is built into the program.

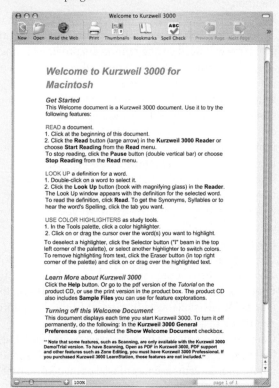

Note: Used with permission from Kurzweil Education, a division of Cambium Learning Technologies.

One potential drawback of the Kurzweil software is its cost. At fall 2009 prices, the professional version needed by the teacher to scan print materials is more than $1,000. Single learner stations for students are approximately $400 each. Lab packs containing multiple copies of the learner stations are available to reduce the cost per student.

Kurzweil 3000 is available for both Window and Macintosh computers, although the two versions differ in some ways. To learn more about this program, visit the website of Kurzweil Educational Systems, a Cambium Learning Technologies Company (*http://www.kurzweiledu.com*). This website includes resources and research on the Kurzweil 3000, and visitors can download a 30-day trial copy of the software at no cost.

such as those that appear in Figure 12-5 for surveying textbooks and textbook chapters.
- Group students together for completing individual assignments. Reinforce the group if all members finish their work and meet the criterion for accuracy.
- Make a list of materials needed to complete an assignment, and have students assemble these before beginning work. Later, require that students prepare such a list before they start an assignment. Grade both the list and the assignment itself.

- Encourage parents to set aside quiet time—with no television, radio, or telephone—each evening for their children to study and complete assignments.
- Work with parents in setting up a home program to reinforce studying. Parents can talk with the teacher each week or sign a check sheet to report whether the student has spent the appropriate time studying at home.

Other sources of information about teaching organizational skills to students with special needs, particularly those in

FIGURE 12-5   Guidelines to Help Students Survey Textbooks and Chapters

Surveying Your Textbook
1. Name of textbook
2. Author(s)
3. List two things you can tell about the book by its title.
4. List three points that the author makes in the introduction.
5. Look at the table of contents. List three things you know about the textbook by reading the chapter titles.
6. Does the textbook contain an index, glossary, and appendix? If so, how will you use each of them?

Surveying a Textbook Chapter
1. Title of chapter
2. List two things that the chapter title suggests.
3. Read the first and last paragraphs and the boldface headings in the chapter. What do you think the author wants you to learn?
4. What graphic aids does the chapter contain?

_____ maps   _____ italics
_____ graphs   _____ questions
_____ charts   _____ definitions
_____ illustrations   _____ bold print
_____ diagrams   _____ other

5. What other clues does the chapter have that might help you understand it?

Note: Teaching Children and Adolescents with Special Needs (5th ed.) (p. 311) by J. L. Olson, J. C. Platt, and L. A. Dieker. Copyright 2008 by Pearson Education, Inc. Reprinted with permission.

middle school and high school, are *Teaching Children and Adolescents with Special Needs* by Olson, Platt, and Dieker (2008), and *Adolescents and Adults with Learning Disabilities and ADHD: Assessment and Accommodation* by N. Gregg (2009).

Increasing Accuracy

Inaccurate responses occur for many reasons. For students with behavioral disorders, a rapid response rate is one common cause. In this instance, students work quickly, without taking time to think about their answers or check them for accuracy. In class discussions, these students may blurt out a response before carefully considering the question. Such students are characterized by the speed with which they work and the resulting high number of incorrect responses; a term used to describe this behavior is *impulsivity*. To help hasty students increase the accuracy of their work, teachers can try one of the strategies described here.

■ When giving assignments, remind students that part of the task is checking for accuracy, and reinforce students for completing this step. Teachers can observe students to see whether they are checking their work, or reinforcement can be contingent on a continual decrease in the number of errors.

■ Provide reinforcement for accurate responses. For example, students might earn tokens for each correct response.

■ Model appropriate proofreading procedures. Show the class examples of work containing errors, and review how to make corrections. Students may be taught to use a proofreading strategy such as COPS, in which students

check Capitalization, Overall Appearance, Punctuation, and Spelling (Schumaker, Nolan, & Deshler, 1985).

■ Carefully design instructional materials to achieve high rates of student success, which is associated with higher levels of student learning. Poorly designed instruction leads to student frustration and poor levels of performance.

■ Teach students strategies for taking tests and examinations. An example of a program to improve test-taking skills appears in Figure 12-6; teachers might also be interested in the article "Improving Test-Taking Skills of LD Adolescents" by Markel (1981).

■ Encourage students to think before they speak. For example, after asking a question, require students to observe a short 5- to 10-second "thinking time" before responding. As students learn to deliberate before answering, gradually reduce the structure of this requirement.

■ Use a cognitive training technique to help students learn to direct their own problem solving. Consult the accompanying "Inclusion Tips for the Teacher" for information about the self-instructional training program described by Finch and Spirito (1980).

■ Kauffman (2001) suggests that careless student errors can be reduced through the use of response cost procedures. That is, when errors are made, students lose something, such as part of their recess time. The procedure can be made more effective by adding a provision that students must complete an additional question or problem correctly for each error made.

FIGURE 12-6 How to Be a Better Test-Taker

To the Student:

If you have ever studied for a test only to find your efforts didn't pay off in a good grade because you didn't study efficiently, this packet can help. Follow the suggestions in the order presented. Read each item carefully. Review wherever you feel necessary. Begin!

1. When taking a test, don't panic! Be prepared with a pencil (with eraser), pen, and paper.
2. Carefully examine the entire test before starting to answer any questions. It is very important that you understand what you are to do in response to the test. Knowing whether the teacher wants one word answers or discussion responses, for example, makes a difference in the correctness of your response.
3. After you have looked at the number of questions and the type of response required, estimate how much time you are going to devote to each question or area. Pay particular attention to the weight each question carries. An essay question worth 25 points out of a 100 possible points must be given more time than two multiple-choice questions of 2 points each.
4. Answer first those questions you feel most confident of the answers.
5. When you are responding to an essay question, it is a good idea to write down the key ideas or main points in brief form. This will help you include everything you feel is of importance in your answer.
6. It is a good idea to try to answer all the questions in a test (unless you're told that you could be penalized for wrong answers). If you are really stumped on a question, go on to another. Sometimes another question will help you to remember the answer to the question you have been struggling with.
7. Write clearly. You are likely to lose points if the teacher has great difficulty reading your writing.
8. Leave time to reread your paper before you hand it in. Pay attention to punctuation and spelling. Most importantly, ask yourself if you wrote what you intended.
9. In objective tests, don't waste time on questions that are confusing to you.
10. Once you have made a guess to a question you are unsure of, you should not change it; first guesses are usually best.

Note: From *Mainstreaming the Learning Disabled Adolescent* (p. 35) by D. M. Woodward, 1981, Austin, TX: PRO-ED. Copyright 1981 by PRO-ED, Inc.

Inclusion Tips for the Teacher

Self-Instructional Training

According to Finch and Spirito (1980), self-instructional training is a procedure in which students learn a step-by-step system for attacking a problem by means of specific verbalizations. That is, students learn specific strategies to talk themselves through problem situations; they themselves give the instructions.

Finch and Spirito (1980) describe the four general types of verbal messages used in the program:

1. Problem definition ("What is it I should do in this situation?")
2. Focusing of attention ("I have to concentrate and do what I'm supposed to do.")
3. Coping statements ("Even though I made a mistake, I can continue more slowly.")
4. Self-reinforcement ("Great! I did it! That was good.")

Students learn this strategy by observing the teacher, who models completion of a task using the verbalization procedures. Then students perform the task and begin by instructing themselves out loud. Next, they perform the task using only whispered instructions. Eventually, the instructions are internalized, and students are able to direct their own problem-solving behavior.

 Use peer tutors to help students correct work or practice correct responses. For instance, the teacher might provide tutors with questions likely to be asked in class, and the tutor and student can then practice those questions. Tutors should be reminded to encourage students to think before they respond.

In this chapter, you have learned ways to handle disruptive behavior in the general education classroom and improve the study skills of students with behavioral disorders and others with similar needs. Check "Things to Remember" to review strategies used to meet the needs of students identified as having behavioral disorders.

Things to Remember

- The most common areas in which adaptations must be made for students with behavioral disorders are social skills and classroom behavior. Although these students usually require assistance in academic instruction, the most urgent needs are generally control of disruptive behaviors and acquisition of appropriate social and study skills.

- The major indicators of behavioral disorders are actions that deviate significantly in frequency, intensity, and duration from those expected of the student's typical peers of the same age and gender.

- Many students with behavioral disorders have academic needs that closely resemble those of students with learning disabilities and require the use of similar instructional interventions.

- Assessment of behavioral disorders is most useful when data are gathered about the current status of students' problem behaviors.

- Typical disruptive behaviors of students include tardiness, verbal outbursts and other acting-out behaviors, inappropriate physical activity, and poor social relationships.

- In the area of study skills, students with behavioral disorders experience difficulty maintaining attention, organizing work, and responding with accuracy.

- Students with behavioral disorders are capable of learning to act appropriately; their school conduct and work habits can be improved with proper instructional and behavioral management techniques.

ACTIVITIES

1. Observe a student who has been identified as having a behavioral disorder in a general education classroom. Describe how this student's behavior differs from that of typical class peers. How does the teacher treat this student? How do classmates react? For this student and one or two typically developing students, try to get a count of the number of positive and negative interactions with the teacher and with other students; compare your data. Look back through this chapter for intervention ideas that might be appropriate for the student. Select one and defend your choice.

2. Interview a special educator who works with students with behavioral disorders. Ask that teacher for recommendations of appropriate techniques to use in the general education classroom. In the teacher's view, what are the important differences between students with behavioral disorders who succeed in the general education program and those who require a special class? Write a summary of your interview, and discuss any of the teacher's points with which you disagree.

3. Read two articles that discuss techniques for working with students with behavioral disorders. *Behavioral Disorders, Beyond Behavior, Teaching Exceptional Children,* and *Education and Treatment of Children* are journals in which such articles often appear. Carefully consider the articles you have read, and describe how these techniques could be used in a general education class.

4. Survey your local community for agencies that provide services to students with behavioral disorders. These agencies may deal with acting-out or withdrawn students, drug abuse, or suicide prevention. Local school districts or mental health organizations may be able to provide the names of some appropriate agencies. Contact two agencies and find out what types of services they offer. How do these programs differ from school programs? Are services offered to parents and family members? In your view, how useful are these programs?

5. Assume that you have been selected to explain behavioral disorders to another teacher. Prepare an outline of your presentation, including the benefits of these students being included in the general education program. Formulate four questions that you anticipate the teacher is likely to ask, and prepare answers for these questions.

6. Watch a film about individuals who have unusual or disordered behavior. If you can't think of any recent examples, do a Google search to locate older films such as *To Sir with Love, Rain Man,* or *Blackboard Jungle.* Describe the behaviors portrayed in terms that would be meaningful in planning for the individual's educational needs. Explain how a general education teacher could accommodate a school-aged individual with similar needs in his or her classroom. What type(s) of special support or services might be needed by the student? By the teacher? Discuss any questions you would have about the feasibility and appropriateness of the placement.

CHAPTER
THIRTEEN

Teaching Students with Communication Disorders

Elaine, Jeff, and Rocky

There are three children with communication problems in Ms. Ranson's first grade class. Despite their speech and language difficulties, these students participate in all general education class activities. Each also receives individual help twice each week from the speech–language pathologist. We will look more closely at the special education needs of two of these children—Elaine and Rocky—later in the chapter.

Elaine speaks clearly and distinctly but has difficulty producing the /r/ sound. Because of this articulation problem, she calls her teacher Ms. Wanson.

Jeff's speech is like that of a much younger child. He mispronounces some sounds, omits others, and speaks hurriedly and indistinctly. Jeff's teacher and classmates often find it difficult to understand what he is saying.

Rocky speaks intelligibly but makes many grammatical errors. He uses incomplete sentences and may mix plural nouns with singular verbs ("boys runs"). In addition, his speaking vocabulary is limited, and his knowledge of word meanings is poor for his age.

Willy

Willy stutters. He is in 10th grade and is a good student. On written reports, assignments, and exams, Willy excels. However, because of his dysfluency in speech, he is reluctant to answer questions in class, participate in discussions, or give oral reports. Willy has several close friends around whom he is comfortable speaking, but he is hesitant to talk with people he does not know well. Although he attends general education classes for all his academic work, Willy receives special education services from the speech–language pathologist. This specialist is working with Willy to reduce his dysfluency and to overcome his embarrassment in speaking. She also consults with Willy's general education teachers to help them provide a nonthreatening classroom environment in which Willy will feel comfortable and will practice speaking in front of others.

LOOKING AHEAD

There are many different types of communication disorders, and the adaptations required in general education classrooms vary from student to student. As you will learn in this chapter, the two major strategies involve encouraging oral communication and teaching new language skills. Think about these questions as you read.

- Compare the communication problems of the three first graders, Elaine, Jeff, and Rocky. Which are speech problems? Language problems? What dimensions of language are involved?
- From what you know about Willy the 10th grader, what are his strengths? Also, what challenges does he face because of his communication problems?
- What strategies could you use to create a classroom environment where students like Elaine, Jeff, Rocky, and Willy would feel comfortable practicing their communication skills?

When children enter school, they are expected to be able to communicate. This expectation may not be realized in students with speech and language impairments. Communication disorders, one of the most common of all disabilities, affect a student's ability to interact with teachers and classmates. Students with speech problems may mispronounce words or sounds, speak with dysfluency, or have an unusual voice quality; as a result, their speech is difficult for the listener to understand. Students with language problems may fail to understand the speech of others and may have trouble expressing their own thoughts in words. Although communication disorders can accompany other disabilities such as learning disabilities, intellectual disabilities, and hearing impairment, most students with speech and language impairments remain in the general education classroom. Special services are provided to them on a part-time basis by professionals such as speech–language pathologists.

The special needs of students with communication problems fall in the areas of academic and social performance. In instruction, the general education teacher may need to make minor adaptations in order to stress language, listening, and speaking skills for such students. Creating an accepting classroom environment is also important. Students with communication impairments are more likely to practice verbal interactions with others if their classmates and teachers are tolerant, accepting, and supportive.

TABLE 13-1 Simulations of Speech and Language Impairments

Communication Situation	Type of Disorder	Suggested Simulation
You are speaking to a group of teachers and parents. Describe the instructional program in your classroom.	Delayed speech	Deliver your speech without talking. You may gesture.
You have just met your new principal. Introduce yourself and welcome him or her to your school.	Articulation	Introduce yourself after you have placed one or two saltine crackers in your mouth. Don't chew.
You are reporting to the school board about the new parent involvement program at your school.	Poor voice quality	Tape record your speech and then play it back at the wrong speed.
You are chatting with the parents of several of your students about the upcoming school play.	Dysfluency or stuttering	S-say th-the f-first s-sound o-of e-each w-word, th-then th-the w-word i-it s-self.

This chapter describes the characteristics of students with communication disorders and suggests methods for the general education teacher to use in gathering data, teaching listening and speaking skills, and creating an accepting classroom environment. To become more familiar with speech and language impairments and their impact on communication, try one of the simulations described in Table 13-1.

INDICATORS OF COMMUNICATION DISORDERS

Because students with communication disorders typically remain members of general education classrooms for their entire educational careers, the general education teacher is an important member of the inclusion team. It is the general education teacher who notes signs of communication difficulties, refers individual students for special education assessment, helps gather assessment information, and later coordinates students' classroom instruction with special speech and language services.

Communication disorders are of two types: those that affect language and those that affect speech. **Language** is the ability to communicate using symbols; it includes both oral and written communication and requires both expression and reception of ideas. **Speech** is one aspect of oral language; it is the vehicle by which thoughts are expressed in oral communication.

According to the American Speech-Language-Hearing Association (ASHA) (n.d.), language and speech disorders can be differentiated as follows.

A *language disorder* is characterized by an inability to use the symbols of language through (a) proper use of words and their meanings, (b) appropriate grammatical patterns, and (c) proper use of speech sounds.

A *speech disorder* is characterized by difficulty in (a) producing speech sounds (articulation), (b) maintaining speech rhythm (fluent speech), and (c) controlling vocal production (voice). (p. 1, italics added)

The National Information Center for Children and Youth with Disabilities (1997b) includes as characteristics of language disorders "improper use of words and their meanings, inability to express ideas, inappropriate grammatical patterns, reduced vocabulary, and inability to follow directions" (p. 1). Thus, students with language disorders experience difficulty understanding or expressing ideas appropriate to their age. Those with speech impairments show poor speech sound production, fluency, or voice quality for their age.

Most speech problems are detected at an early age; articulation disorders are most commonly found among children in the first few grades of school. Language disorders are also identified in young children, but can persist throughout the elementary and secondary years. Speech disorders are usually obvious to the listener. In fact, Van Riper (1978) maintained that one criterion for identifying a communication disorder is

WINDOW ON THE WEB

American Speech-Language-Hearing Association

The American Speech-Language-Hearing Association (ASHA) is the major professional organization in the field of communication disorders. As such, it serves speech–language pathologists, audiologists, and others interested in speech, language, and hearing development and disorders in children and in adults. The ASHA website offers features for several categories of visitors including the public, audiologists, speech–language pathologists, and current and prospective students. The public section of the website provides online information about topics such as "Hearing

Assessment and Screening," "Child Speech and Language," "Speech Sound Disorders," and "Stuttering." The student segment of this site focuses on information about careers, graduate programs, and certification. Information is also available on the ASHA website about careers, certification, publications, events, advocacy efforts, and research.

http://www.asha.org

Recognizing Speech Problems

Perhaps the best way to determine whether a person has a speech problem is to ask yourself the following questions.

1. *Can I understand this person?* This is the simplest judgment you will have to make. If you cannot understand or can understand only with difficulty what a person is saying, she has a communication disorder.

2. *Does this person sound strange?* If you can understand someone, but he doesn't sound like you expect him to, he has a problem. An adult who sounds like Elmer Fudd, a 200-pound adult male who sounds like a nine-year-old girl, and a person who has a flat, expressionless manner of speaking all have communication problems.

3. *Does this person have any peculiar physical characteristics when speaking?* A person who has distracting mannerisms that interfere with his message has a problem. These mannerisms might include unnecessary or unexpected movements of the lips, tongue, nostrils, arms, legs, or posture.

4. *Is the communication in a style inappropriate to the situation?* We do not expect the president of the United States to greet Congress before his annual State of the Union address by saying, "Hey, baby, what's happenin'?". . . . Our point is that we normally shift our style of communication to fit a given situation. A speaker unable to do this may have a problem.

5. *Do I enjoy listening to this speaker?* This is a judgment we all feel comfortable making. If the reason we don't enjoy a speaker is that we don't like her message, the speaker doesn't have a problem. If, on the other hand, we don't enjoy a speaker for one of the reasons mentioned here, she probably does have a problem. . . . Speakers who can alienate people merely by introducing themselves need help.

6. *Is the speaker damaging his communication mechanisms?* Like most other parts of the body, the organs used in communication can be misused. Although diagnoses of physiological abuse can only be made by specialists, listeners can often detect signs of strain in a speaker. Teachers should always refer to professionals children they think may be injuring their voices. An unnecessary referral hurts no one, but overlooking a symptom can have disastrous consequences.

7. *Does the speaker suffer when attempting to communicate?* This is difficult to judge, because a listener cannot usually determine how a person feels about her efforts to communicate. Many people considered normal communicators by their peers suffer emotionally as a result of shortcomings they imagine. Communication problems such as these that do not have obvious symptoms are among the most difficult to treat.

Note: From *An Introduction to Special Education* (2nd ed.) by William H. Berdine and Edward Blackhurst. Published by Allyn & Bacon. Copyright © 1985 Pearson Education. Reprinted by permission of the publisher.

speech unusual enough to bring attention to itself. *Unusual,* however, is not a very precise description of a possible problem. The questions in the "Inclusion Tips for the Teacher" box can assist in obtaining more specific information.

 ASSESSMENT PROCEDURES

When communication disorders are suspected, the assessment team meets to prepare an assessment plan. One important consideration is the student's hearing; the school nurse is consulted to determine whether a hearing loss is contributing to poor speech or language performance. If the problem appears to be a minor speech disorder, the speech–language pathologist takes primary responsibility for assessment. If more serious difficulties are suspected, several specialists participate in gathering assessment information. Formal assessment begins when the parents of the referred student have given written consent.

 Go to the Assignments and Activities section of Topic *Communication Disorders* in the MyEducationLab for your course and complete the activity entitled *Norm-Referenced Speech and Language Assessment.*

In evaluating a student's speech, the speech–language pathologist can administer a standardized measure such as the *Goldman-Fristoe Test of Articulation*–2 (Goldman & Fristoe,

2000). The specialist also talks with the student in an informal setting in order to evaluate speech fluency and voice quality. The classroom teacher may be asked to contribute observations concerning the usual speech patterns of the student.

Figure 13-1 presents a checklist that the teacher can use to evaluate the speech of young elementary children. Voice quality, speech fluency, and sound production are included. The checklist also indicates the ages at which students are expected to produce various speech sounds; these are general guidelines and should be used with caution when evaluating the performance of an individual child.

Most children have mastered the sounds of the English language by the age of 8. Some, however, progress more slowly. Consider Elaine, the first grader introduced at the beginning of this chapter, who has yet to master the /r/ sound. Her articulation error is one of substitution; she replaces the /r/ sound with the /w/ sound. Other types of articulation errors are omissions, distortions, and additions of sounds.

The assessment of language disorders requires the expertise of several disciplines. In addition to the general education teacher and the speech–language pathologist, the assessment team may include the school nurse, an audiologist or other specialist in the detection of hearing losses, the school psychologist, and the special education teacher. The student is evaluated in many areas: hearing, intellectual performance, academic achievement, and language skills.

FIGURE 13-1   Speech Checklist

Student _____ Age _____ Grade _____
Teacher _____ Date of Evaluation _____

1. **Voice Quality** (check all that are appropriate)
   The student's *usual* voice quality is
   —— pleasant to listen to   —— monotone
   —— unpleasant to listen to   —— very high-pitched
   —— hoarse or husky   —— very low-pitched
   —— like a whisper   —— very loud
   —— nasal   —— very soft

2. **Speech Fluency** (check one)
   The student's *usual* speech is
   —— very fluent
   —— generally fluent with occasional hesitations, repetitions, and/or prolongations of sounds and syllables
   —— frequently dysfluent and characterized by hesitations, repetitions, and/or prolongations of sounds and syllables

3. **Sound Production** (check each sound that the student *usually* produces clearly and correctly)*
   Sounds expected by age 5[†]
   —— /p/ as in *pal*   —— /g/ as in *goat*   —— /n/ as in *not*   —— /t/ as in *tap*
   —— /m/ as in *map*   —— /d/ as in *dog*   —— /b/ as in *ball*   —— /ng/ as in *ring*
   —— /f/ as in *fat*   —— /h/ as in *hit*   —— /k/ as in *kill*   —— /y/ as in *year*
   Sounds expected by age 6[†]
   —— /r/ as in *rag*   —— /l/ as in *lad*
   Sounds expected by age 7[†]
   —— /ch/ as in *church* —— /sh/ as in *ship*   —— /j/ as in *junk*
   —— /th/ (voiceless) as in *thank*
   Sounds expected by age 8[†]
   —— /s/ as in *son*   —— /z/ as in *zoo*   —— /v/ as in *very*
   —— /th/ (voiced) as in *this*
   Sounds expected after age 8[†]
   —— /zh/ as in *azure* or *pleasure*

*Only consonant sounds are listed because most children are able to produce vowel and diphthong sounds upon entry to school.
[†]Age norms derived from Sander (1972).

Language assessment typically focuses on both reception and expression. The student's ability to receive and understand information from language is evaluated; likewise, the student's skill in using the symbols of language to express thoughts is assessed. One standardized measure that looks at both of these dimensions is the *Test of Language Development–Primary* (3rd ed.) (Newcomer & Hammill, 1997), an individual test appropriate for students aged 4 to 9. This test assesses three important features of language: **semantics,** the meaningful aspects of language; **syntax,** the grammatical aspects of language; and **phonology,** the sound system of language.

Figure 13-2 presents a portion of the assessment report for Rocky, the first grader with grammar and vocabulary problems who was described at the beginning of this chapter. The results of the *Test of Language Development–Primary* show that Rocky understands language well but has difficulty in expression, particularly in semantics and syntax.

Many other measures are available to the speech–language pathologist or special education teacher responsible for language assessment. Examples include the *Test of Language Development–Intermediate* (3rd ed.) (Hammill &

Newcomer, 1997) for students aged 8 to 13, the *Clinical Evaluation of Language Fundamentals–4* (Semel, Wiig, & Secord, 2003) for students aged 5 to 21, and the *Test of Adolescent and Adult Language* (4th ed.) (Hammill, Brown, Larsen, & Wiederholt, 2007) for individuals aged 12 to 25. These measures concentrate on semantics, syntax, and phonology.

To assess the fourth dimension of language, pragmatics, professionals often rely on informal procedures. **Pragmatics** is the use of language, that is, how language functions in the various situations in which communication occurs. Clearly, language use varies according to the purpose of communication, audience, and setting. For example, when the message to be communicated is that today's homework has not been completed, the language a student uses to communicate that message to the teacher is likely to differ from that used with a classmate.

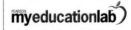
Go to the Assignments and Activities section of Topic *Communication Disorders* in the MyEducationLab for your course and complete the activity entitled *Informal Expressive Language Assessment.*

FIGURE 13-2   Special Education Assessment Results

Student: Rocky   **Age:** 6 years, 2 months   **Grade:** 1

Classroom Performance

Ms. Ranson, Rocky's first-grade teacher, reported that Rocky is experiencing difficulty in classroom language tasks. According to Ms. Ranson's observations, Rocky appears to be a bright child but one who has not yet learned the grammatical rules and vocabulary expected of a first-grade student. Rocky's progress in math is adequate, but he makes mistakes in oral reading that reflect his problems with grammar. Also, he has difficulty expressing his thoughts when speaking in class and in play situations with the other children.

Hearing

Results of a routine hearing screening at the beginning of the school year indicated that Rocky's hearing is adequate.

Intellectual Performance

Mr. Scott, the school psychologist, administered the *Wechsler Intelligence Scale for Children—Fourth Edition* to Rocky. All subtest and IQ scores were within the average range, which indicates adequate intellectual performance.

Oral Language Skills

To learn more about Rocky's oral language skills, Mrs. Putnam, the speech–language pathologist, administered the *Test of Language Development—Primary* to Rocky. This test includes measures of both receptive and expressive language. On the receptive language tests, Rocky scored within the average range; he shows adequate skills in understanding the semantic, syntactical, and phonological aspects of language.

Expressive language tasks were more difficult for Rocky, as the following results indicate. (Average performance is indicated by standard scores of 85 to 115.)

Language Area	Subtest	Standard Score
Expressive Semantics	Oral Vocabulary	78
Expressive Syntax	Sentence Imitation	80
Expressive Syntax	Grammatic Completion	76
Expressive Phonology	Word Articulation	95

Expressive phonology, assessed by the Word Articulation subtest, was within the average range. However, other expressive skills fell within the low average range of performance. Rocky's major areas of need are expressive semantics and syntax. Rocky's oral vocabulary is more typical of a 4- or 5-year-old child than a first grader, and his command of grammatical structures is limited for his age.

A student's parents and general education teacher are valuable sources of information about language performance. These team members have observed the student over long time periods and can comment on the student's usual facility with language tasks. By observing typical classroom activities, the teacher can gather data about the student's performance of language skills such as

- understanding oral directions,
- speaking in complete sentences,
- using age-appropriate vocabulary in oral communication, and
- using correct grammar in speech.

SPECIAL SERVICES

As with all individuals with disabilities, the special services provided to students with communication disorders depend on the severity and extent of the students' educational needs. For many students with speech problems, only minor educational adaptations are necessary. Such students are members of general education classrooms and fully capable of participation in instructional activities. They leave the classroom only for short periods of time to receive special services from the speech–language pathologist on a daily or weekly basis. Elaine, the first grader introduced earlier, is an example of a student with a speech disorder who is successfully included in general education. Elaine's problem was identified early in her school career, and she is receiving the special help she needs to overcome her problem.

 Go to the Building Teaching Skills and Dispositions section of Topic *Communication Disorders* in the MyEducationLab for your course and complete the activity entitled *Collaborating with the Speech Language Pathologist.*

Other types of communication disorders may require more extensive special programming. Rocky, the first grader with difficulty in expressive language, requires special help to learn better language skills. Figure 13-3 shows that his IEP

FIGURE 13-3 IEP Goals and Services for Rocky

Annual Goals

1. By the end of the school year, Rocky will speak in grammatically correct sentences with agreement in number between subjects and verbs.
   Person responsible: Speech–language pathologist
2. By the end of the school year, Rocky will increase his speaking vocabulary by at least 100 words.
   Person responsible: Speech–language pathologist
3. Rocky will successfully complete all requirements for first grade reading, language arts, math, and other academic subjects.
   Person responsible: First grade teacher

Amount of Participation in General Education
Rocky will attend the general education first grade class for all academic instruction.

Special Education and Related Services

1. Rocky will receive special education services from the speech–language pathologist (annual goals 1 and 2) for 30 minutes daily.
2. The speech–language pathologist will provide consultation to Rocky's first grade teacher as necessary.

 For Your Information

Students with Communication Disorders

- Students with communication disorders are estimated to make up almost 2% of the school-aged population. Communication disorders are the second most prevalent disability, accounting for 18.8% of the students served by special education (U.S. Department of Education, 2009).
- The most typical types of communication disorders in school-aged children are articulation problems and language impairments (American Speech-Language-Hearing Association, 2008; Heward, 2006; Smith, 2004).
- Speech and language problems are most often found in young children. The prime time for identification of communication disorders is the first and second grades.
- Expectations for communication skills are related to the age of the child. For example, young preschool children are expected to pass through a developmental stage in which dysfluencies are

common (American Speech-Language-Hearing Association, 1997; Swift, 1988).
- The great majority of school-aged children with communication disorders remain in general education, and only a very few receive special services in a special class or school; in fall 2004, almost 95% of students with speech or language impairments were educated in the general education classroom for the majority of the school day (U.S. Department of Education, 2009).
- Every child and adult who speaks makes articulation errors, and everyone's speech at one time or another is marked by dysfluencies. Deviations in speech are considered communication disorders only when they become frequent and severe enough to interfere with the ability to communicate.
- Speech characterized by an accent or dialect is different, but it is not considered disordered.

---

goals focus on improvement of expressive vocabulary and grammar. However, Rocky remains with his first grade class for instruction in all academic subjects.

Some students with communication disorders also have social needs. Because of their speech or language problems, they have difficulty interacting with others and may feel isolated or disliked. Willy, the 10th grade student described at the beginning of this chapter, is keenly aware of his dysfluent speech and, as a result, remains silent throughout most of the school day. The IEP for Willy stresses not only more fluent speech but also an increased number of interactions with teachers and classmates.

The general education classroom is the most typical placement for students with speech and language impairments. If communication problems are related to other disabilities such as learning disabilities, resource services may be provided. If more severe disabilities such as intellectual disabilities or a hearing impairment are present, the intensive

services available in a special class setting may be needed. Most students, however, remain in the general education classroom and receive special services only on a part-time basis. The general education teacher provides all academic instruction and receives consultant help from the speech–language pathologist as necessary. To learn more about individuals with communication disorders, consult the accompanying "For Your Information" material.

 ## CLASSROOM ADAPTATIONS

The general education teacher usually does not have to make major classroom adaptations in order to meet the special needs of students with communication disorders. Even though characterized by speech or language problems, these students are generally able to participate in all aspects of the general education curriculum. Special attention is needed in only two areas: speech and language skills and social acceptance.

myeducationlab Go to the Assignments and Activities section of Topic *Communication Disorders* in the MyEducationLab for your course and complete the activity entitled *1-1 Speech and Language Intervention*

Students with speech impairments may need to improve articulation, voice quality, or fluency. To meet these needs, an individualized special education program is provided by the speech–language pathologist. The major goal in the general education classroom becomes practice of oral communication. Students require a nonthreatening environment in which to try out the new speech skills they are learning in their special education program. By collaborating with the speech–language pathologist, the general education teacher can target these skills for reinforcement in the general education classroom. The classroom teacher assists by encouraging the students' participation and ensuring that their attempts at oral communication are accepted with tolerance and support by classmates.

Students with language impairments experience difficulty in the reception and expression of oral communication. Again, although the speech–language pathologist takes primary responsibility for instruction in the areas of educational need, students should have opportunities within the general education classroom to practice the new language skills they are learning. The general education teacher also assists by modeling appropriate grammar, stressing vocabulary development in all curriculum areas, and modifying the language aspects of classroom activities and assignments.

The following sections include methods for teaching students with communication disorders, ways to encourage practice of oral communication by students with speech disorders, and suggestions for teaching language skills to students with grammar and vocabulary needs.

► ENCOURAGING ORAL COMMUNICATION

For students with speech impairments, the general education classroom should be a place where they can hear correct speech and feel comfortable enough to practice their newly learned communication skills. To accomplish this, the general education teacher must provide good speech models, an accepting environment, and opportunities for practicing oral communication skills.

myeducationlab Go to the Assignments and Activities section of Topic *Communication Disorders* in the MyEducationLab for your course and complete the activity entitled *Encouraging Participation*.

Students with speech or language disorders require good models of oral communication. The teacher is the primary model and should be careful to speak clearly, fluently, and with appropriate articulation. Sunderland (2004) also suggested that teachers monitor the rate of their speech, the length and

complexity of their sentences, and the number of directions given at any one time. Classmates are also able to help. By demonstrating appropriate speech, they, too, serve as important models for students with communication disorders and those with other special needs.

How the teacher and classroom peers react to speech errors made by students with communication disorders is a major factor in encouraging oral communication. It is crucial that the communication attempts of students with speech disorders be treated with respect and tolerance. If the teacher and peers are accepting listeners, then students with special communication-related needs will feel comfortable enough to practice oral communication. Guidelines for establishing a tolerant classroom climate are identified here.

- When students with speech problems speak, the teacher should listen with full attention and ensure that other students listen.
- Speech errors should not be criticized by the teacher or classmates. However, the teacher may wish to demonstrate correct speech for the student by repeating what was said. For example, if the student says, "The story was about a wittle wabbit," the teacher might say, "Right! The story was about a little rabbit."
- The teacher should not call attention to speech errors. If the teacher accepts misarticulations and dysfluencies and attends to the content of what the student is saying, peers are more likely to do the same. This approach is particularly important with dysfluency problems that may become much more serious if attention is called to them.
- Peers should not be allowed to ridicule or make fun of speech errors. The teacher should make it clear that this is not appropriate behavior. One way to help peers understand the problems of students with special needs is by using simulations. Table 13-1 earlier in this chapter presented ways to experience simulated oral communication problems.

- The teacher should take care when placing students with speech problems in situations in which their communication difficulties might interfere. For example, if class members are reading tongue twisters aloud, "six silly snakes" should be reserved for the student who can articulate the /s/ sound. In other words, the teacher should carefully consider which oral classroom activities are appropriate to assign to students who are unsure of their communication abilities or embarrassed by speaking.

- Changing the nature of the communication situation can sometimes improve stuttering problems. Shames and Ramig (1994) reported that dysfluencies often decrease (or, in some cases, disappear) when students sing, read aloud in unison with another person, whisper, speak in a monotone, speak in a higher or lower pitch than usual, or speak in time to a metronome.

- For some students with communication problems, speech is slow and labored. A stutterer may take a long time to produce a single sentence, a student with cerebral palsy may make facial grimaces as he or she struggles to articulate

each word, and a person who communicates by means of a communication board or an electronic communication aid may require several seconds to select the message he or she wants to convey to the listener. Such students require patient listeners. Attempts to hurry them will likely result in slower, not faster, communication; finishing their sentences for them will discourage and frustrate them further.

The teacher should model appropriate listening skills for the class and also attempt to sensitize students to the need to wait quietly and listen while others speak. In some situations, the teacher may want to speed communication by phrasing questions to students with speech problems so that only short responses are required. In other situations, these students should be encouraged to express their thoughts and opinions more fully. The "Spotlight on Technology" feature provides additional information on alternative methods of communication such as communication boards and electronic communication devices.

SPOTLIGHT ON TECHNOLOGY

Augmentative Communication

When students do not talk or their speech is not intelligible, an **augmentative communication** system may be used to increase their ability to communicate. There are many types of augmentative communication systems. For example, if you have a cold and find it difficult to talk, you might augment your usual means of communication by using more gestures or even writing notes rather than speaking. In classrooms, two types of systems are used most often with students with communication disorders: communication boards and electronic communication devices.

Communication Boards

Communication boards are considered a "low" technology. According to Lewis (1993),

> A communication board can be as simple as a piece of paper or cardboard with two photographs pasted on it, or as elaborate as a notebook filled with pages of messages for a variety of different communication situations. The essential elements are the "board" itself, which may be composed of paper or a sturdier material, and the choices depicted on the board by photos, drawings, or some kind of symbol system. (p. 383)

To use a communication board, the student simply points to one of the choices. For some students, all choices are depicted by photos or drawings. Other students are able to use communication boards with letters, words, and phrases.

Computers can be used to make communication boards with programs such as *Boardmaker* from DynaVox Mayer-Johnson (*http://www.mayer-johnson.com*). This program contains more than 4,500 picture symbols from the Mayer-Johnson Picture Communication Symbol collection (Johnson, 1981, 1985, 1992). *Boardmaker* is easy to use. The teacher has full control over the choice of symbols included on the board and the number, size,

Note: The Picture Communication Symbols™ © 1981–2004 by Mayer-Johnson LLC. All rights reserved worldwide. Used with permission.

and spacing of the symbols. Boards can be printed in black and white or color, and the print labels accompanying each symbol are available in more than 40 languages.

News-2-You is a weekly online newspaper for students with special needs. As this sample page from the color edition illustrates, it provides information about current events via both words and symbols.

Several different editions of the paper are available: regular, higher, simplified, advanced, and Spanish. The regular edition is about 20 pages long with news, a joke, a game page, a puzzle page, a recipe, and pages for review and word study.

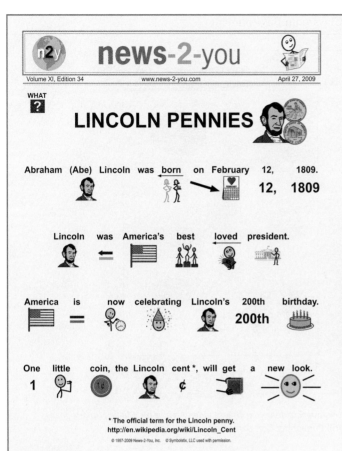

news-2-you

Volume XI, Edition 34   www.news-2-you.com   April 27, 2009

WHAT?

LINCOLN PENNIES

Abraham (Abe) Lincoln was born on February 12, 1809.

12, 1809

Lincoln was America's best loved president.

America is now celebrating Lincoln's 200th birthday.

200th

One little coin, the Lincoln cent *, will get a new look.

1

* The official term for the Lincoln penny.
http://en.wikipedia.org/wiki/Lincoln_Cent

© 1997-2009 News-2-You, Inc. © Symbolstix, LLC used with permission.

Note: From *news-2-you*, Volume XI, Edition 34, April 27, 2009. Used with permission.

Note: Courtesy of Attainment Company.

All editions have the ability to talk. To subscribe—and then download issues weekly—visit the website at *http://www.news-2-you.com*. Subscribers have access to all editions as well as communication boards and worksheets for each issue. Additional features are access to Joey's Locker, a collection of weekly add-on activities, and one or more world news articles each week.

Electronic Communication Devices

Electronic communication devices "talk." Because of this capability, they are sometimes called *voice output communication aids*, or VOCAs. Some electronic devices use prerecorded speech, others contain speech synthesizers, and still others use both technologies.

The Go Talk 9+ from Attainment Company (*http://www.attainmentcompany.com*), shown above (right), is an example of a relatively inexpensive communication device. On the surface of the Go Talk are touch-sensitive "keys"; when the student presses a key, a prerecorded message plays. At the top is a row of three keys designed to contain messages that stay the same in all communication settings. Those keys on the example Go Talk contain messages of greeting, thanks, and "I don't know." The nine keys below are designed to communicate information in one communication setting. Five levels can be recorded for each key, for a total of 45 messages. The key area is covered by an overlay with photos, drawings, words, or phrases that illustrate the messages. The Go Talk unit can store up to 9 minutes of prerecorded speech. Thus, this device can be set up so that, as students move from one activity to another during the school day, messages are available for each class or school activity.

Devices such as the Go Talk, although inexpensive, may not be appropriate for a more advanced student because they can store only a limited number of messages. More sophisticated (and more expensive) devices may be required. Examples are the VMax and the V from DynaVox Technologies (*http://www.dynavoxtech.com*). These augmentative communication devices offer two types of high-quality speech: digitized (recorded) and synthesized (both adult and child voices). Screen displays are in color, and users touch the screen to make selections; the choices shown can be customized to fit individual needs. The display is dynamic; once one choice is made, the screen changes and other choices appear. They are, in effect, computers that can store thousands of messages, which makes them very versatile communication devices.

Note: Courtesy of DynaVox Systems LLC, Pittsburgh, PA (866-DYNAVOX).

In addition to providing good speech models and an accepting environment, the classroom teacher should ensure that students with speech impairments have frequent opportunities to practice their communication skills. McCormick (1986) recommended that practice take place in a variety of contexts throughout the school day. Oral communication can be incorporated into most areas of the curriculum. Whether the subject is reading, math, or social studies, students can practice speaking with the teacher, in small work groups, and during class discussions. Lunchtime, work breaks, and recess create natural opportunities for socialization and talking with others, as do many free-time activities in the classroom. Culatta and Culatta (1993) provided these suggestions for creating communication opportunities.

FIGURE 13-4   Traditional and Modified Classroom Environments

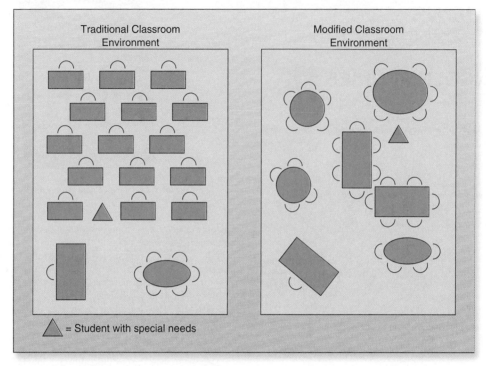

Traditional Classroom
Environment

Modified Classroom
Environment

 = Student with special needs

Note: Adapted with permission of Merrill, an imprint of Macmillan Publishing Company, from *Language Arts for the Mildly Handicapped* (pp. 201, 203) by S. B. Cohen and S. P. Plaskon. Copyright © 1980 Merrill Publishing Company, Columbus, Ohio.

■ *Do not anticipate needs.* A child who is given paper without crayons or who is provided with only a small amount of juice at a time is encountering the need to communicate.

■ *Arrange for unusual or novel events to occur.* A child who sees a box of cereal taped to the wall is likely to want to share that event and seek information about it. Language can also be evoked by engaging in such actions as "inadvertently" throwing away toys, wearing clothes that are too big, and trying to eat soup with a fork.

■ *Arrange for the child to convey information to others.* In the cafeteria the child may be asked to direct others to their seats, describe the menu, convey the location of utensils, and report the acceptability of the food to the cook. Many opportunities to convey experiences to others can be created throughout the day.

■ *Provide the child with choices.* During a snack activity, the child can decide what to drink, where to sit, whether to use a napkin or a paper plate, and who should be responsible for cleaning up. Each decision requires communication. (pp. 251–252)

An important goal of any inclusion program is the participation of students with special needs in as many classroom activities as possible. For students with speech problems, both social and academic activities should be considered. One way to promote acceptance while maximizing communication opportunities is to seat the student with special needs in the midst of several typical peers. In traditional classrooms, students with special needs are usually seated near the teacher in an arrangement that does not encourage student interaction (see Figure 13-4). Instead, the classroom environment should be modified so that the student is surrounded by good speech models and has natural opportunities for communication.

▶ TEACHING LANGUAGE SKILLS

Students with language impairments receive individualized help from the speech–language pathologist. They may require assistance in the development of receptive language skills and/or expressive language skills; instruction focuses on the area of need, whether it is grammatical construction (syntax) or vocabulary development (semantics). The general education teacher can help students with language problems by modeling appropriate grammar, by helping expand their listening and speaking vocabularies, and by modifying classroom activities and assignments that require language skills.

PEARSON **myeducationlab** Go to the Assignments and Activities section of Topic *Communication Disorders* in the MyEducationLab for your course and complete the activity entitled *Promoting Communication in the Classroom*

For students with difficulty in the area of syntax, the classroom teacher must provide a consistent model of grammatically correct speech. The teacher should correct students' grammatical errors by demonstrating the proper construction. If, for instance, a student comments, "It's funner to swim than to water ski," the teacher can respond, "It's more fun to swim? Why?" With this approach, the student hears the grammatically correct version of the statement without being criticized for poor language.

Some students with language disorders need help in vocabulary development. They may not be familiar with the words their classmates and teachers use; they may fail to express themselves in the vocabulary expected of their age level. The classroom teacher can help these students with special needs increase their receptive and expressive vocabularies by following these suggestions.

- Encourage students to ask about the meanings of words they do not understand.
- Use demonstration to teach the meanings of some words. Because prepositions and action verbs are often hard to explain in words, *show* students their meanings.
- Use definitions, explanations, and examples to teach other words. For example, define *container* as something that holds something else; then give examples of objects that are containers and objects that are not.
- Provide multiple examples of word meanings. For example, if students are learning the word *break,* they might "break cookies and crackers, encounter objects that keep falling apart, break spaghetti in order to glue the pieces on a picture, and break carrot sticks for lunch" (Culatta & Culatta, 1993, p. 252).
- Include vocabulary instruction in all curriculum areas. Teach the meanings of new reading words, math terms, and new vocabulary in science, social studies, and art.
- Teach students to use regular or picture dictionaries to discover the meanings of unfamiliar words.
- Give students opportunities throughout the school day to practice the new vocabulary they are learning.
- Sunderland (2004) added: "Encourage the child to elaborate (e.g., 'That's very interesting! Tell me more!')" (p. 212).

In addition to helping students with language impairments acquire correct grammar and new word meanings, the general education teacher may need to make adaptations in classroom activities and assignments. With students who have difficulty listening with understanding, directions for school tasks should be brief, to the point, and in simple language. With students who find it hard to express themselves,

questions that require a yes or no response are easier to answer than open-ended questions. For example, "Is the platypus a mammal?" may be an easier question for a student with a language disorder than "What type of animal is the platypus?"

Some students may require direct instruction in listening skills. Bauwens and Hourcade (1989) suggested teaching the LISTEN strategy to improve students' ability to attend and listen to oral directions. LISTEN is an acronym for a six-step procedure: "Look, Idle your motor, Sit up straight, Turn to me, Engage your brain, Now . . ." (p. 61). The teacher models this strategy, and students practice it to mastery. The goal is for students to internalize the strategy so that they follow each step automatically whenever the teacher says, "Listen."

Older students may benefit from instruction in the skills needed for listening to lectures in content-area classes. One activity for developing these skills uses tape recordings of news broadcasts (Forster & Doyle, 1989). The teacher prepares an outline of the news items, including major points, but leaves space for students to add supporting details; the outline also lists background concepts and vocabulary with which students might be unfamiliar. Students begin the activity by reviewing the outline, and the teacher explains any terms or concepts that students do not recognize or understand. As students listen to the tape, they underline key points on the outline and add details. Students have the opportunity to ask questions before taking a quiz on the information presented in the news broadcast.

The general education teacher plays an important role in the education of students with communication disorders. When these students are provided with a classroom environment that encourages the learning and practice of speech and language skills, their chances for successful performance in school (and in life) increase. Many speech and language problems are developmental in nature; they appear in young children and, with maturation and appropriate treatment, may disappear. The special education program is only part of the appropriate treatment for students with communication disorders. Another important component is the instruction and support received from the teacher in the general education classroom.

Students who leave the classroom to visit the speech–language pathologist or resource teacher may return to discover that the class has moved on to a different activity. To help these students feel more a part of their classroom, see the "Inclusion Tips for the Teacher."

In this chapter, you have learned ways to teach language skills to students with communication disorders. You have also learned methods for creating a classroom climate that encourages the practice of speaking skills. Before going on, check "Things to Remember" to review ways to help students with speech and language disorders succeed in general education.

Inclusion Tips for the Teacher

When Students Leave the Classroom for Special Services

Many students with special needs leave the general education classroom for a short time each day to visit a special education teacher. While they are gone, the activities of the classroom continue. When they return, they may feel lost, confused, and unsure of what they should be doing. To help students reenter the classroom and regain their bearings quickly and easily, try these suggestions.

1. Work with the special education teacher to arrange the best time for each student to leave the classroom. Usually, it is better for students to receive special education services when their class is working on
   - independent practice rather than direct instruction,
   - the student's best rather than worst subject, or
   - the student's least liked rather than favorite activity.
2. Maintain a regular daily schedule so that you and the student know what will be missed each day.
3. Help the student take responsibility for leaving the classroom for special education services at the appropriate time. One

method is to provide the student with a drawing of a clock showing the time to leave.

4. Arrange a communication system so that when the student returns, he or she knows how to find out what to do. The student might
   - go directly to the teacher for directions,
   - look for a note on the board,
   - check in the work folder on his or her desk, or
   - consult a classmate who has been assigned as a buddy.
5. Do not penalize the student for leaving the class for special education help. Avoid scheduling treats and special activities during the time the student is out of the room. Do not double the workload by requiring the student to keep up with the current class activity as well as make up what was missed during his or her absence.

Things to Remember

- The primary areas of need for students with communication disorders are speech and language; because of their communication difficulties, these students may also require assistance in social interactions.

- Major indicators of speech impairments are misarticulations of speech sounds, dysfluent speech, and unusual voice quality.

- Major indicators of language impairments are problems in reception or expression of grammatical constructions and vocabulary.

- In assessment of communication disorders, information is gathered about a possible hearing loss, current performance in speech and language, and, for serious problems, general intellectual performance.

- Students with communication disorders receive individualized special education from the speech–language pathologist.

These students remain in the general education class and take part in special services for only short periods each day or several times each week.

- Major instructional adaptations are usually not necessary to accommodate the needs of students with communication disorders in the general education classroom.

- For students with speech impairments, the general education teacher provides an accepting classroom environment in which students can feel comfortable practicing newly acquired communication skills.

- For students with language impairments, the general education teacher assists their acquisition of language skills by modeling appropriate grammar and helping them expand their listening and speaking vocabularies. Classroom activities and assignments that require language skills may need to be modified.

ACTIVITIES

1. Interview a speech–language pathologist to find out more about students with communication disorders. Ask this professional to describe his or her caseload. How many students does he or she serve? What are their ages and typical problems? Do most students participate in general education classes for the majority of the day? If so, what effects do their speech and language disorders have on their performance in the general education classroom?

2. Locate one of the journals that deals primarily with communication disorders. You might select the *American Journal of Speech–Language Pathology; Journal of Speech, Language, and Hearing Research;* or *Language, Speech, and Hearing Services in the Schools.* Look through recent issues for articles that present suggestions for encouraging oral communication and teaching language skills. Do you find any ideas that could be used by general education teachers?

3. The major professional organization in the field of communication disorders is the American Speech-Language-Hearing

Association (ASHA). Visit its website at http://www.asha.org to find out more about this organization. Or visit with a speech–language pathologist or audiologist who is an ASHA member.

4. Communication disorders can be found in people of any age. Survey your community to locate agencies that provide services to adults with speech and language problems. What services are available? How do these differ from the services offered by the public schools to children and adolescents?

5. In a group, try one or more of the communication disorder simulations described in Table 12-1. Afterward, respond to the following questions: What were the feelings of the person with the simulated speech or language disorder? Did he or she feel frustrated? Anxious? Angry? How did the listeners feel? Were they sympathetic? Impatient? Embarrassed? What recommendations can the group make to teachers of students with communication disorders?

Laura J. Hall
San Diego State University

CHAPTER
FOURTEEN

Teaching Students with Autism Spectrum Disorder

Dan

Dan is currently included in a K–1 class where he excels in his reading abilities. He has a large receptive vocabulary and will speak readily and specifically about Spiderman, particularly with adults. He recalls and imitates the part of Spiderman from the movies and will be found reciting lines to himself during play activities. He enjoys drawing and has difficulty with transitions, especially when he is leaving preferred activities such as art.

Mario

Mario is in a middle school classroom. There is an aide assigned during literacy periods to assist him with academic skills. Although he can complete most tasks, he is easily frustrated and tantrums if he makes errors. Math is an area of strength. Mario speaks in full sentences, but his voice prosody is atypical and he rarely initiates conversations unless he can talk about cars and their capacity for speed. He has been interested in cars since he was very young and he would like to work on a race track in the future.

LOOKING AHEAD

Throughout this chapter, you will see examples of strategies used in the general education classroom to more fully include students like Dan and Mario. As you learn more about teaching students with autism spectrum disorder, keep these questions in mind.

- What are Dan's and Mario's areas of strength? How could their teachers make use of those strengths in the instructional program?
- Would you expect Dan to have special needs in the area of classroom behavior? Social acceptance?
- What about Mario? In what areas do you think he will need the most support in the general education classroom?

utism became a distinct category within special education in 1990 with the passage of PL 101–476, part of the amendments to the original Education for All Handicapped Children Act. Autism is a developmental disability described as significantly affecting verbal communication, nonverbal communication, and social interaction, thereby influencing the child's educational performance. Students classified with **autism spectrum disorder (ASD)** can exhibit a range of characteristics, from severe delays to giftedness. In fact, the same student may have some skills that are delayed, such as social or language skills, and others, such as math, that are well advanced for his or her age. Even in those areas that are, by definition, impaired for students with this disorder (communication, social interaction, behavior), the severity of this impairment varies by individual. Because of the range and variation in the skills and impairments presented, autism is referred to as a *spectrum disorder*.

Although this variation of skills presents an added challenge for the classroom teacher, there are some strategies that work well for most individuals on the spectrum. These strategies will be featured in this chapter. Consultation with specialists is frequently recommended, depending on the area and severity of delay. Consultation with parents is highly recommended because consistency across environments is especially important for students with this disorder. Although the characteristics of one child with autism spectrum disorder may be different from the characteristics of another, some preferences and behaviors occur frequently for these students, and the students described in Students' Stories represent two common profiles.

INDICATORS OF AUTISM SPECTRUM DISORDER

Autism spectrum disorder, or *autistic disorder*, is one of the classifications within the category of Pervasive Developmental Disorders (PDD), according to the fourth edition text revision of the *Diagnostic and Statistical Manual of Mental Disorders* (*DSM–IV–TR*) (American Psychiatric Association, 2000), the manual commonly used to diagnose and describe neurological and psychological disorders. Qualitative impairments are evident for individuals with autism in three areas:

1. Social interaction (nonverbal behavior, peer relationships, socioemotional reciprocity)
2. Communication (delays in spoken language, inability to initiate or sustain conversation, repetitive use of language, and lack of make-believe or imaginative play)

WINDOW ON THE WEB

Autism Society of America

The Autism Society of America, founded in 1965 by parents of children with autism, currently has chapters in many states throughout the United States. Information for individuals with autism spectrum disorder and their families can be found at the organization's website. This information is available in English ("About Autism") and in Spanish ("Information general sobre el autismo"). This website lists resources for parents and professionals, conferences organized and supported by ASA, and information about new and relevant legislation and research activities pertaining to autism.

http://www.autism-society.org

3. Restrictive, repetitive, and stereotyped patterns of behavior (preoccupation with an interest, compulsive adherence to routine, motor mannerisms, and occupations with parts of objects)

Consult the "For Your Information" feature for descriptions of the common characteristics of autism.

 To enhance your understanding of Autism Spectrum Disorder, go to the IRIS Center Resources section of Topic *Autism Spectrum Disorders* in the MyEducationLab for your course and complete the Module entitled *What Do You See? Perceptions of Disability*.

If the student has impairments in social interaction and restrictive, repetitive, and stereotyped patterns of behavior—and not in the area of communication and language—then the student is diagnosed with **Asperger's syndrome** (Atwood, 1998). These students typically have age-appropriate communication and language skills, but have difficulties with social relationships and are usually focused on one topic or activity at a time. Students diagnosed with Asperger's syndrome do not have significant delays in cognitive development compared with students with autism, who also may have intellectual disabilities (Myles, 2005).

In 1993 Catherine Maurice published a book about her struggle to obtain a diagnosis and find effective treatment for her two children with autism. Her book, *Let Me Hear Your Voice*, was influential in encouraging parents to search for educators with knowledge and skills in applied behavior analysis. Books and articles written by other parents (e.g., Koegel & LaZebnik, 2004;

Sicile-Kira, 2004) and by adults with autism (e.g., Edmonds & Beardon, 2008; Grandin, 1995; Grandin & Barron, 2005) have provided important perspectives that are relevant for educators working with students with autism spectrum disorders and their families. Working in collaboration with families results in many benefits for the student (Turnbull, Turnbull, Erwin, & Soodak, 2006). To learn more about an important organization for families and others interested in autism, review the "Window on the Web" material.

 ## IDENTIFICATION AND PROGRESS MONITORING PROCEDURES

Delays in at least one of the three focal areas for students with autism occur prior to age 3. Diagnosis is typically made by a physician or other professional experienced in the use of diagnostic instruments or by those trained to use diagnostic tools created specifically for autism spectrum disorder such as the *Autism Diagnostic Observation Schedule (ADOS)* (Lord, Rutter, DiLavore, & Risi, 2001) and *Autism Diagnostic Interview Revised* (Rutter, LeCouteur, & Lord, 2003).

Consistent with good assessment practices, multiple measures for determining a diagnosis are recommended and may include one or more instruments. Several rating scales are available that are frequently used as one of the diagnostic tools, and teachers who suspect that a student may have autism spectrum disorder (ASD) may be asked to complete one of these scales. The *Childhood Autism Rating Scale (CARS)* (Schopler,

FIGURE 14-1   Sample Items from the *Childhood Autism Rating Scale*

· CARS Rating Sheet ·

Directions: For each category, use the space provided below each scale for taking notes concerning the behaviors relevant to each scale. After you have finished observing the child, rate the behaviors relevant to each item of the scale. For each item, circle the number which corresponds to the statement that best describes the child. You may indicate the child is between two descriptions by using ratings of 1.5, 2.5, or 3.5. Abbreviated rating criteria are presented for each scale. See chapter 2 of the Manual for detailed rating criteria.

	I. RELATING TO PEOPLE		III. EMOTIONAL RESPONSE
1	**No evidence of difficulty or abnormality in relating to people** · The child's behavior is appropriate for his or her age. Some shyness, fussiness, or annoyance at being told what to do may be observed, but not to an atypical degree.	1	**Age-appropriate and situation-appropriate emotional responses** · The child shows the appropriate type and degree of emotional response as indicated by a change in facial expression, posture, and manner.
1.5		1.5	
2	**Mildly abnormal relationships** · The child may avoid looking the adult in the eye, avoid the adult or become fussy if interaction is forced, be excessively shy, not be as responsive to the adult as is typical, or cling to parents somewhat more than most children of the same age.	2	**Mildly abnormal emotional responses** · The child occasionally displays a somewhat inappropriate type or degree of emotional reactions. Reactions are sometimes unrelated to the objects or events surrounding them.
		2.5	
2.5	**Moderately abnormal relationships** · The child shows aloofness (seems unaware of adult) at times. Persistent and forceful attempts are necessary to get the child's attention at times. Minimal contact is initiated by the child.	3	**Moderately abnormal emotional responses** · The child shows definite signs of inappropriate type and/or degree of emotional response. Reactions may be quite inhibited or excessive and unrelated to the situation; may grimace, laugh, or become rigid even though no apparent emotion-producing objects or events are present.
3			
3.5	**Severely abnormal relationships** · The child is consistently aloof or unaware of what the adult is doing. He or she almost never responds or initiates contact with the adult. Only the most persistent attempts to get the child's attention have any effect.	3.5	**Severely abnormal emotional responses** · Responses are seldom appropriate to the situation; once the child gets in a certain mood, it is very difficult to change the mood. Conversely, the child may show wildly different emotions when nothing has changed.
4		4	
	Observations:		Observations:

Note: Sample items from *The Childhood Autism Rating Scale* by E. Schopler, R. J. Reichler, and B. R. Renner. Copyright 1988 by Western Psychological Services. Reprinted by permission of WPS, 12031 Wilshire Boulevard, Los Angeles, CA 90025 (*www.wpspublish.com*). All rights reserved.

Reichler, & Renner, 1988) is a 15-item behavior scale that was one of the first developed to screen for ASD. Figure 14-1 depicts a portion of the *CARS* Rating Sheet and provides two examples of items and how each should be rated on a scale of 1 (within normal limits for age) to 4 (severely abnormal for that age).

The *Gilliam Autism Rating Scale* (GARS–2) (Gilliam, 2006) includes 42 items that closely match the *DSM–IV–TR* diagnostic categories; items are rated from 0 (never observed) to 3 (frequently observed). The second version of this scale includes suggested objectives that can be used by educators when students score differently from the norm group. This scale can be completed by anyone who has direct and sustained contact with the individual and includes suggested instructional objectives to target. Gilliam (2001) also created the *Gilliam Asperger's Disorder Scale (GADS)*, with 32 items in four categories that can be completed by a parent or professional who knows the child.

Teachers also may be asked to complete the *Autism Screening Instrument for Educational Planning* (Krug, Arick, & Almond, 1980), which contains five subtests that include an interaction assessment, an educational or functional skills assessment, a vocal sample, a learning rate indicator, and a behavior checklist. Another assessment tool that is used for targeting educational objectives is the *Assessment of Basic Language and Learning Skills (ABLLS–R)*. The tool contains assessment and skills tracking grids along with information that guides the development of Individualized Education Program (IEP) goals for a child (Partington, 2006). ABLLS–R items are scored 0 through 4 according to established criteria for 554 items distributed across the categories of basic learner skills (e.g., cooperation, imitation, receptive language, requests, play and leisure, follow classroom routines), academic skills (reading, math, writing, and spelling), self-help skills (dressing, eating, grooming, and toileting), and motor skills (fine and gross) (Partington, 2006). The number of items under the 25 categories varies from between 6 and 57.

The *Psychoeducational Profile*, currently in the 3rd edition (PEP–3), was designed to identify the strengths and weaknesses in skills of individuals with autism spectrum disorders ages 6 months through 7 years for the purpose of educational planning (Schopler, Lansing, Reichler, & Marcus, 2005). The assessment is to be conducted in two parts. The first, the Caregiver Report, is a new component in this third version of the PEP (Schopler et al., 2006). Caregivers are asked to identify their child's diagnostic categories and the degree to which each interferes with the child's development. The second component, the Performance Profile, is comprised of 10 subtests, 6 that measure developmental abilities and 4 focused on maladaptive behaviors (Schopler et al., 2006). An educator can purchase a test kit with all of the materials needed to administer the performance

FIGURE 14-2   Assessment Results for Dan

Student: Dan   **Age:** 5 years, 8 months   **Grade:** K-1

Classroom Performance

Dan participates well in those activities that he enjoys such as art and reading readiness. He has a very long attention span for these tasks. He is able to communicate well about topics of interest, although his speech can be difficult to understand at times due to its speed and lack of articulation for some sounds. It is clear that Dan does not prefer large-group activities such as circle time, especially during music activities. He is able to transition from activities and stay with circle time with the use of an individualized token system. Skills in math and social interaction with peers are priority areas for Dan.

Measures of Characteristics Related to Autism

Several measures were used to determine if there was a match between Dan's performance and the characteristics typically found in students with autism spectrum disorder.

Childhood Autism Rating Scale (CARS)
Total score = 36, mild to moderately autistic

Psychoeducational Profile–Third Version (PEP-3)

Developmental Area	Percentile Rank
Cognitive Verbal/Preverbal (CVP)	58
Expressive Language (EL)	75
Receptive Language (RL)	81
Fine Motor (FM)	90
Gross Motor (GM)	90
Visual Motor Imitation (VMI)	86
Affective Expression (AE)	38
Social Reciprocity (SR)	59
Characteristic Motor Behavior (CMB)	80
Characteristic Verbal Behavior (CVB)	65

Results indicate a high probability of mild to moderate autism. Results of the *PEP-3* indicate that fine- and gross-motor skills are areas of strength for Dan. He enjoys drawing and putting items together and can engage in these activities for long periods of time. He prefers to be left alone during these activities and, when asked to imitate the drawings of others or build a structure like a model, he frequently walks away from the task. Sorting and matching tasks were areas of weakness and he was not able to give two, then six, blocks to the examiner. It was observed that he did not consistently use pronouns correctly and did not have age-appropriate speech articulation. His facial displays were not always relevant to the context. When he was engaged in choice activities (e.g., drawing Spiderman), he rarely smiled and did not attempt to share the process or finished product with the examiner.

---

measures. Through a series of test items and activities, the test administrator scores a possible 172 items as 0 (failing), 1 (emerging), or 2 (passing).

The *Adolescent and Adult Psychoeducational Profile (AAPEP)* was designed for the purpose of developing individualized treatment goals for adolescents over age 12 and adults with autism spectrum disorders (Mesibov, Schopler, Schaffer, & Landrus, 1988). The tool is comprised of a direct observation scale and two interviews that include a home scale and school/work scale. Each scale addresses six functional areas: functional communication, leisure skills, vocational skills, vocational behavior, interpersonal behavior, and independent functioning (Mesibov et al., 1988). Figure 14-2 presents a portion of the assessment results for Dan, including a report of the results from the *PEP–3*.

Incorporating student preferences and developing a system that supports student motivation are key to creating a successful educational experience for a student with autism

spectrum disorder (Dyer, 1989). Student preferences for activities, topics, academic subjects, and form and intensity of sensory stimulation may be obtained by asking parents, caregivers, and previous teachers. For some students, a more formal preference assessment may need to be conducted.

Mason, McGee, Farmer-Dougan, and Risley (1989) adapted a reinforcer assessment for nonverbal students with autism. They presented an array of objects (edibles, vibrating toys, music boxes) and activities (hugs, spinning in the air, clapping hands) and assessed preferences for pairs of items by noting which item was reached for within 5 seconds of presentation. Following the identification of a group of preferred items, students choose several items from this group each day to use as rewards for completing educational activities. Incorporating these preferred items increased attention to task and decreased problem behaviors. DeLeon and Iwata (1996) found that presenting an array of seven items and having the

Incorporating a Motivational System

- Identify preferred activities/items through formal or informal assessments.
- Assure that culturally relevant and meaningful activities/items are included in preference assessments.
- Arrange the student's schedule so that preferred activities/items follow less preferred activities (Sulzer-Azaroff & Mayer, 1991).
- Clearly state these contingencies with the student: "First *X*, then *Y*" (Mesibov & Howley, 2003).
- Use identified preferred activities as part of a formal behavior management plan.

- Have students who can read sign a written contract that describes the rewards to be given contingent on appropriate behavior for a select period of time.
- Embed preferred topics, items, and materials into educational activities.
- Establish a formal token system that allows tokens to be traded by the student for preferred activities once the required number of tokens have been obtained by the student (Alberto & Troutman, 2006).

student choose one item at a time was an effective method of determining preferences. In this method, the item chosen by the student is not replaced and the remaining items of the array are rearranged. Researchers have confirmed that this method is effective for determining the preferences of students with autism (Carr, Nicholson, & Higbee, 2000). To learn more about incorporating rewards into the instructional program for students with autism spectrum disorder, consult the "Inclusion Tips for the Teacher" box.

Once a student's strengths, preferences, and targeted educational objectives have been identified, it is the educator's responsibility to monitor progress and make the necessary adjustments to the curriculum and instruction in order to maximize the opportunities for success. Curriculum-based assessment is a methodology where educational success is evaluated by students' progress across key indicators in the curriculum with the primary purpose of determining students' instructional needs (Shapiro & Elliott, 1999). Ongoing data collection (daily, weekly, biweekly) on specific goals and objectives to evaluate intervention strategies and monitor progress is integral to curriculum-based assessment (Wolery, 2004).

A four-step model describing an integrated curriculum-based approach was outlined by Shapiro and Elliott (1999). Step 1 involves assessing the academic environment to determine its effect on successes or failures (e.g., Is the room crowded?). The next step is to assess the curriculum placement or determine if the curriculum materials are a good match for the learner with ASD or if they are too difficult or too easy. In step 3, modifications to instructional information are made, such as including visual supports. The final step is progress monitoring of both short- and long-term outcomes (Shapiro & Elliott). Designing forms for data collection and implementing ongoing progress monitoring are often challenges for general educators, and consultation with special educators with knowledge and skills in progress-monitoring systems may be helpful.

▶ SPECIAL SERVICES

It is highly likely that the general education teacher will be working with a special educator who can help modify curriculum to meet the learning needs of the individual with autism spectrum disorder. Special education teachers can also help design a motivational system for the included student if one is necessary and assist in setting up the physical arrangement of the classroom environment to help facilitate social interaction, maximize student participation in activities, and decrease the likelihood of problem behavior.

> **PEARSON myeducationlab**) Go to the Assignments and Activities section of Topic *Autism Spectrum Disorders* in the MyEducationLab for your course and complete the activity entitled *Classroom Aides*.

Special educators assist in adapting curriculum. For example, Mario, one of the students introduced at the start of this chapter, is motivated to read text on the topics of automobiles and racing. He is also motivated to acquire those vocational skills that are helpful in preparing him for positions working with cars, such as conducting safety tests. Spiderman is a winning context for Dan. It is important not to overuse this topic so it does not lose the power to facilitate engagement. It is also important to aim to expand his areas of interest. During the early years of education, educators should begin to build skills that will be used for future employment. If educators wait until high school, it will be too late and students will be challenged to obtain gainful employment (Harvey, 2008).

Federal (National Research Council, 2001) and state (New York State Department of Health Early Intervention Program, 1999) task forces commissioned to determine effective approaches to the instruction of children with autism spectrum disorder and reviewers of the research literature (Simpson, 2005) have recommended that strategies based on **applied behavior analysis** be included in any program. To provide additional assistance to general education teachers, school districts may employ an autism specialist who knows how to use effective teaching strategies based on the principles of applied behavior analysis, such as discrete trial teaching (Anderson, Taras, & Cannon, 1996) or incidental teaching approaches (Fenske, Krantz, & McClannahan, 2001). Information about applied behavior analysis and strategies used for individuals with autism can be found in the textbook by Cooper, Heron, and Heward (2007) and at *http://www.behavior.org* under the autism section.

A strategy that has been demonstrated as effective for teaching a delay in obtaining preferred items or activities is the

FIGURE 14-3 Token Systems for Dan and Mario

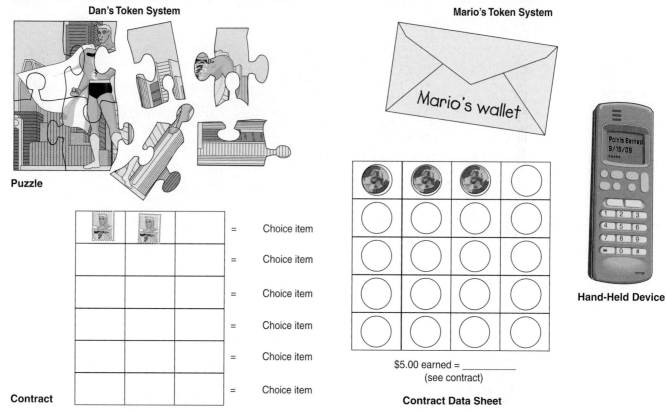

Dan's Token System

Puzzle

			=	Choice item
			=	Choice item
			=	Choice item
			=	Choice item
			=	Choice item
			=	Choice item

Contract

Mario's Token System

Mario's wallet

$5.00 earned = _____
(see contract)

Contract Data Sheet

Points Earned
9/15/09
*****

Hand-Held Device

use of a token system. Meaningful tokens (such as Spiderman pictures for Dan or real coins for Mario) can be used by educators when desirable behavior and skills are demonstrated, such as working on task, or when undesirable behaviors do not take place (such as displays of tantrums by Mario). Using a token system well requires a good understanding of schedules of reinforcement and the power of effective motivational systems. See Alberto and Troutman (2006) and Cooper et al. (2007) for more complete descriptions of token economies. Students can learn to self-administer their own token systems at a young age, and there are clear advantages to implementing self-management programs. In addition, by using real coins, students learn the value of saving money and buying items or activities, and working for pay will have meaning when they reach the age of employment. Figure 14-3 illustrates examples of a token systems that could be used with Dan and Mario.

A common 504 accommodation used in general education settings is the hiring of a paraprofessional, also called a paraeducator, to assist the student with ASD in completing more challenging tasks or through periods in the day when behavioral issues arise. Because paraprofessionals do not receive any formal training prior to being hired, it is the responsibility of the classroom teacher to provide information about student strengths, targeted objectives, and the forms of curriculum and instruction that are most effective. An effective aide can be an asset to the classroom and an ineffective paraprofessional can demand the teacher's time and deter the student's progress with academic

and social goals. See Hall (2009) for a thorough discussion of effective coaching for paraprofessionals working with students with autism spectrum disorders.

Because many students with ASD have some form of communication impairment, the services of specialists in speech and language are commonly sought. Speech–language pathologists may provide educators with strategies to assist with the articulation of words or the formation of complete sentences. These specialists also are familiar with activities that can strengthen the oral-motor muscles that support spoken language. Speech–language pathologists, along with assistive technology specialists, can design augmentative or alternative communication systems and provide training for staff in the use of such systems. Collaboration with the speech–language pathologist is vital because any communication system works only if it is used consistently throughout the day.

It is not uncommon for an occupational therapist to be part of the IEP team with a focus on the sensory challenges that may face individuals with autism. Sensory-stimulating activities such as spinning objects and playing with light by flicking fingers in front of the eyes can be part of the behaviors seen in individuals diagnosed with autism spectrum disorder. Sensory-avoidance activities such as toe walking, tantrums at bath time, or covering the ears during music activities also may be qualities of the student with ASD. The sensory systems are considered the domain of the occupational therapist and, following consultation with this specialist, activities or a "sensory diet" may be recommended. Although occupational therapists

Annual Goals

1. By the end of the school year, Dan will demonstrate the math skills of one-to-one correspondence for 10 small objects by counting each object out loud correctly for four out of five math sessions.
   Person responsible: Special education teacher, grade K-1 teacher

2. By the end of the school year, with the inclusion of a token system, Dan will participate in circle time activities for 10 minutes by staying in his chair and attending to the teacher for four out of five circle time activities.
   Person responsible: Special education teacher, grade K-1 teacher

3. By the end of the school year, Dan will initiate a conversation with at least one peer per day for 8 out of 10 school days by looking at the peer and saying the peer's name plus question/comment so that he can be understood by others.
   Person responsible: Speech–language pathologist

Amount of Participation in General Education

Dan will attend the general education K–1 grade class for all instruction.

Special Education and Related Services

1. The special education teacher will consult with the classroom teacher on a weekly basis to address curriculum design, evaluate the effectiveness of the token system, and assist with classroom adaptations to increase social interaction with peers.

2. Twice a week the speech–language pathologist will work in Dan's classroom to model how to effectively arrange the environment to address his language and social skills and prompt for conversation with Dan.

---

are well established in school systems and their suggested activities are widely used, it is important to note that there is little research supporting the use of sensory activities to address the atypical behaviors of individuals with autism (Baranek, Parham, & Bodfish, 2005; Dawson & Watling, 2000; Ottenbacher, Tickle-Degnen, & Hasselkus, 2002).

Myles and Simpson (1998b) recommended the implementation of their Autism Inclusion Collaboration Model for successful inclusion of students with ASD in the general education environment. Collaboration among parents and professionals of all disciplines is at the center of this model. The environmental and curricular modifications and general education classroom supports also necessary according to these researchers are: (a) availability of appropriately trained support personnel, (b) reduced class size, (c) accessibility to collaborative problem-solving relationships, (d) adequate teacher planning time, (e) availability of paraprofessionals, and (e) inservice training (Myles & Simpson, 1998b). These authors stated that "societal and social changes will require that general and special educators work together more effectively to serve the needs of *all* students, including those with autism" (p. 253).

Figure 14-4 identifies some of the goals selected for Dan by the IEP team, which includes his parents, special education consultant, speech–language pathologist, occupational therapist, and the general education, or classroom, teacher.

 ## CLASSROOM ADAPTATIONS

Several forms of classroom adaptations are likely to be needed to make the educational experience for the student with ASD successful. Almost all students with autism spectrum disorder benefit from a schedule of daily activities (Schopler, Mesibov, &

Hearsey, 1995). The schedule may take the form of a visual sequence of photographs or picture symbols placed on the student's desk, near the coat closet, or in some central location of the classroom to be evident during transitions (Hodgdon, 1998). It may be a written list of activities or the commonly used daily planner for those students who can read. Knowing what will come next and when transitions are likely to occur increases the student's understanding of the environment and decreases the likelihood of stress and challenging behavior during uncertain transition periods. In the chapter entitled *Tools to Give Information*, Linda Hodgdon (1995) listed several suggestions for how teachers can use visual materials to create schedules.

Go to the Assignments and Activities section of Topic *Autism Spectrum Disorders* in the MyEducationLab for your course and complete the activity entitled *Individual Instruction*.

Generally speaking, students with autism spectrum disorder like to follow a routine and like to know what is happening next. For this reason, it is often a good idea to prepare students with ASD for transitions by informing them prior to their occurrence. Some teachers have found that using a visual timer such as a kitchen timer or setting the timer on a watch or handheld PDA to indicate when an activity will end has been helpful.

Organizing schedules is a key component of the *structured teaching* approach that has been used with students with autism spectrum and other communication disorders for more than 20 years (Schopler et al., 1995). To facilitate increased flexibility for students, teachers could add a question mark or a choice of activities in the schedule. Photographs of preferred items or activities can be placed on a choice board for selection by the student (McClannahan & Krantz, 1999).

Inclusion Tips for the Teacher

Facilitating Smooth Transitions

- Incorporate a transition warning system such as a reminder, timer, or cleanup or transition song.
- Use visual strategies, such as items from the next activity or photos of the area for the next activity, to give to the student just prior to the transition (Hodgdon, 1998).
- Identify an area where transitional objects or photographs should be placed. Possibilities are an envelope or a box (Schopler et al., 1995).

- Promote independence by asking students to "Check your schedule" to determine the next activity.
- Review the schedule for the day at a specified period each day.
- Use video-priming for especially difficult periods in the day (Schreibman et al., 2000).
- Consider designing a Social Story (see "Window on the Web" feature later in this chapter) to address appropriate behavior for waiting in line or going to an assembly (Gray, 2000).

If the student with ASD likes videos and movies, like Dan, then the use of video-priming may be a strategy that can be helpful for those activities that are particularly difficult for the student. Let's take going to the mall as an example. The process includes taking a 1- to 4-minute video of someone walking from the car into the mall entrance, walking to one or two stores, and then returning to the car. The student with ASD would watch this tape prior to going to the mall. Video-priming has been demonstrated as helpful for some students with autism spectrum disorder (Schreibman, Whalen, & Stahmer, 2000). See "Inclusion Tips for the Teacher" for ideas on helping students make smooth transitions.

Both Dan and Mario have classroom adaptations to facilitate smooth transitions. Mario carries a daily planner on a hand-held device that he programs himself and he selects leisure activities for earned breaks. His daily schedule is reviewed by the teacher each morning. When he was younger, he had a posted schedule with photographs depicting his daily routine. Eventually these were reduced in size and then replaced by drawings. He now can follow a written schedule with small drawings or pictures placed for activities with new vocabulary words.

Dan would often tantrum when it was time to finish preferred activities such as drawing or time in the book corner. A token system (Alberto & Troutman, 2006) was developed and reviewed with Dan. Each time he moved from one activity to another appropriately he received a token, or one part of a puzzle, that when complete was the face of Spiderman. When he had a complete Spiderman face, he could trade the puzzle in for 10 minutes of watching his favorite part of the Spiderman movie. This system has been working very well, and the IEP team has been discussing the benefits of changing the token system to pennies so that Dan can learn about the value of money.

Authors have found that time and a place to work independently is something that is preferred by students with autism (Schopler et al., 1995). In fact, group work where interactions with peers are required will be more of a challenge for these students. It is a good idea to include both forms of activities throughout the day so that students are not overwhelmed by group work, but at the same time are challenged to work on the areas that are most difficult for them, such as social interaction skills. A strategy that can be used to help Mario during group work activities is to provide a clearly

defined role for Mario that he does not have to negotiate with his peers. For example, Mario could be the person who looks up facts on the Internet or measures and calculates components for a project. Prior to working with groups of peers, Mario's teachers can review with him the rules of social engagement and the importance of being friendly with others. This should take place somewhere away from his peers so they do not hear this special instruction.

Attention to irrelevant stimuli or overattention to parts of objects is one of the diagnostic characteristics of this disorder (APA, 2000). For example, during a calendar activity Dan may be focusing on the shape of a cloud used on the weather board instead of on the day of the week or the current weather conditions. During a lesson about the main characters in a story, Mario may be focusing on a small but irrelevant car in the background of an illustration. It is important for general educators to be aware that students with autism spectrum disorder can be distracted by the items hanging on the walls and bulletin boards of the classroom. Students also may attend to the irrelevant details of the educational materials presented for instruction. Educational materials may need to be adapted so that they are clear of distracting information when a concept is first introduced.

Photographic Activity Schedules

In their book *Activity Schedules for Children with Autism*, McClannahan and Krantz (1999) described how they teach students with autism spectrum disorder to first obtain picture/object correspondence and then to follow photographic cues. They teach the students to turn the pages of a book, point to the photograph, and then complete the activity represented in the photograph. Students need to be able to complete all the activities depicted before those activities are included in the schedule. An important aspect of the activity schedules is the method used to teach the students. Most-to-least prompts (e.g., hand-over-hand) are administered from behind the student so that the student does not learn to wait for an adult cue, but rather follows what is in the photographic schedule independently. Text is added to the activity schedules and eventually the photographs are faded, resulting in the student following a schedule in text as would a typical student. Here are some examples of photographs with text that can be used for a choice board or in an activity schedule.

Note: Photograph from p. 84 of *Activity Schedules for Children with Autism* by L. E. McClannahan and P. J. Krantz. Copyright 1999 by Lynn E. McClannahan and Patricia J. Krantz.

Some students with autism spectrum disorder do not respond well to oral instructions by teachers. Some students with ASD do not attend to the words spoken or have difficulty determining the meaning of the instruction. Importantly, some students develop a dependency on prompts from adults. Students may learn that they do not have to attend to and comprehend what the teacher is saying because someone will repeat the instruction for them or provide some other cue. It would be important for the teacher in Mario's classroom to provide guidance to the paraprofessional working with Mario regarding when to offer assistance and when to require that he complete the task independently.

An effective strategy used to avoid such prompt dependency (MacDuff, Krantz, & McClannahan, 2001) is the incorporation of photographic activity schedules (McClannahan & Krantz, 1999). The researcher-practitioners who developed this strategy have found that even young children can be taught to independently follow picture cues in a book format. Schedules can be made for older students to facilitate completion of vocational activities. For more information about photographic activity schedules, see the "Spotlight on Technology" feature.

A strength for many individuals with ASD is that they are good rule followers. They like rules because rules provide structure and guide action. However, they can have difficulty if rules are broken or changed and if they are required to adapt to situations where the rules may be different from the norm (e.g., it is permissable to remove clothing when visiting the doctor) (Howlin, 2004). In fact, they may be so interested in following rules that they tell or tattle on others who violate them, leading to a breakdown in social relationships (Howlin, 2004).

Curriculum adaptations can be made that focus on the visual strengths of students with autism and Asperger syndrome.

Myles and Simpson (1998a) recommended the use of a Venn diagram as a visual means of teaching concepts such as *alike* and *different*, with the overlapping oval containing the items that are the same between two concepts. They also used flow charts as a visual aide for mapping categories and descriptors (Myles & Simpson). Additional visual strategies include providing a visual representation of a chapter's organization with a graphic organizer, providing a visual timeline for events that occur in sequence over time, and providing boxes to depict cause and effect with boxes in the left column describing causes and followed by an arrow to a box in the right-hand column describing the effect (Hubbard, 2005).

Deciding whether or not to assign homework and how to adapt assignments for individuals with autism spectrum disorders can be a challenge for general educators. Hubbard (2005) provided a checklist of considerations for the educator in regard to homework. Included in this checklist are considerations about whether students write down their own assignments (e.g., teacher will fill in details omitted), aspects of a home routine for homework completion (e.g., there is a designated time when homework is completed), and indication for a plan to monitor the completion and submission of assignments.

TEACHING COMMUNICATION AND LANGUAGE

How a communication system will be adapted for use throughout the day is a key consideration when selecting the form and type of communication system for a student (Rowland & Schweigert, 2000). A communication system is only valuable if it can be used frequently and easily by the student. If a student uses an augmentative or alternative system, it is

CHAPTER
FIFTEEN

Teaching Students with Physical and Health Impairments

Tim

Tim is a 16-year-old high school sophomore with spastic cerebral palsy. He is quite mobile with the aid of his braces and crutches; he is able to move from class to class, use the restroom, and eat in the lunchroom without assistance. Tim attends all general education classes during the day (except for adapted physical education) and is maintaining a B average this semester. He does not receive resource services, but the special education teacher is available to assist Tim's teachers when necessary. In class, Tim uses a laptop computer and word processing program because his handwriting is poor; however, he is expected to complete assignments and exams within the usual time limits. Tim has been in general education classes since the first grade and has several friends at his high school. This semester he is taking the driver's education course, and he's very excited about getting his driver's license.

Maxine

Maxine is 10 years old and in the fourth grade. She enjoys school and has many friends both at school and in her neighborhood. Every day Maxine must take the medication that has helped to control her epileptic seizures for the past 3 years. Despite this medication, she has generalized tonic-clonic seizures (formerly called grand mal seizures) at school about once a month. Mrs. Emerick, Maxine's teacher, knows what to do when a seizure occurs, and she and the school nurse have explained the nature of Maxine's condition to the other students in the class. Although her classmates are quite understanding, Maxine worries about what they think when seizures occur. In the past year she has become more concerned about this problem, and she visits the school counselor once a week to talk about her feelings. In all other respects, Maxine is typical. She is a good student. She performs well in all school subjects and is particularly interested in science and math.

Hank

Hank is 13 years old and attends Madison Middle School. When he was in the first grade, he suffered a spinal injury in a bike accident and now travels by wheelchair. He is able to get to all of his classes because some of the school's architectural barriers have been removed; for instance, a ramp has been built so that he can bypass the three steps up to the door of his English classroom. Hank missed a lot of school during his elementary years and had difficulty acquiring reading skills. At present, he attends general education classes for the majority of the school day but continues to visit the special education teacher for assistance in reading. Hank is a sports enthusiast who keeps up with all the high school and professional teams. He attends an adapted physical education class but is often frustrated because he is not able to participate in many of the athletic activities in which he is interested. Hank has a small circle of close friends, and he is well liked by his teachers. He's an active participant in class discussions and usually maintains at least a C average. This semester he has had several medical appointments that have caused him to miss school at least one day each week; his grades have not yet suffered, but he is beginning to fall behind in some of his classes.

LOOKING AHEAD

Later in this chapter, we will take a look at part of Hank's IEP to see the types of special services he might require to support his success in the general education program. Among the topics discussed in this chapter are strategies for meeting the physical and health needs of students like Hank, Tim, and Maxine; ways to modify the physical environment; and how to adapt instructional materials. As you read, keep these questions in mind.

- Although all are identified as having some type of physical or health problem, Tim, Maxine, and Hank pose quite different challenges to their teachers. Compare and contrast the major strengths of these students.
- If you were Tim's teacher, how might you adapt classroom learning activities so that he could participate?
- If you were Hank's teacher, how might you adapt the physical environment of the classroom?
- What types of modifications would be needed if Maxine was a student in your classroom?

Students with physical and health impairments are an extremely heterogeneous group with a wide variety of conditions and diseases; **cerebral palsy**, paralysis, **epilepsy**, clubfoot, asthma, polio, **diabetes**, and allergies are just a few. Some physical and health impairments are **congenital**, that is, present at birth; others are acquired after birth through disease or injury. Physical and health problems can have grave, little, or no effect on school performance. Some students with physical and health impairments require no special adaptations; others need only modification of the physical environment. For others, it is necessary to adapt instructional activities in the general education classroom or to provide special instruction in areas of

Students with Physical and Health Impairments

- It is estimated that students with physical and health impairments make up approximately 0.9% of the school-aged population; they account for only about 10% of the students with disabilities who receive special education services (U.S. Department of Education, 2009).

- The presence of a medical condition does not automatically signal the need for special education services. As Reynolds and Birch (1982) suggested, "for every 20 children with medically significant conditions, perhaps 4 or 5 of them will be in need of special educational programming" (p. 301).

- Heward (2006) reported that 1 out of 500 students of school age is hospitalized each year because of a traumatic head injury. In addition, "traumatic brain injury is the leading cause of death in children . . . and the most common acquired disability in childhood (Brain Injury Association, 2001)" (p. 477).

- Cerebral palsy is one of the most complex of all physical impairments; because it results from damage to the brain, other areas of functioning including speech, vision, hearing, and intelligence can also be affected. However, there is no relationship between the extent of physical impairment and intellectual performance; individuals with severe motor involvement may be intellectually gifted (Bowe, 2000).

- By the end of 2000, more than 9,000 children under the age of 13 and more than 7,000 in the age range of 13 to 19 had been diagnosed as having acquired immunodeficiency syndrome (AIDS) in the United States (Centers for Disease Control and Prevention, 2009). Byrom and Katz (1991) reported that about 80% of these children were infected by their mothers during pregnancy and about 19% received contaminated blood products during transfusions. The rights of students with HIV/AIDS to an appropriate education have been protected by the provisions of federal special education laws and by the courts (Zirkel, 1989).

- For children, the most common chronic illness is asthma (Friend, 2008).

- According to the Juvenile Diabetes Research Association (Wolff, 2008), in the United States 15,000 children are diagnosed with diabetes each year; "that's 40 children per day" (p. 8).

- Different, and relatively new, diseases such as Lyme disease, Tourette syndrome, or Reye's syndrome appear periodically (Sklaire, 1989). Lyme disease, which results from the bite of a deer tick, was first noticed in the 1970s. It starts with a rash and can lead to swollen joints and stiffness; complications can affect the heart and nervous system. Tourette syndrome is a rare neurobiological disorder that typically affects children between the ages of 2 and 15. While its cause is not known, it appears to be related to a metabolic imbalance. Prestia (2003) explains that "tics are the defining feature of the disorder" (p. 67); tics are involuntary movements that can be motor or vocal in nature. Reye's syndrome can result from administering aspirin to children and youth with flu or chicken pox, and it can be fatal. Education regarding the use of alternatives to aspirin has led to a reduction in the number of cases of Reye's syndrome.

- Most students with physical and health impairments spend the majority of the school day in the general education classroom; many of these students also receive special education services from a resource teacher or other specialist(s), such as a physical therapist, occupational therapist, or adapted physical education teacher.

- Many famous people have had physical and health impairments, including several presidents of the United States: Theodore Roosevelt (asthma), Franklin Delano Roosevelt (polio), and John F. Kennedy (back problems).

need, such as mobility, communication, and basic skills. A few of these students may have multiple disabilities with various medically related needs that require extensive services from the school nurse or other trained individuals. Students with similar impairments may have very different special needs; one student with lower limb paralysis may be active and outgoing, whereas another may be withdrawn and unwilling to interact with others.

Teachers often believe that they should create a protective environment for students with physical and health impairments. However, such an environment discourages the development of skills necessary for independence. Dependency is one of the greatest problems of these students, and teachers must take care not to add to this difficulty. Expectations for students with physical and health impairments should be realistic and geared toward the actual capabilities of individual students. The goal is the same as that for any other students: the development of skills that lead to independence.

This chapter describes the characteristics of students with physical and health impairments who are included in the general education program and presents methods for the general education teacher to use in gathering assessment data and modifying classroom procedures and activities to meet special needs. Consult the "For Your Information" box to learn more about physical and health impairments.

 ## INDICATORS OF PHYSICAL AND HEALTH IMPAIRMENTS

General education teachers are important members of the teams that assist in planning for students with physical and health impairments. Depending on the nature of the student's problem, the general education teacher may be involved in a variety of activities. He or she can help identify a physical or health impairment, provide the prereferral or assessment team with information about the student's current classroom performance, or take primary responsibility for the education and management of the student. In the general education classroom, a range of possible adaptations may be necessary; these include additional instruction for students with frequent absences, modification of the physical environment to allow mobility, and adaptations of instructional materials and activities.

 Go to the Assignments and Activities section of Topic *Physical Disabilities and Health Impairments* in the MyEducationLab for your course and complete the activity entitled *An Inclusive Neighborhood School.*

Some students with physical and health impairments begin their school careers with an identified disability. With others, the problem is first noted after they enter school, or it may result from an accident or disease that occurs during the school years. Because students in this group may have many different physical disabilities and health problems that can serve as impairments, it is not possible to make a single list of signs or symptoms that identify this group. The glossary of terms provided in the "For Your Information" box describes several of the most common physical and health impairments. For more in-depth information, visit the website of Gillette Children's Specialty Healthcare (*www.gillettechildrens.org*) to download brochures on specific illnesses and conditions such as epilepsy, mild traumatic brain injury, and spina bifida.

Knowledge about a student's physical or health problem does not provide educators with much information about instructional programming. As Reynolds and Birch (1988) pointed out:

a. The names of the medical conditions give few clues to individual special education needs;

b. only a minority of children with these conditions have any special education needs at all; and

---

 For Your Information

Glossary of Medical Terms

Reynolds and Birch (1988) discussed several of the physical impairments and health problems that can be found in general education classrooms. Following is a list of the medical terms for these disabilities and a brief description of each.

Allergies

Adverse sensitivities or low tolerances to specific substances that are not problems to people in general. Reactions may take many forms; the most common are watering eyes, sneezing, nasal discharge, itching, or rash.

Arthritis

Inflammation of a joint, making motion difficult, painful, and limited.

Asthma

Repeated occurrence of wheezing coughs, difficult breathing, and feeling of constriction because of bronchial contractions.

Cerebral palsy

Several forms of paralysis due to damage to the brain. The most common forms are ataxia, shown by marked inability to coordinate bodily movements; athetosis, appearing as slow, repeated movements of the limbs; and spasticity, characterized by abrupt contractions of muscles or muscle groups, producing interference with and distortion of movement. All forms involve involuntary movements, and they appear in various combinations in different body locations depending on the nature and sites of the brain damage.

Congenital anomaly

Any body organ or part existing in an abnormal form from the time of birth. It can include, for example, the whole body, as in dwarfism (unusually small size) or albinism (absence of pigmentation); can be limited to one part (absence of an arm or a leg); can be clefts (cleft lip or palate); or can affect internal parts like the spine or spinal cord (spina bifida) or the heart.

Diabetes

Disorder of metabolism of carbohydrates that is indicated by excessive amounts of glucose in the blood or urine.

Epilepsy

Disorder of the brain sometimes resulting in convulsive movements and periods of unconsciousness lasting several minutes and sometimes in brief lapses of consciousness (up to 10 seconds) or feelings of unreality, dizziness, or semiconsciousness.

Hemophilia

A condition in which the normal blood clotting procedure is defective, with consequent difficulty in stopping bleeding when it occurs for any reason on the surface or within the body.

Leukemia

A form of cancer affecting the balance of cells in the blood and, therefore, the normal functioning of the blood.

Muscular dystrophy

A group of chronic inherited disorders characterized by progressive weakening and wasting of voluntary skeletal muscles.

Poliomyelitis

A viral infection that can result in the paralysis of body parts or systems, depending on the parts of the nervous system attacked.

Rheumatic fever

A disease that is characterized by fever, inflammation, and pain around the joints and inflammation of the muscle and valves of the heart.

Spina bifida

An anomaly characterized by a defect in the bone that encases the spinal cord.

Traumatic injuries

Impairments that result from accidents. They include a great variety of conditions ranging through amputations, paralyses, and limitations of body functions.

Note: Excerpted from *Adaptive Mainstreaming: A Primer for Teachers and Principals*, 3/e, by Maynard C. Reynolds and Jack W. Birch. Published by Allyn and Bacon, Boston, MA. Copyright © 1988 by Pearson Education. Reprinted by permission of the publisher.

c. there is no educational justification for grouping these children in school by their medical diagnoses. (p. 269)

As with other students with special needs, it is necessary to go beyond the label and consider the individual needs of the student.

The special needs of students with physical and health impairments are almost as diverse as their physical disabilities. Some require no special assistance in school, others need minor modifications, and a few benefit from extensive special education services. One frequent area of need for students with physical impairments is mobility; for many, the major school adaptation necessary is proper arrangement of the physical environment. Some students also receive services from occupational therapists (e.g., to assist in the development of independent physical daily living skills) or physical therapists (e.g., ambulation training, assistance with mobility, positioning and transfer skills) (Neal, Bigby, & Nicholson, 2004).

Other students may experience difficulty in learning academic skills because of excessive absences, fatigue attributable to a medical condition or medication, or learning problems similar to those of pupils with learning disabilities, behavioral disorders, and intellectual disabilities. Social skill development is often impeded by restricted opportunities to interact with others. Another possible area of need is social acceptance; teachers and peers may be hesitant to interact with a student whose disability is immediately obvious or with one whose condition seems strange and somewhat frightening. For example, the student with epilepsy who experiences seizures may be alarming to the observer unless this condition is understood. Figure 15-1 presents about this disorder.

 FIGURE 15-1   Epilepsy

What Is Epilepsy?
Epilepsy is a disorder of the brain.

A child's brain contains billions of nerve cells. They communicate with each other through tiny electrical charges that fire on and off in random fashion. When some or all of these cells suddenly begin to fire together, a wave of electrical energy sweeps through the brain, causing a seizure.

Seizures interfere with the brain's normal functions. They can cause a child to have sudden changes in consciousness, movement, or sensation.

Some people use the term *seizure disorder* instead of *epilepsy* to describe this condition. In fact, both words mean the same thing—an underlying tendency to experience seizures.

Having a single seizure does not mean a child has epilepsy—epilepsy is the name for seizures that happen more than once without a known treatable cause such as fever or low blood sugar.

Types of Seizures
Children with epilepsy, like adults, have seizures that can be divided into two broad groups: generalized seizures and partial seizures.

When the electrical disturbance involves the whole brain, the seizure is called generalized. When only part of the brain is affected, it is called partial. If the electrical disturbance starts in one part of the brain and then spreads, it is called a partial seizure secondarily generalized.

Some children have just one type of seizure, [while] others have two or more.

For More Information
Visit the website of the Epilepsy Foundation of America (*www.epilepsyfoundation.org*) to learn more about these types of seizures: generalized tonic clonic (Grand Mal), absence, atonic (also called drop attack), myoclonic, and simple and complex partial seizures.

Note: Copyright © 2009 Epilepsy Foundation of America, Inc. Reprinted with permission.

FIGURE 15-2 Classroom Signs of Diabetes and Epilepsy

Diabetes

The American Diabetes Association (n.d.) provides these guidelines for identifying possible signs of diabetes in school-aged individuals:

Often diabetes goes undiagnosed because many of its symptoms seem so harmless. Recent studies indicate that the early detection of diabetes symptoms and treatment can decrease the chance of developing the complications of diabetes.
Some diabetes symptoms include:

- Frequent urination
- Excessive thirst
- Extreme hunger
- Unusual weight loss
- Increased fatigue
- Irritability
- Blurry vision

If you have one or more of these diabetes symptoms, see your doctor right away.

Epilepsy

In 2000, the Epilepsy Foundation of America issued a press release urging parents and other caregivers to be aware of the hidden signs of epilepsy:

Seizures are the most common neurological disorder of childhood. But not all seizures are convulsions, and symptoms can be difficult to recognize. Many of the "hidden" signs mimic normal behavior. Recognition of these signs is important in the early diagnosis and treatment to avoid learning disabilities, social problems and safety risks associated with epilepsy in young children. Early diagnosis offers the child with epilepsy a better chance of treatment success and a future free of seizures. . . .
The "hidden signs" of seizures in children include:

- Short attention blackouts that look like daydreaming.
- Sudden falls for no reason.
- Lack of response for brief periods.
- Dazed behavior.
- Unusual sleepiness and irritability when wakened from sleep.
- Head nodding.
- Rapid blinking.
- Frequent complaints from the child that things look, sound, taste, smell or feel "funny."
- Clusters of "jackknife" movements by babies who are sitting down.
- Clusters of grabbing movements with both arms in babies lying on their backs.
- Sudden stomach pain followed by confusion and sleepiness.
- Repeated movements that look out of place or unnatural.
- Frequent stumbling or unusual clumsiness.
- Sudden repeated episodes of fear for no apparent reason.

Note: From "Diabetes Symptoms" on the website of the National Diabetes Association (n.d.) and from "The Epilepsy Foundation Urges Caregivers, Parents of Young Children to Know the Hidden Signs of Epilepsy" on the website of the Epilepsy Foundation of America (2000). Copyright © 2004 American Diabetes Association. Reprinted with permission from the American Diabetes Association.

The general education teacher may be the first professional to identify the possible physical and health problems of students included in the general education program. Teachers should be aware of the general health status of their students and take note of any changes, whether sudden or gradual. With many physical and medical problems, it is possible to look for specific signs and symptoms. As Figure 15-2 illustrates, several student behaviors can be indicative of the conditions of diabetes and epilepsy. If a physical or health impairment is suspected, the teacher should contact the school nurse or physician for further information.

An increasing number of children with extensive health management or medical needs are entering the educational system because medical technology has allowed them to survive early medical crises and to be capable of attending school. Many of these students are considered to be **medically fragile,** and their participation in a school setting requires the use of technology (e.g., heart monitors, oxygen tanks, or suctioning units), medical support (e.g., consultation or special emergency strategies), and other related services to survive and/or participate in the educational program (Pendergast, 1995; Rapport, 1996).

With the movement toward including a greater number of students with more severe special needs or multiple disabilities in general education, an increasing number of students who are medically fragile are likely to be placed in the general education classroom. Teachers in these general education

Inclusion Tips for the Teacher

Universal Precautions to Prevent Infection in the Classroom

Heward (2003) advised that "all teachers and school personnel must be trained in *universal precautions* for dealing with blood and bodily fluids from any child (e.g., how to safely administer first aid for a cut or tend to a child's nose bleed)" (p. 454). In their article on preventing infection in the classroom, Edens, Murdick, and Gartin (2003) identified several essential skills for teachers:

> At minimum, teachers must know the proper method of gloving, clean-up procedures for potential biohazard areas that might occur in the classroom, and proper hand-washing techniques. (p. 62)

Edens et al. (2003) suggested that teachers carry with them vinyl gloves; latex gloves are not recommended because of the possibility of latex allergy. Before putting on gloves, teachers should remove any jewelry that might cause a puncture. When removing gloves, it is necessary to avoid touching the outside surfaces with unprotected hands. Contaminated gloves should be discarded.

The next step is washing the hands. Edens et al. (2003) provided detailed procedures.

1. Roll out two paper towel sections. One is to dry your hands and the other is to turn off the faucet.

2. Turn on the faucet.

3. Wet hands under water (warm or hot).

4. Apply liquid soap to the hands. A generous amount should be used to work up a good lather.

5. Rub hands in a circular motion, covering the front and back of the hands as well as between the fingers. If needed, a brush may be used to scrub under the fingernails.

6. Each area is to be rubbed with soap ten times or for 10–30 seconds with 30 seconds suggested for health care workers.

7. Rinse hands thoroughly.

8. Dry hands thoroughly on the paper towel rolled out in the beginning of the hand washing process.

9. Discard in a receptacle.

10. Turn off the faucet using the dry paper towel (a dry paper towel spreads germs less than a moist paper towel).

11. Use this dry paper towel to open the door to exit.

12. If only hot air dryers are available, use a tissue, a newspaper or magazine page, or even clothing to turn off the faucet and then open the door. (p. 63)

School or district policies should be followed when cleaning up potential biohazard areas in the classroom. For more information, contact your school principal or nurse.

Note: From Edens, R.M.; Murdick, N. L., and Gortin, B.C. in *Teaching Exceptional Children*, Copyright 2003 by Council for Exceptional Children (VA). Reproduced with permission of Council for Exceptional Children in the Formats Textbooks and Other Book via Copyright Clearance Center.

---

classrooms should participate in the IEP meetings for the student and have a clear understanding of their specific responsibilities when the student is placed in their classroom. In addition, they should be provided information on the full range of related services required to meet the student's educational and medical needs and be aware of the other professionals and support personnel who are assigned the responsibility for implementing this part of the IEP. Another important consideration is the use of **universal precautions** when handling blood or other bodily fluids in the classroom. See the "Inclusion Tips for the Teacher" box for more information.

 ASSESSMENT PROCEDURES

Because of the diverse nature of the problems exhibited by students with physical and health impairments, the teams considering these students must take care to select appropriate assessment devices to gather information about educational needs. The procedures used differ from student to student, and in many cases health professionals and other specialists must be included as part of the assessment team. For example, physical therapists, occupational therapists, adapted physical education teachers, and school nurses and physicians may provide important information about the effects of a disability on school performance. Other team members who play critical roles in assessment are the general education teacher, special educators, speech–language pathologist, and school psychologist.

Students with physical and health impairments often require classroom adaptations to help them function successfully in general education settings. To obtain the information needed to design and implement these adaptations, the assessment team collects assessment data about current levels of performance in important skills. Sirvis (1988) suggested that assessment should focus on the following areas.

- *Activities of daily living.* Assessment of current and potential skills in self-help and daily living (e.g., eating, toileting, personal hygiene, cooking, travel on public transportation).
- *Mobility.* Current ability and potential to move from place to place and to become independent. Special equipment or assistive devices such as special wheelchairs or support devices may be required to facilitate mobility.
- *Physical abilities and limitations.* Identification of the effect of physical factors on the student's present and future plans for schooling, employment, recreation, and independent functioning.
- *Psychosocial development.* Study of factors that interfere with social and emotional development and with the student's ability and opportunities to interact with others.
- *Communication.* Evaluation of the student's ability to understand and express language. May lead to the use of various communication devices such as computers, communication boards, augmentative communication devices, or other aids.
- *Academic potential.* While the academic assessment may be similar to that used with other students, it is essential that the

WINDOW ON THE WEB

Websites About Physical and Health Conditions

A number of websites provide information about physical and health impairments. Several of these sites focus on one condition (e.g., epilepsy), while others are more general in nature.

Websites Focusing on Specific Conditions

- AIDS.ORG (*www.aids.org*)
- American Cancer Society (*www.cancer.org*)
- American Diabetes Association (*www.diabetes.org*)
- Arthritis Foundation (*www.arthritis.org*)
- Asthma and Allergy Foundation of America (*www.aafa.org*)
- Brain Injury Association of America (*www.biausa.org*)
- Christopher & Dana Reeve Foundation (*www.christopherreeve.org*)
- Cystic Fibrosis Foundation (*www.cff.org*)
- Epilepsy Foundation of America (*www.epilepsyfoundation.org*)
- Leukemia & Lymphoma Society (*www.leukemia.org*)

- Muscular Dystrophy Association (*www.mdausa.org*)
- National Institute of Diabetes & Digestive & Kidney Diseases (*www.niddk.nih.gov*)
- National Resource Center for Traumatic Brain Injury (*www.neuro.pmr.vcu.edu*)
- Sickle Cell Disease Association of America (*www.sicklecelldisease.org*)
- Spina Bifida Association of America (*www.sbaa.org*)
- United Cerebral Palsy (*www.ucp.org*)

More General Websites

- American Academy of Pediatrics (*www.aap.org*)
- American Lung Association (*www.lungusa.org*)
- Centers for Disease Control and Prevention (*www.cdc.gov*)
- Easter Seals (*www.easter-seals.org*)
- National Rehabilitation Information Center (*www.naric.com*)

---

students are not penalized because of their physical limitations. This may require adaptations such as modifications in the physical setup, elimination of timed tasks, or alternative response modes such as verbal rather than written responses.

- *Adaptations for learning.* Enhancement of the potential for independence by identifying needed classroom academic and physical adaptations for the student.
- *Transition skills.* Identification of the factors necessary for a successful transition from school to living and working in the community. This is not limited to assessing job skills but should include other factors that will affect post-school performance.

Sirvis (1988) warned that standardized tests should be used cautiously with students with physical impairments. Communication problems or poor motor coordination can affect a student's ability to respond within the test's time limits or to provide adequate verbal responses. Sirvis also contended that students with physical impairments can be at a disadvantage when responding to norm-referenced tests because their physical problems may restrict their ability to explore the world around them.

Criterion-referenced tests that compare a student's performance to the goals of the curriculum rather than to the performance of others are especially useful with this group of students with special needs. Criterion-referenced measures provide a way to evaluate a student's current level of performance and progress without the limitation of standardized tests. They also supply the teacher with information that is helpful in the design of instructional/ management programs.

Direct observation is another useful technique. The teacher can collect data on a variety of student behaviors, such as academic performance, the frequency of seizures, the time taken to complete assignments, the types of interactions with others, and the frequency of inappropriate classroom behaviors. Classroom observation data provide the teams serving students with special needs with important information about current school

performance and can also be useful to medical personnel responsible for management of physical or health problems.

The general education teacher should review the assessment results of other professionals who aid in the evaluation of a student with physical or health impairments. The information gathered in assessment can be extremely useful for the teacher working with the student in the general education classroom. If portions of the assessment reports are unclear, the teacher should seek assistance from the school nurse, special educator, physician, other appropriate professionals, or the student's parents. For a classroom program that develops the independence as well as the academic and behavioral skills of students, a clear picture of their capabilities and limitations is imperative.

 myeducationlab To enhance your understanding of teaching students with health impairments, go to the IRIS Center Resources section of Topic *Physical Disabilities and Health Impairments* in the MyEducationLab for your course and complete the Module entitled *Working with Your School Nurse: What General Education Teachers Should Do to Promote Educational Success for Students with Health Needs.*

▶ SPECIAL SERVICES

When assessment is complete, an IEP is developed by the IEP team for each student found eligible for special education services. For students with physical or health impairments, IEP goals may address several areas and involve services from a wide variety of professionals—for example, general education teachers, special education teachers, physical or occupational therapists, school nurses, social workers, counselors, speech and language specialists, adapted physical education teachers, and vocational counselors. Figure 15-3 shows portions of the IEP for Hank, the middle school student introduced at the beginning of this chapter. Although Hank is

FIGURE 15-3 IEP Goals and Services for Hank

Annual Goals

1. By the end of the school year, Hank will demonstrate the basic skills necessary to participate in two group-oriented recreational activities.
   Person responsible: Adapted physical education teacher
2. By the end of the school year, Hank will participate in 4 hours of self-directed recreational activity each week.
   Person responsible: Adapted physical education teacher
3. By the end of the school year, Hank will read materials at the sixth-grade level with adequate word recognition and comprehension.
   Person responsible: Resource teacher
4. Hank will successfully complete eighth-grade math, English, social studies, and science.
   Persons responsible: Eighth-grade teachers

Amount of Participation in General Education

Hank will attend eighth-grade general education classes in math, English, social studies, and science.

Special Education and Related Services

1. Hank will receive special education services from the adapted physical education teacher (annual goals 1 and 2) for one period per day.
2. Hank will receive special education services from the resource teacher (annual goal 3) for one period per day.
3. The resource teacher, adapted physical education teacher, and school nurse will provide consultation to Hank's eighth-grade teachers as needed.

included in the general education program for the majority of the school day, he receives help in reading from the resource teacher, and he is learning leisure time skills in adapted physical education.

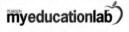

Go to the Assignments and Activities section of Topic *Physical Disabilities and Health Impairments* in the MyEducation-Lab for your course and complete the activity entitled *Paraprofessionals and Children with Physical Disabilities.*

Most students with physical and health impairments spend the majority of their day in the general education classroom and only attend a resource room for academic assistance or visit a specialist for some other type of necessary service. Special classes and schools are available for students with severe or multiple disabilities; these placements are usually reserved for individuals with complex physical needs accompanied by severe learning problems. As noted earlier in this chapter, increased attention has been aimed at including students who are medically fragile and those with more severe disabilities in the general education program whenever it is appropriate to meet their special educational needs. When students cannot attend school because of prolonged illness or the need for extensive medical services, home and hospital services can be provided. Consultant services are also available to the general education teacher from a variety of specialists who attempt to assist the teacher in making classroom adaptations to facilitate the successful inclusion of students with health and physical impairments.

 ## CLASSROOM ADAPTATIONS

When students with physical and health impairments enter the general education classroom, one of the teacher's first tasks is to learn about their disabilities. Other students must also become aware of the problems of these students with special needs and learn about possible ways of helping them function as independently as possible. In addition, it may be necessary to adapt portions of the general education program to allow full participation of students with physical and health impairments. The areas in which modifications are usually required are the arrangement of the physical environment and the format and structure of instructional activities and assignments.

 Go to the Assignments and Activities section of Topic *Physical Disabilities and Health Impairments* in the MyEducationLab for your course and complete the activity entitled *Benefits of Including Students with Physical or Health Impairments in the Inclusion Classroom.*

The following sections of this chapter describe methods for meeting physical and health needs of special students in the general education classroom, modifying the physical environment, and adapting instructional activities. Reynolds and Birch (1988)

pointed out that students with physical and health impairments "seldom need to be taught material that is outside the curriculum for all other pupils" (p. 281). That is, the general education curriculum with its emphasis on academic skills is appropriate. However, several additional curriculum areas may benefit students with physical and health impairments. Mobility training (instruction in planning travel within the school building) may help some students conserve their limited energy. For secondary students, continued instruction in writing skills (handwriting, typing, or using computers and word processors) may be necessary. Other possible areas of benefit are driver's training, recreation and use of leisure time, and sex education. In many cases, these additions to the general education curriculum are offered as part of the student's special education program.

 ## MEETING PHYSICAL AND HEALTH NEEDS

Students' physical and health needs are an important area of concern to any teacher. Students with identified physical and health impairments often require special diets, have restrictions placed on their physical activities, take medication during the school day, or require other health-related services (e.g., seizure, nutrition, or glucose monitoring; transfer and lifting) that are provided by the school nurse or other qualified person (Bigby, 2004; Mukherjee, Lightfoot, & Sloper, 2000). Often misconceptions arise about the needs of students with disabilities; an example of these is provided in the accompanying "Inclusion Tips for the Teacher" material.

Go to the Assignments and Activities section of Topic *Physical Disabilities and Health Impairments* in the MyEducationLab for your course and complete the activity entitled *Building Physical Independence.*

Inclusion Tips for the Teacher

Misconceptions About Students with Diabetes

Although everyone has heard of juvenile diabetes, and many think they understand the disease, there are still many classic misconceptions regarding the manifestations of the symptoms and the effect on learning and classroom behavior. The following is a list of classic myths.

Misconception 1: The student will tell you when he or she is either high or low. This is not always true. Some students do not know when they are high or low. Even when they do know, students want to be the same as everyone else and do not want to draw attention to their condition. They are sometimes embarrassed to say that they are having a diabetic reaction. They would rather just ask quietly to go to the nurse. Also, students may not realize that the particular set of symptoms they are feeling is related to the diabetes.

Misconception 2: Diabetes is affected only by food intake, and if a student eats properly, the diabetes will be under control. This is definitely not true. The level of the student's blood sugar is always a

balancing act between the amount of activity, such as a basketball game or dancing, and food intake. In some students, activity can make their blood sugar level lower for up to 12 hours, whereas in others the sugar levels may get higher. In other words, one day the student may have close to normal sugar levels, yet even within the same day, the sugar level may change by 300 points due to a bad food choice or a strenuous activity.

Misconception 3: Bathroom and nurse privileges can wait a few minutes. This is an emphatic, NO, they cannot wait! By the time a student is aware that he or she is low, the minutes of waiting may be crucial, and the student may soon go into a diabetic coma. As long as a student is astute enough to know the feelings of being low, then that is the time to go to check and take care of their needs. Conversely, the symptoms of high blood sugar are just as important to eradicate. Little learning can take place while that dry mouth is present, or while a student has to go to the bathroom.

Note: From Misconceptions about Students with Diabetes by the Juvenile Diabetes Research Foundation, n.d., New York: Author.

FIGURE 15-4   Questions to Ask About Physical and Health Needs

Medical Concerns
- In addition to the child's primary disorder, does the child have additional problems such as seizures or diabetes? Does the child have any sensory disorders?
- Does the child take medication? How frequently, and in what amounts?
- If medication is taken, is the school authorized to administer the medication during school hours?
- What are the expected side effects of the medication? What are the other possible side effects?
- What procedures should be followed in the event of a seizure, insulin shock, diabetic coma, or other problem, with regard to contacting the child's parents or medical personnel?
- Should the child's activities be restricted in any way?

Travel
- How will the child be transported to school?
- Will the child arrive at the usual time?
- Will someone need to meet the child at the entrance to the school to provide assistance in getting the child on and off the vehicle?
- Will the child need special accommodations to travel within the school building or the classroom?

Transfer and Lifting
- What methods are used to get the child on and off the school bus?
- What is the preferred way to lift and transfer the child out of a wheelchair and onto a chair or to the floor?
- What cautions or limitations are there regarding transfer and lifting?
- How much help does the child really need with movement and transfer?

Communication
- If the child does not communicate verbally, what particular or unique means of communication does the child use?
- Does the child have a speech or language problem?
- Does the child use gestures? If so, what are they? Is a pointer used? Does the child use the same signal consistently for *yes, no,* or other common words?
- Can the child write? Type? How?
- Is an electronic communication aid used? If so, are there any special instructions necessary for the child to use it or for the teacher to understand and maintain it? Are fresh batteries or a charger needed?
- Can the child make his or her needs known to the teacher? How?

Self-Care
- What types of help does the child need with self-care activities such as feeding, dressing, toileting, and so forth?
- What equipment, such as a special feeding tray, does the child need?

Positioning
- What positioning aids or devices (braces, pillows, wedges, etc.) does the child use?
- What particular positions are the most useful for specific academic activities? What positions for resting?
- What positions are best for toileting, feeding, dressing, and other activities?
- Are there any other special aids or devices that I should know about?

Educational Needs
- What is the child's current level of achievement and of developmental and vocational functioning?
- What are the child's strengths and weaknesses?
- To what extent is achievement in school affected by physical disabilities?
- What medical considerations must be taken into account (that is, to what extent is the child able to participate in classroom activities)?
- What physical modifications to the classroom need to be made?
- What special equipment must be acquired?
- What related services will be needed?

Note: William H. Berdine and Edward Blackhurst, *An Introduction to Special Education,* 3rd ed. Published by Allyn & Bacon, Boston. MA. Copyright © 1993 by Pearson Education. Reprinted by permission of the publisher.

The teacher's first step in meeting special physical and health needs is to learn as much as possible about each student's limitations and capabilities. One source of information is the assessment data collected by the assessment team. Recent evaluations will describe the current functioning levels of the student in important areas such as mobility, communication, academic achievement, classroom behavior, and social skills. Cross (1993) suggested that teachers contact the student's parents and the professionals who have worked with that student in the past to determine the best ways to meet physical and health needs. Figure 15-4 lists

Inclusion Tips for the Teacher

What to Do for Seizures

When tonic-clonic (also known as grand mal) seizures occur in the classroom, the teacher should remain calm, assist the child with the seizure, and assure the other students that their classmate is not in pain and that the seizure will last only a few minutes.

The Epilepsy Foundation of America (n.d.) has suggested that teachers take the following steps to safeguard the student having a tonic-clonic seizure.

First aid for a convulsive seizure protects the child from injury while the seizure runs its course. The seizure itself triggers mechanisms in the brain to bring it safely to an end. There are no other first aid steps that can hasten that process.

When this type of seizure happens, the teacher should:

- Keep calm. Reassure the other children that the child will be fine in a minute.
- Ease the child gently to the floor and clear the area around him of anything that could hurt him.
- Put something flat and soft (like a folded jacket) under his head so it will not bang against the floor as his body jerks.
- Turn him gently onto his side. This keeps his airway clear and allows any fluid in his mouth to drain harmlessly away. DON'T try to force his mouth open. DON'T try to hold on to his

tongue. DON'T put anything in his mouth. DON'T restrain his movements.
- When the jerking movements stop, let the child rest until full consciousness returns.
- Breathing may have been shallow during the seizure, and may even have stopped briefly. This can give the child's lips or skin a bluish tinge, which corrects naturally as the seizure ends. In the unlikely event that breathing does not begin again, check the child's airway for any obstruction. It is rarely necessary to give artificial respiration.

Some children recover quickly after this type of seizure; others need more time. A short period of rest, depending on the child's alertness following the seizure, is usually advised.

However, if the child is able to remain in the classroom afterwards, he or she should be encouraged to do so. Staying in the classroom (or returning to it as soon as possible) allows for continued participation in classroom activity and is psychologically less difficult for the child.

If a child has frequent seizures, handling them can become routine once teacher and classmates learn what to expect. One or two of the children can be assigned to help while the others get on with their work.

---

questions that teachers can ask to find out more about a student's specific requirements.

Medical personnel such as the school nurse and the student's physician are another excellent source of information (Bigby, 2004). Typically the school nurse helps the assessment and IEP teams interpret medical reports and translate medical findings into educationally relevant information. The nurse might explain why certain students have activity restrictions, how different medications affect students' classroom behavior, and what the reasons are for medical treatments and procedures. The nurse can also help teachers learn to deal with unusual medical situations, such as seizures in the classroom. If teachers are aware of the proper procedures to follow should a seizure occur, they will face the situation more calmly and be of more assistance to the student and the student's peers. To learn about what to do in case of a seizure, see the "Inclusion Tips for the Teacher" box.

When teachers are fully aware of the needs of students with physical and health impairments, the next step is consideration of what information to provide to other students in the class. This issue should be discussed with the prereferral and IEP teams, including the student's parents and, if appropriate, the student. In some cases, parents and students may be reluctant to have teachers inform students in the general education class about the specific nature of the problem. However, with disabilities and conditions that are obvious to a student's peers, the general education teacher or the school nurse should prepare the class by explaining the impairment and the ways in which it will affect the student's participation in class activities. Older students with special needs may want to give this explanation themselves. This approach

should be encouraged because these students, as adults, will often have occasion to explain their disabilities to friends, acquaintances, and potential employers.

Information about physical and health needs of students should be presented factually, with emphasis not only on the student's problems but also on her or his abilities. Any questions peers might have should be answered openly and accurately. This sharing of information is particularly important with young students, who may wonder whether needing to ride in a wheelchair is contagious or whether being naughty causes seizures. The teacher should anticipate such concerns and attempt to quell apprehensions with a matter-of-fact explanation.

One subject that many teachers find difficult to discuss with their students is death. If there is a child or adolescent in the class with a terminal illness, this discussion may become necessary. Some thoughts on helping students deal with the death of a classmate are presented in Figure 15-5. Another resource that may be of interest is "Death in My Classroom?" by Postel (1986); others are the article about students with cancer by Spinelli (2004) and "Coping with Grief: Guidelines and Resources for Assisting Children" (Heath et al., 2008).

To accommodate the physical and health needs of students with special needs who are included in the general education classroom, alterations in some classroom routines and procedures may be necessary. These students should not be automatically excused from classroom activities simply because they have a disability. However, if they do have medical restrictions that prevent participation or if their disabilities truly impose limits, then classroom standards should be changed. Examples of appropriate modifications appear here.

FIGURE 15-5 When a Classmate Dies

The Compassionate Friends is a nonprofit organization dedicated to providing support to those who have lost a child. The website of The Compassionate Friends offers these suggestions to teachers of children who have lost a brother, sister, or classmate:

When a student or a brother or sister of a student dies, teachers should examine their own feelings about death and grief. Share your feelings with the children within your class. Know that it's okay to cry, be sad or angry, and even smile. Children cannot be shielded from death and grief, and a thoughtful approach taken in the classroom can help them in the future.

If a student seeks you out to talk, be available and really listen. Hear with your ears, your eyes, and your heart. A warm hug says, "I know what happened and I care. I am here if you need me."

Be open and honest with your feelings. Create an atmosphere of open acceptance that invites questions and fosters confidence that you are concerned.

Encourage children to express their grief openly, but in ways that are not disruptive to the class or damaging to other students. Acknowledge the reality that grief hurts, but do not attempt to rescue the child (or the class, or yourself) from that pain. Be supportive and available to classmates who may want to know how they can help.

Provide a quiet, private place where a student may go whenever he or she feels a need to be alone. Almost anything that happens in the classroom may trigger tears. Respect the need that students have to grieve while helping classmates realize that grief is a natural and normal reaction to loss.

Help students to recognize that death is a natural part of life. Use such opportunities as a fallen leaf, a wilted flower, and the death of an insect, bird, or class pet to discuss death as a part of the life cycle. Explore feelings about death, loss, and grief through books while fostering discussions as a classroom family.

Note: From *Suggestions for Teachers and School Counselors* by The Compassionate Friends. Copyright by the Compassionate Friends, USA. Retrieved November 6, 2009, from *www.compassionatefriends.org/Brochures/suggestions_for_teachers_and_school_counselors.aspx*

- If students in wheelchairs or those with mobility problems travel slowly, they can be dismissed a few minutes early from class so that they can arrive at their next class or activity on time.
- Students should be allowed to take breaks during the day if these are necessary for rest, a visit to the bathroom, medication, or a special diet.
- Classroom procedures should be put in place for emergency situations. For example, in the case of a fire drill, someone should be assigned the responsibility of making certain that students with mobility problems are assisted in leaving the classroom quickly.
- For some students, it is hard to follow dietary or activity restrictions. The student who is on a low-carbohydrate diet may want to eat candy; one who is restricted to short exercise periods may want to join the others playing football at recess. These students should be provided with attractive alternatives to help them adhere to their medical regimens. For instance, instead of snacks for classroom rewards, activities can be used as reinforcers; or if students are unable to play sports, they can be appointed coaching assistants to the teacher.

Students with physical and health impairments may require some assistance, but it is equally important that these students be offered opportunities to learn to function independently. Often it is quicker and easier for the teacher or peers to do things for these students rather than allow them to do things for themselves. For example, a student may take 5 minutes to put on a jacket, whereas, with assistance, only a few seconds are required. However, such skills are acquired only with practice, and another's help may actually hinder learning.

MODIFYING THE PHYSICAL ENVIRONMENT

One major consideration in the education of students with physical and health impairments is the physical environment of the classroom and school. For some students with mobility problems, this may be the prime area in which modifications must be made. The following guidelines should help ensure that the physical environment is suitably arranged to accommodate students with disabilities.

 myeducationlab Go to the Building Teaching Skills and Dispositions section of Topic *Physical Disabilities and Health Impairments* in the MyEducationLab for your course and complete the activity entitled *Identifying and responding to the Needs of Students with Physical Disabilities in the Inclusive Classroom*

- Evaluate the school and classroom for accessibility. Architectural barriers that restrict the travel of students in wheelchairs or students with physical limitations may prevent their full participation in the educational program. The most brilliant student cannot benefit from the best of programs if stairs are the only route to the classroom and the student uses a wheelchair. Use the checklist in the accompanying "Inclusion Tips for the Teacher" box to evaluate the accessibility of your school building. If problems are evident, bring these to the attention of the

Inclusion Tips for the Teacher

Checking Your School for Accessibility

Sidewalks

Are there curb cuts which provide access?
Is there a width of at least 48"?
Are they level, without irregular surfaces?
Is there a level area 5' by 5' if the door swings in?

Ramps

Are handrails present (32" high)?
Is the grade of the ramp less than a 1" rise in every 12" length?
Does it have a nonslip surface in all types of weather?

Doors (including elevator)

Is there an opening of at least 32" when the door is open?
Are floors level for 5' in both directions of the door?
Are the thresholds navigable (1/2")?

Floor

Do hallways, stairs, and class areas have carpeting or some other non-slip surface?

Toilets

Is one stall 3' wide by 4' 8" deep with handrails 33" high?
Is the toilet seat 20" high and urinals 19" from floor?
Are sinks, towel dispensers, mirrors, etc. 36–40" from floor?

Water fountains

Are the controls hand operated?
Is the spout in the front of the unit?
Are they mounted 26–30" from the floor?

Note: From "Environmental Alternatives for the Physically Handicapped" by B. B. Greer, J. Allsop, and J. G. Greer in *Implementing Learning in the Least Restrictive Environment* (pp. 128–129) by J. W. Schifani, R. M. Anderson, and S. J. Odle (Eds.), 1980, Austin, TX: PRO-ED. Copyright 1980 by PRO-ED. Reprinted by permission.

school principal and the teams working with students with special needs.

■ Arrange the classroom to facilitate mobility. Be sure sufficient room is allowed for students in wheelchairs or those who use crutches to travel from one work area to another.

■ Make all areas and activities within the general education classroom accessible to students with mobility problems. This includes chalkboards, bookcases, storage cupboards, coat racks, art supplies, bulletin boards, display cases, computers, audiovisual equipment, activity centers, and so on.

■ Consider the seating arrangements for students with special needs. Students in wheelchairs may need a special table or lapboard on which to write. Others may require special chairs that provide extra support; for instance, arm- or footrests can help students maintain an upright position for reading and writing activities. Check with the school nurse, special education teacher, or physical therapist for specific information about the positioning needs of each student.

■ Provide storage space for students' aids and equipment. For example, crutches should be within their owner's easy

The IntelliKeys Keyboard

IntelliKeys is a versatile and easy-to-use alternative keyboard. The current version, IntelliKeys USB, works with both Windows and Macintosh computers by plugging into the USB port. When IntelliKeys is installed, the standard keyboard and mouse remain operational.

Note: Used with permission of IntelliTools, Inc.

Note: Used with permission of IntelliTools, Inc.

IntelliKeys is called "the keyboard with a changing face." IntelliKeys comes with several standard "smart" overlays that fit on its surface. To use an overlay, the teacher simply places it on the keyboard; a bar code on the back of the overlay tells IntelliKeys which standard overlay is in place. Among the standard overlays included with the keyboard are an ABC overlay with the letters in alphabetical order, a QWERTY overlay with the letters arranged in standard keyboard format, a basic writing overlay, a math access overlay, one to manipulate the mouse, and one for Web access.

The Set-Up overlay is used to configure IntelliKeys for students with special physical needs. Several adjustments are

possible, including changing the response rate and repeat rate of keys. Also, keys such as Shift can be set so that the student presses them in sequence, not simultaneously (e.g., press Shift, then press the key of the letter to be capitalized). This helps students who have difficulty pressing two keys on the keyboard at the same time.

If the standard overlays do not meet the needs of a particular student, the teacher can easily create a new overlay and reprogram the IntelliKeys keyboard. The *Overlay Maker* program is used for this purpose. For more information, go to the IntelliTools website (*http://www.intellitools.com*).

---

reach without presenting a hazard to others moving about the classroom. One method is to use crutch holders on the back or sides of a student's chair.
- Be sure that special equipment is kept in good working order. For example, check wheelchairs periodically for proper fit, comfort, and good repair. If there is need for modification or repair, notify the student's parents or the special educator who works with the student.
- For students with crutches, Glazzard (1982) suggested chairs with wheels to facilitate movement about the classroom; an office chair on rollers is appropriate. In rooms without carpets, crutches can slip when students use them to help themselves up from a sitting position. If assistance is needed, show their peers in the general education class how to use one of their feet as a brace to prevent the crutch from slipping.
- Students with limited strength or poor coordination may need easy access to work equipment. Desks with open storage space are preferable to those with a lid that must be raised. Pencil grooves on the desk top or a small box to hold pencils, pens, and erasers can help keep work materials close at hand.

▶ ADAPTING INSTRUCTIONAL ACTIVITIES

In addition to meeting physical and health needs and modifying the classroom environment, it may also be necessary to adapt instructional activities and procedures. Glazzard (1982) suggested several ideas for assisting students with poor coordination or inadequate muscle control.

- Tape the student's paper to the desk with a piece of masking tape applied to the top and bottom of the paper.
- Attach one end of a string to a pencil and the other end to the desk with a thumbtack or masking tape so that a student can easily retrieve a dropped pencil.
- Appoint a student to bring teacher handouts to the student's desk.
- Allow students to answer questions orally, or have them record answers for later evaluation. It is often laborious for some . . . students [with disabilities] to write their answers. If they have poor muscle control in their hands they must exert much more energy than the . . . [typical] students to write their answers.

Switch Access

Because of physical impairments, some students cannot grip a pencil or pen, hold a book or turn its pages, or play with toys designed for typical children. However, students can access these activities if they have voluntary control over at least one type of motor movement. That movement can involve any part of the body: lifting a finger, raising an eyebrow, moving a hand outward from the body, pressing downward with a foot, or blowing through a tube. Movements such as these allow students to operate a switch, and switches can control a number of different devices.

Many types of switches are available, but each requires only a single action. With some switches, the student pushes or pulls; with others, he or she pinches or squeezes, sucks or blows, changes the position of a body part, or makes a small muscle movement such as flexing the muscles in a hand. Switches requiring a pushing motion are most common; see the photo for examples of push switches.

Note: Photo courtesy of Ablenet Inc.

Students who are switch users can control toys, appliances, and even the lights in their home or classroom. Here are some examples.

- *Battery-operated devices* can be converted for switch use by adding a device called a battery adapter. One source of battery adapters and similar assistive devices is AbleNet Inc. (*http://www.ablenetinc.com*).
- Some battery-operated devices already *adapted for switch use* are also available. Companies such as Enabling Devices/Toys for Special Children (*http://www.enablingdevices.com*) offer toys for switch users, while AbleNet Inc. offers battery-operated scissors, digital cameras, and clip-on fans.
- *Electrical appliances* can be accessed by switch with a device such as the AbleNet PowerLink® 3 control unit. The appliance and the switch are plugged into the control unit and it in turn is plugged into a wall socket. With this configuration, a student could press the switch to turn on a television, blender, hair dryer, or fan.
- *Automatic pageturners* hold a book or magazine, then turn its pages when the user presses a switch.
- Some *environmental control devices* can be operated by switch. Options these devices offer include turning on lights and appliances, automatically dialing the telephone, and automatically releasing a door lock.
- Some *electronic communication devices* accept switch input. To select a message, the student presses a switch rather than a key on the device's keyboard.
- *Computers* can also be adapted for switch use.

- Make a copy of your lecture notes for the child with disabilities who writes slowly or with difficulty. It would also be simple for a classmate to insert a sheet of carbon paper under his or her paper so that a duplicate set of notes can be supplied to the . . . student [with disabilities].
- Provide . . . students [with disabilities] with plastic or wooden rulers to use as bookmarks. They are easier to manipulate than paper markers.
- A . . . child [with disabilities] may use a shoulder bag to carry books and supplies from class to class. The book bag leaves arms free to handle crutches. (pp. 7–8)

Be creative, but remember that simple modifications are sometimes all that's necessary. Don't use clamps and tape if a paperweight will work just as well.

myeducationlab Go to the Assignments and Activities section of Topic *Physical Disabilities and Health Impairments* in the MyEducationLab for your course and complete the activity entitled *Instructional Strategies*

Many of the technological aids available to assist students with physical and health impairments in the general education program help compensate for the effects of their disabilities on mobility, communication, and academic learning. See the "Spotlight

on Technology" feature for more information about switches and how these simple devices can provide access to a wide variety of activities in the classroom, at home, and in the community.

Some students with physical and health impairments may require further adaptations in instruction in order to keep pace in the general education classroom. When students miss school because of illness or medical treatment, extra instruction should be provided so that they do not fall far behind. For those who work slowly, the teacher can alter requirements for assignments and exams; more time can be allowed, or the amount of work can be reduced. If students have difficulty speaking or writing, other response modes can be substituted. For example, instead of writing, a student might type, tape-record, or dictate a response to a peer. By adapting instruction in these ways, the general education teacher creates a learning environment in which students with special needs have every chance for success. For more information about adaptations for one group of students with physical and health impairments, those with traumatic brain injuries, see the "Inclusion Tips for the Teacher" box.

When a child or adolescent receives a head injury, the first interventions will be medical. It is likely that the student will be hospitalized for some period of time, then continue rehabilitation

Inclusion Tips for the Teacher

Working with Students with Traumatic Brain Injury

Students with traumatic brain injury (TBI) may have special needs in a variety of areas including physical, academic, socioemotional, and behavioral performance. Although teachers expect students who have received serious head injuries to experience difficulty with learning tasks (and, depending on the injury, with tasks requiring physical skills), they often do not anticipate the socioemotional consequences that can accompany this disability. Tucker and Colson (1992) described the types of behaviors that some students with TBI may show.

- *Overestimates abilities*—Student brags to friends that he or she is still the fastest runner or will win the spelling bee.
- *Lowered social inhibition and judgment*—Student tries to touch and hug everyone.
- *Lowered impulse control*—Student interrupts teachers and peers at inappropriate times.
- *Faulty reasoning*—Student confronts peers and teachers with unfair accusations.
- *Lowered initiative*—Student will not begin a task without a reminder or assistance.
- *Depression*—Student appears uninterested and passive, even in activities once considered highly enjoyable. The emotional stress of the injury may be prolonged and can be overwhelming.
- *Fatigue*—This can be a result of both the injury and medication. Sleep disorders are common.
- *Acting-out behavior*—Student may yell or curse about being asked to do a task he or she doesn't want to do. He or she may walk out of class or knock over a desk.
- *Impulsivity*—Student may be unable to wait his or her turn at a drinking fountain or in the cafeteria. He or she may talk out during a test or speak before being called on.
- *Rigidity*—Student may be unable to adapt to changes in schedule or routine. Student may be unwilling to go to an assembly if it is scheduled during the regular math period.
- *Flat affect*—Student seems to have no voice inflections. Face seems expressionless, eyes seem vacant, he or she doesn't laugh or smile appropriately.

- *Low motivation*—What appears as low motivation may be confusion and inability to conceptualize and plan how to do the task.
- *Agitation and irritability*—Varying degrees of agitation and irritability may manifest themselves, such as becoming annoyed over picky things to becoming aggressive toward self or teachers.

The following recommendations should be considered when dealing with the student with traumatic brain injury in the school setting (National Information Center for Children and Youth with Disabilities, 1997a).

It will be important to determine whether the child needs to relearn material previously known. Supervision may be needed (i.e., between the classroom and restroom) as the child may have difficulty with orientation. Teachers should also be aware that, because the child's short-term memory may be impaired, what appears to have been learned may be forgotten later in the day. To work constructively with students with TBI, educators may need to:

- Provide repetition and consistency;
- Demonstrate new tasks, state instructions, and provide examples to illustrate ideas and concepts;
- Avoid figurative language;
- Reinforce lengthening periods of attention to appropriate tasks;
- Probe skill acquisition frequently and provide repeated practice;
- Teach compensatory strategies for increasing memory;
- Be prepared for students' reduced stamina and increased fatigue and provide rest breaks as needed; and
- Keep the environment as distraction-free as possible.

Initially, it may be important for teachers to gauge whether the child can follow one-step instructions well before challenging the child with a sequence of two or more directions. Often attention is focused on the child's disabilities after the injury, which reduces self-esteem; therefore, it is important to build opportunities for success and to maximize the child's strength.

Note: From "Traumatic Brain Injury: An Overview of School Re-Entry" by B. F. Tucker and S. E. Colson, 1992, *Intervention in School and Clinic,* 27, p. 201. Copyright 1992 by PRO-ED, Inc. Adapted with permission. Also from *Traumatic Brain Injury,* p. 2, National Information Center for Children and Youth with Disabilities, 1997a, Washington, DC. Not copyrighted.

---

on an outpatient basis with professionals such as occupational and physical therapists. Depending on the length of hospitalization, the student may attend hospital school; once back at home, he or she may receive educational services from a teacher who visits several times a week. Planning the student's return to school requires a team approach; Mira and Tyler (1991) recommended collaboration among hospital staff, school personnel, and the student and his or her family. Consider, for example, the reentry plan developed for Barbara, a 16-year-old who sustained a severe head injury in an auto accident.

1. *Reduce course load:* Barbara enrolled in a limited number of academic courses with the understanding that others could be added.
2. *Special scheduling:* Barbara took her most taxing courses early in the day, when she was most alert.

3. *Resource room:* Barbara would begin and end the day in the resource room with an aide present to provide assistance.
4. *Rest breaks:* Barbara was allowed to rest in the nurse's office when she became fatigued.
5. *Adaptive physical education:* Barbara would receive adaptive PE with an aide present to assist her at all times, because of the danger of her falling.
6. *Student aide:* One of her friends would assist her in moving from one class to the next.
7. *Extra set of books:* Barbara was given an extra set of books to keep at home, to avoid having to carry them back and forth.
8. *Lunch room provisions:* Because Barbara was still physically unsteady, someone would carry her lunch tray and have her seated before the lunchroom crowds arrived.

9. *Counseling:* Meetings were scheduled with the school counselor, and she was given the option for other meetings as needed.

10. *Other modifications:* Barbara would be allowed to have someone take notes for her in her class and tape her lectures, and she would be able to take her exams in a setting other than the regular classroom, with extra time allowed. She also would have use of a computer to complete assignments. (p. 7)

In this chapter, you have learned about the special needs of students with physical and health impairments. Methods for accommodating their disabilities within the general education classroom, modifying the physical environment, and adapting instructional activities have been suggested. Consult the "Things to Remember" section to review the major points of this chapter.

Things to Remember

- The special needs of students with physical and health impairments are diverse and vary with each individual. Some students require no educational adaptations, some require modification of the physical environment because they have limited energy or mobility, and others require modification of instructional activities. Medically fragile students may have special health management needs. However, the major goal for all of these students is circumvention of the restrictions imposed by their physical or health impairments.

- There are a great many conditions that can produce special physical and health needs. Among the most common are traumatic brain injuries, epilepsy, cerebral palsy, diabetes, and asthma.

- Some physical and health impairments are congenital, whereas others occur after birth and are due to injury, accident, or disease.

- The primary purpose of assessing physical and health impairments is to gather information about the impact of the disabilities on educational performance and participation in instructional activities. It is also important to consider the effect of the disabilities on the development of social, vocational, and leisure skills. Medical information is useful only when it is interpreted in relation to classroom functioning and special health needs.

- One primary need of students with physical and health impairments is the opportunity to develop independence. Students should be encouraged to learn the skills necessary to assume responsibility for their own needs.

- In the general education classroom, the teacher provides for physical and health needs, ensures an accessible environment, and accommodates learning difficulties by adapting instruction.

ACTIVITIES

1. Use the checklist provided in "Inclusion Tips for the Teacher: Checking Your School for Accessibility" to check the accessibility of one of your local public schools. Also consider whether instructional activities within the classroom are accessible. Can a student in a wheelchair write on the chalkboard? Remove a book from the bookcase? Hang up a coat? Use the classroom computer? If possible, borrow a wheelchair and travel through the school and several classrooms to gain a better understanding of what environmental features can act as barriers.

2. Visit a school with a special education program for students with physical and health impairments. Talk with the teacher and find out what types of disorders the students have. Are most of the students included in the general education program? How are these students accepted by their peers? What adaptations are necessary in the general education classroom?

3. Interview a young person or adult with a physical or health impairment. What impact does this condition have on daily life? That is, how does it affect routine tasks such as eating, dressing, shopping, traveling, and working? How do others react to the disability, and how does the person with a disability deal with these reactions?

4. Identify a school setting that has a medically fragile student included in the general education program. Visit the school and observe the student's educational program, talk with the teachers involved, and review any concerns that may arise in implementing the program. Prepare a short report on your findings related to the appropriateness of the program and its success.

5. Learn more about agencies that provide services to those with physical and health impairments by visiting the websites of the United Cerebral Palsy, Epilepsy Foundation of America, Brain Injury Association of America, American Diabetes Association, or others mentioned in this chapter's "Window on the Web" feature. Several of these organizations provide information on branches in your community and can help you locate their local office. Determine what services these agencies offer and the information they provide for parents, teachers, and individuals with physical or health impairments. How does one go about obtaining additional information or services?

6. Locate journal articles that present suggestions for including students with physical and health impairments in the general education program. Good places to look include special education journals such as *Teaching Exceptional Children* or *Intervention in School and Clinic.*

Kristina M. English
University of Akron

CHAPTER
SIXTEEN

Teaching Students with Visual and Hearing Impairments

Marco

Marco is an 11-year-old fifth grader who lost his right eye at the age of 3 from a tumor on the retina (retinoblastoma). He has a prosthetic for that eye, and subsequent chemotherapy caused significant damage to his left eye. With correction, his left eye has a visual acuity of 20/120, which means he cannot read the writing on the classroom blackboard from the first row. His teacher therefore uses the board only minimally, and when she does, she reads everything aloud and also has the classroom aide enter the information into a computer to develop printouts in large type. Worksheets are also designed with large type, as are labels identifying the activities and equipment in the room. Marco uses a desk level magnifier to read material in smaller print. His reading skills are at grade level, but he is 2 years behind in math skills. His handwriting is fairly illegible, so he is learning keyboarding skills with a "talking" computer program. He is a sociable child and liked by his peers, but recently he has been withdrawing from playground activity; because of his monocular vision, he is becoming wary of the increasingly unpredictable actions of unstructured play.

Beverly

Beverly is a 17-year-old junior in high school who has been blind since birth. She has attended general education classes since the first grade. She also has been active in choir, plays the guitar, and is in the drama club. This year, she attends general education classes for all of her academic subjects. In the regular physical education class, she excels in swimming and gymnastics. Beverly uses an electronic device to take class notes in Braille, transfers those notes to her computer, and completes her assignments with a talking word processor. In math, she uses a talking calculator and, when materials for her classes are not available in tape-recorded or Braille formats, two of her fellow students act as readers so that she can keep up with her reading assignments. Beverly receives special services from a mobility instructor who is helping her develop the skills needed to use public transportation to travel around town. An itinerant teacher of students with visual impairments provides assistance and special instructional materials to Beverly and also to her teachers when needed.

Ahmeer

Ahmeer is a 5-year-old boy with a moderate hearing loss in both ears, acquired at the age of 6 months from bacterial meningitis. He wears hearing aids on both ears and with them he can hear most speech sounds, if the environment is quiet. However, even low levels of noise will interfere with his ability to hear and concentrate. His language development is about a year behind his peers. A psychological assessment indicated his nonverbal intelligence to be within normal range. His speech is 50% intelligible to his teachers and 30% intelligible to unfamiliar listeners. His social skills are immature but are improving. He is not yet informing adults when the batteries in his hearing aids are dead; instead, adults first observe inattentive behaviors and then check and replace the batteries.

Carly

Carly is a high school junior who has a congenital profound hearing loss in both ears. She has worn hearing aids since her loss was diagnosed at the age of 2; even though these are "power aids," she can only hear very loud sounds with them.

LOOKING AHEAD

You'll see portions of the IEPs for two of these students, Marco and Ahmeer, later in this chapter. Consider the questions that follow and look for possible answers as you read about strategies for arranging the learning environment and modifying instructional procedures for students with visual and hearing impairments.

- What are the educational strengths of each of these students?
- If you were Marco's teacher, what strategies would you use to encourage his participation in playground games?
- Identify the types of support that Beverly uses to be a successful high school junior. What do you think her needs will be when she enters college?
- One of Ahmeer's educational needs is language development. What activities would you recommend to help this kindergartener practice classroom listening and speaking skills?
- Carly, like Beverly, is a junior this year. What supports is she using now? Would you predict that she'd need the same types of assistance in college?

People's voices are almost imperceptible to her, and she cannot understand anyone without using speechreading. She is mainstreamed in a small rural school, and has a full-time interpreter who uses the Signed Exact English (SEE) method. She is a strong student in many subjects, but does not enjoy math. She is an effective speechreader, and her speech is fairly intelligible, although soft and nasal. She has several close friends, all of whom learned to sign to communicate with her. At the age of 16, she obtained a cochlear implant for her right ear and is receiving auditory training to learn how to interpret auditory information. Carly plans to attend college on a softball scholarship.

Each of the students introduced in the "Students' Stories" has a specific and different hearing or visual impairment. They all, however, share a sensory loss. Such students can exhibit a wide range of abilities and can experience a variety of problems in school. Their visual and hearing impairments can be mild, moderate, or severe. Although their performance in most areas falls within a range similar to that of typical students, their school achievement is generally poorer than that expected for their age and grade. Students with visual impairments have difficulty with mobility and with reading print or other visual materials (Hazekamp & Huebner, 1989); those with hearing impairments experience problems in language development and oral communication (Luetke-Stahlman & Luckner, 1991). Many students with visual and hearing disabilities are also in need of social skills training (Eaton & Wall, 1999; Loeding & Greenan, 1999; Luckner & Carter, 2001; McGaha & Farran, 2001; Webster & Roe, 1998) and have other disabilities (e.g., learning disabilities) that often go undiagnosed (Easterbrooks, 1999; Layton & Lock, 2001). Both the degree of the disability and the specific characteristics of the student influence the nature and extent of the impairment.

Special education for students with sensory impairments may be provided in a special class or resource room; in many cases, students remain in the general education class and receive special instruction, materials, or equipment to supplement or enrich their educational program. The goal of special education for students with visual and hearing impairments is the same as it is for other students with disabilities—facilitation of learning. This may require teaching students to make use of remaining sensory abilities or helping them learn to use other abilities to compensate for their disabilities.

Students with visual impairments are taught to rely on unaffected senses, such as hearing and touch. For example, they may learn to read **Braille,** to develop their listening skills, and to travel using **orientation** and **mobility** skills. For students with visual impairments with some usable vision, the educational program may include instruction in the use of **low-vision aids,** such as magnification devices, large-print reading materials, and new technological devices (Hasselbring & Glaser, 2000). Students with hearing impairments may require instruction in speech and language, training in other communication systems such as **speechreading** and **sign language,** or assistance in learning to use and care for **amplification devices** such as hearing aids and cochlear implants. It is generally necessary to provide **auditory training** to students with hearing impairments in order for them to develop listening skills by learning to use their residual hearing. In addition to the specific sensory needs of these students, adaptations in the general education classroom may be needed to give them the opportunity to participate in instructional activities and social interactions.

The characteristics of students with visual and hearing impairments, methods for adapting the classroom environment, and instructional procedures for the general education teacher are described in this chapter. The "For Your Information" feature provides readers with background information on individuals with sensory impairments and helps to familiarize teachers with the problems these students may encounter.

▶ INDICATORS OF VISUAL AND HEARING IMPAIRMENTS

The general education teacher plays an important role on the various teams assigned to assist students with visual and hearing impairments. Many of these students are initially identified and referred for consideration for special education services by the general education classroom teacher. In addition, general education teachers assist in collecting information about their students' classroom performance and in coordinating the services provided by various specialists.

PEARSON **myeducationlab**) Go to the Assignments and Activities section of Topic *Visual Impairments* in the MyEducationLab for your course and complete the activity entitled *Effect of Visual Impairments on Daily Life.*

Visual and hearing impairments can be **congenital** (present at birth) or **adventitious.** An adventitious impairment is one that is acquired as a result of illness or accident. Students with severe impairments are generally identified by parents or a physician prior to entrance into school; those with impairments that are milder or that result from illness or accident may be identified during the school years. Students who acquire impairments after they have experienced normal vision or hearing (with normal development of speech and language) are usually affected less adversely than those whose impairments are present at birth.

The extent of a vision or hearing loss is determined only after all possible corrections have been made. If a sensory impairment can be corrected so that the student has adequate vision or hearing, then the student is not considered to have a disability and be in need of special education. If impairments remain after corrections have been made (e.g., eyeglasses, hearing aids, and all possible medical treatments, including surgery), then the student is considered to have a disability.

For Your Information

Students with Sensory Impairments

- The number of students with sensory impairments is small when compared to numbers in other disability groups. In fall 2004, students with visual impairments made up 0.4% of all students receiving special education services; those with hearing impairments made up 1.2% (U.S. Department of Education, 2009).
- About 1 student in 1,000 has a highly significant, noncorrectable visual impairment (Bowe, 2000), but only about 3 out of 10 of these students are considered blind for educational purposes (Reynolds & Birch, 1988).
- The loss of vision can slow the pace of intellectual and social development because it limits access to the normal range and variety of experiences (Caton, 1993).
- Students with visual impairments may be somewhat below grade level in school because of factors such as school absences for medical reasons and the difficulty of acquiring adequate instructional materials in Braille or large print (Caton, 1993).
- About 8 out of every 100 children in the United States have what is termed an *educationally significant hearing loss* (U.S. Public Health Service, 1990).
- Hearing losses are measured in decibels (dB) and can be categorized by severity; individuals with losses in the speech range may have a mild (20–40 dB), moderate (40–60 dB), severe (60–80 dB), or profound (80 dB or greater) hearing impairment.
- Amplification of unintelligible sounds may do nothing for the person with a hearing impairment except make the unintelligible sound louder.

- American Sign Language (called Ameslan or ASL) is the fourth most-used language in the United States (after English, Spanish, and Italian). It employs both fingerspelling and signs, with its own system and rules for formation of signs; it is not merely a manual form of English (Cartwright, Cartwright, & Ward, 1995).
- Speechreading (or lipreading) is a system of interpreting a speaker's words and message without hearing the speaker's voice. The speechreader watches the lips, mouth, tongue, gestures, and facial movements of the speaker in order to decode the message. This approach is difficult because many words are identical in appearance. For example, the words *pie* and *buy* appear the same on the lips. According to Green and Fischgrund (1993), "only 30% to 40% of the sounds in our language are produced with visible lip movements, so the speechreader has many gaps to fill in" (p. 293).
- Approximately 70% of students with visual impairments and 65% of those with hearing impairments spend most of their school day in the general education classroom; graduation rates for these groups are 73.4% and 67.6% respectively (U.S. Department of Education, 2002).
- It is incorrect to presume that persons with sensory losses develop extraordinary perceptions with unimpaired senses. That is the "myth of sensory compensation."

Students with visual impairments may be **blind** or **partially sighted**. These designations are based on measures of visual acuity (the ability to resolve very fine detail) and may have little educational relevance, just as an IQ score is not always an accurate predictor of academic achievement. Students who are blind are defined legally as (1) those whose visual acuity is 20/200 or less in the better eye with the best possible correction or (2) those whose field of vision is restricted to an arc of 20 degrees or less at its widest point (National Information Center for Children and Youth with Disabilities, 2001b). A larger group is made up of students who are partially sighted, whose vision in the best eye is between 20/70 and 20/200 after correction. The designation of 20/200 roughly indicates that the individual can see at 20 feet what a person with normal vision can see at 200 feet. Grayson (n.d.) indicates that "the American Foundation for the Blind prefers that the term blindness be reserved for a complete loss which can accurately be determined by ophthalmic measurements" (p. 1).

Legal terminology to describe visual impairments often lacks meaning for the educator. Instead, teachers are primarily concerned with a child's functional use of residual vision and how it is used when light, locations, and contrasts change. Teachers need to know whether the student's remaining vision will allow learning with visually presented material, whether learning must be through other senses, or what combination of these approaches will be most beneficial (Corn & Webne, 2001). Many students who are legally blind are not considered **educationally blind**. Some are able to read regular print; oth-

ers can read print that is enlarged typographically or viewed through a magnifying device. Because of the limited educational relevance of the legal terms and acuity scores, teachers should be aware that it is important to acquire information about the visual functioning of students included in the general education program; assumptions regarding their ability to use their vision should not be based on a label or acuity score.

Students with visual impairments who have not been identified before entering school are often located as a result of the periodic vision screening conducted for all students in a school. The general education teacher can play an important role by carefully observing students in the classroom. The signs and symptoms of vision problems listed in Figure 16-1 can alert the teacher to students in need of further investigation.

Students with hearing impairments may be **deaf** or **hard of hearing**. Students who are deaf (about 10% of those with hearing loss) are not able to use their hearing to understand speech, even with a hearing aid. Students who are hard of hearing (90% of those with hearing loss) have a significant hearing loss in one or both ears that requires some special adaptations; they are able to use hearing to understand speech, often through the use of hearing aids (Heward, 2006).

Conductive hearing losses are caused by interference with the transmission of sound from the outer ear to the inner ear; this interference can occur in either the outer or the middle ear. Individuals with this type of loss are usually treated by medication or surgery, but occasionally hearing aids are prescribed. An impairment to the auditory nerve or inner ear results in a

FIGURE 16-1   Signs of Possible Vision Problems

Prevent Blindness America (2001) urges teachers and parents to watch for these signs that a child might be experiencing vision problems.

Behavior
- Rubs eyes excessively.
- Squints, shuts, or covers one eye.
- Tilts or thrusts head forward, or holds head in unusual angles while reading.
- Has difficulty with reading or other close-up work.
- Holds objects close to eyes.
- Blinks more than usual or is irritable when doing close-up work.
- Moves head rather than eyes while reading.
- Is unable to see distant things clearly.
- Demonstrates aversion to glare or bright light.
- Has difficulty copying from blackboard and books.

Appearance
- Crossed or maligned eyes
- Red-rimmed, encrusted, or swollen eyelids
- Inflamed or watery eyes
- Recurring styes (infections) on eyelids
- Color photos of eyes show white reflection instead of typical red or no reflection
- Uncontrolled eye movements or drooping eyelids

Complaints
- Eyes itch, burn, or feel scratchy
- Cannot see well
- Dizziness, headaches, nausea following close-up work
- Blurred or double vision

If students exhibit any of these problems for a period of time, they should be referred to the school nurse or appropriate special education personnel. Regular eye exams are important because some eye problems have no signs or symptoms.

sensorineural hearing loss. Surgery and medication are generally less effective in treating this type of loss; most individuals with a sensorineural hearing loss will benefit from the use of hearing aids. A mixed hearing loss involves both conductive and sensorineural impairments. Functional hearing losses have no known organic origin, can be due to emotional factors, and are generally not improved by sound amplification (National Information Center for Children and Youth with Disabilities, 2001a).

The types of hearing losses described above usually occur in both ears; however, some children have a **unilateral hearing loss,** with normal hearing in one ear and a hearing loss in the other. For years, conventional wisdom assumed that "one good ear was enough"; however, research has shown that children with unilateral hearing loss are 10 times more likely to fail a grade by age 10 than children without hearing loss (Bess, Dodd-Murphy, & Parker, 1998); therefore, it is now considered best practice to keep these children on a watch list in order to identify problems as soon as they develop (English & Church, 1999).

 FIGURE 16-2 Signs of Hearing Problems

The American Academy of Otolaryngology (1995) provides these indicators of possible hearing problems.

Behavior
- Does not accurately turn in the direction of a soft voice on the first call.
- Is not alert to environmental sounds.
- Does not respond to sound or does not locate where sound is coming from.
- Does not sound like or use speech like other children of similar age.
- Does not show consistent growth in the understanding and the use of words to communicate.
- Seems consistently inattentive; says "what?" or "huh?" more than other children.
- Misunderstands verbal directions.

Appearance
- Drainage or blood from ears
- Continual tugging of ears
- Mouth breathing

Complaints
- Cannot hear well
- Tired

Hearing loss is frequently called an "invisible disability" because the usual site of damage is beyond the eardrum, and indicators are more behavioral than physical. As with suspicions about visual impairment, refer children exhibiting these symptoms to the school nurse or appropriate special education personnel. Regularly scheduled hearing screenings are usually required by state law because hearing loss can be difficult to detect.

Frequency and intensity are two of the physical characteristics of sound used in measuring hearing loss. Frequency, or pitch, is expressed in a unit called hertz (Hz). An example of pitch is the musical scale; as the voice ascends the scale, pitch or frequency increases. Intensity, or loudness, is measured in decibels (dB). These symbols often appear on reports of students' hearing losses, with a loss indicated in decibels at each hertz level. It is important for the educator to consider a hearing loss in relation to speech sounds. Most speech is between 500 and 2,000 Hz in frequency and between 40 and 65 dB in intensity (Green & Fischgrund, 1993). A student with a 75- to 80-dB loss in the 1,000- to 4,000-Hz range would have a severe loss that would affect his or her ability to understand speech.

In most parts of the United States, congenital hearing losses are detected via newborn screening procedures. Acquired hearing loss and hearing loss not identified at birth are usually diagnosed during the preschool years by parents or physicians. Finally, hearing losses are often detected during annual school hearing screenings. By carefully observing the behaviors of students, the classroom teacher can be alert to signs and symptoms that indicate possible hearing impairments. Warning signals to watch for are listed in Figure 16-2 these and other indicators of visual or hearing impairments may be noticed by the teacher. Students who do not respond normally to visual or auditory stimuli are potential candidates for special education assessment.

ASSESSMENT PROCEDURES

When students are suspected of having visual or hearing impairments, they are referred to the prereferral team to determine if appropriate interventions can be implemented in the general education classroom. If this team determines that a more extensive review is needed, a referral is made to the special education assessment team. An assessment plan is then developed and presented to the parents, who must grant permission before it is implemented. This assessment should determine the student's intellectual functioning, academic achievement, and communicative status. It must be conducted in an appropriate mode of communication (e.g., Braille or sign language when appropriate) and must assess all areas that relate to the suspected sensory impairment. The assessment should determine the student's capabilities and identify factors that are interfering with school performance.

Assessments of students with visual and hearing impairments can be conducted by a variety of professionals. Several—such as special education teachers of students with visual or hearing impairments, ophthalmologists, and audiologists—may assess only this type of special student. Many instruments commonly used to evaluate the ability or achievement of other students with disabilities may be inappropriate for students with sensory impairments. To obtain accurate and reliable information about these individuals, measures must be selected carefully and, if necessary, adapted to allow students to circumvent their disabilities.

The intellectual functioning of pupils with visual and hearing impairments can be assessed with adapted, modified, or specially designed measures. Verbal portions of the *Wechsler Intelligence Scale for Children* have been used to assess students with visual impairments. In addition, some measures have been specifically designed to provide an indication of the capability of students with visual or hearing impairments. For example, the *Perkins–Binet Intelligence Scale* (Davis, 1980) is designed for students with visual impairments who are ages 2 to 22. This adaptation of the *Stanford–Binet Intelligence Scale* has two forms, one for those with nonusable vision and another for those with usable vision. Approximately 25% to 30% of the items are performance based, and the test yields both mental age and intelligence quotients. The *Hiskey–Nebraska Test of Learning Aptitude* (Hiskey, 1966) is a measure of the learning aptitude of individuals between the ages of 3 and 16 who are deaf.

Many academic assessment instruments for sighted or hearing students can be administered with little or no modification to individuals who are partially sighted or hard of hearing. Students with more severe impairments may require adaptations, such as communicating in sign language or transcribing portions of the test into Braille. In addition, students can be allowed extra time to finish portions of a test if this is necessary to reflect their skill levels adequately. However, if modifications have been made in the administration procedures of standardized tests, they must be noted in the assessment report.

Vision and hearing assessments are normally conducted by specially trained individuals. These assessments can be useful in indicating the extent of an impairment and determining possible remedies (e.g., glasses, low-vision aids, hearing aids) that can reduce the impact of the impairment on the student's educational performance. Students who are partially sighted should be encouraged to have their vision rechecked frequently because their visual efficiency may improve and adjustments may be needed in their optical aids or the type size used for their materials (Harley & Lawrence, 1984). Ophthalmologists are medical doctors who specialize in the diagnosis and treatment of defects and diseases of the eye. An optometrist is a nonmedical practitioner licensed to measure refractive errors and eye muscle

disturbances. Both of these professionals measure vision and prescribe corrective lenses, but only the ophthalmologist may perform surgery, prescribe medication, and administer other medical treatments. Medical doctors concerned with hearing impairments are the otolaryngologist (who diagnoses and treats ear, nose, and throat disorders) and the otologist (who specializes in the treatment of ear diseases and disorders).

The **Snellen chart** is commonly used for vision screening of students; its purpose is to identify students with possible visual acuity problems who are in need of a more thorough evaluation by a vision specialist. The chart is composed of rows of letters of various sizes, which students must identify from a preset distance. For young children, the Snellen chart contains only the letter E in various sizes and orientations; this allows the child to point in the direction the E is facing rather than name various letters. Hearing is assessed with a device called an **audiometer.** The student listens to tones or speech delivered via air or bone conduction at a variety of frequencies and intensities.

A mobility specialist may meet with students with visual impairments to assess their orientation and mobility skills and to determine their need for training in these areas. Other specialists may evaluate students' ability to use low-vision aids or read printed material. For students with hearing impairments, the speech–language pathologist is the professional who determines current functioning in oral communication and language development. The educational audiologist is responsible for ensuring that hearing aids and other amplification systems are functioning properly.

Direct observation and informal assessment by the teacher can provide a great deal of information for the prereferral and assessment teams. Much of the data needed to determine a student's requirements for special services and to prepare the goals for the IEP can most effectively be gathered by the teacher or specialists while the student is performing under typical conditions in the general education classroom.

SPECIAL SERVICES

Information gathered through the assessment process is used by the IEP team to develop a student's IEP. The IEPs of students with visual and hearing impairments usually contain several goals. Students with visual impairments often have goals in the use of vision aids, improvement of listening skills, development of Braille reading and writing ability, notetaking, mobility, and academic skill areas. Figure 16-3 shows portions of an IEP for Marco, one of the students introduced at the beginning of this chapter. Marco is a fifth grader who is partially sighted.

 myeducationlab Go to the Assignments and Activities section of Topic *Hearing Loss and Deafness* in the MyEducationLab for your course and complete the activity entitled *Audiologist/Speech Pathologist*

Students with hearing impairments may have goals in speechreading, speech and language, auditory training, sign language, and the use of amplification devices. Ahmeer, the kindergarten student described at the start of this chapter, has a moderate bilateral hearing loss that resulted from a disease in early childhood. A portion of Ahmeer's IEP appears in Figure 16-4.

 myeducationlab To enhance your understanding of teaching students with visual impairments, go to the IRIS Center Resources section of Topic *Visual Impairment* in the MyEducationLab for your course and complete the Module entitled *Serving Students with Visual Impairments: The Importance of Collaboration.*

The majority of students with sensory impairments spend some portion of their school day included in the general education program. Many receive services from an itinerant special education teacher to supplement the activities provided in the general education class. For those spending the entire day in the general education classroom, teacher consultants may work with the general education teacher to help design needed classroom adaptations and provide special materials or equipment. Other students may attend a resource room. Very young students or those with multiple or more severe disabilities may

FIGURE 16-3 IEP Goals and Services for Marco

Annual Goals

1. By the end of the year, Marco will achieve 90% accuracy levels in keyboarding skills, in order to take notes throughout the day with a laptop computer.
   Person responsible: Resource teacher

2. By the end of the year, Marco will decrease his math errors by correcting his work with a talking calculator.
   Person responsible: Resource teacher

3. By the end of the year, Marco will increase his participation in physical education within the context of a predictable team-sport activity.
   Person responsible: Adaptive physical education teacher

4. By the end of the year, Marco will successfully complete all requirements for fifth grade.
   Persons responsible: General education teacher, resource teacher

Amount of Participation in General Education
Marco will attend the entire day in the fifth grade with the exception of one hour per day in the special education program.

Special Education and Related Services

1. Marco will receive special education services from the resource teacher (annual goals 1, 2, and 4) for one hour daily.

2. Marco will receive special education services from the adaptive physical education teacher (annual goal 3) during regularly scheduled PE classes.

FIGURE 16-4 IEP Goals and Services for Ahmeer

Annual Goals

1. By the end of the year, Ahmeer will demonstrate language skills appropriate for his age.
   Persons responsible: General education teacher, speech-language pathologist, and itinerant teacher for children who are deaf and hard of hearing.

2. By the end of the year, Ahmeer will use speech with 80% intelligibility as rated by familiar listeners.
   Person responsible: Speech-language pathologist.

3. By the end of the year, Ahmeer will assume responsibility for the maintenance of his hearing aids and his classroom FM system, including checking batteries and replacing dead batteries (a fundamental self-advocacy skill).
   Persons responsible: General education teacher, speech-language pathologist, educational audiologist.

4. By the end of the year, Ahmeer will successfully complete all kindergarten requirements.
   Persons responsible: General education teacher, speech-language pathologist, itinerant teacher.

Amount of Participation in General Education
Ahmeer will spend the entire day in the kindergarten classroom with the exception of one hour a day in special education and related services.

Special Education and Related Services

1. Ahmeer will receive special education services from the speech-language pathologist (annual goals 1-4) for one hour, 3 days a week.

2. Ahmeer will receive special education services from the itinerant teacher (goals 1 and 4) for one hour, 2 days a week.

3. The educational audiologist will provide inservicing and equipment maintenance for all amplification devices across the school year, and will teach Ahmeer how to manage these systems (annual goal 3).

Websites About Sensory Impairments

Websites About Visual Impairments

- American Council of the Blind (*http://www.acb.org*)
- American Foundation for the Blind (*http://www.afb.org*)
- American Printing House for the Blind, Inc. (*http://www.aph.org*)
- Blindness Resource Center (*http://www.nyise.org/blind.htm*)
- Family Connection (*http://www.FamilyConnect.org*)
- National Association for Visually Handicapped (*http://www.navh.org*)
- National Eye Institute (*http://www.nei.nih.gov*)
- National Federation of the Blind (*http://www.nfb.org*)
- National Library Service for the Blind and Physically Handicapped (NLS), The Library of Congress (*http://www.loc.gov/nls*)

Websites About Hearing Impairments

- Alexander Graham Bell Association for the Deaf and Hard of Hearing (*http://www.agbell.org*)
- American Society for Deaf Children (*http://www.deafchildren.org*)
- Beginnings for Parents of Children who are Deaf or Hard of Hearing (*http://www.ncbegin.org*)
- Educational Audiology Association (*http://www.edaud.org*)
- Hearing Loss Association of America (*http://www.shhh.org*)
- Laurent Clerc National Deaf Education Center, Gallaudet University (*http://www.clerccenter.gallaudet.edu*)
- National Association of the Deaf (*http://www.nad.org*)
- National Institute on Deafness and Other Communication Disorders (*http://www.nidcd.nih.gov*)

---

spend the majority of their school day in a special class and participate in general education classroom activities when there is some assurance that they can have successful involvement and progress in the general curriculum. Students with sensory impairments receive services from a variety of specialists, such as speech–language pathologists, adapted physical education teachers, and vocational rehabilitation counselors. The school system or outside agencies may offer these students special programs, such as instruction in daily living skills or recreational activities. The special services required for different students with similar impairments may vary considerably. For information on Internet resources about students with sensory impairments, see the "Window on the Web."

In making decisions about including students with disabilities in the general education program, the views of parents and those of students themselves must be considered. In the past few years, for example, many members of the Deaf community have become advocates for special schools for students who are deaf. This position reflects a growing awareness of Deaf culture and the Deaf community's pride in that culture. For example, in 1988, students at Gallaudet University, a university for students who are deaf, staged a protest until trustees named a person who was deaf as president. Another example is the testimony given by Jesse Thomas, a 15-year-old who is deaf, before the National Council on Disabilities:

> I think I have to explain that I am not disabled, I'm just deaf. Deaf persons are a minority group. They use American Sign Language (ASL) and are part of the Deaf Culture. One of the main reasons that mainstreaming is not good is because mainstreaming lacks Deaf Culture and ASL. I can't really explain Deaf Culture. I do know that Deaf Culture makes me proud of who I am—DEAF. (as cited in Heward, 2000, p. 396)

myeducationlab Go to the Assignments and Activities section of Topic *Visual Impairments* in the MyEducationLab for your course and complete the activity entitled *Orientation and Mobility Instructors*

▶ CLASSROOM ADAPTATIONS

Students with visual or hearing impairments who are in the general education program frequently require adaptations in the arrangement of the learning environment and in the structure of instructional procedures. Extensive curricular adaptations are typically not needed. Although additional hands-on experiences may be beneficial for students with sensory impairments, other adjustments correspond to those generally provided for typical students.

myeducationlab Go to the Assignments and Activities section of Topic *Visual Impairments* in the MyEducationLab for your course and complete the activity entitled *Assistive Technology for Students with Visual Impairments.*

The idea of adapting instruction for students with visual and hearing impairments is not new. In 1900, for example, Helen Keller wrote specifications for her own classroom adaptations. Much has been written about the obviously gifted Helen Keller, who had severe impairments in both hearing and vision. Her familiar story and struggle to adapt to a world she could neither see nor hear is captured in the letter she wrote to the chairman of the academic board at Radcliffe College. In this letter, she asks for adaptations to the regular, not special, college classroom.

> Dear Sir:
> As an aid to me in determining my plans for study the coming year, I apply to you for information as to the possibility of my taking the regular courses in Radcliffe College.
> Since receiving my certificate of admission to Radcliffe last July, I have been studying with a private tutor, Horace, Aeschylus, French, German, Rhetoric, English History, English Literature and Criticism, and English Composition.
> In college I should wish to continue most, if not all, of these subjects. The conditions under which I work require the presence of Miss Sullivan, who has been my teacher and companion for thirteen years, as an interpreter of oral speech and as a reader of examination papers. In college, she, or possibly in some subjects someone else, would of necessity be with me in

the lecture room and at recitations. I should do all my written work on a typewriter, and if a Professor could not understand my speech, I could write out my answers to his questions and hand them to him after the recitation.

Is it possible for the College to accommodate itself to these unprecedented conditions, so as to enable me to pursue my studies at Radcliffe? I realize that the obstacles in the way of my receiving a college education are very great—to others they may seem insurmountable; but, dear Sir, a true soldier does not acknowledge defeat before the battle. (Keller, 1965, p. 151)

The classroom adaptations for students with visual and hearing impairments are similar to those required for students with health and physical impairments. The teacher should be sure to explain the special student's impairment(s) to the other students in the general education class. A careful explanation facilitates the acceptance of students with disabilities by their peers. However, teachers and students should be careful not to become overprotective of students with disabilities; they must be encouraged to develop independence.

ARRANGING THE LEARNING ENVIRONMENT

Students with sensory impairments may require adaptations in the arrangement of the classroom, seating patterns, and other factors related to lighting, sound transmission, and proximity to activities. The following are suggestions for general education classroom teachers working with students with visual impairments.

- Use a clock orientation to help students become familiar with the room and to clarify locations: for example, the teacher's desk is at 12 o'clock, the bookshelves are at 3 o'-clock, computers are at 6 o'clock, the door is at 11 o'clock (Smith, Polloway, Patton, & Dowdy, 1998)

- Be sure students' tables or desktops are large enough for Braillewriters and other equipment (Maron & Martinez, 1980).
- Copyholders, easels, and adjustable tops on desks help students to maintain good posture for close-eye activities (Harley & Lawrence, 1984).
- Provide an accessible storage area with adequate space for large pieces of equipment such as optical devices or reading stands and Braille or large-print books (Torres & Corn, 1990).
- Do not place students who are partially sighted where they must face the glare of a primary source of light, such as a window (Pasanella & Volkmor, 1981). However, lighting should be adequate; some students may need additional light from a source such as a desk lamp or a window.
- Seat students so that they are able to participate in activities with other class members. A flexible seating arrangement will allow students to be close to different classroom activities or to adjust the amount of light available as needed. For example, a student might relocate to obtain a better view of the teacher, the chalkboard, or the projection screen, or to obtain a greater amount of light for a particular activity.
- Use copy machines to enlarge print materials for students with visual impairments (Torres & Corn, 1990).
- Allow students to become oriented to the classroom; permit them to explore (Maron & Martinez, 1980).
- Attend to the auditory environment. Children with visual impairment depend on what they hear to compensate for what they do not see, so reduce or eliminate auditory distractions (squeaks from a hamster wheel, buzzing from a loose fluorescent light bulb, etc.). Wait until classroom noise subsides before giving oral instructions. Identify fixed noise sources (for example, the ticking of a clock) to help the child's orientation to the physical space (Webster & Roe, 1998).
- Prepare and rehearse procedures for emergency situations (fire drill evacuations, etc.).
- Ask the child what assistance or help is needed.

PEARSON
myeducationlab) Go to the Assignments and Activities section of Topic *Hearing Loss and Deafness* in the MyEducationLab for your course and complete the activity entitled *Sign Language Interpretation*.

Other suggestions for developing the mobility skills of students with visual impairments are listed in the "Inclusion Tips for the Teacher" section.

Students with hearing impairments require other types of adaptations to facilitate their successful inclusion in the general education program:

- The student's seat should be away from noise and close to the area where instruction takes place.
- Seating arrangements should permit the student to face the teacher and other students. Teachers should take care not to turn their back to students with hearing impairments while speaking. During a class discussion, it may be necessary to allow the student to move around the room to be able to see those who are speaking (Reynolds & Birch, 1988).

Inclusion Tips for the Teacher

Mobility Skills for Students with Visual Impairments

For students who are blind, or those with limited vision, the orientation and mobility specialist provides instruction in how to travel from one place to another. According to Mandell and Fiscus (1981), "*Orientation* refers to the ability to understand the relationship between self and environment through intact sensory input. *Mobility* refers to one's ability to travel safely and independently through the physical environment" (p. 209, emphasis added). Independent travel is an important skill for individuals who are blind, and several types of travel aids are available: a long cane, a guide dog (for older students and adults), and electronic devices that signal the presence of obstacles in the path of travel. The general education teacher can support and supplement the training provided by the mobility specialist, as Craig and Howard (1981) suggested:

■ Eliminate unnecessary obstacles; inform students of changes in room arrangement or of any temporary obstacles, such as a portable movie screen.
■ Keep doors completely closed or completely open to eliminate the possibility of the student running into a partially open door.
■ Initially, allow the student to travel with a companion to frequently used rooms, such as the library, restroom, and auditorium. Discuss the route, pointing out right and left turns and any distinguishing landmarks.
■ Allow the student to move about freely until he has familiarized himself with the room or route.

■ Discourage reliance upon sighted guides once the student has demonstrated the ability to travel independently.
■ If necessary, make provisions for a sighted guide for fire drills, field trips, assemblies, and seating in rooms that ordinarily have unassigned seating. (p. 191)

Recommendations for persons who will act as sighted guides are provided by the Arkansas Enterprises for the Blind (n.d.):

■ When offering assistance to a . . . person [who is blind], be direct. Speak in a normal tone. Simply ask: "May I be of help?" Address him directly; this helps him locate you.
■ Never "grab" . . . [the] arm [of a person who is blind]; he can't anticipate your movements if you do. Permit him to take your arm and say: "Here's my left arm" or the right, as the case may be. He knows, then, how to take your arm and he will respond to your motion much as a dancer follows a partner.
■ In walking with a . . . person [who is blind] proceed at a normal pace; hesitate slightly before stepping up or down; don't drag him over the curb. After crossing a street, see that he is started in the direction he wants to take, and caution him of any unusual obstructions ahead.
■ In showing a . . . person [who is blind] to a chair, place his hand upon the back of it; don't try to push him into it. His touch will tell him the type, width and height of the chair. (p. 2)

■ If an interpreter is provided, that individual should be seated near the student. The student and the interpreter should have some flexibility in where they choose to sit.
■ Speakers should avoid standing with a direct light behind them; if the teacher stands in front of a window, it may not be possible to see what he or she is saying (English, 1995).
■ Keep classroom and background noise to a minimum; when students wear hearing aids, all sounds are amplified (Reynolds & Birch, 1988).
■ Verify that fire alarm/emergency signals have a visual component (for example, strobe light) in addition to the customary auditory component.
■ Label items in the classroom to help in the development of vocabulary for the young student. This practice can also help other students in learning to read (Glazzard, 1980).

For many students with sensory impairments, special assistive aids and equipment are helpful, and students should be encouraged to use the special devices that have been provided. Become acquainted with one type of device designed to help students with visual impairments communicate with others by consulting the "Spotlight on Technology" feature on page 309.

 Go to the Building Teaching Skills and Dispositions section of Topic *Hearing Loss and Deafness* in the MyEducationLab for your course and complete the activity entitled *Using Visual Teaching Techniques.*

Other adaptations are often required to meet the individual needs of students. Special educators, the students' parents, and often the students themselves can give suggestions for

such adaptations. Careful observation of students in a classroom setting provides information on how the educational environment can best be modified.

▶ MODIFYING INSTRUCTIONAL PROCEDURES

When students with visual or hearing impairments are present in the general education classroom, it may be necessary for the teacher to modify instructional procedures. These adaptations depend on the individual needs and capabilities of the students with special needs and vary from minimal to extensive. Specialists are generally available to assist the teacher in developing and implementing modified instructional strategies.

myeducationlab Go to the Assignments and Activities section of Topic *Visual Impairment* in the MyEducationLab for your course and complete the activity entitled *Using Large Print, Braille, and Braille Notes.*

Students with visual impairments who are included in the general education program may require instruction from a specialist to acquire the skills needed to use low-vision aids or to read and write Braille. In addition, some students need special materials or equipment; others use only those materials available in the classroom. Suggestions for teachers working with students with visual impairments in a general education setting are listed here.

■ Change instructional procedures only when absolutely necessary. Curricular goals should remain the same for typical and special students (Blankenship & Lilly, 1981).

Accessible Text
- Bookshare (*www.bookshare.org*)

Large-Print Materials
- American Printing House for the Blind, Inc. (*www.aph.org*)
- National Association for Visually Handicapped (*www.navh.org*)
- Read How You Want (*www.readhowyouwant.com*)

Braille Materials
- American Printing House for the Blind, Inc. (includes Chrissy's Collection, combined print and Braille books for children) (*www.aph.org*)
- Library of Congress National Library Service for the Blind and Physically Handicapped (*www.loc.gov/nls*)

Tape-Recorded Materials
- American Printing House for the Blind, Inc. (*www.aph.org*)
- Library of Congress National Library Service for the Blind and Physically Handicapped (*www.loc.gov/nls*)
- Recording for the Blind and Dyslexic (*www.rfbd.org*)

E-Text (Electronic Text)
- Project Gutenberg (*www.gutenberg.org*)
- Worditude.com (*www.worditude.com*)

Captioned Films and Videos
- Described and Captioned Media Program (*www.dcmp.org*)
- National Captioning Institute (*www.ncicap.org*)

▦ Many of the print materials used in the general education classroom may be available in other formats. Work with the student's special education teacher to locate large-print, Braille, or tape-recorded texts. Digital text may also be available through sources such as Bookshare. When materials are needed in accessible formats, it is wise to start looking well ahead of the time when materials are needed to ensure their availability. For information about sources of materials for students with visual (and hearing) impairments, see Figure 16-5.

▦ Use descriptive language to interpret events that involve facial expressions or gestures; students will be less likely to be off task (Spenciner, 1992).

▦ Allow adequate time for students with visual impairments to complete reading assignments; some students may need extra time to locate their materials, find the starting place, and complete the task (Spenciner, 1992). Some teachers report needing to provide 50% to 100% more time to complete some assignments (Mastropieri & Scruggs, 2004).

▦ Encourage students to use a word processor or to type communications that must be read by sighted individuals; examples include written reports, homework assignments, and personal correspondence. The special education teacher may provide word processing and typing instruction; the general education teacher can help by allowing students access to a computer or a typewriter in the classroom (Hasselbring & Glaser, 2000).

▦ Say aloud material that is being written on the chalkboard or on the overhead projector (Spenciner, 1992). Abstract concepts such as time, distance, quantity, or estimation may require experiential components (Webster & Roe, 1998).

▦ Avoid using glossy paper or white boards, if possible, because these produce glare.

▦ Provide students with instruction and experiences that develop critical listening skills; individuals with visual impairments do not automatically have better listening skills (Blankenship & Lilly, 1981).

▦ Occasionally provide tape-recorded materials to students who read Braille or large print in order to vary the presentation of reading material (Spenciner, 1992).

▦ Arrange for vigorous physical exercise to help students with visual impairments in the development of balance, spatial orientation, and eye–hand coordination. Encourage them to compete with sighted peers whenever possible (Reynolds & Birch, 1988).

Become familiar with the various types of special equipment used by the students with visual impairments in your class. Let the special education teacher know immediately of any necessary replacement or repairs. Perkins **Braillewriters** are small machines that are often used to write (type) material in Braille; the **slate and stylus** is a small handheld device also used to write Braille. Devices such as an abacus, Braille ruler, or raised relief map are also useful for students. To learn more about the Braille system, consult Figure 16-6.

In addition to the special equipment available for students with visual impairments, the teacher can use general education classroom materials more effectively by adapting them. Glazzard (1980) suggested several ideas for the modification of materials.

- Use a heavy black marking pen on dittoed worksheets. It makes them easier to see.
- Use a marking pen to delineate lines on writing paper or purchase heavy-lined paper.

FIGURE 16-6 Braille: Tactile Communication for Individuals Who Are Blind

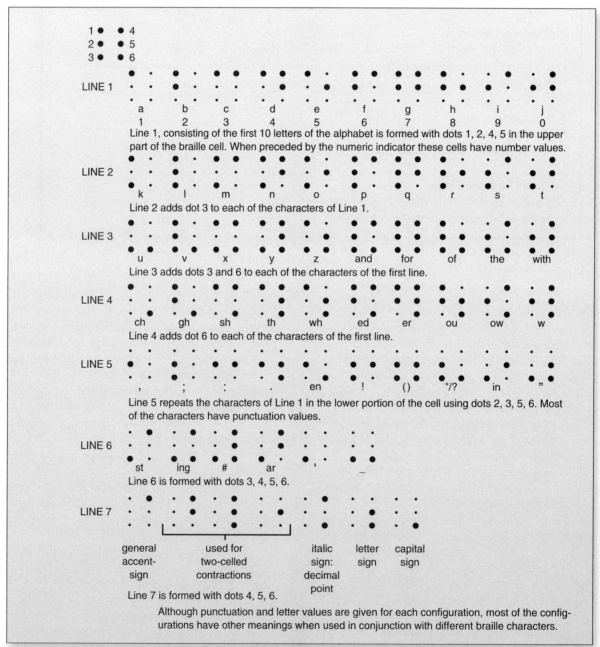

Note: From *Understanding Braille* by the American Foundation for the Blind, 1969, New York: Author. Reprinted by permission.

Braille Personal Notetakers

Braille personal notetakers are portable electronic devices that allow students who are blind to take notes in class, complete written assignments, and write answers to exam questions. One example is the BrailleNote family of devices from Humanware (www.humanware.com). The basic model, the BrailleNote mPower BT 18, shown below, is lightweight (2.2 pounds), quite small (9.9" × 6.1" × 2"), and is powered by a battery.

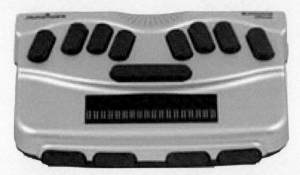

This version of the BrailleNote comes with a Braille keyboard (the top half of the device) and Braille output (the bottom half). Its nine-key keyboard is designed for typing Braille, not standard text. Three keys are used for commands. The other six correspond to the six dots found in Braille; the student presses one, two, three, or more keys depending on the Braille character he or she wants to type.

The Braille output of the BrailleNote is a dynamic Braille display. This is a tactile display; small pins corresponding to the dots in the Braille cell are raised electronically to form Braille characters. Eighteen Braille cells are displayed at a time on the BrailleNote. This type of Braille is called paperless or refreshable Braille. It does not need to be printed on paper, and it can be reused (or refreshed) by lowering the pins and then arranging them to form a different set of Braille characters. The BrailleNote mPower BT is also available with a 32-cell Braille display. This larger display allows the student to review more material at one time.

The BrailleNote provides speech output in addition to Braille output. Its built-in speech synthesizer allows students to hear text read aloud. Also, with the built-in microphone, students can record voice memos.

The BrailleNote comes in several different configurations to fit the needs of different users. These include options for a standard keyboard instead of a Braille keyboard, different lengths for the Braille display, and a model with a standard keyboard and no Braille display.

Visitors to the Humanware website can download "The World of BrailleNote: An Educational Resource Guide" designed for teachers and parents. The diagram below, from the Guide, provides labels for the various parts of the device. The Guide also describes the features available on all BrailleNote models. These features include:

- Word processing to create, edit, and store documents; convert documents to Braille or text formats; print documents
- Internet access via WiFi or a Bluetooth cellphone
- Media player compatible with many formats including MP3 files
- Voice memos
- Web browser and e-mail
- Daily planner
- Address book
- Book reader for e-books in Braille or text format
- Stopwatch and scientific calculator
- Ability to connect to a visual display and with PCs

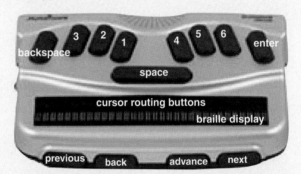

Note: Images of BrailleNote mPower BT 18 used by permission of HumanWare, *www.humanware.com/education*.

- Write chalkboard directions on a separate piece of paper for the child with poor vision. Keep copying work for the . . . student to a minimum.
- Ask parents or other students to read reference material or lengthy reading assignments to the . . . student [with visual impairments].
- Record reading material or other assignments for the . . . child [with visual impairments]. Aides, parents, volunteers, or other students are possible sources of help for recording assignments.
- A magnifying glass may be helpful for enlarging the print of regular class materials. It is less tiring for some . . . students [with visual impairments] to use such an aid. (pp. 27–28)

Pasanella and Volkmor (1981) provided additional suggestions that general education teachers might find helpful in communicating with students with visual impairments.

- Use a vocabulary that is related to sight, such as the words *see* and *look* . . . [P]ersons [with visual impairments] use those words, too.
- Call the student by name when you are speaking to him.
- Talk directly to the student. Look him in the face and remind classmates to do the same.
- Some . . . students [with visual impairments] develop unusual mannerisms. Gently remind them about more appropriate behaviors.
- Tell the student who you are when you approach him or her and tell him when you leave.
- Encourage the student to use any adaptive aids s/he needs and to explain their use to other classmates. (pp. 186–187)

Students with hearing impairments may also require adaptations in the general education classroom. Specialists provide many of these students with instruction in speechreading,

FIGURE 16-7 The Manual Alphabet

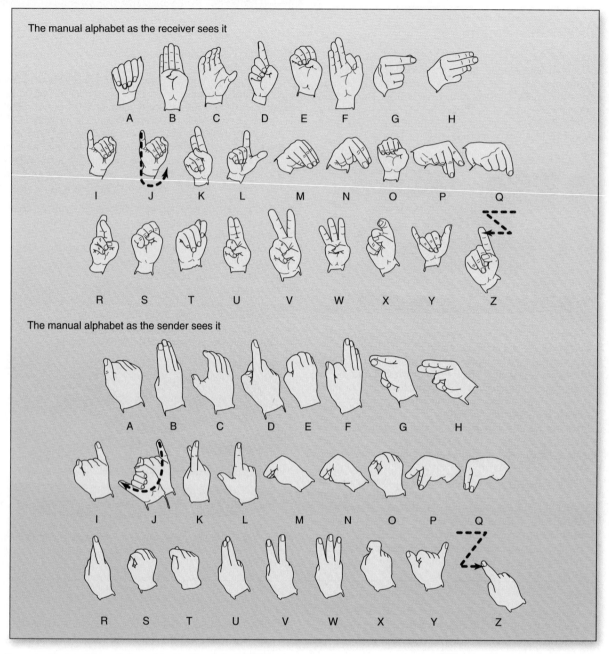

The manual alphabet as the receiver sees it

A B C D E F G H
I J K L M N O P Q
R S T U V W X Y Z

The manual alphabet as the sender sees it

A B C D E F G H
I J K L M N O P Q
R S T U V W X Y Z

Note: From the National Association of the Deaf, n.d. Copyright by the National Association of the Deaf. Reprinted by permission.

fingerspelling, and sign language. Educators of students with hearing impairments do not agree on the most appropriate communication method for this group, but many professionals advocate **total communication.** This approach combines the oral/aural method of communication (speech, speechreading, and audition) with the manual method (fingerspelling and sign language). The manual alphabet, shown in Figure 16-7, allows students to fingerspell names and technical terms that are not available in sign language. The following suggestions can help the teacher work with students with hearing impairments who are included in the general education program.

■ Teachers and students should speak naturally, use natural gestures, and maintain face-to-face contact when speaking with a student with a hearing impairment (Reynolds & Birch, 1988).

■ Encourage students with hearing impairments to use their hearing aids and/or cochlear implant at all times.

■ Find out the best seating position for the student to speechread the teacher's verbal presentations to the class by discussing this with the student (Rees, 1992).

■ An overhead projector permits a teacher to write material that can be seen by all students while the teacher continues

Classroom Amplification Devices

Students with hearing impairments benefit from technological devices that amplify sounds in order to optimize residual hearing. Some amplification systems also overcome the problem of listening in noisy situations.

Hearing Aids

Hearing aids differ in shape and style, but all operate on the same principles. Sound is picked up by a microphone, amplified, and delivered to a receiver in the canal of the ear. Unfortunately, all sounds are amplified, making it difficult for the user to discriminate between conversation and all other noises in the background. In the classroom, a student with a hearing impairment will likely find it difficult to follow a teacher's instructions in the presence of competing noise (rustling paper, shuffling feet, pencil sharpeners, aquarium motors, heating systems, etc.).

The hearing aid user is also affected by two other factors: distance and direction. As distance between the speaker and the hearing aid user increases, the intensity of the speaker's voice decreases. To a person with a hearing impairment, this decrease has a significantly negative impact on speech perception. As a speaker turns away from a hearing aid user, the speech signal again becomes weaker and sometimes distorted. To overcome these limitations of a hearing aid, a teacher would need to directly face the student with a hearing impairment at all times, and speak at a distance of approximately 12 inches from the hearing aid microphone. Obviously, this strategy is not a practical recommendation.

FM Technology

Fortunately, technology is available to address these hearing aid limitations. FM technology is used in an instrument specially designed to address the problems of noise, distance, and direction (Flexer, Wray, & Ireland, 1989; Maxon, Brackett, & van den Berg, 1991). To use an FM system (previously called an *auditory trainer*), the classroom teacher wears a wireless microphone and the student wears a wireless receiver. Some receivers look and operate like personal stereos. Recently, receivers have also been designed to be worn as behind-the-ear hearing aids. This new type of receiver is a preferred choice among students if cosmetic concerns become an issue.

Note: Photo courtesy of Phonak

The FM system has three advantages:

1. The teacher's voice is amplified 12 to 15 decibels above the classroom noise;
2. the teacher's voice is transmitted at an even intensity across a distance of up to 100 feet; and
3. the teacher's voice is not affected by direction.

This threefold "FM advantage" has helped make the FM system standard equipment in special classrooms for students with hearing impairments for many years. Because the FM system is easy to use, it has been introduced into general education settings with much success. However, because there is a real risk of over-amplification, FM systems must be fitted and monitored by an audiologist.

Another amplification system used in classrooms is called *sound field amplification.* FM technology is used to transmit the teacher's voice by a microphone to one or more speakers placed around the classroom. The teacher's voice is slightly amplified and conveyed to the whole room (that is, the sound field); students in the back of class hear the teacher's voice as loudly as the students in front. If there is a student in the classroom with a hearing impairment, he or she may wear either an FM receiver or his or her personal hearing aids, depending on the audiologist's recommendation. Research indicates that all members in the class can benefit from sound field amplification; for example, students have demonstrated significant academic gains and an increase in on-task behavior. Teachers also report a noticeable reduction in vocal fatigue (Berg, 1987; Sarff, 1981; Zabel & Tabor, 1993).

Cochlear Implants

Finally, another type of amplification showing up in increasing numbers in the general classroom is called a **cochlear implant.** Part of this device is surgically implanted in the child's inner ear to bypass the sensory organ and to stimulate the auditory nerve directly. Another component of the device is a hearing-aid-looking component that rests on the outer ear. Its microphone picks up sound; a small processor converts the sound to electrical energy, and then a magnet carries that energy through the skull to the implant. Like hearing aids, implants do not "cure" hearing loss; users still have to contend with the adverse effects of background noise and will typically need therapy to learn how to interpret the auditory input. To help with localization, some children use a hearing aid on the non-implanted side. If a student has a cochlear implant, the teacher will want to meet with the educational audiologist or the implant center's audiologist for information and support. For more information, visit this website: *www.utdallas.edu/~loizou/cimplants/tutorial.*

to face the class (English, 1995). However, the projector must have a quiet fan. Also remember that when the projector is being used, the room is typically dark, which means the student who depends on speechreading will not be able to see the teacher's face. Work with the student to determine the most helpful strategy.

■ Provide copies of the teacher's notes or those of two other students when material is presented in lecture format; it is not possible to speechread and take notes simultaneously. Write assignments, outlines of lectures, and public address announcements on the board (Reynolds & Birch, 1988).

■ Use **captioned films** whenever possible. Many films and videotapes used in the classroom are available in a captioned version. (See Figure 16–5 for information about sources for captioned films and videos.)

■ Maximize the use of other visual teaching strategies such as using bulletin boards and materials that include pictures, illustrations, artifacts, slides, and computer graphics (Luckner, Bowen, & Carter, 2001).

■ Hearing aids should be checked daily. Consult with a speech–language pathologist or educational audiologist to determine who will assume this responsibility. The "Spotlight on Technology" feature describes the use of hearing aids and classroom amplification devices with students with hearing impairments.

■ Question students with hearing impairments to determine whether they understand information presented in class. Do not assume that students understand the material.

■ Clearly explain concepts being taught. Use visual examples whenever possible, and keep terminology consistent.

■ Do not talk when distributing handouts because the student with a hearing impairment cannot look for papers and watch the teacher at the same time (Rees, 1992).

■ Talk in full sentences. Avoid the use of single words, and rephrase the entire sentence if it was not understood; content and meaning are easier to grasp in context (Reynolds & Birch, 1988).

■ Provide assignments both orally and in writing to avoid confusion (Rees, 1992).

■ Speechreading and attending to auditory stimuli with deficient hearing can be tiring tasks; watch for student fatigue.

■ Start lectures with an outline of material to be presented and end the lecture with a summary of the key points (Rees, 1992).

■ During class discussions, allow only one person to speak at a time and signal who is talking so the student with hearing impairment knows where to look (Rees, 1992).

■ The academic problems of many students are related to their language impairments, not to a lack of intelligence. Closely monitor their achievement (Blankenship & Lilly, 1981).

■ Classmates of a student with a hearing impairment may wish to learn sign language. Arrange for instruction in this area if it is appropriate (Blankenship & Lilly, 1981).

■ Encourage independence in students with hearing impairments and help them develop skills to act as their own advocates. English (1997) and Marttila and Mills (1995) designed self-advocacy curriculums for students with hearing losses.

■ Work closely with specialists to ensure that students with hearing impairments are provided with appropriate experiences in the general education classroom.

Specific suggestions for working with students who are hard of hearing are presented in the "Inclusion Tips for the Teacher" box. In addition, Harrington (1976) made the following recommendations about communicating with a student with a hearing impairment:

(a) If you have difficulty understanding the child, ask him to repeat; (b) Do not call attention to the child's speech errors in the classroom. Record and share them with the speech clinician; (c) Realize that the child may have limited vocabulary and syntax, both receptively and expressively. His/her failure to understand may be related to this language deficit as well as the inability to hear normally. (p. 25)

General education teachers ordinarily are not required to become proficient in specialized techniques, such as Braille or sign language. However, they must be aware of students' needs and be familiar with the specialists who provide assistance in adapting instructional procedures for students with sensory impairments. Teachers must also appreciate how visual and hearing impairments increase the demands on students' ability to concentrate and process information. With both kinds of sensory impairments, students must work harder to keep pace with their peers. The effort involved in expending this extra energy has been called **vigilance,** akin to functioning at 110% capacity for long periods of time. This heightened state of attention obviously will be fatiguing, so students often "recharge their batteries" by withdrawing their attention from instruction or conversation—younger children even take short naps. This is a legitimate coping strategy called **respite,** an understandable mental health choice (Gottlieb, 1997). However, these behaviors can be misinterpreted to imply rudeness or lack of interest, and children are frequently scolded for conserving or restoring their energy in this way. Teachers can help students understand how they expend and conserve cognitive and physical energy by discussing different respite strategies and how to use them effectively.

This chapter has presented information on adapting the classroom environment and instructional procedures for students with visual and hearing impairments. Many such students are fully capable of spending the majority of the school day in the general education classroom when appropriate adaptations are introduced.

Students Who Are Hard of Hearing

Hearing Aid Basics

- Do not expect a hearing aid to "correct" hearing impairments like glasses correct visual impairments. The instrument will make sounds louder but not necessarily clearer. In addition, a conventional hearing aid amplifies all sounds; it cannot sort out the teacher's instruction from the general background noise. Recent advances in electronics allow some hearing aids to be "programmed" to reduce speech-in-noise problems; however, these are relatively expensive and not often recommended for children's use.

- If the aid "whistles" or produces feedback while in the child's ear, check the earpiece (or earmold) to see whether it has been inserted properly. Feedback will naturally occur if the aid is covered with a hand or a hat, or if the student leans close to a wall or turns the volume too high. However, if the earmold is fully in the ear, if the aid is not covered, and if the volume is at the appropriate setting, and feedback still occurs, the earmold may be too small and need to be replaced. Inform the parent of the situation. Reducing the volume is only a temporary solution.

- Obtain a battery tester and a hearing aid stethoscope from the school audiologist and request training in conducting a hearing aid check. Hearing aids must be checked every day.

- Ask parents to provide spare batteries to keep at school, and let them know when dead batteries are replaced.

- Encourage the student to develop self-management skills for hearing aid care. Students should be able to check their own hearing aid batteries by third grade. If a battery dies during the school day, students should advise their teachers immediately; reinforce these self-advocacy skills.

Classroom Acoustic Considerations

Noise has a detrimental effect on the listening abilities of all students, but particularly students with hearing impairments (American Speech-Language-Hearing Association, 1995). New standards in classroom acoustics have been developed by the Acoustical Society of America, providing easy directions about how to evaluate and improve a classroom's auditory environment (*http://asa.aip.org/classroom/booklet.html*).

A classroom's acoustical environment can be immediately improved by reducing or eliminating noise sources. A careful "listening inspection" of the classroom will help the teacher identify noise sources that most adults have learned to ignore but most children find distracting; examples are fish tank filters, computers, printers, and fans from overhead projectors. If noise sources cannot be eliminated or reduced, the student with a hearing impairment should work away from noise as much as possible.

In addition to conducting a "listening inspection," teachers can request the following environmental modifications to significantly reduce noise and reverberation problems:

- Carpeting, acoustic ceiling tile, and walls covered with bulletin board or similar materials, which absorb rather than reflect noise.

- Acoustic treatments for noise sources such as rumbling plumbing, rattling window blinds, and buzzing fluorescent lights. Noise from heating, ventilation, and air conditioning systems can be reduced with inexpensive baffles.

- Acoustic modifications to a classroom can generally be accomplished by the site custodial staff at little cost and will result in an environment conducive for learning for students with normal hearing as well as those with hearing impairments.

Strategies to Optimize Visual Information

Students with hearing impairments need as much visual cueing as possible. Comprehension increases significantly when a student can watch the teacher's face in order to lipread or, more accurately, speechread. Here are some suggestions to improve speechreading conditions.

- Speak in a normal fashion, without exaggeration or an increase in volume. Speak in phrases, at a normal pace. If there is a misunderstanding, rephrase rather than repeat.

- As often as possible, directly face a student with a hearing impairment, at eye level. Proximity is also very important; it is too difficult to speechread beyond 10 feet.

- When the room is darkened for films or slides, have another student take notes; the student will not be able to speechread the teacher.

- Be aware that some people are naturally better speechreaders than others and that, even for the best speechreaders, only one-third of English speech sounds are visible. Speechreading becomes more difficult when the speaker has a foreign accent or a mustache that covers the mouth.

Other Teaching Strategies

- Students with hearing impairments often have some language deficits as a result of inconsistent auditory input. Pre-tutoring helps a student develop familiarity with new vocabulary and concepts before they are presented in class. Have the student read ahead on a subject to allow for extra time to consider new material. This can be accomplished as a homework assignment or with a resource teacher.

- As often as possible, write page numbers, homework assignments, public address announcements, key vocabulary, and so forth, on the chalkboard.

- Routinely check comprehension with questions that require more than yes or no answers. When simply asked, "Do you understand?" a student with a hearing impairment may prefer to nod his or her head rather than volunteer that he or she does not fully understand.

- For older students, it is helpful to have another student act as a notetaker. If the notes are made on NCR (no carbon required) paper, a copy can also be provided for a notebook available to any class member who may have missed information during class lectures. A student with a hearing impairment will then have a copy without conspicuously requiring special assistance.

Things to Remember

- Students with visual or hearing impairments commonly require modification of the learning environment and adaptation of instructional procedures to facilitate their performance in the general education classroom.

- Students with severe visual and hearing impairments are typically identified before they enter school. Milder impairments may be identified as a result of school screening programs or teacher observation and referral.

- Sensory impairments may be congenital, or they may occur as a result of illness or accident.

- Legal definitions of visual impairment have little educational relevance. Educators need to know whether students can use their remaining vision to learn or whether they must rely on other senses.

- An educator needs to know the effects of a hearing loss on a student's ability to use and understand speech. Speech and language are the most significant areas in which hearing impairments affect students educationally.

- Students with visual or hearing impairments can learn to use other senses to compensate for their disabilities. Individuals who are blind can develop tactile reading skills and improve their listening skills; persons with hearing impairments can learn to speechread and to communicate manually. Students with visual impairments may also need orientation and mobility training to facilitate independent travel in the school and community.

- Many technological developments have improved the opportunities for students with sensory impairments to communicate with others; examples include FM classroom amplification systems for students with hearing impairments and Braille notetakers that provide speech or tactile output for students who are blind.

- Special educators are generally available to assist general education teachers in making classroom adaptations and obtaining appropriate materials for students with sensory impairments who are included in the general education classroom.

▶ ACTIVITIES

1. Observe the classroom behavior of a student with a visual or hearing impairment. Keep a record of the adaptations made by the student and by others. What problems, if any, are encountered? Can the student adjust as unexpected events occur? What reactions do you observe from other students? From teachers? Write a brief summary of your observations.

2. Interview the parents of a student with a sensory impairment. When were they first aware of the disability? How did they react? Does the student encounter any difficulties at home or in the neighborhood? Has inclusion in the general education program been a positive experience for the student? Are the parents apprehensive about the student's eventual adulthood? How do they encourage their child to become independent? Describe your impressions of the interview.

3. Read two articles about students with sensory impairments, one about visual impairments and one about hearing losses. The *Journal of Visual Impairment and Blindness* and the *Sight-Saving Review* provide articles related to visual impairments; *American Annals of the Deaf, Volta Review,* and *Language, Speech, and Hearing Services in Schools* discuss hearing impairments. Summarize each article's relevance for the general education teacher.

4. Contact a large and a small school district to determine what services they offer to students with visual and hearing impairments. Are all the services needed by these students provided within the district, or must services be contracted from another district? What personnel are employed to provide instruction for these students? Is the percentage of students with sensory impairments about the same in both districts? What services are provided for general education teachers?

5. Write a short report describing one of the new electronic devices being used by persons who are blind or deaf. You can find information about assistive technology by visiting the sites highlighted in this chapter's "Window on the Web" feature. Choose a device, explain how it works, its advantages and disadvantages, cost, and special benefits to the user. If possible, interview an individual who actually uses the device. Find out how this person evaluated the device and include this information in your report. Determine whether the device is available for students in a local school district.

6. Two new technologies have recently become available for students with hearing impairments. One, called the Audi-See, uses a tiny head-mounted camera aimed at the teacher's face (*www.audisoft.net*). The image of the face is transmitted to a laptop computer so that the student can easily speechread the teacher from any seat in the classroom. Another electronic device is the iCommunicator (*www.icommunicator.com*). It uses a head-mounted microphone to pick up the teacher's voice and transmit it to a laptop computer, then converts speech into text and also sign language. The text can be saved as lecture notes. Visit the websites, then prepare a brief report explaining how each device works. Include a discussion of the potential advantages of these technologies for students included in the general education classroom.

Methods for Teaching Students with Other Types of Special Needs

PART IV

Margie K. Kitano
San Diego State University

CHAPTER
SEVENTEEN

Teaching Students Who Are Gifted and Talented

Kay

Kay is a high school junior who was identified in the second grade as gifted. Since that time, special adaptations have been provided in much of her education, especially in the area of mathematics. Her current program allows her to complete a 3-year high school curriculum in 2 years, and she plans to enroll as a full-time college student at age 16. At present, she is taking courses in calculus and computer programming at the local junior college, in addition to her regular high school program. In her after-school hours, she plays on the school golf team, serves as president of the math club, and has helped with set designs for several of the drama club's plays.

Luis

Luis is a 6-year-old first grader who has recently been identified as gifted. He was able to read when he entered kindergarten and now is in an advanced reading group in the school's resource program for students who are gifted. The resource teacher assists the general education teacher by providing Luis with individualized assignments in most academic areas; Luis has already mastered much of the material appropriate for his classmates. Math is an exception; Luis's performance in this area is only average. Although assessment results indicate that Luis is quite capable, his interest in math is low. His teacher hopes to engage his interest in mathematics by helping him explore relationships between math and music. Luis possesses a passion for music and has learned to play both the piano and the guitar; he takes music lessons twice a week at the local recreation center.

Johnny

Johnny is a sixth grader with special talent in writing. Although he did not learn to read until he entered school, he began to write short stories and poems in first grade. Several of his pieces have been published in children's magazines. Although his spelling is not always the best, his vocabulary and ability to use words are far beyond those expected of a 12-year-old student. Johnny's school has no special programs for students who are talented, and he does not qualify for the gifted program because his achievement is average in all areas except writing. Despite the lack of special services, Johnny's teacher is interested in helping him progress and maintain his interest in writing. She allows him to select his own topics for classroom writing assignments, reads and critiques any poems or stories he brings to her, and is investigating ways to help Johnny enroll in the creative writing course offered at the high school in the summer.

LOOKING AHEAD

Later in this chapter we will take a look at the goals and services from Luis's individualized education program. This chapter suggests strategies for providing educational options to gifted and talented students, developing creativity and problem-solving skills, and assisting students who are underachieving. As you read, think about these questions.

- Kay, Luis, and Johnny present quite different pictures of extraordinary ability. Compare and contrast their strengths.
- If you were Kay's high school English teacher, what types of activities could you introduce to challenge her higher level thinking skills?
- Luis excels in some but not all school subjects. Would you consider Luis an underachiever? What strategies (besides making connections with music) could the first grade teacher use to pique Luis's interest and improve his performance in math?
- What advice would you offer Johnny's sixth grade teacher for nurturing his writing ability?

Students who are gifted and talented exist at all ages and grade levels within the school system. They are distinguished by their exceptional ability, can be female or male, and come from all economic, ethnic, cultural, and language backgrounds. Students can have both disabilities and gifts and talents, making them "twice exceptional." Gifted and talented individuals are among the most neglected of all groups of students with special needs. Most "spend their school days without attention paid to their special learning needs" (U.S. Department of Education, 1993, p. 2) because these needs are not universally recognized. Potentially gifted children who live in poverty are especially underserved, as are English learners and children from African American, Latino, Native American, and some Asian groups.

Many teachers and parents do not clearly understand the needs of students who are gifted and talented. Some educators continue to believe that these students, because of their exceptional abilities, are capable of realizing their maximum potential without the benefit of specially designed educational adaptations or programs. Colangelo and Davis (2003) explained:

> One common argument against special educational programs for the gifted is the belief that these students "will make it on their own." A corollary is "Give the help to students who really need it." However, many students labeled *gifted* do *not* make it on their own. Inadequate curriculum, unsupportive educators, social and emotional difficulties, peer pressures, and inadequate parenting all can extinguish the potentially high accomplishment of gifted children and adolescents. (p. 5)

Students who are gifted and talented have special learning needs that are not fully met by the general education program. Such students should be identified in order to adapt the general education program or provide special educational services. In this way, it is possible to help them achieve at a level commensurate with their potential (Clark, 2008; Culross, 1997; Parker, 1989).

This chapter examines the characteristics of students with special gifts and talents who are included in the general education program and also describes methods for the general education teacher to use in gathering data and designing and implementing program adaptations.

▶ DEFINITIONS

A 1972 report to Congress on the education of the gifted and talented, now called the Marland Report for then U.S. Commissioner of Education Sydney Marland, brought national recognition to the plight of gifted and talented students. The report (U.S. Department of Health, Education, and Welfare, 1972) indicated that 3% to 5% of the nation's students could be considered gifted and that schools were not meeting most of their needs. The report provided a federal definition for gifted and talented that was used with modification in subsequent federal legislation (PL 95-561, The Gifted and Talented Children's Act of 1978; PL 100-297, The Jacob K. Javits Gifted and Talented Students Education Act of 1988; PL 107-110, the No Child Left Behind Act of 2001).

A 1993 report by the U.S. Department of Education, titled *National Excellence: A Case for Developing America's Talent,* reiterated concern that the nation was "squandering" its precious resource of talented students by not challenging them to excel. The report also emphasized the needs of gifted students from economically and culturally diverse backgrounds: "This problem is especially severe among economically disadvantaged and minority students, who have access to fewer advanced educational opportunities and whose talents often go unnoticed" (p. 1). This report reaffirmed and updated the Marland definition of the gifted and talented, emphasizing "talent" to connote a developing ability:

> Children and youth with outstanding talent perform or show the potential for performing at remarkably high levels of accomplishment when compared with others of their age, experience, or environment.
>
> These children and youth exhibit high performance capability in intellectual, creative, and/or artistic areas, possess an unusual leadership capacity, or excel in specific academic fields. They require services or activities not ordinarily provided by the schools.
>
> Outstanding talents are present in children and youth from all *cultural* groups, across all economic strata, and in all areas of human endeavor. (p. 26)

Experts have offered other definitions and conceptualizations of the terms **giftedness** and **talented.** For example, based on studies of eminent individuals, Renzulli (1978) derived a three-ring definition requiring above-average ability, high creativity, and strong task commitment. Recent theories of intelligence, most notably Gardner's multiple intelligences and Sternberg's triarchic conceptions, have broadened our notions beyond a single dimension and suggest that intelligence can be enhanced. Gardner has proposed nine categories of intelligence: linguistic, logical–mathematical, musical, spatial, bodily–kinesthetic, interpersonal, intrapersonal, naturalist, and existential (von Károlyi, Ramos-Ford, & Gardner, 2003). Sternberg's (2003) theory of successful intelligence includes three main types of abilities: analytic, synthetic, and practical.

Although universal agreement has not been reached concerning a definition of this group of students, some form of the federal definition is often cited, and a majority of states continue to use the term *gifted and talented* (Stephens & Karnes, 2000).

A major purpose of the Marland and *National Excellence* definitions was to expand the concept of giftedness beyond IQ. By specifying a range of domains as well as both performance and potential, an expected outcome would be greater inclusion. Yet in practice, IQ tests, teacher recommendations, grades, and standardized achievement tests are most frequently used to identify students as gifted. Such measures screen out many gifted students who have the highest needs for special services: those who are culturally and linguistically diverse, twice exceptional, economically disadvantaged, or highly creative (Richert, 2003).

As a result, students in these categories continue to be underrepresented in programs for the gifted relative to their proportions in the total school population. Table 17-1 shows national projections for general enrollments and enrollments in gifted and talented programs by ethnic, English learner, and disability groups for the year 2006 (Office for Civil Rights, 2008). These data indicate, for example, that while African American students constitute 17.13% of the general enrollment, they comprise only 9.15% of enrollment in programs for the gifted. The term *Asian or Pacific Islander* includes a large number of diverse ethnic, cultural, and language groups, some of whom also are underrepresented in programs for the gifted and talented (Kitano & DiJiosia, 2002).

TABLE 17-1 National Projections for Enrollment in Gifted/Talented Programs by Race/Ethnicity, English Learner Status, and Disability

	American Indian or Alaskan Native (%)	Asian or Pacific Islander (%)	Hispanic (%)	Black, not Hispanic (%)	White, not Hispanic (%)	English Learners (%)	Students with Disabilities (%)
Enrollment in School	1.24	4.81	20.41	17.13	56.42	9.39	12.82
In Gifted/ Talented Programs	0.97	9.40	12.79	9.15	67.69	2.00	2.10
Mathematics Advanced Placement	0.45	15.47	11.53	5.49	67.06	2.29	1.07
Science Advanced Placement	0.54	15.57	12.04	6.83	65.01	2.06	1.08

Note: From *Office for Civil Rights Elementary and Secondary School Survey* (2006), retrieved from *http://ocrdata.ed.gov/ocr2006rv30/xls/2006Projected.html*

Until we resolve the decades-long underrepresentation of some students of color in programs for the gifted, many of these students will receive services in general education settings. In fact, regular classroom teachers "are most often relied upon to meet the diverse educational needs" of the nation's gifted children and youth. Yet most states (37) do not require general education teachers to have training to meet their needs (National Association for Gifted Children, 2008).

 ## INDICATORS OF TALENT AND GIFTEDNESS

Some students who are gifted and talented have highly unusual abilities that are identified early in life by their parents. For most students, however, it is the classroom teacher who first notices their special abilities. Students who are gifted and talented can be identified at any time during their school careers, but they are most likely to come to their teachers' attention during the elementary school years.

Giftedness and talent have several indicators that teachers might look for. However, Heward (2000) cautioned that general descriptions of group characteristics are not always effective in the identification of individuals; students may be gifted or talented and display several or none of the specific characteristics included on a list. As with all special individuals, the student's unique needs must be considered.

The accompanying "Inclusion Tips for the Teacher" material summarizes some of the major indicators of giftedness and talent that can be observed in the general education classroom. Although these students do not generally display all these signs, the presence of one or two of them is cause for a teacher to consider further assessment. Heward (2000) pointed out that even though descriptions of students who are gifted usually emphasize only positive characteristics, these students can also display less attractive behaviors. Figure 17-1 presents both sides of the giftedness coin.

School districts differ in procedures and measures used to identify students who are gifted and talented. Procedures may include one or more of the following steps: referral, screening, assessment, and identification. The referral process involves nominating students for further testing or for special services. Referrals can come from teachers, parents, peers, or students themselves. Screening permits large numbers of students to be considered for further, more individual assessment. Some districts screen all students, while others screen only those referred, typically using group measures of achievement or intellectual performance and observation of special academic or creative achievements. Screening every student for potential gifts and talents—for example, through a culture-fair group measure—may be one strategy for decreasing the number of potentially gifted students who are overlooked through referral. Although teachers are the most common source of referrals, their accuracy as identifiers is questionable, especially with

Signs of Giftedness and Talent

There are numerous lists of characteristics or distinguishing features and attributes of gifted and talented children. Teachers and parents should interpret any single list, including this one, as only an example of possible traits.

Few gifted children will display all of the characteristics in a given list; however, when clusters of these characteristics are present, they do serve as fairly reliable indicators. Giftedness may exist in only one area of academic learning, such as mathematics, or may be quite general across the school curriculum. These characteristics are signals to indicate that a particular child might warrant closer observation and could require specialized educational attention, pending a more comprehensive assessment.

General Behavioral Characteristics

- Many typically learn to read earlier with a better comprehension of the nuances of the language. As many as half of the gifted and talented population have learned to read before entering school. They often read widely, quickly, and intensely, and have large vocabularies.
- They commonly learn basic skills better, more quickly, and with less practice.
- They are frequently able to pick up and interpret nonverbal cues and can draw inferences that other children have to have spelled out for them.
- They take less for granted, seeking the "hows" and "whys."
- They display a better ability to work independently at an earlier age and for longer periods of time than other children.
- They can sustain longer periods of concentration and attention.
- Their interests are often both widely eclectic and intensely focused.
- They frequently have seemingly boundless energy, which sometimes leads to a misdiagnosis of "hyperactive."
- They are usually able to respond and relate well to parents, teachers, and other adults. They may prefer the company of older children and adults to that of their peers.
- They are willing to examine the unusual and are highly inquisitive.
- Their behavior is often well organized, goal directed, and efficient with respect to tasks and problems.
- They exhibit an intrinsic motivation to learn, find out, or explore and are often very persistent. "I'd rather do it myself" is a common attitude.
- They enjoy learning new things and new ways of doing things.
- They have a longer attention and concentration span than their peers.

Learning Characteristics

- They may show keen powers of observation, exhibit a sense of the significant, and have an eye for important details.

- They may read a great deal on their own, preferring books and magazines written for youngsters older than themselves.
- They often take great pleasure in intellectual activity.
- They have well-developed powers of abstraction, conceptualization, and synthesizing abilities.
- They generally have rapid insight into cause–effect relationships.
- They often display a questioning attitude and seek information for the sake of having it as much as for its instrumental value.
- They are often skeptical, critical, and evaluative. They are quick to spot inconsistencies.
- They often have a large storehouse of information regarding a variety of topics they can recall quickly.
- They show a ready grasp of underlying principles and can often make valid generalizations about events, people, and objects.
- They readily perceive similarities, differences, and anomalies.
- They often attack complicated material by separating it into its components and analyzing it systematically.

Creative Characteristics

- They are fluent thinkers, able to produce a large quantity of possibilities, consequences, or related ideas.
- They are flexible thinkers able to use many different alternatives and approaches to problem solving.
- They are original thinkers, seeking new, unusual, or unconventional associations and combinations among items of information. They also have an ability to see relationships among seemingly unrelated objects, ideas, or facts.
- They are elaborative thinkers, producing new steps, ideas, responses, or other embellishments to a basic idea, situation, or problem.
- They show a willingness to entertain complexity and seem to thrive in problem situations.
- They are good guessers and can construct hypotheses or "what if" questions readily.
- They often are aware of their own impulsiveness and the irrationality within themselves and show emotional sensitivity.
- They have a high level of curiosity about objects, ideas, situations, or events.
- They often display intellectual playfulness, fantasize, and imagine readily.
- They can be less intellectually inhibited than their peers in expressing opinions and ideas and often exhibit spirited disagreement.
- They have a sensitivity to beauty and are attracted to aesthetic dimensions.

Note: From "Characteristics of Intellectually Gifted Children" (Digest 344) by J. R. Whitmore, 1985, *Digests on the Gifted* (Reston, VA: The Council for Exceptional Children), pp. 1–2. Material is in the public domain.

younger children (Smutny, 2000) and students from diverse ethnic, cultural, or linguistic groups (Ford, Harris, Tyson, & Trotman, 2002). Training increases teachers' reliability as nominators (Piirto, 2007), though some still tend to look for the stereotypical student who is gifted—one who is highly motivated and adjusted to school—and often overlook the unique student with a set of unusual skills and abilities. The "Inclusion Tips for the Teacher" box provides information on some popular myths about gifted students and some truths found by professionals working with gifted students.

FIGURE 17-1 Two Sides of Gifted Behavior

List A: Positive Aspects
1. Expresses ideas and feelings well
2. Can move at a rapid pace
3. Works conscientiously
4. Wants to learn, explore, and seek more information
5. Develops broad knowledge and an extensive store of vicarious experiences
6. Is sensitive to the feelings and rights of others
7. Makes steady progress
8. Makes original and stimulating contributions to discussions
9. Sees relationships easily
10. Learns material quickly
11. Is able to use reading skills to obtain new information
12. Contributes to enjoyment of life for self and others
13. Completes assigned tasks
14. Requires little drill for learning

List B: Not-So-Positive Aspects
1. May be glib, making fluent statements based on little or no knowledge or understanding
2. May dominate discussions
3. May be impatient to proceed to the next level or task
4. May be considered nosey
5. May choose reading at the expense of active participation in social, creative, or physical activities
6. May struggle against rules, regulations, and standardized procedures
7. May lead discussions "off the track"
8. May be frustrated by the apparent absence of logic in activities and daily events
9. May become bored by repetitions
10. May use humor to manipulate
11. May resist a schedule based on time rather than task
12. May lose interest quickly

Note: Reprinted with the permission of Prentice-Hall, Inc., from *Exceptional Children,* 6th ed., by William L. Heward. Copyright © 2000 by Merrill/Prentice-Hall, Inc.

 ## Inclusion Tips for the Teacher

Common Myths and Truths About Gifted Students

Myths About Gifted Students

- Gifted students do not need help. If they are really gifted, they can manage on their own.
- Gifted students have fewer problems than others because their intelligence and abilities somehow exempt them from the hassles of daily life.
- The future of a gifted student is assured: A world of opportunities lies before the student.
- Gifted students are self-directed; they know where they are heading.
- The social and emotional development of the gifted student is at the same level as his or her intellectual development.
- Gifted students are nerds and social isolates.
- The primary value of the gifted student lies in his or her brain power.
- The gifted student's family always prizes his or her abilities.
- Gifted students need to serve as examples to others and they should always assume extra responsibility.
- Gifted students make everyone else smarter.
- Gifted students can accomplish anything they put their minds to. All they have to do is apply themselves.
- Gifted students are naturally creative and do not need encouragement.
- Gifted children are easy to raise and a welcome addition to any classroom.

Truths About Gifted Students

- Gifted students are often perfectionistic and idealistic. They may equate achievement and grades with self-esteem and self-worth, which sometimes leads to fear of failure and interferes with achievement.
- Gifted students may experience heightened sensitivity to their own expectations and those of others, resulting in guilt over achievements or grades perceived to be low.
- Gifted students are asynchronous. Their chronological age, social, physical, emotional, and intellectual development may all be at different levels. For example, a 5-year-old might be able to read and comprehend a third grade book but might not be able to write legibly.
- Some gifted children are "mappers" (sequential learners), while others are "leapers" (spatial learners). Leapers may not know how they got a "right answer." Mappers may get lost in the steps leading to the right answer.
- Gifted students may be so far ahead of their chronological age mates that they know more than half the curriculum before the school year begins! Their boredom can result in low achievement and grades.
- Gifted children are problem solvers. They benefit from working on open-ended, interdisciplinary problems; for example, how to solve a shortage of community resources. Gifted students often refuse to work for grades alone.
- Gifted students often think abstractly and with such complexity that they may need help with concrete study and test-taking skills. They may not be able to select one answer in a multiple choice question because they see how all the answers might be correct.
- Gifted students who do well in school may define success as getting an "A" and failure as any grade less than an "A." By early adolescence, they may be unwilling to try anything for which they are not certain of guaranteed success.

Note: ERIC Clearinghouse on Disabilities and Gifted Education (2000). *Common Myths About Gifted Students* and "College Planning for Gifted Students" by Sandra Berger, 1998, published by the Council for Exceptional Children.

Behavior checklists or rating scales can prove helpful to the teacher. For example, the *Scales for Rating the Behavior Characteristics of Superior Students* (Renzulli, Smith, White, Callahan, & Hartman, 2001) is used by a teacher to rate a student's performance in the areas of learning, motivation, and creativity. This type of scale provides information on a student's strengths and is useful for both identification and educational planning.

Special attention should be paid to the inclusion of students from diverse ethnic, cultural, or linguistic groups (Castellano, 2003) and those with disabilities (Besnoy, 2005) in programs for students who are gifted and talented. See the "Inclusion Tips for the Teacher" box for characteristics that may assist in identifying gifted students from low-income backgrounds.

Although there has been an increasing awareness of the needs of gifted students who also have other exceptionalities such as ADHD (e.g., Flint, 2001; Zentall, Hall, & Grskovic, 2001), learning disabilities (e.g., Fetzer, 2000; Shaywitz et al., 2001), behavioral disorders (e.g., Morrison & Omdal, 2000), or physical or sensory impairments (e.g., Cline & Schwartz, 1999), many students with these disabilities have been precluded from being identified as gifted because of the difficulties involved in correctly identifying their abilities and educational needs. Total reliance on standardized tests should be avoided; norm-referenced measures can lead to the exclusion of many such students who are excellent candidates for programs for students who are gifted and talented. Educators should use several different measures, rather than only one or two (Feldhusen, 2001; Masse, 2001) and stress procedures

---

Inclusion Tips for the Teacher

Characteristics of the Gifted Student from a Low-Income Background

- Has high mathematical abilities
- Is curious; has varied interests
- Is independent
- Has good imagination
- Is fluent in nonverbal communication
- Improvises when solving problems
- Learns quickly through experience
- Retains and uses information well

- Shows a desire to learn in daily work
- Is original and creative
- Uses language rich in imagery
- Responds well to visual media and concrete activities
- Shows leadership among peers; is responsible
- Shows relationships among unrelated ideas
- Is entrepreneurial
- Has a keen sense of humor

Note: From Johnsen, S. K. (2004a, p 18). Definitions, models, and characteristics of gifted students. In S. K. Johnsen (Ed.), *Identifying gifted students: A practical guide* (pp. 1–21). Waco, TX: Prufrock Press. Reprinted with permission.

---

i For Your Information

Students Who Are Gifted and Talented

- Although the earliest federal program on gifted education was created in 1931, it was the post–World War II threat of communism that stimulated major federal interest in the gifted. The successful launching of the Sputnik satellite in 1957 spurred development of programs, especially in science and mathematics (Wickstrom, 2004).

- As of 2006, only 27 states of 43 reporting had a state mandate for gifted education (Council of State Directors of Programs for the Gifted and the National Association for Gifted Children, 2007).

- A nationwide poll (Rose, Gallup, & Elam, 1997) indicates that "a small majority (52%) of the public supports the placement of gifted and talented students in separate classes. This response takes added significance from the fact that 66% of poll respondents also said they believe that grouping students according to ability will improve student achievement a great deal or quite a lot" (p. 53).

- Many students who are gifted may have high levels of activity in the classroom because of boredom or intense interest in an activity and may be considered to be hyperactive (e.g., have ADHD) and in need of special education services. This possibility should be carefully evaluated before decisions are made regarding changes in their programs (Webb & Latimer, 1993).

- Highly effective teachers of the gifted and talented prefer abstract themes and concepts, are open and flexible, and value logical analysis and objectivity. They display enthusiasm, self-confidence, high energy, and an achievement orientation. Additionally, at the secondary level, they tend to possess a strong background in an academic discipline and passion for their subject matter (Mills, 2003).

- Girls are well represented in programs for the gifted. They report high self-efficacy, high aspirations, and accurate self-perceptions. Their attitudes toward and interest in science and mathematics may affect the courses they select (Kitano, 2008).

- Gifted males tend to experience heightened emotional sensitivity and empathy for others. If peers, teachers, and family members disparage their sensitivity, gifted males may stifle their feelings and withdraw emotionally. Gifted males benefit from teachers who validate and help them express their feelings (Hébert, 2002).

- Professionals and parents interested in gifted education are concerned that the school reform movement designed to increase the inclusion of students with disabilities in general education programs will also lead to a reduction in the opportunities to provide specialized programs for students who are gifted and talented (Culross, 1997).

that reduce the potential bias that may interfere with identifying students from these populations (Clark, 2008; Cline & Schwartz, 1999; Joseph & Ford, 2006; Piirto, 2007). To learn more about students with special gifts and talents, consult the "For Your Information" material.

IDENTIFICATION PROCEDURES

When referral and/or screening identifies a student as a potential candidate for special education services for students who are gifted and talented, the next step is a comprehensive assessment. The purpose is to gather information about the learning needs and abilities of the student in order to assist in planning appropriate educational modifications. Both formal and informal measures are used. Examples of possible informal procedures are direct observation, inventories, checklists, and analysis of various types of work samples. There is agreement in the field that identification should be based on multiple criteria. A recent survey of states indicated that 21 of the 43 responding states require specific identification criteria or methods, and 18 of these use a multiple criteria model to identify gifted students (Council of State Directors of Programs for the Gifted and the National Association for Gifted Children, 2007). In some states, there are specific guidelines for determining eligibility for special education programs for gifted and talented pupils; in others, this decision is left to the discretion of the local school district. In any case, identification measures and procedures must be consistent with the district or state definition of giftedness (Borland, 2008).

In the past, many programs for students who are gifted relied almost exclusively on norm-referenced tests of intelligence for assessment. Measures such as the *Wechsler Intelligence Scale for Children–Fourth Edition (WISC–IV)* (Wechsler, 2003) and the *Stanford–Binet Intelligence Scales, Fifth Edition* (Roid, 2003) remain in use today, particularly for identification of students who are academically talented. Practices vary widely regarding minimum scores for eligibility for services for students who are gifted; a *WISC–IV* score of IQ 115 may qualify a student in one

state or school district, whereas a score of 130 or 135 may be necessary in another.

Although individual IQ tests such as the *WISC* and the *Stanford–Binet* are considered the single most reliable indicator of intellectual giftedness, they have many drawbacks. They are expensive to use and can be administered only by special personnel. They are biased in favor of middle- and upper-class students and discriminate against those students who have disabilities or come from diverse ethnic, cultural, or linguistic groups. Nonverbal ability measures, such as the *Naglieri Nonverbal Ability Test,* the *Universal Nonverbal Intelligence Test,* and *Raven Progressive Matrices* demonstrate reduced bias and increased inclusion of culturally and linguistically diverse students and students from low-income backgrounds. The *DISCOVER* system (Maker, 2001), based on problem solving and multiple intelligences, demonstrates effectiveness in identifying giftedness among culturally and linguistically diverse elementary through high school students.

Intelligence tests, including those that are less culturally biased, fail to assess such important abilities as creativity, leadership, and specific talents. Measures such as the *Torrance Tests of Creative Thinking* (Torrance, 1966) can be used to assess creativity. Such tests help identify divergent thinkers who may be

overlooked on intelligence tests. In describing these instruments, Gay (1981) noted that

> one such test asks the individual to list as many uses as he or she can think of for an ordinary brick. Think about it and list a few. If you listed uses such as build a school, build a house, build a library, etc., then you are not very creative; all of those uses are really the same, namely, you can use a brick to build something. Now, if you are creative, you listed different uses such as break a window, drown a rat, and hit a robber on the head. (p. 128)

Creativity test results should be supplemented with information from other sources, such as analysis of students' creative products and performances and direct observation of student behavior.

Observation techniques help to objectively assess and describe a student's academic and social performance in the classroom. For example, a teacher can observe the amount and reading levels of material the student reads each week, the number of social interactions per class period, or the time taken to complete an assignment. Information such as this not only helps to determine the student's current performance levels but also assists in the development of program modifications.

Analysis of work samples is conducted somewhat differently with students who are gifted and talented. Instead of searching for error patterns, the purpose is to discover a student's strengths and potential for further achievement. In the area of academics, a teacher looks for advanced school skills or competence in a subject matter not normally taught in the general education curriculum. Examples include the precocious kindergartner who reads and understands fourth grade material and the second grader who has special knowledge in botany and zoology. For information about specific talents, the teacher should consider a wide variety of student products, such as writings, artwork, musical compositions, and inventions; other possibilities are dramatic or musical performances. A teacher can analyze these work samples or ask for assistance from others. Subject matter experts and practicing artists, musicians, or writers may be better able to judge whether students' work is exceptional and whether students have the potential to benefit from advanced study in the area.

In addition to the strengths of students who are gifted and talented, areas of relative weakness should also be considered. This is particularly important for students with major discrepancies between ability and achievement and those who excel in one or two areas but not in others. The assessment procedures suggested for students with learning disabilities and behavioral disorders are appropriate for gathering information about academic achievement and school conduct. Typically, Individualized Education Programs (IEPs) are not required for students who are gifted and talented. However, it is good practice to develop a written educational plan. Figure 17-2 presents portions of the IE plan for Luis, the first grader introduced at the beginning of this chapter.

Johnsen (2004b) suggested that identification procedures for students with gifts and talents should ensure that instruments

FIGURE 17-2 Individualized Education Goals and Services for Luis

Annual Goals

1. By the end of the school year, Luis will read fifth grade material on a topic of his choice, demonstrating depth of comprehension through oral, written, or visual extensions or syntheses to be shared with his classmates (e.g., retelling from a different perspective, a song, storyboard, brochure, or diorama).
   Person responsible: Resource teacher

2. By the end of the school year, Luis will write short reports on topics of his choice. The written products will demonstrate correct spelling and sentence structure and higher level thinking, for example, detailed descriptions, comparisons, diverse points of view, original ideas.
   Persons responsible: First grade teacher, resource teacher

3. By the end of the school year, Luis will successfully complete all requirements for first-grade math.
   Person responsible: First grade teacher

4. By the end of the school year, Luis will successfully play a series of songs on both the guitar and the piano.
   Person responsible: Parent

Amount of Participation in General Education

Luis will attend the regular first grade class for all subjects except reading.

Special Education and Related Services

1. Luis will receive special education services from the resource teacher for students who are gifted (annual goals 1 and 2) for 1 hour daily.

2. The resource teacher will provide consultation to Luis's first grade teacher as needed.

match student characteristics and program services. To ensure an effective identification process, she recommended the following questions be used as guidelines.

1. Is the procedure based on best research and recommendations?
2. Does it match the district's definition and program options?
3. Do all students have an equal opportunity to be nominated?
4. Are special populations considered in the nomination process?
5. Are all students able to demonstrate their strengths?
6. Are assessments fair to student cultures?
7. Are all students able to demonstrate their abilities in classroom activities?
8. Are multiple sources of information used?
9. Are all data considered during the selection phase?
10. Are the students' data evaluated objectively?

11. Are all students who need a differentiated education being identified?
12. Do identified students perform well in the program that matches their gifts and talents? (pp. 114–115)

▶ CLASSROOM ADAPTATIONS

Given their higher intelligence and more rapid learning rate, gifted students require services different from those offered by the regular program. **Differentiation** of the curriculum and instruction can occur in the general classroom or in special settings. Undifferentiated, the regular school curriculum does not provide the challenge needed by gifted students. Many gifted children have already mastered up to one-half of the standard elementary curriculum, and teachers typically do not make accommodations for their learning needs (U.S. Department of Education, 1993). With appropriate support, some highly gifted students can acquire a year's worth of advanced content in just three weeks (Colangelo, Assouline, & Gross, 2004)!

Classrooms adaptations must be made in curriculum and instruction for students who are gifted and talented. The following sections of this chapter address ways in which the general education teacher can select appropriate educational options, promote the development of creativity and problem solving, and assist underachieving students in better realizing their capabilities.

Individualized programs can be delivered in several ways to students who are gifted and talented. In many of these options, the student remains in the general education classroom with age peers. Special instruction can be provided within this class by the general education teacher, on a part-time basis by a special teacher in a special class or resource room, or in a setting outside the school when school is not in session.

As for any learner with exceptional needs, identifying the appropriate educational option begins with diagnostic testing. Diagnostic Testing and Prescriptive Instruction (DT/PI) is a useful model for this purpose and involves four steps:

1. Assess student knowledge. Teachers use formal or informal measures (e.g., end-of-unit assessments; concept maps) to determine students' knowledge and skills with respect to the target content. Students who demonstrate mastery of 85 percent or more should be excused from that content and provided options for acceleration or enrichment.
2. Write goals for instruction based on the assessment outcomes. Based on assessment outcomes, the teacher identifies new goals for instruction, such as moving to the next standards for the content area or pursuing the student's interests.
3. Deliver instruction based on the modified goals.
4. Re-assess student knowledge. (VanTassel-Baska & Stambaugh, 2006)

Following DT/PI, general education teachers can accommodate the needs of gifted learners in their classrooms through implementation of differentiated program, instructional, and curriculum models.

Differentiated Program Models

Three program adaptations are recommended for gifted and talented learners either alone or in combination: acceleration, enrichment, and grouping. While we can distinguish these three options conceptually, they overlap in practice.

Acceleration refers to changing the pace of instruction, moving faster through the regular education curriculum. Students may be admitted to school at a younger than usual age or be allowed to skip one or more grades. Accelerating high school students through the use of advanced placement into selected college coursework provides these students with an opportunity for accelerated learning regarding advanced concepts (VanTassel-Baska, 2001). Acceleration within the general education classroom can take several forms (Southern & Jones, 2004):

- *Continuous Progress:* As a student masters material, he or she progresses to the next level.
- *Self-Paced Instruction:* Similar to continuous progress, the student proceeds through instructional activities but at a self-selected pace.
- *Content or Partial Acceleration:* Students attend a higher grade for a specific subject area, for example, a third grade student attends a fifth grade classroom just for science.
- *Telescoping Curriculum:* The course of study for one grade might be compressed into one semester, or two years into one.
- *Curriculum compacting:* Instruction reduces introductory activities, drill, and practice and/or eliminates content already mastered. The time gained permits introduction of more advanced content or enrichment activities. This option will be discussed in more detail later in this chapter.

Enrichment typically means providing richer and more varied educational experiences through increased depth and breadth in content, instructional strategies requiring higher level thinking skills, and instructional resources that go beyond the typical curriculum (Davis & Rimm, 2004). Enrichment activities may address such goals as increasing creativity or critical thinking, encouraging students to pursue their own interests in depth, engaging students in research, and involving them in independent or small-group projects. To learn more about the available educational options for providing enrichment and acceleration, consult the list of programs described in Figure 17-3.

Grouping brings gifted students together for part or all of the day. Grouping is a structural accommodation that typically involves acceleration or enrichment. By grouping students who are gifted in mathematics, for example, teachers can offer the math curriculum at a more rapid pace. Within the general education classroom, teachers "cluster" gifted (and high-achieving) students together to engage them in more challenging activities.

A large body of research supports acceleration as (a) the most effective intervention for gifted students, (b) having long-term academic and social benefits, and (c) costing virtually nothing. Yet many educators discount acceleration despite profuse effectiveness research—so much so that a national report on acceleration for the gifted was titled "A Nation Deceived" to emphasize the fact that we deceive ourselves, our brightest students,

FIGURE 17-3 Options for Providing Enrichment and Acceleration

Acceleration
- Subject matter acceleration—remaining at grade level while advancing in specific subject areas (e.g., advanced placement classes).
- Telescoping—covering more than a full year's work in a given year (e.g., multiage grouping).
- Grade skipping—bypassing at least one year of instruction (e.g., early graduation).
- Early entrance—entering school at least one year younger than the norm (e.g., early admission to kindergarten or college).

Enrichment in the Regular Classroom
- Individualized programming
- Independent study
- Ability grouping
- Cluster grouping—all students who are gifted at a grade level are placed with one teacher to facilitate differentiated instruction.
- Flexible scheduling—students attend class less often than peers, perhaps for only 4 days each week.
- Use of faster paced, higher level materials
- Field trips
- Use of community resource persons at school

Special Classes
- Honors classes and seminars
- Advanced Placement
- Extra coursework
- Special course offerings (e.g., Junior Great Books)
- Use of a resource room or itinerant teacher on a weekly basis
- Segregated "pull-out" program for part of the day or week
- Full-time placement in a special class
- Special study centers
- Magnet schools—one may specialize in science, another in language arts. Students choose to enroll in a school that will serve them best.
- School within a school—a portion of the school is reserved for specialized classes for students who are gifted.
- Specialized school for students who are gifted (e.g., Bronx High School of Science)
- International Baccalaureate

Flexible Scheduling (i.e., Offerings Outside the School Day)
- Extracurricular clubs
- Early-bird classes—special classes held before school
- Extended day
- Extended school year
- Saturday or after-school workshops, classes, excursions
- Summer courses
- Evening courses
- Online courses

Off-Campus Options
- Mentorships
- Individual study with a community member
- Internships—working in the field with a specialist
- Outreach activities—programs developed for students who are gifted at local museums, colleges, businesses, etc.
- Residential summer institutes
- Community-based career education
- Student exchange programs
- Credit for educational experiences outside school (e.g., travel)

From: "Gifted and Talented" by L. K. Silverman in *Exceptional Children and Youth* (3rd ed., pp. 281–283) by E. L. Meyer and T. M. Skritic (Eds.), Denver: Love. Copyright 1988 by Love. Adapted by permission.

and the nation when we deny that these students would benefit from acceleration (Colangelo et al., 2004). Moreover, findings across multiple studies indicate that grouping of gifted students for advanced or accelerated instruction is more effective than grouping without acceleration. Students who are grouped for acceleration outperform their nonaccelerated peers by about one year. Students grouped together for enrichment outperform regular mixed-ability groups by the equivalent of 4 months (Kulik, 2003). Additional research (Delcourt, Cornell, & Goldberg, 2007) indicates that for gifted students from mainstream and diverse backgrounds, grouping (special schools, separate classes, pullout) results in higher levels of academic achievement across subject areas compared to general education classrooms that do not differentiate the curriculum. These studies demonstrate the critical importance of general education teachers' appropriate implementation of acceleration and differentiated instructional practices for gifted students.

Differentiating Instructional Models

Among the most commonly recommended models for accommodating gifted and talented learners in the general education classroom are curriculum compacting, tiered assignments, and problem-based learning.

Curriculum compacting is one method of adapting general education programs for students who are gifted and talented. The goal of **curriculum compacting** is to expand the amount of time academically capable students have to work on more challenging material by "either eliminating work that has been mastered previously or streamlining work that may be mastered at a pace commensurate with the student's ability" (Feldhusen, Van Winkle, & Ehle, 1996, p. 50). This permits the student to replace unnecessary repetition of the basics with enriched and accelerated learning activities (Kennedy, 1995). The curriculum compacting technique also ensures that the gifted students cover the essential elements of the general education curriculum and it "is a powerful technique for adapting and developing curriculum for talented students in the regular classroom" (Heward, 2000, p. 560).

Winebrenner (2001) has identified five steps to successful compacting.

1. Identify the learning objectives or standards all students must learn.
2. Offer a pretest opportunity to volunteers who think they may have already mastered the content, OR plan an alternate path through the content for those students who can learn the required material in less time than their age peers.
3. Plan and offer curriculum extensions for students who are successful with the compacting opportunities.
4. Eliminate all drill, practice, review, or preparation for state or standardized tests for students who have already mastered such things.
5. Keep accurate records of students' compacting activities. (p. 32)

Research on gifted learners in general elementary classrooms indicates that curriculum compacting enables teachers to eliminate between 40% and 50% of the curriculum across content areas without negatively affecting students' achievement test scores. Students maintain their achievement scores even when the replacement activities are not in the same content area (Reis, Westberg, Kulikowich, & Purcell, 1998). These findings suggest that curriculum compacting permits gifted students to pursue their special interests beyond the regular curriculum without decreasing their subject matter knowledge.

Tiering assignments refers to the practice of differentiating tasks within a classroom based on student readiness levels. Typically, all students receive assignments that address the same content objective or topic (e.g., understanding a sonnet) with specific activities varying in degree of difficulty. This method is especially useful in the general education classroom, where current performance levels vary from below grade level to well above grade level, as is the case for many gifted students. "This instructional strategy allows a teacher to accomplish two critical things at once. First, tiering allows the teacher to keep all students focused on the same essential learning goals. Second, tiering enables the teacher to develop student tasks and products that are at appropriate levels of complexity for the varied learners in the classroom" (Tomlinson, 2001, p. 37). Consider an example provided by Heacox (2002) in which the goal for all students in the classroom is to acquire knowledge about rain forests through the development of a brochure. Depending on readiness level, students create a brochure on rain forests to (a) inform audiences about an environmental issue, (b) describe different points of view on an environmental issue, or (c) present a convincing argument after determining their own position on an issue related to rain forests. The three tasks require different levels of complexity from factual to analytic to persuasive. Depending on unit goals and learner needs, the teacher can tier by challenge level, complexity, resources, outcome, process, or product (Heacox). The "Inclusion Tips for the Teacher" presents a sample tiered activity in a 12th grade English class.

Problem-based learning is a strategy that simulates real-world problem finding and problem solving by engaging students as stakeholders in situations with undefined problems and incomplete information. Students define issues, create hypotheses, conduct investigations, evaluate earlier hypotheses, develop and justify solutions, and consider ethical implications. As in the real world, they move forward, hit dead ends, revisit data, revise their thinking, choose new paths, and move on (Stepien & Pyke, 1997). The teacher develops the engagement scenario to ensure students cover preidentified knowledge and concepts, identifies resources, monitors student progress, provides supporting lessons as needed, and debriefs. General education teachers can implement problem-based learning for the whole classroom, with modifications for the gifted that include advanced content, complexity, interdisciplinary connections, higher order thinking skills, and ethical dilemmas (Gallagher, 2001). This strategy can also be used with a gifted student cluster. Problem-based learning is well matched to gifted learners' greater adeptness at problem finding and conceptual reasoning (Gallagher, 2001). The "Inclusion Tips for the Teacher" presents a sample lesson that includes a problem-based learning activity used to extend the curriculum for gifted students whose social studies curriculum has been compacted.

Inclusion Tips for the Teacher

A Sample Tiered Lesson in 12th Grade English

Brett Weiss, a talented 12th grade English teacher, used tiering to accommodate her students' range of readiness levels for literary analysis. At one extreme, some students demonstrated superficial reading and difficulty grasping the logic of analytical argument. At the other extreme, students had mastered the skills of close textual analysis and analytic writing. She identified three groups based on readiness levels.

Ms. Weiss maintained high standards for all students by holding to common expected outcomes. All students would:

- analyze how the poets' styles affect thematic meaning and
- develop generalizations regarding the human struggle against mortality and the ability of the written word to bestow immortality.

Tiering occurred through the level and complexity of the poems provided to the three groups for comparative analysis as well as the amount of scaffolding. Across groups, students responded to the same writing prompts:

- Identify and compare the devices of style and how they contribute to the poets' thematic arguments.

- Evaluate the strengths and weaknesses of the thematic arguments.
- Discuss how the thematic arguments compare with your own ideas about the ability of verse to ensure immortality.

Group 1 compared Shakespeare's Sonnets 55 and 65. Both follow the form of Elizabethan sonnets and offer relatively simple relationships between stylistic devices and meaning. Students in this group received a list of study questions to support their identification of images, metaphors, personification, and their relationship to thematic meaning.

Group 2 received Shakespeare's Sonnet 65 and Percy Bysshe Shelley's "Ozymandias." Here, the poets' tone and structure differ, and Shelly's poem presents a more complex form and argument than Shakespeare's.

Group 3 analyzed Shakespeare's Sonnet 55 and Archibald MacLeish's "Not Marble Nor the Gilded Monuments." The latter is more complicated thematically and stylistically, communicating a combative and cynical tone.

Inclusion Tips for the Teacher

A Sample Lesson Integrating Curriculum Compacting, Problem-Based Learning, and Multicultural Curriculum

This sample lesson (adapted from Kitano & Pedersen, 2002) illustrates how curriculum compacting, problem-based learning, and a multicultural curriculum can be integrated for gifted learners.

Fifth grade teacher Candace Perkins used curriculum compacting and problem-based learning to enrich the social studies curriculum of gifted students in her general education classroom. She created the problem-based learning scenario to encourage students to investigate diverse perspectives. She began by giving all students as a pretest the end-of-unit test on the American Revolution. Students who achieved 98% on the pretest had already mastered the core content. These students were given the opportunity to engage in a problem-based learning activity (Stepien & Pyke, 1997) on the same subject. Ms. Perkins presented the following engagement scenario:

> The year is 1775. Sentiment among the colonists is hostile toward the King of England. Many patriots are in favor of becoming independent of British rule. As trusted advisors, you are asked to gather information to help assess whether independence would be a realistic goal. Your reports will be presented at the Second Continental Congress.

Participating students assumed the roles of experts (e.g., domestic advisor, international advisor, sociologist) preparing reports to be presented at the Continental Congress (to be held in class). They conducted their research in small groups using multiple sources (encyclopedias, textbooks, videos, Internet) while Ms. Perkins led the rest of the class through the core unit on the American Revolution.

Some of the students working on the scenario required no support from the teacher. A few experienced difficulty organizing their research. Ms. Perkins provided these students with a matrix graphic that helped the students to summarize material from several sources addressing the same issue and to synthesize their findings.

A gifted African American girl shared her enthusiasm: "I'm working on slavery and blacks during the American Revolution. I think this is the best thing I've done so far in school for social studies. I've put a lot of effort into it and take my time at home instead of playing. Like I ask my Grandma questions about what she knows. I love to study. I love to study what happens to slaves and blacks and what our history was. My questions are did the slaves fight in the Revolutionary War? What side were they on? What happened to them after the war?"

Another student investigated women's roles in the Revolutionary War. The students' collective presentations to the Second Continental Congress (i.e., the class) enriched all students' knowledge of the historical events of the period and enabled them to grasp a broader truth.

Note: Adapted from "Multicultural Content Integration in Gifted Education: Lesson from the Field," by M. K. Kitano and K. S. Pedersen (2002), *Journal for the Education of the Gifted,* 25(3), 269–289. Reprinted with permission.

Differentiated Curriculum Models

General education teachers can select from an array of curriculum models developed for gifted students (Davis & Rimm, 2004; VanTassel-Baska, 2001). Earlier emphasis on differentiation through higher order thinking skills in isolation has shifted to emphasis on content and depth of disciplinary knowledge while integrating thinking skills. One goal of gifted education is to enable gifted students to become "experts" as opposed to "novices" in the disciplines. Experts display a depth of content knowledge, skill in applying the methods of the discipline, ability to perceive meaningful patterns, rapid speed and accuracy in problem solving within the discipline, and automaticity of mental processing (Gallagher, 2003).

VanTassel-Baska's (2003) Integrated Curriculum Model (ICM) combines advanced content, high-level thinking processes, and core themes and ideas in teaching a discipline (e.g., language arts, science, social studies). Research supports the effectiveness of ICM units with gifted students in a variety of educational settings. For example, gifted students from both economically disadvantaged and advantaged backgrounds showed significant gains in literary analysis and persuasive writing skills using the ICM language arts units. Problem-based science units enhanced students' integration of higher order thinking skills in science, and ICM social studies units supported concept development, critical thinking, and content mastery (VanTassel-Baska & Brown, 2007).

Sternberg's (2003) theory of successful intelligence serves as the basis for curriculum development that involves teaching for analytical, creative, and practical thinking as well as for traditional memory learning. For example (Sternberg, 1997), in art, students might compare and contrast how Rembrandt and Dali used light in their paintings (analytical), draw a beam of light (creative), and determine how the lighting in a given painting could be re-created in the classroom (practical). Research suggests that students taught for successful intelligence outperform students taught in traditional ways (Sternberg & Grigorenko, 2000, 2002).

The Parallel Curriculum Model (Tomlinson et al., 2002) constitutes an emerging practice. It synthesizes several approaches to curriculum for the gifted by proposing that teachers help gifted learners explore a discipline in four ways. The first is through the core curriculum—the framework of knowledge and skills defining a discipline. The Curriculum of Connections expands the core by enabling students to make connections within or across disciplines, times, cultures, and places. The Curriculum of Practice guides students in functioning like an expert in the discipline would function by applying concepts, skills, and methods of the discipline. The Curriculum of Identity helps students understand their own skills, interests, and values with respect to the discipline.

Integration of multicultural content and high-level thinking has been recommended as a strategy for engaging diverse and mainstream gifted learners. Ford and Harris's (1999) framework for multicultural gifted curriculum integrates increasingly transformative multicultural goals with higher level cognitive strategies. They viewed multicultural gifted curriculum as a

promising strategy for engaging gifted students of color and providing needed opportunities to identify and connect with the curriculum. Kitano and Pedersen (2002) argued that all gifted students, irrespective of background, benefit from a challenging multicultural curriculum that integrates multicultural content, strategies appropriate for gifted students (e.g., problem-based learning), and culturally consonant instruction (accommodations for differences in approaches to communication and learning). The sample lesson presented earlier in the "Inclusion Tips for the Teacher" section provides an example of this integration.

An easy way to summarize accommodations for gifted students is to think of four types of differentiation: content, process, product, and environment (Maker & Nielson, 1996; Winebrenner, 2001). Gifted students require more advanced and complex content and materials that offer greater depth. Process differentiation can occur through instruction that is more open ended and appropriately paced and that encourages higher-level thinking, creativity, and pursuit of interests. Products enable students to demonstrate their understanding and can range from written reports to exhibitions, performances, or poems developed for real audiences. Environmental differentiation can include changes in the physical setting (library, lab), atmosphere (learner centered), or schedule. Time limits can be flexible to permit pursuit of in-depth research.

▶ PROMOTING CREATIVITY AND PROBLEM SOLVING

When students who are gifted and talented are included in the general education classroom, their teacher is responsible for making program adaptations that facilitate maximum growth and development. Reynolds and Birch (1982) presented six principles to help teachers provide appropriate educational experiences for this group of students.

1. Teach pupils to be efficient and effective at independent study, instilling and polishing the skills called for in self-directed learning and in analyzing and solving problems on one's own.

2. Help pupils to invoke and apply complex cognitive processes such as creative thinking, critiques, and pro and con analyses.
3. Encourage pupils to press discussions of questions or issues all the way to the culminating activity of decision making and to clear communication to others of plans, status reports, or solutions based on the decisions.
4. Establish the human interaction skills necessary to work smoothly with groups of all ages and of all levels of cognitive development.
5. Aid pupils in acquiring respect for all other humans whatever their gifts or talents and in understanding themselves in relation to all others.
6. Build pupils' positive expectations about careers and about lives as adults that optimize their talents and gifts. (p. 185)

Creativity and problem solving are two important areas in which students who are gifted and talented may require special attention and instruction. No single accepted definition of **creativity** exists (Coleman & Cross, 2005). Cropley and Urban (2000) suggested that novelty serves as the common element and offered the following definition: "the production of relevant and effective novel ideas" (p. 486) promoting the common good. They argued that a combination of intelligence and creativity defines giftedness because research suggests that productively gifted adults evidence both. Additionally, there is increasing evidence that creativity may be domain specific (Coleman & Cross, 2005), such that creativity in music, for example, is different from creativity in physics.

According to Davis (2003), creative adults show both creative abilities (e.g., fluency, flexibility, originality, elaboration, sensitivity to missing information, critical and analogical thinking) and creative personality traits. Personality traits related to creativity in adults include:

- original, imaginative, and unconventional;
- aware of own creative ability;
- independent, self-confident, unconcerned about impressing others;
- risk taking; not afraid to try something new;
- motivated, adventurous, spontaneous;
- curious, inquisitive, questioning;
- playful, sense of humor;
- likes complexity, novelty, ambiguity, incongruity;
- artistic;
- open-minded, receptive to new ideas, experiences, and viewpoints;
- reflective and introspective, needing time alone; and
- intuitive, perceptive.

Teachers can enhance creativity in children. Goals for creativity training should focus on fostering creative consciousness and attitudes, improving understanding of creativity, exercising creative abilities, teaching creative thinking techniques, and involving students in creative activities (Davis, 2003). Teachers need to create a psychologically safe classroom environment; help students become aware of their creativity; encourage fantasy and imagination; give positive, constructive evaluations; help students resist peer pressure to conform; encourage questions, humor, risk taking, and original responses; and beware that difficult behavior can be a manifestation of creativity (p. 320).

One component of creativity is divergent thinking. According to Silverman (1988), divergent thinking can result in several solutions to one problem. Four factors are important to divergent thought processes:

- *Fluency*—the ability to generate many responses.
- *Flexibility*—the ability to change the form, modify information, or shift perspectives.
- *Originality*—the ability to generate novel responses.
- *Elaboration*—the ability to embellish an idea with details. (Silverman, 1988, p. 276)

For ideas about ways to encourage creative thinking in gifted and talented students, consider the following suggestions.

- Provide regular opportunities for creative thinking. Creativity can be incorporated into most school subjects as soon as basic skills are acquired. Do not, however, accept novelty when accuracy is the goal. For example, spelling is one of the areas in which creativity should not be encouraged.
- Develop fluency with brainstorming sessions. Present a problem and see how many possible solutions can be suggested within a certain period of time. While students are brainstorming, do not evaluate the proposed solutions; instead, encourage a high rate of response. Younger students can practice with problems such as how to finance a trip to the toy department of a favorite store; older students might wish to suggest solutions for societal problems, such as how to provide proper health care for senior citizens or funding for public education. As for all the strategies, fluency should be integrated with curriculum content, for example, asking students to think of many ways to produce the number 32. In this example, solutions require evaluation.
- Encourage flexibility by considering various perspectives on an event. For example, in studying rain forests, have students imagine, and then confirm through research, the perspectives of all stakeholder groups, including the animals. Have students list solutions to a school problem from their own point of view. In literature, students can rewrite or visually depict the story from a different character's perspective.
- Develop original thinking by providing opportunities for its occurrence. Suggest problems or needs and direct students to come up with novel solutions. For example, in physical education, students might consider developing a new game or adapting a traditional one to equitably include peers with various disabilities.
- In elaboration, ideas are expanded and made more detailed. Give students practice in elaborative thinking by presenting simple statements that they must expand. Use quotations or

WebQuests and Web Inquiry Projects

WebQuests and Web Inquiry Projects (WIPs) are strategies designed to enable teachers to effectively use Internet resources in the classroom to support student learning of subject matter and skills in virtually any discipline (Molebash, Dodge, Bell, Mason, & Irving, 2004). Together, they offer inquiry opportunities appropriate for gifted students that range from structured (WebQuests) to open (WIPs).

WebQuests, created by Bernie Dodge and Tom March, typically engage students in a problem scenario, assign roles as stakeholders in the scenario, and provide links to Internet sources giving information critical to problem solution. Dodge (1995) lists as critical attributes a stage-setting introduction, an interesting task, a set of information sources embedded in the WebQuest as links, steps for accomplishing the task, guidance on organizing the information, and a conclusion. WebQuests are considered structured inquiry in that the teacher presents the problem and prescribes procedures students will use for investigating. WebQuests can serve as scaffolding to more open-ended WIPs.

Web Inquiry Projects provide students with a snippet of information called a "hook," intended to arouse student interest and curiosity. Students are encouraged to ask questions, determine the types of data needed to answer their questions, identify procedures for collecting data, locate and analyze the data, and report their findings, which often lead to new questions. Thus, WIPs involve students in more open inquiry in which they formulate questions and determine for investigation.

Examples of WebQuests can be accessed at *http://www.webquest.org/index.php*; examples of WIPs are available at *http://www.webinquiry.org/*

At the top of the next column is the introduction to a WebQuest titled "A Forest Forever" designed by Michelle Bergey for fifth grade science, social studies, and language arts.

At the bottom of the next column is a "hook" from a Web Inquiry Project designed by Philip Molebash based on an activity by Cheryl Mason and Alice Carter. The teacher page for this WIP appears at *http://www.webinquiry.org/examples/garber/index.htm*

Introduction

You will be working with a team of four people who have been selected to decide the fate of a forest designated as a National Forest.

Should it be used for recreation? Set aside as a wilderness? Logged for timber? Or a combination of things?

Your team will explore all of the different uses of our National Forests and the laws that regulate them. You will prepare a persuasive paper to convince the others in your team to take your position. Then together you will prepare a PowerPoint presentation at a "public hearing" of your entire class to inform them of your final recommendations for the use of the National Forest.

Good Luck! The public is trusting you to make the best use of their land!

WEB INQUIRY PROJECTS
CIVIL WAR AND THE SOUTHERN FAMILY

Hook | Questions | Procedures | Data Investigation | Analysis | Findings | New Questions

Student Page

Hook

The student page contains the hook only. It is intended to spark interest in the topic and lead students to ask questions or make predictions.

Have you ever wondered what life would have been like for you had you lived during another era?

What era intrigues you?

How could we learn what it was like during that time?

Read aloud with your classmates or by yourself a letter that was written August 15, 1862. What was happening in the United States during the early 1860s?

The letter was written by Thomas Garber to his sister Addie. From reading the letter what have we learned about Thomas and Addie? Can you answer any of the following questions based on what you read in the letter?

- Do you think Thomas was afraid?
- Do you think Thomas missed his family?
- What do you think was Thomas' job in the army?
- How old do you think Thomas was when he wrote this letter?

---

sayings, such as "All's well that ends well" and "All people are created equal." Or consider one of the novel responses produced in an original thinking exercise; have students expand the idea to include directions for implementation, ways of evaluating effectiveness, potential advantages, and possible disadvantages.

The "Spotlight on Technology" feature describes two web-based strategies for promoting higher level thinking skills, creativity, and problem solving. These strategies are WebQuests and Web Inquiry projects.

Problem solving is an extension of divergent thinking. It is important for students to become sensitive to the fact that

problems exist and that they possess the skills required to develop appropriate solutions for these problems (Feldhusen, 1989). In his structure of intellect model, Guilford (1967) describes five types of mental operations: cognition, memory, divergent production, convergent production, and evaluation. Cognition and memory relate to the gathering of information about a specific problem. In divergent thinking, several solutions are proposed; in convergent thinking, one "best" solution is selected. The final step is evaluation, in which the success of the selected solution is assessed; if the result is unsatisfactory, another solution can be chosen.

These different types of mental operations relate closely to the problem-solving model suggested by Gordon (1974). In this approach, conflicts are resolved by means of a six-step process:

1. defining the problem
2. generating possible solutions
3. evaluating the solutions
4. deciding which solution is best
5. deciding how to implement the solution
6. assessing how well the solution solved the problem. (p. 228)

In the second step, all possible solutions are specified (divergent production). Then the solutions are considered, and one is selected (convergent production). The process ends with implementation and evaluation of the chosen alternative.

The Gordon model is one that can be taught to students included in the general education program and then used for the solution of classroom problems. It is also useful as a general strategy for attacking any problem situation. To students who are gifted and talented, it represents a powerful tool to guide analysis, synthesis, and evaluation activities.

▶ ASSISTING STUDENTS WHO ARE UNDERACHIEVING

Underachieving students who are gifted and talented are one of the great tragedies of education. Because their potential for achievement is so high, their failure to thrive in school represents a double loss. The reasons for underachievement are many and complex and include factors related to the school, home, student, and peers (Peters, Grager-Loidl, & Supplee, 2000).

Some—particularly students from diverse ethnic, cultural, or linguistic groups and those with disabilities—may simply be overlooked. Hallahan and Kauffman (1988) address this issue and others in their recommendations to general education teachers.

1. The teacher should periodically review the characteristics of all the pupils in the class in order not to overlook any child who may be gifted. Which students in the class show particular ability, creativity, and task commitment? Are there pupils in the class, especially pupils who are economically disadvantaged or . . . ? [from a diverse ethnic, cultural, or linguistic] group, whose abilities may be less obvious according to white middle-class standards or who may be masking their abilities because of peer pressure for conformity?
2. The teacher must analyze and adjust his or her educational requirements for gifted pupils. Is the gifted child turned off to education because the work is not challenging or is not suitable for his [or her] superior intellectual powers? Is the gifted child underachieving simply because he [or she] is not being given appropriate work? Especially with the disadvantaged or culturally different gifted, it is important to present specific educational tasks in a structured environment with the firm and consistent expectation that they will be completed. . . .

3. The teacher must seek out and employ the resources of the school and community that can be used to the advantage of gifted children. Are there other teachers or older students with knowledge of the problems and methods of inquiry in a field of special interest who can help the child in independent study or small-group activities? Are there residents of other communities with special expertise who are willing to tutor the child or use him as an assistant?
4. The teacher should support whatever movement there may be in the school system toward establishing special programs for the gifted. Are there parents of gifted children whose pleas for special programs should be encouraged? Are there workshops for teachers? Does the school system employ resource teachers or specialists who will help . . .? [general education] teachers find methods, materials, community resources? (pp. 453–454)

Olenchak and Reis's (2002) recommendations for gifted students with learning disabilities include several that can be implemented by the general education teacher:

- focusing on strengths as opposed to deficits, acceleration in areas of academic strength;
- an IEP that addresses both strengths and needs;
- interest-based independent studies; and
- advanced-level courses (online or in person) in areas of strength for gifted students with learning disabilities in middle and high schools.

Pendarvis (1993) presented several ideas from various sources for removing the barriers to achievement.

- Don't give the students lectures or "pep talks" to get them to try harder. This has been shown to have detrimental effects on achievement.
- Show support and respect for the students' efforts.
- Establish appropriate standards and provide the instruction, guidance, and support to help students meet them.
- Encourage cooperation, rather than competition, in the classroom.
- Reward small gains in achievement, and don't expect quick success. (p. 583)

Coleman and Cross (2005) described underachievement among gifted students as "likely to be one means of camouflaging competence" (p. 199). They noted that, without early identification and guidance, a supportive teacher or counselor, and remedial-skills training in a sympathetic atmosphere, underachievement is resistant to intervention. Recent research has suggested that underachieving gifted students are not a homogeneous group, and interventions must be tailored to the individual student. McCoach and Siegle (2003) found that many underachieving gifted students see no benefits to schooling. These authors recommended that interventions include creating classrooms and assignments that are more enjoyable and intrinsically motivating as well as activities that encourage students to value learning tasks or the outcome of those tasks for their future. Several suggestions

Promoting Appropriate Instruction for Gifted Students

Kennedy (1995) provided several suggestions for general education teachers to consider when reviewing their classroom practices with gifted students.

1. *Resist policies requiring more work of those who finish assignments quickly and easily.* Instead, explore ways to assign different work that may be more complex, more abstract, and both deeper and wider. Find curriculum compacting strategies that work, and use them regularly.

2. *Seek out supplemental materials and ideas that extend, not merely reinforce, the curriculum.* Develop interdisciplinary units and learning centers that call for higher level thinking. Don't dwell on comprehension-level questions and tasks for those who have no problems with comprehension. Encourage activities that call for analysis, synthesis, and critical thinking, and push beyond superficial responses.

3. *De-emphasize grades and other extrinsic rewards.* Encourage learning for its own sake, and help perfectionists establish realistic goals and priorities. Try to ensure that the self-esteem of talented learners does not rest solely on their products and achievements.

4. *Encourage intellectual and academic risk-taking.* The flawless completion of a simple worksheet by an academically talented student calls for little or no reward, but struggling with a complex, open-ended issue should earn praise. Provide frequent opportunities to stretch mental muscles.

5. *Help all children develop social skills to relate well to one another.* For gifted children this may require special efforts to see things from other viewpoints. Training in how to "read" others and how to send accurate verbal and nonverbal messages may also be helpful. Tolerate neither elitist attitudes nor anti-gifted discrimination.

6. *Take time to listen to responses that may at first appear to be off-target.* Gifted children often are divergent thinkers who get more out of a story or remark and have creative approaches to problems. Hear them out, and help them elaborate on their ideas.

7. *Provide opportunities for independent investigations in areas of interest.* Gifted children are often intensely, even passionately, curious about certain topics. Facilitate their in-depth explorations by teaching research skills as needed, redirecting them to good resources, and providing support as they plan and complete appropriate products.

8. *Be aware of the special needs of gifted girls.* Encourage them to establish realistically high-level educational and career goals, and give them additional encouragement to succeed in math and science (pp. 233–234).

 ## WINDOW ON THE WEB

Websites About Giftedness and Talent

Organizations Related to Gifted and Talented Education

- GT World(*http://www.gtworld.org*)
- National Association for Gifted Children (NAGC) (*http://www.nagc.org*)
- National Foundation for Gifted and Creative Children (*http://www.nfgcc.org*)
- The Association for the Gifted (*http://www.cectag.org*)
- World Council for Gifted and Talented Children (*http://www.worldgifted.org*)
- Supporting the Emotional Needs of the Gifted, Inc. (*http://www.SENGifted.org*)

Web Resources

- Hoagies' Gifted Education Page (*http://www.hoagiesgifted.org*)
- Uniquely Gifted: Resources for Gifted Children with Special Need (*http://www.uniquelygifted.org/*)
- Odyssey of the Mind (*http://www.odysseyofth-emind.com*)

Special Programs and Research Centers

- Connie Belin and Jacqueline N. Blank International Center for Talented & Gifted Education, University of Iowa (*http://www.education.uiowa.edu/belinblank/*)
- Northwestern University Center for Talent Development (*http://www.ctd.northwestern.edu*)
- Duke University Talent Identification Program (TIP) (*http://www.tip.duke.edu*)
- Jacob K. Javits Gifted and Talented Students Education Program (*http://www.ed.gov/programs/javits/index.html*)
- National Consortium for Specialized Secondary Schools of Mathematics, Science, and Technology (*http://www.ncsssmst.org*)
- National Research Center on Gifted and Talented at the University of Connecticut (*http://www.gifted.uconn.edu/NRCGT.html*)
- The Center for Talented Youth at the Johns Hopkins University (*http://www.jhu.edu/~gifted*)
- College of William and Mary Center for Gifted Education (*http://www.cfge.wm.edu*)

for whetting students' appetites for learning appear in the following "Inclusion Tips for the Teacher" material. Additional resources are Winebrenner's (2001) *Teaching Gifted Kids in the Regular Classroom,* Karnes and Bean's (2005) *Methods and Materials for Teaching the Gifted,* and Gross, Sleap, and Pretorius's (1999) *Gifted Students in Secondary Schools: Differentiating the Curriculum.* The "Window on the Web" provides websites for organizations, resources, and special programs that offer more information about giftedness and talent.

In this chapter, you have learned about some of the characteristics of students who are unusually bright and those with special gifts and talents. Methods for identifying appropriate educational options, promoting creativity and problem solving, and assisting underachievers have been suggested. Consult "Things to Remember" to review this chapter's major points.

Things to Remember

- For achievement to be commensurate with potential, students who are gifted and talented require special educational adaptations in the general education class or in separate programs.

- Students who are gifted and talented are characterized by their above-average ability. Their gift or talent can be in intellectual performance, creativity, academic achievement, leadership potential, or special areas of endeavor such as art or music.

- This group of students is composed of both males and females and individuals representing all socioeconomic strata and cultures. As a group, students who are gifted and talented are more verbal, learn more rapidly, and are better adjusted than their typical class peers.

- The major educational adaptations for students who are gifted and talented are acceleration, enrichment, and grouping for challenging instruction. General education teachers can use curriculum compacting to reduce the coverage of material already mastered. Tiered assignments and problem-based learning also can be used in the general education classroom to differentiate instruction for gifted students.

- One important goal in the education of this group of students is to provide opportunities to develop disciplinary and interdisciplinary expertise through a challenging curriculum.

- Teachers can support gifted students' development of creativity and problem-solving skills by engaging them in divergent thinking and convergence and evaluation as they encounter unanswered questions, problems, and issues in their studies.

- Students who are gifted and talented do not all excel in school; some, considered underachievers, remain unidentified or lack sufficient motivation to perform near their potential.

- Most students who are gifted and talented remain in the general education program for the majority of their school careers. To meet their special learning needs, educators must adapt the instructional procedures in the general education classroom.

- It is not necessary to be gifted or talented to be an effective teacher of such students. It is more important to be passionate about knowledge acquisition, self-confident, open, and an adept facilitator of learning.

ACTIVITIES

1. Observe a general education classroom in which one or more students have been identified as gifted or talented. Are these pupils involved in any special programs outside the classroom or school? What special provisions are made in the general education classroom? Are techniques such as curriculum compacting used to eliminate the need for students to work on material they have already mastered or to streamline the pace at which they master other materials? Do the behaviors of these students differ in any way from those of their peers? Are they well accepted by their classmates and teacher?

2. Interview children or young adults who have been identified as gifted or talented. What are their current interests? What do they like and dislike about school? Ask them to suggest ways in which the school experience could be made more valuable to them.

3. Locate articles that discuss education of pupils who are gifted and talented. *G/T/C (Gifted/Talented/Creative), Gifted and Talented International, Roeper Review, Journal of Creative Behavior, Journal for the Education of the Gifted, Gifted Child Today, Journal of Advanced Academics,* and *The Gifted Child Quarterly* are possible sources. Can you find suggestions for general education class adaptations? For assisting underachievers? For students from diverse ethnic, cultural, or linguistic groups?

4. Contact local schools to find out what services are available for youngsters who are gifted and talented. What procedures are used to identify students? Are there special classes? Early admission? Resource services? Enrichment

programs to augment the general education classroom? What assistance is available to the general education teacher? Are students with disabilities enrolled in the program?

5. Ask several members of your community to define the terms *gifted* and *talented*. You might select teachers, students, school administrators, parents of school-aged children, and others with no current connection with the public school system. Compare their definitions to see whether there is any consensus. Use the information you have collected to prepare a set of local definitions meaningful to the persons in your community. Be clear and concise, and use language understandable to both educators and the general public.

CHAPTER EIGHTEEN

Teaching English Learners

Xiong

Xiong is a first grade student whose Hmong family came to the United States when he was an infant from the Chinese province of Guizhou through the sponsorship of a local church. He is the youngest member of his family, and he has four older siblings. He lives with his parents, maternal grandparents, and several other extended family members. Xiong's family does not speak English at home, and both his teacher for students learning English as a second language (ESL) and his first grade teacher are worried about his slow academic progress and classroom behavior. The educators are especially concerned because of their difficulty in communicating with Xiong's family. His parents clearly cherish this youngest child, and they do not seem to believe that a problem exists. Even when the teachers address Xiong's apparent disrespect for others' belongings, his parents do not seem to understand. The teachers are beginning to suspect that Xiong may have a learning or intellectual disability. When they discussed this possibility with their school's intervention assistance team, Ms. Klein, the social worker who has worked extensively with community agencies helping families such as Xiong's, explained that some of the concerns may be related to cultural differences (Friend, 2008, p. 69).

Nico

Nico is a 10th grader who was born in Guatemala. He moved to Southern California in the second grade. Before coming to this country, he was a good student and learned to read and write in Spanish. When he began school in the United States, he was placed in a bilingual classroom where he received some native-language support before transitioning into English instruction. Now in high school, he is performing at or above grade level in mainstream classes. Because Nico can speak, read, and write well in both languages, Nico's teacher is considering him for the gifted program at his school (Echevarria & Graves, 2007, p. 2).

Luisa

Born in an urban U.S. city, Luisa is a friendly 15-year-old who sits quietly in class giving the impression that she understands everything. When written assignments are given, she writes down the assignment and begins to work. Her writing, however, is illegible, and her spelling is extremely poor. Spanish is her first language, although her family speaks a mix of English and Spanish at home. She writes in English in a knowledge-telling mode without recognizable structure in her sentences or paragraphs. Luisa can converse quite well in both languages, but for some reason has not made academic progress in either language. Although she is popular in school, she is at risk of dropping out because of consistent underachievement (Echevarria & Graves, 2007, p. 3).

LOOKING AHEAD

This chapter is about students like Xiong, Nico, Luisa, and others who speak languages other than English, the language of the classroom in the United States. Think about these questions as you read this chapter.

- If you were Xiong's teacher, what steps could you take to make him and his family feel welcome in your classroom?
- What strategies would you recommend to help students like Xiong develop English language skills in a classroom where English is the only language of instruction?
- Nico and Luisa speak both English and Spanish. Would you consider them both to be bilingual? Why or why not?
- What types of classroom modifications could you make to help English learners learn content areas such as science and social studies?

Students who speak languages other than English are called many things. If they have command of both English and another language like Nico, they are called bilingual. If they do have not acquired any English skills at all or are still in the process of learning English, they may be called a variety of terms including **English learners,** the term used in this book. Other labels that appear in the literature include *English language learners, limited English proficient, linguistically diverse,* and *speakers of other languages.*

According to reports of recent research about teacher preparation (Lee, 2009; Wright, 2009), teaching English learners is one of the areas in which general educators feel they could benefit from more training. This chapter addresses this important need by describing the typical instructional needs of students who are English learners, the ways in which these students are identified

For Your Information

and assessed, available services, and strategies for adaptations in the general education classroom. Among the topics covered are techniques for assisting English learners with vocabulary development and the acquisition of content area subjects. Take a look at the "For Your Information" section to learn more about this heterogeneous group of students.

INDICATORS OF THE NEED FOR ENGLISH LANGUAGE INSTRUCTION

When parents bring their child to a new school either as a beginning kindergartener or as a student in a higher grade, one of the first things that happens is that they are asked to provide information about the language or languages spoken in the home. If parents indicate that a language other than English is spoken at home, this alerts the school to the possibility that the student also speaks this language. When this occurs, parents are asked to complete a language background survey or participate in an interview. Figure 18-1 presents a sample home language survey.

It is important to note that, as Payan (1989) commented, "The types of questions commonly presented in language background questionnaires will not directly identify the language the child commands readily" (p. 132). However, parents can provide information about the child's **heritage language** or home language, which helps the school decide whether further assessment is needed. Possibilities include homes where English is the only language spoken, another language is the only one spoken, two or more languages including English are spoken, and two or more languages other than English are spoken.

---

myeducationlab To enhance your understanding of teaching English learners, go to the IRIS Center Resources section of Topic *Cultural and Linguistic Diversity* in the MyEducationLab for your course and complete the Module entitled *Cultural and Linguistic Differences: What Teachers Should Know.*

The purpose of further assessment is to determine the student's language proficiency in the heritage language (often called Language 1 or L1), in any other language spoken in the home (which may be L2 or L3), and also in English, the language of the school. In some cases, English is L1 for students. It can also be L2 (or L3), or it may not be one of a student's languages at all. See "For Your Information" for assistance with the many terms (e.g., L1, L2) related to English learners.

Teachers play a role in the identification of students who would benefit from English language instruction by observing language in the classroom and other school settings. One important aspect of this is understanding the nature of language proficiency. McLoughlin and Lewis (2008) contended:

> Language proficiency is not a simple, unitary skill. According to Cummins (1981), there are two major dimensions of language proficiency. *Basic interpersonal communication skills (BICS)* are the spoken skills of the language community and are acquired by almost all community members. *Cognitive/academic language proficiency (CALP)*, in contrast, is the set of language skills needed to function in the academic environment of school" (emphasis added, p. 471).

Basic interpersonal communication skills are typically developed first, usually within a period of two years; the higher level skills involved in cognitive/academic learning proficiency require more time, up to five to seven years of school training (Gollnick & Chinn, 2006).

Figure 18-2 presents a case study that illustrates the differences between these two types of language proficiencies. As you read, identify which of the language skills described are basic interpersonal communication skills and which represent cognitive/academic language proficiency.

FIGURE 18-1   Sample Parent–Home Language Survey

What language did/does your child . . .

       speak when beginning to talk?   English _____ Other language _____

       speak *most often* at home?   English _____ Other language _____

       speak *most often* with friends?   English _____ Other language _____

What language do you . . .

       use *most often* when speaking to your child?   English _____ Other language _____

       use *most often* when speaking to your friends? English _____ Other language _____

What language do other family members in your

       home *usually* use when speaking to each other? English _____ Other language _____

Family Member	Native Language	Language Used at Home	Second Language Fluency		
Father	_____	_____	None ____	Emerging ____	Mastery ____
Mother	_____	_____	None ____	Emerging ____	Mastery ____
Siblings	_____	_____	None ____	Emerging ____	Mastery ____
Others in home	_____	_____	None ____	Emerging ____	Mastery ____
Peers	_____	_____	None ____	Emerging ____	Mastery ____

Student's use of second language	None	Occasional	Frequent	Total
	_____	_____	_____	_____

	Speaking	Writing	Reading
Age began . . .	_____	_____	_____

Student's English fluency

    _____ Uses basic nouns and verbs

    _____ Uses conjugated verbs, nouns, and adjectives

    _____ Speaks in full sentences and uses form and structure inconsistently

    _____ Speaks fluently with good usage, form, and structure

Student's dominant language _____ Language of preference _____

Language parents prefer for school instruction _____

Student's school experience:

Native language instruction _____ Bilingual instruction _____ All English instruction _____

                       _____ Bilingual aide _____ ESL Teacher _____ Regular Education Teacher _____

Note: From C. G. Spinelli, *Classroom Assessment for Students in Special and General Education* (2nd ed.), "Sample Parent-Home Language Survey", (p. 207). Copyright © 2006. Reproduced by permission of Pearson Education, Inc.

FIGURE 18-2   Case Study: Language Skills Needed for the First Day of School

You're five years old. At five you're quite competent in the use of English with other kids. You may still have much to learn, but basically, you understand what people say to you and you can communicate with others.

    For a while now, your parents have been talking about the fact that you have to learn to read and write, and that soon, you'll be going to school. You're a little afraid and very excited. On the first day of school, your mother makes sure that you've wearing a nice outfit. You have a backpack filled with blank notebooks, pencils, and crayons. You know that those are the implements you will be using to learn how to read and write. As you walk into the classroom, the teacher begins to give instructions to the class. She calls out the children's names but she can't pronounce yours. The other children seem to know what's going on. They all know what to do, except for you. Are they laughing at you? Tears roll down your cheeks.

    Suddenly, you realize that learning is going to be much more difficult than you ever imagined.

Note: Reprinted by permission of Bank Street College of Education from its "Bank Street's Guide to Literacy and Tutors," in the section, "English Language Learners," *http://www.bankstreet.edu/literacyguide/ell.html.* Copyright Bank Street College of Education.

For Your Information

Terms Related to the Instruction of English Learners

Díaz-Rico (2004, p. 6) includes a glossary early in her book *Teaching English Learners*. Some of the most common terms and their definitions appear here.

English learners, EL students	Anyone learning to speak English whose native language is not English
English as a second language (ESL)	Learners whose primary language is not English, yet who live in places where English has some sort of special status or public availability
English as a foreign language	Learners of English who live in places where English is, by and large, an academic subject, functioning narrowly in that culture as a tool for communicating with outsiders
First language (L1)	The language learned at home from the primary caregivers (mother tongue, primary language, or native language)
Second language (L2)	Any language (whether third or twentieth) that is learned after the first language
ELL	English-language learner (English learner)
Fluent-English-proficient (FEP), or Fluent-English speaker (FES)	English learner who is ready for redesignation (mainstreaming)
Limited-English-proficient (LEP), or Limited-English speaker (LES)	English learner who is not yet ready for redesignation
Non-English-proficient (NEP), or Non-English speaker (NES)	English learner who is in the first stages of learning English

Note: From L.T. Diaz-Rico, *Teaching English Learners,* Excerpt from glossary terms (p. 6). Copyright © 2004. Reproduced by permission of Pearson Education, Inc.

 ## IDENTIFICATION AND ASSESSMENT PROCEDURES

Identification of students in need of English language instruction requires determination of language proficiency in English as well as in any other languages spoken. This may take place at the entry to school or as part of Response to Intervention if students experience difficulty in school (Rinaldi & Samson, 2008). One of the main concerns is differentiating between problems due to the acquisition of a second language and those due to a disability such as a learning disability (Hardman, Drew, & Egan, 2005; National Center for Culturally Responsive Educational Systems, 2006–2008; Salend, 2008). Consult the "Inclusion Tips for the Teacher" section to learn about questions to ask about language acquisition issues versus learning disabilities.

 Go to the Building Teaching Skills and Dispositions section of Topic *Inclusive Practices* in the MyEducationLab for your course and complete the activity entitled *Creating a Supportive Classroom Climate*.

Durán (2008) reported that all states rely on home language surveys to identify students who live in homes where a language other than English is spoken; in most states, students from such homes are then assessed to determine which initial classification is most appropriate: English proficient or English language learner. Language proficiency is typically assessed with formal measures such as the *Basic Inventory of Natural Language, Language Assessment*

Scales, and *Idea Proficiency Test* (Díaz-Rico, 2004; Echevarria & Graves, 2007; McLoughlin & Lewis, 2008). Durán also pointed out that most states allow local districts to use additional types of information in making decisions about language proficiency and that there is consideration variation across states in the standards for defining and assessing English language learners.

Teachers can assist in the assessment of language proficiency by observing students in academic settings and in the more social situations of school such as recess and lunch. Echevarria and Graves (2007) presented an informal observation form to help teachers structure their observations of English learners. That form, the *Student Oral Language Observation Matrix* or *SOLOM,* appears in Figure 18-3.

The *SOLOM* guides teacher to observe the student in question in five language skill areas: comprehension, fluency, vocabulary, pronunciation, and grammar. In each area, five ratings are possible. The first, 1, indicates the lowest level of proficiency and the last, 5, indicates the highest level of proficiency. For example, in the area of comprehension, a rating of 1 indicates "cannot understand even simple conversation," whereas a rating of 5 indicates "understands everyday conversation and normal classroom discussions without difficulty." In most skill areas, ratings of 4 and 5 indicate English proficiency.

SERVICES FOR ENGLISH LEARNERS

The services available for English learners vary widely from state to state and from district to district. Bilingual education programs

FIGURE 18-3 Teacher Observation Form for Oral Language

Student's Name: _____

Language Observed: _____

Teacher Observation
Student Oral Language Observation Matrix (SOLOM)

Grade: _____ Examiner: _____

Date: _____

LEVEL	1	2	3	4	5
(A) Comprehension	Cannot understand even simple conversation.	Has great difficulty following what is said. Can comprehend only "social conversation" spoken slowly and with frequent repetitions.	Understands most of what is said at slower than normal speed with repetitions.	Understands nearly everything at normal speed, although occasional repetition may be necessary.	Understands everyday conversation and normal classroom discussions without difficulty.
(B) Fluency	Speech is so halting and fragmentary as to make conversation virtually impossible.	Usually hesitant; often forced into silence by language limitations.	Speech in everyday conversation and classroom discussions is frequently disrupted by the student's search for the correct manner of expression.	Speech in everyday conversation and classroom discussion is generally fluent, with occasional lapses while searching for the correct manner of expression.	Speech in everyday conversation and classroom discussion is fluent and effortless, approximating that of a native speaker.
(C) Vocabulary	Vocabulary limitations so extreme as to make conversation virtually impossible.	Misuse of words and very limited vocabulary make comprehension quite difficult.	Frequently uses the wrong words; conversation somewhat limited because of inadequate vocabulary.	Occasionally uses inappropriate terms and/or must rephrase ideas because of lexical inadequacies.	Use of vocabulary and idioms approximates that of a native speaker.
(D) Pronunciation	Pronunciation problems so severe as to make speech virtually unintelligible.	Very hard to understand because of pronunciation problems. Must frequently repeat in order to make him/herself understood.	Pronunciation problems necessitate concentration on the part of the listener and occasionally lead to misunderstanding.	Always intelligible though one is conscious of a definite accent and occasional inappropriate intonation patterns.	Pronunciation and intonation approximates that of a native speaker.
(E) Grammar	Errors in grammar and word order so severe as to make speech virtually unintelligible.	Grammar and word order errors make comprehension difficult. Must often rephrase and/or restrict him/herself to basic patterns.	Makes frequent errors of grammar and word order, which occasionally obscure meaning.	Occasionally makes grammatical and/or word order errors, which do not obscure meaning.	Grammatical usage and word order approximates that of a native speaker.

The student oral language observation matrix (SOLOM) has five (5) categories on the left: A. Comprehension, B. Fluency, C. Vocabulary, D. Pronunciation, and E. Grammar. It also has five numbers along the top, one (1) being the lowest mark to five (5) being the highest mark. According to your observation, indicate with an (X) across the square in each category which best describes the child's abilities. Those students whose checkmarks (Xs) are to the right of the darkened line will be considered for reclassification, if test scores and achievement data also indicate English proficiency.

Note: From J. Echevarria and A. Graves, *Sheltered Content Instruction, 3e,* "Teacher Observation Form for Oral Language" (p. 15). Copyright © 2007 Reproduced by permission of Pearson Education, Inc.

Inclusion Tips for the Teacher

Prereferral Considerations for English Language Learners

Rinaldi and Samson (2008) offer the questions that follow to guide you through the three tiers of the Response-to-Intervention model. These questions can help you to differentiate between students who may benefit from English language instruction and those who may also need additional assistance because of a learning disability.

RTI Tier 1, Interpersonal English Language Acquisition Difficulties?

- What is the student's level of interpersonal English language proficiency?
- What is the student's interpersonal native language proficiency?
- Have bilingual education or ESL personnel made recommendations (Ortiz & Yates, 2001)? If so, are these recommendations being monitored using informal measures?

RTI Tier 2, Academic Language Difficulties?

- Is the student receiving instruction that addresses his language needs based on bilingual or ESL professional recommendations?

- What is the rate of progress and level of English language proficiency since implementation of ESL instructional strategies (Ortiz & Yates, 2001)?
- What is the student's academic language proficiency?
- What is the student's rate and level of reading and comprehension in the native language compared to English?

RTI Tier 3, Learning Disability?

- Has the student received evidence-based instruction and intervention to meet his academic needs?
- Is there evidence of failure to respond to intervention (learning rate and level of performance)?
- Is the data-driven progress monitoring addressing the student's needs effectively in the native language and in English?

Note: ESL = English as a second language.

Note: From C. Rinaldi & J. Samson in *Teaching Exceptional Children,* Copyright © 2008 by Council for Exceptional Children (VA). Reproduced with permission of Council for Exceptional Children in the formats Textbook and Other Book via Copyright Clearance Center.

that include both heritage language and English instruction have become less common, and programs focusing on English language development have become more common. One reason for this is practical and relates to the heterogeneity of the languages in some locales. If 5, 10, or even 15 heritage languages are spoken by English learners in one elementary or secondary school, it would be difficult if not impossible to provide a bilingual program for speakers of each different language. Another reason is political: in the past two decades, the "English only" movement has led to an upsurge in the number of states in which English has been

designated as the official language (Garcia, 2006) and a corresponding decline in the number of English learners receiving bilingual education (Gollnick & Chinn, 2006; Hardman, Drew, & Egan, 2005).

Table 18-1 provides information on the types of program options available today for English learners. The first option, Sheltered Instruction, is likely the most common mode of providing instruction to this group of students, particularly in schools where a number of different heritage languages are spoken.

TABLE 18-1   Program Options for English Language Learners

Sheltered Instruction	Promotes use of techniques and strategies for making grade-level content comprehensible for ELL's while promoting their English development. Although native language may be used for clarification, English is the medium of instruction.
Transitional Bilingual Education	Teaching in students' native language provides support as they transition into English instruction, usually within 2 to 3 years. Sheltered instruction is used during instruction in English to scaffold students' understanding.
Developmental Bilingual Education	With the goal of bilingualism and biliteracy, students are taught in two languages for multiple years. Sheltered instruction techniques and strategies assist students' comprehension in English.
Two-Way Immersion	English language learners and English-speaking students are taught together in two languages. Students communicate in authentic, meaningful ways that promote dual-language development for both groups. Sheltered instruction techniques are utilized when teaching content through the second language.
Newcomer Programs	The goals of newcomer programs are to acculturate immigrant students with limited English proficiency to U.S. schools, to assist students in acquiring beginning English language skills, and to develop core academic skills and knowledge.

Note: From J. Echevarria and A. Graves, *Sheltered Content Instruction,* 3e, "Program Options for English Language Learners", (p. 7). Copyright © 2007. Reproduced by permission of Pearson Education, Inc.

Whichever approach is selected for the language instruction of English learners, the general education teacher is likely to encounter as members of the class students who are learning a new language. The likelihood of this is highest in the western states. In the West, English learners make up at least 25% of school population in 19% of public schools (National Center for Education Statistics, 2004). In the nation as a whole, however, English learners make up less than 1% of the student body in more than half the schools.

Teachers of English to Speakers of Other Languages, or TESOL, is an organization of professionals interested in the education of students who are English learners. TESOL has developed a set of standards for pre-kindergarten through grade 12 students in relation to language development. Those standards appear in Table 18-2. TESOL's website provides information about how each of the standards applies to different age groups (e.g., grades pre-K–3, grades 4–8). Among the types of information available are descriptors of the language

TABLE 18-2 Standards for English Learners from TESOL

Goal 1: To use English to communicate in social settings	
Standard 1	Students will use English to participate in social interactions
Standard 2	Students will interact in, through, and with spoken and written English for personal expression and enjoyment
Standard 3	Students will use learning strategies to extend their communicative competence
Goal 2: To use English to achieve academically in all content areas	
Standard 1	Students will use English to interact in the classroom
Standard 2	Students will use English to obtain, process, construct, and provide subject matter information in spoken and written form
Standard 3	Students will use appropriate learning strategies to construct and apply academic knowledge
Goal 3: To use English in socially and culturally appropriate ways	
Standard 1	Students will use the appropriate language variety, register, and genre according to audience, purpose, and setting
Standard 2	Students will use nonverbal communication appropriate to audience, purpose, and setting
Standard 3	Students will use appropriate learning strategies to extend their sociolinguistic and sociocultural competence

Note: From *ESL Standards for Pre-K–12 Students* by TESOL. Copyright © 2006 by Teachers of English to Speakers of Other Languages. Reproduced with permission of Teachers of English to Speakers of Other Languages in the formats Textbook and Other book via Copyright Clearance Center.

WINDOW ON THE WEB

Websites About English Learners

Colorín Colorado

Colorín Colorado is "a bilingual site for families and educators of English language learners." The site is available in English and in Spanish. The portion of the site for educators offers several sets of resources such as Reaching Out to Hispanic Students and Families, Placement and Assessment, Teaching Reading, and Teaching Content Areas. Information for parents includes topics such as "What You Can Do at Home" and "Helping Your Child Succeed at School." The site also offers one-page "Reading Tip Sheets" for parents for many grade levels and in 11 languages (e.g., Arabic, Haitian Creole, Navajo, and Tagalog). Several e-mail newsletters for both parents and teachers are available at no charge. Visit the site to find out what its name, "Colorín Colorado," means.

www.colorincolorado.org/

TESOL

The Teachers of English to Speakers of Other Languages, Inc. is an organization of more than 11,000 members interested in how best to teach English learners. This site contains information about the organization as well as news, advocacy alerts, and valuable resources such as the TESOL standards. Some resources are available to members only.

www.tesol.org/s_tesol/index.asp

NABE

NABE is the National Association for Bilingual Education. According to its website, it is the "only national professional organization devoted to representing Bilingual Learners and Bilingual Education professionals." Among the resources on this site are sections on Research (e.g., Bilingual Education, Demography), Advocacy, Publications (e.g., *Bilingual Research Journal*), and the NABE Store.

http://nabe.org/

Other websites that may be of interest to teachers are:

- NCCREST, the National Center for Culturally Responsive Educational Systems (*www.nccrest.org*)
- OELA, the Office of English Language Acquisition (*www.ed.gov/about/offices/list/oela/index.html*)
- NCELA, the National Clearinghouse for English Language Acquisition & Language Instruction Educational Programs (*www.ncela.gwu.edu/*)
- Equity Alliance at ASU (*www.equityallianceatasu.org/*)

behaviors pertinent to the age group, sample progress indicators, and a teaching vignette that describes the students, the teacher, and the instructional sequence. For information about TESOL's website and other with valuable resources for teachers of English learners, consult "Window on the Web."

CLASSROOM ADAPTATIONS

The adaptations for English learners in the general education classroom revolve around language instruction and the need to make academic learning easier for students who must acquire the language of the classroom at the same time they are attempting to learn new skills and content subjects. Several principles guide the process of making classroom adaptations for English learners, including those related to learning a second language, teaching English learners, and culturally responsive instruction.

Go to the Assignments and Activities section of Topic *Inclusive Practices* in the My-EducationLab for your course and complete the activity entitled *Cultural, Linguistic, and Other Factors that Influence Participation.*

Principles of Culturally Responsive Instruction

The principles of culturally responsive instruction (Brown, 2007; Gay, 2000; Gollnick & Chinn, 2006) are the most basic principles underlying the education of English learners and all others in the general education classroom. It is crucial that instruction in the general education classroom be culturally responsive to all types of diversity. Callins (2006) identifies these elements of culturally responsive pedagogy:

- Communicate high expectations.
- Use active teaching methods.
- Facilitate learning.
- Have positive perspectives on parents and families of culturally and linguistically diverse students.

- Demonstrate cultural sensitivity.
- Reshape the curriculum.
- Provide culturally mediated instruction.
- Promote student-controlled classroom discourse.
- Include small group instruction and cooperative learning. (p. 63) *

Principles of Language Instruction

When English learners are the concern, it is important to take into consideration principles related to language. Salend (2008) presents these research-based principles underlying second language learning for students.

- Students who have been educated in their native language often progress faster in learning a new language than those who have not had a formal education (Collier & Thomas, 2002; Rodriguez & Higgins, 2005).
- Students who speak languages that are similar to English tend to learn English faster than those whose first language is very different from English. It also is very common for students to attempt to apply the rules of their first language to their second language, which can affect students' pronunciations (e.g., students say *share* for *chair*), syntax (e.g., in Spanish, adjectives follow the noun . . .), and spelling (Tiedt & Tiedt, 2006).
- As some students learn a second language, they may experience language loss or arrested language development in their native languages (Wrigley, 2004).
- Children who simultaneously learn two languages from birth may initially experience some temporary language delay in achieving developmental language milestones and some language mixing, which tends to disappear over time (Fierro-Cobas & Chan, 2001). (p. 125)

Goldenberg (2008) also looked at the research on language learning, but focused on the instructional implications for classroom teachers. Here are his three summary points:

1. Teaching students to read in their first language promotes higher levels of reading achievement *in English;*
2. What we know about good instruction and curriculum in general holds true for English learners as well; but
3. When instructing English learners in English, teachers must modify instruction to take into account students' language limitations (p. 14).

In other words, students' language skills do make a difference for teachers of general education classrooms. However, effective instruction for English learners shares the same characteristics as effective instruction for all students (Echevarria & Graves, 2007; Gersten, Baker, Haager, & Graves, 2005).

The sections that follow discuss strategies for two important areas of concern for teachers of English learners: building English

---

vocabulary and teaching content area subjects. In each area, teachers are challenged to communicate clearly in order to help students build meaning. For students to learn, the input they receive from teachers and other aspects of the instructional program must be understandable. Comprehensible input, as Krashen (1987) calls it, is necessary for students to be able to begin to acquire new meanings and vocabulary, including both basic interpersonal and cognitive/academic language skills. To build meaning, teachers activate students' background knowledge or, if necessary, help them acquire the necessary background knowledge. Learning is contextualized to make it more meaningful, and scaffolding support is provided by the teacher as needed (Echevarria & Graves, 2007).

Building English Vocabulary

Vocabulary development is one of the most important ways that general education teachers can assist English learners to succeed in classroom activities. In discussing the importance of vocabulary development, the Colorín Colorado website (2007c) notes that children who are native English speakers enter kindergarten with a vocabulary of 5,000 or more words. English learners, in contrast, may know an equivalent number of words in their heritage language, but only a few words in English.

> **myeducationlab** To enhance your understanding of teaching English learners, go to the IRIS Center Resources section of Topic *Cultural and Linguistic Diversity* in the MyEducationLab for your course and complete the Module entitled *RTI (Part 5): A Closer Look at Tier 3.*

Numerous authors provide suggestions for how to assist English learners in vocabulary development. Several of these suggestions follow.

- Provide students who are English learners with opportunities to hear, say, read, and write new words (Swanson & Howerton, 2007).
- Make the classroom a comfortable place for students to practice their new language skills (Swanson & Howerton).
- Allow students to be silent when they are first learning a new language (Rodriguez & Higgins, 2005). This stage of

language learning is called the *preproduction* or *silent period*, and it is a time when students learn by listening rather than speaking (Salend, 2008).

- In the first stages of language learning, students can respond by pointing, drawing, gesturing, and other nonverbal techniques (Salend).
- Rodriguez and Higgins (2005) recommended that teachers "use gestures as much as possible when describing or explaining things to students. For example, when teaching big and small, use your arms to demonstrate" (p. 241).
- Use systematic instruction to teach vocabulary directly (Graves, Gersten, & Haager, 2004).
- Integrate vocabulary development into as many teaching activities as possible (Gersten et al., 2005).
- Use pictures and other visuals, manipulatives, real objects, gestures, demonstrations, role playing, and modeling to teach new vocabulary (Brown & Doolittle, 2008; Colorín Colorado, 2007c; Gersten et al., 2005).
- Try the Total Physical Response strategy for teaching new words and phrases. With this technique, teachers model and students mimic whole-body responses while speaking new vocabulary. Colorín Colorado (2007a) gives this example of a script that teachers could use to help students practice new vocabulary: "Take out your math book. Put it on your desk. Put it on your head. Put it under the chair. Hold it in your left hand."
- Take advantage of cognates when available (Swanson & Howerton, 2007). *Cognates* are words that are related in origin and may look, sound, and mean the same in two languages. Table 18-3 presents examples of some of the

TABLE 18-3 Spanish–English Cognates

These cognates were selected from a five-page list that appears on the Colorín Colorado (2007b) website. To see the entire list, go to *http://www.colorincolorado.org/educators/background/cognates*

English	Spanish
active	activo/activa
adventure	aventura
allergic	alérgico/alérgica
arithmetic	aritmética
biography	biografía
camera	camera
color	color
confusing	confuso
different	diferente
family	familia
history	historia
information	información
memory	memoria
paper	papel
September	septiembre
television	televisión

Note: Adapted from Calderón, M., August, D. Durán, D., Madden, N., Slavin, R. and M. Gil. (2003). *Spanish to English Transitional Reading: Teacher's Manual.* Baltimore, MD: The Success for All Foundation.

Software to Assist Language Learners

Software is available to help students (and adults) learn new languages. Lowdermilk, Fielding, Mendoza, García de Alba, and Simpson (2008) differentiate between English language acquisition technology (ELAT) and software that provides a translation from one language to another. Language acquisition software is designed to develop skills in individuals interested in language learning. Lowdermilk et al. provide an example of how software such as this might be used in a general education classroom:

> Ms. Flores is preparing for her next period class in which she has a new student, Leticia, who has recently emigrated from Mexico. Leticia is presently in the third grade and speaks very little English. Ms. Flores has decided to use an ELAT to introduce Leticia to basic concepts such as numbers, colors, family relations, household items, common signs, and body parts. Ms. Flores begins by showing Leticia how to open the ELAT at Level One. A quadrant appears with a number in each square. A woman's voice is heard saying, "four." Ms. Flores demonstrates to Leticia how to move the pointer to the number four, and she clicks on it. Applause and a ringing bell are heard. The next screen appears. This time Ms. Flores encourages Leticia to try. The voice says, "two." Leticia carefully moves the pointer and clicks on the correct number. Applause and a ringing bell are heard. (p. 2)

Note: Lowdermilk, J., Fielding, C., Mendoza, R. Garcia de Alba, R. & Simpson, C. (2009). Selecting English language acquisition technology. In J. Castellani & C. Warger (Eds.), *Accommodating students with disabilities: Instructional and assistive technology tools that work* (pp. 13-16). Arlington, VA: Technology and Media Division of the Council for Exceptional Children (TAM).

There are many language software options. A classic program, *Jumpstart Languages* from Knowledge Adventure, provides activities for younger students in four languages: French, Japanese, Spanish, and English. *KidSpeak* and the *Learn Language Now* series from Transparent Language offer instruction for older elementary students, teens, and adults in a range of languages including Chinese, French, German, Hebrew, Indonesian, Italian, Japanese, Korean, and Spanish. However, English is not one of the choices.

Perhaps the best known software for learning English and other languages are the Rosetta Stone programs (*http://www.rosettastone.com*). This company provides programs in more than 30 languages,

including both American and British English. The screen below comes from an interactive demo on the Rosetta Stone website. The learner hears the Swedish words pronounced and must then click on the appropriate photo in the bottom row. Rosetta Stone offers classroom versions for K–12 students and those in higher education. More than 20 languages are available, including two versions of English and two of Spanish (Latin American and Spain). Teachers with students in their classroom who speak Filipino (Tagalog), Russian, Farsi, or Vietnamese could use Rosetta Stone software to begin learning one of these languages.

Note: Used with permission from Rosetta Stone, Ltd.

English learners can also find language activities on the web. Here are a few examples of websites for students (and teachers)

- Interesting Things for ESL Learners: A Fun Study Site for Learners of English as a Second Language (*http://www.manythings.org/*)
- Everything ESL (*http://www.everythingesl.net/*) and Elementary Web Sites for English Language Learners (*http://www.everythingesl.net/inservices/elementary_sites_ells_71638.php*)
- Activities for ESL Students (*http://www.a4esl.org*)

---

cognates of English and Spanish. However, be aware that some words that appear to be cognates may instead be false cognates. Many a beginning Spanish student has been chagrined to find the Spanish word *embarazada* means pregnant, not embarrassed.

- Be aware that idioms are not universal across languages (Swanson & Howerton, 2007). *Idioms* are expressions in which words do not carry their literal meanings. Dictionary.com provides these examples of English idioms: *kick the bucket* and *hang one's head*.
- Another method for helping students learn English is through technology support. Visit the "Spotlight on Technology" to learn about software programs that teach English skills and skills in many other languages.

Teaching Content Area Subjects

Building English vocabulary continues to be a concern when teaching content area subjects. The sheltered English approach (e.g., Echevarria & Graves, 2007) incorporates the teaching of English language skills within instruction related to specific content-area knowledge (California Teachers of English to Speakers of Other Languages, 1992; Hoover & Patton, 2005; Northcutt & Watson, 1986). To do this, the teacher analyzes the content of the lesson to identify key concepts and vocabulary. Then, he or she systematically teaches those concepts and vocabulary by using instructional techniques designed to maximize students' ability to comprehend English language input (Krashen, 1987). These techniques

Teaching Content Subjects using Sheltered English

Echevarria (1995) suggested that teachers follow six steps when presenting sheltered English instruction to English learners.

1. *Target vocabulary.* Select several terms or words critical to the lesson. Define those words at the outset of the lesson and keep them posted for visual reference for the students. The vocabulary then becomes part of a word bank to which words are continually added. As previous lessons are built upon, the word banks serve to orient students and create a context for greater understanding.

2. *Select a main concept.* Most chapters or lessons can be summarized by one or two key concepts. Focus on the main concept, with the lesson's goal being attainment of that concept. Chapter readings can be outlined or reduced to manageable parts, making the content more comprehensible. A unit of study is more valuable when students fully understand the main ideas and have developed the related academic vocabulary rather than covering every detail with only a cursory understanding.

3. *Create a context.* This is where the teacher's creativity is put to work. Anything and everything should be used to provide a context for the information to make it more understandable: visuals, sketches on an overhead, gestures, real objects (realia), facial expressions, props, manipulatives, bulletin boards, and the like. Demonstrate what the book is talking about; provide the students with the requisite experiences to add meaning to the topic. If they have difficulty understanding the story's reference to a phrase like "Her attitude

was as sour as a lemon," give them the experience of tasting a lemon; if the lesson involves learning the name and function of the teeth, give each child a slice of apple to test out the function of each tooth (e.g., incisor cuts and bicuspid crushes).

4. *Make connections.* Provide the students with opportunities to relate their background experiences to the topic at hand. The teacher may need to facilitate this process by asking probing questions and then relating the students' comments to the topic. Being able to identify with the topic makes instruction more meaningful to students.

5. *Check for understanding.* Second-language learners require repetition, clarification, and elaboration. Check frequently for understanding by reviewing target vocabulary and concepts. Use different types of questions to elicit responses and assess understanding in a variety of ways. Above all, maintain a supportive atmosphere in which students are comfortable asking for clarification and participating in the lesson.

6. *Encourage Student-to-Student Interaction.* Because sheltered instruction is highly interactive in nature, it provides students with an optimum opportunity to practice the language they are acquiring. Planning needs to include cooperative activities and projects that group native speakers of English with non-native speakers. For example, partners might work together with a globe to locate specific areas. Cooperative groups might complete a worksheet together, or small groups might plan and execute role playing of the topic.

Note: From "Sheltered Instruction for Students with Learning Disabilities Who Have Limited English Proficiency" by J. Echevarria, 1995, *Intervention in School and Clinic, 30,* p. 303. Copyright 1995 by PRO-ED, Inc. Reprinted by permission.

---

include linking new information to students' background knowledge; use of clear, consistent language with many repetitions; and incorporation of extralingual cues such as visual aids, media, props, realia (i.e., real objects), demonstrations, dramatizations, and so forth (Freeman & Freeman, 1988; Gersten & Jiménez, 1998; Ratleff, 1989; Towell & Wink, 1993). If the teacher or aide speaks the language of the student, key concepts can be pretaught in that language prior to the start of the lesson.

The "Inclusion Tips for the Teacher" section presents recommendations for using sheltered English techniques in the teaching of content area subjects. Note that the first step is identification of target vocabulary.

A similar approach is SDAIE or Specially Designed Academic Instruction in English. In discussing this approach, Díaz-Rico (2004) commented that SADAIE teachers focus instruction on content subject objectives, support development of academic English language skills through the use of visual cues and props, and simplify their oral language so that English learners can understand them better.

Echevarria and Graves (2007) also suggest that teachers modify their own oral language when working with English learners. Among their recommendations are controlling sentence length and complexity, speaking at a slower rate with clear enunciation, avoiding idioms, and choosing high-frequency vocabulary when that is feasible. Also, student participation should be encouraged; the teacher's voice should not be the only one that is heard. Figure 18-4 contains two versions of the same lesson, the first taught in a traditional approach and the second using sheltered English. Compare the versions to determine the ratio of teacher to student talk in each.

A recent study (Shyyan, Thurlow, & Liu, 2008) asked both teachers and English learners to share their view on the importance of various instructional strategies for learning the content area of science. The strategies rated as most important by teachers were hands-on, active participation; using visuals; and using pictures to demonstrate steps (e.g., in an experiment). Students agreed with one of these: the use of visuals. Students, however, also identified these strategies as

[Traditional] Mainstream Lesson

Teacher: Look at the piece of clothing at the bottom. It says (*he reads*), "This shirt is flame-resistant," which means what?

Student: Could not burn.

Student: Won't catch fire.

Teacher: It will not burn, won't catch fire. Right. (*Continues reading.*) "To retain the flame-resistant properties"—what does it mean "to retain"?

Student: (*unintelligible*)

Teacher: To keep it. All right. "In order to keep this shirt flame-resistant (*he reads*), wash with detergent only." All right (*he reads*). "Do not use soap or bleach. Tumble dry. One hundred percent polyester." Now, why does it say, "Do not use soap or bleach"?

Student: 'Cause it will take off the . . .

Teacher: It'll take off the what?

Students: (*fragmented responses*)

Teacher: It'll take off the flame-resistant quality. If you wash it with soap or bleach, then the shirt's just gonna be like any old shirt, any regular shirt, so when you put a match to it, will it catch fire?

Student: No.

Teacher: Yes. 'Cause you've ruined it then. It's no longer flame resistant. So the government says you gotta tell the consumer what kind of shirt it is and how to take care of it. If you look at any piece of clothing: shirt—it doesn't come on your underwear or your socks—but on your pants, your shirts, um, your skirts, anything. There's always going to be a tag on these that says what it is made of and how you're going to take care of it. OK. And that's for your protection so you won't buy something and then treat it wrong. So labeling is important.

Sheltered Instruction

Teacher: Most clothing must have labels that tell what kind of cloth was used in it, right? Look at the material in the picture down there (*points to picture in text*). What does it say, the tag right there?

Student: The, the, the. . .

Teacher: The tag right there.

Student: Flame-resis. . .

Teacher: Resistant.

Student: Flame-resistant. To retain the flame-resistant properties, wash with detergent only. Do not use soap or bleach. Use warm water. Tumble dry.

Teacher: One hundred percent.

Student: Polyester.

Teacher: Now, most clothes carry labels, right (*pointing to the neck of her sweater*), explaining how to take care of it, like dry clean, machine wash, right? Why does this product have to be washed with a detergent and no soap or bleach?

Student: Because clothes. . .

Teacher: Why can't you use something else?

Students: (*Several students mumble answers.*)

Student: (*says in Spanish*) Because it will make it small . . .

Teacher: It may shrink, or (*gestures to a student*) it may not be . . . what does it say?

Student: It's not going to be able to be resistant to fire.

Teacher: Exactly. It's flame resistant, right? So if you use something else, it won't be flame resistant any more.

Note: J. Echevarria and A. Graves, *Sheltered Content Instruction, 3e*, "One Lesson Taught In Two Ways: Traditional versus Sheltered English", (adapted from pp. 153-155). Copyright © 2007. Reproduced by permission of Pearson Education, Inc.

important: preteaching vocabulary, peer tutoring, and teaching students how to find the main idea. Visuals were chosen as the most used and the most feasible strategy by teachers.

In summary, this chapter and the other chapters in this book have discussed and described the wonders and the challenges that diversity brings to a classroom. That diversity includes students with identified disabilities, those with special gifts and talents, and those whose language or culture may diverge from that of the school and community. The "Things to Remember" section reviews the main points of this chapter. The major points of this book—that diversity is good and inclusion should be part of the everyday fabric of our lives—can be summed up in this description of the 2009 inauguration of President Barack Obama:

The president's elderly stepgrandmother brought him an oxtail fly whisk, a mark of power at home in Kenya. Cousins journeyed from the South Carolina town where the first lady's great-great-grandfather was born into slavery, while the rabbi in the family came from the synagogue where he had been commemorating Martin Luther King's Birthday. The president and first lady's siblings were there, too, of course: his Indonesian-American half-sister, who brought her Chinese-Canadian husband, and her brother, a black man with a white wife. . .

For well over two centuries, the United States has been vastly more diverse than its ruling families. Now the Obama family has flipped that around, with a Technicolor cast that looks almost nothing like their overwhelmingly white, overwhelmingly Protestant predecessors in the role. The family that produced Barack and Michelle Obama is black and white and Asian, Christian, Muslim and Jewish. They speak English; Indonesian; French; Cantonese; German; Hebrew; African languages including Swahili, Luo and Igbo; and even a few phrases of Gullah, the Creole dialect of the South Carolina Lowcountry. Very few are wealthy, and some—like Sarah Obama, the stepgrandmother who only recently got electricity and running water in her metal-roofed shack—are quite poor (Kantor, 2009).*

Things to Remember

- English learners come to school speaking the family's heritage language; they may know little, some, or no English.

- In U.S. schools, more than 350 languages other than English are spoken by students.

- When languages other than English are spoken at home, families take part in home language surveys or interviews to help schools understand students' language prowess in English and the heritage language or languages.

- Proficiency in a language must include both basic interpersonal communication skills and cognitive/academic learning proficiency.

- The most common program option today for English learners is sheltered instruction; bilingual education programs have become less popular, in part because of the increase in the number of languages spoken in any one school.

- The principles of culturally responsive instruction apply to the education of English learners and to that of their general education peers.

- Effective instruction for English learners shares the same characteristics as effective instruction for all students; however, teachers must also make adaptations because of students' needs in the area of English language learning.

- Strategies for building English vocabulary include teaching vocabulary directly; providing opportunities for practice; techniques such as gesturing, the use of visuals and real objects, and modeling and demonstrations; and in the first stages of language learning, allowing students to respond by pointing, drawing, or some other non-verbal technique.

- In sheltered English, the teacher provides instruction in a content area subject in English; to aid the students' comprehension of English, the teacher activates background knowledge, uses clear and consistent language, and incorporates cues such as visual aids.

- Students who are English learners add to the wonders and challenges that diversity brings to a classroom. Instruction that is responsive to diversity honors its value while meeting students' individual needs.

ACTIVITIES

1. Observe in a classroom where some of the students are English learners. What techniques does the teacher use to make English more comprehensible to these students? How well do the English learners attend to instruction? Do they participate in classroom discussions as much as their peers?

2. Review the brief case study in Figure 18-2 about the five-year-old who is entering school with some English skills. Explain the differences between basic interpersonal communication skills and cognitive/academic learning proficiency for this child. Give examples of some of the academic words and phrases that might prove difficult for this English learner.

3. Review Figure 18-4 and the two methods of teaching the same lesson. Critique the traditional lesson, explaining how that lesson could be improved. Also critique the sheltered English lesson, pointing out what the teacher did right.

4. Contact a local school district to find out what languages are spoken by students in that district. Also investigate the programs offered to students who enter school as English learners. Compare your results with those of a classmate who studied a different district.

5. Write a brief paper describing your philosophy of inclusion. You may choose to discuss inclusion in relation to education or in a broader context. Be sure to include your ideas about diversity.

GLOSSARY

504 accommodation plan. A plan for educational adaptations within the general education classroom for students found eligible under Section 504 of the Rehabilitation Act rather than IDEA.

Academic problems. Difficulties encountered in the acquisition, maintenance, and generalization of basic school skills and content-area subjects.

Acceleration. Progress through the curriculum at an increased rate.

Access. Ease of entry to and travel from place to place within a building or location.

Acquisition. The initial learning of information or skills.

Adapted physical education teacher. A specialist who modifies physical education instruction to meet the needs of students with special needs.

Adaptive behavior. The individual's ability to change in order to cope with the demands of the environment; also called *social competence.*

Advance organizers. Information presented to students prior to an instructional task as a preview or overview.

Adventitious. Acquired after birth, often as a result of illness or accident.

Algorithm. A procedure used to perform an operation in mathematics.

Amplification device. Anything that increases the volume of sound.

Antecedent. The event or condition that occurs immediately before a behavior of interest. See also *Consequence.*

Application. In technology, a program that runs on a computer or other device.

Applied behavior analysis. A system for the understanding and improvement of human behavior focusing on objectively defined and measurable behaviors of social significance.

Architectural barriers. Obstructions in the physical environment that prevent access.

Asperger's syndrome. A disorder characterized by qualitative impairments in social interaction and restrictive or repetitive patterns of behavior without significant delays in cognitive development or adaptive behavior other than social interaction.

Assessment team. Required by federal law, the purpose of this team is determining whether students meet eligibility requirements for special education services.

Assessment. The process by which information is gathered about students in order to make educational decisions.

Assistive technology specialist. Individual responsible for advising the team serving students with special needs regarding the selection, acquisition, or use of assistive technology devices that can increase, maintain, or improve the functional capabilities of students with a disability.

Assistive technology. Any technology designed specifically for individuals with disabilities; includes add-ons to computer systems and stand-alone devices.

Attention deficit hyperactivity disorder (ADHD). A term used in psychiatric classification systems to describe individuals who show poor attention, impulsivity, and sometimes hyperactivity.

Audiologist. A specialist trained in the evaluation and remediation of hearing losses.

Audiometer. A device to assess hearing ability.

Auditory training. Instruction to improve listening skills by teaching individuals with hearing impairments to use as much of their residual hearing as possible.

Augmentative communication. Any system or device designed to enhance the communication abilities of individuals who are nonverbal or whose speech is difficult to understand.

Autism spectrum disorder. A pervasive developmental disorder with qualitative impairments in communication, social interaction, and restrictive or repetitive patterns of behavior that first occur prior to age 3.

Autism. See *Autism spectrum disorder.*

Automaticity. In skill learning, the ability to perform a skill both accurately and quickly without thought.

Baseline data. Information collected about a behavior before an intervention is implemented.

Basic skills. The "tool" subjects of listening, speaking, reading, writing, spelling, and mathematics.

Behavioral disorder. A disability in which students are characterized by inappropriate school behavior.

Behavioral intervention plan (BIP). Also called a *positive behavioral support plan,* this plan describes the positive interventions and supports to be provided to students with behaviors that interfere with their own or others' learning.

Behavioral support. Refers to strategies for manipulating the instructional environment to encourage appropriate behavior; a modern term for *behavior management.*

Bilingual education. Programs emphasizing both the language of the home and English.

Bipolar disorder. A psychiatric disorder characterized by severe changes in mood and behavior.

Blind. A legal designation, often with little educational relevance, that indicates (1) visual acuity of 20/200 or less in the better eye with the best possible correction or (2) a field of vision restricted to an angle subtending an arc of 20 degrees or less.

Blindness. The condition in which so little information is received through the eye that other senses must be used for learning.

Blog. An online journal; also called a *web log.*

Braille. A system of raised dots that can be decoded by touch.

Bullying. Behavior in which one student threatens or attempts to intimidate another.

Captioned film. A film adapted for viewers who are deaf; dialogue appears in print superimposed on the screen.

Career education. Instruction in the application of basic skills and content-area information to problems of daily life, independent living, and vocational independence.

Cerebral palsy. A motor impairment due to damage to the brain, usually occurring before, during, or shortly following birth.

Choral responding. An instructional technique in which groups of students answer the teacher's question in unison.

Classroom conduct problems. Inappropriate school behaviors that interfere with classroom instruction, impede social interaction with teachers and peers, or endanger others.

Clinical teaching. An instructional technique in which data are gathered both before and during the implementation of an intervention in order to evaluate the effectiveness of that intervention.

Cloze procedure. A method used to determine whether reading material is appropriate for a particular student.

Cochlear implant. An amplification device that uses electrodes surgically inserted in the inner ear and other hearing-aid-type components that pick up and transmit sound to the electrodes.

Code-emphasis approach. An approach to reading instruction in which decoding skills are taught first, then comprehension skills.

Cognitive training. The behavior change method that attempts to teach students new thinking strategies for controlling their own behavior.

Compensation. The instructional technique in which a student's weaknesses are bypassed.

Conductive hearing loss. A hearing loss caused by damage or disease in the outer or middle ear.

Congenital. Present at birth.

Consequence. The event or condition that occurs after a behavior of interest. See also *Antecedent*.

Content-area subjects. Bodies of knowledge in the academic curriculum; for example, English and other languages, the sciences, mathematics, and the social sciences.

Contingency contract. A written agreement between a student and a teacher that states what the student must do to earn a specific reward.

Cooperative learning. The instructional model in which students work together as a team to complete activities or assignments (in contrast to competitive learning, in which each student works alone).

Correction procedure. The instructional technique of making students aware of errors, then helping them produce correct responses.

Creativity tool. A type of computer program that aids in the design, development, and presentation of creative products including those in art, music, video, and website design.

Creativity. The process of generating novel solutions or products.

Criterion-referenced test. An informal assessment device that measures whether students have mastered the educational goals stated in instructional objectives.

Culturally and linguistically diverse students. Students whose home cultures (and perhaps languages) differ from that of the school. Such students may require special assistance to succeed in general education.

Culturally responsive instruction. Instruction designed to meet the needs of students from culturally diverse backgrounds.

Culture. A subgroup of the population that shares beliefs, values, practices, and language.

Curriculum compacting. Eliminating instruction on content or skills already mastered so that gifted students can move to more challenging material.

Curriculum-based assessment. The use of current classroom performance as the basis for determining students' educational needs.

Curriculum-based measurement. A type of curriculum-based assessment in which the teacher takes frequent, brief samples of student performance in important skill areas to evaluate progress toward curricular goals. See also *Curriculum-based assessment*.

Database program. A type of computer program that facilitates the storage of information and its retrieval.

Deaf. See *Deafness*.

Deafness. The condition in which so little information is received through the sense of hearing that other senses must be used for learning.

Delicious. A web-based storage area for online bookmarks where users can add tags to describe each website.

Demonstration. The instructional procedure in which a new skill is modeled.

Diabetes. A disorder of metabolism.

Differentiated instruction. Instruction within the general education setting that is varied to meet the needs of different learners.

Differentiation. Providing services different from those offered in the general program; see also *Differentiated instruction*.

Direct teaching. The teacher's demonstration of appropriate strategies for the performance of a learning task, encouragement of maximal student response opportunities, and provision of frequent systematic feedback on task performance; also called *direct instruction* or *active teaching*.

Discovery learning. An instructional technique in which the teacher presents students with opportunities for learning; skills are not taught directly.

Distractibility. Difficulty in maintaining attention.

Divergent thinking. The production of several solutions to one problem.

Duration recording. The system of recording observation data in which the length of time a behavior occurs is noted.

Dysfluency. Difficulty in the production of fluent, rhythmic speech; for example, stuttering.

Early interventionist. A specialist who provides educational services to infants, toddlers, and preschoolers with special needs and to the families of these children. These services may be provided in the home, school, or other settings.

Educationally blind. Having vision impaired to the extent that tactile or auditory materials must be used for reading.

E-mail mailing list. An electronic mailing list to which a user subscribes to receive e-mail messages related to a specific topic.

E-mail. Electronic mail; the type of mail sent over the Internet.

Engaged time. The actual time during which students are actively involved and participating in instruction.

English learner. An individual who is learning English as his or her second or subsequent language. Also called *English language learner*.

Enrichment. The instructional technique in which something is added to the regular school program in order to enrich it.

Epilepsy. A convulsive disorder of the central nervous system.

Error analysis. The technique in which student work samples are studied for patterns of errors.

E-text. Electronic text such as books downloadable from the Internet.

Ethnic group. A group that shares a common ancestry or native country.

Etiology. Cause.

Event recording. The system of recording observation data in which the number of times a behavior occurs is noted.

Explicit instruction. Systematic and specific instruction in the knowledge or skill area the student is expected to acquire. See also *Direct teaching*.

Extinction. A procedure used to decrease the occurrence of a behavior by removing reinforcers that have previously followed the behavior.

Flexible grouping. A method of instructional grouping in which arrangements of students change frequently and placement decisions are based on a variety of criteria (e.g., skills, interests, proximity).

Flickr. A web-based storage area for still photos where users can add tags to describe each photo.

Fluency. The ability to perform a skill quickly and accurately.

Full inclusion. Full-time integration in general education classrooms of all students with special needs, regardless of the severity of their disabilities. See also *Inclusion*.

Functional behavioral assessment. A systematic process designed to collect data to help educators (1) understand a problem behavior and (2) develop effective methods for modifying the behavior.

Functional skills. Important skills selected for instruction because of their usefulness in everyday life.

Generalization. The application or transfer of learned material to similar situations and problems.

Gifted and talented students. Students with exceptional potential or ability in intellectual, academic, leadership, creative, or artistic domains and who require specialized services to realize their potential.

Giftedness. Superior intellect; it can be accompanied by creative ability.

Grouping. Bringing gifted students together for instruction; can be within a general education classroom or specialized setting.

Guided practice. The performance of a task under supervision; feedback, correction, and confirmation are immediate.

Habilitation. The instructional approach directed toward the development of the critical skills necessary for successful adulthood.

Hard of hearing. Characterized by a condition in which hearing, although impaired, can be used as one of the senses for learning.

Hearing impairment. A disability characterized by a decrease in the ability to hear. See also *Deafness* and *Hard of hearing*.

Heritage language. The language of the student's family and cultural group.

Heterogeneous grouping. A method of instructional grouping that places together students whose instructional needs are somehow dissimilar.

High interest–low vocabulary. Reading materials that appeal to students who read at a lower grade level than that expected for their age.

Hyperactivity. Excessive activity.

Idea processor. A type of computer program that assists in the generation and manipulation of ideas.

Impulsivity. Lack of reflectivity; activity without careful thought and reflection.

Inclusion. Meaningful participation of students with special needs in general education classrooms and programs.

Independent practice. The performance of a skill without supervision; feedback is delayed.

Individualized Education Program (IEP) team. Required by federal law, the purpose of this team is development and monitoring of the instructional plan for students receiving special education services.

Individualized Education Program (IEP). A written educational plan that specifies the current levels of educational performance and annual goals for a student with a disability; prepared by a team that includes the student's parent(s), teacher(s), and, if appropriate, the student.

Individualized instruction. Instruction designed to meet the needs of each student; it can be group instruction or tutorial as long as a high proportion of correct responses is maintained.

Informal assessment. The process of gathering information about students with measures and techniques such as inventories, criterion-referenced tests, and observation; teachers often design their own informal assessment strategies.

Informal reading inventory. An informal assessment device that aids in determining a student's instructional reading level.

Information processing. The method by which persons receive, store, and express information; also called *psychological processing*.

Instruction. The teaching process. See also *Direct teaching* and *Individualized instruction*.

Instructional environment. In the context of the classroom, the procedures, materials, and equipment used by the teacher to increase student performance.

Instructional unit. See *Unit approach*.

Intellectual disability. A disability characterized by comprehensive learning problems due to subaverage general intellectual functioning and deficits in adaptive behavior; a modern term for *mental retardation*.

Internet. A worldwide computer network that includes e-mail, the World Wide Web, and other resources.

Interval recording. The system of recording observation data in which the occurrence or nonoccurrence of a behavior within a specific time interval is noted.

Inventory. An informal assessment device that samples a variety of skills within a subject matter area; for example, an informal reading inventory.

Itinerant teacher. A professional who travels from school to school rather than providing instruction at one school site.

Knowledge of results. Information provided to students about the accuracy of their responses.

Language. The ability to communicate using symbols.

Learning center. An area of the classroom designed for use of self-instructional materials for independent practice.

Learning disability. A disorder in the ability to process information that can result in attention, perception, or memory deficits. Students with learning disabilities experience difficulty in school learning despite adequate hearing, vision, and intelligence.

Learning strategies. Methods students use to acquire, rehearse, organize, and recall information.

Least Restrictive Environment (LRE). The most appropriate educational placement that is closest to general education.

Low vision. The condition in which vision, although impaired, can be used as one of the senses for learning.

Low-vision aid. Any device that aids vision by magnification.

Mainstreaming. The inclusion of students with special needs in the general educational program for any part of the school day. See also *Inclusion*.

Maintenance. The recall of information previously learned.

Meaning-emphasis approach. An approach to reading instruction in which decoding skills are taught with common words and comprehension is emphasized from the start.

Mediated instruction. Any instructional procedure that includes the use of media.

Medically fragile. Students with a chronic medical condition that requires ongoing medical management and accommodation during the school day.

Mental retardation. See *Intellectual disability.*

Mobility. The ability to move from place to place.

Modeling. The reinforcement of another individual, the model, for exhibiting the desired behavior in the presence of the target student. When the target student imitates the desired behavior, he or she is then reinforced.

Multicultural education. The instructional approach that emphasizes the value of diverse cultures.

Narrative recording. A system of observation in which the observer describes all behaviors that occur.

Negative attention. Use of a negative verbal or nonverbal response (e.g., "Stop" or a frown) that indicates disapproval of a student's behavior. The procedure attempts to reduce the behavior quickly without interfering with ongoing classroom activities.

Negative reinforcement. A procedure used to increase the occurrence of a behavior by following it with the removal of an aversive event or condition.

NIMAS. Required by law, the National Instructional Materials Accessibility Standard mandates that print instructional materials for students with disabilities be available in accessible formats.

Norm-referenced test. A test designed to compare the performance of one student with that of students in the norm group of the same age or grade; used to determine whether students have significant problems in relation to peers.

Occupational therapist. A specialist who provides therapy and instruction to students with motor disabilities.

Orientation. The determination of one's position in space, especially in relation to objects or reference points in the environment.

Partially sighted. Having vision that is impaired but can be used as one of the senses for learning.

Peer tutor. A student who provides instruction to another student.

Permanent product recording. The system of recording observation data in which permanent products (such as written assignments, videotapes, and audiotapes) are evaluated.

Personal digital assistant. A small handheld device used to store, organize, and retrieve information electronically.

Phonics. The word recognition strategy in which print letters (graphemes) are converted to letter sounds (phonemes).

Phonological awareness. The ability to recognize individual sounds within words.

Phonology. The sound system of language.

Physical and health impairments. Physical disabilities and medical conditions that result in chronic health problems.

Physical environment. In the context of the school, the classroom and its furnishings.

Physical therapist. A specialist who provides treatment under the supervision of a physician to students with motor disabilities.

Podcast. A series of audio or video files recorded about one topic or subject.

Portfolio assessment. The process of gathering information about students by assembling samples of their work over time.

Positive reinforcement. A procedure used to increase the occurrence of a behavior by following it with a pleasant or positive event.

Practice. The performance of a learned skill. See also *Guided practice* and *Independent practice.*

Pragmatics. The use of language; language within the context of communication.

Premack principle. The practice of providing a reinforcement after the completion of a less desired task; for example, if Joan takes out the garbage, then she may watch television.

Prereferral intervention team. The purpose of this team is to assist educators to solve instructional and behavioral problems within the general education classroom.

Prereferral interventions. Modifications to the general education program designed to promote a student's success in the regular classroom and prevent referral for services such as special education.

Presentation tool. A type of computer program used to share information with audiences via slides, other visuals, and sometimes sound.

Problem solving. The process of attempting to resolve a question or problem.

Problem-based learning. Instructional strategy engaging students in problem identification, inquiry/research, and problem solving based on a real or realistic scenario.

Program modifications and/or supports for school personnel. One of the types of service available to students with IEPs; includes any change made in the general education program to support the successful progress of a student with disabilities; also include services provided to teachers and other school employees, rather than to students.

Programmed instruction. A method of instruction in which learners progress at their own pace through small incremental steps that provide immediate feedback about response accuracy.

Prompt. Any feature added to learning tasks that assists students in task performance. Prompts can be verbal, visual, or physical.

Psychosis. A type of emotional disturbance characterized by lack of contact with reality.

Punishment. A procedure used to decrease the occurrence of a behavior by following it with the presentation of an aversive event.

Race. A social construction that relates to a person's family origins; among the racial categories recognized in the U.S. Census are American Indian or Alaska Native, Asian, Black or African American, Native Hawaiian or Other Pacific Islander, and White.

Readability measure. A method of determining the reading level of a given material.

Reading fluency. The ability to read quickly and accurately.

Reciprocal teaching. An approach to teaching reading comprehension skills in which teachers engage students in dialogues about texts.

Referral. The process by which a student is identified for study; it can result in consideration for special education services.

Reinforcement menu. A listing of reinforcers and the number of points or tokens needed to purchase each; it is used in a token economy system.

Reinforcement. Anything that increases the probability of occurrence of a behavior. See also *Negative reinforcement* and *Positive reinforcement.*

Related services. Auxiliary services such as psychological services for assessment, transportation, or physical therapy that are available to help students with disabilities derive maximum benefit from special education.

Remediation. The instructional approach that focuses on correcting the weaknesses of the student.

Repeated readings. An instructional technique in which students read a passage several times to increase comprehension.

Resource room. A service arrangement in which special education is provided to students for a portion of the school day. Typically the student is placed in a general education classroom and visits the resource room only for short periods.

Respite. A coping strategy used by individuals with disabilities after they have exerted a great deal of energy and need to withdraw temporarily.

Response cost. A mild form of punishment in which an inappropriate behavior is followed by the loss or withdrawal of earned reinforcers or privileges.

Response-to-intervention (RTI). An approach to identification of students for special education services which looks at how well students progress in the school curriculum when presented with high-quality instruction.

Rubric. An assessment tool for evaluating curricular progress; provides brief descriptions of student performance at various levels.

Scanning. In technology, the process by which a user looks at a set of choices, then selects one; the first selection may lead to another set of choices as, for example, when pressing the number 4 on a phone leads to a choice of the letters G, H, and I.

Schoolwide positive behavior supports. An approach to school discipline which attempts to prevent problems or identify them quickly and offer interventions.

Screening. A method for gathering information about large number of persons to identify those who may be in need of further study.

Seizure. The loss or alteration of consciousness due to a convulsive disorder.

Self-correcting materials. Instructional materials that provide the student with the correct response so that answers can be checked for accuracy.

Self-instruction. A procedure in which students learn specific strategies to talk themselves through problem situations.

Self-monitoring. Observing, recording, and evaluating one's own behavior; for example, students might observe/record the number of times they leave their chairs, graph the data, and then review the graph daily to determine whether they are improving.

Semantics. The aspects of language related to meaning.

Sensorineural hearing loss. A hearing loss caused by impairment of the auditory nerve.

Sequence analysis. A system of observation in which the observer describes each behavior and attempts to identify its antecedent and consequence.

Shaping. The reinforcement of successive approximations or small progressive steps toward a desired behavior.

Sheltered English. A teaching technique for students learning English in which content-area lessons include systematic instruction in English language skills.

Sign language. The system of manual communication in which gestures express thoughts.

Skill-specific group. A homogeneous instructional group made up of students who require instruction in the same area.

Snellen chart. A measure used in screening for visual acuity problems.

Social networking sites. Web-based sites designed to promote social interactions among users.

Sociometric measure. An assessment device used to determine how students perceive their peers.

Special class. A service arrangement in which students with special needs are grouped together in a self-contained class; students may leave the special class for short periods to participate in general education activities.

Special education. Instruction that is specially designed to meet the unique educational needs of students with disabilities.

Special educator. A professional educator trained to meet the instructional needs of students with special needs; usually an educator who serves students with disabilities or gifted and talented students.

Speech and language impairments. Disabilities characterized by deficits in speech, receptive language, and/or expressive language.

Speech. The vehicle by which thoughts are expressed in oral communication.

Speech–language pathologist. A specialist who serves students with speech and language impairments.

Speechreading. The process of decoding speech by watching the speaker's face.

Spreadsheet. A type of computer program used to manipulate and analyze numerical information.

Students at risk for school failure. General education students who show poor achievement and/or are likely to drop out of school.

Students with disabilities. Students with special learning needs due to physical, sensory, cognitive, or emotional impairments. Included are students with learning disabilities, intellectual disabilities, behavioral disorders, speech and language impairments, physical and health impairments, vision impairments, hearing impairments, autism spectrum disorder, traumatic brain injury, and multiple disabilities.

Students with special needs. Those students who require instructional adaptations in order to learn successfully; includes students with disabilities, gifted and talented students, culturally and linguistically diverse students, and students at risk for school failure.

Study skill problems. Inappropriate classroom behaviors that interfere with the student's own academic performance or with the teacher's ability to assess academic progress.

Substance abuse. The voluntary intake of chemicals (e.g., alcohol, narcotics) that can produce adverse social and physical consequences.

Supplementary aids and services. Supports provided to students with disabilities to enable them to participate in general education programs.

Syntax. The grammatical aspects of language.

Talented. Having a special ability in an area such as music or leadership.

Task analysis. The process of breaking down a task into smaller subtasks.

Technology. See *Assistive technology*.

Text messaging. Sending and receiving information in text format via a device such as a cell phone.

Thematic unit. A method of organizing the curriculum by themes; also called *instructional unit* when those themes address important life skills.

Tiering assignments. Differentiation strategy that matches task to student readiness level while enabling all students to achieve the general content goal.

Time management. The organization and scheduling of time for its most effective use.

Time-out. A mild form of punishment in which either the individual is removed from an event that is reinforcing or reinforcement is withdrawn for a specified period of time.

Token economy. A behavior change system in which students are presented with tokens rather than reinforcers after the occurrence of a desired behavior; the tokens can be cashed in for reinforcers at a later time.

Total communication. A method of communication combining oral techniques (speech and speechreading) and manual techniques (fingerspelling and sign language).

Transition. Process of preparing students to meet the challenges of adulthood including those involved in postsecondary education, vocational pursuits, and home and community.

Traumatic brain injury. A disability caused by injury or accident involving damage to the brain.

Twitter. A web-based communication system in which users send and receive brief text messages.

Unilateral hearing loss. A condition involving only one ear, the other ear having no hearing loss.

Unit approach. A method of organizing the curriculum by important life themes.

Universal design. The principle by which all environments are designed for all users, including those with disabilities.

Universal precautions. Procedures recommended for use when handling blood or other bodily fluids to prevent spread of infection.

Vigilance. A coping strategy used by individuals with disabilities when they want to sustain a high level of energy for a long period of time.

Visual impairment. A limitation in the ability to see.

Vocational rehabilitation counselor. A specialist who assists individuals with disabilities in obtaining employment.

Volunteer. A classroom assistant from the community.

Web-based conferencing. Real-time conferencing over the World Wide Web; usually video-based but can be sound-based only.

Wikipedia. A web-based encyclopedia where content is provided by site users.

Word processor. A type of computer program that facilitates written composition by making it easy to manipulate text.

World Wide Web (WWW). That portion of the Internet in which information is presented not only in text but also in graphics; audio, video, and other multimedia features are sometimes available.

YouTube. A web-based storage area for videos where users can add tags to describe the contents of each video.

REFERENCES

Abramowitz, A. J., & O'Leary, S. G. (1991). Behavior interventions for the classroom: Implications for students with ADHD. *School Psychology Review, 20,* 221–235.

Adams, G., & Carnine, D. (2003). Direct instruction. In H. L. Swanson, K. R. Harris, & S. Graham (Eds.), *Handbook of learning disabilities* (pp. 403–416). New York: Guilford Press.

Adamson, L. B., & Chance, S. E. (1998). Coordinating attention to people, objects & language. In A. M. Wetherby, S. F. Warren, & J. Reichle, (Eds.), *Transitions in prelinguistic communication* (pp. 15–37). Baltimore: Brookes.

Adelson, R. (2004). Instruction versus exploration in science learning. *Monitor on Psychology, 35*(6), 34–36.

Affleck, J. Q., Lowenbraun, S., & Archer, A. L. (1980). *Teaching the mildly handicapped in the regular classroom* (2nd ed.). Columbus, OH: Merrill/Prentice Hall.

Aiello, B. (1979). Hey, what's it like to be handicapped? *Education Unlimited, 1*(2), 28–31.

Airasian, P. W. (1996). *Assessment in the classroom.* New York: McGraw-Hill.

Alberto, P. A., & Troutman, A. C. (2006). *Applied behavior analysis for teachers* (7th ed.). Columbus, OH: Prentice Hall.

Algozzine, B., Christenson, S. L., & Ysseldyke, J. E. (1982). Probabilities associated with the referral to placement process. *Teacher Education and Special Education, 5*(3), 19–23.

Alliance for Technology Access. (n.d.). *Web accessibility.* Retrieved June 7, 2007, from http://www.ataccess.org/rresources/webaccess.html

Allsopp, D. H., Santos, K. E., & Linn, R. (2000). Collaborating to teach prosocial skills. *Intervention in School and Clinic, 35,* 141–146.

Altieri, J. L. (2008). Fictional characters with dyslexia: What are we seeing in books? *Teaching Exceptional Children, 41*(1), 48–54.

Alves, A. J., & Gottlieb, J. (1986). Teacher interactions with mainstreamed handicapped students and their nonhandicapped peers. *Learning Disability Quarterly, 9,* 77–83.

America 2000. (1990). Washington, DC: U.S. Department of Education.

America by the numbers. (2006, October 30). *Time, 168*(18), 41–54.

American Association of Colleges for Teacher Education, Commission on Multicultural Education. (1973). No one model American. *Journal of Teacher Education, 24,* 264–265.

American Association on Mental Retardation. (2002). *Mental retardation: Definition, classification, and systems of support* (10th ed.). Washington, DC: Author.

American Federation of Teachers. (2009). *A call for national standards.* Retrieved November 27, 2009 from http://www.aft.org/topics/sbr/index.htm

American Psychiatric Association. (1994). *Diagnostic and statistical manual of mental disorders* (4th ed.). Washington, DC: Author.

American Psychiatric Association. (2000). *Diagnostic and statistical manual of mental disorders* (4th ed., text revision). Washington, DC: Williams & Wilkins.

American Speech-Language-Hearing Association. (1995, March). Position statement and guidelines for acoustics in educational settings. *ASHA, 37* (Suppl. 14), 15–19.

American Speech-Language-Hearing Association. (1997). *American Speech-Language-Hearing Association answers questions about stuttering.* Retrieved December 13, 1997, from http://www.asha.org/consumers/brochures/stuttering.htm

American Speech-Language-Hearing Association. (2008). *2008 Schools Survey summary report: Number and type of responses.* Rockville, MD: Author. Retrieved August 25, 2009, from http://www.asha.org/research/memberdata/2008SchoolsSurvey.htm

American Speech-Language-Hearing Association. (n.d.). *Speech and language disorders and the speech-language pathologist.* Rockville, MD: Author.

Andersen, M. L., & Taylor, H. F. (2002). *Sociology: Understanding a diverse society.* Belmont, CA: Wadsworth.

Andersen, M., Nelson, L. R., Fox, R. G., & Gruber, S. E. (1988). Integrating cooperative learning and structured learning: Effective approaches to teaching social skills. *Focus on Exceptional Children, 20*(9), 1–8.

Anderson, S. R., Taras, M., & Cannon, B. O. (1996). Teaching new skills to young children with autism. In C. Maurice, G. Green, & S. Luce (Eds.), *Behavioral intervention for young children with autism: A manual for parents and professionals* (pp. 181–193). Austin, TX: PRO-ED.

Annie E. Casey Foundation. (2008). *2008 kids count data book.* Baltimore, MD: Author.

Aragon, J. (1973). Cultural conflict and cultural diversity in education. In L. A. Bransford, L. M. Baca, & K. Lane (Eds.), *Cultural diversity and the exceptional child* (pp. 24–31). Reston, VA: The Council for Exceptional Children.

Aragon, J., & Marquez, L. (1973). Highlights of Institute on Language and Culture: Spanish-speaking component. In L. A. Bransford, L. M. Baca, & K. Lane (Eds.), *Cultural diversity and the exceptional child* (pp. 20–21). Reston, VA: The Council for Exceptional Children.

Arc, The. (2002). *Information about mental retardation and related topics.* Silver Springs, MD: Author. Retrieved September 18, 2004, from http://www.thearc.org/infomr.html

Archer, A. L. (1992). *Advanced skills for school success.* North Billerica, MA: Curriculum Associates.

Archer, A. L., & Gleason, M. M. (1989). *Design and delivery of lessons.* Paper presented at the annual meeting of the Council for Exceptional Children, San Francisco.

Archer, A. L., & Gleason, M. M. (1994). *Skills for school success.* North Billerica, MA: Curriculum Associates.

Archer, A. L., & Gleason, M. M. (1995). Skills for school success. In P. T. Cegelka & W. H. Berdine (Eds.), *Effective instruction for students with learning difficulties* (pp. 227–263). Boston: Allyn & Bacon.

Archer, A. L., Gleason, M. M., Englert, C. S., & Isaacson, S. (1995). Meeting individual instructional needs. In P. T. Cegelka & W. H. Berdine (Eds.), *Effective instruction for students with learning difficulties* (pp. 195–225). Boston: Allyn & Bacon.

Arkansas Enterprises for the Blind. (n.d.). *10 rules of courtesy to the blind.* Little Rock: Author.

Artiles, A. J., & Trent, S. C. (1994). Overrepresentation of minority students in special education: A continuing debate. *Journal of Special Education, 27,* 410–437.

Asher, S. R., & Taylor, A. R. (1981). Social outcomes of mainstreaming: Sociometric assessment and beyond. *Exceptional Education Quarterly, 1*(4), 13–30.

Ashton, T. M. (1997). *Making technology work in the inclusive classroom.* Unpublished manuscript, San Diego State University.

Ashton-Coombs, T. M., & James, H. F. (1995). Including all of us: A K–8 bibliography. *California English, 31*(2), 12–13, 26–27.

Atwood, T. (1998). *Asperger's syndrome: A guide for parents and professionals.* London: Jessica Kingsley Publishers.

Autism Society of America. (2008). *What is autism?* Retrieved June 16, 2008, from http://www.autism-society.org/site/

Axelrod, S., Hall, R. V., & Tams, A. (1972). *A comparison of common seating arrangements in the classroom.* Paper presented at the meeting of the Kansas Symposium on Behavior Analysis in Education, Lawrence.

Baca, L. M., & Almanza, E. (1991). *Language minority students with disabilities.* Reston, VA: The Council for Exceptional Children.

Bacon, E. H., & Schulz, J. B. (1991). A survey of mainstreaming practices. *Teacher Education and Special Education, 14,* 144–149.

Ballantyne, K. G., Sanderman, A. R., & Levy, J. (2008) *Educating English language learners: Building teacher capacity; Volume I, Teacher education and professional development for mainstream teachers of English language learners.* Washington, DC: National Clearinghouse for English Language Acquisition. Retrieved September 3, 2009, from http://www.ncela.gwu.edu/development/

Bank Street College of Education. (n.d.). *English language learners: Working with children for whom English is a new language.* Retrieved September 2, 2009, from http://www.bankstreet.edu/literacyguide/ell.html

Banks, J. A. (2006). *Cultural diversity and education* (5th ed.). Boston: Pearson.

Baranek, G. T., Parham, D., & Bodfish, J. W. (2005). Sensory and motor features in autism: Assessment and intervention. In F. Volkmar, R. Paul, A. Klin, & D. Cohen (Eds.), *Handbook of autism and pervasive developmental disorders* (pp. 831–857). Hoboken, NJ: John Wiley & Sons.

Barnhill, G. P. (2005). Functional behavioral assessment in schools. *Intervention in School and Clinic, 40,* 131–143.

Bauwens, J., & Hourcade, J. J. (1989). Hey, would you just LISTEN. *Teaching Exceptional Children, 21*(4), 61.

Becker, W. C., Englemann, S., & Thomas, D. R. (1975). *Teaching 2: Cognitive learning and instruction.* Chicago: Science Research Associates.

Beery, K. E., & Beery, N. A. (2004). *Developmental test of visual-motor integration* (5th ed.). Minneapolis, MN: NCS Pearson, Inc.

Beery, K. E., & Beery, N. A. (2006). *Addendum: Beery VMI adult norms.* Minneapolis, MN: NCS Pearson, Inc.

Bender, W. N., & Mathes, M. Y. (1995). Students with ADHD in the inclusive classroom: A hierarchical approach to strategy selection. *Intervention in School and Clinic, 30,* 226–234.

Berdine, W. H., & Blackhurst, A. E. (Eds.). (1981). *An introduction to special education* (2nd ed.). Boston: Little, Brown.

Berdine, W. H., & Cegelka, P. T. (1980). *Teaching the trainable retarded.* Columbus, OH: Merrill/Prentice Hall.

Berg, F. (1987). *Facilitating classroom listening: A handbook for teachers of normal and hard of hearing students.* Austin, TX: PRO-ED.

Besnoy, K. D. (2005). *Successful strategies for twice-exceptional students.* Practical strategies series in gifted education. Waco, TX: Prufrock Press.

Bess, F., Dodd-Murphy, J., & Parker, R. (1998). Children with minimal sensorineural hearing loss: Prevalence, educational performance, and functional status. *Ear and Hearing, 19,* 339–354.

Bettinger, M. M. (1989). Educating the pregnant teen. *CTA Action, 28*(2), 9.

Biddle, B. J. (1997). Foolishness, dangerous nonsense, and real correlates of state differences in achievement. *Phi Delta Kappan, 79,* 9–13.

Bigby, L. M. (2004). Medical and health-related services: More than treating boo-boos and ouchies. *Intervention in School and Clinic, 39*(4), 233–235.

Biklen, D. (1985). *Achieving the complete school.* New York: Teachers College Press.

Binkard, B. (1985). A successful handicap awareness program—run by special parents. *Teaching Exceptional Children, 18*(1), 12–16.

Blankenship, C., & Lilly, M. S. (1981). *Mainstreaming students with learning and behavior problems.* New York: Holt, Rinehart & Winston.

Bolt, S. A., & Thurlow, M. L. (2004). Five of the most frequently allowed testing accommodations in state policy: Synthesis of research. *Remedial and Special Education, 25,* 141–152.

Bondy, A., & Frost, L. (2002). *A picture's worth. PECS and other communication strategies in autism.* Bethesda, MD: Woodbine House.

Borland, J. H. (2008). Identification. In J. A. Plucker & C. M. Callahan (Eds.), *Critical issues and practices in gifted education: What the research says* (pp. 261–280). Waco, TX: Prufrock Press.

Bormuth, J. R. (1968). The cloze readability procedure. *Elementary English, 45,* 429–436.

Bossert, S. T., & Barnett, B. G. (1981). *Grouping for instruction. A catalog of arrangements.* San Francisco: Far West Laboratory for Educational Research and Development. (ERIC Document Reproduction Service No. ED-201–052)

Bowe, F. (2000). *Physical, sensory, and health disabilities: An introduction.* Upper Saddle River, NJ: Merrill/Prentice Hall.

Bower, E. M. (1969). *Early identification of emotionally handicapped children in school* (2nd ed.). Springfield, IL: Thomas.

Brady, M. P., & McEvoy, M. A. (1989). Social skills training as an integration strategy. In R. Gaylord-Ross (Ed.), *Integration strategies for students with handicaps* (pp. 213–231). Baltimore: Brookes.

Brigance, A. H. (1999). *BRIGANCE® diagnostic comprehensive inventory of basic skills—Revised.* North Billerica, MA: Curriculum Associates.

Brinker, R. P. (1985). Interactions between severely mentally retarded students and other students in integrated and segregated public school settings. *American Journal of Mental Deficiency, 89,* 587–594.

Brolin, D. E. (1986). *Life centered career education: A competency based approach* (rev. ed.). Reston, VA: The Council for Exceptional Children.

Brophy, J. E., & Good, T. L. (1986). Teacher behavior and student achievement. In M. C. Wittrock (Ed.), *Handbook of research on teaching* (3rd ed., pp. 328–375). New York: Macmillan.

Brown, J. E., & Doolittle, J. (2008). A cultural, linguistic, and ecological framework for response to intervention with English language learners. *Teaching Exceptional Children, 40*(5), 66–72.

Brown, L., & Hammill, D. D. (1990). *Behavior rating profile* (2nd ed.). Austin, TX: PRO-ED.

Brown, M. R. (2007). Educating all students: Creating culturally responsive teachers, classrooms, and schools. *Intervention in School and Clinic, 43,* 57–62.

Brown, M. S., Ilderton, P., & Taylor, A. (2001). Include a student with an attention problem in the general education classroom. *Intervention in School and Clinic, 37*(1), 50–52.

Bruininks, R. H. (1977). *Manual for the Bruininks–Oseretsky test of motor proficiency.* Circle Pines, MN: American Guidance Service.

Bruininks, R. H., Thurlow, M. L., & Gilman, C. J. (1987). Adaptive behavior and mental retardation. *Journal of Special Education, 21*(1), 69–88.

Bruininks, R. H., Woodcock, R. W., Weatherman, R. F., & Hill, B. K. (1996). *Scales of independent behavior–Revised.* Chicago: Riverside Publishing.

Bryan, T. (1997). Assessing the personal and social status of students with learning disabilities. *Learning Disabilities Research & Practice, 12,* 63–76.

Bryan, T. H., & Bryan, J. H. (1977). The social-emotional side of learning disabilities. *Behavioral Disorders, 2,* 141–145.

Bryen, D. N. (1974). Special education and the linguistically different child. *Exceptional Children, 40*(8), 589–599.

Buck, G. H., Polloway, E. A., Smith-Thomas, A., & Cook, K. W. (2003). Prereferral intervention processes: A survey of state practices. *Exceptional Children, 59,* 349–360.

Buffington, D. M., Krantz, P. J., McClannahan, L. E., & Poulson, C. L. (1998). Procedures for teaching appropriate gestural communication skills to children with autism. *Journal of Autism & Developmental Disorders, 28*(6), 535–545.

Bulgren, J. A., & Carta, J. J. (1992). Examining the instructional contexts of students with learning disabilities. *Exceptional Children, 59,* 182–191.

Burns, M. K., & Symington, T. (2002). A meta-analysis of prereferral intervention teams: Student and systemic outcomes. *Journal of School Psychology, 40,* 437–447.

Burron, A., & Claybaugh, A. L. (1977). *Basic concepts in reading instruction* (2nd ed.). Columbus, OH: Merrill/Prentice Hall.

Bush, G. W. (2001). *No child left behind.* Washington, DC: U.S. Department of Education. Retrieved June 1, 2001, from http://www.ed.gov/inits/nclb/index.html

Bushaw, W. J., & Gallup, A. M. (2008). *Americans speak out—Are educators and policy makers listening? The 40th Annual Phi Delta Kappa/Gallup Poll of the public's attitudes toward the public schools.* Retrieved July 9, 2009, from http://www.pdkintl.org/kappan/kpollpdf.htm

Byrom, E., & Katz, G. (Eds.). (1991). *HIV prevention and AIDS education: Resources for special educators.* Reston, VA: The Council for Exceptional Children.

Caffrey, E., & Fuchs, D. (2007). Differences in performance between students with learning disabilities and mild mental retardation: Implications for categorical instruction. *Learning Disabilities Research & Practice, 22*(2), 119–128.

California Governor's Committee on Employment of People with Disabilities and the Employment Development Department. (2005). *Language guide on disability* (rev. 6). Retrieved January 25, 2008, from http://www.edd.ca.gov/gcepdpub.asp

California Newsreel. (2003). *RACE—The power of an illusion.* Retrieved July 1, 2008, from http://www.pbs.org/race/

California Teachers of English to Speakers of Other Languages. (1992). *CATESOL position paper on specially-designed academic instruction in English (sheltered instruction).* Retrieved December 16, 1997, from http://www.catesol.org/shelter.html

Callins, T. (2006). Culturally responsive literacy instruction. *Teaching Exceptional Children, 39*(2), 62–65.

Campbell, N. J., Dodson, J. E., & Bost, J. M. (1985). Educator perceptions of behavior problems of mainstreamed students. *Exceptional Children, 51,* 298–303.

Campbell, P. H. (1989). Students with physical disabilities. In R. Gaylord-Ross (Ed.), *Integration strategies for students with handicaps* (pp. 53–76). Baltimore: Brookes.

Carbone, E. (2001). Arranging the classroom with an eye (and ear) to students with ADHD. *Teaching Exceptional Children, 34,* 72–81.

Carr, J. E., Nicholson, A. C., & Higbee, T. S. (2000). Evaluation of a brief multiple-stimulus preference assessment in a naturalistic context. *Journal of Applied Behavior Analysis, 33,* 353–357.

Carroll, D. (2001). Considering paraeducator training, roles, and responsibilities. *Teaching Exceptional Children, 34*(2), 60–64.

Cartledge, G., & Kourea, L. (2008). Culturally responsive classrooms for culturally diverse students with and at risk for disabilities. *Exceptional Children, 74,* 351–371.

Cartledge, G., & Milburn, J. F. (1995). *Teaching social skills to children: Innovative approaches* (3rd ed.). Boston: Allyn & Bacon.

Cartledge, G., Frew, T., & Zaharias, J. (1985). Social skill needs of mainstreamed students: Peer and teacher perceptions. *Learning Disability Quarterly, 8,* 132–140.

Cartwright, G. P., Cartwright, C. A., & Ward, M. E. (1995). *Educating special learners* (4th ed.). Belmont, CA: Wadsworth.

CAST. (1999–2009). *About CAST.* Retrieved April 15, 2009, from http://cast.org/about/index.html

Castellano, J. A. (2003). *Special populations in gifted education: Working with diverse gifted learners.* Boston: Allyn and Bacon.

Casto, G., & Mastropieri, M. A. (1986). The efficacy of early intervention programs: A meta-analysis. *Exceptional Children, 52,* 417–424.

Caton, H. R. (1993). Students with visual impairments. In A. E. Blackhurst & W. H. Berdine (Eds.), *An introduction to special education* (3rd ed., pp. 313–349). New York: HarperCollins.

Cavanaugh, T. W. (2006). *The digital reader: Using e-books in K–12 education.* Eugene, OR: International Society for Technology in Education.

Cawley, J. F., Foley, T. E., & Miller, J. (2003). Science and students with learning disabilities: Principles of universal design. *Intervention in School and Clinic, 38,* 160–171.

Cegelka, P. T. (1988). Multicultural considerations. In E. W. Lynch & R. B. Lewis (Eds.), *Exceptional children and adults* (pp. 545–587). Glenview, IL: Scott, Foresman.

Cegelka, P. T. (1995a). An overview of effective education for students with learning problems. In P. T. Cegelka & W. H. Berdine (Eds.), *Effective instruction for students with learning difficulties* (pp. 1–17). Boston: Allyn & Bacon.

Cegelka, P. T. (1995b). Structuring the classroom for effective instruction. In P. T. Cegelka & W. H. Berdine (Eds.), *Effective instruction for students with learning difficulties* (pp. 135–160). Boston: Allyn & Bacon.

Center for Applied Technology. (2003). *Summary of universal design for learning concepts.* Boston: Author. Retrieved August 18, 2004, from http://www.cast.org/udl/index.cfm?i=7

Center for Research on Education, Diversity and Excellence. (2002). *The five standards for effective pedagogy.* Retrieved October 16, 2004, from http://www.crede.ucsc.edu/standards/standards.html

Center for Universal Design. (2004). *Learning about universal design.* Raleigh: North Carolina State University. Retrieved August 18, 2004, from http://www.udeducation.org/learn/index.asp

Centers for Disease Control and Prevention. (2009). *HIV/AIDS surveillance report, 2007. Vol. 19.* Atlanta: U.S. Department of Health and Human Services, Centers for Disease Control and Prevention.

Chalfant, J. C., & Pysh, M. (1989). Teacher assistance teams: Five descriptive studies on 96 teams. *Remedial and Special Education, 10*(6), 49–58.

Chall, J. S. (1967). *Learning to read: The great debate.* New York: McGraw-Hill.

Chall, J. S. (1977). *Reading 1967–1977: A decade of change and promise.* Bloomington, IN: Phi Delta Kappa Educational Foundation.

Chall, J. S. (1983). *Learning to read: The great debate* (updated ed.). New York: McGraw-Hill.

Chall, J. S. (1989). Learning to read: The Great Debate 20 years later—A response to "Debunking the great phonics myth." *Phi Delta Kappan, 70,* 521–538.

Chall, J. S. (2000). *The academic achievement challenge.* New York: Guilford Press.

Chan, S., & Lee, E. (2004). Families with Asian roots. In E. W. Lynch & M. J. Hanson, *Developing cross-cultural competence* (3rd ed., pp. 219–298). Baltimore, MD: Paul H. Brookes.

Chandler, M. A. (2007). Waiting too late to test? *Washington Post.* Retrieved January 27, 2008, from http://www.washingtonpost.com/wp-dyn/content/article/2007/12/30/AR2007123002447.html

Charlop, M. H., & Milstein, J. P. (1989). Teaching autistic children conversational speech using video-modeling. *Journal of Applied Behavior Analysis, 23,* 275–285.

Charlop, M. H., & Walsh, M. E. (1986). Increasing autistic children's spontaneous verbalizations of affection: An assessment of time delay and peer modeling procedures. *Journal of Applied Behavior Analysis, 19,* 307–314.

Charlop-Christy, M. H., Carpenter, M., Le, L., LeBlanc, L. A., & Kellet, K. (2002). Using the Picture Exchange Communication System wth children with autism: Assessment of PECs acquisition, speech, social-communicative behavior, and problem behavior. *Journal of Applied Behavior Analysis, 35,* 213–231.

Cheng, L. L. (1991). *Assessing Asian language performance.* Oceanside, CA: Academic Communication Associates.

Child Trends DataBank—Family structure. (n.d.). Retrieved July 14, 2008, from http://ww.childtrendsdatabank.org/indicators/59Family Structure.cfm

Child Trends DataBank—Foster care. (n.d.). Retrieved July 14, 2008, from http://ww.childtrendsdatabank.org/indicators/12FosterCare.cfm

Child Trends DataBank—Percentage of births to unmarried women. (n.d.). Retrieved July 14, 2008, from http://ww.childtrendsdatabank.org/indicators/75Unmarriedbirths.cfm

Chinn, P. C., & Hughes, S. (1987). Representation of minority students in special education classes. *Remedial and Special Education, 8*(4), 41–46.

Chitiyo, M., & Wheeler, J. J. (2009). Challenges faced by school teachers in implementing positive behavior support in their school systems. *Remedial and Special Education, 30,* 58–63.

Christenson, S. L., & Ysseldyke, J. E. (1986). *Academic responding time as a function of instructional arrangements.* Paper presented at the annual meeting of the American Educational Research Association, San Francisco. (ERIC Document Reproduction Service No. ED-271–917).

Clark, B. (2008). *Growing up gifted* (7th ed.). Upper Saddle River, NJ: Pearson.

Clark, F. L. (2000). The strategies instruction model: A research-validated intervention for students with learning disabilities. *Learning Disabilities: A Multidisciplinary Journal, 10,* 209–217.

Cline, S., & Schwartz, D. (1999). *Diverse populations of gifted students.* Upper Saddle River, NJ: Merrill/Prentice Hall.

Close, D. W., Irvin, L. K., Taylor, V. E., & Agosta, J. (1981). Community living skills instruction for mildly retarded persons. *Exceptional Education Quarterly, 2*(1), 75–85.

Cochran, C., Feng, H., Cartledge, G., & Hamilton, S. (1993). The effects of cross-age tutoring on the academic achievement, social behaviors, and self-perceptions of low-achieving African-American males with behavioral disorders. *Behavioral Disorders, 18,* 292–302.

Cohen, S. B., & Hart-Hester, S. (1987). Time management strategies. *Teaching Exceptional Children, 20*(1), 56–57.

Colangelo, N., & Davis, G. A. (Eds.). (2003). *Handbook of gifted education* (3rd ed.). Boston: Allyn & Bacon.

Colangelo, N., Assouline, S. G., & Gross, M. U. M. (2004). *A nation deceived: How schools hold back America's brightest students* (Vol. 1). Iowa City, IA: University of Iowa.

Colarusso, R. P., & Hammill, D. D. (2003). *Motor-free visual perception test* (3rd ed.). Novato, CA: Academic Therapy.

Cole, C. M., Waldron, N., & Majd, M. (2004). Academic progress of students across inclusive and traditional settings. *Mental Retardation, 42,* 136–144.

Coleman, L. J., & Cross, T. L. (2005). *Being gifted in school: An introduction to development, guidance, and teaching* (2nd ed.). Waco, TX: Prufrock Press.

Coleman, M. C. (1986). *Behavior disorders.* Upper Saddle River, NJ: Prentice Hall.

Colorín Colorado. (2007a). *Oral language development for beginners.* Retrieved September 9, 2009, from http://www.colorincolorado.org/educators/content/oral

Colorín Colorado. (2007b). *Using cognates to develop comprehension in English.* Retrieved September 9, 2009, from http://www.colorincolorado.org/educators/background/cognates

Colorín Colorado. (2007c). *Vocabulary development.* Retrieved September 9, 2009, from http://www.colorincolorado.org/educators/teaching/vocabulary

Condon, E. C., Peters, J. Y., & Sueiro-Ross, C. (1979). *Special education and the Hispanic child: Cultural perspectives*. Philadelphia: Temple University, Teacher Corps Mid-Atlantic Network.

Cook, B. G. (2001). A comparison of teachers' attitudes toward their included students with mild and severe disabilities. *Journal of Special Education, 34,* 203–213.

Cook, E. H. (1998). Genetics of autism. *Mental Retardation and Developmental Disabilities Research Reviews, 4*(2), 113–120.

Cooper, J., Heron, T., & Heward, W. (2007). *Applied behavior analysis* (2nd ed.). Upper Saddle River, NJ: Pearson, Merrill, Prentice Hall.

Cooper, P. M. (2003). Effective white teachers of black children: Teaching within a community. *Journal of Teacher Education, 54*(5), 413–427.

Corn, A. L., & Webne, S. L. (2001). Expectations for visual function: An initial evaluation of a new clinical instrument. *Journal of Visual Impairment & Blindness, 95,* 110–116.

Correa, V. I., & Heward, W. L. (2003). Special education in a culturally diverse society. In W. L. Heward, *Exceptional children* (7th ed., pp. 86–119). Upper Saddle River, NJ: Merrill/Prentice Hall.

Council for Children with Behavioral Disorders. (2000). *Draft position on terminology and definition of emotional or behavioral disorders.* Reston, VA: Author, a Division of the Council for Exceptional Children. Retrieved April 9, 2008, from http://www.ccbd.net/advocacy/index.cfm?categoryID=668947C8-C09F-1D6F-F9375EDC805102B3

Council for Exceptional Children. (2007). *NCLB—A law under fire.* Retrieved January 22, 2008, from http://www.cec.sped.org/AM/Template.cfm?Section=Search&template=/CM/HTMLDisplay.cfm&ContentID=9314

Council for Exceptional Children. (1993a). *Career education and transition.* Retrieved November 29, 1997, from http://www.cec.sped.org/pp/cec_pol.htm#14

Council for Exceptional Children. (1993b). CEC policy on inclusive schools and community settings. *Teaching Exceptional Children, 25*(4) supplement.

Council for Exceptional Children. (2006–2007). *Differentiated instruction.* Retrieved August 28, 2008, from http://www.cec.sped.org/AM/Template.cfm?Section=Differentiated_Instruction&Template=/TaggedPage/TaggedPageDisplay.cfm&TPLID=24&ContentID=4695

Council of State Directors of Programs for the Gifted and the National Association for Gifted Children. (2007). *State of the states in gifted education 2006–2007.* Washington, DC: National Association for Gifted Children.

Craig, R., & Howard, C. (1981). Visual impairment. In M. L. Hardman, M. W. Egan, & D. Landau (Eds.), *What will we do in the morning?* (pp. 180–209). Dubuque, IA: Brown.

Cronin, M. E., & Patton, J. R. (1993). *Life skills for students with special needs.* Austin, TX: PRO-ED.

Cropley, A. J., & Urban, K. K. (2000). Programs and strategies for nurturing creativity. In K. A. Heller, F. J. Monks, R. J. Sternberg, & R. F. Subotnik (Eds.), *International handbook of giftedness and talent* (2nd ed., 485–498). Oxford: Elsevier Science, Ltd.

Cross, D. P. (1993). Students with physical and health-related disabilities. In A. E. Blackhurst & W. H. Berdine (Eds.), *An introduction to special education* (3rd ed., pp. 350–397). New York: HarperCollins.

Cross, T. L. (2004). *On the social and emotional lives of gifted children* (2nd ed.). Waco, TX: Prufrock Press.

Cuenin, L. H., & Harris, K. R. (1986). Planning, implementing, and evaluating timeout interventions with exceptional students. *Teaching Exceptional Children, 18,* 272–276.

Culatta, B. K., & Culatta, R. (1993). Students with communication problems. In A. E. Blackhurst & W. H. Berdine (Eds.), *An introduction to special education* (3rd ed., pp. 238–269). New York: HarperCollins.

Cullinan, D. (2002). *Students with emotional and behavioral disorders: An introduction for teachers and other helping professionals.* Upper Saddle River, NJ: Merrill/Prentice Hall.

Culross, R. R. (1997). Concepts of inclusion in gifted education. *Teaching Exceptional Children, 29*(3), 24–26.

D'Alonzo, B. J., D'Alonzo, R. L., & Mauser, A. J. (1979). Developing resource rooms for the handicapped. *Teaching Exceptional Children, 11,* 91–96.

D'Antonio, M. (1993, November 21). Sound & fury. *Los Angeles Times Magazine,* 44–48, 60–63.

Dale, E., & Chall, J. S. (1948). A formula for predicting readability. *Educational Research Bulletin, 27,* 11–20.

Davies, S., & White, R. (2000). Self-management and peer-monitoring within a group contingency to decrease uncontrolled verbalizations of children with attention-deficit/hyperactivity disorder. *Psychology in the Schools, 37,* 135–147.

Davis, C. (1980). *Perkins–Binet intelligence scale.* Watertown, MA: Perkins School for the Blind.

Davis, G. A. (2003). Identifying creative students, teaching for creative growth. In N. Colangelo & G. A. Davis (Eds.), *Handbook of gifted education* (3rd ed., pp. 311–324). Boston: Allyn and Bacon.

Davis, G. A., & Rimm, S. B. (2004). *Education of the gifted and talented* (5th ed.). Boston: Allyn & Bacon.

Dawson, G., & Watling, R. (2000). Interventions to facility auditory, visual, and motor integration in autism: A review of the evidence. *Journal of Autism and Developmental Disorders, 30,* 415–421.

de Grandpre, B. B., & Messier, J. M. (1979). Helping mainstreamed students stay in the mainstream. *The Directive Teacher, 2*(2), 12.

De Navas-Walt, C., Proctor, B. D., & Smith, J. (2007). *Income, poverty, and health insurance coverage in the United States: 2006.* U.S. Census Bureau, Current Populations Report, P60-233. Washington, DC: U.S. Government Printing Office. Retrieved January 23, 2008, from http://www.census.gov/hhes/www/poverty/poverty06.html

DeBell, M., & Chapman, C. (2003a). *Computer and Internet use by children and adolescents in 2001: Statistical analysis report.* Washington, DC: U.S. Department of Education, National Center for Education Statistics. Retrieved August 17, 2004, from http://nces.ed.gov/pubsearch/pubsinfo.asp?pubid=2004014

DeBell, M., & Chapman, C. (2003b). *Internet access in U.S. public schools and classrooms: 1994–2002.* Washington, DC: U.S. Department of Education, National Center for Education Statistics. Retrieved August 17, 2004, from http://nces.ed.gov/pubsearch/pubsinfo.asp?pubid=2004011

Decano, P. (1979). Asian and Pacific-American exceptional children: A conversation. *Teacher Education and Special Education, 2*(4), 33–36.

Delcourt, M. A. B., Cornell, D. G., & Goldberg, M. D. (2007). Cognitive and affective learning outcomes of gifted elementary school students. *Gifted Child Quarterly, 51*(4), 359–381.

DeLeon, I. G., & Iwata, B. A. (1996). Evaluation of a multiple-stimulus presentation format for assessing reinforcer preferences. *Journal of Applied Behavior Analysis, 29,* 519–533.

Deno, S. L. (1985). Curriculum-based measurement: The emerging alternative. *Exceptional Children, 52,* 219–232.

Deno, S. L. (1987). Curriculum-based measurement. *Teaching Exceptional Children, 20*(1), 41–42.

Deno, S. L., & Fuchs, L. S. (1987). Developing curriculum-based measurement systems for data-based special education problem solving. *Focus on Exceptional Children, 19*(8), 1–16.

Diana v. State Board of Education. Civ. No. C-70 37 RFP (N. D. Cal. 1970, 1973).

Díaz-Rico, L. T. (2004). *Teaching English learners.* Boston: Pearson Allyn and Bacon.

Dinkes, R., Kemp, J., & Baum, K. (2009). *Indicators of school crime and safety: 2008.* National Center for Education Statistics, U. S. Department of Education, and Bureau of Justice Statistics, U. S. Department of Justice. Washington, DC. Retrieved July 9, 2007, from http://nces.ed.gov/programs/crimeindicators/crimeindicators2008/

Diplomas count 2008: School to college, executive summary. (2008). *Education Week.* Retrieved June 10, 2008, from http://www.edweek.org/ew/articles/2008/06/05/40execsum.h27.html

Dodge, B. (1995). *Some thoughts about WebQuests.* Retrieved September 25, 2009, from http://webquest.sdsu.edu/about_webquests.html

Dolch, E. W. (1953). *The Dolch basic sight word list.* Champaign, IL: Garrard.

Donaldson, J. (1980). Changing attitudes toward handicapped persons: A review and analysis of research. *Exceptional Children, 46,* 504–514.

Donaldson, J., & Martinson, M. C. (1977). Modifying attitudes toward physically disabled persons. *Exceptional Children, 43,* 337–341.

Doorlag, D. H. (1989). Students with learning handicaps. In R. Gaylord-Ross (Ed.), *Integration strategies for students with handicaps* (pp. 33–52). Baltimore: Brookes.

Doyle, W. (1986). Classroom organization and management. In M. C. Wittrock (Ed.), *Handbook of research on teaching* (3rd ed., pp. 392–431). New York: Macmillan.

Drabman, R. S., & Patterson, J. N. (1981). Disruptive behavior and the social standing of exceptional children. *Exceptional Education Quarterly, 1*(4), 45–56.

Drew, C. J., Logan, D. R., & Hardman, M. L. (1992). *Mental retardation* (5th ed.). New York: Merrill/Macmillan.

Dunn, L. M. (1968). Special education for the mildly retarded—Is much of it justifiable? *Exceptional Children, 35,* 5–22.

Durán, R. P. (2008). Assessing English-language learners' achievement. *Review of Research in Education, 32,* 292–327.

Dwyer, K., & Osher, D. (2000). *Safeguarding our children: An action guide.* Washington, DC: U.S. Department of Education. Retrieved August 21, 2009, from http://www.ed.gov/admins/lead/safety/actguide/index.html

Dwyer, K., Osher, D., & Warger, C. (1998). *Early warning, timely response: A guide to safe schools.* Washington, DC: U.S. Department of Education. Retrieved August 21, 2009, from http://www.nasponline.org/resources/crisis_safety/

Dyches, T. T., & Burrow, E. (2004). Using children's books with characters with disabilities. *CEC Today, 10*(6), 13.

Dyer, K. (1989). The effects of preference on spontaneous verbal requests in individuals with autism. *Journal of the Association for Persons with Severe Handicaps, 14,* 184–189.

Easterbrooks, S. (1999). Improving practices for students with hearing impairments. *Exceptional Children, 65,* 537–554.

Eaton, M. D., & Hansen, C. L. (1978). Classroom organization and management. In N. G. Haring, T. C. Lovitt, M. D. Eaton, & C. L. Hansen (Eds.), *The fourth R: Research in the classroom* (pp. 191–217). Columbus, OH: Merrill/Prentice Hall.

Eaton, S. B., & Wall, R. S. (1999). A survey of social skills instruction in preservice programs for visual disabilities. *RE:view, 31,* 40–45.

Echevarria, J. (1995). Sheltered instruction for students with learning disabilities who have limited English proficiency. *Intervention in School and Clinic, 30,* 302–305.

Echevarria, J., & Graves, A. (2007). *Sheltered content instruction: Teaching English language learners with diverse abilities* (3rd ed.). Boston: Pearson Allyn and Bacon.

Edens, R. M., Murdick, N. L., & Gartin, B. C. (2003). Preventing infection in the classroom: The use of universal precautions. *Teaching Exceptional Children, 35*(4), 62–66.

Edgar, E., & Davidson, C. (1979). Parent perceptions of mainstreaming. *Education Unlimited, 1*(4), 32–33.

Edmonds, G., & Beardon, L. (2008). *Asperger syndrome and employment: Adults speak out about Asperger syndrome.* London: Jessica Kingsley Publishers.

Educating refugees: Understanding the basics. (1989). *NCBE Forum, 12*(3), 1, 3.

Education. (2009). Retrieved June 22, 2009, from http://www.whitehouse.gov/issues/education/

Edyburn, D. L. (2000). Assistive technology and students with mild disabilities. *Focus on Exceptional Children, 32*(9), 1–24.

Edyburn, D. L. (2003). Rethinking assistive technology. *Special Education Technology Practice, 5*(4), 16–22.

Edyburn, D. L. (2004). Key ingredients of an accessible curriculum. *Special Education Technology Practice, 6*(1), 17–22.

Ehly, S. W., & Larsen, S. C. (1980). *Peer tutoring for individualized instruction.* Boston: Allyn & Bacon.

Ellett, L. (1993). Instructional practices in mainstreamed secondary classrooms. *Journal of Learning Disabilities, 26,* 57–64.

Elliott, S. N., & Gresham, F. M. (1993). Social skills interventions for children. *Behavior Modification, 17,* 287–313.

Elliott, S. N., Kratochwill, T. R., & Gilbertson, A. (1998). *The assessment accommodation checklist.* Monterey, CA: CTB/McGraw-Hill.

Emmer, E. T. (1981). *Effective management in junior high math classes* (Report No. 6111). Austin: University of Texas, Research and Development Center for Teacher Education.

Emmer, E. T., Evertson, C. M., Sanford, J. P., Clements, B. S., & Worsham, M. E. (1989). *Classroom management for secondary teachers* (2nd ed.). Upper Saddle River, NJ: Prentice Hall.

England, P., & Edin, K. (2007). *Unmarried couples with children: Why don't they marry? How can policy-makers promote more stable relationships?* A briefing paper prepared for the Council on Contemporary Families. Retrieved July 14, 2008, from http://www.contemporaryfamilies.org/subtemplate.php?t=BriefingPapers&ext=unmarriedcouples

Englert, C. S. (1984). Measuring teacher effectiveness from the teacher's point of view. *Focus on Exceptional Children, 17*(2), 1–14.

Englert, C. S., & Raphael, T. E. (1988). Constructing well-formed prose: Process, structure, and metacognitive knowledge. *Exceptional Children, 54,* 513–520.

English, K. M. (1995). *Educational audiology across the lifespan: Serving all learners with hearing impairment.* Baltimore: Brookes.

English, K. M. (1997). *Self-advocacy for students who are deaf and hard of hearing.* Austin, TX: PRO-ED.

English, K. M., & Church, G. (1999). Unilateral hearing loss in children: An update for the 1990s. *Language, Speech, and Hearing Services in Schools, 30*(1), 26–31.

Epilepsy Foundation of America. (n.d.). Managing seizures at school. Retrieved September 23, 2009, from http://www.epilepsyfoundation.org/living/children/education/managing.cfm

Epstein, M., Atkins, M., Cullinan, D., Kutash, K., & Weaver, R. (2008). *Reducing behavior problems in the elementary school classroom: A practice guide* (NCEE #2008-012). Washington, DC: National Center for Education Evaluation and Regional Assistance, Institute of Education Sciences, U.S. Department of Education. Retrieved July 18, 2009, from http://ies.ed.gov/ncee/wwc/publications/practiceguides/

Erickson, R., Ysseldyke, J., Thurlow, M., & Elliott, J. (1998). Inclusive assessments and accountability systems. *Teaching Exceptional Children, 31*(2), 4–9.

Evans, J., & Guevara, A. E. (1974). Classroom instruction for young Spanish speakers. *Exceptional Children, 41,* 16–19.

Evertson, C. M., Sanford, J. P., & Emmer, E. T. (1981). Effects of class heterogeneity in junior high school. *American Educational Research Journal, 18,* 219–232.

Fad, K. S., Ross, M., & Boston, J. (1995). Using cooperative learning to teach social skills to young children. *Teaching Exceptional Children, 27*(4), 29–34.

Falvey, M. A., Grenot-Scheyer, M., & Bishop, K. (1989). Integrating students with severe handicaps. *California State Federation/CEC Journal, 35*(3), 8–10.

Farmer, T. W., & Cadwallader, T. W. (1999). Social interactions and peer support for problem behavior. *Preventing School Failure, 44,* 105–109.

Fass, S., & Cauthen, N. K. (2007). *Who are America's poor children? The official story.* National Center for Children in Poverty. Retrieved July 19, 2008, from http://www.nccp.org/publications/pub_787.html

Feldhusen, J. F. (1989). Thinking skills for the gifted. In J. F. Feldhusen, J. VanTassel-Baska, & K. Seeley (Eds.), *Excellence in educating the gifted* (pp. 239–259). Denver: Love.

Feldhusen, J. F. (2001). *Talent development in gifted education.* Arlington, VA: The Council for Exceptional Children. (ERIC Clearinghouse on Disabilities and Gifted Education, ERIC EC Digest No. E610).

Feldhusen, J. F., Van Winkle, L., & Ehle, D. A. (1996). Is it acceleration or simply appropriate instruction for precocious youth? *Teaching Exceptional Children, 28*(3), 48–51.

Feldman, K., & Denti, L. (2004). High-access instruction: Practical strategies to increase active learning in diverse classrooms. *Focus on Exceptional Children, 36*(7), 1–12.

Fenske, E. C., Krantz, P. J., & McClannahan, L. E. (2001). Incidental teaching: A not-so-discrete-trial teaching procedure. In C. Maurice, G. Green, and R. M. Foxx (Eds.), *Making a difference: Behavioral intervention for autism* (pp. 75–82). Austin, TX: PRO-ED.

Fetzer, E. A. (2000). The gifted/learning disabled child: A guide for teachers and parents. *Gifted Child Today, 23*(4), 44–50.

Fiedler, C. R., & Simpson, R. L. (1987). Modifying the attitudes of nonhandicapped students toward handicapped peers. *Exceptional Children, 53,* 342–349.

Finch, A. J., & Spirito, A. (1980). Use of cognitive training to change cognitive processes. *Exceptional Education Quarterly, 1*(1), 31–39.

Flesch, R. (1951). *How to test readability.* New York: Harper & Row.

Flett, A., & Conderman, G. (2001). Enhance the involvement of parents from culturally and linguistically diverse backgrounds. *Intervention in School and Clinic, 37*(1), 53–55.

Flexer, C., Wray, D., & Ireland, J. C. (1989). Preferential seating is not enough: Issues in classroom management of hearing-impaired students. *Language, Speech, and Hearing in Schools, 20,* 11–21.

Flint, L. J. (2001). Challenges of identifying and serving gifted children with ADHD. *Teaching Exceptional Children, 33*(4), 62–69.

Flower, A., Burns, M. K., & Bottsford-Miller, N. A. (2007). Meta-analysis of disability simulation research. *Remedial and Special Education, 28,* 72–79.

Food and Nutrition Service. (2008). *National school lunch program.* United States Department of Agriculture. Retrieved July 20, 2008, from http://www.fns.usda.gov/cnd/Lunch/

Ford, D. Y., & Harris III, J. J. (1999). *Multicultural gifted education.* New York: Teachers College Press.

Ford, D. Y., Grantham, T. C., & Whiting, G. W. (2008). Another look at the achievement gap: Learning from the experiences of gifted black students. *Urban Education. 43*(2), 216–239.

Ford, D. Y., Harris III, J. J., Tyson, C. A., & Trotman, M. F. (2002). Beyond deficit thinking: Providing access for gifted African American students. *Roeper Review, 24*(2), 52–58.

Ford, M. P. (2005). *Differentiation through flexible grouping: Successfully reaching all readers.* Naperville, IL: Learning Points Associates/North Central Regional Educational Laboratory. (ERIC Document Reproduction Service No. ED489510).

Forest, M., & Lusthaus, E. (1989). Promoting educational equality for all students. In S. Stainback, W. Stainback, & M. Forest (Eds.), *Educating all students in the mainstream of regular education* (pp. 43–57). Baltimore: Brookes.

Forness, S. R., & Kavale, K. A. (1993). Strategies to improve basic learning and memory deficits in mental retardation: A meta-analysis of experimental studies. *Education and Training in Mental Retardation, 28,* 99–110.

Forness, S. R., Walker, H. M., & Kavale, K. A. (2003). Psychiatric disorders and treatments: A primer for teachers. *Teaching Exceptional Children, 36*(2), 42–49.

Forster, P., & Doyle, B. A. (1989). Teaching listening skills to students with attention deficit disorders. *Teaching Exceptional Children, 21*(2), 20–22.

Forum on Child and Family Statistics. (2008). *America's children in brief: Key national indicators of well-being, 2008—Health care.* ChildStats.gov. Retrieved July 19, 2008, from http://childstats.gov/americaschildren/care.asp

Foster, S. L., Inderbitzen, H. M., & Nangle, D. W. (1993). Assessing acceptance and social skills with peers in childhood. *Behavior Modification, 17,* 255–286.

Fox, C. L. (1989). Peer acceptance of learning disabled children in the regular classroom. *Exceptional Children, 56,* 50–59.

Foyle, H. C., & Lyman, L. (1990). *Cooperative learning: What you need to know.* Washington, DC: National Education Association.

Franklin, M. E. (1992). Culturally sensitive instructional practices for African-American learners with disabilities. *Exceptional Children, 59,* 115–122.

Freedman, S. W. (1982). Language assessment and writing disorders. *Topics in Language Disorders, 2*(4), 34–44.

Freeman, D., & Freeman, Y. (1988). *Sheltered English instruction.* Washington, DC: ERIC Clearinghouse on Languages and Linguistics. (ERIC Document Reproduction Service No. ED-301–070).

Friend, M. (2008). *Special education* (2nd ed.). Boston: Allyn and Bacon.

Frost, L. A., & Bondy, A. S. (2002). *The picture exchange communication system: Training manual* (2nd ed.). Newark, DE: Pyramid Educational Consultants, Inc.

Fry, E. (1968). A readability formula that saves time. *Journal of Reading, 11,* 513–516, 575–577.

Fry, E. (1977). Fry's readability graph: Clarifications, validity, and extension to level 17. *Journal of Reading, 21,* 242–252.

Fuchigami, R. Y. (1980). Teacher education for culturally diverse exceptional children. *Exceptional Children, 46,* 634–641.

Fuchs, D., Fuchs, L. S., & Burish, P. (2000). Peer-assisted learning strategies: An evidence-based approach to promote reading achievement. *Learning Disabilities Research and Practice, 15,* 85–91.

Fuchs, D., Fuchs, L. S., Thompson, A., Yen, L., Al Otaiba, S., Nyman, K., Svenson, E., et al. (2001). Peer-assisted learning strategies in reading: Extensions for kindergarten, first grade, and high school. *Remedial and Special Education, 22,* 15–21.

Fuchs, D., Mock, D., Morgan, P. L., & Young, C. L. (2003). Responsiveness-to-intervention: Definitions, evidence, and implications for the learning disabilities construct. *Learning Disabilities Research & Practice, 18,* 157–171.

Fuchs, L. S. (1986). Monitoring progress among mildly handicapped pupils: Review of current practice and research. *Remedial and Special Education, 7*(5), 5–12.

Fuchs, L. S. (1987). Program development. *Teaching Exceptional Children, 20*(1), 42–44.

Gable, R. A., Hester, P. H., Rock, M. L., & Hughes, K. G. (2009). Back to basics: Rules, praise, ignoring, and reprimands revisited. *Intervention in School and Clinic, 44,* 195–205.

Gable, R. A., Laycock, V. K., Maroney, S. A., & Smith, C. R. (1991). *Preparing to integrate students with behavioral disorders.* Reston, VA: The Council for Exceptional Children.

Gable, R. A., Strain, P. S., & Hendrickson, J. M. (1979). Strategies for improving the status and social behavior of learning disabled children. *Learning Disability Quarterly, 2*(3), 33–39.

Gallagher, J. J. (2003). Issues and challenges in the education of gifted students. In N. Colangelo & G. A. Davis (Eds.), *Handbook of gifted education* (3rd ed., pp. 11–23). Boston: Allyn & Bacon.

Gallagher, S. A. (2001). Adapting problem-based learning for gifted students. In F. A. Karnes & S. M. Bean (Eds.), *Methods and materials for teaching the gifted* (pp. 369–394). Waco, TX: Prufrock Press.

Gans, K. D. (1985). Regular and special educators: Handicap integration attitudes and implications for consultants. *Teacher Education and Special Education, 8,* 188–197.

Ganz, J. B., & Simpson, R. L. (2004). Effects on communicative requesting and speech development of the Picture Exchange Communication System in children with characteristics of autism. *Journal of Autism and Developmental Disorders, 34,* 395–409.

Garcia, R. L. (1978). *Fostering a pluralistic society through multi-ethnic education.* Bloomington, IN: Phi Delta Kappa Educational Foundation.

Garcia, R. L. (2006). Language, culture, and education. In J. A. Banks (Ed.), *Cultural diversity and education* (5th ed., p. 266–291). Boston: Allyn and Bacon.

Garrett, M. K., & Crump, W. D. (1980). Peer acceptance, teacher preference, and self-appraisal of social status of learning disabled students. *Learning Disability Quarterly, 3*(3), 42–48.

Gartner, A., & Riessman, F. (1977). *How to individualize learning.* Bloomington, IN: Phi Delta Kappa Educational Foundation.

Gastright, J. F. (1989, April). Don't base your dropout program on somebody else's problem. *Phi Delta Kappa Research Bulletin,* pp. 1–4.

Gay, G. (2000). *Culturally responsive teaching: Theory, research, and practice.* New York: Teachers College Press.

Gay, L. R. (1981). *Educational research* (2nd ed.). Columbus, OH: Merrill/Prentice Hall.

Gena, A., & Kymissis, E. (2001). Assessing and setting goals for the attending and communicative behavior of three preschoolers with autism in inclusive kindergarten settings. *Journal of Developmental and Physical Disabilities, 13*(1), 11–26.

Gersten, R., & Dimino, J. (1993). Visions and revisions: A special education perspective on the whole language controversy. *Special Education and Remedial Education, 14*(4), 5–13.

Gersten, R., & Jiménez, R. (1998). Modulating instruction for language minority students. In E. J. Kameenui & D. W. Carnine (Eds.), *Effective teaching strategies that accommodate diverse learners* (pp. 161–178). Upper Saddle River, NJ: Merrill/Prentice Hall.

Gersten, R., Baker, S. K., Haager, D., & Graves, A. W. (2005). Exploring the role of teacher quality in predicting reading outcomes for first-grade English learners. *Remedial and Special Education, 26,* 197–206.

Giangreco, M., Cloninger, C., & Iverson, V. (1990). *C.O.A.C.H.— Cayuga-Onondaga assessment for children with handicaps* (6th ed.). Stillwater: Oklahoma State University.

Gickling, E. E., & Thompson, V. P. (1985). A personal view of curriculum-based assessment. *Exceptional Children, 52,* 205–218.

Gilliam, J. E. (2001). *Gilliam Asperger's disorder scale (GADS).* Austin, TX: PRO-ED.

Gilliam, J. E. (2006). *Gilliam Autism rating scale–Second Edition (GARS-2).* Austin, TX: PRO-ED.

Gillung, T. B., & Rucker, C. N. (1977). Labels and teacher expectations. *Exceptional Children, 43,* 464–465.

Glass, G. V., & Smith, M. L. (1978). *Meta-analysis of research on class size and achievement.* Boulder: University of Colorado, Laboratory of Educational Research.

Glazzard, P. (1980). Adaptations for mainstreaming. *Teaching Exceptional Children, 13,* 26–29.

Glazzard, P. (1982). *Learning activities and teaching ideas for the special child in the regular classroom.* Upper Saddle River, NJ: Prentice Hall.

Goldenberg, C. (2008). Teaching English language learners: What the research does—and does not—say. *American Educator, 32*(2), 8–23, 42–44.

Goldman, R., & Fristoe, M. (2000). *Goldman–Fristoe test of articulation— Second edition.* Circle Pines, MN: American Guidance Service.

Goldstein, A. P., & McGinnis, E. (1997). *Skillstreaming the adolescent: New strategies and perspectives for teaching prosocial skills.* Champaign, IL: Research Press.

Gollnick, D. M., & Chinn, P. C. (2006). *Multicultural education in a pluralistic society* (7th ed.). Upper Saddle River, NJ: Merrill Prentice Hall.

Goodman, L. (1978). Meeting children's needs through materials modification. *Teaching Exceptional Children, 10,* 92–94.

Goodwin, M. W. (1999). Cooperative learning and social skills: What skills to teach and how to teach. *Intervention in School and Clinic, 35,* 29–33.

Goral, R., & Lenburg, J. (2001). *Website evaluation form.* Madison Metropolitan School District, Madison, Wisconsin. Retrieved November 6, 2004, from http://www.madison.k12.wi.us/tnl/detectives/evalform.htm

Gordon, T. (1974). *Teacher effectiveness training.* New York: Wyden.

Gorman, C. (2003, July 28). The new science of dyslexia. *Time, 162*(4), 52–57.

Gottlieb, B. (1997). *Coping with chronic stress.* New York: Plenum.

Gottlieb, J., & Leyser, Y. (1981). Facilitating the social mainstreaming of retarded children. *Exceptional Education Quarterly, 1*(4), 57–70.

Grady, E. (1992). *The portfolio approach to assessment.* Bloomington, IN: Phi Delta Kappa Educational Foundation.

Graham, S., & Harris, K. R. (1989). Improving learning disabled students skills at composing essays: Self-instructional strategy training. *Exceptional Children, 56,* 201–214.

Graham, S., & Johnson, L. A. (1989). Teaching reading to learning disabled students: A review of research-supported procedures. *Focus on Exceptional Children, 21*(6), 1–12.

Graham, S., & Miller, L. (1979). Spelling research and practice: A unified approach. *Focus on Exceptional Children, 12*(2), 1–16.

Graham, S., Harris, K. R., & Reid, R. (1998). Developing self-regulated learners. In R. J. Whelan (Ed.), *Emotional and behavioral disorders: A 25 year focus* (pp. 205–228). Denver: Love.

Graham, S., Murphy, P., Harris, K. R., Fink-Chorzempa, B., Saddler, B., Moran, S., & Mason, L. (2008). Teaching spelling in the primary grades: A national survey of instructional practices and applications. *American Educational Research Journal, 45,* 796–825.

Grandin, T. (1995). *Thinking in pictures and other reports from my life with autism.* New York: Vintage Books.

Grandin, T., & Barron, S. (2005). *Unwritten rules of social relationships: Decoding social mysteries through the unique perspectives of autism.* Arlington, TX: Future Horizons, Inc.

Graves, A. W., Gersten, R., & Haager, D. (2005). Literacy instruction in multiple-language first-grade classrooms: Linking student outcomes to observed instructional practice. *Learning Disabilities Research & Practice, 19,* 262–272.

Gray, C. (2000). *The new social story book.* Arlington, TX: Future Horizons, Inc.

Grayson, D. (n.d.). *Facts about blindness and visual impairment.* New York: American Foundation for the Blind.

Grayson, J. (2007). Children of incarcerated parents. *Virginia Child Protection Newsletter, 81,* 1–3, 5–6, 8, 24.

Green, W. W., & Fischgrund, J. E. (1993). Students with hearing loss. In A. E. Blackhurst & W. H. Berdine (Eds.), *An introduction to special education* (3rd ed., pp. 271–311). New York: HarperCollins.

Gregg, N. (2009). *Adolescents and adults with learning disabilities and ADHD: Assessment and accommodation.* New York: Guilford Press.

Gresham, F. M. (1984). Social skills and self-efficacy for exceptional children. *Exceptional Children, 51,* 253–261.

Grieco, E. M., & Cassidy R. C. (2001). *Overview of race and Hispanic origin, Census 2000 brief.* Washington, DC: U.S. Census Bureau. Retrieved June 1, 2001, from http://www.census.gov/prod/2001pubs/c2kbr01-1.pdf

Grosenick, J. K., & Huntze, S. L. (1980). *National needs analysis in behavior disorders: Adolescent behavior disorders.* Columbia: University of Missouri at Columbia, Department of Special Education.

Gross, M. U. M., Sleap, B., & Pretorius, M. (1999). *Gifted students in secondary schools: Differentiating the curriculum.* Sydney: A Gerric Publication.

Grossman, H. J. (Ed.). (1983). *Classification in mental retardation* (1983 revision). Washington, DC: American Association on Mental Retardation.

Guetzloe, E. (1999). Inclusion: The broken promise. *Preventing School Failure, 43,* 92–98.

Guilford, J. P. (1967). *The nature of human intelligence.* New York: McGraw-Hill.

Gumpel, T. P., & Frank, R. (1999). An expansion of the peer-tutoring paradigm: Cross-age peer tutoring of social skills among socially rejected boys. *Journal of Applied Behavior Analysis, 32,* 115–118.

Guralnick, M. J. (1981). Programmatic factors affecting child-child social interactions in mainstreamed preschool programs. *Exceptional Education Quarterly, 1*(4), 71–92.

Gutstein, S. E., & Sheely, R. K. (2002). *Relationship development intervention with young children.* New York: Jessica Kingsley Publishers.

Hadley, A. M., Hair, E. C., & Moore, K. A. (2003). *Assessing what kids think about themselves: A guide to adolescent self-concept for out-of-school time program participants. Research-to-practice brief no. 2008-32.* Retrieved October 19, 2008 from http://www.childtrends.org.

Hall, L. J. (2009). *Autism spectrum disorders: From theory to practice.* Upper Saddle River, NJ: Pearson Merrill Prentice Hall.

Hall, L. J., & McGregor, J. A. (2000). A follow-up study of the peer relationships of children with disabilities in an inclusive school. *The Journal of Special Education, 34,* 114–126.

Hall, L. J., & Smith, K. L. (1996). The generalization of social skills by preferred peers with autism. *Journal of Intellectual and Developmental Disability, 21,* 313–330.

Hall, T., Strangman, N., & Meyer, A. (2003). *Differentiated instruction and implications for UDL implementation.* Wakefield, MA: National Center on Accessing the General Curriculum. Retrieved September 9, 2008, from http://www.cast.org/publications/ncac/ncac_diffinstructudl.html

Hallahan, D. P., & Kauffman, J. M. (1988). *Exceptional children* (4th ed.). Upper Saddle River, NJ: Prentice Hall.

Hammill, D. D. (1998). *Detroit tests of learning aptitude* (4th ed.). Austin, TX: PRO-ED.

Hammill, D. D., & Bartel, N. R. (1986). *Teaching students with learning and behavior problems* (4th ed.). Austin, TX: PRO-ED.

Hammill, D. D., & Bryant, B. R. (1998). *Learning disabilities diagnostic inventory.* Austin, TX: PRO-ED.

Hammill, D. D., & Newcomer, P. L. (1997). *Test of language development—3, Intermediate.* Austin, TX: PRO-ED.

Hammill, D. D., Brown, V. L., Larsen, S. C., & Wiederholt, J. L. (2007). *Test of adolescent and adult language* (4th ed.). Austin, TX: PRO-ED.

Hammill, D. D., Pearson N. A., & Voress, J. K. (1993). *Developmental test of visual perception* (2nd ed.). Austin, TX: PRO-ED.

Hamre-Nietupski, S., McDonald, J., & Nietupski, J. (1992). Integrating elementary students with multiple disabilities into supported regular classes: Challenges and solutions. *Teaching Exceptional Children, 24*(3), 6–9.

Handlers, A., & Austin, K. (1980). Improving attitudes of high school students toward their handicapped peers. *Exceptional Children, 47,* 228–229.

Hardman, M. L., Drew, C. J., & Egan, M. W. (2005). *Human exceptionality* (8th ed.). Boston: Pearson Allyn and Bacon.

Harley, R. K., & Lawrence, G. A. (1984). *Visual impairment in the schools.* Springfield, IL: Thomas.

Harrington, J. D. (1976). Hard-of-hearing pupils in the mainstream: Educational needs and services. In *Serving hard-of-hearing pupils: Alternative strategies for personnel preparation* (pp. 16–31). Minneapolis: University of Minnesota, Leadership Training Institute/Special Education.

Harvey, G. (2008). Employment for people with Asperger's syndrome: What's needed? In G. Edmonds, & L. Beardon (Eds.), *Asperger syndrome and employment: Adults speak out about Asperger syndrome* (pp. 19–30). London: Jessica Kingsley Publishers.

Harvey, S., & Goudvis, A. (2000). *Strategies that work: Teaching comprehension to enhance understanding.* Portland, ME: Stenhouse.

Hasazi, S. B., Furney, K. S., & Hull, M. (1995). Additional preparation for adulthood: Transition planning. In P. T. Cegelka & W. H. Berdine (Eds.), *Effective instruction for students with learning difficulties* (pp. 419–443). Boston: Allyn & Bacon.

Hasselbring, T. S., & Glaser, C. H. W. (2000). Use of computer technology to help students with special needs. *The Future of Children, 10,* 102–122.

Hasselbring, T. S., Goin, L. I., & Bransford, J. D. (1987). Developing automaticity. *Teaching Exceptional Children, 19*(3), 30–33.

Hazekamp, J., & Huebner, K. M. (Eds.). (1989). *Program planning and evaluation for blind and visually impaired students: National guidelines for educational excellence.* New York: American Foundation for the Blind.

Heacox, D. (2002). What do students need? Tiered assignments. In D. Heacox (Ed.), *Differentiating instruction in the regular classroom: How to reach and teach all learners, grades 3–12.* Minneapolis: Free Spirit Press.

Heath, M. A., Leavy, D., Hansen, K., Ryan, K., Lawrence, L., & Sonntag, A. G. (2008). Coping with grief: Guidelines and resources for assisting children. *Intervention in School and Clinic, 43,* 259–269.

Hébert, T. P. (2002). Gifted males. In M. Neihart, S. M. Reis, N. M. Robinson, & S. M. Moon (Eds.), *The social and emotional development of gifted children: What do we know?* (pp. 137–144). Waco, TX: Prufrock Press.

Heflin, L. J., & Bullock, L. M. (1999). Inclusion of students with emotional/behavioral disorders: A survey of teachers in general and special education. *Preventing School Failure, 43,* 103–111.

Hemphill, B. (1997). *Taming the paper tiger.* Washington, DC: Kiplinger Washington Editors.

Henker, B., Whalen, C. K., & Hinshaw, S. P. (1980). The attributional contexts of cognitive intervention strategies. *Exceptional Education Quarterly, 1*(1), 17–30.

Heron, T. E., & Harris, K. C. (1993). *The educational consultant* (3rd ed.). Austin, TX: PRO-ED.

Heron, T. E., & Harris, K. C. (2001). *The educational consultant: Helping professionals, parents, and students in inclusive classrooms* (4th ed.). Austin, TX: PRO-ED.

Heron, T. E., Heward, W. L., & Cooke, N. L. (1980). *A classwide peer tutoring system.* Paper presented at the Sixth Annual Meeting of the Association of Behavior Analysis, Dearborn, MI.

Heward, W. L. (1996). *Exceptional children: An introduction to special education* (5th ed.). Upper Saddle River, NJ: Merrill/Prentice Hall.

Heward, W. L. (2000). *Exceptional children* (6th ed.). Upper Saddle River, NJ: Merrill/Prentice Hall.

Heward, W. L. (2003). *Exceptional children* (7th ed.). Upper Saddle River, NJ: Merrill/Prentice Hall.

Heward, W. L. (2006). *Exceptional children* (8th ed.). Upper Saddle River, NJ: Merrill Prentice Hall.

Heward, W. L., & Orlansky, M. D. (1992). *Exceptional children* (4th ed.). New York: Merrill/Macmillan.

Heward, W. L., Courson, F. H., & Narayan, J. S. (1989). Using choral responding to increase active student response. *Teaching Exceptional Children, 21*(3), 72–75.

Heward, W. L., Gardner, R. I., Cavanaugh, R. A., Courson, F. H., Grossi, T. A., & Barbette, P. M. (1996). Everyone participates in this class: Using response cards to increase active student responses. *Teaching Exceptional Children, 28,* 4–11.

Hiskey, M. (1966). *Hiskey–Nebraska test of learning aptitude.* Lincoln, NE: Union College Press.

Hobbs, N. (1975). *The futures of children.* San Francisco: Jossey-Bass.

Hobbs, N. (1976). *Issues in the classification of children.* San Francisco: Jossey-Bass.

Hocutt, A. M. (1996). Effectiveness of special education: Is placement the critical factor? *The Future of Children, 6*(1), 77–102.

Hodgdon, L. (1998). *Visual strategies for improving communication. Volume 1.* Troy, MI: QuirkRoberts Publishing.

Hodgdon, L. A. (1995). *Visual strategies for improving communication: Practical supports for school and home.* Troy, MI: QuirkRoberts Publishing.

Hodgkinson, H. (1993). American education: The good, the bad, and the task. *Phi Delta Kappan, 74,* 619–623.

Hoefer, M., Rytina, N., & Campbell, C. (2007). *Estimates of the unauthorized immigrant population residing in the United States: January 2006.* Population Estimates from the U. S. Department of Homeland Security, Office of Immigration Statistics. Retrieved July 8, 2008, from http://www.dhs.gov/ximgtn/statistics/

Hollinger, J. D. (1987). Social skills for behaviorally disordered children as preparation for mainstreaming: Theory, practice, and new directions. *Remedial and Special Education, 8*(4), 17–27.

Hoover, J. J., & Patton, J. R. (2005). Differentiating curriculum and instruction for English-language learners with special needs. *Intervention in School and Clinic, 40,* 231–235.

Hosp, J. L., & Reschly, D. J. (2003). Referral rates for intervention or assessment: A meta-analysis of racial differences. *Journal of Special Education, 37*(2), 67–80.

Howell, K. W., Fox, S. L., & Morehead, M. K. (1993). *Curriculum-based evaluation* (2nd ed.). Pacific Grove, CA: Brooks/Cole.

Howlin, P. (2004). *Autism and Asperger syndrome: Preparing for adulthood* (2nd ed.). London: Routledge.

Hubbard, A. (2005). Academic modifications. In B. S. Myles (Ed.), *Children and youth with Asperger syndrome: Strategies for success in inclusive settings* (pp. 35–58). Thousand Oaks, CA: Corwin Press.

Hughes, C. (1999). Identifying critical social interaction behaviors among high school students with and without disabilities. *Behavior Modification, 23,* 41–60.

Hunt, P., & Goetz, L. (1997). Research on inclusive educational programs, practices, and outcomes for students with severe disabilities. *Journal of Special Education, 31,* 3–29.

Idol, L. (1993). *Special educator's consultation handbook* (2nd ed.). Austin, TX: PRO-ED.

Idol, L., & West, J. F. (1991). Educational collaboration: A catalyst for effective schooling. *Intervention in School and Clinic, 27*(2), 70–78, 125.

Intervention Central. (n.d.). *Time out from reinforcement*. Retrieved July 16, 2009, from http://www.interventioncentral.org/htmdocs/interventions/behavior/timeout.php

Isaacson, S. L. (1987). Effective instruction in written language. *Focus on Exceptional Children, 19*(6), 1–12.

Israelson, J. (1980). I'm special too—A classroom program promotes understanding and acceptance of handicaps. *Teaching Exceptional Children, 13*, 35–37.

Janesick, V. J. (1995). Our multicultural society. In E. L. Meyen & T. M. Skrtic (Eds.), *Special education and student disability* (4th ed., pp. 713–727). Denver: Love.

Jenkins, J. R., & Jenkins, L. (1985). Peer tutoring in elementary and secondary programs. *Focus on Exceptional Children, 17*(6), 1–12.

Jenkins, J. R., Heliotis, J. D., Stein, M. L., & Haynes, M. C. (1987). Improving reading comprehension by using paragraph restatements. *Exceptional Children, 54*, 54–59.

Joe, J. R., & Malach, R. S. (2004). Families with American Indian roots. In E. W. Lynch & M. J. Hanson (Eds.), *Developing cross-cultural competence* (3rd ed., pp. 109–139). Baltimore, MD: Paul H. Brookes.

Johnsen, S. K. (2004a). Definitions, models, and characteristics of gifted students. In S. K. Johnsen (Ed.), *Identifying gifted students: A practical guide* (pp. 1–21). Waco, TX: Prufrock Press.

Johnsen, S. K. (2004b). Making decisions about placement. In S. K. Johnsen (Ed.), *Identifying gifted students: A practical guide* (pp. 107–131). Waco, TX: Prufrock Press.

Johnson, D. D. (1971). The Dolch list reexamined. *The Reading Teacher, 24*, 455–456.

Johnson, D. W., Johnson, R. T., & Stanne, M. B. (2000). *Cooperative learning methods: A meta-analysis*. Minneapolis, MN: Cooperative Learning Center, University of Minnesota. Retrieved July 25, 2009, from http://www.co-operation.org/pages/ cl-methods.html

Johnson, D. W., & Johnson, R. T. (1980). Integrating handicapped students into the mainstream. *Exceptional Children, 47*, 90–98.

Johnson, D. W., & Johnson, R. T. (1984). Classroom learning structure and attitudes toward handicapped students in mainstream settings. In R. L. Jones (Ed.), *Attitudes and attitude change in special education* (pp. 118–142). Reston, VA: The Council for Exceptional Children.

Johnson, D. W., & Johnson, R. T. (1989). Cooperative learning and mainstreaming. In R. Gaylord-Ross (Ed.), *Integration strategies for students with handicaps* (pp. 233–248). Baltimore: Brookes.

Johnson, L. J., & Pugach, M. C. (1990). Classroom teachers' views of intervention strategies for learning and behavior problems: Which are reasonable and how frequently are they used? *Journal of Special Education, 24*, 69–84.

Johnson, N. (2009). *Nielsen online December 2008 search engine share rankings*. Retrieved May 13, 2009, from http://searchenginewatch.com/3632382

Johnson, R. (1981). *The picture communication symbols: Book I*. Solana Beach, CA: Mayer-Johnson Co.

Johnson, R. (1985). *The picture communication symbols: Book II*. Solana Beach, CA: Mayer-Johnson Co.

Johnson, R. (1992). *The picture communication symbols: Book III*. Solana Beach, CA: Mayer-Johnson Co.

Johnson, R. (1995). *The picture communication symbols guide*. Solana Beach, CA: Mayer-Johnson Co.

Jones, F. H., & Eimers, R. C. (1975). Role playing to train elementary teachers to use a classroom management "skill package." *Journal of Applied Behavior Analysis, 8*, 421–433.

Jones, F. H., & Miller, W. H. (1974). The effective use of negative attention for reducing group disruption in special elementary school classrooms. *Psychological Record, 24*, 435–448.

Joseph, L. M., & Ford, D. Y. (2006). Nondiscriminatory assessment: Considerations for gifted education. *Gifted Child Quarterly, 50*(1), 42–51.

Kalyanpur, M., & Harry, B. (1999). *Culture in special education*. Baltimore: Brookes.

Kameenui, E. J., & Simmons, D. C. (1990). *Designing instructional strategies*. New York: Merrill/Macmillan.

Kantor, J. (2009, January 21). A portrait of change: In first family, a nation's many faces. *New York Times*. Retrieved January 21, 2009, from http://www.nytimes.com/2009/01/21/us/politics/21family.html

Kantrowitz, B., & Scelfo, J. (2006, November, 27). What happens when they grow up? *Newsweek*, pp. 47–53.

Kapoun, J. (1998, July/August). Teaching undergrads web evaluation: A guide for library instruction. *College & Research Libraries News, 59*(7), 522–523. Retrieved August 28, 2004, from http://www.library.cornell.edu/olinuris/ref/webcrit.html

Karnes, F. A., & Bean, S. M. (Eds.). (2005). *Methods and materials for teaching the gifted* (2nd ed.). Waco, TX: Prufrock Press.

Karweit, N. L., & Slavin, R. E. (1981). Measurement and modeling choices in studies of time and learning. *Educational Research Journal, 18*(2), 157–171.

Kauffman, J. M. (1997). *Characteristics of emotional and behavioral disorders of children and youth* (6th ed.). Upper Saddle River, NJ: Merrill.

Kauffman, J. M. (2001). *Characteristics of emotional and behavioral disorders of children and youth* (7th ed.). Upper Saddle River, NJ: Merrill/Prentice Hall.

Kaufman, M. J., Gottlieb, J., Agard, J. A., & Kukic, M. D. (1975). Mainstreaming: Toward an explication of the construct. In E. L. Meyen, G. A. Vergason, & R. J. Whelan (Eds.), *Alternatives for teaching exceptional children* (pp. 35–54). Denver: Love.

Kavale, K. A. (2005). Identifying specific learning disability: Is responsiveness to intervention the answer? *Journal of Learning Disabilities, 39*, 553–562.

Kavale, K. A., & Mostert, M. P. (2003). River of ideology, islands of evidence. *Exceptionality, 11*(4), 191–208.

Keefe, C. H., & Keefe, D. R. (1993). Instruction for students with LD: A whole language model. *Intervention in School and Clinic, 28*, 172–177.

Keller, H. (1965). *The story of my life*. New York: Airmont.

Kennedy, C. H., & Horn, E. M. (Eds.). (2004). *Including students with severe disabilities*. Boston: Allyn & Bacon.

Kennedy, D. M. (1995). Plain talk about creating a gifted-friendly classroom. *Roeper Review, 17*, 232–234.

Kerr, M. M., & Nelson, C. M. (2002). *Strategies for addressing behavior problems in the classroom* (4th ed.). Upper Saddle River, NJ: Merrill/Prentice Hall.

Killu, K., & Crundwell, M. A. (2008). Understanding and developing academic and behavioral interventions for students with bipolar disorder. *Intervention in School and Clinic, 43*, 244–251.

Kim, A., & Yeh, C. J. (2002). *Stereotypes of Asian American students*. ERIC Digest 172. Retrieved October 13, 2009 from *http://www.eric.ed.gov/ERICWebPortal/custom/portlets/recordDetails/detailmini.jsp?_nfpb=true&_&ERICExtSearch_SearchValue_0=EJ616350&ERICExtSearch_SearchType_0=no&accno=EJ616350*.

King-Sears, M. E. (1997). Best academic practices for inclusive classrooms. *Focus on Exceptional Children, 29*(7), 1–22.

King-Sears, M. E. (2007). Designing and delivering learning center instruction. *Intervention in School and Clinic, 42,* 137–147.

Kinnaman, D. E. (1992). 2.5 million strong—and growing. *Technology &Learning, 13*(1), 67.

Kirk, S. A., & Gallagher, J. J. (1979). *Educating exceptional children* (3rd ed.). Boston: Houghton Mifflin.

Kirk, S. A., Kliebhan, J. M., & Lerner, J. W. (1978). *Teaching reading to slow and disabled readers.* Boston: Houghton Mifflin.

Kitano, H. (1973). Highlights of Institute on Language and Culture: Asian component. In L. A. Bransford, L. M. Baca, & K. Lane (Eds.), *Cultural diversity and the exceptional child* (pp. 14–15). Reston, VA: The Council for Exceptional Children.

Kitano, M. K. (1991). A multicultural educational perspective on serving the culturally diverse gifted. *Journal for the Education of the Gifted, 15*(1), 4–19.

Kitano, M. K. (2008). Gifted girls. In J. A. Plucker & C. M. Callahan (Eds.), *Critical issues and practices in gifted education: What the research says* (pp. 225–240). Waco, TX: Prufrock Press.

Kitano, M. K., & DiJiosia, M. (2002). Are Asian and Pacific Americans over-represented in programs for the gifted? *Roeper Review, 24*(2), 76–80.

Kitano, M. K., & Pedersen, K. S. (2002). Action research and practical inquiry. Multicultural content integration in gifted education: Lessons from the field. *Journal for the Education of the Gifted, 25*(3), 269–289.

Knitzer, J. (1989). *Invisible Children Project: Final report and recommendations of the Invisible Children Project.* Alexandria, VA: National Mental Health Association.

Koegel, L. K., & LaZebnik, C. (2004). *Overcoming autism: Finding the answers, strategies, and hope that can transform a child's life.* New York: Viking.

Koegel, R. L., Koegel, L. K., & Carter, C. M. (1999). Pivotal teaching interactions for children with autism. *School Psychology Review, 28,* 576–594.

Kohl, F. L., Moses, L. G., & Stettner-Eaton, B. A. (1983). The results of teaching fifth and sixth graders to be instructional trainers with students who are severely handicapped. *Journal of the Association for the Severely Handicapped, 8*(4), 32–40.

Kokaska, C. J. (1980). A curriculum model for career education. In G. M. Clark & W. J. White (Eds.), *Career education for the handicapped: Current perspectives for teachers* (pp. 35–41). Boothwyn, PA: Educational Resources Center.

Kokaska, C. J., & Brolin, D. E. (1985). *Career education for handicapped individuals* (2nd ed.). New York: Merrill/Macmillan.

Kollins, S. H., Barkley, R. A., & DuPaul, G. J. (2001). Use and management of medications for children diagnosed with attention deficit hyperactivity disorder (ADHD). *Focus on Exceptional Children, 33*(3), 1–24.

Kolstoe, O. P. (1976). *Teaching educable mentally retarded children* (2nd ed.). New York: Holt, Rinehart, & Winston.

Kominski, R., Shin, H., & Marotz, K. (2008). *Language needs of school-age children.* Paper presented at the annual meeting of the Population Association of America, New Orlean, LA. Retrieved September 3, 2009, from http://www.census.gov/population/www/socdemo/lang_use.html

Konrad, M., Helf, S., & Itoi, M. (2007). More bang for the book: Using children's literature to promote self-determination and literacy skills. *Teaching Exceptional Children, 40*(1), 64–71.

Krantz, P. J., & McClannahan, L. E. (1993). Teaching children with autism to Initiate to peers: Effects of a script-fading procedure. *Journal of Applied Behavior Analysis, 26,* 121–132.

Krashen, S. D. (1987). *Principles and practice in second language acquisition.* New York: Prentice Hall.

Kroeger, S. D., & Bauer, A. M. (2004). *Exploring diversity.* Upper Saddle River, NJ: Merrill Prentice Hall.

Kroth, R. (1981). Involvement with parents of behaviorally disordered adolescents. In G. Brown, R. L. McDowell, & J. Smith (Eds.), *Educating adolescents with behavior disorders* (pp. 123–139). Columbus, OH: Merrill/Prentice Hall.

Krouse, J., Gerber, M. M., & Kauffman, J. M. (1981). Peer tutoring: Procedures, promises, and unresolved issues. *Exceptional Education Quarterly, 1*(4), 107–115.

Krug, D. A., Arick, J. R., & Almond, P. J. (1980). *Autism screening instrument for educational planning (ASIEP).* Austin, TX: PRO-ED.

Kulik, J. A. (2003). Grouping and tracking. In N. Colangelo & G. A. Davis (Eds.), *Handbook of gifted education* (pp. 268–281). Boston: Allyn & Bacon.

Kurzweil Technologies, Inc. (2009). *Companies founded by Ray Kurzweil.* Retrieved August 24, 2009, from http://www.kurzweiltech.com/companies_flash.html

Lake, C., & Miguelez, J. M. (2003). Comparative analysis of microprocessors in upper limb prosthetics. *Journal of Prosthetics & Orthotics, 15*(2), 48–65.

Lambert, N., Nihira, K., & Leland, H. (1993). *AAMR adaptive behavior scale—School* (2nd ed.). Austin, TX: PRO-ED.

Lamers, K., & Hall, L. J. (2003). The response of children with autism to preferred prosody during instruction. *Focus on Autism and Other Developmental Disabilities, 18*(2), 95–104.

Landau, J. K., Vohs, J. R., & Romano, C. A. (1998). *All kids count.* Boston: Federation for Children with Special Needs. Excerpted on LDOnline: http://www.ldonline.org/ld_indepth/assessment/assessment.html

Landi, M. A. G. (2001). Helping students with learning disabilities make sense of word problems. *Intervention in School and Clinic, 37*(1), 13–18, 30.

Lane, K. L. (1999). Young students at risk for antisocial behavior: The utility of academic and social skills interventions. *Journal of Emotional and Behavioral Disorders, 7,* 211–223.

Lane, K. L., Barton-Arwood, S. M., Nelson, J. R., & Wehby, J. (2008). Academic performance of students with emotional and behavioral disorders placed in a self-contained setting. *Journal of Behavioral Education, 17*(1), 43–62.

Lane, K. L., Pierson, M. R., Robertson, F. E., & Little, A. (2004). Teachers' views of prereferral interventions: Perceptions of and recommendations for implementation support. *Education and Treatment of Children, 27,* 420–439.

Lapp, D., & Flood, J. (1992). *Teaching reading to every child* (3rd ed.). New York: Macmillan.

Larry P. v. Riles. C-71-2270-RFP (N. D. Cal. 1972), 495 F. Suppl. 96 (N. D. Cal. 1979) Aff'r (9th Cir. 1984), 1983–84 EHLR DEC. 555:304.

Laushey, K. M., & Heflin, J. L. (2000). Enhancing social skills of kindergarten children with autism through the training of multiple peers as tutors. *Journal of Autism and Developmental Disorders, 30*(3), 183–193.

Layton, C. A., & Lock, R. H. (2001). Determining learning disabilities in students with low vision. *Journal of Visual Impairment & Blindness, 95,* 288–298.

Lee, S. (2009, July 24). Evaluating teacher ed. *Inside Higher Education.* Retrieved July 25, 2009, from http://www.insidehighereducation.com/news/2009/07/24/teachered

Leffert, J., & Siperstein, G. N. (2003, Fall). A focus on social skills instruction for students with learning disabilities. *Current Practice Alerts, Alert Issue 9.* Retrieved from http://www.teachingld.org/ld_resources/alerts/

Leinhardt, G., & Pallay, A. (1982). Restrictive educational settings: Exile or haven? *Review of Educational Research, 52,* 557–578.

Lenz, B. K. (2006). Creating school-wide conditions for high-quality learning strategy classroom instruction. *Intervention in School and Clinic, 41,* 261–266.

Lerner, J. (2003). *Learning disabilities* (9th ed.). Boston: Houghton Mifflin.

Lerner, J. W., & Lowenthal, B. (1993). Attention deficit disorders: New responsibilities for special educators. *Learning Disabilities: A Multidisciplinary Journal, 4*(1), 1–8.

Lerner, J. W., Cousin, P. T., & Richeck, M. (1992). Critical issues in learning disabilities: Whole language learning. *Learning Disabilities Research & Practice, 7,* 226–230.

Lerner, J. W., Lowenthal, B., & Lerner, S. R. (1995). *Attention deficit disorders.* Pacific Grove, CA: Brooks/Cole.

Lerner, J., & Johns, B. (2009). *Learning disabilities and related mild disabilities* (11th ed.). Boston: Houghton Mifflin Harcourt.

Lewis, R. B. (1993). *Special education technology: Classroom applications.* Pacific Grove, CA: Brooks/Cole.

Lewis, R. B. (1998). Assistive technology and learning disabilities: Today's realities and tomorrow's promises. *Journal of Learning Disabilities, 31,* 16–26, 54.

Lewis, R. B. (2000). Musing on technology and learning disabilities on the occasion of the new millennium. *Journal of Special Education Technology, 15*(2), 5–12.

Lewis, R. B., Ashton, T., & Kieley, C. (1996). Word processing and individuals with learning disabilities: Overcoming the keyboard barrier [Computer software]. In *Eleventh Annual Conference on Technology for People with Disabilities, California State University, Northridge, submitted papers, 1996.* Newport Beach, CA: Rapidtext.

Lewis, R. B., Dell, S. J., Lynch, E. W., Harrison, P. J., & Saba, F. (1987). *Special education technology in action: Teachers speak out.* San Diego, CA: San Diego State University, Department of Special Education.

Lloyd, J. W., & Carnine, D. W. (Eds.). (1981). Foreword to structured instruction: Effective teaching of essential skills. *Exceptional Education Quarterly, 2*(1), viii–ix.

Lloyd, J. W., & Keller, C. E. (1989). Effective mathematics instruction: Development, instruction, and programs. *Focus on Exceptional Children, 21*(7), 1–10.

Lloyd, J. W., Crowley, E. P., Kohler, F. W., & Strain, P. S. (1988). Redefining the applied research agenda: Cooperative learning, prereferral, teacher consultation, and peer-mediated interventions. *Journal of Learning Disabilities, 21,* 43–52.

Lloyd, J. W., Kauffman, J. M., Landrum, T. J., & Roe, D. L. (1991). Why do teachers refer pupils for special education? An analysis of referral records. *Exceptionality, 2,* 115–126.

Loeding, B. L., & Greenan, J. P. (1999). Relationship between self-ratings by sensory impaired students and teacher's ratings of generalizable skills. *Journal of Visual Impairment & Blindness, 93,* 716–727.

Lord, C., Rutter, M., DiLavore, P. C., & Risi, S. (2001). *Autism diagnostic observation schedule: Manual (ADOS).* Los Angeles: Western Psychological Services.

Lovaas, O. I., & Newsom, C. D. (1976). Behavior modification with psychotic children. In H. Leitenberg (Ed.), *Handbook of behavior modification and behavior therapy* (pp. 303–360). Upper Saddle River, NJ: Prentice Hall.

Lowdermilk, J., Fielding, C., Mendoza, R., García de Alba, R., & Simpson, C. (2008). Selecting English language acquisition technology. *Technology in Action, 3*(2), 1–4.

Lowenbraun, S., & Thompson, M. D. (1986). Hearing impairments. In N. G. Haring & L. McCormick (Eds.), *Exceptional children and youth* (4th ed., pp. 357–395). New York: Merrill/Macmillan.

Luckner, J. L., & Carter, K. (2001). Essential competencies for teaching students with hearing loss and additional disabilities. *American Annals of the Deaf, 146,* 7–15.

Luckner, J., Bowen, S., & Carter, K. (2001). Visual teaching strategies for students who are deaf or hard of hearing. *Teaching Exceptional Children, 33*(3), 38–44.

Luetke-Stahlman, B., & Luckner, J. (1991). *Effectively educating students with hearing impairments.* White Plains: NY: Longman.

Luftig, R. L. (1989). *Assessment of learners with special needs.* Boston: Allyn & Bacon.

Lusthaus, E. & Forest, M. (1987). The kaleidoscope: A challenge to the cascade. In M. Forest (Ed.), *More education integration* (pp. 1–17). Downsview, Ontario: G. Allan Roeher Institute.

Lynch, E. W. (1981). *But I've tried everything! A special educator's guide to working with parents.* San Diego, CA: San Diego State University.

Lynch, E. W. (2004a). Conceptual framework: From culture shock to cultural learning. In E. W. Lynch & M. J. Hanson (Eds.), *Developing cross-cultural competence* (3rd ed., pp. 19–39). Baltimore: Brookes.

Lynch, E. W. (2004b). Developing cross-cultural competence. In E. W. Lynch & M. J. Hanson (Eds.), *Developing cross-cultural competence* (3rd ed., pp. 41–77). Baltimore: Brookes.

Lynch, E. W., & Hanson, M. J. (Eds.). (2004). *Developing cross-cultural competence* (3rd ed.). Baltimore: Brookes.

Maag, J. W., & Webber, J. (1995). Promoting children's social development in general education classrooms. *Preventing School Failure, 39*(3), 13–19.

MacArthur, C. A. (2009). Reflections on research on writing and technology for struggling writers. *Learning Disabilities Research & Practice, 24,* 93–103.

MacArthur, C. A., Graham, S., Haynes, J. B., & DeLaPaz, S. (1996). Spelling checkers and students with learning disabilities: Performance comparisons and impact on spelling. *Journal of Special Education, 30,* 35–57.

MacDuff, G. S., Krantz, P. J., & McClannahan, L. E. (2001). Prompts and prompt-fading strategies for people with autism. In C. Maurice, G. Green, & R. Foxx (Eds.), *Making a difference: Behavioral intervention for autism* (pp. 37–50). Austin, TX: PRO-ED.

Madden, N. A., & Slavin, R. E. (1983). Mainstreaming students with mild handicaps: Academic and social outcomes. *Review of Educational Research, 53,* 519–569.

Madsen, C. H., Becker, W. C., & Thomas, D. R. (1968). Rules, praise, and ignoring: Elements of elementary classroom control. *Journal of Applied Behavior Analysis, 1,* 139–151.

Mager, R. F. (1984). *Preparing instructional objectives* (rev. ed.). Belmont, CA: Pitman Learning.

Maginnis, G. (1969). The readability graph and informal reading inventories. *The Reading Teacher, 22,* 534–538.

Maheady, L., Harper, G. F., & Mallette, B. (2003, Spring). A focus on class wide peer tutoring. *Current Practice Alerts, Alert Issue 8.* Retrieved from http://www.teachingld.org/ld_resources/alerts/

Maheady, L., Sacca, M. K., & Harper, G. F. (1988). Classwide peer tutoring with mildly handicapped high school students. *Exceptional Children, 55,* 52–59.

Maker, C. J. (2001). DISCOVER: Assessing and developing problem solving. *Gifted Education International, 15*(3), 232–51.

Maker, C. J., & Nielson, A. B. (1996). *Curriculum development and teaching strategies for gifted learners* (2nd ed.). Austin, TX: PRO-ED.

Mandell, C. J., & Fiscus, E. (1981). *Understanding exceptional people.* St. Paul, MN: West.

Manning, M. L., & Baruth, L. G. (1995). *Students at risk.* Boston: Allyn & Bacon.

Manzo, K. K. (1996). Slow progress in reaching goals for 2000 reported. *Education Week, 16*(13), 6.

Markel, G. (1981). Improving test-taking skills of LD adolescents. *Academic Therapy, 16,* 333–342.

Markow, D., & Martin, S. (2005). *Transitions and the role of supportive relationships: A survey of teachers, principals and students.* Retrieved July 9, 2009, from http://www.metlife.com/about/corporate-profile/citizenship/metlife-foundation/metlife-survey-of-the-american-teacher.html

Markwardt, F. C. (1998). *Peabody individual achievement test—Revised/normative update.* Circle Pines, MN: American Guidance Service.

Maron, S. S., & Martinez, D. H. (1980). Environmental alternatives for the visually handicapped. In J. W. Schifani, R. M. Anderson, & S. J. Odle (Eds.), *Implementing learning in the least restrictive environment* (pp. 149–198). Baltimore: University Park Press.

Martin, E. W. (1974). Some thoughts on mainstreaming. *Exceptional Children, 41,* 150–153.

Martin, J. E., Marshall, J. H., & Sale, P. (2004). A 3-year study of middle, junior high, and high school IEP meetings. *Exceptional Children, 70,* 285–297.

Marttila, J., & Mills, M. (1995). *Knowledge is power.* Bettendorf, IA: Mississippi Bend Area Education Agency.

Mason, S., McGee, G. G., Farmer-Dougan, V., & Risley, T. (1989). A practical strategy for ongoing reinforcer assessment. *Journal of Behavior Analysis, 22,* 171–179.

Masse, L. (2001). Direction of gifted education in the first decade of the 21st century: A step back, continuity, and new direction. *Journal of Secondary Gifted Education, 12,* 170–173.

Mastropieri, M., & Scruggs, T. (2004). *The inclusive classroom: Strategies for effective education* (2nd ed.). Upper Saddle River, NJ: Merrill/Prentice Hall.

Mather, N. (1992). Whole language reading instruction for students with learning disabilities: Caught in the cross fire. *Learning Disabilities Research & Practice, 7,* 87–95.

Mathews, J. (2009). Favorite education blogs of 2008. *The Washington Post.* Retrieved May 23, 2009, from http://www.washingtonpost.com/wp-dyn/content/article/2008/04/07/AR2008040700387.html

Mathews, R. (2000). Cultural patterns of South Asian and Southeast Asian Americans. *Intervention in School and Clinic, 36,* 101–104.

Maurice, C. (1993). *Let me hear your voice.* London: Robert Hale.

Maxon, A., Brackett, D., & van den Berg, S. (1991). Classroom amplification use: A national long-term study. *Language, Speech, and Hearing Services in Schools, 22,* 242–253.

Mayer, R. E. (2004). Should there be a three-strikes rule against pure discovery learning? *American Psychologist, 59,* 14–19.

McCarney, S. B., & Arthaud, T. J. (2005). *Behavior evaluation scale—Third edition.* Columbia, MO: Hawthorne Educational Services.

McClannahan, L. E., & Krantz, P. J. (1999). *Activity schedules for children with autism: Teaching independent behavior.* Bethesda, MD: Woodbine House.

McClannahan, L. E., & Krantz, P. J. (2005). *Teaching conversation to children with autism.* Bethesda, MD: Woodbine House.

McCoach, D. B., & Siegle. D. (2003). Factors that differentiate underachieving gifted students from high-achieving gifted students. *Gifted Child Quarterly, 47*(2), 144–154.

McCormick, L. (1986). Keeping up with language intervention trends. *Teaching Exceptional Children, 18*(2), 123–129.

McCormick, L. (1990). Cultural diversity and exceptionality. In N. G. Haring & L. McCormick (Eds.), *Exceptional children and youth* (5th ed., pp. 46–75). New York: Merrill/Macmillan.

McDonnell, J. (1987). The integration of students with severe handicaps into regular public schools: An analysis of parents' perceptions of potential outcomes. *Education and Training in Mental Retardation, 22,* 98–111.

McGaha, C. G., & Farran, D. C. (2001). Interactions in an inclusive classroom: The effects of visual status and setting. *Journal of Visual Impairment & Blindness, 95,* 80–94.

McGinnis, E., & Goldstein, A. P. (1997). *Skillstreaming the elementary school child: New strategies and perspectives for teaching prosocial skills.* Champaign, IL: Research Press.

McIntosh, R., Vaughn, S., & Zaragoza, N. (1991). A review of social interventions for students with learning disabilities. *Journal of Learning Disabilities, 24,* 451–458.

McLoughlin, J. A., & Lewis, R. B. (2008). *Assessing students with special needs* (7th ed.). Upper Saddle River, NJ: Merrill Prentice Hall.

McNamara, K., & Hollinger, C. (2003). Intervention-based assessment: Evaluation rates and eligibility findings. *Learning Disabilities Research & Practice, 18,* 181–193.

Medley, D. M. (1982). Teacher effectiveness. In H. E. Mitzel (Ed.), *Encyclopedia of educational research* (5th ed., pp. 1894–1903). New York: Free Press.

Meisgeier, C. (1981). A social/behavioral program for the adolescent student with serious learning problems. *Focus on Exceptional Children, 13*(9), 1–13.

Mercer, C. D., & Mercer, A. R. (1989). *Teaching students with learning problems* (3rd ed.). New York: Merrill/Macmillan.

Mercer, C. D., & Mercer, A. R. (1993). *Teaching students with learning problems* (4th ed.). New York: Merrill/Macmillan.

Mercer, C. D., & Mercer, A. R. (2005). *Teaching students with learning problems* (7th ed.). Upper Saddle River, NJ: Merrill/Prentice Hall.

Mercer, C. D., & Pullen, P. C. (2005). *Students with learning disabilities* (6th ed.). Upper Saddle River, NJ: Merrill/Prentice Hall.

Mercer, J. R. (1973). *Labeling the mentally retarded.* Berkeley: University of California Press.

Mesibov, G. B., Schopler, E., Schaffer, B., & Landrus, R. (1988). *Adolescent and Adult Psychoeducational Profile (AAPEP): Volume IV.* Austin, TX: PRO-ED.

Mesibov, G. B., Shea, V., & Schopler, E. (2004). *The TEACCH approach to autism spectrum disorders.* New York: Springer.

Mesibov, G., & Howley, M. (2003). *Accessing the curriculum for pupils with autistic spectrum disorders.* London: David Fulton Publishers.

Meyen, E. L. (1981). *Developing instructional units* (3rd ed.). Dubuque, IA: Brown.

Migliore, E. T. (2003). Eliminating bullying in your classroom. *Intervention in School and Clinic, 38*(3), 172–176.

Miller, A. K., & Chandler, K. (2003). *Violence in U.S. public schools: 2000 school survey on crime and safety.* Washington, DC: U.S. Department of Education, National Center for Education Statistics.

Miller, M. (2003). Students' views of least restrictive environment: A pilot study. *Learning Disabilities, 12,* 85–88.

Mills, C. J. (2003). Characteristics of effective teachers of gifted students: Teacher background and personality styles of students. *Gifted Child Quarterly, 47*(4), 272–281.

Mills, P. J. (1979). Education within the mainstream: Suggestions for classroom teachers. *The Directive Teacher, 2*(2), 16.

Mira, M. P., & Tyler, J. S. (1991). Students with traumatic brain injury: Making the transition from hospital to school. *Focus on Exceptional Children, 23*(5), 1–12.

Molebash, P. E., Dodge, B., Bell, R. L., Mason, C. L., & Irving, K. E. (2004.) Promoting student inquiry: WebQuests to web inquiry projects (WIPs). Retrieved June 13, 2008, from http://webinquiry.org/WIP_Intro.htm

Monroe, C. R., & Obidah, J. E. (2004). The influence of cultural synchronization on a teacher's perception of disruption: A case study of an African American middle-school classroom. *Journal of Teacher Education, 55*(3), 256–268.

Montague, M. (1992). The effects of cognitive and metacognitive strategy instruction on the mathematical problem-solving of middle school students with learning disabilities. *Journal of Learning Disabilities, 25,* 230–248.

Montague, M., Warger, C., & Morgan, T. H. (2000). Solve it! Strategy instruction to improve mathematical problem solving. *Learning Disabilities Research & Practice, 15,* 110–116.

Montgomery, M. D. (1978). The special educator as consultant: Some strategies. *Teaching Exceptional Children, 10,* 110–112.

Montgomery, W. (2001). Creating culturally responsive, inclusive classrooms. *Teaching Exceptional Children, 33*(4), 4–8.

Morrison, G. M., & Polloway, E. A. (1995). Mental retardation. In E. L. Meyen & T. M. Skrtic (Eds.), *Special education and student disability* (4th ed., pp. 212–269). Denver: Love.

Morrison, W. F., & Omdal, S. N. (2000). The twice exceptional student. *Reclaiming Children and Youth, 9*(2), 103–106.

Morsink, C. V., & Lenk, L. L. (1992). The delivery of special education programs and services. *Remedial and Special Education, 13*(6), 33–43.

Mukherjee, S., Lightfoot, J., & Sloper, P. (2000). The inclusion of pupils with a chronic health condition in mainstream school: What does it mean for teachers? *Educational Research, 42,* 59–72.

Munson, S. M. (1986). Regular education teacher modifications for mainstreamed mildly handicapped students. *Journal of Special Education, 20,* 489–502.

Murdick, N. L., & Petch-Hogan, B. (1996). Inclusive classroom management: Using preintervention strategies. *Intervention in School and Clinic, 31,* 172–176.

Myles, B. S. (2005). *Children and youth with Asperger syndrome: Strategies for success in inclusive settings.* Thousand Oaks, CA: Corwin Press.

Myles, B. S., & Simpson, R. L. (1998a). *Asperger syndrome: A guide for educators and parents.* Austin, TX: PRO-ED.

Myles, B. S., & Simpson, R. L. (1998b). Inclusion of students with autism in general education classrooms: The autism inclusion collaboration model. In R. L. Simpson & B. S. Myles (Eds.), *Educating children and youth with autism: Strategies for effective practice* (pp. 241–256). Austin, TX: PRO-ED.

National Advisory Committe on Handicapped Children. (1968). *Special education for handicapped children* [First annual report]. Washington, DC: U.S. Department of Health, Education, and Welfare.

National Association for Gifted Children. (2008). *State of the nation. A summary of the 2006–2007 State of the States report.* Retrieved April 11, 2008, from http://www.nagc.org/index.aspx?id=1051

National Association of State Directors of Special Education. (1991). *An overview of standards and policy on the use of time-out as a behavior management strategy.* Alexandria, VA: Author. (ERIC Document Reproduction Service No. ED389118).

National Association of the Deaf. (2000). *Cochlear implants: NAD position statement.* Retrieved June 7, 2009, from http://www.nad.org/ciposition

National Center for Culturally Responsive Educational Systems. (2006–2008). Mission & outcomes. Retrieved September 4, 2009, from http://www.nccrest.org/about/mission.html

National Center for Education Statistics, U.S. Department of Education. (2004). *Issue brief: English language learner students in U.S. public schools: 1994 and 2000.* Retrieved September 7, 2009, from http://nces.ed.gov/pubs2004/2004035.pdf

National Center for Education Statistics, U.S. Department of Education. (2006). *Fast facts.* From Public elementary and secondary students, staff, schools, and school districts: School year 2003-04. Retrieved September 3, 2009, from http://nces.ed.gov/fastfacts/display.asp?id=96

National Center for Education Statistics, U.S. Department of Education. (2009). *State education reforms.* Retrieved September 3, 2009, from http://nces.ed.gov/programs/statereform/tab3_6.asp

National Center for Education Statistics. (2007a). *Fast facts: Back to school statistics.* Retrieved August 22, 2007, from http://nces.ed.gov/fastfacts/display.asp?id=372

National Center for Education Statistics. (2007b). *Digest of education statistics: 2006.* Washington, DC. Retrieved January 23, 2008, from http://nces.ed.gov/programs/digest/d06/tables/dt06_003.asp?referrer=report

National Center for Education Statistics. (2007c). *Status and trends in the education of racial and ethnic minorities.* Washington, DC. Retrieved January 23, 2008, from http://nces.ed.gov/pubs2007/minoritytrends/#1

National Center for Education Statistics. (2007d). *Status in trends in the education of racial and ethnic minorities: Highlights.* Retrieved July 2, 2008, from http://nces.ed.gov/pubs2007/minoritytrends/

National Center for Education Statistics. (2007e). *Status in trends in the education of racial and ethnic minorities: Indicator 28: Median Income.* Retrieved July 2, 2008, from http://nces.ed.gov/pubs2007/minoritytrends/ind_7_28.asp

National Center for Health Statistics. (2008). *Child health.* Retrieved July 19, 2008, from http://www.cdc.gov/nchs/fastats/children.htm

National Center for Learning Disabilities, Inc. (2007). *Learning disabilities checklist*. Retrieved June 30, 2009, from http://www.ncld.org/publications-a-more/checklists-worksheets-a-forms/ld-checklist-of-signs-and-symptoms

National Center for Learning Disabilities. (2001). *LD at a glance*. Retrieved September 4, 2004, from http://www.ld.org/LDInfoZone/InfoZone_FactSheet_LD.cfm#

National Center on Response to Instruction. (2008). *What is RTI?* Retrieved February 18, 2008, from http://www.rti4success.org

National Clearinghouse for English Language Acquisition and Language Instruction Educational Programs. (2007a). *NCELA frequently asked questions: What are the most common language groups for ELL students?* Retrieved July 10, 2008, from http://www.ncela.gwu.edu/expert/faq/05toplangs.html

National Clearinghouse for English Language Acquisition and Language Instruction Educational Programs. (2007b). *The growing numbers of English proficient students: 1995/96-2005/06*. Washington, DC. Retrieved January 23, 2008, from http://www.ncela.gwu.edu/stats/2_nation.htm

National Coalition of Advocates for Students. (1985). *Barriers to excellence: Our children at risk*. Boston: Author.

National Commission on Excellence in Education. (1983). *A nation at risk: The imperative for educational reform*. Washington, DC: U.S. Government Printing Office.

National Council of Teachers of Mathematics. (1989). *Curriculum and evaluation standards for school mathematics*. Reston, VA: Author.

National Council of Teachers of Mathematics. (2000). *Principles and standards for school mathematics*. Retrieved August 21, 2003, from http://standards.nctm.org

National Education Association. (2007). *'No Child Left Behind' Act/ESEA*. Retrieved January 22, 2008, from http://www.nea.org/esea/policy.html

National Education Goals Panel. (1997). *Commonly asked questions*. Retrieved from http://www.negp.gov/caq/html

National Information Center for Children and Youth with Disabilities. (1997a). *General information about traumatic brain injury: Fact sheet number 4*. Washington, DC: Author.

National Information Center for Children and Youth with Disabilities. (1997b). *Speech and language disorders*. Washington, DC: Author.

National Information Center for Children and Youth with Disabilities. (2001a). *General information about deafness and hearing loss: Fact sheet number 3*. Washington, DC: Author.

National Information Center for Children and Youth with Disabilities. (2001b). *General information about visual impairments: Fact sheet number 13*. Washington, DC: Author.

National Institute on Deafness and Other Communication Disorders. (2007a). *Cochlear implants*. Retrieved June 7, 2009, from http://www.nidcd.nih.gov/health/hearing/coch.asp

National Institute on Deafness and Other Communication Disorders. (2007b). *Hearing aids*. Retrieved June 7, 2009, from http://www.nidcd.nih.gov/health/hearing/hearingaid.asp

National Joint Committee on Learning Disabilities. (1994). *Collective perspectives on issues affecting learning disabilities*. Austin, TX: PRO-ED.

National Research Council. (1997). *Executive summary. Educating one & all: Students with disabilities and standards-based reform*. Washington, DC: National Academy Press.

National Research Council. (2001). *Educating children with autism*. Committee on Educational Interventions for Children with Autism, Division of Behavioral and Social Sciences and Education. Washington, DC: National Academy Press.

Neal, J., Bigby, L., & Nicholson, R. (2004). Occupational therapy, physical therapy, and orientation and mobility services in public schools. *Intervention in School and Clinic, 39*(4), 218–222.

Nelson, C. M. (1988). Social skill training for handicapped students. *Teaching Exceptional Children, 20*(4), 19–23.

Nelson, C. M. (1993). Students with behavioral disorders. In A. E. Blackhurst & W. H. Berdine (Eds.), *An introduction to special education* (3rd ed., pp. 528–561). New York: HarperCollins.

Nelson, J. R., Benner, G. J., Lane, K., & Smith, B. W. (2004). Academic achievement of K–12 students with emotional and behavioral disorders. *Exceptional Children, 71*, 59–73.

Nelson, J. R., Stage, S., Duppong-Hurley, K., Synhorst, L., & Epstein, M. H. (2007). Risk factors predictive of the problem behavior of children at risk for emotional and behavioral disorders. *Exceptional Children, 73*, 367–379.

New York State Department of Health Early Intervention Program. (1999). *The guideline technical report: Autism/pervasive developmental disorders*. Albany: New York State Department of Health.

Newcomer, P. L., & Hammill, D. D. (1997). *Test of language development–3, Primary*. Austin, TX: PRO-ED.

Nietupski, J., Hamre-Nietupski, S., Curtin, S., & Shrikanth, K. (1997). A review of curricular research in severe disabilities from 1976 to 1995 in six selected journals. *Journal of Special Education, 31*, 36–55.

Nirje, B. (1969). The normalization principle and its human management implications. In R. B. Kugel & W. Wolfensberger (Eds.), *Changing patterns in residential services for the mentally retarded* (pp. 231–240). Washington, DC: U.S. Government Printing Office.

Norris, C., & Soloway, E. (2009). *Get cell phones into schools*. Retrieved May 1, 2009, from http://www.businessweek.com/technology/content/jan2009/tc20090114_741903.htm

Norris, W. C. (1977). Via technology to a new era in education. *Phi Delta Kappan, 58*, 451–453.

Northcutt, L., & Watson, D. (1986). *Sheltered English teaching handbook*. San Marcos, CA: AM Graphics & Printing.

O'Conor, R. E., White, A., & Swanson, H. L. (2007). Repeated reading versus continuous reading: Influences on reading fluency and comprehension. *Exceptional Children, 74*, 31–46.

Odom, S. L., McConnell, S. R., & Chandler, L. K. (1994). Acceptability and feasibility of classroom based social interaction interventions for young children with disabilities. *Exceptional Children, 60*, 226–236.

Office for Civil Rights. (2008). *Office for Civil Rights Elementary and Secondary School Survey, 2006*. Retrieved May 30, 2008, from http://ocrdata.ed.gov/ocr2006rv30/xls/2006Projected.html

Olenchak, F. R., & Reis, S. M. (2002). Gifted students with learning disabilities. In M. Neihart, S. M. Reis, N. M. Robinson, & S. M. Moon (Eds.), *The social and emotional development of gifted children: What do we know?* (pp. 177–191). Waco, TX: Prufrock Press.

Olson, J. L., & Platt, J. M. (1996). *Teaching children and adolescents with special needs* (2nd ed.). Upper Saddle River, NJ: Merrill/Prentice Hall.

Olson, J. L., Platt, J. C., & Dieker, L. A. (2008). *Teaching children and adolescents with special needs* (5th ed.). Upper Saddle River, NJ: Merrill Prentice Hall.

Olson, L. (2004). Enveloping expectations. [Special issue: *Quality counts 2004: Count me in.*] *Education Week, 23*(17), 8–21.

Olson, M. L. (2006). A decade of effort. *Education Week, 25*(17), 8–16.

Orr, L. E., Craig, G. P., Best, J., Borland, A., Holland, D., Knodel, H., Lehman, A., et al. (1997). Exploring developmental disabilities through literature: An annotated bibliography. *Teaching Exceptional Children, 29*(6), 14–17.

Osguthorpe, R. T., & Scruggs, T. E. (1986). Special education students as tutors: A review and analysis. *Remedial and Special Education, 7*(4), 15–26.

Ottenbacher, K. J., Tickle-Degnen, L., & Hasselkus, B. R. (2002). Therapists awake! The challenge of evidence-based occupational therapy, *The American Journal of Occupational Therapy, 56*(3), 247–249.

Overview, four pillars of NCLB. (2004). Retrieved January 21, 2009, from http://www.ed.gov/nclb/overview/intro/4pillars.html

Pacchiano, D. M. (2000). A review of instructional variables related to student problem behavior. *Preventing School Failure, 4,* 174–178.

Padrón, Y. N., Waxman, H. C., & Rivera, H. H. (2002). *Educating Hispanic students: Obstacles and avenues to improved academic achievement.* Santa Cruz: Center for Research on Education, Diversity and Education, University of California, Santa Cruz.

Palinscar, A. S., & Brown, A. L. (1988). Teaching and practicing thinking skills to promote comprehension in the context of group problem solving. *Remedial and Special Education, 9*(1), 53–59.

Palmer, D. S., Fuller, K., Arora, T., & Nelson, M. (2001). Taking sides: Parent views on inclusion for their children with severe disabilities. *Exceptional Children, 67,* 467–484.

Pang, V. O., & Park, C. D. (2003). Examination of the self-regulation mechanism: Prejudice reduction in pre-service teachers. *Action in Teacher Education, 25*(3), 1–11.

Papalia-Berardi, A., & Hall, T. E. (2007). Teacher assistance team social validity: A perspective from general education teachers. *Education and Treatment of Children, 30,* 89–110.

Parette, H. P., & Petch-Hogan, B. (2000). Approaching families: Facilitating culturally/linguistically diverse family involvement. *Teaching Exceptional Children, 33*(2), 4–10.

Park, A. (2008, June 2) How safe are vaccines? *Time* (pp. 36–41).

Parker, J. P. (1989). *Instructional strategies for teaching the gifted.* Boston: Allyn & Bacon.

Parson, L. R., & Heward, W. L. (1979). Training peers to tutor: Evaluation of a training package for primary learning disabled students. *Journal of Applied Behavior Analysis, 12,* 309–310.

Partington, J. W. (2006). *The assessment of basic language and learning skills (ABLLS-R Protocol): An assessment, curriculum guide, and skills tracking system for children with autism and other developmental disabilities.* Pleasant Hill, CA: Behavior Analysts, Inc.

Pasanella, A. L., & Volkmor, C. B. (1981). *Teaching handicapped students in the mainstream* (2nd ed.). Columbus, OH: Merrill/Prentice Hall.

Patrick, J. L., & Reschly, D. J. (1982). Relationship of state educational criteria and demographic variables to school-system prevalence of mental retardation. *American Journal of Mental Deficiency, 86,* 351–360.

Patton, J. E., Snell, J., Knight, W. J., & Gerken, K. (2001). *A survey study of elementary classroom seating designs.* Paper presented at the Annual Meeting of the National Association of School Psychologists (Washington, DC, April 17–21, 2001). (ERIC Document Reproduction Service No. ED454194).

Pavri, S., & Luftig, R. (2000). The social face of inclusive education: Are students with learning disabilities really included in the classroom? *Preventing School Failure, 45,* 8–14.

Payan, R. M. (1989). Language assessment for the bilingual exceptional child. In L. M. Baca & H. T. Cervantes (Eds.), *The bilingual special education interface* (pp. 125–152). Columbus, OH: Merrill.

Pemberton, J. B. (2003). Communicating academic progress as an integral part of assessment. *Teaching Exceptional Children, 35*(4), 16–20.

Pendarvis, E. D. (1993). Students with unique gifts and talents. In A. E. Blackhurst & W. H. Berdine (Eds.), *An introduction to special education* (3rd ed., pp. 563–599). New York: HarperCollins.

Pendergast, D. E. (1995). Preparing for children who are medically fragile in educational programs. *Teaching Exceptional Children, 27*(2), 37–41.

Pepper, F. C. (1976). Teaching the American Indian child in mainstream settings. In R. L. Jones (Ed.), *Mainstreaming and the minority child* (pp. 133–158). Reston, VA: The Council for Exceptional Children.

Perske, R., & Perske, M. (1988). *Circles of friends: People with disabilities and their friends enrich the lives of one another.* Nashville, TN: Abington.

Peters, W. A. M., Grager-Loidl, H., & Supplee, P. (2000). Underachievement in gifted children and adolescents: Theory and practice. In K. A. Heller, F. J. Mönks, R. J. Sternberg, & R. F. Subotnik (Eds.), *International handbook of giftedness and talent* (2nd ed., 609–620). Oxford: Elsevier Science Ltd.

Pew Research Center. (2007). *What Americans pay for—and how: "Information age bills keep piling up."* Retrieved April 30, 2009, from http://pewsocialtrends.org/pubs/407/what-americans-pay-for—and-how

Phelan, P. (1996). *High interest easy reading: An annotated booklist for middle school and senior high school* (7th ed.). Urbana, IL: National Council of Teachers of English.

Pierce, C. D., Reid, R., & Epstein, M. H. (2004). Teacher-mediated interventions for children with EBD and their academic outcomes: A review. *Remedial and Special Education, 25*(3), 175–188.

Piirto, J. (2007). *Talented children and adults: Their development and education* (3rd ed.). Upper Saddle River, NJ: Merrill/Prentice Hall.

Platt, J. M., & Platt, J. S. (1980). Volunteers for special education: A mainstreaming support system. *Teaching Exceptional Children, 13,* 31–34.

Polloway, E. A., & Patton, J. R. (1993). *Strategies for teaching learners with special needs* (5th ed.). New York: Merrill/Macmillan.

Polloway, E. A., Patton, J. R., & Serna, L. (2008). *Strategies for teaching learners with special needs* (9th ed.). Upper Saddle River, NJ: Pearson Prentice Hall.

Postel, C. A. (1986). Death in my classroom? *Teaching Exceptional Children, 18,* 139–143.

Posth, M. A. (1997, March). Why the Web? *Mac Home Journal,* 36–37.

Prasad, S. (1994). Assessing social interactions of children with disabilities. *Teaching Exceptional Children, 26*(2), 23–25.

Prater, M. A. (1994). Improving academic and behavior skills through self-management procedures. *Preventing School Failure, 38*(4), 5–9.

Prater, M. A., & Dyches, T. T. (2008). Books that portray characters with disabilities: A top 25 list for children and young adults. *Teaching Exceptional Children, 40*(4), 32–38.

Prater, M. A., Dyches, T. T., & Johnstun, M. (2006). Teaching students about learning disabilities through children's literature. *Intervention in School and Clinic, 42,* 14–24.

President's Committee for People with Intellectual Disabilities. (2004). *Frequently asked questions.* Washington, DC: Author.

Retrieved September 18, 2004, from http://www.acf.hhs.gov/programs/pcpid/

President's Committee on Mental Retardation. (1969). *The six hour retarded child.* Washington, DC: U.S. Department of Health, Education, and Welfare.

President's Committee on Mental Retardation. (1975). *The problem of mental retardation.* Washington, DC: U.S. Department of Health, Education, and Welfare.

Prestia, K. (2003). Tourette's syndrome: Characteristics and interventions. *Intervention in School and Clinic, 39*(2), 67–71.

Prizant, B. M., Wetherby, A. M., & Rydell, P. J. (2000). Communication intervention issues for children with autism spectrum disorders. In A. M. Wetherby & B. M. Prizant (Eds.), *Autism spectrum disorders: A transactional developmental perspective* (pp. 193–224). Baltimore: Brookes.

Puckett, K. S. (2004). Process ACCESS: Field testing an assistive technology toolkit for students with mild disabilities. *Journal of Special Education Technology, 19*(2), 5–17.

Pumpian, I. (1988). Severe multiple handicaps. In E. W. Lynch & R. B. Lewis (Eds.), *Exceptional children and adults* (pp. 180–226). Glenview, IL: Scott, Foresman.

Putnam, J. M. (1992). Teaching students with severe disabilities in the regular classroom. In L. G. Cohen (Ed.), *Children with exceptional needs in regular classrooms* (pp. 118–142). Washington, DC: National Education Association.

Quality Education Data, Inc. (1985). *Microcomputer usage in schools, 1984–1985.* Denver: Author.

Quay, H. C. (1979). Classification. In H. C. Quay & J. S. Werry (Eds.), *Psychopathological disorders of childhood* (2nd ed.). New York: Wiley.

Quinn, B., S., Behrmann, M., Mastropieri, M., Bausch, M. E., Ault, M. J., & Chung, Y. (2009). Who is using assistive technology in schools? *Journal of Special Education Technology, 24*(1), 1–13.

Quinn, M. M., Rutherford, R. B., & Leone, P. E. (2001). *Students with disabilities in correctional facilities.* ERIC Digest. Arlington, VA: ERIC Clearinghouse on Disabilities and Gifted Education. (ERIC Document Reproduction Service No. ED461958). Retrieved April 8, 2008, from http://www.ericec.org

Raison, S. B. (1979). Curriculum modification for special needs at the secondary level. *Education Unlimited, 1*(3), 19–21.

Rapport, J. K. (1996). Legal guidelines for the delivery of special health care services in schools. *Exceptional Children, 62,* 537–549.

Ratleff, J. E. (1989). *Instructional strategies for crosscultural students with special education needs.* Sacramento, CA: Resources in Special Education.

Ray, B. M. (1985). Measuring the social position of the mainstreamed handicapped child. *Exceptional Children, 52,* 57–62.

Rees, T. (1992). Students with hearing impairments. In L. G. Cohen (Ed.), *Children with exceptional needs in regular classrooms* (pp. 98–117). Washington, DC: National Education Association.

Reeve, R. E. (1990). ADHD: Facts and fallacies. *Intervention in School and Clinic, 26,* 70–78.

Reid, D. K., Hresko, W. P., & Swanson, H. L. (Eds.). (1996). *Cognitive approaches to learning disabilities* (3rd ed.). Austin, TX: PRO-ED.

Reid, R. (1996). Research in self-monitoring with students with learning disabilities: The present, the prospects, the pitfalls. *Journal of Learning Disabilities, 29,* 317–331.

Reis, S. M., Westberg, K. L., Kulikowich, J. M., & Purcell, J. H. (1998). Curriculum compacting and achievement test scores: What does the research say? *Gifted Child Quarterly, 42*(2), 123–129.

Renzulli, J. S. (1978). What makes giftedness? Re-examining a definition. *Phi Delta Kappan, 60,* 180–184.

Renzulli, J. S., Smith, L., White, A., Callahan, C., & Hartman, R. (2001). *Scales for rating the behavioral characteristics of superior students* (rev. ed.). Manual and nine rating scales. Mansfield Center, CT: Creative Learning Press.

Reschly, D. J., & Lamprecht, M. J. (1979). Expectancy effects of labels: Fact or artifact? *Exceptional Children, 46,* 55–58.

Research and Training Center on Independent Living. (2001). *Guidelines for reporting and writing about people with disabilities* (6th ed.). University of Kansas. Retrieved January 25, 2008, from http:// www.lsi.ku.edu/lsi/internal/guidelines.html

Reynolds, C. R., & Bigler, E. D. (1994). *Test of memory and learning.* Austin, TX: PRO-ED.

Reynolds, M. C., & Birch, J. W. (1982). *Teaching exceptional children in all America's schools* (rev. ed.). Reston, VA: The Council for Exceptional Children.

Reynolds, M. C., & Birch, J. W. (1988). *Adaptive mainstreaming* (3rd ed.). New York: Longman.

Reynolds, M. C., Zetlin, A. G., & Wang, M. C. (1993). 20/20 analysis: Taking a close look at the margins. *Exceptional Children, 59,* 294–300.

Rich, H. L., & Ross, S. M. (1989). Students' time on learning tasks in special education. *Exceptional Children, 55,* 508–515.

Richardson, R. C. (2000). Teaching social and emotional competence. *Children & Schools, 22,* 246–251.

Richert, E. S. (2003). Excellence with justice in identification and programming. In N. Colangelo & G. A. Davis (Eds.), *Handbook of gifted education* (3rd ed., pp. 146–158). Boston: Allyn & Bacon.

Rieth, H., & Evertson, C. M. (1988). Variables related to the effective instruction of difficult-to-teach children. *Focus on Exceptional Children, 20*(5), 1–8.

Rinaldi, C., & Samson, J. (2008). English language learners and Response to Intervention. *Teaching Exceptional Children, 40*(5), 6–14.

Rivera, B. D., & Rogers-Adkinson, D. (1997). Culturally sensitive interventions: Social skills training with children and parents from culturally and linguistically diverse backgrounds. *Intervention in School and Clinic, 33,* 75–80.

Roberts, S. (2007, November 17). In U.S. name count, Garcias are catching up with Jones. *New York Times,* pp. A1, A13.

Robinson, N. M., Reis, S. M., Neihart, M., & Moon, S. M. (2002). Social and emotional issues facing gifted and talented students: What have we learned and what should we do now? In M. Neihart, S. M. Reis, N. M. Robinson, & S. M. Moon (Eds.), *The social and emotional development of gifted children* (pp. 267–289). Waco, TX: Prufrock Press.

Robinson, S., & Deshler, D. D. (1995). Learning disabled. In E. L. Meyen & T. M. Skrtic (Eds.), *Special education and student disability* (4th ed., pp. 170–211). Denver: Love.

Rockefeller, N. A. (1976, October 16). Don't accept anyone's verdict that you are lazy, stupid, or retarded. *TV Guide,* pp. 12–14.

Rodriguez, C. D., & Higgins, K. (2005). Preschool children with developmental delays and limited English proficiency. *Intervention in School and Clinic, 40,* 236–242.

Rodriguez, R. C., Cole, J. T., Stile, S. W., & Gallegos, R. L. (1979). Bilingualism and biculturalism for the special education classroom. *Teacher Education and Special Education, 2*(4), 69–74.

Roid, G. (2003). *Stanford-Binet intelligence scales, Fifth edition*. Itasca, IL: Riverside Publishing.

Roland, P. (1989, August). A parent speaks to special educators. *Exceptional Times*, p. 3.

Romero, A. P., Baumie, A. K., Badgett, M. V. L., & Gates, G. J. (2007). *Census snapshot United States*. Retrieved July 14, 2008, from http://www.law.ucla.edu/williamsinstitute/publications/USCensusSnapshot.pdf

Rose, L. C., & Gallup, A. M. (2007). The 39th Annual Phi Delta Kappa/Gallup Poll of the Public's Attitudes Toward the Public Schools. *Phi Delta Kappan, 89*, 33–48. Retrieved January 22, 2008, from http://www.pdkintl.org/kappan/kpollpdf.htm

Rose, L. C., Gallup, A. M., & Elam, S. M. (1997). The 29th annual Phi Delta Kappa/Gallup poll of the public's attitudes toward the public schools. *Phi Delta Kappan, 79*, 41–56.

Rosenkoetter, S. E., & Fowler, S. A. (1986). Teaching mainstreamed children to manage daily transitions. *Teaching Exceptional Children, 19*(1), 20–23.

Rosenshine, B., & Stevens, R. (1986). Teaching functions. In M. C. Wittrock (Ed.), *Handbook of research on teaching* (3rd ed., pp. 376–391). New York: Macmillan.

Rowland, C., & Schweigert, P. (2000). *Tangible symbol systems*. Portland, OR: OHSU Center on Self-Determination.

Rubin, R. A., & Balow, B. (1978). Prevalence of teacher identified behavior problems: A longitudinal study. *Exceptional Children, 45*, 102–111.

Ruiz, N. T. (1989). An optimal learning environment for Rosemary. *Exceptional Children, 56*, 130–144.

Rutter, M., LeCouteur, A. L., & Lord, C. (2003). *Autism diagnostic interview revised manual (ADI-R)*. Los Angeles: Western Psychological Services.

Ryan, A. L., Halsey, H. N., & Matthews, W. J. (2003). Using functional assessment to promote desirable student behavior in school. *Teaching Exceptional Children, 35*(5), 8–15.

Ryan, J. B., Reid, R., & Ellis, C. (2008). Special educators' knowledge regarding psychotrophic interventions for students with emotional and behavioral disorders. *Remedial and Special Education, 29*, 269–279.

Ryder, R. J., Graves, B. B., & Graves, M. F. (1989). *Easy reading: Book series and periodicals for less able readers* (2nd ed.). Newark, DE: International Reading Association.

Sabornie, E. J., & Kauffman, J. M. (1985). Regular classroom sociometric status of behaviorally disordered adolescents. *Behavioral Disorders, 10*, 268–274.

Sabornie, E. J., Cullinan, D., Osborne, S. S., & Brock, L. B. (2005). Intellectual, academic, and behavioral functioning of students with high-incidence disabilities: A cross-categorical meta-analysis. *Exceptional Children, 72*, 47–63.

Sabornie, E. J., Evans, C., & Cullinan, D. (2006). Comparing characteristics of high-incidence disability groups. *Remedial and Special Education, 27*, 95–104.

Saddler, B. (2004). 20 ways to improve writing ability. *Intervention in School and Clinic, 39*, 310–314.

Safran, S. P., & Safran, J. S. (1996). Intervention assistance programs and prereferral teams: Directions for the twenty-first century. *Remedial and Special Education, 17*, 363–369.

Sailor, W., Gee, K., & Karasoff, P. (1993). Full inclusion and school restructuring. In M. E. Snell (Ed.), *Instruction of students with severe disabilities* (4th ed., pp. 1–30). New York: Merrill/Macmillan.

Sale, P., & Carey, D. M. (1995). The sociometric status of students with disabilities in a full-inclusion school. *Exceptional Children, 62*, 6–19.

Salend, S. J. (1987). Group-oriented behavior management strategies. *Teaching Exceptional Children, 19*(1), 53–55.

Salend, S. J. (2008). *Creating inclusive classrooms* (6th ed.). Upper Saddle River, NJ: Merrill Prentice Hall.

Salend, S. J., & Duhaney, L. M. G. (2002). Grading students in inclusive settings. *Teaching Exceptional Children, 34*(3), 8–15.

Samuels, C. A. (2008). 'Response to intervention' sparks interests, questions. *Education Week*. Retrieved January 27, 2008, from http://www.edweek.org/ew/articles/2008/01/23/20rtireact.h27.html?tmp=824727498

Sarff, L. (1981). An innovative use of free field amplification in regular classrooms. In R. Roesser & M. Downs (Eds.), *Auditory disorders in school children* (pp. 263–272). New York: Thieme Stratton.

Sasso, G., & Rude, H. A. (1988). The social effects of integration on nonhandicapped children. *Education and Training in Mental Retardation, 23*, 18–23.

Schelvan, R. L., Swanson, T. C., & Smith, S. M. (2005). Making each year successful: Issues in transition. In B. S. Myles (Ed.), *Children and youth with Asperger syndrome: Strategies for success in inclusive settings* (pp. 127–157). Thousand Oaks, CA: Corwin Press.

Schilit, J., & Caldwell, M. L. (1980). A word list of essential career/vocational words for mentally retarded students. *Education and Training of the Mentally Retarded, 15*, 113–117.

Schlosser, L. Y., & Algozzine, B. (1980). Sex, behavior, and teacher expectancies. *Journal of Experimental Education, 48*, 231–236.

Schopler, E., Lansing, M. D., Reichler, R., & Marcus, L. M. (2005). *Psychoeducational profile (third edition)(PEP-3): TEACCH individualized psychoeducational assessment for children with autism spectrum disorders*. Austin, TX: PRO-ED.

Schopler, E., Mesibov, G. B., & Hearsey, K. (1995). Structured teaching in the TEACCH system. In E. Schopler & G. B. Mesibov (Eds.), *Learning and cognition in autism* (pp. 243–268). New York: Plenum Press.

Schopler, E., Reichler, R. J., & Renner, B. R. (1988). *The childhood autism rating scale*. Los Angeles: Western Psychological Services.

Schreibman, L., Whalen, C., & Stahmer, A. C. (2000). The use of video priming to reduce disruptive transition behavior in children with autism. *Journal of Positive Behavior Interventions, 2*(1), 3–11.

Schrock, K. (2009). Teacher helpers: Critical evaluation information. Retrieved May 18, 2009, from http://school.discoveryeducation.com/schrockguide/eval.html

Schubert, M., Glick, H., & Bauer, D. (1979). *The least restrictive environment and the handicapped student*. Dayton, OH: Wright State University.

Schulte, A. C., Osborne, S. S., & McKinney, J. D. (1990). Academic outcomes for students with learning disabilities in consultation and resource programs. *Exceptional Children, 57*, 162–172.

Schultz, J. B., & Torrie, M. (1984). Effectiveness of parenthood education materials for mainstreamed vocational home economics classes. *Journal of Vocational Education Research, 9*(1), 46–56.

Schulz, J. B., & Turnbull, A. P. (1983). *Mainstreaming handicapped students* (2nd ed.). Boston: Allyn & Bacon.

Schumaker, J. B., & Hazel, J. S. (1984). Social skills assessment and training for the learning disabled: Who's on first and what's on second? Part I. *Journal of Learning Disabilities, 17*, 422–431.

Schumaker, J. B., Nolan, S. M., & Deshler, D. D. (1985). *Learning strategies curriculum: The error monitoring strategy.* Lawrence: University of Kansas.

Scruggs, T. E., Mastropieri, M. A., & McDuffie, K. A. (2007). Co-teaching in inclusive classrooms: A metasynthesis of qualitative research. *Exceptional Children, 73,* 392–416.

Searcy, S. (1996). Friendship interventions for the integration of children and youth with learning and behavior problems. *Preventing School Failure, 40*(3), 131–134.

Seroussi, K. (2000, February). We cured our son's autism. *Parents, 75*(2), 118–125.

Shames, G. H., & Ramig, P. R. (1994). Stuttering and other disorders of fluency. In G. H. Shames, E. H. Wiig, & W. A Secord (Eds.), *Human communication disorders* (4th ed., pp. 336–386). New York: Merrill/Macmillan.

Shanker, J. L., & Ekwall, E. E. (2000). *Ekwall/Shanker reading inventory* (4th ed.). Boston: Allyn & Bacon.

Shanker, J. L., & Ekwall, E. E. (2002). *Locating and correcting reading difficulties* (8th ed.). Upper Saddle River, NJ: Merrill/Prentice Hall.

Shapiro, E. S., & Elliott, S. N. (1999). Curriculum-based assessment and other performance-based assessment strategies. In C. R. Reynolds & T. B. Gutkin (Eds.), *The handbook of school psychology* (3rd ed., pp. 383–408). New York: John Wiley & Sons, Inc.

Shaywitz, S. (2003). *Overcoming dyslexia.* New York: Knopf.

Shaywitz, S. E., Holahan, J. M., Freudenheim, D. A., Fletcher, J. M., Makuch, R. W., & Shaywitz, B. A. (2001). Heterogeneity with the gifted: Higher IQ boys exhibit behaviors resembling boys with learning disabilities. *Gifted Child Quarterly, 45,* 16–23.

Sheehan, S. (2003, December 1). The autism fight. *The New Yorker,* pp. 76–87.

Shinn, M. R., & Hubbard, D. D. (1993). Curriculum-based measurement and problem-solving assessment: Basic procedures and outcomes. In E. L. Meyen, G. A. Vergason, & R. J. Whelan (Eds.), *Educating students with mild disabilities* (pp. 221–253). Denver: Love.

Shyyan, V., Thurlow, M. L., & Liu, K. K. (2008). Instructional strategies for improving achievement in reading, mathematics, and science for English language learners with disabilities. *Assessment for Effective Instruction, 33,* 145–155.

Sicile-Kira, C. (2004). *Autism spectrum disorders: The complete guide to understanding autism, Asperger's syndrome, pervasive developmental disorder, and other ASDs.* New York: The Berkley Publishing Group.

Sierra, V. (1973). Learning style of the Mexican American. In L. A. Bransford, L. M. Baca, & K. Lane (Eds.), *Cultural diversity and the exceptional child* (pp. 42–49). Reston, VA: The Council for Exceptional Children.

Silvaroli, N. J., & Wheelock, W. H. (2004). *Classroom reading inventory* (10th ed.). Boston: McGraw Hill.

Silverman, L. K. (1988). Gifted and talented. In E. L. Meyen & T. M. Socratic (Eds.), *Exceptional children and youth: An introduction* (3rd ed., pp. 263–291). Denver: Love.

Simms, R. S., & Falcon, S. C. (1987). Teaching sight words. *Teaching Exceptional Children, 20*(1), 30–33.

Simonsen, B., Sugai, G., & Negron, M. (2008). Schoolwide positive behavior supports: Primary systems and practices. *Teaching on Exceptional Children, 40*(6), 2–40.

Simpson, R. L. (1980). Modifying the attitudes of regular class students toward the handicapped. *Focus on Exceptional Children, 13*(3), 1–11.

Simpson, R. L. (2005). *Autism spectrum disorders: Interventions and treatments for children and youth.* Thousand Oaks, CA: Corwin Press.

Sindelar, P. T. (1987). Increasing reading fluency. *Teaching Exceptional Children, 19*(2), 59–60.

Siperstein, G. N., Parker, R. C., Bardon, J. N., & Widaman, K. F. (2007). A national study of youth attitudes toward the inclusion of students with intellectual abilities. *Exceptional Children, 73,* 435–455.

Sirvis, B. (1982). The physically disabled. In E. L. Meyen (Ed.), *Exceptional children and youth* (2nd ed., pp. 382–405). Denver: Love.

Sirvis, B. (1988). Physical disabilities. In E. L. Meyen & T. M. Skrtic (Eds.), *Exceptional children and youth: An introduction* (3rd ed., pp. 387–411). Denver: Love.

Sklaire, M. (1989). Today's kids face different diseases. *NEA Today, 7*(8), 9.

Slate, J. R., & Saudargas, R. A. (1986). Differences in learning disabled and average students' classroom behaviors. *Learning Disability Quarterly, 9*(1), 61–67.

Slavin, R. E. (1987). *Cooperative learning: Student teams.* Washington, DC: National Education Association.

Slavin, R. E. (1995). *Cooperative learning: Theory, research, and practice* (2nd ed.). Boston: Allyn & Bacon.

Slavin, R. E., Madden, N. A., & Leavey, M. (1984). Effects of cooperative learning and individualized instruction on mainstreamed students. *Exceptional Children, 50,* 434–443.

Smith, D. D. (2004). *Introduction to special education in an age of opportunity* (5th ed.). Boston: Allyn & Bacon.

Smith, F. (1982). *Writing and the writer.* New York: Holt, Rinehart & Winston.

Smith, R. M., Neisworth, J. T., & Greer, J. G. (1978). *Evaluating educational environments.* Columbus, OH: Merrill/Prentice Hall.

Smith, T. E. C., Finn, D. M., & Dowdy, C. A. (1993). *Teaching students with mild disabilities.* Fort Worth, TX: Harcourt Brace Jovanovich.

Smith, T. E. C., Polloway, E. A., Patton, J. R., & Dowdy, C. A. (2008). *Teaching students with special needs in inclusive settings* (5th ed.). Boston: Pearson Allyn and Bacon.

Smith, T. E. C., Polloway, E. A., Patton, J. R., & Dowdy, C. A. (1998). *Teaching students with special needs in inclusive settings* (2nd ed.). Boston: Allyn & Bacon.

Smutny, J. F. (2000). *Teaching young gifted children in the regular classroom.* Arlington, VA: The Council for Exceptional Children. (ERIC Clearinghouse on Disabilities and Gifted Education, EC Digest No. 595).

Snell, M., & Brown, F. (1993). Instructional planning and implementation. In M. Snell (Ed.), *Instruction of students with severe disabilities* (4th ed., pp. 99–151). New York: Merrill/Macmillan.

Snow, C. E., Burns, S., & Griffin, P. (Eds.). (1998). *Preventing reading difficulties in young children.* Washington, DC: National Academic Press.

Southern, W. T., & Jones, E. D. (2004). Types of acceleration: Dimensions and issues. In N. Colangelo, S. G. Assouline, & M. U. M. Gross (Eds.), *A nation deceived: How schools hold back America's brightest students* (Vol. II, pp. 5–12). Iowa City, IA: University of Iowa.

Spache, G. (1953). A new readability formula for primary-grade reading materials. *The Elementary School Journal, 53,* 410–413.

Spalding, R. B., & Spalding, W. T. (1986). *The writing road to reading* (3rd ed.). New York: Morrow.

Spear-Swerling, L., & Sternberg, R. J. (2001). What science offers to teachers of reading. *Learning Disabilities Research & Practice, 16*(1), 51–57.

Special needs, common goals. (2004). *Education Week, 33*(17), 7.

Spenciner, L. J. (1992). Mainstreaming the child with a visual impairment. In L. G. Cohen (Ed.), *Children with exceptional needs in regular classrooms* (pp. 82–97). Washington, DC: National Education Association.

Spinelli, C. G. (2004). Dealing with cancer in the classroom: The teacher's role and responsibilities. *Teaching Exceptional Children, 36*(4), 14–21.

Stahl, S. A., & Miller, P. D. (1989). Whole language and language experience approaches for beginning reading: A quantitative research synthesis. *Review of Educational Research, 59*, 87–116.

Stainback, S., & Stainback, W. (1988). Educating students with severe disabilities. *Teaching Exceptional Children, 21*(1), 16–19.

Stainback, S., & Stainback, W. (1992). *Curriculum considerations in inclusive classrooms.* Baltimore: Brookes.

Stainback, S., & Stainback, W. (Eds.). (1985). *Integrating students with severe handicaps into regular schools.* Reston, VA: The Council for Exceptional Children.

Stainback, S., Stainback, W., & Forest, M. (1989). *Educating all students in the mainstream of regular education.* Baltimore: Brookes.

Stainback, S., Stainback, W., & Slavin, R. (1989). Classroom organization for diversity among students. In S. Stainback, W. Stainback, & M. Forest (Eds.), *Educating all students in the mainstream of regular education* (pp. 131–142). Baltimore: Brookes.

Stainback, W., & Stainback, S. (Eds.). (1990). *Support networks for inclusive schooling.* Baltimore: Brookes.

Stainback, W., Stainback, S., & Froyen, L. (1987). Structuring the classroom to prevent disruptive behaviors. *Teaching Exceptional Children, 19*(4), 12–16.

Stainback, W., Stainback, S., & Wilkinson, A. (1992). Encouraging peer supports and friendships. *Teaching Exceptional Children, 24*(2), 6–11.

State-wide assessment programs. (1998, Spring). Research connections in special education (No. 2). Reston, VA: ERIC/OSEP Special Project, ERIC Clearinghouse on Disabilities and Gifted Education, Council for Exceptional Children.

Stephens, K. R., & Karnes, F. A. (2000). State definitions for the gifted and talented revisited. *Exceptional Children, 66*(2), 219–38.

Stephens, T. M. (1980). Teachers as managers. *The Directive Teacher, 2*(5), 4.

Stepien, W. J., & Pyke, S. L. (1997). Designing problem-based learning units. *Journal for the Education of the Gifted, 20*(4), 380–400.

Sternberg, R. J. (1997). A triarchic view of giftedness: Theory and practice. In N. Colangelo & G. A. Davis (Eds.), *Handbook of gifted education* (2nd ed., pp. 43–53). Boston: Allyn & Bacon.

Sternberg, R. J. (2003). Giftedness according to the theory of successful intelligence. In N. Colangelo & G. A. Davis (Eds.), *Handbook of gifted education* (3rd ed., pp. 88–99). Boston: Allyn & Bacon.

Sternberg, R. J., & Grigorenko, E. L. (2000). *Teaching for successful intelligence to increase student learning and achievement.* Arlington Heights, IL: SkyLight Professional Development.

Sternberg, R. J., & Grigorenko, E. L. (2002). The theory of successful intelligence as a basis for gifted education. *Gifted Child Quarterly, 46*(4), 265–277.

Stevens, M., Washington, A., Rice, C., Jenner, W., Ottolino, J., Clancy, K., Whitney, J., et al. (2007). *Prevalence of the autism spectrum disorders (ASDs) in multiple areas of the United States, 2000 and 2002.* Atlanta, GA: Centers for Disease Control and Prevention.

Stevens, R., & Rosenshine, B. (1981). Advances in research on teaching. *Exceptional Education Quarterly, 2*(1), 1–9.

Stichter, J. P., & Conroy, M. A. (2006). *How to teach social skills for and plan for peer social interaction.* Austin, TX: PRO-ED.

Stitt, B. A., Erekson, T. L., Hofstrand, R. K., Loepp, F. L., Minor, C. W., Perreault, H. R., et al. (1988). *Building gender fairness in schools.* Carbondale: Board of Trustees, Southern Illinois University.

Stone, B., Cundick, B. P., & Swanson, D. (1988). Special education screening system: Group achievement test. *Exceptional Children, 55*, 71–75.

Stormont, M. A. (2008). Increase academic success for children with ADHD using sticky notes and highlighters. *Intervention in School and Clinic, 43*, 305–308.

Stowitschek, J. J., Gable, R. A., & Hendrickson, J. M. (1980). *Instructional materials for exceptional children.* Germantown, MD: Aspen Systems.

Strain, P. S. (1981a). Peer-mediated treatment of exceptional children's social withdrawal. *Exceptional Education Quarterly, 1*(4), 93–105.

Strain, P. S. (Ed.). (1981b). *The utilization of peers as behavior change agents.* New York: Plenum.

Strickland, B. B., & Turnbull, A. P. (1993). *Developing and implementing individualized education programs* (3rd ed.). New York: Merrill/Macmillan.

Sugai, G., & Lewis, T. J. (1996). Preferred and promising practices for social skills instruction. *Focus on Exceptional Children, 29*(4), 1–16.

Sugai, G. M., & Tindal, G. A. (1993). *Effective school consultation: An interactive approach.* Pacific Grove, CA: Brooks/Cole.

Sulzer-Azaroff, B., & Mayer, G. R. (1977). *Applying behavior-analysis procedures with children and youth.* New York: Holt, Rinehart & Winston.

Sulzer-Azaroff, B., & Mayer, R. (1991). *Behavior analysis for lasting change.* Fort Worth, TX: Holt, Rinehart & Winston.

Sunderland, L. C. (2004). Speech, language, and audiology services in public schools. *Intervention in School and Clinic, 39*(4), 209–217.

Sutherland, K. S., & Wehby, J. H. (2001). Exploring the relationship between increased opportunities to respond to academic requests and the academic and behavioral outcomes of students with EBD. *Remedial and Special Education, 22*, 113–121.

Swanson, E. A., & Howerton, D. (2007). Influence vocabulary acquisition for English language learners. *Intervention in School and Clinic, 42*, 209–294.

Swanson, H. L., & Cooney, J. B. (1996). Learning disabilities and memory. In D. K. Reid, W. P. Hresko, & H. L. Swanson (Eds.), *Cognitive approaches to learning disabilities* (3rd ed., pp. 287–314). Austin, TX: PRO-ED.

Swanson, H. L., & Malone, S. (1992). Social skills and learning disabilities: A meta-analysis of the literature. *School Psychology Review, 21*, 427–443.

Swift, C. A. (1988). Communication disorders. In E. W. Lynch & R. B. Lewis (Eds.), *Exceptional children and adults* (pp. 318–351). Glenview, IL: Scott, Foresman.

Tarver, S., & Hallahan, D. P. (1976). Children with learning disabilities: An overview. In J. M. Kauffman & D. P. Hallahan (Eds.),

Teaching children with learning disabilities: Personal perspectives (pp. 2–57). Columbus, OH: Merrill/Prentice Hall.

Taylor, B. A. (2001). Teaching peer social skills to children with autism. In C. Maurice, G. Green, & R. Foxx (Eds.), *Making a difference: Behavioral intervention for autism* (pp. 83–96), Austin, TX: PRO-ED.

Taylor, B. A., & Jasper, S. (2001). Teaching programs to increase peer interaction. In C. Maurice, G. Green, & R. Foxx (Eds.), *Making a difference: Behavioral intervention for autism* (pp. 97–162). Austin, TX: PRO-ED.

Taylor, B. A., & McDonough, K. A. (1996). Selecting teaching programs. In C. Maurice, G. Green, & S. Luce (Eds.), *Behavioral intervention for young children with autism: A manual for parents and professionals* (pp. 63–177). Austin, TX: PRO-ED.

Taylor, B. A., Levin, L., & Jasper, S. (1999). Increasing play-related statements in children with autism toward their siblings: Effects of video-modeling. *Journal of Developmental and Physical Disabilities, 11,* 253–264.

Taylor, O. (1986). Language differences. In G. H. Shames & E. H. Wiig (Eds.), *Human communication disorders* (2nd ed., pp. 385–413). New York: Merrill/Macmillan.

Teachers of English to Speakers of Other Languages, Inc. (1996-2007). *ESL standards for Pre-K–12 students, online edition.* Retrieved September 1, 2009, from http://www.tesol.org/s_tesol/seccss.asp?CID=113&DID=1583

The Epilepsy Foundation urges caregivers, parents of young children to know the hidden signs of epilepsy. Retrieved October 2, 2004, from http://www.epilepsyfoundation.org/epilepsyusa/media/n110100.cfm

Thomas, C. H., & Patton, J. R. (1990). Mild and moderate retardation. In J. R. Patton, M. Beirne-Smith, & J. S. Payne (Eds.), *Mental retardation* (3rd ed., pp. 197–226). New York: Merrill/Macmillan.

Thousand, J. S., & Villa, R. A. (1990). Strategies for educating learners with severe disabilities within their local home schools and communities. *Focus on Exceptional Children, 23*(3), 1–24.

Thurber, D. N. (2001). *D'nealian handwriting cursive connections.* Tucson, AZ: GoodYear Books.

Thurlow, M., House, A., Boys, C., Scott, D., & Ysseldyke, J. (2000). *State participation and accommodation policies for students with disabilities: 1999 update* (Synthesis Rep. No. 33). Minneapolis, MN: University of Minnesota, National Center on Educational Outcomes.

Tomlinson, C. A. (2000). *Differentiation of instruction in the elementary grades.* Champaign, IL: ERIC Clearinghouse on Elementary and Early Childhood Education. (ERIC Document Reproduction Service No. ED-443–572).

Tomlinson, C. A. (Winter, 2001). Tiered lessons: What are their benefits and implications? *Gifted Education Communicator,* 37–39.

Tomlinson, C. A., Kaplan, S. N., Renzulli, J. S., Purcell, J., Leppien, J., & Burns, D. (2002). *The parallel curriculum.* Thousand Oaks, CA: Corwin Press.

Tompkins, G. E., & Friend, M. (1986). On your mark, get set, write! *Teaching Exceptional Children, 18*(2), 82–89.

Tomsho, R. (2007). Is an early-help program shortchanging kids? *The Wall Street Journal Online.* Retrieved January 27, 2008, from http://online.wsj.com/article/SB118721849477198989.html?mod=dist_smartbrief

Torgesen, J. K. (1977). The role of nonspecific factors in the task performance of learning disabled children: A theoretical assessment. *Journal of Learning Disabilities, 10,* 27–34.

Torrance, E. P. (1966). *Torrance tests of creative thinking.* Princeton, NJ: Personnal.

Torres, I., & Corn, A. L. (1990). *When you have a visually handicapped child in your classroom: Suggestions for teachers.* New York: American Foundation for the Blind.

Tournaki, N., & Criscitiello, E. (2003). Using peer tutoring as a successful part of behavior management. *Teaching Exceptional Children, 36*(2), 22–29.

Towell, J., & Wink, J. (1993). *Strategies for monolingual teachers in multilingual classrooms.* Turlock: California State University, Stanislaus. (ERIC Document Reproduction Service No. ED-359–797).

Trout, A. L., Lienemann, T. O., Reid, R., & Epstein, M. H. (2007). A review of non-medication interventions to improve the academic performance of children and youth with ADHD. *Remedial and Special Education, 28,* 207–226.

Truscott, S. D., Cohen, C. E., Sams, D. P. , Sanborn, K., & Frank, A. J. (2005). The current state(s) of prereferral intervention teams: A report from two national surveys. *Remedial and Special Education, 26,* 130–140.

Tucker, B. F., & Colson, S. E. (1992). Traumatic brain injury: An overview of school re-entry. *Intervention in School and Clinic, 27,* 198–206.

Tur-Kaspa, H., & Bryan, T. (1994). Social information processing skills of students with learning disabilities. *Learning Disabilities Research and Practice, 9,* 12–23.

Turnbull, A. P., & Schulz, J. B. (1979). *Mainstreaming handicapped students.* Boston: Allyn & Bacon.

Turnbull, A., Turnbull, R., Erwin, E. & Soodak, L. (2006). *Families, professionals, and exceptionality* (5th ed). Upper Saddle River, NJ: Merrill/Prentice Hall.

Turnbull, R., Turnbull, A., Shank, M., & Smith, S. J. (2004). *Exceptional lives* (4th ed.). Upper Saddle River, NJ: Merrill/Prentice Hall.

U.S. Census Bureau. (2000). *Profile of general demographic characteristics: 2000.* Washington, DC: Author. Retrieved June 1, 2001, from http://factfinder.census.gov/servlet/BasicFactsServlet

U. S. Census Bureau. (2001). *Census 2000 briefs and special reports.* Retrieved July 2, 2008, from http://www.census.gov/population/www/cen2000/briefs.html

U. S. Census Bureau. (2003). *Married-couple and unmarried-partner households: 2000.* Retrieved July 18, 2008, from http://www.census.gov/prod/2003pubs/censr-5.pdf

U. S. Census Bureau. (2005). *Number, timing, and duration of marriages and divorces: 2001.* Retrieved July 19, 2008, from http://www.census.gov/prod/2005pubs/p70-97.pdf

U. S. Census Bureau. (2008). *American community survey (ACS).* Retrieved July 10, 2008, from http://www.census.gov/acs/www/

U.S. Department of Education, Office of Educational Research and Improvement. (1993). *National excellence: A case for developing America's talent.* Washington, DC: Author.

U.S. Department of Education, Office of Special Education and Rehabilitative Services, Office of Special Education Programs. (2008). *Identifying and treating attention deficit hyperactivity disorder: A resource for school and home.* Washington, DC: Author.

U.S. Department of Education. (1991, September 16). *Memorandum: Clarification of policy to address the needs of children with attention deficit disorders within general and/or special education.* Washington, DC: Office of Special Education and Rehabilitative Services.

U.S. Department of Education. (1996). *Eighteenth annual report to Congress on the implementation of the Individuals with Disabilities Education Act*. Washington, DC: Author.

U.S. Department of Education. (2002). *Twenty-fourth annual report to Congress on the implementation of the Individuals with Disabilities Education Act*. Washington, DC: Author.

U.S. Department of Education. (2007). *Twenty-seventh annual report to Congress on the implementation of the Individuals with Disabilities Education Act, 2005, Vol. 1*. Washington, DC: Author.

U.S. Department of Education. (2009). *Twenty-eighth annual report to Congress on the implementation of the Individuals with Disabilities Education Act, Volume. 1*. Washington, DC: Author.

U.S. Department of Health, Education, and Welfare. (1972). *Education of the gifted and talented*. Washington, DC: Author.

U. S. Office of Homeland Security. (2007). *Yearbook of immigration statistics: 2006*. Washington, DC: U. S. Department of Homeland Security, Office of Immigration Statistics.

U.S. Public Health Service. (1990). *Healthy people 2000*. Washington, DC: U.S. Government Printing Office.

Utley, C. A., Mortweet, S. L., & Greenwood, C. R. (1997). Peer-mediated instruction and interventions. *Focus on Exceptional Children, 29*(5), 1–23.

VanRiper, C. (1978). *Speech correction*. Upper Saddle River, NJ: Prentice Hall.

VanTassel-Baska, J. (2001). The role of advanced placement in talent development. *Journal of Secondary Gifted Education, 12*, 126–132.

VanTassel-Baska, J. (2003). What matters in curriculum for gifted learners: Reflections on theory, research, and practice. N. Colangelo & G. A. Davis (Eds.), *Handbook of gifted education* (pp. 174–183). Boston: Allyn & Bacon.

VanTassel-Baska, J., & Brown, E. F. (2007). Toward best practice: An analysis of the efficacy of curriculum models in gifted education. *Gifted Child Quarterly, 51*(4), 342–358.

VanTassel-Baska, J., & Stambaugh, T. (2006). *Comprehensive curriculum for gifted learners* (3rd ed.). Boston: Pearson.

Vandercook, T., & York, J. (1990). A team approach to program development and support. In W. Stainback & S. Stainback (Eds.), *Support networks for inclusive schooling* (pp. 95–122). Baltimore: Brookes.

Vandercook, T., York, J., & Forest, M. (1989). The McGill Action Planning System (MAPS): A strategy for building the vision. *Journal of the Association for Persons with Severe Handicaps, 14*, 205–215.

Vaughn Gross Center for Reading and Language Arts at The University of Texas at Austin. (2005). *Introduction to the 3-tier reading model* (4th ed.). Austin, TX: Author.

Vaughn, S. R. (1995, July). *Responsible inclusion for students with learning disabilities*. Paper presented at the conference of the International Academy for Research in Learning Disabilities, Phoenix, AZ.

Vaughn, S., & Fuchs, L. S. (2003). Redefining learning disabilities as inadequate response to instruction: The promise and potential problems. *Learning Disabilities Research & Practice, 18*, 137–146.

Vaughn, S., Bos, C. S., & Schumm, J. S. (2003). *Teaching exceptional, diverse, and at-risk students* (3rd ed.). Boston: Allyn & Bacon.

Vaughn, S., Gersten, R., & Chard, D. J. (2000). The underlying message in LD intervention research: Findings from research syntheses. *Exceptional Children, 67*, 99–114.

Vaughn, S., Linan-Thompson, S., & Hickman, P. (2003). Response to instruction as a means of identifying students with reading/learning disabilities. *Exceptional Children, 69*, 391–409.

Vergason, G. A., & Anderegg, M. L. (1991). Beyond the regular education initiative and the resource room controversy. *Focus on Exceptional Children, 23*(7), 1–7.

Voeltz, L. M. (1980). Children's attitudes toward handicapped peers. *American Journal of Mental Deficiency, 84*, 455–464.

Voeltz, L. M. (1982). Effects of structured interactions with severely handicapped peers on children's attitudes. *American Journal of Mental Deficiency, 86*, 380–390.

Voltz, D. L., Brazil, N., & Ford, A. (2001). What matters most in inclusive education: A practical guide for moving forward. *Intervention in School and Clinic, 37*(1), 23–30.

von Károlyi, C., Ramos-Ford, V., & Gardner, H. (2003). Multiple intelligences: A perspective on giftedness. In N. Colangelo & G. A. Davis (Eds.), *Handbook of gifted education* (3rd ed., pp. 100–112). Boston: Allyn & Bacon.

Wagner, S. (1999). *Inclusive programming for elementary students with autism*. Arlington, TX: Future Horizons.

Walker, H. M. (1995). *The acting out child: Coping with classroom disruption* (2nd ed.). Longmont, CO: Sopris West.

Walker, H. M., McConnell, S., Holmes, D., Todis, B., Walker, J., & Golden, N. (1988). *The Walker social skills curriculum: The ACCEPTS program*. Austin, TX: PRO-ED.

Walker, H. M., Todis, B., Holmes, D., & Horton, G. (1988). *The Walker social skills curriculum: The ACCESS [Adolescent Curriculum for Communication and Effective Social Skills] program*. Austin, TX: PRO-ED.

Walker, J. L. (1988). Young American Indian children. *Teaching Exceptional Children, 20*(4), 50–51.

Wallis, C. (2006, May 15). Inside the autistic mind. *Time*, pp. 42–51.

Walsh, J. M., & Jones, B. (2004). New models of cooperative teaching. *Teaching Exceptional Children, 36*(5), 14–20.

Wayman, K. I., Lynch, E. W., & Hanson, M. J. (1990). Home-based early childhood services: Cultural sensitivity in a family systems approach. *Topics in Early Childhood Special Education, 10*, 65–66.

Wayne, T. (2009, May 18). Social networks eclipse e-mail. *The New York Times*, p. B3.

Webb, J. T., & Latimer, D. (1993). ADHD and children who are gifted. *Exceptional Children, 60*, 183–184.

Webster, A., & Roe, J. (1998). *Children with visual impairment: Social interaction, language, and learning*. London: Routledge.

Wechsler, D. (2003). *Wechsler intelligence scale for children–Fourth edition*. San Antonio, TX: Psychological Corporation.

Wehman, P. (1997). *Exceptional individuals in school, community, and work*. Austin, TX: PRO-ED.

Weil, M. L., & Murphy, J. (1982). Instruction processes. In H. E. Mitzel (Ed.), *Encyclopedia of educational research* (5th ed., pp. 890–917). New York: Free Press.

Weiner, J., & Harris, P. J. (1997). Evaluation of an individualized, context-based social skills training program for children with learning disabilities. *Learning Disabilities Research & Practice, 12*, 40–53.

Weinstein, C. S. (1979). The physical environment of the school: A review of research. *Review of Educational Research, 49*, 577–610.

Wells, J., & Lewis, L. (2006). *Internet access in U.S. public schools and classrooms: 1994–2004* (NCES 2007-020). U.S. Department of

Education, National Center for Education Statistics: Washington, DC. Retrieved March 18, 2009, from http://nces.ed.gov/pubsearch/pubsinfo.asp?pubid2007020

Werts, M. G., Wolery, M., Snyder, E. D., & Caldwell, N. K. (1996). Teachers' perceptions of the supports critical to the success of inclusion programs. *JASH, 21,* 9–21.

Westby, C. E. (1992). Whole language and learners with mild handicaps. *Focus on Exceptional Children, 24*(8), 1–16.

Whelan, R. J. (1995). Emotional disturbance. In E. L. Meyen & T. M. Skrtic (Eds.), *Special education and student disability* (4th ed., pp. 270–336). Denver: Love.

White, K. R., Bush, D., & Casto, G. (1986). Let the past be prologue: Learning from previous reviews of early intervention efficacy research. *Journal of Special Education, 19,* 417–428.

Whitt, J., Paul, P. V., & Reynolds, C. J. (1988). Motivate reluctant learning disabled writers. *Teaching Exceptional Children, 20*(3), 37–39.

Whittaker, C. R., Salend, S., & Elhoweris, H. (2009). Religious diversity in schools: Addressing the issues. *Intervention in School and Clinic, 44,* 314–319.

Wickstrom, C. D. (2004). Give us the best and brightest, but . . . A historical review of U.S. national policy on education for the highly capable. In D. Boothe & J. C. Stanley (Eds.), *In the eyes of the beholder: Critical issues for diversity in gifted education* (pp. 263–274). Waco, TX: Prufrock Press.

Wiedmeyer, D., & Lehman, J. (1991). "The House Plan" approach to collaborative teaching and consultation. *Teaching Exceptional Children, 23*(10), 7–10.

Wikipedia. (2009). *World Wide Web.* Retrieved May 13, 2009, from http://en.wikipedia.org/wiki/World_wide_web

Willis, W. O. (2004). Families with African American roots. In E. W. Lynch & M. J. Hanson (Eds.), *Developing cross-cultural competence* (3rd ed., pp. 141–177). Baltimore: Brookes.

Winebrenner, S. (2001). *Teaching gifted kids in the regular classroom* (2nd ed.). Minneapolis: Free Spirit Publishing.

Winget, P., & Kirk, J. (1991). *California programs and services for students with serious emotional disturbances.* Sacramento, CA: Resources in Special Education.

Winston, S. (1995). *Stephanie Winston's best organizing tips.* New York: Simon & Schuster.

Wolery, M. (2004). Monitoring children's progress and intervention implementation. In M. McLean, M. Wolery, & D. B. Bailey (Eds.), *Assessing infants and preschoolers with special needs* (3rd ed., pp. 545–584). Columbus, OH: Pearson Merrill Prentice Hall.

Wolfberg, P. J. (2003). *Peer play and the autism spectrum: The art of guiding children's socialization and imagination.* Shawnee Mission, KS: Autism Asperger Publishing Company.

Wolfe, P. S., & Hall, T. E. (2003). Making inclusion a reality for students with severe disabilities. *Teaching Exceptional Children, 35*(4), 56–61.

Wolfensberger, W. (1972). *The principle of normalization in human services.* Toronto: National Institute on Mental Retardation.

Wolff, H. (2008). *School advisory toolkit for families.* New York: Juvenile Diabetes Research Association.

Woodcock, R. W., McGrew, K., & Mather, N. (2001). *Woodcock–Johnson III.* Itasca, IL: Riverside.

Woods, M. L., & Moe, A. J. (2007). *Analytical reading inventory* (8th ed.). Upper Saddle River, NJ: Pearson.

Woodward, J. (2004). Mathematics education in the United States: Past to present. *Journal of Learning Disabilities, 37,* 16–31.

Wormeli, R. (2003). *Differentiating instruction: A modified concerto in four movements.* LD Online. Retrieved July 9, 2004, from http://www.ldonline.org/ld_indepth/teaching_techniques/modified_concerto.htm/

Wright, A. (2009, August 19). Programs to prepare teachers for some student populations lack oversight, GAO says. *The Chronicle of Higher Education.* Retrieved August 19, 2009, from http://chronicle.com/article/Programs-to-Prepare-Teachers/48060/

York, J., Doyle, M. B., & Kronberg, R. (1992). A curriculum development process for inclusive classrooms. *Focus on Exceptional Children, 25*(4), 1–16.

York, J., Vandercook, T., MacDonald, C., Heise-Neff, C., & Caughey, E. (1992). Feedback about integrating middle-school students with severe disabilities in general education classes. *Exceptional Children, 58,* 244–258.

Ysseldyke, J. E., Algozzine, B., & Thurlow, M. L. (1992). *Critical issues in special education* (2nd ed.). Boston, MA: Houghton Mifflin.

Ysseldyke, J. E., Thurlow, M. L., Wotruba, J. W., & Nania, P. A. (1990). Instructional arrangements: Perceptions from general education. *Teaching Exceptional Children, 22*(4), 4–8.

Zabel, H., & Tabor, M. (1993). Effects of soundfield amplification on spelling performance of elementary school children. *Educational Audiology Monograph, 3,* 5–9.

Zaragoza, N., Vaughn, S., & McIntosh, R. (1991). Social skills interventions and children with behavior problems: A review. *Behavioral Disorders, 16,* 260–275.

Zentall, S. S. (1983). Learning environments: A review of physical and temporal factors. *Exceptional Education Quarterly, 4*(2), 90–115.

Zentall, S. S., Hall, A. M., & Grskovic, J. A. (2001). Learning and motivational characteristics of boys with ADHD and/or giftedness. *Exceptional Children, 67,* 499–519.

Zirkel, P. A. (1989). AIDS: Students in glass houses? *Phi Delta Kappan, 70,* 646–648.

Zirkel, P. A., & Krohn, N. (2008). RTI after IDEA: A survey of state laws. *Teaching Exceptional Children, 40*(3), 71–73.

Zirpoli, T. J., & Melloy, K. J. (2001). *Behavior management: Applications for teachers* (3rd ed.). Upper Saddle River, NJ: Merrill/Prentice Hall.

Zuniga, M. E. (2004). Families with Latino roots. In E. W. Lynch & M. J. Hanson (Eds.), *Developing cross-cultural competence* (3rd ed., pp. 179–217). Baltimore: Brookes.

NAME INDEX

Johnson, N., 171
Johnson, R., 258, 274
Johnson, R. T., 134, 139, 141
Johnstun, M., 140
Jones, B., 47
Jones, E. D., 325
Jones, F. H., 123
Joseph, L. M., 323
Juvenile Diabetes Research
    Association, 280, 287

Kalyanpur, M., 76
Kantor, J., 349
Kantrowitz, B., 277
Kapoun, J., 172
Karasoff, P., 48
Karnes, F. A., 318, 333
Karweit, N. L., 97
Kathy Schrock's Guide for Educators, 171
Katz, G., 280
Kauffman, J. M., 31, 54, 59, 64, 112, 132,
    135, 142, 160, 213, 233, 235, 247, 332
Kaufman, M. J., 4
Kavale, K. A., 4, 38, 213, 233
Keefe, C. H., 93
Keefe, D. R., 93
Keller, C. E., 95
Keller, H., 138, 304–305
Keller, K., 274
Kemp, J., 112
Kennedy, C. H., 224
Kennedy, D. M., 327, 333
Kennedy, J. F., 280
Kerr, M. M., 234
Kids on the Block, 138
Kieley, C., 201
Killu, K., 235
King-Sears, M. E., 93, 158
Kinnaman, D. E., 164
Kirk, J., 142
Kirk, S. A., 4, 191, 213
Kitano, M. K., 72, 318, 322, 328, 329
Kliebhan, J. M., 191
Knight, W. J., 151
Knitzer, J., 233
Koegel, L. K., 266, 274
Koegel, R. L., 274
Kohl, F. L., 224
Kohler, F. W., 34
Kokaska, C. J., 217, 221, 222, 223
Kollins, S. H., 116, 233
Kolstoe, O. P., 222
Kominski, R., 338
Konigsburg, E. L., 140
Konrad, M., 140
Koorland, M. A., 118
Kourea, L., 80
Kozleski, E., 93
Krantz, P. J., 269, 271, 273, 274, 276
Krashen, S. D., 345, 346
Kratochwill, T. R., 107
Krementz, J., 139

Kroeger, S. D., 80
Krohn, N., 25
Kronberg, R., 224
Kroth, R., 145
Krouse, J., 142, 160
Krug, D. A., 267
Kukic, M. D., 4
Kulik, J. A., 327
Kulikowich, J. M., 327
Kurzweil, R., 246
Kurzweil Computer Products, 246
Kurzweil Educational Systems, 178, 246
Kurzweil Technologies, 246
Kutash, K., 121
Kymissis, E., 275

Lake, C., 179
Lakein, A., 159
Lambert, N., 215
Lamers, K., 275
Lamprecht, M. J., 132
Landau, J. K., 107
Landi, M. A. G., 203
Landrum, T. J., 31
Landrus, R., 268
Lane, K. L., 32, 55, 112, 135
Lansing, M. D., 267
Lapp, D., 156, 194
Larry P. v. Riles, 7
Larsen, S. C., 160, 254
Lasker, J., 139
Latimer, D., 322
Laushey, K. M., 275
Lawrence, G. A., 302, 305
Laycock, V. K., 144
Layton, C. A., 298
LaZebnik, C., 266
LD OnLine, 187, 188
LD OnLine Newsletter, 187
LD Resources, 187
Le, L., 274
Learning Disabilities Association of
    America (LDA), 7, 49, 187
Leavey, M., 140
LeBlanc, L. A., 274
LeBoeuf, M., 159
LeCouteur, A. L., 266
Lee, E., 72, 74, 77
Lee, S., 337
Leffert, J., 132, 142
Lehman, J., 47
Leinhardt, G., 10
Leland, H., 215
Lenburg, J., 172, 173
Lenk, L. L., 93
Leno, J., 193
Lenz, B. K., 52
Leonardo da Vinci, 193
Leone, P. E., 54
Lerner, J., 187, 193, 194, 198
Lerner, J. W., 58, 93, 191, 206, 207
Lerner, S. R., 58, 206

Levin, L., 276
Levy, J., 338
Lewis, L., 164, 167, 170
Lewis, R. B., 18, 24, 36, 39, 65, 108, 116,
    117, 119, 135, 136, 163, 182, 188,
    191, 194, 200, 201, 213, 221, 258,
    338, 340
Lewis, T. J., 136, 142, 233
Leyser, Y., 132, 139, 140
Libertarian Party, 175
Lienemann, T. O., 206
Lightfoot, J., 287
Lilly, M. S., 125, 306, 307, 312
Linan-Thompson, S., 188
Linn, R., 131
Litchfield, A. B., 139
Little, A., 32
Liu, K. K., 347
Lloyd, J. W., 31, 34, 89, 95
Lock, R. H., 298
Loeding, B. L., 298
Logan, D. R., 213
Lord, C., 266
Lovaas, O. I., 59
Lowdermilk, J., 346
Lowenbraun, S., 105, 156, 180, 195
Lowenthal, B., 58, 206, 207
Luckner, J., 298
Luckner, J. L., 298, 312
Luetke-Stahlman, B., 298
Luftig, R., 132, 136
Lusthaus, E., 224, 225, 226
Lyman, L., 139
Lynch, E. W., 73, 74, 75, 76, 77, 78, 200

Maag, J. W., 131, 132, 139, 142
MacArthur, C. A., 200, 202
MacDonald, C., 133
MacDuff, G. S., 273
Madden, N., 345
Madden, N. A., 10, 140
Madison Metropolitan School District,
    Wisconsin, 172
Madsen, C. H., 158
Mager, R. F., 93, 94
Maginnis, G., 191
Maheady, L., 142, 160
Mainzer, R. W., 93
Majd, M., 57
Maker, C. J., 323, 329
Malach, R. S., 72, 74, 77
Mallette, B., 160
Malone, S., 131
Mandell, C. J., 306
Manzo, K. K., 17
March, T., 331
Marcus, L. M., 267
Markel, G., 247
Markow, D., 112
Markwardt, F. C., 189, 214, 236
Maron, S. S., 305
Maroney, S. A., 144

Curriculum-based measurement (CBM), 65, 102, 103
Curriculum compacting, 325, 327, 328
Curriculum overlapping, 226

Database programs, 168
Data collection
  about instruction, 100–104
  on classroom behavior, 116–120
  during interventions, 120
  methods for, 158
  in prereferral stage, 32
  to promote social acceptance, 135–136
  teaching efficiency and, 66
Deaf students, 59, 299
Death, of students, 290
Delicious, 174–175
Demonstration, 95
Demonstration-prompt-practice model, 94–96
Developmental Test of Visual-Motor Integration (5th ed.), 189
Developmental Test of Visual Perception (2nd ed.), 189
Diabetes, 279–281, 283, 287
Diagnostic Testing and Prescriptive Instruction (DT/PI), 325
Diagnostic tools. *See also* Assessment; Tests
  for autism spectrum disorder, 266–268
  for English learners, 340
  for gifted and talented students, 323, 324
  for speech and language disorders, 253, 254
Differential grading, 221
Differentiation
  curriculum models for, 329
  explanation of, 89, 325
  function of, 91
  instructional models for, 156, 327
  program models for, 325, 327
Direct observation
  to assess behavior, 236
  to assess social skills, 136
  of English learners, 340, 341
  frequency of, 119–120
  of gifted and talented students, 324
  guidelines for, 120
  of language skills, 255
  methods of, 117–119
  for students with physical and health impairments, 285
  of students with sensory impairments, 302
Direct teaching, 90, 95
Disabilities, 52. *See also* Students with disabilities; *specific disabilities*
DISCOVER system, 323
Discovery learning, 91, 93
Disruptive behavior, 240–242. *See also* Behavior
Divergent thinking, 330

Diversity. *See also* Culturally and linguistically diverse students.
  in culture, ethnicity, and race, 70–75
  family income and, 78–80
  in family make-up, 77–78
  in general education classrooms, 69–70
  linguistic, 75–76
  overview of, 71–72
  promoting acceptance of, 80–83
  religious, 77
  in U.S. schools, 70, 72
  websites about, 74
Dominant culture, 70, 74
Draft:Builder program, 200
Duration recording, 118

Early interventionists, as team members, 29
Echolalic speech, 59
Edible reinforcers, 124
Edmark Reading Program, 219
Educationally blind students, 299
Educational reform, trends in, 16–18
Educational technology, 163. *See also* Technology
Education for All Handicapped Children Act of 1975, 8, 265
Education specialists, 10–11
Education World, 171
Electronic communication aids, 178, 259. *See also* Assistive technology (AT)
E-mail, 172
Emotional disturbances, 55. *See also* Behavioral disorders
Engaged time, 97–98
English language acquisition technology (ELAT), 346
English learners
  culturally responsive instruction for, 344
  explanation of, 75
  identification and assessment procedures for, 340, 341
  language instruction needs for, 338–339
  overview of, 337–338
  principles of language instruction for, 344–345
  services for, 340, 342–344
  teaching content area subjects to, 346–349
  terms related to instruction of, 340
  vocabulary building for, 345–346
  websites about, 343
Enrichment, 325, 326
Environment. *See* Instructional environment; Physical environment
Epilepsy, 279, 281–283, 289
Error analysis, 102, 104
Ethnic groups. *See also* Culturally and linguistically diverse students; Diversity; Race

explanation of, 71
gifted and talented programs and, 318, 319
Etiology, of learning problems, 60–61
Event recording, 118
Excessive activity, 241–242
Explicit instruction, 90
Extinction, 115, 243

Families, trends in, 77–78
FASTT Math, 239
Federal Resources for Educational Excellence (FREE), 171
Feedback, 99, 123
Flexible grouping, 156
Flickr, 175–176
FM technology, 311
Friendship
  as goal of full inclusion, 224–226
  strategies to promote, 142
  for students with autism spectrum disorder, 275
Full inclusion
  explanation of, 4
  for students with severe intellectual disabilities, 224, 226, 228
Functional academics, 217–221
Functional behavior assessment (FBA)
  explanation of, 113, 116
  methods for, 117
Functional skills, 218
Furniture, appropriate, 151

General education classrooms
  activities for special students in, 39
  adaptations for, 32–34
  assistive technology in, 176–181
  conduct problems in, 128
  co-teaching in, 47
  English learners in, 344–349
  gifted and talented students in, 61, 325–329
  instructional environment in, 155–158
  instructional personnel for, 160, 161
  introducing students with disabilities to, 144
  learning materials for, 159–160
  management strategies for, 149–150
  modifications for, 32, 64
  overview of, 211–212
  physical environment in, 150–155
  placement options for, 45–48
  profile of, 69–70
  resources available for, 34
  special services for, 12
  students with attention deficit hyperactivity disorder in, 208–209
  students with autism spectrum disorder in, 271–273
  students with behavioral disorders in, 235, 238

Instruction (*Continued*)
    for students with physical and health
        impairments, 292–295
    for students with sensory impairments,
        306–313
    universal design and, 89–90
    use of systematic, 94–96
Instructional environment
    behavior guidelines and, 158
    curriculum organization and, 155–156
    explanation of, 155
    groupings methods and, 156
    monitoring systems and, 156–158
    record-keeping procedures and, 158
    for students with sensory impairments,
        305–306
Instructional materials
    to assist in teaching of social skills, 143
    commercial, 159–160
    modifications of, 104–105
    selection of, 159
    self-instructional, 156, 157
    for students with sensory impairments,
        307–309
Instructional objectives, 94
Instructional personnel, 160, 161
Instructional technologies
    explanation of, 164 (*See also*
        Technology)
    selection of, 167–168
    types of, 167, 168
Integrated Curriculum Model (ICM), 329
Intellectual disabilities. *See also* Students
    with mild intellectual disabilities;
    Students with severe intellectual
    disabilities
    assessment of, 213–215
    explanation of, 56–57
    indicators of, 212–213
    severe, 223–224, 226, 228
    websites about, 212
Intelligence quotient (IQ), 56, 188, 323
Intelligence tests, 56, 187–188, 214–215,
    323–324
IntelliKeys, 292
Internet. *See also* Technology
    accessibility to, 181
    communication tools on, 172, 174
    evaluating material on, 172, 173
    information management on, 174–175
    information sources on, 174
    as instructional tool, 170
    networking sites on, 175–176
    search strategies for, 170–171
    WebQuests and Web Inquiry Projects
        on, 331
Interpreters, in classrooms with deaf
    children, 59
Interval recording, 118–119
Intervention strategies, 33
Inventories, 101
Itinerant teachers, 28, 47

Jigsaw, 141
Joint attention, 275
Jumpstart Languages, 346

Kathy Schrock's Guide for Educators, 171
Keller, Helen, 304–305
Knowledge of results, 99
Kurzweil 3000, 246

Labeling, effects of, 132
Language. *See also* English learners
    explanation of, 252
    heritage, 75, 76, 338
    interdependence of culture and, 65
    spoken in U.S. schools, 75–76
Language Assessment Scales, 340
Language disorders. *See also*
    Communication disorders
    assessment of, 253–255
    explanation of, 252, 260–261
Latinos, 75
Learning
    causes of problems in, 60–61
    cooperative, 80, 139–141
    engaged time for, 97–98
    factors that facilitate, 92
    gifted and talented students and, 320
    problem-based, 327, 328
    process of, 66
    strategies for, 187
Learning centers, 156–157
Learning disabilities. *See also* Students with
    learning disabilities
    assessment of, 187–191
    definitions of, 53, 186
    facts about, 193
    indicators of, 186–188
    overview of, 52, 185
    websites about, 187
*Learning Disabilities Diagnostic
    Inventory,* 187
Learning Disability Evaluation Scale, 187
Learning tasks
    altering requirements for, 106–107
    analyzing reasons for failure of, 102, 104
    broken into teachable
        subcomponents, 94
    correcting errors in, 105
    directions for, 98
    finding alternate, 106–107
    selection of, 90, 93–94
    speed and accuracy in, 96–97
    successful performance of, 99
Learning together approach, 141
Learn Language Now series, 346
Least Restrictive Environment (LRE), 12, 16
Let Me Hear Your Voice (Maurice), 266
Leukemia, 281
Limited English proficiency, 18
Linguistically diverse students, 61, 75–76.
    See also Culturally and linguistically
    diverse students; English learners

LISTEN strategy, 261
Listservs, 174
Literature, to promote understanding of
    disabilities, 138–140
Low-vision students
    aids for, 298, 306, 307
    explanation of, 59
Lyme syndrome, 280

Mainstreaming, 3–4. *See also* Inclusion
Maintenance
    acquisition and, 99–100
    checking for, 99–100
    explanation of, 87
Management adaptations, 34
Mapping, 201, 202
MAPS (Making Action Plans), 114
Math Blaster series, 239
Math skills
    for students with behavioral
        disorders, 239
    for students with learning disabilities,
        202–203, 205
Maurice, Catherine, 266
Mayer-Johnson Picture Communication
    Symbols, 258
Meaning-emphasis approach, 194
Mediated instruction, 156
Medically fragile students, 283
Mental retardation, 56
Metropolitan Achievement Tests, 100
Microcultures, 70
Minorities, 71–72
Mobility skills, 298, 306
Modeling, 126
Motivation, 268–269
Motor-Free Visual Perception Test
    (3rd ed.), 189
Multicultural curriculum, 328
Multicultural education
    explanation of, 71
    implication for classroom of, 73–75
Muscular dystrophy, 281

Naglieri Nonverbal Ability Test, 56, 188, 323
Narrative recording, 117
*National Excellence: A Case for Developing
    America's Talent* (Department of
    Education), 318
*A Nation at Risk: The Imperative for
    Educational Reform* (National
    Commission on Excellence in
    Education), 16
Negative attention, 123
Negative reinforcement, 115, 124
Networking sites, 175–176
News-2-You, 258
No Child Left Behind Act (NCLB),
    17, 93
Nomination method, 136
Norm-referenced tests, 65
Nutrition, 79–80